| DATE DUE | | | |
|---|---|---|---|
| May 23 '72 | Oct 7 79 | | |
| Aug 15 '72 | Mar 10 80 | | |
| Dec 13 '72 | | | |
| Mar 15 '73 | | | |
| Nov 12 '73 | | | |
| Dec 3 '73 | | | |
| Apr 24 74 | | | |
| May 14 '74 | | | |
| Oct 16 '74 | | | |
| Dec 15 '76 | | | |
| Oct 19 78 | | | |
| Dec 6 78 | | | |

*The*
*American Population*
*Debate*

# The
# American Population
# Debate

EDITED BY
**DANIEL CALLAHAN**

Doubleday & Company, Inc.   Garden City, New York
1971

Library of Congress Catalog Card Number 79–144256
Copyright © 1971 by Daniel Callahan

# Acknowledgments

1) Lawrence A. Mayer, "U.S. Population Growth: Would Fewer Be Better?" Reprinted from the June 1970 issue of Fortune Magazine by special permission; © Time Inc.

2) Paul R. Ehrlich and John P. Holdren, "Population and Environment," which originally appeared in The Saturday Review as "The People Problem," July 4, 1970, "Hidden Effects of Overpopulation," August 1, 1970, "Deceptive Birth Rates," October 3, 1970. Copyright 1970 Saturday Review.

3) Frank Notestein, "Zero Population Growth: What Is It?" *Population Index* (October–December 1970). Reprinted by permission of Office of Population Research, Princeton University, and *Family Planning Perspectives* (June 1970, Vol. 2, No. 3), where the article first appeared.

4) Donald J. Bogue, "The End of the Population Explosion," *The Public Interest.* © 1967 by National Affairs, Inc.

5) Frank Pollara, "Trends in U.S. Population," *AFL-CIO American Federationist* (June 1970). Reprinted with permission of the *AFL-CIO American Federationist.*

6) This was a mimeographed handout, with no copyright. Permission was asked from the address given on the handout, but the letter was returned with a postoffice note that they were not there.

7) Marston Bates, "Crowded People," from *A Jungle in the House* by Marston Bates. Copyright © 1970 by Marston Bates. Reprinted by permission of the publisher, Walker & Co., New York.

8) Morris K. Udall, "Standing Room Only on Spaceship Earth," *Arizona Magazine* (July 27, 1969). Reprinted with permission of *Arizona Magazine,* The Arizona Republic.

9) Ben Wattenberg, "The Nonsense Explosion," *The New Republic* (April 4 & 11, 1970). © 1970 by Harrison-Blaine of New

Jersey, Inc., reprinted by permission of the Harold Matson Company, Inc.

10) William and Paul Paddock, "Today Hungry Nations, Tomorrow Starving Nations," Chapter Two of *Famine—1975! America's Decision: Who Will Survive?* by permission of Little, Brown and Co. Copyright © 1967 by William and Paul Paddock, and by permission of George Weidenfeld & Nicolson, Ltd.

11) Jean Mayer, "Toward a Non-Malthusian Population Policy." Reprinted from the Columbia FORUM, Summer 1969, Vol. XII, No. 2. Copyright © 1969 by the Trustees of Columbia University in the City of New York.

12) Kenneth S. Norris, "The Third Fish," *The New Republic* (May 9, 1970). Reprinted by permission of The New Republic, © 1970, Harrison-Blaine of New Jersey, Inc.

13) Wayne H. Davis, "Overpopulated America," *The New Republic* (January 10, 1970). Reprinted by permission of the author. Copyright © by Wayne H. Davis.

14) Ansley J. Coale, "Man and His Environment," *Science,* Vol. 170, pp. 132–136, October 9, 1970. Reprinted with permission of *Science.* Copyright © 1970 by the American Association for the Advancement of Science.

15) Robin Elliott, Lynn C. Landman, Richard Lincoln and Theodore Tsuruoka, "U.S. Population Growth and Family Planning: A Review of the Literature," *Family Planning Perspectives* (October 1970, Vol. 2, No. 4). Reprinted by permission of *Family Planning Perspectives.*

16) Kingsley Davis, "Population Policy: Will Current Programs Succeed?" *Science,* Vol. 158, pp. 730–739, November 10, 1967. Reprinted with permission of author and publisher. Copyright 1967 by the American Association for the Advancement of Science.

17) Garrett Hardin, "Multiple Paths to Population Control," *Family Planning Perspectives,* Vol. 2, No. 3, June 1970. Reprinted by permission of *Family Planning Perspectives.*

18) Larry Bumpass and Charles F. Westoff, "Unwanted Births and U.S. Population Control," *Family Planning Perspectives,* Vol. 2, No. 4, October 1970. Reprinted with permission of *Family Planning Perspectives.*

19) Edgar Chasteen, "The Case for Compulsory Birth Control," *Mademoiselle* Magazine (January 1970). Reprinted with permission of the author. Copyright 1970 Edgar Chasteen.

20) Melvin M. Ketchel, "Fertility Control Agents as a Possible Solution to the World Population Problem," *Perspectives in Biology and Medicine* (Summer, 1968). Reprinted by permission of

the University of Chicago Press. Copyright © 1968 by the University of Chicago.

21) Judith Blake, "Population Policy for Americans: Is the Government Being Misled?" *Science,* Vol. 164, pp. 522–529, May 2, 1969. Reprinted with permission of *Science.* Copyright 1969 by the American Association for the Advancement of Science.

22) Oscar Harkavy, Frederick S. Jaffe, Samuel M. Wishik, "Family Planning and Public Policy: Who Is Misleading Whom?" *Science,* Vol. 165, pp. 367–373, July 25, 1969. Reprinted by permission of *Science.* Copyright 1969 by the American Association for the Advancement of Science.

Judith Blake, Reply to above article, *Science,* Vol. 165, pp. 372–373, July 25, 1969. Reprinted with permission of *Science.* Copyright 1969 by the American Association for the Advancement of Science.

23) Arthur J. Dyck, "Population Policies and Ethical Acceptability," from *Rapid Population Growth: Some Consequences and Some Public Policy Implications* (Johns Hopkins Press, 1971). Reprinted with permission of Johns Hopkins Press.

# Contents

Introduction                                                    xi

PART I. DOES THE UNITED STATES HAVE A POPULA-
TION PROBLEM?

1. U.S. Population Growth: Would Fewer Be Better?
   *Lawrence A. Mayer*                                          3

2. Population and Environment  *Paul R. Ehrlich
   and John P. Holdren*                                         21

3. Zero Population Growth: What Is It?  *Frank
   Notestein*                                                   31

4. The End of the Population Explosion  *Donald J.
   Bogue*                                                       44

5. Trends in U.S. Population  *Frank Pollara*                   55

6. ZPG: A Fascist Movement! *A Progressive Labor
   Party Position*                                              68

7. Crowded People  *Marston Bates*                             77

8. Spaceship Earth—Standing Room Only  *Morris
   K. Udall*                                                    84

9. The Nonsense Explosion  *Ben Wattenberg*                     96

10. Today Hungry Nations, Tomorrow Starving Na-
    tions  *William and Paul Paddock*                           110

11. Toward a Non-Malthusian Population Policy
    *Jean Mayer*                                          135

12. The Third Fish   *Kenneth S. Norris*                  154

13. Overpopulated America   *Wayne H. Davis*              161

14. Man and His Environment   *Ansley J. Coale*           168


PART II. WHAT IS THE SOLUTION TO THE PROBLEM?

15. U.S. Population Growth and Family Planning: A
    Review of the Literature   *Robin Elliott, Lynn
    C. Landman, Richard Lincoln and Theodore
    Tsuruoka*                                             185

16. Population Policy: Will Current Programs Suc-
    ceed?   *Kingsley Davis*                              227

17. Multiple Paths to Population Control   *Garrett
    Hardin*                                               259

18. Unwanted Births and U.S. Population Growth
    *Larry Bumpass and Charles F. Westoff*               267

19. The Case for Compulsory Birth Control   *Edgar
    Chasteen*                                             274

20. Fertility Control Agents as a Possible Solution
    to the World Population Problem   *Melvin M.
    Ketchel*                                              279

21. Population Policy for Americans: Is the Gov-
    ernment Being Misled?   *Judith Blake*               298

22. Family Planning and Public Policy: Who Is Mis-
    leading Whom?   *Oscar Harkavy, Frederick S.
    Jaffe, and Samuel M. Wishik* (*with a reply from
    Judith Blake*)                                        325

23. Population Policies and Ethical Acceptability
    *Arthur J. Dyck*                                      351

Notes on Contributors                                     378

# Introduction

The purpose of this book can be directly stated. It is meant to bring together a variety of statements, analyses, and positions on American population growth and its implications for the quality and future of American life. There exists little public or professional agreement on the issues, other than on the perhaps non-revelatory proposition that the population of the United States cannot continue to grow indefinitely at its present rate. Otherwise, the issues are open to argument; and argument there is. Indeed, it is proper to speak of a "population debate" in the United States. It is not to be confused with earlier debates over the morality and legality of the distribution and sale of contraceptives or the establishment of voluntary family planning programs. That debate has waned. Nor is it to be confused with the argument that raged in the fifties, concerning the propriety of the United States Government providing funds for foreign population limitation and family planning programs. Those earlier debates were premised on the dual assumption that (1) many individuals, couples and families in the United States desired family planning information and the availability of contraceptives—but that the United States had no problem as such with excessive population growth; and (2) that many foreign nations, particularly in the underdeveloped parts of the world, had both a family planning and a population problem—and therein differed significantly from the United States and other developed countries.

Both assumptions, particularly the first, have now been called into serious question. Could it be—possibly, shock-

ingly—that the United States itself has a population problem?
That not just the poorest nation in the world, but also the
richest is suffering from too many children being born too
fast taxing too many resources which are being consumed
too fast? That it is time for this country to stop preaching
to others and to do something about its own population
growth? Not long ago, these questions would have seemed
ridiculous, even bizarre. That is no longer the case.

In short, the debate referred to in the title of this book
focuses on the question of whether the United States has a
population problem; and if it does, how serious is the problem; and if the problem is serious, what can be done about
it? That is a long question, and the different parts of it need
to be distinguished. What is meant by a "population problem"? Too many people *now?* Too rapid a *rate* of population
growth? Too many people, or too rapid a rate of growth in
terms of available space and food supply? Or too many people and too rapid a rate of growth in terms of the rapidity
with which an affluent people consumes its resources and
despoils its environment? And what is meant when and if
we say the problem (once identified) is a "serious" one?
Serious at *this* moment, disaster *now?* Or likely to be serious
in the near—or far?—future if something is not done soon?
If we can agree on all that, what would it mean to "do" something about the problem? Change laws, change policy, change
attitudes? How?

These are the kinds of questions dealt with by the authors in
this book. That they do not see eye-to-eye will quickly become evident. Just why they differ, however, is far more interesting. Part of the dispute turns on different interpreta-
tions of the same data; the same facts do not always mean
the same thing to different specialists. Part of the dispute
turns on the weight given to different groups of data; what
seems highly relevant to some seems relatively unimportant to
others. Finally, though less obviously, there are different em-
phases given to different values. For some, the preservation
of freedom is a more critical issue than insuring survival.
For others, civil and social justice loom as the over-arching
concern. Still another source of disagreement stems from the
basic frame of reference employed. It makes a great deal of

difference if the problem of population is predicated on the continuing desirability of technological affluence, with all that means in terms of more cars, more roads, more consumer goods. A critique of that affluence and the predication of a very different, simpler kind of social order casts the population problem in a different light. Moreover, to take another source of conflict, a biologist or ecologist looking at population in terms of the entire eco-sphere is often likely to come out with a different conclusion than a demographer or social scientist whose attention is fixed on social and political systems. It seems to me critical that the distinctive value and professional premises, the disparate starting points, be discerned. If they are missed, it will often be difficult to understand why the same facts can mean quite different things to different people and groups.

A number of remarks should be made about the articles collected here. First, a certain amount of repetition of data is present. This seemed unavoidable in the collection of articles, as much as anything because, as mentioned above, much of the debate turns not on the meaning of incommensurable data but on the meaning of data accepted by all. If the repetition leads to a certain amount of yawning on the part of the reader, we can hope that he will come awake when he sees the way in which radically different kinds of conclusions can be drawn from that data. Second, while the focus of this collection is on the United States, it seemed desirable to include at least a few articles that deal primarily with the world population picture; they help to provide a larger framework in which to place the American problem. Third, this collection aims at a presentation of the spectrum of positions which has emerged as the debate has developed. Inevitably, some excellent studies had to be omitted.

Fairness was sought. Unfortunately, one man's idea of fairness is likely to be another man's notion of bigotry. The sharp-eyed critic will undoubtedly detect some bias or other operating in the choice and positioning of the articles collected here. I can save that critic some trouble, at least in part. I am happier with those who would increase and implement the range of free choice—what might be termed the voluntarist position—than I am with those who move in the direction of coercion. At the same time, I am sobered enough by the demographic and environmental data to realize that the possibility of something less than individual free choice must be seriously considered. Fortunately, the debate is fairly fresh. There is still some time—just how much, of course, is part of the debate—to think and to weigh. I have tried to present a decent range of opinion, rich and sufficient enough so that the reader can come away from the book with a sense of what the issues are, where the sources of difference lie, and what the options are for analysis and action.

The plan of the book is relatively simple. It is divided into two parts, the first concerned with the question "Does the United States Have a Population Problem?" and the second with the question "What Is the Solution to the Problem?" To be sure, the question posed for the second part begs the question posed for the first part. But as will be seen, there is considerable agreement (with a few exceptions) among the authors represented in the first part that the United States does have *some* kind of population problem. It will also be seen that, while the book is divided into two parts, there is considerable overlap between them. Some authors in the first part deal also with possible solutions, and some authors in the second part also concern themselves with whether or not there is a problem. This is only to say that authors do not always write articles to fit into the neat categories editors might like to devise for collections. One cannot complain about that. My original intention was to divide the book into a plethora of parts, breaking the issues down into a variety of technical categories (e.g., American population growth and the availability of natural resources, projected land use, etc.). This proved unworkable, primarily because there are comparatively few such specialized articles available, and those which are available proved to be either too long or too technical. It seemed best, then, to use two general categories only. As the reader will discern, however, a large number of specialized issues are dealt with *passim* in this collection.

The preparation of this volume called for combing through a great mass of literature. I would like to thank two colleagues and friends for their assistance and wise counsel: Robert

Veatch, Associate for Medical Ethics at the Institute of Society, Ethics and the Life Sciences, and Stephen Viederman, Assistant Director of the Demographic Division, The Population Council. Where this book suffers from a lack of balance, that is to be attributed to me.

Daniel Callahan

Institute of Society, Ethics and the Life Sciences
Hastings-on-Hudson, New York

# PART I

*Does the United States Have a
Population Problem?*

# 1. U.S. Population Growth:
# Would Fewer Be Better?

## LAWRENCE A. MAYER

The movement to curb population growth in the U.S. has come into prominence, curiously enough, at a time when the birth rate is close to its all-time low. The actual low in the U.S. birth rate came in 1968, at 17.5 per thousand. While the rate rose a bit to 17.7 last year—the first increase in more than a decade—it was still lower than at any point during the great depression of the Thirties. And though the number of births last year was up 2 percent to 3,570,000, that total was about 700,000 below the all-time peak reached in 1957.

The U.S., then, appears to have already moved in the direction that proponents of population stability advocate. But it's not at stability yet. Even at the recent reduced birth rates, the population has been growing 1 percent a year, and that is enough to double it in a single lifetime of seventy-two years. Moreover, birth rates are now bound to go higher, at least for some years to come. One important reason has to do with the changing numbers of women aged twenty to thirty-four, who account for about three-quarters of all births. The size of this group remained practically constant at about 18 million between 1955 and 1965, but from 1965 to 1970 it grew by three million, and in the next fifteen years it will increase ten million more. This wave of younger women is the result, of course, of the baby boom that followed World War II.

While the number of young women began to increase markedly in the years following 1965, the number of births did not. The women who had reached at least the age of twenty-five by around 1965 had borne most of their children by that time, and births to them naturally slowed down drastically thereafter. At the same time, women who were then just moving into the childbearing ages delayed having children (see "Why the U.S. Population *Isn't* Exploding," FORTUNE, April, 1967). This delay should partly be made up at later ages, however, and meanwhile the ranks of the twenty- to thirty-four-year-olds will increase rapidly. These two factors virtually guarantee that there will be a rise in births during the years directly ahead.

How boomy this baby boom will turn out to be is a question that perplexes demographers. Those at the Census Bureau who made four alternative population projections in 1967 have already discarded the highest as virtually impossible. What's more, it has become clear that the second highest is improbable. Up to this moment, it is the lowest that is on target with a figure of 205 million for 1970.[1] At any rate Census will soon issue a new, lower set of projections.

In the present era of changing mores and social upheavals, it is even more difficult than usual to forecast the probable course of U.S. population growth. Just about everything known, however, suggests to Census demographers that a range of projections for the year 2000 should at the outside be no higher than 325 million (the old Census high was 361 million). Even the 300 million people still commonly said to be inevitable by 2000 are no longer inevitable at all.

### Some distance from zero

Population projections have to be built on many assumptions. One key assumption has to do with how large a family the average woman eventually will have. And nobody knows what that figure will be for the young women who will soon begin to bear children, or have recently begun. Surveys have shown that women expect what averages out as about 3.2 children. Demographers largely agree that at present it looks as if today's young women would have fewer children than that. But it would take a drop all the way down to an average of 2.1 children per woman (a bit more than 2.2 per married woman) to bring population growth to a halt. The 2.1 figure is sometimes referred to as the "zero population growth" rate. Obviously it takes two children to replace a set of parents. The extra 0.1 compensates for the girls who die before maturity and takes account of the fact that fewer girls than boys are born. (The 2.1 figure ignores net immigration, which has been contributing 0.2 percent a year to U.S. population growth.)

An important clue to future family size is the total fertility rate. This is the combined rate at which, in any particular year, women of all reproductive ages bear children. The figure for 1969 suggested women were building families at a rate that, if sustained, would give them an average of about 2.5 children by the end of their childbearing careers. This rate is very close to that underlying the present Census low projection. But the total fertility rate at any point in time may be an unreliable indicator. For example, the rate hit 3.7 per woman in the late 1950's, a figure demographers rightly suspected was too high to last. Many experts think the present 2.5 is too low to last.

Donald J. Bogue, a demographer at the University of Chicago, argues that the present fertility rate is *not* misleading. The rise in fertility that followed World War II, he believes, was merely a prolonged interruption of the decline in the U.S. birth rate that got started early in the nineteenth century. He thinks it quite significant that by 1968 white women were bearing children at a rate of only 2.37 per woman, 1.26 fewer than in 1957 and not so very far from the stability rate of 2.1. Childbearing by black women (who account for about 17 percent of all births) has come down by about the same proportion, and was at a rate of 3.2 per woman in 1968. Moreover, Bogue thinks the black rate may go below the white rate by the end of this century. He points out, for example, that the percentage of black women who bear five or more children has halved since 1957. Moreover, college-educated black women expect fewer children than college-educated white women expect.

Accordingly, Bogue sees comparatively moderate growth in the U.S. population by the year 2000. The low of about 280 million in the Census Bureau's 1967 projection is the top of Bogue's high range. Bogue's low goes down to 220 million.

## The big little difference

A view quite different from Bogue's is advanced by Arthur A. Campbell, a widely respected government demographer now at the National Institutes of Health. He believes that the total fertility rate is probably giving off a false signal. He takes the depression years, when all measures of births were extremely low, as his bench mark. At that time, women born in 1909 were in their peak childbearing years. By age twenty-six (in 1935) they had given birth to but 1.05 children on average, and they finally produced the smallest American families on record, 2.23 children. By contrast, when women born in 1943 were twenty-six years old (in 1969), they had already averaged 1.57 children. It now looks as if these younger women would eventually have an average of close to three. Recent patterns suggest that 90 percent of today's young women will have at least one child; in contrast, nearly 25 percent of the women born in 1909 never had any children at all.

In short, Campbell believes that much of the recent decline in birth rates reflects a delay in childbearing by young women. And even though such delays tend to reduce the eventual size of families ("Later means less," demographers say), he still thinks current reproductive behavior is consistent with an average of 2.8 children per woman rather than 2.5. This seemingly insignificant difference has large implications. If sustained over thirty years to 2000, the higher figure would mean 25 million more Americans.

As surer means of birth control come into use, it becomes more important for demographers to know how many children people really want. One kind of information bearing on this question is what proportion of births represents unwanted children. In a recent paper, Professors Larry Bumpass of Wisconsin and Charles F. Westoff of Princeton maintain that 16 percent of the births to women who were nearing the end of their childbearing years in 1965—when the last national fertility survey was taken—were unwanted. They conclude that these women, on average, would have had only

2.5 children if they had been able to exercise perfect control over their fertility.

This is astounding, since whenever surveys have directly asked women how many children they wanted or expected, the average has always come out a little over three. Bumpass and Westoff, however, went back over the 1965 questionnaires to ascertain what parents said about wanting *each successive child*. In this way the two demographers arrived at their 2.5 figure. And this result could well be conservative. It can be imagined that parents find it difficult to describe children who may literally be sitting in the adjoining room as "unwanted."

By extending their analysis to the entire population, Bumpass and Westoff conclude that in the 1960's one-fifth of all births were unwanted—meaning about 700,000 annually in the past few years. The extra births are more widely spread among social classes than might be supposed. The poor and near-poor, of course, contributed more than their proportionate share, *but more than half* of the unwanted children were born to parents who were not considered poor. (A family of four that had an income of at least $4,000 in 1964 was classified as "nonpoor.")

The implications of these findings are quite far reaching. If the number of children that couples really want averages 2.5 rather than three or so, it might not require very extensive social alterations to attain population stability, assuming the availability of perfect contraception.

### The *"popullution"* problem

A sense that population growth is becoming a burden rather than a boon has taken hold in the U.S. with surprising swiftness. Last July, only a year after President Johnson's restrained advocacy of family planning and his hesitant mention of "population change," President Nixon spoke out forthrightly about the "pressing problems" associated with population growth. In keeping with Mr. Nixon's request, Congress has established a Commission on Population Growth and the American Future.

All the attention to population has arisen from several interwoven concerns having to do with crowding, pollution, and deterioration of the environment. The U.S. is confronting a "popullution" problem, observes S. Fred Singer, Deputy Assistant Secretary of the Interior and director of that department's research on environmental quality. Also, it is disturbing to some that the U.S. is chewing up a disproportionate share of the earth's limited stock of natural resources.

Population growth, of course, is not the only villain in these matters. Under present arrangements, the nation's productive system provides high levels of consumption but also throws off inordinate amounts of pollution, waste, and discomfort. The uneven distribution of the population also affects the quality of life.

It is often said that the U.S. doesn't really have a population problem, because there are only fifty-five people per square mile (sixty-five excluding Alaska). Density in some European countries runs more than ten times as high. But the over-all density figure for the U.S. is misleading, because two-thirds of the population lives in metropolitan areas, where density is much greater. And nearly half of the people in metropolitan areas live in central cities, where the density averages around 7,000 per square mile (and a lot higher than that in city cores). It is true that these urban areas are becoming decentralized, but the continuing helter-skelter growth of suburbs is causing new problems of traffic, water supply, and pollution.

If the U.S. rationally altered the distribution of people, it is often contended, there would be no reason for concern about the size of the population. This is more easily proposed than done. Schemes to distribute the population differently are up against what appears to be an iron law of urbanization: in a technologically advancing society the bigger cities tend to grow in perpetuity. Public authorities have tried over the years to halt the growth of London, Paris, Tokyo, and Moscow. None has succeeded, not even the authoritarian government of the U.S.S.R.

Another often-mentioned possibility is to build new towns. Britain has carried out the largest endeavors along this line, having started twenty-seven new towns—new cities, really—

since 1946. But they contain only about 1 percent of the total population. Most observers give Britain's new towns at least passing marks, in large part because they have preserved a lot of open space, especially around London. However, the towns have failed to improve conditions within London; the inferior housing that was evacuated filled up again with newcomers.

Only a few communities that really qualify as new towns have been built in the U.S., and those few are not very populous. Recently the federal government gave its first real support to a new town in more than thirty years by issuing a loan guarantee to Jonathan, about twenty miles from Minneapolis. The location of Jonathan supports those who contend that new towns can succeed only within the ambit of established cities. If that is true, then although new towns prevent haphazard development, they don't really do much redistributing. A number of experts think some redistribution could be accomplished if new towns were built around existing ones and used facilities already in place. They have in mind cities in the Middle West that could stand revival—cities with 20,000 to 40,000 people that have stopped growing or are losing population.

One way to try to get new cities built is for the federal government to grant tax incentives to business, an approach that a number of studies and some bills in Congress advocate. Other measures that Washington or local governments could try include selective placement of procurement contracts, provision of inter-area job information, and special channeling of assistance to home building. This spring the Nixon Administration was considering several alternative approaches to a new-town program.

### Romantic nonsense

Many economists take a quite different approach to the problems of population distribution. Attempts to use subsidies and special assistance to get people and companies to relocate in less crowded parts of the country are "romantic nonsense," according to Dick Netzer, an urban-economics specialist at New York University. Of the many underlying reasons, perhaps the most important is that the key decisions about location are ordinarily not made by individuals seeking amenities, but by business organizations that cluster together in places they find economically advantageous.

The sensible way to change present patterns of distribution, Netzer and other economists maintain, is to make organizations and individuals pay the full costs of their activities. The argument is that if business, for one, was forced to pay for all the pollution, waste disposal, and traffic congestion resulting from its activities, and for all the benefits it gets from airports, highways, and other public facilities, the distribution of industry and people would be a lot different and the condition of the environment a lot better. In other words, the costs of producing and distributing goods and services should reflect the "externalities." The additional costs would, in many cases, be passed on to consumers. (See "The Economics of Environmental Quality," FORTUNE, February 1970.)

Another way to reduce adverse effects of population growth on the environment is to reduce standards of consumption. It has been calculated that an attempt to get pollution in 1965 back to the levels of 1940 would have required reductions of 50 percent in the number of cars on the road, 50 percent in consumption of paper, 70 percent in generation of electric power, and 87 percent in the use of nitrogen fertilizer.

Still another set of troublesome questions connected with population has to do with the future adequacy of resources. The answers are by no means certain, though judging by the past alone there is nothing much to worry about. Important new materials such as petroleum and aluminum have been brought into use in the past century, and others, such as synthetic fibers and plastics, have emerged from laboratories. Additional reserves of minerals and fuels keep coming along. Better conservation methods have also added to supplies, as in the case of lumber. And improved technology has in some instances played an important role in holding down the consumption of materials. In 1968, electric utilities burned 480 million tons of fuel, measured in coal equivalents; Hans H. Landsberg of Resources for the Future calculates that 740 million tons would have been burned if the technology of 1940 had still been in use.

In principle there are only four real resources: the earth

and its minerals, air, water, and fossil fuels. The first three can be constantly repurified or recycled in one way or another, maintains Roger Revelle of Harvard. But the fossil fuels—coal and petroleum—are irrecoverable once consumed, and are bound to run out within a few hundred years. However, most energy experts expect that, before the present century is over, breeder reactors to supply energy will be available, and some believe that controlled fusion will also prove feasible.

The world, of course, is a long way from ideal utilization and recycling of materials. Moreover, if one extrapolates demand on the assumption that most or all countries will become industrially advanced, then it is possible to arrive at enormously large estimates of future global requirements for resources. Changes in technology and patterns of resource use will temper these requirements, but even so, demand for materials will certainly rise far above present levels.

The U.S. is already a large user and importer of a long string of raw materials from antimony to zinc. With only 6 percent of the world's population, the U.S. gobbles up about one-third of the world's materials. At present the high U.S. rate of imports helps provide underdeveloped countries with badly needed foreign exchange, but as they achieve a high degree of industrialization they may ration their exports of resources.

### An eventual halt

It seems feasible, in theory at least, to mitigate problems arising from the distribution of population, environmental pollution, and scarcity of resources by altering government regulations, taxes, and subsidies, re-allocating costs, and adopting different technologies and life styles. But such measures, even if society is willing to accept the costs, will not enable the U.S. to postpone indefinitely facing questions about population growth. Eventually, growth will have to come to a halt. Though no one can formulate them with any precision, there must be limits to how many people the earth, or any nation, can hold. Accordingly, it might be wise to begin thinking now about ways to stabilize the population. If society waits until limitation becomes a matter of desperate urgency, it may be too late for humane, noncoercive policies, and in any event the quality of life will have been severely and perhaps irreparably impaired.

The economic and social consequences of population stability merit a great deal more research and thought than they have received. Still, it is possible now to foresee some of the effects. Whether the effects seem beneficial or not depends to some extent on individual values and tastes; at any rate, a lot of things would be different.

It was once believed by businessmen and by many economists that population growth was necessary to sustain national prosperity. Nowadays hardly any economist would argue in favor of that view. Despite a widely held assumption to the contrary, big business seems to have swung around too. A FORTUNE-Yankelovich survey of chief executives of the 500 largest corporations (February 1970) showed that almost eight in ten favor some sort of effort that would curb further population growth.

### THE U.S. APPETITE FOR RESOURCES

*U.S. Consumption as Percent of World Production*

| | | | |
|---|---|---|---|
| Natural Gas | 67% | Gypsum | 29% |
| Silver | 58 | Mercury | 28 |
| Molybdenum | 50 | Chromium | 28 |
| Sulphur | 48 | Antimony | 27 |
| Magnesium | 43 | Zinc | 27 |
| Cobalt | 41 | Crude Petroleum | 26 |
| Lead | 37 | Tin | 26 |
| Platinum | 35 | Nickel | 25 |
| Bauxite | 30 | Coal | 21 |
| Copper | 29 | Iron Ore | 21 |

The size of the gross national product would be smaller with population stability than with continued growth. More women would presumably go to work if there were fewer children, but once employment of women reached a ceiling there would be no further growth in the labor force. From then on the economy could grow only as fast as the average output per worker. This means that if productivity is still rising at 3 percent or so a year with the population stabilized, the economy's potential rate of growth would be 3 percent a year rather than the present rate of more than 4 percent.

The average standard of living is nevertheless likely to be higher with population stability. When population is rising, some proportion of national product must go to provide consumer goods and services and social overhead for additional people. With stability, the U.S. could use the freed resources to increase both private and public investment per capita. Because each member of the labor force would then be working with a larger or more advanced stock of capital, there would be more output and income *per worker*. And since workers would, on average, belong to smaller families, income *per person* would rise even faster. The income position of young families—with fewer children living at home than their counterparts of today—would benefit the most. It thus turns out that businessmen are confronted with a trade-off: a growing population would mean larger markets, and a stationary population would mean richer markets.

Markets would also be affected by the changed age composition of the population. By the year 2000, according to some assumptions, a population moving toward stability would have roughly the same number of people of each age up to about fifty. Several decades later, with population growth actually zero, all age groups except the very old would be approximately the same size. On the particular assumptions used to construct that chart, people under twenty-five would constitute one-third of the population compared to more than 45 percent at present, and the median age would be thirty-eight compared to twenty-eight. The market would thus be far more oriented toward older people and far less toward younger ones than is the case today. Apart from the different marketing strategies this implies, some industries would stand to gain, relatively, and others to lose.

With higher incomes and fewer children, young families could afford to spend more for travel, recreation, adult clothing, and home goods. The businesses that, on the whole, would presumably do worst are those with a kind of fundamental dependence on growth in numbers of people. Purveyors of goods and services for infants, producers of staple foods such as bread, sugar, and canned goods, bottlers of beer and soft drinks, construction, building-supply, and real-estate companies; and manufacturers of such tobacco products as are still being sold—all these could very well be stuck with relatively stagnant markets.

Population stability would also bring with it a somewhat less flexible economy, though it would not necessarily be less efficient. A growing population makes it easier to maintain opportunities for members of all occupations, and for business to make adjustments to changing tastes and technologies. Because markets grow faster, marginal investments are more likely to succeed and obsolete industries to hold on.

Stability is not likely to entail higher production costs. The U.S. market is already large enough to make it possible for most industries to enjoy maximum economies of scale, or it certainly will be by the time population growth levels out. At least one burden would grow, however. Social-security taxes and pension costs are bound to go up as stable population conditions are reached, because of the increase in the ratio of people receiving benefits to those paying.

## Will youth be disserved?

Among the social benefits of population stability would be some reduction in poverty because there would be few large families. And smaller families would make for more education per child. That, in turn, implies a more highly skilled labor force and enhanced ability to innovate or to cope with advanced technology. The less the population grows, the less the need for increases in governmental expenditures in such areas as education, health, recreation, and water supply. Indeed, there would be less need for government regulation or intervention of many kinds. With relatively fewer young people around, there would presumably be less juvenile delinquency. With fewer drivers on the road, control of traffic would be less onerous. With fewer families looking for homes, there would be less pressure to alter the zoning of land.

Some people who have considered the matter maintain that population stability would bring some social disadvantages. Ansley Coale of Princeton has pointed out that when

there are about as many older as younger people, the average
age of those who run things will be greater, and advancement
in business, in politics, or in any other form of organized activity will perforce be slower, a situation that will be frustrating to oncoming generations. Things might not work out quite
that way, however: a relatively smaller demand for the services of young people would be partially balanced by a relatively smaller supply. In general, it may be misleading to
project today's attitudes into tomorrow's world. A changed
population structure would have many interacting consequences that might affect the morale and outlook of both
young people and their elders in ways difficult to foresee. At
any rate, it is not certain that youth would be served any less
well in a stable population than it is now.

The most sweeping attack on population stability comes
from the pen of Alfred Sauvy. This distinguished French demographer's textbook has finally been published in English
(*General Theory of Population,* Basic Books), and may well
play an important role in future debate about population.
Sauvy presents a long catalogue of social, cultural, and economic ailments that France has experienced from early in
the nineteenth century to the present, and he attributes them
largely or exclusively to the virtual stagnation of the population during most of that time. The argument is long and
rich, but cause and effect are scarcely ever conclusively demonstrated, and there is a noticeable absence of the statistical
analysis one might expect. Sauvy's main explanation is that
when population stops growing, society loses a sort of creative pressure that stimulates and adds healthy ferment to
all of its aspects. This sort of generalization is perhaps more
persuasive to French readers than to others, for concern over
slow population growth is widespread in France and has been
of long-standing concern to the government. Surely there are
other reasons for difficulties that the French are bothered
about. Coale likes to point out, for example, that just as the
Industrial Revolution in England was getting under way,
France, under Napoleon, was undertaking a series of ultimately unproductive military adventures.

### *Assigned to motherhood*

A society that wants to stabilize its population runs up against the puzzle of how to go about doing it. One difficulty is that little is known in any systematic way about the psychological and social motivations that impel people to become parents or to have large families. For example, to what degree are decisions to have children consciously arrived at and to what degree are they subconscious? Knowledge about such matters may be an important prerequisite for devising a population policy that would work.

Of course, if Bogue is correct that the U.S. is already moving toward a halt in population growth, there isn't any puzzle to solve. Or if Bumpass and Westoff are correct that the number of children women really want averages out to around 2.5, then perhaps a reasonably uncontroversial program might be able to reduce that number to 2.1 Such a program would include an educational campaign about the long-run consequences of continued population growth; a system for making means of contraception available to all women; elimination of obstacles to abortion; and greatly intensified research efforts to discover more reliable and acceptable contraceptive methods. (At the moment, research is under way on some three dozen or so.) These steps would amount to a broadening and intensification of present family planning. Complete freedom of choice would be left to the individual.

But suppose Bumpass and Westoff are wrong, and people really still want three children? Then intensified family planning, though helpful, would be insufficient. Family planning in the U.S. has traditionally been put forward as a way of widening individual options, not of implementing a population policy. Some claim that family planning is incapable of fulfilling the latter role. The heart of the argument is that what demographers call "pro-natalist" influences are far too strong and deeply embedded to be counteracted solely by voluntary family planning.

Government tax and subsidy policies are at least implicitly pro-natalist. The examples that come to mind most easily are tax exemptions for children and, because of the split-income provision, higher tax rates for single than for married people. FHA and VA assistance to buyers of single-family homes has done a great deal to encourage the growth of all those child-centered suburbs. In many ways, customs and social arrangements operate to favor motherhood—a situation that some women are now vigorously protesting. Many people who advocate smaller families maintain that childbearing cannot be reduced substantially until women have real and satisfying alternatives to motherhood as a primary role. Perhaps nothing would do more to ensure the prevalence of small families than widespread success for the "women's liberation movement."

It will, of course, be somewhat easier to make a go of any limitationist policy once biologists learn just how to predetermine the sex of a child. In the U.S., as well as in other countries, many couples with one or more daughters decide to have additional children in the hope of having a son. However, if choosing the sex of children were to bring an appreciable change in the ratio of male to female births, that would not only enormously complicate population policy, but would also have other far-reaching social consequences.

### A problem never faced before

There is some question whether a government can deliberately curtail a nation's population growth. Official approval apparently contributed to the postwar decline in Japan's population growth, but otherwise there is no direct evidence that government policies work. And the indirect evidence is negative. Some countries have consciously tried *pro*-natalist policies —France for the past thirty years, Germany under Hitler, Italy under Mussolini—with little success.

A great many proposed methods, some of them quite fanciful, have been put forward. Bernard Berelson, president of the Population Council, has listed twenty-nine different proposals to limit population growth apart from family planning. (Some really apply only to underdeveloped countries.) They include adding temporary sterilants—as yet undevised—to water-supply systems; licensing childbearing through permits that could be bought and sold on the open market, raising the legal age of marriage, and, of course, changing the tax system. The difficulty is to devise programs that are both feasible and effective. Measures that rank high on ethics, such as educational campaigns, might not be very effective. Deliberate changes in social institutions might eventually work, but they could have unforeseen side effects and would be hard to bring about.

Everyone who thinks about these matters is groping for answers to a problem that no democratic society has squarely faced before. The root question is how to reconcile long-run collective interest in limiting the growth of population with the desires of those who want to have more than two children. Uncomfortable choices will be involved if at some point society decides that it is desirable to curtail freedom to reproduce in order to preserve other freedoms or to preserve valued amenities.

Until recently almost all Americans took it for granted that the right to have as many children as one wants should not be abridged in any way. The number of people who openly disagree is a lot larger now than it was a few years ago, as is evidenced by the sudden emergence of the Zero Population Growth movement. The right to have children is not absolute, argues Judith Blake Davis, chairman of the department of demography at the University of California. She points out that much of the cost of the satisfaction enjoyed by families with many children is willy-nilly subsidized by others who must pay for the additional schooling and public services. The freedom to have children, she says, does not exist in a vacuum but in a context where the tax laws, the status of women, and various other social arrangements have a pro-natalist bias.

### Symbolic commitment

It seems obvious that any population policy would have to meet certain ethical criteria. It should permit a maximum of individual freedom and diversity. It should not in any way impair the welfare of "extra" children. Also, it should not be used to practice selective coercion against any special group within the population.

The history and ways of Americans suggest that the fiscal

system, which is impersonal and has long been used to accomplish social and economic ends, would come into play early in any effort to limit population growth. For example, there might be some form of bonus for not having more than a specified number of children. Or various kinds of tax disincentives might be enacted.

A proposal along these lines has been introduced in Congress by Senator Robert Packwood of Oregon. The bill would take effect in 1973 and would provide exemptions of $750 each for a family's first two children and none for any subsequent children. (Those born before the effective date of the act would not fall under this limitation, nor would adopted children.) Under tax provisions that were enacted last year and will take full effect in 1973, a family of four will get exemptions of $3,000 and a standard deduction of at least $1,000, so families below the poverty line won't be paying federal taxes anyway. The Packwood bill would therefore have no impact on large families among the poor. Nor would it have much impact on the well-to-do. The effect on people in middle-income brackets is uncertain, and Packwood, among others, suspects it wouldn't be great. "I don't regard a tax incentive per se as a key to population stabilization," he declares. "The important thing is that a tax-incentive bill, if passed, is a government commitment to make an effort to achieve stabilization. It would be symbolic."

Whatever the time or the circumstances, any policy of deliberately limiting population growth should be suffused with respect for the quality of individual life. This view was well expressed by Catherine S. Chilman, dean of the faculty at Hood College, in a paper recently presented at the New York Academy of Sciences. "We must care as a society," she said, "about the fulfillment and well-being of individuals as whole people, not just as potential reproducers . . . While a humane population policy would recognize the need to motivate people to have no or very few children, it would lead from a social and psychological base rather than one that is exclusively material and technological. It would emphasize that there are many ways of being a respected, successful person other than having a large family; that there are many benefits, other than economic ones, alone, to be gained from controlling family size. It would build on and enhance the human need to love, cherish, nurture, and protect."

## Footnote

[1] If this year's Census picked up the number of people thought to have been missed in the Census of 1960, the official figure for 1970 will finally be reported as about 210 million.

# 2. *Population and Environment*
## PAUL R. EHRLICH AND JOHN P. HOLDREN

### *The people problem*

Opposite points of view concerning the relationship in this country between population size and the environment have recently been expressed. According to one view, the United States is one of the most overpopulated countries in the world. That conclusion is based on the enormous stress our affluent population exerts on the environment and on the Earth's store of resources. The other view, espoused by some economists and demographers and at least one prominent biologist, holds that environmental deterioration in the United States is due primarily to the misuse of technology, with population growth having only a minor effect. The implied conclusion is that the current concern with population size and growth rate in the United States is misdirected.

We wish the environmental problem (which is only one of many reasons for halting population growth in the United States) were really this simple, but it is not. Rather, if there is to be any chance of success, we must mount *simultaneous* assaults on many fronts. We must curb extravagant affluence (for example, 300-horsepower automobiles), economic growth for growth's sake (planned obsolescence), the accelerating conversion of resources into waste ("disposable" everything), the application of massive technology toward ill-considered goals (the California water project, the SST), ecologically absurd practices (present fertilizer and pesticide abuses), *and* population growth itself. The contention that it will suffice to attack any one of these areas alone, or any combination not including the last, is naïve and misleading.

We will discuss here three of the fallacious assumptions on which that contention rests.

Assumption I. *A 1 per cent increase in population generates a 1 per cent increase in man's impact on the environment.* The proponents of the "no-population-problem" position are mesmerized by statistics demonstrating that some forms of pollution in the United States have increased by several hundred per cent since 1940, while population has increased only about 55 per cent. Presumably, they would conclude that if population had remained stationary since 1940, pollution would be reduced by "only" 35 per cent from today's level ($55/155 = 35$ per cent). But 35 per cent of the 1970 impact is, in absolute terms, an enormous load on the environment. So, even if Assumption I were correct, it is clear that complacency about the population-pollution relationship is unjustified.

In fact, however, an increment of population growth in today's industrial nations has a highly *magnified* impact on the environment. For example, urban areas tend to expand into adjacent prime agricultural land, ultimately leading to more intensive farming of more remote and less suitable regions. This means increases in *per capita* use of fertilizers and pesticides, and more transportation systems for these manufactured inputs and the produce. Other essentials of existence must be extracted from resources already past the point of diminishing returns. One pertinent example is the disproportionate amount of dollars, energy, and environmental havoc associated with supplying water to an increment of population anywhere in the southwestern United States; others include moving to ever lower grades of mineral ores (chewing up more earth per pound of metal required), and perilously extracting oil from geologically or ecologically unstable regions (the Santa Barbara Channel, Alaska's North Slope).

Simple "thought-experiments" demonstrating the absurdity of Assumption I are also readily devised. Imagine two cities of a million inhabitants each, connected by ten miles of freeway. Suppose a 50 per cent population increase in the area is absorbed in the form of a third city of the same size, ten miles equidistant from each of the other two. If the obvious additional freeways are built, we see that a 50 per cent increase in population has stimulated a 200 per cent increase in freeway mileage. The real world, of course, is more complicated than this.

Assumption II. *Adverse effects of man's activities can be reduced virtually to zero.* Pollution can be said to be the result of multiplying three factors: population size, per capita consumption, and an "environmental impact" index that measures, in part, how wisely we apply the technology that goes with the consumption. The wiser we are, the smaller the index. Those who contend that environmental deterioration is unrelated to population growth can only do so by claiming that this index (and hence the total pollution by a population of any size) can be reduced for all practical purposes to zero. Since this is demonstrably impossible, the case against the importance of population size collapses on this account alone.

To begin with, the ways in which we can reduce our impact (for example, changes in power sources, transport systems, sewage treatment, and the use of fertilizers and pesticides) are far from perfect; most attempts to eliminate pollution really only shift and redistribute it. For instance, the switch from fossil-fueled to nuclear electrical generating plants replaces conventional air pollutants with low-level emissions of radioactivity, and it results in an additional burden of incredibly toxic, concentrated wastes to be disposed of. Similarly, the incinerating of garbage pollutes the air, smog-control additives and devices normally increase some emissions while reducing others, and a return to reusable containers will increase use of polluting detergents. Moreover, there is an ultimate and inescapable pollutant associated with man's activities, for the laws of thermodynamics dictate that all the energy we consume will ultimately be degraded to waste heat. The ecological and climatological consequences of this problem are already important in cities and areas near power plants, and will eventually become globally significant. We emphasize in this connection that the technological control of other forms of pollution has a cost in energy, and the cost increases sharply as one tries to reduce the pollutant concentrations to arbitrarily low levels. Clearly, even if we knew enough about the intricacies of the ecosystem to do everything right (which we do not), a finite impact—proportional to population—would still remain.

Elementary biological considerations lead to the same conclusion. As organisms with needs for food, air, water, and waste disposal, we *must* interact with our environment, and whether these interactions produce unacceptable changes in the biosphere depends on the adequacy of natural systems to buffer them. In other words, pollution is a quantitative as well as a qualitative problem: Having biodegradable effluents will buy us nothing once the capacity of the available "bios" is exhausted. Abundant evidence of malfunction in the world's ecosystems suggests we are already perilously close to that point.

Assumption III. *Of all the possible attacks on pollution, population control will be the slowest to take effect; it should therefore be assigned lowest priority.* Because of the enormous inertia in human attitudes, and because of the high proportion of young people in the United States (the ranks of persons in the reproductive ages will soon swell), it is true that even dramatic advances in population control will be slow to bring the growth rate to zero. But to argue that this means we should defer action on population control is twisted logic at best. Precisely because population control is the slowest and most difficult to yield among the components of environmental deterioration, we must start on it at once and with vigor. Such action need not divert attention from the necessary broadside attack on the symptoms of pollution; we must find the resources and the skills to do both, for any success with the symptoms increases the odds that the ecosystem can endure the lag between initiation and success of measures to stabilize population. But to ignore population control today because the problem is a tough one is to commit ourselves to even gloomier prospects twenty years hence, when most of the "easy" tricks to reduce per capita impact on the environment will have been exhausted. The desperate measures for population control that might be contemplated then are reasons in themselves to proceed with foresight and alacrity today.

## Hidden effects of overpopulation

Several subtle aspects of the relationship between population growth and environmental degradation operate to make man's predicament even more perilous than superficial analyses indicate. Four to be considered here are *synergisms, threshold effects, trigger effects,* and *time-lag effects.*

A *synergism* is the interaction (constructive or destructive) of two or more factors that yield a total effect greater than would occur if the factors operated independently. In colloquial terms, it is a situation in which the whole exceeds the sum of its parts. A suspected synergism in environmental health is the interaction of sulphur dioxide (from coal-burning power plants) and asbestos particles (from automobile brake linings) in inducing lung cancer. The sulphur dioxide interferes with the process by which foreign particles are expelled from the lungs; that, in turn, increases the residence time of the carcinogenic asbestos and hence the chances of contracting the disease. Many other destructive synergisms are known, and one can speculate about even more ominous ones yet to be identified—perhaps an interaction between low-dose radiation and persistent pesticides, which could affect vital components of the ecosystem or man directly.

The connection of such effects to population growth is clear. As populations grow and the associated technologies increase in power and variety, a broadening array of biologically active wastes is distributed in ever more overlapping spheres of influence. Substances that previously rarely came in contact with each other now commonly occur together. Fertilizer residues and oil spills now pollute coastal waters once devoid of either, and pesticides, toxic lead compounds, and man-made radionuclides move simultaneously through important food chains.

A second aspect of the response of environmental systems to the wastes generated by human populations involves *threshold effects.* At levels or rates below a threshold, many sorts of impact are buffered by the environment without adverse effects. Manure is naturally processed into humus by microorganisms in the soil, and organic matter introduced into rivers is decomposed in a similar way. Increases in atmospheric carbon dioxide are partly self-correcting because they stimulate an increase in the rate of carbon dioxide-consuming photosynthesis (and part of any excess is absorbed by the oceans). Unfortunately, such systems are all too easily overloaded—the thresholds can be exceeded—with consequences ranging from nuisance odors to potential climatological disaster.

Perhaps the classic example is the plight of many of the rivers of the developed world, whose capacity to absorb sewage and industrial wastes has long since been exceeded. Although a thousand people may dump their raw sewage into a stream with impunity, ten thousand may hopelessly pollute it; activities that appear entirely innocuous when carried on by a small population may be disastrous for a larger one. We understand only a few natural systems well enough to identify their thresholds quantitatively, but we continue to play the game of growth, a procedure guaranteed to find them all by experiment. The demise of so many of our rivers does not seem to have taught us the lesson; perhaps that of the oceans will.

A related third possibility, usually overlooked by those who insist that the population/environment crisis has been exaggerated, is the *trigger effect,* in which an environmental balance is upset by a relatively small man-made input. A little-known example is the triggering of earthquakes as a result of filling the reservoirs behind large dams—dams that are built to supply the water and power needs of growing populations. The stress associated with the weight of the water impounded by the dam may lead to fault slippage, which releases far more energy than man put in. Hundreds of seismic events, with magnitudes up to 5.0 on the Richter scale, resulted from the filling of Lake Mead in the years 1935–39, and an earthquake of magnitude 6.4, caused by the filling of the Kogna Dam, killed 200 people in India in 1967. Less bizarre and perhaps much more serious trigger effects may intrude wherever the environmental status quo is maintained by opposing forces in balance: in predator-prey relationships that affect the human food supply, in the soil and water conditions that encourage or inhibit the growth of certain viruses and other agents of disease, in the chemical reactions of the upper atmosphere that maintain the Earth's protective screen against ultraviolet radiation.

The difficulties in predicting, identifying, and alleviating any of the phenomena discussed above—synergisms, threshold effects, and trigger effects—are compounded because they may operate in conjunction with a fourth factor: *time delay*. Time delay refers to situations in which causes may precede their effects by years or even decades. This can come about in a number of ways. With many persistent pesticides, the process of concentration consumes time as the substances move from level to level up the food chains. This results in a substantial lag between the original application at low concentration and the appearance of pathological effects high in the food web. For reasons not entirely understood, induction of various forms of cancer by exposure to radiation is characterized by "latency periods" ranging up to thirty years. Particulate pollution, more than 50 per cent of it dust from agricultural activities, is cooling the Earth and bringing on climatic changes. The full consequences of this trend may not be apparent for decades or longer.

Many other conditions associated with man's environmental meddling are also characterized by dormant stages preceding the appearance of identifiable symptoms (e.g., certain parasitic diseases and genetic effects associated with various chemical pollutants). Usually such a time lag means that when the symptoms finally appear, corrective action is ineffective or impossible. If *all* use of persistent pesticides were stopped tomorrow, the concentrations of these substances in many critical organisms—and the associated damage—would continue to increase for some years to come.

Consideration of the four classes of phenomena discussed here—synergisms, threshold effects, trigger effects, and time-delay effects—suggests that population growth today is committing us to a degree of environmental degradation not yet fully apparent.

*Deceptive birth rates*

Informed demographers and ecologists have recently been surprised to see the end of the population explosion celebrated in a spate of newspaper editorials and columns. Headlines such as FALSE PROPHETS OF DOOM, ridiculing those scientists concerned about population problems, have greeted readers across the nation. The stimulus for this outpouring has been preliminary reports of the 1970 census, projecting an increase in the American population of "as little as" 75 million people by the year 2000. We do not quarrel with these figures themselves; the census has only reinforced conclusions accepted in the demographic literature for several years. But it is difficult for us to understand how a population increase of some 35 per cent in an already overpopulated country can be regarded as the conclusion of the population explosion, especially when the demographic situation contains the potential for substantial additional growth in the next century. The optimists should note that even if the reproductive rate drops to the replacement level by 1980, the population of the United States will level off at more than 300 million in 2045. If we should not reach the replacement level until the year 2000, population growth will stop in 2065, with a final population size of more than 350 million people.

The replacement level would correspond to each female infant born today ultimately producing, on average, one female offspring (that is, replacing herself). Reaching this situation, defined by demographers as NRR (Net Reproductive Rate) $=1.0$, would not lead to zero population growth (ZPG) at once, because of persons still living who were born when the NRR exceeded 1.0. It will take sixty-five to seventy years (roughly the life expectancy) following the achievement of replacement reproduction to reach ZPG in the United States. The ballyhoo about the end of the population explosion notwithstanding, we have not yet even reached NRR $=1.0$ (the 1967 figure was 1.213). Moreover, if the NRR reaches unity, there is no guarantee that it will remain there.

Much attention in the press has been focused on the birth rate, at best, a crude index of fertility and an incomplete indicator of the demographic situation. The difference between the birth rate (number of people being born per thousand people in the population per year) and the death rate (number per thousand dying) gives the natural rate of increase for that year. Adding migration to the calculation gives the overall growth rate. Some demographers, who should know better, compound the public's confusion both by continuing to focus attention on the birth rate alone and by erroneously stating that it is now at an all-time low. The fact is the *Monthly Vital Statistics Reports* of the U.S. Public Health Service show a bottoming of the birth rate in late 1968 or early 1969, and a subsequent and continuing increase. This came as no surprise to those familiar with the age structure of the population (the relative numbers of people in different age groups). Specifically, the low birth rates of the middle 1960s were due in part to the small number of women in the reproductive years. They were the scarce wartime babies. Now the abundant World War II boom babies have grown into women who are moving into their peak reproductive years. This age-structure effect is causing a predictable rise in the birth rate. In view of the disconcerting lack of public awareness regarding these matters, one can draw three conclusions: It is irresponsible for any demographer to mislead the public about the present birth rates; it is unprofessional to discuss birth rates outside the context of the age structure; it is inexcusable to omit from the discussion the all-important relationship between birth rate and death rate in determining the growth rate.

At the "all-time" low birth rate, the U.S. population was growing at about 1 per cent per year, with 80 per cent of the growth contributed by the difference between birth and death rates, and 20 per cent by immigration. This "slow" growth rate, if continued, would double the population in about seventy years. A little elementary arithmetic shows that such a rate is unsustainable for any considerable period, even if ecological and social factors are ignored. But, of course, these factors cannot be ignored. Most of our environmental problems and many of our social problems have been and will continue to be exacerbated by population growth. That a 50 per cent increase in population will stimulate a disproportionate deterioration in many of these problem areas adds to the urgency of moving rapidly to zero population growth and, ultimately, to a declining population size.

The "responsible, orderly approach" to NRR=1 advocated by many conservative demographers and sociologists in fact consists of a go-slow program that condemns us to perhaps another century of population growth, as should be apparent from the above discussion relating NRR and ZPG. This attitude is defended by references to relatively easily managed social problems arising from seeking a stable population, and by a naïve underestimation of problems in resources and environment. If these individuals are successful in preventing our society and others from taking enlightened voluntary steps toward population control, the most likely outcome is that population will be "controlled" automatically by a massive rise in the death rate brought about by war, plague, famine, ecosystem collapse, or some combination of these. Alternatively, by delaying intelligent steps now, the go-slow contingent increases the chances that governments awakening too late will institute repressive, racist, or otherwise socially repugnant measures.

To prevent such outcomes, we should press by all acceptable means to reduce the NRR *below* 1.0 as soon as possible, in the hope of achieving ZPG by the end of the century. Those journalists who describe us in this advocacy as "prophets of doom" would do well to learn enough elementary ecology and demography to be able to discriminate prophets of doom from those working to avoid it.

# 3. Zero Population Growth: What Is It?

## FRANK NOTESTEIN

Zero population growth, as platitude, sales slogan or urgent goal, has caught the public by storm—and included in that public are many biologists and economists, as well as a considerable number of sociologists and demographers.

From one point of view, favoring zero population growth is somewhat like favoring the laws of motion. Anyone who knows how to use a table of logarithms must be aware that in the long run the average rate of population growth will approach zero as a limit. If, for example, the world's population had grown at its present rate since the beginning of the Christian era, the water content of the human race would fill a sphere having a radius more than ten times that of the earth. Zero growth is, then, not simply a desirable goal, it is the only possibility in a finite world. One cannot object to people who favor the inevitable.

There is another group that values zero population growth because it is a powerful sales slogan. They are willing to accept—even to promote—the slogan despite its ambiguity, because of the energy and resources it brings to the subject of population. Some of these supporters foster the popular impression that population growth could be stopped quickly by acceptable means if only the public were alerted to the dangers of the situation; and a few of them advance this line despite their private opinions to the contrary. They justify this lack of candor on the grounds that egregious overstatement is necessary to arouse public interest. They seem to feel that it takes massive advertising to sell both soap and the ecological necessity for a prompt end to population growth.

With that I am inclined to agree. But it is a sad day when we see professionally expert distortions of the truth peddled to the public under the highest scientific auspices, as if truth can be fostered best by untruth. When scientists become concerned with reform, as I think duty indeed requires, they will at their peril abandon the ardent respect for truth that lies at the basis of their professions. It is hard enough to stick to the truth when one tries. Fortunately, this huckstering group is only a small part of those who see zero population growth as a slogan that arouses interest in objectives perceived to be both timely and important. To this there can be no objection. It is our obligation to stick to the truth, but we are not compelled to be dull about it.

Many of its most earnest advocates obviously see zero population growth as more than a slogan, and more than a platitude about long-run objectives. They want, or at least some of them want, zero growth, if not yesterday, at least now. They want it moreover, if not on any terms, at least with the sense of urgency that makes them willing to accept many second and third order effects without careful examination. It is to these questions that we must turn our most careful attention. This means that we must ask with what urgency it is necessary to seek zero growth under varying circumstances. What are the advantages and disadvantages of attaining the goal with varying speeds, and what are the advantages and disadvantages of using various methods for its attainment? The assessment of the means is quite as important as the assessment of the goal.

There may be different answers for the technologically more developed and less developed countries, because of differences in the severity of the problem as well as differences in the availability of means for their solution. Let us consider first the problem in developed countries, and particularly the United States.

### ZPG in the developed regions

Here the ecologists take the hardest line. Some of them seem to be saying that we now stand in mortal danger if our population continues to grow; indeed, that we already have too much population and should start reducing the size. On matters of resources, energy and ecology I am outside of my professional field, but I have read some and listened more and find these ecologists' case wholly unpersuasive. There are no substantial limits in sight either in raw materials or in energy that alterations in the price structures, product substitution, anticipated gains in technology and pollution control cannot be expected to solve.\* Subject to one condition, my statement seems to be in agreement with the overwhelming weight of professional opinion. The limitation arises from the fact that on the side of resources and technology we can only look ahead about a generation in terms of specific technology and known raw materials. Obviously our human interests run much farther into the future; but we cannot spell out the nature of a technology not yet developed. One can, however, on the assumption of an ordered world, reasonably predict immensely powerful developments based on cheap and virtually unlimited energy, and, thanks partly to that, on an enormously expanded availability of conventional and new raw materials.

Much of the pessimistic argument is based on the idea that there are non-renewable resources in our finite world. This seems to me to miss the point. Basically resources are not material; they are socially defined. Coal did not become a resource until a few centuries ago. It is barely one hundred years since petroleum had any but medical and magical uses. Nuclear energy is only beginning to become a resource although it has almost unlimited prospects. We talk of diminishing returns with non-renewable resources, but so far as I

---

\* The very extensive literature is summarized in a nutshell by R. Philip Hammond in a letter to *Science*, 167:1439, 1970, reading in part as follows: "Even 20 x $10^9$ people, each producing 20 kilowatts of heat (twice the U.S. average), would add only 1/300 of the present atmospheric heat load. This would raise the average temperature of the earth by about $0.25°$ . . . At an energy budget of 20 kilowatts per person, we could maintain a worldwide living standard near the present U.S. level even when we have exhausted our high-grade mineral resources. We could do this without placing an impossible heat load on the earth for a very large population, but not for an 'unlimited' one."

know almost all materials usually put in that category have declined in relative worth. Even with modern machinery it no longer pays to clear land in the United States. Indeed, land has never been so abundant. The fact is that basically we have only one non-renewable resource, and that is space. Otherwise mankind's basic resources are knowledge and skill, mainly of the organizational kind.

Nor do I share in that ocean of guilt now flooding the literature because our small fraction of the world's population consumes the lion's share of the world's resources. I hope our share becomes smaller as others gain, but I do not want a reduction of our per capita consumption. Thanks, indeed, to the high consumption of the developed world we have generated the knowledge and techniques that have greatly expanded both the supplies and the reserves of such raw materials in the world. There has often been outrageous waste but, on balance, our heavy use is expanding the world's resources, not diminishing them. We can get into intricate discussions about whether the more developed regions have paid enough for the raw materials they have purchased from the less developed regions,* but we cannot fail to see that substantial reductions of our purchases from those regions would bring them to economic chaos and greatly retard their development. Our sin is not use. Instead, it is the failure to pay the costs of use by avoiding pollution and by recycling minerals instead of further degrading them. I think it is time that social scientists look at resources in the same dynamic terms with which they have become accustomed recently to study population.

If we consider the evidence, not just the inchoate fears, there is not the slightest indication that per capita income in the United States would be consequentially different if we had 50 or 100 million more people than we have, or 50 or 100 million fewer people. At present, the costs of both energy and raw materials represent such a small proportion of

---

* By more developed regions, I mean Europe, the Soviet Union, Japan, Northern America, temperate South America, Australia and New Zealand. The remainder of the world comprises the less developed regions.

our total costs that they could be drastically increased with a negligible effect on per capita income.

Moreover, the current excitement about the size of population as a cause of pollution is almost completely without merit, save in the sense that there can be no pollution without polluters. That there is severe pollution is all too evident; but it is equally evident that pollution is related almost exclusively to mismanagement and to our high standard of living. It is related negligibly to our numbers. If we had half the population and the same per capita income, we would have much the same kind of urban concentration, and much the same local pollution. Australia is sparsely populated but has 80 percent of its people concentrated in huge cities, and has much the same kind of smog and other pollution as do we.

Moreover, it is silly to suggest that reductions in population would drastically help in attacking pollution while we continue to raise our per capita incomes. There has been a vast increase in use of electricity in this country since World War II—a fact which has worried those concerned with heat and air pollution. But if we wished to achieve the per capita use of electricity of 1960 without increasing the total produced above the 1940 level we would need to reduce our U.S. population below 25 million. Pollution control of all kinds will involve social and economic changes of considerable magnitude, but manipulation of the numbers of people in the society to solve this problem is probably not a realistically open option.

Nor, incidentally, does the exhortation that people should stop aspiring to lift their standards of living come gracefully from college professors, already sitting comfortably in the top ten percent of the income distribution of the richest nation on earth. I doubt that we members of the international jet set will be very effective in telling others that they should not aspire to live half as well as we do lest pollution destroy our narrowly balanced ecology.

In political terms, relating pollution to population may have done harm to a serious attack on both pollution and on population growth. It weakens interest in the present by concentrating on a distant goal. The effective approach to pollution is to make the polluters pay, and to start doing so as soon as possible. This will cost all of us money, for we are all polluters. We also need research on a vastly increased scale. That, too, is expensive. Particularly, we need research in ecology. It is time for some solid information to replace the bad dreams of the enthusiasts, their yearnings for traditional biological equilibria and their reasoning by analogy. It is a distraction from an immediate attack on pollution to concentrate attention on the importance of stopping population growth in, say, 20, 30 or 50 years. Similarly, it is a distraction from legitimate concern for the nation's population policy to base the attack on ecological ghost stories instead of the actual inhumanities of our reproductive process. The present population-pollution axis, by raising false issues, deters rather than helps realistic and urgently needed efforts in both fields.

### We don't need more people

My own interest in speeding the end of population growth in the United States is based on much less urgent problems than the constraints of dwindling resources and energy or the risk of insoluble ecological problems. It is clear that growth must stop sometime, both here and in the world as a whole. It does not seem that we are likely to grow in national effectiveness by virtue of increasing numbers. At least I have difficulties thinking of any national need for which we do not have enough population to provide the economies of large scale production. On esthetic grounds it seems to me that we should avoid becoming a highly crowded nation. Europe is much more densely settled, but we are a more mobile people and more space will almost certainly add to our enjoyment. I would like to come to zero population growth, but with no great haste and without making important sacrifices in the process of accomplishing it.

It is also clear that some costs will be entailed if we come to an end of growth. I shall not detail them, because they are well set out in the pre-war literature on stagnation. I doubt that the costs of stopping growth will be nearly as high as then envisioned. Much has since been learned about managing the level of economic activity. But some adjustments will have to be made. Our entire economy has developed in a period of population growth with the relatively young populations that high birth rates produce. Nevertheless, this is an adjustment that must be made sometime unless we start lifting the death rates of the oldsters drastically—a proposal with which I have an understandable lack of sympathy. In short, I would like to see population growth come to a gradual end in the United States. But my lack of a sense of great urgency makes me unwilling to accept drastic means such as those often proposed by the people to whom the problems of energy, resources and ecological protection have high saliency.

I would be happy if, for example, we could reach replacement level of reproduction in 10 or 15 years and stay there until the end of the century. After that I would have no objection to an intrinsic rate of natural decrease of a quarter of one percent for a time. If we did this we would still come to a maximum population of something like 300 millions in some 70 to 90 years. These to me are acceptable goals as to numbers. They are not very important, however, compared to the means for their attainment.

The rates of population change and the factors determining them are very much more important than the *size* of the population. Family planning represents a new and important freedom in the world. It will surely be a happy day when parents can have and can avoid having children, as they see fit. We are coming close to realization of that goal—a goal that has given new dignity and new importance to the individual. We have not yet arrived at it. Bumpass and Westoff[1] have shown that the proportion of unwanted births was substantial in the first half of the 1960s. It was very much higher in the lower educational groups, in the lower income groups and, partly as a consequence of this, among Negroes. It is a matter of major importance that this kind of new freedom to choose, now existing for the bulk of the population, should be extended to its most disadvantaged parts. If it were extended, reproduction would be brought fairly close to the replacement level. However, I would advocate the right to choose even if I thought the demographic consequences would be highly adverse, because it will always remain possible to manipulate the environment in which the choice is made.

I happen also to favor the repeal of laws against abortion in the belief that parents should control the destiny of the non-viable products of their bodies. I do not favor it on demographic grounds, and hope that when abortion becomes legal no one will advocate it as anything but the personal tragedy which it inevitably is. One may expect, however, that easy abortion will further reduce the birth rate.

It is not at all beyond belief that, with contraceptives of ever increasing efficiency and legal abortion, fertility may fall below the replacement level. And, of course, it also may not. But, lacking a sense of urgency in matters of population size and believing in the importance of voluntary parenthood as a human freedom, I hope we do not accept drastic proposals to reward or penalize reproduction. We should wait at least until all of the population has ready access to effective contraception, and we can see under these conditions how the trend is going.

It seems to me dangerous to endeavor to penalize reproduction by various economic constraints because almost certainly the political process would result in maximum pressures on the most defenseless sectors of the population. There is too often willingness on the part of the bulk of the population to blame its troubles on the poor and ignorant minorities. But economic sanctions taken against the poor to compel a reduction of fertility seldom work. Generally, fertility does not fall in response to the lash of poverty. The most fertile sectors of the population will reduce their fertility with maximum speed if they can have easy access to competent contraception and the kind of support that brings them into the mainstream of the economy and society. At least in the present temper of the times, I would rather accept growth than step up the constraints which we have reason to expect would fall most heavily on the poor and their children.

It must also be recognized that the actual adoption of drastic programs designed to restrict fertility would, if they were successful, contain the seeds of their early reversal. If we could imagine a program that would drop the crude birth rate to the crude death rate in five years, we would have, as Frejka[2] has shown, to imagine a net reproduction rate of less than 0.6—not a two-child, but a one-child family—which if maintained for a few years would evoke the specter of rapid population decline, cries of race suicide and a turn-about. It is to be noted that no nation, however heavily populated and poor, has adopted a policy for population decline. At best they want to bring the rates of growth down to two or even one percent, and just possibly to become stationary in the long run. It is interesting to note that Japan is already talking of the dangers of slow growth, that Rumania repealed its liberal abortion law because of plummeting birth rates, and that in Hong Kong one hears a great deal of talk about a labor shortage. Quickly successful policies of a drastic nature would certainly contain the seeds of their own reversal. I think there is every reason to believe that the quick way to a stationary population is the gentle one, both in action and in propaganda. And herein lies the weakness of the hucksters. Their line is successful until people realize that they have been misled. Then even sensible discussion suffers, for people once burned are twice cautious.

## ZPG and the less developed regions

The situation of that two-thirds of the world's population living in the less developed regions contrasts sharply with that of the United States. In general, in the less developed regions the economy rests heavily on subsistence agriculture and other extractive industries; per capita income and literacy are very low, birth rates are very high and death rates range from the world's highest to the world's lowest, as does the density of population. Rates of growth vary from a little under two percent to well over three percent. Moreover, where the increase is relatively low, as in parts of Africa, it is clear that it will rise as soon as rudimentary health protection can be introduced.

It is evident that most of these populations are already too large to rise from poverty on the basis of a traditional subsistence agriculture. Their only hope of achieving reasonable per capita incomes, literacy and health lies in the modernization of their economies. Such modernization entails heavy investment in productive equipment, transport, education and health. Rapid progress in this direction is considerably deterred by the necessity of meeting the costs of rapid population growth at the same time. Indeed, I think that there is grave danger that population growth will so retard economic transformation and the improvement of living conditions that there will be a breakdown of civil order in a number of large countries. This risk gravely threatens the lives of tens, perhaps scores, of millions of people.

It seems difficult to exaggerate the importance of reducing the rate of population growth as soon as possible throughout most of the less developed regions. Indeed, even the areas now viewed as too sparsely populated might well benefit from the reduction of the rate of increase. In these circumstances, wisdom may enjoin favoring development at the expense of population growth where possible. This is not the place to discuss the issue, but it is my impression that there are extremely few places in the less developed regions that would not be aided in their struggle for modernization by a slower rate of population growth.

From my point of view, then, the need for slowing population growth is vastly greater in the less developed than in the more developed regions. A rapid decline of fertility for some decades until there is even a small negative rate of increase would be desirable. But zero growth, as a meaningful proposal in the near term, is idle talk. It could only be achieved by a rise in the death rate, which no one will accept as a goal of policy for his own people. During the next century, for theoretical purposes, zero growth is not low enough and, for practical purposes, it is too low. Although the problems of the less developed regions are much greater, unfortunately the opportunities for relevant action are far fewer than in the rest of the world.

A rather large and growing number of countries in the less developed regions have national policies designed to foster the reduction of the birth rate and thereby a slowing of population growth. But even in these countries there would be minimal support for zero population growth. Policies in support of family planning have been widely adopted because the provision of services to the citizens who want them entails few political risks, and much of the top leadership realizes that the unprecedented speed of growth is blocking efforts at development. It is one thing to favor a reduction of the pace of population increase, and another thing to ask for a complete stop. When one begins to talk about growth rates less than one percent, attention quickly shifts to the rate of growth of the traditional enemy or rival. Israel's victories in the Six-Day War did much to devalue large populations as a source of power; but the rivalry of numbers remains. It is possible that, among small countries, Hong Kong and Singapore would be content to stop growing fairly soon; and, among large countries, India and Pakistan might accept the idea at the level of top leadership. I can think of no other countries where this position would be accepted. Even where leadership agreed on the long-run objective, it would almost certainly wish not to advertise that fact, because more limited objectives would be expected to attract more widespread political support and serve program needs as well.

A number of scholars have been critical of people of my persuasion who advocate voluntarism through family planning as a means of slowing population growth and who have concentrated efforts on contraceptive methods, information and service. They hold that since the difficulty lies in the lack of motivation for restriction, it makes little sense to concentrate on the means while failing to strengthen the motives.

Naturally, I think that my approach represents the first and most effective step in strengthening the motivation for fertility restriction. Obviously, there are large numbers of people who are behaving in the traditional manner, governed by the values of the traditional society. But the number is larger in the minds of the leadership than it is in reality. Surveys, trials and national experiences show that major proportions—often, indeed, a heavy majority—of the population expresses an interest in limiting their fertility. To be sure, they generally want more children than are needed to maintain a stationary population. To be sure also, many aspects of their society still foster the ideal of the large family. I am aware that values influence behavior, but I am also aware that behavior influences values. It seems to me that the example of successful fertility limitation set by those now motivated is probably the most effective means of fostering both new values and innovative behavior. Moreover, I am greatly impressed by the speed with which the restrictive behavior has spread where family planning programs have been skillfully introduced.

I am happier than the critics with the progress that has been made, possibly for two reasons. On the one hand, I view the ultimate constraints to population growth as less narrowly drawn than they do. On the other hand, in the light of the situation a decade ago, I think there has been great and accelerating progress. By contrast, I am much less hopeful than are the critics of voluntarism about the feasibility of using more drastic measures to lift incentives for the restriction of fertility. The leadership would accept them in very few countries. Indeed, even in many of the countries having policies to foster family planning, the opposition in influential parts of the leadership group remains substantial—more substantial, I think, than among the people. In the near term more drastic means will be entirely unacceptable almost everywhere.

In the less developed regions, moreover, it would, simply for administrative reasons, be impossible to introduce even such measures as fiscal sanctions and rewards. Even now, weak administration is proving more of an obstacle to the spread of family planning than lack of public interest. Almost all of the governments are far too poor and weak to carry out a drastic program. Few of them can even count the number of their births and deaths, or have more than rudimentary medical services and facilities, or social security systems. It is hard to remember how poor they are. Canada, for example, with some 21 million people, has a larger national income and federal budget than the Government of India with more than 500 million people. It is at best idle to talk of governments in this position drastically coercing their people's reproductive behavior. They are governments that can do something to educate and lead, but, save in the most primitive matters of public order, they cannot coerce.

The inability to coerce is perhaps fortunate in this field. I think we have reason to believe that voluntarism through education and service is the most direct route, as it is certainly the most civilized.

My own reaction to zero population growth, therefore, comes out about the same way for the less developed regions as for the more developed regions. The countries that could apply drastic constraints to human fertility do not need to; the countries that need drastic constraints cannot apply them; and in any case, the path of voluntarism through family planning is likely to be both more efficient and civilized.

If zero population growth means the down-grading of voluntarism and the strident demand for a quick end to population growth, then it will do more harm than good. If on the other hand it is taken as an organizing focus for research and educational efforts concerning the importance of a worldwide trend to a stationary population and the means by which it is ultimately to be achieved, then it should be enthusiastically welcomed.

## References

1. L. Bumpass and C. F. Westoff, "The 'Perfect Contraceptive' Population: Extent and Implications of Unwanted Fertility in the U.S.," *Science.*
2. T. Frejka, "Reflections on the Demographic Conditions Needed to Establish a U.S. Stationary Population Growth," *Population Studies,* 22:379, 1968.

# 4. *The End of the Population Explosion*
## DONALD J. BOGUE

Recent developments in the worldwide movement to bring runaway birth rates under control are such that it now is possible to assert with considerable confidence that the prospects for success are excellent. In fact, it is quite reasonable to assume that *the world population crisis is a phenomenon of the 20th century, and will be largely if not entirely a matter of history when humanity moves into the 21st century*. No doubt there will still be problematic areas in the year 2000, but they will be confined to a few nations that were too prejudiced, too bureaucratic, or too disorganized to take action sooner, or will be confined to small regions within some nations where particular ethnic, economic, or religious groups will not yet have received adequate fertility control services and information. With the exception of such isolated remnants (which may be neutralized by other areas of growth-at-less-than-replacement), it is probable that by the year 2000 each of the major world regions will have a population growth rate that either is zero or is easily within the capacity of its expanding economy to support.

The implications of these assertions for the feeding of the human race are obvious. Given the present capacity of the earth for food production, and the potential for additional food production if modern technology were more fully employed, mankind clearly has within its grasp the capacity to abolish hunger—within a matter of a decade or two. Furthermore, it is doubtful whether a total net food shortage for the entire earth will ever develop. If such a deficit does develop, it will be mild and only of short duration. The really critical problem will continue to be one of maldistribution of food among the world's regions.

These optimistic assertions are not intended to detract from the seriousness of the present population situation. Some years of acute crisis lie immediately ahead for India, China, the Philippines, Indonesia, Pakistan, Mexico, Brazil, Egypt, and other nations. Severe famines quite probably will develop within local areas of some of these nations unless emergency international measures are taken. My purpose here is to emphasize that the engineers and the agricultural technicians striving to increase the output of material goods in these nations are not working alone. Paralleling their activity is a very ambitious international fertility control program which is just starting to "pay off."

These remarks are certainly not intended to cause the participants in this international fertility control program to relax their efforts and be lulled into complacency. The successful outcome anticipated above is not one that will come automatically, but only as a result of a continued all-out "crash program" to make the widest and most intensive use of the medical, sociological and psychological knowledge now available, and of the practical experience that has recently emerged from experimental family planning programs. It also anticipates a continued flow of new research findings and enriched practical experience that is promptly fed back into programs of fertility reduction.

This view is at variance with the established view of many population experts. For more than a century, demographers have terrorized themselves, each other, and the public at large with the essential hopelessness and inevitability of the "population explosion." Their prophecies have all been dependent upon one premise: "If recent trends continue. . . ." It is an ancient statistical fallacy to perform extrapolations upon this premise when in fact the premise is invalid. It is my major point that *recent trends have not continued, nor will they be likely to do so*. Instead, there have been some new and recent developments that make it plausible to expect a much more rapid pace in fertility control. These developments are so new and so novel that *population trends before 1960 are largely irrelevant in predicting what will happen in the future.*

In times of social revolution, it often is fruitless to forecast the future on the basis of past experience. Instead, it is better to abandon time series analysis and study the phenomenon of change itself, seeking to understand it and to learn in which direction and how rapidly it is moving. If enough can be learned about the social movement that is bringing about the change, there is a hope that its eventual outcome can be roughly predicted. This procedure is followed here. The result is subjective and crude, but I believe it to be nearer the future course of demographic history than the official population projections now on record.

## II

Limitations of space permit only a listing of major social developments which, in my view, justify the relatively optimistic prospect I have set forth.

1. Grass roots approval. All over the world, wherever surveys of the attitudes of the public with respect to fertility have been taken, it has uniformly been found that a majority of couples with three living children wish to have no more. Of these, a very large proportion approve of family planning in principle and declare they would like to have more information about it. They also approve of nationwide health service that includes family planning. In other words, active objections among the masses on cultural, moral, or religious grounds are minor rather than major obstacles. This is true both in Asia and Latin America, and seems to be developing rapidly in Africa. Thus, at the "grass roots" level, the attitudinal and cultural conditions are highly favorable. Previously, it had been feared that traditionalism and religious attitudes would prove to be almost insuperable blocks to rapid fertility control. But the more sociologists study the situation, the more they accept as correct the generalization that, in most places where there is a population problem, the attitude toward family planning among the mass of the people is strongly positive.

2. Aroused political leadership. Whereas fertility control was regarded as a subversive, immoral, and sinful program during the 150 years of fertility decline in Europe and the

United States, in the nations with a population problem today the national political leadership openly accepts family planning as a moral and rational solution. Heads of state in India, Pakistan, Korea, China, Egypt, Chile, Turkey, and Colombia, for example, have made fertility control an integral part of the national plan for economic development. In this, they have followed the lead of Japan. The national ministers of health and welfare not only are permitted but are expected to provide family planning services. National health services are adding family planning to their clinic services, financed by public tax funds. The mass media are increasingly carrying official endorsements, public encouragements, and specific information.

3. Accelerated professional and research activity. Professional groups in the developing countries (as well as in the rest of the world) are rapidly losing whatever antipathy or prejudice against family planning they may have had. Everywhere, the medical profession is rapidly giving it a solid endorsement—even in nations where there have been problems of religious objection. Within religious groups where there formerly was a hard inflexible prohibition against the use of chemical or mechanical contraceptive appliances, there is now a great deal of difference of opinion. Gradually, the laity is reaching the belief that the control of natality is a matter for the individual conscience, or a medical matter to be discussed with a physician—but not with the priest. Physicians and priests alike tend to accept this interpretation without forthright challenge.

Universities, both in the United States and abroad, have undertaken large-scale and sustained research activities in the fields of family planning. Their activities cover the entire range of topics—medical, sociological, and psychological. Most of the nations with a national family planning program are sponsoring research into the problem. This includes not only projects to discover new and improved ways of promoting fertility control, but also the evaluation of present programs. These activities are not amorphous, but within a remarkably short time have been coordinated. The process of integration was greatly facilitated by the holding in Geneva in 1965 of an International Conference on Family Planning Programs.

Much of the credit for the development described above is due to the activities of not-for-profit organizations that have taken population control as a focus of their activities: the Ford Foundation, Rockefeller Foundation, Population Council, and International Planned Parenthood are the leaders. The Swedish Government, the Milbank Memorial Fund, the Planned Parenthood Association of America, and the Pathfinder Fund have also been highly important sponsors of these activities. These organizations have provided unprecedented financial and technical support.

4. The slackening of progress in death control. Immediately after World War II, the industrialized nations of the world realized that there was a series of public health and medical programs that could be accomplished quickly and cheaply to bring about a reduction in mortality. These have now been largely carried out—there have been campaigns against malaria, smallpox, cholera, yellow fever, and other diseases that can be brought under control with an injection, a semiannual house spraying, etc. The results have been dramatic, and death rates have tumbled. However, further progress in death control will be slower, because the remaining problems are those for which a solution is more difficult or is as yet unknown. For example, the death rate in Latin America stands at about 14 per thousand now. Modern medicine could bring it, at best, only to about 8 per thousand—a fall of 6 points. But a very much greater investment must be made, and over a considerably longer span of time, to achieve these 6 points than was required to obtain the preceding six points. In Asia the death rate still stands at about 20, even after the advent of the "miracle drugs" and the mass-inoculation and mass-treatment programs. It may be expected to drift lower, but at a slower pace than before.

This slackening of death control has a most important implication—a decline in the birth rate would be more directly reflected in a decline in the rate of population growth. During the past two decades, even if birth rates were declining, death rates were declining still faster, so that the population growth rate increased. That trend now appears to be reaching the end of a cycle: the cycle appears to be on the verge of reversing itself.

5. A variety of sociological and psychological phenomena, previously unknown or underappreciated, are promoting the rapid adoption of family planning by the mass of the people. Here we can only list them, without explanation:

a. Privation is itself a powerful motivating force for fertility control.

b. Private communication about family planning is far greater than had been thought, and can easily be stimulated to attain flood proportions.

c. "Opinion leaders"—indigenous men and women who are knowledgeable about birth control and freely undertake to influence others to adopt it—can be mass-produced cheaply and very rapidly by means of mass media and other action programs. Thus, in this area just as in economic development, there is a "multiplier effect" which, if capitalized upon, can greatly hasten "takeoff" into rapidly declining fertility.

d. It is becoming evident that fathers are very nearly equally as interested and responsible in controlling fertility as are wives. Programs aimed at couples, instead of at females, are highly effective.

e. We are discovering that illiterate rural populations will make use of the traditional methods of family planning—condom, suppositories, etc.—very nearly as readily as urban populations, after a brief period of information and trial. They will also adopt the newer methods as—or even more—readily.

6. Improved technology in contraception promotes massive adoption by uneducated people at a rapid pace. Oral contraceptives and the intra-uterine devices have both proved to be highly acceptable after only short periods of instruction and familiarity. Even illiterate rural villagers make sustained use of these methods where they have been given unprejudiced trial. These developments are only half-a-decade old, but they already have had a profound impact upon fertility control programs and plans. As yet there is still a great deal of prejudice against the oral compounds in Asia, so that the advantages of a two-method assault have not been fully realized there. In Latin American experiments, where the "pills" and intra-uterine devices are used side-by-side as alternative methods, the results are highly impressive.

We are repeatedly being told by the physiologists, however, that our so-called "modern" methods of contraception are crude and barbarous—each with unpleasant side-effects and unsuitable for as much as one quarter of the population. They insist that much superior methods are on the horizon—that soon there will be dramatic improvements, that costs will be cheaper, and that the need for "sustained motivation" to practice contraception will be greatly reduced. Millions of dollars are being poured into experimental research on this front each year. This activity is taking place both in the public and the private sector. The giants of the drug industry know that huge markets can be gained by improving upon present contraceptive technology—and that huge markets will be lost if a competitor discovers and markets a superior product. As a result, all of the leading motives that bring about frenzied activity for progress among scientists have been harnessed and are at work in behalf of improving contraceptive technology—prestige, economic gain, anxiety, compassion.

## III

In order to illustrate the above points, let us take as an example the recent experience of Korea. In 1962, the Republic of Korea formally adopted family planning as one of its national policies. In 1965, a National Survey of Family Planning was conducted. Following are some points from that survey.

1. Eighty-nine percent of the wives and 79 percent of the husbands approved of family planning.
2. The rate of approval was only slightly lower in the rural than in the urban areas (88 percent for rural women and 77 percent for rural men).
3. Of the minority who disapproved, only 8 percent mentioned religion or morals. Traditional resistance was as low in rural as in urban areas.
4. Inability to read was no barrier; 81 percent of those unable to read nevertheless approved of family planning.
5. On the verbal level, the population declared itself willing to practice family planning if given services. Seventy-seven percent of the urban women and 71 percent of the rural

women made such a declaration. Among husbands, 71 percent of the urban and 65 percent of the rural made such a declaration.

6. Unwillingness to practice family planning was concentrated primarily among young couples who had not yet had the number of children they desired and older couples (past 40 years of age) who were approaching the end of their childbearing. Couples in the years of prime importance for birth control, 25–40, were most positive in their attitudes. Moreover, the greater the number of living children, the greater the willingness to practice.

7. As a result of the national information program, 85 percent of the urban and 83 percent of the rural population had heard of family planning. Moreover, 67 percent of the urban and 64 percent of the rural population had knowledge of at least one contraceptive method. Even among the illiterate, 51 percent knew of one method or more. Knowledge of the more reliable methods—oral pill, IUCD, condom—was only very slightly less widespread in rural than in urban areas.

8. At the time of the interview, 21 percent of the urban and 14 percent of the rural couples were practicing family planning. Even among the illiterate population, 10 percent were currently practicing family planning. Although small, these percentages very obviously have sprung from a condition of near-zero within a span of three years. If only 2 percent are added each year, within 35 years population growth would be near zero.

9. The methods used by rural families were equal to or superior to those of the urban population in terms of reliability:

|  | PERCENT OF THOSE USING A METHOD | |
| --- | --- | --- |
| *Method* | *Rural* | *Urban* |
| Condom | 51.1 | 61.1 |
| IUCD | 18.4 | 27.0 |
| Oral Pill | 8.5 | 3.5 |
| Foam tablet | 34.5 | 42.2 |

Note: Figures add to more than 100 because some couples employed more than one contraceptive.

10. In April of 1965 there were 2207 field workers in the national family planning service, stationed in the health centers or in local offices. This is only the first wave of a rapid build-up to a point where there will be one field worker for

each 10,000 population. The medical and social science departments of Seoul National University are actively engaged in research, evaluation, and participation in the national program. A private organization, Planned Parenthood Federation of Korea, has a branch in each province and is providing service and information through its office. Yonsel Medical College is conducting special experiments in rural areas, with assistance from the Population Council.

11. The progress of the national program in giving family planning services is most impressive. The progress that results when a well-designed family planning program is carried out in a population of low education is illustrated by the Sungdong Gu Action-Research Project on Family Planning, Conducted by Seoul National University School of Public Health under the sponsorship of the Population Council. This program started in July, 1964. It included the use of mass media (T.V., radio, newspaper, posters, pamphlets, leaflets), group meetings, and home visiting. During the first 15 months of the program, of a total of 44,900 eligible (married women in the ages 20–44), 9,809 visited the family planning station for family planning information. About 85 percent of these visitors (19 percent of all the eligible women) accepted a method of family planning. Acceptance was divided roughly equally between condoms and other traditional methods and the IUCD's. Within the period, a total of 5,722 insertions (13 percent of the eligible women) were made. Even when allowance is made for the fact that the first year's experience would "skim off" the accumulated group of already-motivated people, the fact that one-fifth of the fertile population could be induced to adopt family planning within such short time is most impressive. It suggests the potential progress that can be made when a well-balanced program of information and service is provided, making use both of the mass media and personal contact.

The above brief notes on the progress of fertility control in Korea are not isolated instances. A recent report from the Pakistan Family Planning Programme suggests that more than one million families in that nation of 100 million (about 5 percent of the eligible population) now are currently contracepted through this program alone. In India, more than a million insertions of IUCD's are being made annually—in addition, the use of other methods of contraception is rising. In Colombia in Latin America, the oral pills and the IUCD both are being accepted at phenomenal rates; it is estimated that more than 120,000 couples in this nation of 18 million persons are using the oral pills alone; this is roughly 3 percent of the eligible population. In addition, large quantities of other methods are known to be used. In Santiago, Chile, the IUCD is so well known and widely used that it is a part of the medical service throughout the metropolitan area.

To summarize: wherever one looks in the underdeveloped segments of the world, one finds evidence of firmly established and flourishing family planning activity. By whatever crude estimates it is possible to make, it is quite clear that a sufficiently large share of the population already is making use of modern contraceptives to have a depressing effect upon the birth rate. Even conservative evaluation of the prospects suggests that *instead of a "population explosion" the world is on the threshold of a "contraception adoption explosion."* Because of lack of adequate vital statistics, the effects of this new "explosion" will not be readily measurable for a few years, but they will start to manifest themselves in the censuses of 1970 and will be most unmistakable in 1980.

*IV*

Given the situation that has just been described, what can be said concerning the future population of the world? If we insist on extrapolating past trends, we are making the unrealistic assertion that conditions have remained and will continue to remain unchanged. If we predict a slow change of the type that was typical of Europe and Northern America before 1960, we are implicitly asserting that the current programs are having zero effect: this assertion is contrary to fact. The course taken here has been to try to comprehend the nature of the change that is taking place, and to predict its probable course and speed, so that its impact may be guessed. As crude and subjective as this procedure is, it appears to offer more valid predictions than conventional population projections.

Looking at the developments listed above, realizing that they are only 5 years old or less, knowing that accomplishments in this area are cumulative and grow by exponential curves, and appreciating that new discoveries and improvements will accrue promptly along all fronts—medical, social, and psychological—both from basic research and from accumulating experience and evaluation—the following generalizations appear to be justified:

*The trend of the worldwide movement toward fertility control has already reached a state where declines in death rates are being surpassed by declines in birth rates. Because progress in death control is slackening and progress in birth control is accelerating, the world has already entered a situation where the pace of population growth has begun to slacken. The exact time at which this "switch-over" took place cannot be known exactly, but we estimate it to have occurred about 1965. From 1965 onward, therefore, the rate of world population growth may be expected to decline with each passing year. The rate of growth will slacken at such a pace that it will be zero or near zero at about the year 2000, so that population growth will not be regarded as a major social problem except in isolated and small "retarded" areas.*

In evaluating these conclusions, it must be kept in mind that the topic is a deadly serious one, and the penalties for misjudgment may be very great. There is one set of penalties that results from overoptimism. But there is another set of penalties that results from overpessimism. It is quite possible that nothing has sapped the morale of family planning workers in the developing countries more than the Malthusian pessimism that has been radiated by many demographic reports. It is like assuring soldiers going into battle that they are almost certain to be defeated. If the comments made here should be so fortunate as to fall into the hands of these same family planning workers, it is hoped that those who read them will appreciate just how close they actually are to success. They have it within their grasp to improve dramatically their countries' fortunes. Coupled with the companion programs of industrialization and modernization, the effects could appear almost miraculous as they unfold in the 1970's and 1980's.

# 5. *Trends in U.S. Population*

## FRANK POLLARA

Prophets abound with predictions of impending doom for the United States unless immediate steps are taken to contain the "population explosion." There is some cause for concern, but some of it is gross exaggeration.

What gives these predictions some validity is that there is undoubtedly some point in the population growth of this country, or of the world, which invites disaster. But what that point is and when it will arrive, no one knows. Certainly this country, with a population estimated at 206 million, does not have a disaster point of 240 million people, or 270 million or 300 million. So the disaster point will not be reached in 10 years or 20 years or even 30 years from now.

Growth creates problems. But there is more to the population problem than growth. The real damage done by the purveyors of disaster resulting from the "population explosion" is that they obscure the more pressing problems of population that demand immediate attention. They would have you believe that if we simply put a stop to population growth, all of our problems would disappear.

We should be concerned not only with population growth but with the structure of population:

Where will the people live? City, suburb or country?

What kind of people will they be? Rich, poor, black, white, old, young?

The answer to these and related questions will affect many of the major decisions on the quality and direction of life in the United States. And they are of much more pressing concern than the question of when are we going to starve ourselves to death from overpopulation.

The world population at the beginning of Christianity was about 250 million. By the middle of the 17th century, or 1,600 years later, the earth's population had doubled to 500 million. It took only 200 years for it to double again, reaching 1 billion in 1840; then 90 years to reach 2 billion in 1930. By 1975 it is expected to double again to 4 billion and by the end of the century the earth's population is projected to be about 7 billion. It will reach 8 billion by 2007.

The bulk of this growth will occur in the underdeveloped areas of the world. In the more advanced countries growth will be at a more modest rate.

It is difficult to assess the urgency of the world population growth problem. Certainly the problem may be more acute in some countries than in others. Some scientists fear famine or near-famine conditions in the near future. Others feel that man through his ingenuity can cope with the problem. Still others are more concerned that the quality of life faces deterioration as the resources of the world become overstrained. They feel that population growth is about to outstrip the earth's capacity to sustain man in affluence and contentment. The debate is on but the correct answers may not be immediately forthcoming.

In this quick overview of world population it is obvious that what happens in the rest of the world may well be of overriding importance in determining U.S. policies and the direction of life in this country. However, there are American population problems independent of world population problems.

The population of the United States will grow at a rate about half as fast as world population in the next 30 years. By the year 2000, U.S. population is predicted to be 308 million, a growth of 102 million over projected population for the year 1970. This growth is almost as much as the total population of the United States in 1920.

However, the rate of growth has declined. It was more than 30 percent each decade until 1860. In the next five decades the rate of growth ranged from 21 to 27 percent. In the five

## U.S. POPULATION, 1790–2000

| YEAR | POPULATION (In Millions) | PER SQUARE MILE | MEDIAN AGE | NEGRO POPULATION (In Millions) | NEGRO PERCENT OF TOTAL |
|------|------|------|------|------|------|
| 1790 | 3.9 | 4.5 | — | .76 | 19.3 |
| 1800 | 5.3 | 6.1 | — | 1.00 | 18.9 |
| 1810 | 7.2 | 4.3 | — | 1.38 | 19.0 |
| 1820 | 9.6 | 5.5 | 16.7 | 1.77 | 18.4 |
| 1830 | 12.9 | 7.4 | 17.2 | 2.33 | 18.1 |
| 1840 | 17.1 | 9.8 | 17.8 | 2.87 | 16.8 |
| 1850 | 23.2 | 7.9 | 18.9 | 3.64 | 15.7 |
| 1860 | 31.4 | 10.6 | 19.4 | 4.44 | 14.1 |
| 1870 | 39.9 | 13.4 | 20.2 | 4.88 | 12.7 |
| 1880 | 50.2 | 16.9 | 20.9 | 6.58 | 13.1 |
| 1890 | 63.0 | 21.2 | 22.0 | 7.49 | 11.9 |
| 1900 | 76.2 | 25.6 | 22.9 | 8.83 | 11.6 |
| 1910 | 92.2 | 31.0 | 24.1 | 9.83 | 10.7 |
| 1920 | 106.0 | 35.6 | 25.3 | 10.46 | 9.9 |
| 1930 | 123.2 | 41.2 | 26.4 | 11.89 | 9.7 |
| 1940 | 132.3 | 44.2 | 29.0 | 12.87 | 9.8 |
| 1950 | 151.7 | 42.6 | 30.2 | 15.05 | 9.9 |
| 1960 | 180.0 | 50.5 | 29.5 | 18.87 | 10.5 |
| PROJECTIONS | | | | | |
| 1970 | 206.0 | 58.2 | 27.6 | 25.40 | 12.3 |
| 1980 | 235.2 | 66.4 | 28.0 | 30.97 | 13.2 |
| 1990 | 270.7 | 76.5 | 28.7 | 38.14 | 14.1 |
| 2000 | 307.8 | 86.9 | — | — | — |

Includes Alaska and Hawaii beginning in 1950. Projections are for nonwhite. Not available for Negroes, separately, who constitute about 92% of nonwhite population.

*Source: U.S. Department of Commerce, Bureau of the Census.*

decades ending in 1960, the rate of growth hovered around 15 to 19 percent each 10 years except for the depression years of the 1930s, when the growth rate plummeted to 7.4 percent.

In the decades to come, population is projected to grow at a rate of 14 to 15 percent, which is below the historical rate. Yet there are some who believe that even this rate overstates population growth and a more likely growth rate is 11 or 12 percent.

The high rate of growth in the early years of this country was largely affected by immigration. In the 1800s, the immigration rate generally ranged from 6 to 10 percent and continued at that level until the immigration law of 1924 took effect. As a result of that law, the rate of immigration declined to under 1 percent during the 1930s and 1940s and averaged 1.5 percent in the 1950s, the rate at which it is expected to continue. Total immigration is expected to be about 400,000 annually in future years. While this is a sizable number, it is less than one-fifth of the total U.S. population growth.

In the 1850s, when America had a population of around 27 million, immigration averaged 260,000 per year. In the 1880s, with a population of 56 million, immigration averaged 520,000 per year and in the first 10 years of this century immigrants entered this country at a yearly rate of 880,-000 compared to a population average of 84 million.

Just the increase in numbers of itself creates problems. It means a proportionate increase in food and drink (unless dieting and teetotaling become ways of life) and a proportionate increase in clothing (unless we all become nudists). It means more factories and more offices, more houses, more automobiles and more highways. It means more depletion of our natural resources. The list is almost endless.

However, we must not forget that we have lived with population growth. Somehow the schools have been built, factories have turned out the goods, hospitals have sprung up and food has been grown to take care of the population growth. Maybe not as well as we would have liked, but nevertheless the needs of a growing population have been met.

This should not lead, however, to a feeling of complacency. Growth will have an extraordinary impact on environment. Problems of air, land and water pollution and the disposal of waste will double and triple and there will be an increasing strain on resources.

Yet growth has its compensations. More people produce

more wealth, even if there is no increase in per capita wealth. And certain costs remain relatively fixed—it costs no more to send a man to the moon whether we have 200 million or 300 million people. Thus a bigger share of a bigger pie becomes available to tackle such problems as race, pollution, housing, poverty and crime. Whether that extra wealth will be used to combat these domestic problems is a question for the American people to decide.

Perfectly stable population is not such an ideal thing, either. A non-growing population tends toward stagnation. Wealth growth would be slowed. We would have a much older population with the median age between 35 and 40 instead of the current median of 27.6.

America is not overcrowded and it will not be in the near future. Currently there is an average of 58 people per square mile. By the year 2000, density may increase to 87 per square mile. Holland has a density rate of almost 1,000 people per square mile; Japan has 700; West Germany 600; Switzerland 400.

In the long run, growth transcends all other aspects of population in importance. But in the long run, we'll all be dead. Of more immediate urgency are the questions of where will they live and who will they be.

Birth and death rates are pretty much the same in all parts of the country. Despite the excess of births over deaths, some areas decline in population because of people moving out. In 1966 about 1,100 U.S. counties, or one-third of the total, had less people than in 1960.

Prior to 1955, the population was shifting from the South to the Great Lakes region. But that migration has abated and both the South and the Great Lakes areas are expected to grow at rates close to the national average in the future.

In recent years the fastest growth has been in those states along the southern perimeter of this country stretching from Florida to California, where the climate is attractive. That trend is expected to continue.

Low rates of growth are projected for the states between the Mississippi and the Rockies and in Pennsylvania and

Kentucky. West Virginia is actually expected to decline in population.

The center of U.S. population has been moving steadily westward since 1800, when it was midway between Washington and Baltimore. It is expected to be 40 miles south of St. Louis in 1980.

Negroes have been moving out of the South in large numbers. More than 75 percent of the U.S. Negro population was concentrated in the South in 1940 but by 1968 that percentage was down to 52. The percent of Negroes living in the North rose from 22 to 41 percent and in the West from 1 to 7 percent in that period.

This trend out of the South will continue, but at a much slower pace. By 1985, the percent of Negroes will decline to 49 percent in the South and to 37 percent in the North and rise to 14 percent in the West.

Coinciding with the movement of Negroes out of the South has been the vast migration from rural to urban areas. In 1790 only 5 percent of the U.S. population lived in the cities; by 1920 it was a little more than 50 percent and today about 67 percent. By 1985, urban residents will constitute 71 percent of the total population.

Almost all of the recent growth in metropolitan areas has been in the outer ring, or suburbs. While it may be too early to predict that today's central cities will be tomorrow's ghost towns, the decline of the central cities is real and, unless positive efforts are made to reverse the slide, the situation could become hopeless.

In 1960, the central cities had a population of 57.8 million and the suburbs had 55.1 million. By 1969 the suburbs had grown to 70.6 million while the central cities remained practically stationary at 58.5 million.

Growth in the central city occurred only among the blacks. From 1960 to 1969, the Negro population in the central city increased by 2.9 million while the white population declined by 2.2 million. In 1960, 18 of every 100 central city residents were nonwhite. In 1969 the number had grown to 23 of every 100.

As for the future, projections prepared for the National

Commission on Urban Problems show that by 1985 the suburbs will double their 1960 population, going from 55.1 million to 112.6 million. The central cities are projected to show a growth from 57.8 million in 1960 to 65.6 million in 1985. The suburbs are growing as projected, but there is a serious question whether the central cities will grow at all.

The central city population has actually declined since those projections were made several years ago. Whether or not this decline will continue is highly speculative. To a large extent it will depend upon whether the country is prepared to commit the necessary effort to revitalizing the central cities.

The central city population growth from 57.8 million in 1960 to the projected 65.5 million in 1985 anticipates a decline of 2.4 million in the white population and a growth of 9.8 million in the nonwhite.

These projections are suspect for the reason noted earlier. From 1964 to 1969, the central city population actually declined 200,000 per year, so all growth in the central city population in the 1960s occurred in the first half of the decade. Possibly the riots of the mid-1960s were largely responsible for the decline in the last half of the 60s. In any case, it would seem logical to expect little or no increase in central city population by 1985; it would seem more likely that this population will actually decline.

Of even more significance is what the mix of that population will be. No one questions that the ratio of blacks to whites will increase by 1985. The only question is the magnitude of that increase.

By 1985 at least 30 of every 100 central city residents are expected to be nonwhite. How much higher than that it will be depends on many variables.

On a national basis, about 12 of 100 are nonwhite. By 1985 this will increase slightly, to 13 or 14 per 100. In the suburban ring where the greatest population growth is projected, the ratio of blacks to whites is expected to remain stationary at around 5 per 100. In non-metropolitan areas the ratio is expected to decline from 11 per 100 in 1960 to about 10 per 100 in 1985. This means that blacks are moving to the suburbs at about the same ratio as whites and they are moving out of the rural areas at a faster rate than whites.

By its very nature the concentration of blacks in the central cities will accentuate polarization of the races; but there is more to it than that.

The people who are leaving the central city, both black and white, are the more affluent. In 1967 dollars, the median family income in 1959 was $6,700 in the central cities and $7,700 in the suburbs. By 1967, the median income increased to $7,800 for central city families and $9,400 for the suburbs. The gap had widened from $1,000 to $1,600 in this 7-year span and there is every likelihood that it will continue to widen.

Even with an increase in central city median income, there has been a narrowing of the tax base and a rising demand for public services.

Businesses have left the city to follow the population to the suburbs. Manufacturing plants found advantages in locations outside the central city. Doctors, lawyers and dentists discovered a bigger clientele in the suburbs. Most new residential construction was in the suburbs.

At the same time the needs for education, welfare and health care have risen. The demand for pollution and crime control has become more pressing. As the city, with its diminished tax base, is less able to afford these services, more people and businesses leave the city, diminishing the supply of good jobs and further narrowing the tax base. The circle is on. No one likes to live in a city that has inferior educational facilities, inadequate hospitals, insufficient safety measures and a similar inadequacy of other necessary community facilities.

Much has been made of the growing youthfulness of the population and its implications. Just as in the scare theories of world and U.S. population, some analysts and commentators have gone overboard in emphasizing the youthfulness of the U.S. population.

In 1970 the median age in the United States was 27.6 years (half the people were less than that age and half more) and the projections indicate a slight upward movement in median age over the next 20 years or so. Over the past 20 years the median age has declined from 30.2 in 1950 to 29.6 in 1960 and 27.8 in 1968. In the years prior to 1950 we find the exact opposite trend—a steady rise in the median age from 16.7 years in 1820 to a 30.2 peak in 1950. Actually, through most of our history the population was younger than it is now.

The recent decline in the median age stems largely from the sharp rise in births from 1940 to 1957. After 1957, the birth rate has declined enough for a slight rise in median age in the years ahead—from 27.6 in 1970 to an expected 28.7 in 1990.

However, within each age group there will be sharp changes. From 1965 to 1985, all age groups will increase except the 45–54 category, which will drop from 22 million to 21.7 million. The rate of increase within each age group will vary sharply. The highest growth rate will occur in the 25–34 age group, which will increase from 22.4 million to 40.7 million. The next highest will be in the 20–24 group, which will increase from 13.7 million to 21.1 million. At the same time, there will be growth at both ends of the age scale.

By and large, a sharp growth is projected for young adults and college- and school-age youths, clearly spelling out the need for expanded educational facilities, especially at the college level.

Total enrollment in all educational institutions is projected to increase from 55.1 million in 1966 to 69.2 million in 1985. The most extraordinary increase will occur at the college level, where enrollments are projected to rise from 6.1 million in 1966 to 11.7 million in 1985.

By the same token the rapid growth of young adults points up the need for an expansion of entry-type jobs requiring little or no experience. The absence of any growth in the number of mature adults points up the leadership gap that may well occur in the face of an expanding population and economy.

The great growth in the group of marriageable age means an increase in the number of marriages: from 1.6 million per year in 1960–1965 to 2.5 million per year by 1985–1990. The number of households will increase from 53 million in 1960 to 84 million in 1985.

Consumption patterns will be affected by the projected age distribution and household formation. The demand for apartments will increase, as will the need for medical services for the aged.

Little change is anticipated in the overall ratio of males to females. In 1965 there were 97 males to 100 females and the change is expected to be negligible in the next 20 years. By and large, there are more males than females under age 25. Thereafter, the ratio of males to females keeps declining until at ages 75 and over there are only 70 males per 100 females.

The nonwhite population (of which 92 percent is black) is growing much faster than the population as a whole. From 1945 to 1955 the nonwhite population grew by 25 percent while the entire population grew by 19 percent.

From 1955 to 1965 the nonwhite grew by 27 percent compared to 17 percent for the entire population. The same trend is projected over the next 20 years, with the nonwhite population growing by 46.5 percent and the entire population by 29.1 percent. The percent of nonwhites in the population has been rising steadily from 10.2 percent in 1930 (Negroes were 9.7 percent of total population) to 11.4 percent in 1960 and is projected to rise to 14.1 percent in 1990. Yet while this growth has occurred in recent years, the ratio of nonwhites to the entire population is still considerably below what it was in the early years of the republic.

In 1790, about 20 percent of the population was nonwhite. (Blacks accounted for 19.3 percent of total population). This ratio declined steadily until 1930 when it reached the low point of 10.2 percent.

The sharp growth in the nonwhite population in recent years stems largely from the considerably higher birth rate among nonwhites. In 1960 this was 27 per 1,000 among nonwhites and 18 per 1,000 among whites. This differential in birth rates will undoubtedly narrow as society becomes more affluent. However, it will not have too much effect on the faster growth rate among nonwhites because the death rate among nonwhites will decline more sharply than among whites over the next 20 years.

In 1966 the death rate among nonwhites was 9.8 per thousand compared to 9.5 for whites. While the death rate among whites is projected to decline by 1990 to 9.1, among nonwhites it is projected to decline to 8.1. That much lower rate stems from the higher birth rate among nonwhites at present, which means they will be a much younger group in 1990 than the whites. Thereafter, this differential should narrow.

The nonwhite population of this country is considerably younger than the white. In 1966, the median age of the white population was 28.7 years compared to 21.4 for the nonwhite. Over the next 20 years little change is anticipated in the median age of the white people. Nonwhites may show the same trend with perhaps a slight increase in the median age. By 1985 nonwhites are expected to constitute 13.7 percent of the total population but about 17 percent of the population under 20 years of age.

Clearly we do have some population problems, but growth is one we can cope with. Inherent in growth is the generation of resources to cope with that problem. The more pressing problems are those which relate to the distribution of population, to the concentration of blacks and the less affluent in the central cities.

By 1985 median family income will have risen to $14,700 from $8,600 in 1968. But because of the growth in families, total family income is expected to rise from $486 billion to $1,137 billion.

The wealth will be there. But will it be used to fulfill our social needs or will it be used to satisfy our materialistic wants?

On our own we can buy a more luxurious car, but we can't buy better mass transit on our own. We can buy a bigger home but not cleaner air. We can buy a motorboat but not pure water.

How this wealth will be spent is a choice the people must make—and on that choice depends the quality of life in America.

*Projections—and how they can vary*

The art of projection in all fields has come a long way in recent years—but projections are still subject to considerable degree of uncertainty and should be used with care.

Sophisticated computers have been utilized to give the art the appearance of scientific infallibility. However, one should not forget that the computer still projects on the basis of assumptions fed into it by human beings—and humans are fallible. Thus, computerized projections are no better or no worse than the assumptions on which they are based.

In regard to population figures, the Bureau of Census exercised a degree of discretion when it calculated four series of projections based on assumptions relating to births, deaths and immigration. The same estimates of deaths and immigration were used for all four series since it can be reasonably assumed that their range will vary only slightly in the future. A slight decline was assumed in the mortality rate and net immigration of 400,000 per year was assumed to continue at the same level. Yet if cures were found for major diseases or immigration quotas were changed, these estimates would be far off. Barring that, they are reasonable.

Birth rates, on the other hand, have a wide possible range. The Bureau of the Census has made four projections of U.S. population, based on four varying assumptions regarding births. These projections are:

| YEAR | SERIES A | SERIES B | SERIES C | SERIES D |
|------|----------|----------|----------|----------|
| (In thousands) | | | | |
| 1970 | 208,615 | 207,326 | 206,039 | 204,923 |
| 1985 | 274,748 | 264,607 | 252,871 | 241,731 |
| 2000 | 361,424 | 335,977 | 307,803 | 282,642 |

The assumptions regarding the average number of children per woman are: Series A—3.350; Series B—3.100; Series C—2.775; Series D—2.450.

Series A projections were based on the fertility rate in 1963, a highly fertile year; Series B on the average level for 1964 and 1965; Series C on 1966 and Series D on the early 1940s.

Series A and B appear unrealistically high. No one uses them any more. Series C may also be too high, but it is the most commonly used and was chosen for this article as the best middle ground—and points up the fact that even with slightly high projections, there is no immediate growth crisis in the United States.

At present, the fertility rate approximates the one used in Series D, based on the early 1940s. The birth rate has been declining since 1957 and at present is at its lowest point since early in the 1940s.

Thus a solid case could be made for use of Series D, or the lowest rate projected by the Bureau of the Census. That would mean that over the next 30 years, the U.S. population would grow about 75 or 80 million, somewhat less than the commonly used figure of 100 million.

The argument for using Series D, or the somewhat smaller projection of the future U.S. population, would be based on these three points; 1) the fertility rate is on a declining trend and will likely continue downward or remain at the current low level; 2) affluent people have less children and society is becoming more affluent; 3) birth control knowledge is becoming more readily available.

# 6. ZPG: A Fascist Movement!
## A PROGRESSIVE LABOR PARTY POSITION

### "Too many people" Racist hysteria

*The essence of the Zero Population Growth (ZPG) move-ment is racist hysteria.* What ZPG leaders like Paul Ehrlich are saying is, in effect, "yellow, black, and brown people are out to get *you*." ZPG says that there are too many people, especially non-white people, in the world, that these people are terrifying and violent, and that their population growth must be stopped—by "coercion" if necessary.

> We are going to be sitting on top of the only food surpluses available for distribution, and those surpluses will not be large. In addition, it is not unreasonable to expect our level of affluence to continue to increase over the next few years as the situation in the rest of the world grows ever more desperate. Can we guess what effect this growing disparity will have on our "ship-mates" in the underdeveloped countries? *Will they starve grace-fully, without rocking the boat/ or will they attempt to over-whelm us in order to get what they consider to be their fair share?*
>
> Ehrlich, *Population Bomb*, pp. 132–3

Racist hysteria is also the tone of Ehrlich's account of how he came to "feel" the overpopulation problem one "stinking hot night in Delhi."

> . . . the streets seemed alive with people. People eating, people washing, people sleeping. People visiting, arguing, and scream-ing. People thrusting their hands through the taxi window, beg-

ging . . . *People, people, people, people . . . Would we ever get to our hotel? All three of us were, frankly, frightened.*

                                            *Population Bomb,* p. 15

According to Ehrlich, the *cause* of starvation, unemployment, urban riots, deteriorating schools and health care, wars of liberation—*is too many working people.*

In the United States, one of the more rapidly growing developing countries, we hear constantly of the headaches *caused by growing population:* not just garbage in our environment, but overcrowded highways, burgeoning slums, deteriorating school systems, rising crime rates, riots, and other related problems.

                                            *Population Bomb,* p. 25

*What this says is that the problem lies with the working people —there are too many of them. The "solution" advanced is a* fascist *one: forcibly sterilize black and third world working people.*

The United States could take effective unilateral action in many cases . . . When [Sripati] Chandrasekhar [Indian minister for family planning] . . . suggested sterilizing all Indian males with three or more children, *we should have applied pressure on the Indian government to go ahead with the plan.* We should have volunteered logistic support in the form of helicopters, vehicles, and surgical instruments . . . *coercion? Perhaps, but coercion in a good cause. I am sometimes astounded at the attitudes of Americans who are horrified at the prospect of our government insisting on population control as the price of food aid.*

                                            *Population Bomb,* p. 166

In other words, what businessmen cannot do with US troops to control revolutions, they should do with the scalpel! The same idea—forced sterilization—is advanced in the "Earth Day Special" of the *Boston Globe,* which suggests an alternative means: "addition of fertility control agents to public water supply or staple foods." Ehrlich combines the crudest male chauvinism with his racist hysteria in order to point out one drawback of this alternative: "Feeding potent male hormones to the whole population might sterilize and defeminize the women, *while the upset in the male population and society as a whole can be well imagined."* (*Population Bomb,* p. 136)

This is not the first time that racist hysteria and fascist practices (including forced sterilization!) have been advocated by capitalist agents.

> Since the inferior is always numerically superior to the best, the worst would multiply so much faster—given the same opportunity to survive and to procreate—that the best would be necessarily pushed into the background. Therefore a correction in favor of the better must be undertaken.
>
> Adolf Hitler, *Mein Kampf,* 1934

### *Super-exploitation the problem, not "Too many people"*

The problem of non-white people, whether outside or inside the United States is super-exploitation and racist oppression, not "overpopulation." In this country black and third world workers are given the hardest jobs at the lowest wages, have the highest unemployment rates, the worst housing, medical care, and schooling. The result of the super-exploitation and oppression of black workers is that white workers are also hurt. By promoting the racist division of the working class, businessmen hope to prevent white workers from uniting with black and third world workers to fight against their common enemy. In addition, black and third world working people are brutalized and murdered by the police, who enforce the bosses' racist practices. Duggan, a Boston city cop who is still "on duty," recently murdered Franklin Lynch, a black patient in Boston City Hospital.

The racist exploitation and oppression of workers in third world countries is even more extreme. The most that workers in Saigon take home is $1.40 a day! At the same time workers and peasants throughout Vietnam, Laos, Cambodia, and Thailand are hunted down and murdered for fighting back against their local landlords and US bosses. *This racist and imperialist oppression also hurts American working people, black and white, who must fight in and pay for wars that are intended to provide bosses with a long-term supply of cheap labor.*

Racist ideology, such as the racist hysteria promoted by ZPG leaders, is used to justify the super-exploitation and oppression of black and third world working people at home and abroad. We are told these "teeming millions" of working people are "our" enemies. This effort to get workers and students in this country to ally with US bosses instead of with their natural allies must be exposed and defeated!

### Black and third world workers lead the fight

Black and third world workers are taking the lead in the sharpening class struggle both at home and abroad. The postal workers' strike was spearheaded by the black workers of local 36 in NYC. These black workers organized a rank and file fight against both the Government and union mis-leaders and were clear on the class nature of the strike. They offered to deliver welfare and workers' pay checks on their own time! Working class troops from Fort Dix, assigned to scab on the strike, also saw that this strike was in the interest of all workers. They sorted out draft notices and destroyed them! The city rebellions against the super-exploitation of black and third world workers were sharply focused in their attacks on the gouging pawn shops, furniture and liquor stores, banks and supermarkets—as well as in their militant battling with police and riot troops. In some cities like Detroit, white workers joined the rioting: exploitation is a class question. As Ehrlich says in a rare moment of truth, "Few Americans could sit in the same room with a child and watch it starve." Neither can Vietnamese workers or peasants.

The heroic fight led by Vietnamese workers and peasants against local landlords and US bosses has helped set the pace for class struggle in the US. Their fight has exposed the desperation with which US businessmen must hold on to S.E. Asia. It has also shown how the US business empire hurts most Americans, especially working people, and profits only US bosses. The growing pro-working class nature of the anti-war movement shows that many students and intellectuals have come to see workers as the leading force for change. Fighting ROTC and counter-insurgency research because they are racist attacks on working people at home and abroad, refusing to ally with liberal politicians, supporting GE strikers on November 15, linking up fights against racism with fights against the war—these are all signs that pro-working class consciousness is growing among other sectors of the population.

### Class struggle is bad environment—for bosses

*This sharpening foreign and domestic class struggle has created a massive environmental problem for the businessmen who own the wealth and control the means of production in the US. US bosses are finding it increasingly hard to breathe. These men are desperately trying to clean up this air of revolution by diverting it through channels like the ZPG and changing it into its opposite—a fascist attack on black and third world working people.*

Many people are honestly concerned about starvation, destruction of the environment, and the extreme misery of working people in most areas of the world, including this country. ZPG leaders, *backed up and built by businessmen* through feature articles in *Life* and the *Boston Globe,* try to make people think the roots of these problems lie in the working people themselves. They blame working people for "breeding" too much, for "consuming" too much, and for "polluting" the environment. They try to convince students and intellectuals to ally with the bosses in fighting this "common enemy." These businessmen hope these racist ideas can be used to turn growing class consciousness into its opposite—a racist attack on the black and third world workers who are leading the fight to overthrow the rule of the businessmen and their politicians who profit from hunger, pollution, disease, and war.

### Population control arguments: "Scientific" racism

The ZPG leaders' racist ideas are dressed up in "scientific" garb. Consider their main arguments. Each one tries to take the blame off the bosses and put it on "the people," especially black and third world workers.

1) *The "ant-heap" argument:*

"If growth continued at its current rate for about 900 years, there would be some 60,000,000,000,000,000 people on the face of the earth." (*Population Bomb,* p. 18)

ZPG leaders seek a bosses' solution to these hysterical figures: they want a constant world population by 1990, enforced by fascist means if necessary. In China, workers and peasants have overthrown their landlords and foreign bosses and are feeding and educating themselves. In contrast to US and British dominated India, China may be the first underdeveloped country to stabilize its growth rate (*China Quarterly*). Indian workers and peasants, led by the new Communist Party of India-Marxist-Leninist, *are not waiting for the ZPG's solutions but have risen up in armed revolt in West Bengal, seizing land and seeking a socialist solution to their exploitation.* (*New York Times,* 3/31/70)

2) *"The people are starving themselves to death" argument:*

"There is not enough food today. How much there will be tomorrow is open to debate." "We are going to be sitting on top of the only food surpluses available for distribution." (*Population Bomb,* p. 44; p. 132)

There is starvation today because US and foreign businessmen burn or let rot enormous food surpluses and keep vast areas of arable land out of production—*to keep food prices and profits up!* Numerous studies by the Rockefeller Foundation and Presidential advisors show that there is now adequate food production in the world and that there will continue to be so for many years to come. The problem is not "too many" working people but *too many bosses whose profit motives control food production and distribution. When US businessmen bring modern agriculture technology to the Third World, they make things worse.* In India, for example, they help wealthy farmers and landlords, subvert land reform programs, and push poor farmers off the land, increasing unemployment and boosting the supply of cheap labor (*NYT* 5/28/69). The food needs of all working people can be satisfied *only if workers and peasants unite to get rid of the landlords and businessmen who profit from hunger and high food prices.* In contrast to India, China's food problem is being solved by the creative efforts of a united working class. From 1949 to 1956, wheat production in China rose over 75%—before the full effects of collectivization and the cultural revolution were felt. Since then, in Hsiaohsien county of Anhwei province, for example, workers and peasants have increased per-*mu* grain production by 500% and cotton production by 400%. It is imperialism that creates starvation, not working people.

3) *"The people are the polluters" argument:*

"The causal chain of the deterioration is easily followed to its source. Too many cars, too many factories, too much detergent, too much pesticide, multiplying contrails, inadequate sewerage treatment plants, too little water, too much carbon dioxide—*all can be traced easily to too many people."* (*Population Bomb*, pp. 66–67)

Here the ZPG leaders' enthusiasm to attack working people leads them into a contradiction: the US has a low population density; even by ZPG calculations, there are not "too many" working people. There are, however, too many businessmen who profit from unsafe flimsy cars; from dirty, dangerous factories in which there are over 14,000 fatal accidents a year; and from cheap waste disposal. *Only when workers seize control of the means of production and destroy the bosses' state will "the common enemy" be eliminated; only then can ecology become a science that serves working people rather than a way of tricking working people into paying the price for cleaning up the bosses' mess.*

4) *"The people eat up capital and stop economic development" argument:*

The argument here is that third world workers and peasants are so numerous that they eat up all the profits that should be reinvested to boost agricultural and industrial production.

In fact, most capital produced in third world countries is either consumed by local landlords and businessmen or exported to the US and other imperialist investors. US corporations each year remove more capital from the rest of the world in profit than they invest. US business' control of world trade as well as of capital in third world countries forces production to serve US businessmen's needs, not the needs of the workers and peasants. *Imperialism is the source of economic under-*

*development, not "too many" working people. Problems of economic development are class problems: working people are the only force that can solve them—by getting rid of "too many" bosses!*

### Zero population level for bosses

Progressive Labor Party thinks that there is an overpopulation problem, if one views it in class terms. It is fine that there are many, many working people. It is terrible that there are "too many" bosses!

*WE ARE OPPOSED TO ZERO POPULATION GROWTH FOR WORKERS!*

*WE WILL FIGHT FOR A ZERO POPULATION LEVEL FOR BOSSES!*

The efforts of US business to push ZPG's racist ideas should be seen as part of a general effort to build racist ideology as a justification for racist practices and the increased repression of black and third world workers, who lead the fight against these bosses. On the ideological level, for example, US "educators" push the debate between Jensen, who says that blacks are genetically inferior, and his liberal opponents, who say that blacks are culturally inferior—but, nevertheless, inferior! In addition to waging an ideological war to build racism, US bosses are attempting to intimidate militant black workers through daily atrocities, like the murder of Franklin Lynch, the Boston City Hospital patient, and the attacks on the Black Panther leadership.

*The student movement must ally with workers to fight this racist oppression and to attack the material basis for racism—the profits US bosses make from the super-exploitation of black workers and from the racist divisions they promote in the working class. We must expose and fight all attempts of businessmen and their politicians to repress such a movement and to divide it from workers.*

*Only a working-class led movement fighting racism can hope to clean the bosses out of our environment, thus stopping at its source the root cause of wars like the war in Vietnam, murders like the murder of Franklin Lynch, and the starvation and pollution that ruins the lives of so many working people.* FIGHT FOR SOCIALISM! ALLY WITH WORKERS!

# 7. *Crowded People*

## MARSTON BATES

In the August–September 1968 issue of *Natural History* I reviewed some of the work that has been done on the effects of crowding on animal behavior. It appears that crowding is often associated with weird behavior—the suicidal migrations of lemmings and locusts, the "behavioral sinks" formed by the rats studied by John Calhoun. What happens to people when they are crowded?

There is plenty of chance for observation, and opportunities for the study of crowding are increasing steadily. The usual present estimate for the population of the world is 3½ billion persons, and the numbers are now increasing at a rate of 2 per cent a year. This means an annual increase of 70 million: the equivalent of a new Chicago metropolitan area every month. Whatever one thinks of Chicago, this seems a little excessive.

Further, there is a tendency almost everywhere for these growing numbers of people to aggregate more and more in cities. This is true of Asia and Africa as well as of industrialized Europe and North America. If the 200 million people of the United States were scattered evenly over the landscape, the density would be 50 persons per square mile. But 70 per cent of this population lives in urban centers. New York City proper has a density of 25,000 persons per square mile —90,000 per square mile on Manhattan Island. Lewis Herber, in his book *Crisis in Our Cities,* calculates that in the residential parts of Manhattan the actual density is 380,000 people per square mile or 136 individuals for every 100-by-100-foot lot. This is achieved, of course, by stacking the residential units.

Here surely are appropriate conditions for the formulation of behavioral sinks, and the rioting and violence of the ghettos would seem to demonstrate that people and rats do act much alike. I doubt, however, that the miseries of the ghetto are purely a consequence of crowding. After all, thousands of men can be crowded on a battleship with no obvious damage to behavior, and conditions in a submarine are even more restrictive. To be sure, the men on a submarine are carefully selected for personality traits; the situation might be very different if the crowded ships included families instead of just men.

There are few detailed studies of the psychological effects of crowding on people. The most thorough and best-known is a three-volume report on an intensive study of the inhabitants of midtown Manhattan by a team of social scientists, entitled *Mental Health in the Metropolis.* The area covered did not include ghettos, although conditions did range from near-slum to luxury apartments. Only 18.5 per cent of the 1,660 people interviewed were found to be free of all but inconsequential symptoms of mental illness. All the rest had some kind of neurotic or psychotic symptoms, although only 2.7 per cent were incapacitated. No hospitalized people were included in the sampling. However, a survey of the hospitals and clinics in the region showed that on an average day eight individuals per thousand were receiving outpatient psychiatric care, and five per thousand were hospitalized. None of this sounds very healthy.

It is difficult to measure mental health because there are so many differences of opinion among psychiatrists and clinical psychologists. Physical health is easier to measure and compare, and here there is no question about the relatively greater risk to health from living in the city, despite the greater availability of medical services there. Lewis Herber, in the book mentioned above, has reviewed a number of studies. Peptic ulcers and coronary attacks are understandably more common in the city and probably have psychosomatic aspects. Lung cancer among non-smokers is eleven times more common in an urban environment than in a rural one—smokers, on the other hand, have about the same rate in both environments. Lung cancer can be explained by air pollution, but curiously, most kinds of cancer are more common in the city than in the country, which makes one wonder whether some element of stress is involved.

Reading about urban conditions one begins to wonder why anyone lives in cities. There is, of course, a tremendous out-migration to the suburbs by people who can afford it, but this is more than balanced numerically by the in-migration from villages, towns, and countryside. These are mostly people at poverty level coming to the city because that is where the jobs are, now that agriculture has become so completely mechanized. Often there are no jobs, or only jobs with inadequate pay; the resulting poverty leads to the deterioration of the inner city, which has lately been causing so much concern.

We have a national conviction that the city is a poor place to raise children. In the midtown Manhattan study, residents were asked, "For growing children, do you think it is better to be brought up on a farm, in a small town, in a small city, or in a big city like New York?" In reply, only 15 per cent preferred a big city like New York. Interestingly enough, native New Yorkers disapproved of their city as an environment for children just as much as parents who had come in from outside. When asked the same question with regard to themselves, about half thought they would be better off away from New York. Yet millions of people continue to live in New York—and to raise families there.

The middle-class parents of midtown Manhattan tend to restrict the size of their families—a large proportion of the couples having only one child or none. In the slums, on the other hand, breeding seems to be unrestricted. In the racist climate that prevails in the United States, Negroes may even resent birth-control propaganda as aimed at restricting their numbers discriminatorily. Urban middle-class couples are thoroughly caught in the rat race of working their way up in the social and economic systems, so that children become a handicap, while many of the slum inhabitants have given up. Perhaps the competitive struggle, rather than the crowding accounts for the poor mental health of urban white-collar workers. In the case of the slums, the deprived environment can be used to explain almost anything, including mass hysteria.

I have been writing mostly about the dismal aspects of the crowded city, yet all through history cities have been the habitat of civilized man, the source of progress in the arts and sciences as well as in industry and commerce. There is something exhilarating about life in a great city, some spirit that compensates for the trials of crowding. Besides, people like crowds. Most people go where other people are—packing beaches, parks, theaters, sidewalks. David Lowenthal documented this nicely in the article entitled "Daniel Boone Is Dead" in the last issue of this magazine [*Natural History*].

The great value of the city lies in its diversity: all kinds of people with all kinds of facilities for filling their varying needs. The very concentration of people provides audiences for the theater, visitors for museums and galleries, readers for books and periodicals, and a market for an immense variety of shops. In the small town, where everyone knows all about everyone else, the pressures for conformity are great. The eccentric, the deviant, the talented, move to the city where they can find more of their own kind. The city is a haven for the artist as well as for the thief.

Cities became possible back about 3000 B.C. with the discovery of methods of transporting and storing foodstuff, so that an agricultural surplus produced by farmers could be used to support other kinds of people—priests, kings, soldiers, smiths, philosophers. The proliferation of occupational niches in the city has continued all through history and is going on in our own day at an accelerating rate. I suspect that this multiplicity of niches is what enables people to survive under crowded conditions—conditions that rats could not tolerate. After all, rats lack the means of avoiding the stress of frequent contact between individuals that occupational diversity provides.

This is the argument of the Chicago sociologist Nathan Keyfitz in an article in the issue of *BioScience* for December, 1966. "If the city is, on the one side, a jungle of potentially infinite and destroying competition, on the other it shows a nearly infinite capacity of its members to differentiate themselves, to become useful to one another, to become needed."

In psychological jargon, the niche gives a feeling of identity. We are engineers, teachers, cab-drivers, physicians, or what have you. We thus belong to a group: but within each group there are numerous sub-groups reflecting the specialized knowledge or skill of each of us. As Keyfitz points out, there may be a hundred specialties within such a field as electronic engineering—the possible specializations within a modern city are truly almost infinite. Also, there are almost endless organizations within the city, sometimes competing, as banks or stores: sometimes providing general service, as the educational or telephone systems. These organizations further pattern space in the city and serve also to reduce stressful contacts among individuals.

The man in the city comes in contact with hundreds of other people every day, but most of these contacts, unlike those between crowded rats, are not stressful. We are not involved in the private life of the cab-driver, the bank clerk, or the reporter for *The New York Times*. We usually know little about our physician or lawyer beyond confidence in his professional skill. As we move between the small world of home and the small world of the office or business place, we pass many hundreds of people, but for the most part this results in no meaningful relationships. We are inured to other people.

This kind of individual support is generally lacking in the ghetto, which is probably one of the causes of ghetto unrest. The unemployed or the underemployed person becomes Ralph Ellison's "invisible man," uncertain about work, not knowing how to get money for rent or groceries or the installment on the television set. Ghetto life has been graphically described in the Kerner report on riots, and in books like the novels of James Baldwin and the report on the life of Puerto Ricans in the United States by Oscar Lewis. Prostitution, alcoholism, drug addiction, and violence become rife. The Kerner report found that 12 per cent of Negro families with incomes of under $3,000 had no father living at home. The ghetto world is in large part a matriarchy—with mother constantly distracted by the problems of survival. The ghetto thus comes to resemble the behavioral sink of Calhoun's rats, except that it continues to reproduce.

Poverty tends to shackle us, and wealth to free us, without much relation to the intensity of crowdedness. This makes me wonder about that "territorial imperative" of Robert Ardrey and others. If the human species is strongly territorial, how did the formation of cities ever get started? I share with Ardrey, Lorenz, and others the feeling that Old Stone Age man lived in social groups, with individuals within the group forming a dominance hierarchy or pecking order and with the whole group occupying a defended territory. But I suspect that with the beginning of settled life and agriculture during the Neolithic period, territoriality started to break down. Cities, city-states, and empires—with their wars and rebellions—represent cultural ideas, rather than territorial instinct.

The "turfs" of the gangs of adolescent hoodlums are the nearest thing to territories in a modern city. I can think of no way of determining whether these represent the arousal of some latent instinct in these youth, or whether they are a secondary development, only analogous to the territories of wild animals. Jane Jacobs, in her thought-provoking book *The Death and Life of Great American Cities,* discusses the extension of the turf idea to exclusive residential areas where no strangers are wanted. This surely is cultural rather than instinctive—as, I think, are all forms of discrimination.

To explain discrimination in terms of pecking order seems to me as far-fetched as to explain war in terms of territoriality. Some vague leftover of inborn aggression may be found in the one, and of dominance in the other, but they are well buried under accumulated ideas. The pecking-order pattern that emerges in prisons, schools, and adolescent gangs may well have an instinctive basis: but this dominance among a group of individuals seems to me different from mass discrimination against Negroes, Jews, Protestants, Indians, et al.

Dominance hierarchy in our society is largely formal: rank in the armed forces, chain of command in business, position within the university, and the like. Whether the drive to become a general in the army is comparable with the drive of a gorilla to become the Old Man of the tribe, I don't know. But in both cases the structuring serves to promote the stability of the group.

The human animal obviously can be crowded into quite dense aggregations without striking physical or mental deterioration—if there are ample resources for support. I tend to think this is partly due to the weakness of our territorial drive and the formality of our system of dominance hierarchy. This is comforting when one looks at those multiplying billions in the years ahead, except that there is always the catch about resources. The vice and misery of the Malthusian propositions will not necessarily persist if we can find food, housing, and some amenities for all of mankind. But it takes considerable optimism to think this possible. Under present conditions crowded people are apt to be miserable people who sometimes act in as bizarre a fashion as Calhoun's rats. The plea of the Kerner report that we must do something about the ghettos in our cities is surely valid if we wish to have a healthy nation.

## 8. Spaceship Earth—Standing Room Only
### MORRIS K. UDALL

In January I sat in the House chamber when Tucsonan Col. Frank Borman and his two companions of Apollo 8 told a joint session of Congress of their pioneering adventure to the moon. They described a space that is black, lifeless, hostile, desperately cold—a kind of celestial desert in which man would perish instantly were it not for the complex life-support systems of the space capsule. Those of you who followed the adventure on television remember this event: As the capsule rounded the dead, white face of the moon last Christmas Eve, Capt. James Lovell looked from it back to the bright blues and rich browns of our little planet riding through the emptiness and said:

> "It's awe-inspiring. It makes you realize just how much you have back there on earth. The earth from here is a grand oasis in the blackness of space."

His words led me to reflect on our country and our world.

* * *

One of America's great strengths has been the fundamental optimism of its people, a kind of national "can-do" attitude about any problems the future might hold. The difficult is done now; the impossible takes a week or two. It is the attitude that might explain, more than anything else, the $500 billion gross national product when I came to Congress and the $900 billion GNP we expect this year.

Yet, for the first time since the early 1930s, America seems to have a serious crisis of the spirit. Large numbers of people are dubious and skeptical, if not pessimistic, about the years ahead. Despite all our material prosperity, there is real questioning about whether life is really going to be better or more tranquil next year, in the next decade, or for our children.

My work takes me to various parts of the country each year. It's often inspiring and rewarding, but gloom and pessimism are much in evidence. The numbers of people jammed into our large cities are increasingly ominous; courtesy is a rarity between strangers; few stop to aid the victim of a robbery or a heart attack. I see long lines at ticket counters, restaurants and rest rooms and I have sweated out a two-hour holding pattern above Chicago's airports. But what I see is the obvious. The problem, we all know, is much deeper.

Crime rates soar and no one really has a solution. Most major cities have schools on double sessions. There is scant progress toward a racially integrated society. There aren't enough facilities for college applicants. Anarchists threaten the very existence of universities.

In just one year, sanitation workers, teachers, subway workers and police strike or go on slowdown protests in New York. Experts question whether the city is "governable" any longer.

At a time when Americans haven't even begun to bring under control the pressing problems of the people already crowded into cities, we have triggered continuing social and economic forces which will shortly jam even more millions into those cities.

Every major river system in the country is polluted with debris, topsoil, chemicals, pesticides and partly treated raw sewage. Lake Erie has been all but choked to death on the pollution of our prosperity. The thin and precious blanket of air that makes Capt. Lovell's oasis possible is pumped full of foulness from automobiles, factories and generating plants.

The people of Los Angeles, already paying record property taxes, were told recently that the rate would triple in five years lacking tax reforms. A "taxpayers' revolt" is talked about as federal, state and local outlays for schools, hospitals, roads, sewage treatment plants and other basic services are overwhelmed with growth. Traffic on a major downtown

freeway in Chicago was so great that it came to a standstill
the day after the new highway opened. In Los Angeles cab-
bies make better time leaving the freeway and picking their
way through local streets to the airport.

I have seen fishing streams and beaches where one had to
stand in line or elbow somebody out of the way to get to the
water. I have known farmers and cattlemen who once took
a host's pride in allowing their lands to be used for hunting,
picnicking or camping survey the trash and damage left behind and tack up "no trespassing" signs. There's more privacy
at Kennedy Airport than at a campground I visited on a North
Carolina beach last summer.

This isn't the whole story of America today. There are
still many places of beauty, quiet and tranquility. There is
still a strong feeling of goodwill and many "welcome" mats
are still out. But the things I outlined do exist. They are the
symptoms of a fundamental disease which must be recognized
and treated or it will get far worse.

*     *     *

If you don't like the picture I have just painted, try this
one. Suppose I told you that I have a plan which would
guarantee to New York and Los Angeles within a few years:

Reduced local, state and federal taxes; less crowded streets,
freeways and hospitals; room at the beaches, streams and ski
slopes; single session schools and shortened waiting lists at
colleges; some genuine hope for lowered crime rates, some
measurable progress against pollution.

You'd be interested, of course. Now, suppose I told you
that it would do these things not just for New York and Los
Angeles, but for Phoenix, Houston, Chicago and every other
area in the country. Suppose I told you further that the plan
would cost almost nothing in public spending and involve absolutely no governmental controls, and very little legislation.
Furthermore, under my plan you might wake up each morning to a newspaper filled with heartening progress rather than
the calamity of the day.

Well, I have such a plan. I can't be optimistic that it will
be adopted very soon. It's entirely voluntary and it runs
counter to some basic attitudes built into our culture. But it

ought to be adopted and soon, because it is directed at the basic, underlying causes of nearly all the problems that trouble America as we move into the 1970s.

Here is my plan:

Americans, voluntarily and openly, must face the fact that most of our tensions and our failures are directly due to an unrestrained, spiraling population growth. Every family with two or more children would make a personal, voluntary decision to have no more children. Every couple with no children or one child would voluntarily agree to stop with the second.

Having done this, we would use science and technology and the resources of government to thin out the cities by making it attractive for industries and people to voluntarily relocate in smaller, middle-sized communities, where people still can be a blessing, not a burden. We would do for this country the one thing which I believe would bring back tranquility and a permanent strength: stabilize our population.

My plan would be helpful on the international scene as well. Our ambassadors abroad tell us that it is hard to sell U.S. supported birth control programs to other nations. One of the criticisms they get from foreign governments is that the U.S. hasn't done very much to solve its own problem, so why should it be peddling programs for others? If we were to stabilize our population, we would be the first nation to show the world that the problem can be solved and that, it seems to me, would give a tremendous uplift to other nations who are approaching the population problem half-heartedly, if at all.

\* \* \*

The dreary statistics of the population explosion have been repeated many times. Some of them were covered in my 1965 newsletter, "A Time Bomb Called Population." Since I wrote that newsletter we have added to our population 9.5 million more Americans. Last year alone there were 3.5 million births and 440,000 added through immigration, more than offsetting 1.9 million deaths for a net increase of 2 million in our population. This is easy to write, but difficult to comprehend. These Americans are not just statistics; they are people. They have children and build houses. They want to go to the mountains or the park and on the same day that you do. They take the freeway to work in the morning and their children want into the same colleges and schools as yours. They get sick, and need doctors and hospitals and at the same time as you do. Each adds 120 gallons a day to the local sewage treatment plant and four pounds of solid wastes to be disposed of and 1.9 pounds of air pollutants. Each throws away 250 cans and 135 bottles or jars a year, and you see some of this production every time you go to a beach or walk in a neighborhood park. You wait for some of them at the golf course, the national park, the local lake, the bus stop or the local supermarket.

Individually, they are mostly fine people. But you never get to know them as friends. They are in your way; they make life a little more difficult. And you and I get in their way and cause them inconvenience in return.

Some scientists are beginning to suspect that dangerous and unknown stresses occur on human beings when they are overcrowded and subjected to the strains of complicated overlapping relationships. They know what happens to animals when they overpopulate their habitat, and the implications for man are ominous. There is reason to believe that much of the increased crime, mental illness and some of the other things I have talked about may be products of an overcrowded and overcomplicated existence.

And the total population spirals upward at an ever accelerating rate. It took us 180 years to go from four million Americans to 200 million. By the year 2000 we will have hit 318 million. Since 1950, the world has added one billion people. And since I wrote that 1965 newsletter, the world's population has increased by at least 250 million, or, put another way, by a number greater than the 1965 population of the Soviet Union, or all of Africa, or all of Latin America.

There was no political reason for comparing four and one half years of growth to the Soviet Union—the two numbers happened to be convenient comparisons—but in looking back over the preceding sentence, I think it does more than I first intended it to do.

It suggests the truly frightening course down which we humans are hurtling.

If an ultimate calamity were to befall mankind—and in nuclear weapons we have the tools to manufacture such a calamity—chances are it will be population, not politics, that will have to be blamed. In short, of the two problems, population and the Soviet Union, population scares me more. If the world could solve, somehow, the problem of overpopulation, our problems with the Soviet Union, or any other country or ideology, would be more easily coped with.

I believe, as a matter of fact, that virtually all of our problems either stem from or are intensified by the sheer numbers of people that are now crowded into the limited living spaces of our earth. For example:

—It does not take much imagination to see that the foundation of war can be laid in the Asian mud of prospective famine.

—The specter that Latin America's hundreds of millions will double within the next generation cannot spell anything but turbulence and misery—the very atmosphere that invites the spread of Castroism—for decades to come.

—It is obvious to me that the destruction of wilderness and natural beauty and the pollution or poisoning of soil, air and water are caused by man's numbers overwhelming, at the very time he needs it most, the delicate base of nature that sustains him.

—In America the problems of poverty, racial strife, transportation; the rotting of our central cities and the formless and ugly sprawl of urbanization—all so debilitating to the individualism that our country cherishes—can be traced directly to the problem of overpopulation.

Yet, while the United States spends billions of dollars at all levels of government and in foreign aid programs in an attempt to grapple with individual problems, we still are doing little to get to the basic problem. I take that basic problem to be:

How can we—humanely and with a regard for basic human rights—stabilize the world's population?

For, if we do not, it will surely stabilize itself through catastrophes that may threaten the very existence of all mankind. One thing is certain: The world's population cannot continue to grow at its present rate. We are not going to put more people on earth than the earth can sustain. If birth rates do not fall, death rates will rise.

There are those who say that science will rescue us, that the world can support almost unlimited numbers of people. Although modern science has done fantastic things, I would answer that there are things it cannot do and will never do: Science cannot add one square foot to the surface of this planet; nor can it add a ton of coal, a pound of uranium, a barrel of oil, or a glass of water.

Experts whose judgment I trust believe that nothing we can do in terms of increased food production will avoid widespread famine in Asia in the next two or three decades. More recently, we have been told that a "green revolution" now going on has so increased crop yields in some of the areas thought to be in danger that it is outdated to speak of famine in the 1970s. Well, that is good news, but if the "green revolution" is not accompanied by dramatic progress in lowering the birth rates in those countries, the problem has only been delayed, not solved. No one can predict what political consequences will arise from this. As for me, I cannot conceive of millions of people—people who through mass communications have been given a new deep thirst for the quality of life you and I enjoy—resigning themselves to starvation without making a fight for life.

\* \* \*

Man is much more than the other animals. His brain is so much larger; he has a soul and a conscience. But man, like the other animals, is a product of earth, subject to her laws, and he must have a continuing relationship with the outdoors, with nature, or he loses sight of his place on earth. He must realize that he can tinker only so much with the delicately tuned machinery of this planet, or he will destroy himself, and the planet.

Let me say it another way: Livestock ecologists long have been guided by the concept of the "carrying capacity" of a given tract of land. They know that a certain acreage will support 10 cattle. Up to that number, the grass will be lush, trees will thrive, water will be produced. Animals and plants are in balance. But put 20, 50 or 100 cattle on that land and the grass goes and the topsoil erodes. The cattle die; the plants die; the productive land itself dies.

The earth has a maximum carrying capacity too. Science does not yet know precisely what it is, but some experts believe that our numbers already exceed the critical point. Let me give you an indicator:

We Americans comprise 6 per cent of the world's population, yet, because of our wealth, technology and enterprise, we use almost 40 per cent of the world's resources. Suppose we could magically bring all the people of the world up to our living standards by tomorrow. A scientist recently computed that the world would then consume about 20 times the iron, copper, sulphur, timber, oil, water it consumed in 1969. Well, the rub is that the planet does not have 20 times its present usable store of resources. In many instances, the margins are very slight. If all the people of the world suddenly began using the same amount of petroleum products used by each American, all the known petroleum reserves in the world would be gone in about six years.

\* \* \*

The situation I describe is critical, but is it hopeless? I talk about it because I think something can be done. A start has been made.

What was once a subject off limits to the public discussion has been brought in the past few years into the open air of legitimate and free debate. Presidents Eisenhower and Kennedy both expressed concern. "Second only to the search for peace," President Johnson said in 1965, "it is humanity's greatest challenge."

Some experts, although they admit to their own optimism, are beginning to detect progress. The birth rate in the United States certainly is dropping dramatically. There are signs that the birth rate is falling off in some Asian and Latin American countries. There is no reason to relax, but there is some room to hope.

A giant step in the area of public debate was taken in 1965 when former Sen. Ernest Gruening of Alaska, a courageous man, opened Senate hearings on his bill to establish offices of population in both the Department of State and the Department of Health, Education and Welfare.

I introduced a companion bill in the House and, although the bills did not pass, both departments reacted by getting deeply involved in the question of population.

Although there is no way to measure the actual effect of the coordination and spending that resulted, the hearings did accomplish that all-important first step: to identify the problem and bring it into the open.

The discussion continues:

—In January, the President's Committee on Population and Family Planning recommended that the federal government expand its family planning services to all American women who want them by 1973. It also recommended that Congress create a permanent Presidential Commission on Population.

—The much publicized debate within the Roman Catholic Church about Pope Paul's continued ban on artificial means of birth control, despite the severity and divisiveness of the debate, is a healthy sign.

What can I do, what can you do, and what can government do about this sensitive and essentially private matter? I don't believe that government can solve this problem, but it can help. I am introducing a bill that would do these main things:

1. Have the Congress and the President declare that it shall be the goal of the United States to encourage by decent, humane and voluntary means, a stabilized United States population. These may sound like meaningless words when actions are needed, but no goal can be reached until a problem is identified and a goal determined.

2. Authorize a new presidentially appointed Assistant Secretary of the Interior to coordinate research and programs having to do with the relationship of population growth and its impact on the natural environment.

3. Create a two-year Commission on Population and the Environment, composed of our most distinguished citizens in private life and public officials, which would, in an impartial, nonpartisan and scientific manner, tell the American people the facts about population growth and its implications, and offer detailed recommendations.

Furthermore, bills introduced by colleagues who share my concern—bills that would increase foreign aid for birth control programs and enable every American, without regard to his religious convictions, to have the means to voluntarily limit his family through birth control—will have my support.

I've talked about some limited things government can do. But no government will, or should, ever undertake to tell people when to have, or not to have children. The solution, if there is one, must come from individuals. If you believe, as I do, that this problem is our chief concern, that it underlies most of the world's major problems, begin to talk about it. You can help change some basic attitudes, for this is where the ultimate answer lies.

We are faced with a formidable set of hostile attitudes. First, we deal with an extremely personal and sensitive area of human relationships, traditionally outside public concern. There are religious attitudes, also, and this is an area I decline to enter. Each American is entitled to be respected for his individual beliefs. Until and unless Catholic doctrine on this subject changes, we can only encourage Catholics to use church-approved methods of birth control and direct some of our research to improving and making more reliable those methods that are sanctioned.

Other people, particularly black militants, see the population control movement as "genocide," directed at minorities. The fact is that uncontrolled population growth will eventually wipe us all out, black, white, yellow and brown. Besides, most of the U.S. population explosion is the result of 180 million whites having two or three children too many rather than 20 million blacks having three or four too many.

Indeed, one of the myths recently exposed is that of the "unwanted child." Planned parenthood movements worked for years on the premise that a solution would occur if we could just insure that every child born was a wanted child. We now know that even if that goal were achieved, the population explosion would not be checked. It is the wanted, sometimes badly wanted, fourth, fifth or eighth child that makes up the bulk of our annual population increase. In fact, an organization called Large Families of America, Inc., actually boasts that 23 per cent of America's families raise over 65 per cent of America's children.

For reasons that are simple and understandable, the large family has a firm place in our history and folklore. As one of six children—and the father of six more—I know the special delights and satisfactions of multiple brothers and sisters, especially in a rural environment. Until this century, the nation was underpopulated. Empty lands awaited exploration and exploitation. When my grandfather first came to Arizona, a family desperately needed a home full of growing boys and girls; a small community grew stronger and better with more people. New settlers and large families were welcomed, encouraged and honored. Our scripture, our literature, our culture—and our tax laws—urged us on.

But, recognizing all of this history, we must also face the fact that the time is rapidly approaching when a large family, whatever its comforts to the home or the ego, may be a disaster to the community, the nation and the world. As James Reston said some years ago, "The history of mankind is strewn with habits and creeds and dogmas that were essential in one age and disastrous in another."

We face another fundamental American attitude also: The myth that growth is good business. For 150 years more people truly meant more prosperity, more markets, more opportunities for everyone. Businessmen and their communities were built on the doctrine that bigger is always better. If Arizona with two million people is good, the reasoning goes, Arizona with 20 million people will be 10 times as good. In terms of quality of life, this kind of thinking is dangerous nonsense. The kind of informal, outdoor, neighborly, spacious life which brings so many people to our state would be an inevitable casualty of unlimited growth. There would be in Arizona more signboards than saguaro, more cars than cottontails, and neon will long have replaced starshine in the desert.

In the last 10 years, the great conservation movement has really come alive. A national wilderness system has been established. We've added millions of acres to our national parks. Seashores and lakeshores have been set aside for recreation and wildlife. A huge federal fund now helps cities and states buy park and recreation lands before they are bulldozed. We have saved a few wild rivers. Despite all this, future generations may never find the outdoor areas every man needs for solitude and recreation and self-awareness unless we somehow bring this population growth to a halt. Perhaps the world can find space for some kind of existence for 10 or even 20 billion people instead of the 3.5 billion we have today. But what of the quality of that life? And the relationship of those people to the earth that supports them?

Which brings me back to Colonel Borman and Captain Lovell and their spaceship to the moon. Scientists call such a craft a "closed system," meaning that everything needed for a long voyage must be carried on board. Nothing can be thrown away. On long voyages everything—even human wastes—must be recycled and reused. The earth is a closed system too. It is our spaceship and it has everything on board that we will ever have, all the air, water, metal, soil and fuel. Unlike Apollo 8, however, our Spaceship Earth takes on more passengers all the time. At some point, it's got to stop taking on passengers, or the trip is going to be a lot shorter than any of us believed.

Somehow, I can't help but believe that if all mankind could see the earth as Lovell saw it from the far side of the moon last Christmas Eve, we'd change our attitudes and our policies.

We would again realize that here, on our "grand oasis in the blackness of space," it is man's relationship to his environment and to all other living things that will determine our survival and our happiness.

# 9. The Nonsense Explosion

## BEN WATTENBERG

As the concern about the environment has swept across the nation, the ghost of the "population explosion"—recently haunting only India and other ugly foreign places—has suddenly been domestically resurrected and we are again hearing how crowded it is in America.

*Life* magazine, for example, chose to launch the new decade with the headline "Squeezing into the '70s," announcing that, because of the crowds, "the despair of yesterday's soup line has been replaced by today's ordeal of the steak line." Two months later *Life* featured a story about a young New Jersey mathematician who had himself sterilized because he is "deeply worried by this country's wildly expanding population."

Crowded, crowded, crowded, we are told. Slums are crowded, suburbs are crowded, megalopolis is crowded and more and more and more people are eating up, burning up and using up the beauty and wealth of America—turning the land into a polluted, depleted sprawl of scummy water and flickering neon, an ecological catastrophe stretching from the Everglades to the Pacific Northwest. Crisis. Crisis. Crisis.

That so very much of this is preposterous, as we shall see, should come as no real surprise to those who follow the fads of crisis in America. There are no plain and simple problems any more. From poverty to race to crime to Vietnam all we face are crises which threaten to bring down the world upon our heads. And now it is ecology/environment—which is a perfectly good problem to be sure—but with its advent comes dragged in by the heels our old friend the super-crisis of the population explosion, which is not nearly as real or immediate a problem in America, and ends up serving unfortunately as a political smokescreen that can obscure a host of legitimate concerns.

While the rhetoric rattles on about where will we ever put the next hundred million Americans, while the President tells us that the roots of so many of our current problems are to be found in the speed with which the last hundred million Americans came upon us, while the more apocalyptic demographers and biologists (like Dr. Paul Ehrlich) are talking about putting still nonexistent birth control chemicals in the water supply, and about federal licensing of babies—the critical facts in the argument remain generally unstated and the critical premises in the argument remain largely unchallenged.

—The critical facts are that America is not by any standard a crowded country and that the American birth rate has recently been at an all-time low,

—The critical premise is that population growth in America is harmful.

In not stating the facts and in not at least challenging the premises, politicians and planners alike seem to be leaving themselves open to both bad planning and bad politics. This happens by concentrating on what the problem is not, rather than on what the problem is. Let's, then, first look at the facts. The current population of the United States is 205 million. That population is distributed over 3,615,123 square miles of land, for a density of about 55 persons per square mile. In terms of density, this makes the United States one of the most sparsely populated nations in the world. As measured by density, Holland is about 18 times as "crowded" (at 975 persons per square mile), England is 10 times as dense (588 persons per square mile), scenic Switzerland seven times as dense (382), tropical Nigeria three times as dense (174) and even neighboring Mexico beats us out with 60 persons per square mile. The US, by international standards, is not a very "crowded" country.

But density in some cases can be very misleading in trying to judge "crowdedness." The Soviet Union, for example, is less dense than the US (29 per square mile), but has millions

of square miles of uninhabitable land, just as does Brazil
and Australia, two other nations also less densely populated
than the US.

Of course, the US also has large areas of land that are
equally uninhabitable: the Rockies, the Western deserts, parts
of Alaska and so on.

But while it is of interest to know that America has some
land that is uninhabitable, what is of far more importance is
that we have in the United States vast unused areas of emi-
nently habitable land, land that in fact was inhabited until very
recently. In the last eight years one out of three counties in
America actually *lost* population. Four states have lost population: North and South Dakota, West Virginia, and
Wyoming; and another two states, Maine and Iowa, gained
less than one percent in the eight years. Furthermore, three
out of five counties had a net out-migration, that is, more
people left the county than came in.

These counties, the net-loss counties and the net-out-
migration counties, are the areas in America where the current hoopla about the population sounds a bit hollow. These
are the areas, mostly rural and small town, that are trying to
attract industry, areas where a smokestack or a traffic jam
signifies not pollution but progress, areas that have more open
space around them for hunting and fishing than before, and
areas where the older people are a little sad because, as they
tell you, "the young people don't stay around here anymore."

This human plaint tells us what has been happening demographically in the United States in recent years. It has not
been a population explosion, but a population redistribution.
And the place people have been redistributing themselves *to*
is a place we call "suburb":

AMERICAN POPULATION BY RESIDENCE

| | Population | | *Increase* |
| --- | --- | --- | --- |
| | 1950 | 1968 | 1950–1968 |
| Residing in Central city | 35% | 29% | 6 million |
| Residing in Suburb | 24% | 35% | 32 million (!) |
| Residing in small cities, towns and rural | 41% | 36% | 9 million |
| | 100% | 100% | 47 million |

In less than two decades the proportion of Americans living in suburbs has gone from less than a quarter to more than a third.

But even the total increase in population—rural, city, and suburb—is misleading. The big gains in population occurred ten and fifteen years ago; today growth is much slower. Thus, in calendar year 1956, the US population grew by 3.1 million, while in calendar year 1968 population went up by 2.0 million—and in a nation with a larger population base.

What has happened, simply, is that the baby-boom has ended. When the GIs came home after World War II, they began begetting large quantities of children, and Americans went on begetting at high rates for about 15 years. The best index of population growth in the US is the fertility rate, that is, the number of babies born per thousand women aged 15–44. In 1940, the fertility rate was 80, just a few points above the 1936 Depression all-time low of 76. Ten years later, in 1950, the baby-boom had begun and the fertility rate had soared to 106, an increase of 32 percent in just ten years. It kept climbing. In 1957, it reached 123, up more than 50 percent in two decades.

But since 1957, the rate has gone steadily down: to 119 in 1960, to 98 in 1965, to 85.7 in 1968, not very much higher now than in Depression times. The estimated fertility rate for 1969 was down slightly to 85.5 and there is no reason now to think it will go up, although, as we shall see, it may sink further.

When measured by another yardstick, the "percent national population growth" (birth plus immigration less deaths), the American population is now growing by about 1.0 percent per year; just a decade ago it was growing by 1.8 percent per year. That may not sound like much of a difference, .8 percent, but in a nation of 200 million people it means 16 million fewer people over a single decade!

With all this, however, comes another important set of facts: our population *is* still growing. At the reduced growth rate there are now about two million people being added to our population each year. This may even go up somewhat in the next few years as the baby-boom babies become young adults and—roughly simultaneously—parents. Moreover, a growing population, even a slowly growing population, grows by larger numbers as it grows. As the two hundred million Americans become two hundred and fifty million Americans there is a proportionately greater number of potential mothers, more babies, and the incremental two million new Americans per year can rise to 2½ or 3 million new Americans even with a relatively low growth *rate*.

The current, most likely projection of the Census Bureau of the US population in the year 2000—three decades hence—hovers somewhere in the 280–290 million range. That means there will be about 75–85 million more Americans than today, which is many millions more indeed, although not quite the round "hundred million" figure everyone is talking about.

It must be stressed, however, that this is only a projection: it could be high, it could be low. The figure is derived from a series of four alternate projections based on different levels of fertility rates issued by the Census Bureau in 1967. Already the highest two projections—calling for 361 million and 336 million—are out of the question. The third projection called for 308 million and that too now seems high, as it called for a fertility rate of 95 in 1970—about 10 points higher than the 1969 rate. The lowest of the four projections calls for a fertility rate of 84.6 in 1970 (roughly where we are) and yields a population of 283 million in the year 2000.

But even that is not an immutable figure by any means. Just as the first three of the alternate projections quickly proved themselves false, so it may be that Series D may prove high. After all, the Hoover Depression, in an era with far less effective birth control technology, brought fertility rates down to 76. What might a Nixon Recession do in an era of pills, loops, diaphragms, liberalized abortion?

Already the Census Bureau—quite properly—is preparing to revise its projections for the future. The new set of alternate projections—which will bracket the newer, lower, fertility rates—will unquestionably be lower, with a low-end possibility in the general area of 265 million for the year 2000. That too will only be a projection, based on assumptions which may or may not prove valid. But if such a low fertility rate does indeed occur, population in the US would then begin to level off after the year 2000 as the last of the baby-boom babies have completed their own families. The US might then be in an era of near-stable population along the lines of many Western European nations.

But even that is sixty million more Americans in just three decades—more than the population of Great Britain today.

Those, then, would seem to be the elementary facts. More Americans, although probably not as many as we may have been led to believe. More Americans, but not necessarily inhabiting a statistically crowded country.

With these facts, we can now turn to the premise set forth by the Explosionists, i.e., more Americans are bad.

Are they? My own judgment is—not necessarily.

There are a number of points made by the Explosionists and they can only be briefly examined here.

Because population growth is currently being linked to environmental problems, we can look there first. The Explosionists say people, and the industry needed to support people, causes pollution. Ergo: fewer people—less pollution.

On the surface, a reasonable enough statement; certainly, population is one of the variables in the pollution problem. Yet, there is something else to be said. People not only cause pollution, but once you have a substantial number of people, it is only people that can solve pollution. Further, the case can be made that *more people* can more easily and more quickly solve pollution problems than can fewer people. For example: let us assume that $60 billion per year are necessary for national defense. The cost of defense will not necessarily be higher for a nation of three hundred million than for a nation of two hundred million. Yet the tax revenues to the government would be immensely higher, freeing vast sums of tax money to be used for the very expensive programs that are necessary for air, water, and pollution control. Spreading constant defense costs over a large population base provides proportionately greater amounts for nondefense spending. The same sort of equation can be used for the huge, one-time capital costs of research that must go into any effective, long-range anti-pollution program. The costs are roughly the same for 200 or 300 million people—but easier to pay by 300 million.

Lake Erie, the Hudson River, the Potomac, are ecological

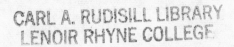

slums today. If the US population did not grow by one person over the current 205 million Americans, these bodies of waters would *still* be ecological slums. These waters, and any others now threatened, will be decent places only if men are willing to devote resources to the job. That is not a function of population growth, but of national will. It can be done if we, as a nation, decide that we want it done and are willing to pay for it. It is as simple as that and it has relatively little to do with whether the national decision involves 200 or 250 or 300 or 350 million Americans. It should also be remembered that pollution occurs in underpopulated places as well: in Sydney, Australia today, in medieval Europe in ancient Rome.

Next, the Explosionists view more people as a crisis because of all the demands they will make upon the society. So many new schools, so many more hospitals, more libraries—services and facilities which we are having difficulty providing right now. Similarly with "new towns." If we are to avoid vast and sprawling megalopolitan swaths, we are told, we must build 100 brand-new towns in 30 years. Unfortunately, we've only been able to construct a few in the last couple of decades—so, alas, what possible chance do we have to make the grade in the years to come?

What this argument ignores, of course, is that it is not governments who really create schools, hospitals, libraries and even new towns. It is *people* who create and build. People pay taxes; the taxes build and staff the schools; the more people, the more need for schools, *and* the more taxes. In an uncanny way it usually works out that every child in America has his own set of parents, and a school to attend. In a nation of a hundred million there were roughly enough schools for the children then present, at two hundred million the same was true and, no doubt, it will hold true at three hundred million. Nor will quality suffer because of numbers; quality suffers if taxpayers aren't willing to pay for quality and it is not harder for 300 million Americans to pay for quality schools for their children than it is for 230 million to buy quality schooling for their offspring.

And those "new towns"? *People* make them too. That's

just what's been happening in America in the last few decades. We call them "suburbs," not "new towns," and as the earlier data showed, 32 million American opted for this "decentralization" over the past eighteen years, long before it became a fashionable, political fad-word. People did this because people are not damn fools and when they had a chance to trade a rural shack or an urban tenement for a green quarter acre in suburbia, they did so, even though the faddists then were saying that suburbia was not "decentralized" (which is allegedly good), but "conformist" (which is allegedly bad). What smug town-planners like to call urban sprawl, represents uncrowded, gracious living for the former residents of city slums and the quality of such suburban life doesn't necessarily deteriorate if another new suburb rises down the road a mile.

Now, suburbs are not identical to the new town concept. The new towns, in theory, are further away from big cities, they are largely self-contained and they are designed from scratch. But, curiously, as many jobs move from the central cities, suburbs are becoming more and more self-contained; as metropolitan areas get larger, the newer suburbs *are* quite far from central cities; and there are some fascinating new start-from-scratch concepts in planning that are now materializing in suburban areas, particularly in some of the massive all-weather, multi-tiered, multi-malled shopping centers.

All this is not to denigrate new towns or the idea of population decentralization. Far from it. The effort here is only to point out that people often act even faster than their governments in seeking their own best interests. If it is new towns near a babbling brook that Americans feel they want, if the country remains prosperous, some patriot will no doubt step forward and provide same, and even have salesmen in boiler rooms phoning you to sell same. The process is mostly organic, not planned/governmental. It works with 200 or 250 or 300 or 350 million Americans.

There is next the "resources" argument. It comes in two parts. Part one: many of our resources are finite (oil, coal, etc.); more people obviously use more resources; the fewer the people, the less the drain on the resources. Part two: we Americans are rich people; rich people use more resources;

therefore, we must cut back population particularly fast, and particularly our rich population.

The resources problem is difficult to assess. A demographer now in his sixties seemed to put it in perspective. "Resources are a serious problem," he said. "We've been running out of oil ever since I was a boy."

The fact is, of course, sooner or later we *will* run out of oil; perhaps in thirty years or fifty years, or a hundred years or two hundred years. So too will we run out of *all* nonrenewable resources—by definition. We will run out of oil even if population growth stops today and we will run out of oil, somewhat sooner, if population growth continues. Whether oil reserves are depleted in 2020 or 2040 or 2140 does not seem to be of critical importance; in any event a substitute fuel must be found—probably nuclear. If no adequate substitute is developed, then we (all us earthmen) will suffer somewhat regardless of numbers.

Part two, that *rich* people are the real menace both resource-wise and pollution-wise, has recently been particularly stressed by Dr. Jean Mayer who advises the President hunger-wise but would not seem to be fully up to date demography-wise.

For the simple fact is that wealthier people generally have far fewer children than poorer people. With current mortality rates, population stability is maintained if the typical woman has on the average 2.13 children. In a 1964 Census Bureau survey among women who had completed their child-bearing years, it was shown that families with incomes of $10,000 and over had 2.21 children, just a trifle over replacement. This compared with 3.53 children for the poorest women. Since 1964, fertility rates have gone down among young women, and it is possible that when these lower rates are ultimately reflected as "completed fertility" we may see that affluent American women of the future just barely replace their own number, if that.

In short, current population patterns show that affluent people do not cause rapid population growth. And if the entire population were entirely affluent, we certainly would not be talking about a population explosion. Further, if the entire population were affluent *and* committed to combatting pollution, we wouldn't be talking about a pollution explosion either.

What then is Dr. Mayer's prescription? Is he against affluent people having babies but not poor people, even though the affluent have relatively few anyway? Or perhaps is it that he is just against the idea of letting any more poor people become affluent people, because they too will then consume too many resources and cause more pollution?

There are two important points that run through most of the above. First is that the simple numbers of people are not in themselves of great importance in the United States. There is no "optimum" population as such for the US, not within population ranges now forecast in any event. Whether we have 250 million people or 350 million people is less important than what the people—however many of them there are—decide to do about their problems. Second the population problem, at least in the United States, is an extremely long-term proposition, and in a country of this size and wealth, there is more flexibility in solving the potential demographic problems than might be assumed from the current rhetoric-of-crisis.

To be sure, much of the concern about population growth is sane, valid, and important. Certainly the concept of family planning—which for years had been a political stepchild—is now coming into the mainstream, and properly so. That every family in America should at least have the knowledge and the technology to control the size of its family as it sees fit seems beyond question. This knowledge and this technology, previously available largely to middle-class and affluent Americans, is now being made available to poorer Americans through growing federal programs. Some of the more militant black leaders have called it "genocide," but that is a rather hollow charge when one realizes a) that the poorest American women now have about 50 percent more children per capita than do middle-class Americans and b) that more-children-than-can-be-properly-provided-for is one of the most classic causes of poverty in America and around the world.

Certainly too, population growth must sooner or later level off. While America could support twice its current population and probably four times its current population—growth can obviously not go on forever and it is wise to understand this fact now rather than a hundred years from now. It is also wise to begin to act upon this knowledge, as indeed we have begun to act upon it. It is, accordingly, difficult to complain about the suggestions for legislation to make conditions easier for women to get and hold decent jobs—the thought being that easier access to employment will slow the birth rate. Our problems in the future probably will be easier to handle with somewhat fewer people than with somewhat greater numbers.

But what is wrong, and dangerous, and foolhardy is to make population a crisis. Doing so will simply allow too many politicians to take their eyes off the ball. When Explosionists say, as they do, that crime, riots, and urban problems are caused by "the population explosion," it is just too easy for politicians to agree and say sure, let's stop having so many babies, instead of saying let's get to work on the real urban problems of this nation. (As a matter of general interest it should be noted that the riot areas, the high-crime areas, the areas of the most acute urban problems *are areas that are typically losing population.* For example, special censuses in Hough and Watts showed population *loss.* Given that kind of data it is hard to accept the Explosionist notion that crowding causes crime.)

When the Explosionists say, as they do, that Yosemite and Yellowstone are crowded and that there is a vanishing wilderness because of too many people—they are wrong again. When visits to national parks have gone up by more than 400 percent in less than two decades, while population growth has gone up by about 30 percent, over the same time, then Yosemite isn't crowded because of population but because of other factors. When you have a nation where a workingman can afford a car, and/or a camper-trailer, when you give him three weeks paid vacation, provide decent roads—there would be something to say for the fact that you have indeed set up the society that Old Liberals, Trade Union Variety, lusted for, and who is to say that is bad? Again, if the population-crisis rhetoric is accepted it becomes too easy to say that the way to an un-crowded Yosemite is to have fewer people, and forget about the hard and far more costly problems of creating more recreation areas, which are needed even if our population does not rise.

When the Explosionists say, as they do, that it's because we have so many people that Lake Erie is polluted then once again we are invited to take our eye off the tens-of-*billions*-of-dollars ball of environmental safety and we are simultaneously invited to piddle around with 25-*million* dollar programs for birth control, which are nice, but don't solve anything to do with Lake Erie.

Finally, we must take note of the new thrust by the Explosionists: population control. Note the phrase carefully. This is specifically not "family planning," where the family concerned does the planning. This is *control* of population by the government and this is what the apocalyptics are demanding, because, they say, family planning by itself will not reduce us to a zero growth rate. The more popular "soft" position of government control involves what is called "disincentives," that is, a few minor measures like changing the taxation system, the school system and the moral code to see if that won't work before going onto outright baby licensing.

Accordingly, the demographer Judith Blake Davis of the University of California (Berkeley) complained to a House Committee: "We penalize homosexuals of both sexes, we insist that women must bear unwanted children by depriving them of ready access to abortion, *we bind individuals to pay for the education of other people's children, we make people with small families support the schooling of others. . . .*" (Italics mine.)

Now, Dr. Davis is not exactly saying that we should go to a private school system or eliminate the tax exemption for children thereby penalizing the poor but not the rich—but that is the implication. In essence, Senator Packwood recently proposed just that: no tax exemptions for any children beyond the second per family, born after 1972.

The strong position on population control ultimately comes around to some form of governmental permission, or licensing, for babies.

Dr. Garrett Hardin, a professor-biologist at the University of California, Santa Barbara, says, "In the long run, volun-

tarism is insanity. The result will be continued uncontrolled
population growth."

Astro-physicist Donald Aiken says, "The government has
to step in and tamper with religious and personal convictions
—maybe even impose penalties for every child a family has
beyond two."

Dr. Melvin Ketchel, professor of physiology at Tufts
Medical School writes in *Medical World News:* "Scientists
will discover ways of controlling the fertility of an entire population . . . the compound . . . could be controlled by adjustments in dosage, [and] a government could regulate the
growth of its population without depending upon the voluntary action of individual couples . . . such an agent might be
added to the water supply."

And Dr. Paul Ehrlich of Stanford: "If we don't do something dramatic about population and environment, and do it
immediately, there's just no hope that civilization will persist.
. . . The world's most serious population-growth problem is
right here in the United States among affluent white Americans. . . ."

What it all adds up to is this: why have a long-range man-
ageable population problem that can be coped with gradually
over generations when, with a little extra souped-up scare
rhetoric, we can drum up a full-fledged crisis? We certainly
need one; it's been months since we've had a crisis. After all,
Vietnam, we were told, was "the greatest crisis in a hundred
years." Piker. Here's a crisis that's a beauty: the greatest crisis
in two billion years: we're about to breed ourselves right into
oblivion.

Finally, look at it all from Mr. Nixon's point of view. It's
beautiful. You (Mr. Nixon) take office and the major
domestic problems, generally acknowledged, are the race
situation and the (so-called) crisis of the cities. They are
tough problems. They are controversial problems. They are
problems that have given way only gradually, painstakingly,
expensively, over the years. Your opponents are in a militant
mood. They have been co-opted in Vietnam and you fully expect them to hold your feet to the fire on these tough domestic
problems.

Apprehensively, you await the onslaught. And what is the slogan? No, it . . . can't be—but yes, it is. It's coming into focus. Read it: "Lower Emission Standards"! And in the next rank is another militant sign; and what does it say? It says, "Our Rivers Stink."

Full circle. The opposition sloganeers have gone from the "New Deal" to the "Fair Deal," to the "New Frontier" to the "Great Society," and now they march to a new banner: "No Shit"!

Beautiful. Of course the environment *is* a real problem, an important problem; we knew that from Senator Muskie. Of course your President will respond to it, particularly since almost everyone is for it, particularly if it takes the heat off elsewhere. But even the environment issue is massively expensive—too expensive to do everything now that ought to be done now.

So wait a minute, you say, your opponents have been good to you so far, let's see how really helpful they'll be. And behold, here comes the cavalry.

And what do they say? The problem of pollution is really the problem of too many people. Let the opponents divide among themselves and let the opponents fight among themselves. Let there be a children's allowance, say some of your opponents. Nay, let there not be a children's allowance, it will encourage population growth. Let there be better public schools, say some of your enemies. Nay, let each family pay for their own schooling to discourage population growth. Let us help the poor, say the opponents; nay, let us penalize the poor for having too many children. Let then the Secretary of HEW go forth to the people and say, "Ask not what your country can do for you, ask what you can do for your country—you shall have two children no more, no less, that is your brave social mission in America."

I imagine there have been luckier Presidents, but I can't think of any.

## 10. Today Hungry Nations, Tomorrow Starving Nations
### WILLIAM AND PAUL PADDOCK

In college I took two courses in statistics. The first I almost understood. The second was incomprehensible, but Professor Josiah Livermore closed the course with a piece of advice I have applied profitably many times: "When the statistics go against your reasoned judgment, throw the statistics out the window!"

I applied this precept when I doubted the optimistic statements and figures in an address given by Secretary of Agriculture Orville L. Freeman at the United Nations Food and Agriculture Organization (FAO) in Rome at the end of 1965. He said: "I should like to unfurl the banner of hope, a hope that arises because it now seems possible to win the war against hunger within the next ten or twenty years. . . . My optimism arises out of the conclusions of a study [which] reveals the startling fact that some newly developing countries are already increasing their agricultural production at rates far higher than those ever achieved by the highly developed nations—including my own."[1] The Secretary then quoted in support of his optimism parts of a statistical study just released by his department, *Changes in Agriculture in 26 Developing Nations 1948–1963,* published in late 1965.[2]

Wide publicity was given to the Secretary's speech; editorials and other comment conveyed the assurance that there is little to worry about regarding food shortages in these nations.

However, when I reviewed this same study, its conclusion did not, in my opinion, ring true. Because my own observations in many of the countries had been exactly the opposite of the statements in this study, I made inquiry concerning its background. It turned out that despite its title dates of "1948–1963" the data did not go beyond 1962, and the figures were merely *averaged out* for the full period 1948–1962. When I broke down these same figures by year, it developed that nearly all the increases in production had occurred from 1948 to 1955. After 1955 per capita production has decreased steadily, thus verifying the trends I had myself noted on the spot—a situation which might have been apparent if the study had indeed included data from 1962 up to the time Freeman addressed the FAO Conference in 1965.

"When the statistics go against your reasoned judgment, throw the statistics out the window!"

Therefore, based on my reasoned judgment, and despite the optimistic statements of Mr. Freeman, whom I greatly admire as one of the most effective officials in Washington, I state flatly that the hungry world will not be able to feed itself ten years from now. If twenty years from now it feeds itself, it will do so either because some now unknown method of improved food production has been discovered (most unlikely!) or because the population has been drastically reduced by famine or war. My statement is based not only on my own experiences and observations abroad but also on the statistics of:

(1) the somersault of export-import food shipments;
(2) the lagging productive capacity of the land in the hungry nations; and
(3) the extent of hunger in the world today.

### The somersault of export-import food shipments

Prior to World War II today's hungry nations were exporters of grain. By the 1950's they had become importers!

In the 1930's Latin America exported more grain than the United States and Canada combined. In 1949 Latin America became a grain importer!

It is not only the sheer bulk size of this change that has caught the world off guard and has left the leaders floundering for remedies. It is the speed at which this somersault has taken place.

The citizens of the nations which so suddenly lost their capacity to export food (and, therefore, had to import it) often did not realize what was happening. Indeed, it took the publication of a report in 1963 (*Man, Land and Food*) by the perceptive young Department of Agriculture economist, Lester R. Brown, to bring this first to the attention of American officials.

Those concerned with calculating the balance of payments in these nations were, however, well aware of the catastrophe that was occurring to their cash flow. If there had been any way, any way whatever, within the bounds of their knowledge and ability to stop this outflow of their cash, the governments would have acted. I hedged, it will be noted, by saying "within the bounds of their knowledge and ability." Now, in retrospect, many officials realize that their surge to create artificial industrialization and their parallel neglect of agriculture were wrong. Wrong, too, were the half-hearted efforts given to agriculture by the aid-givers in contrast to their excessive emphasis on projects which do not increase food production: hospitals, highways, drinking water, urban housing, etc.

Since the war, the United States and Canada have become the principal food exporters. Both have always been important exporters of agricultural products, but only recently have they come to dominate the international market so strikingly. Today's situation is due partly to their own agricultural expansions based on the application of new scientific knowledge. Yet it is also due to the withdrawal of other producers from the international markets; in a sense, our farmers have simply filled the vacuum resulting from this unexpected, sudden somersault within the former exporting nations. The completeness of the somersault is seen in the graph.[3]

The former, prewar suppliers of foodstuffs for the international markets have, one by one, been forced to use their former excess food supplies to feed their own growing populations. Now they must import more than they export.

Before the war I was stationed in the Consulate General at Batavia, Netherlands Indies (now Djakarta, Indonesia). One of my jobs was to prepare periodic reports for the Department of Agriculture on local export crops, such as citronella, rubber, tea, etc. The crop that interested me most was copra. Most

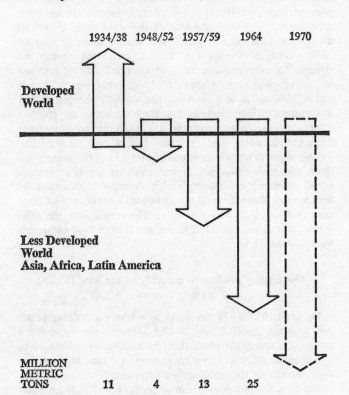

**Somersault in
Net Flow of World Grain**

1934/38   1948/52   1957/59   1964   1970

**Developed
World**

**Less Developed
World
Asia, Africa, Latin America**

MILLION
METRIC
TONS        11        4        13        25

of the others were grown on large company-owned estates. Copra, a source of edible oil from coconuts, usually was raised on peasant-type holdings. The world price was deep in the doldrums and, as I went around the archipelago, it was easy to translate this directly into how it affected the beautiful small islands where the coconut trees were the only evidence of economic activity. The islands were so beautiful with the elegant palms and the gentle life of the people; to the casual visitor it all seemed idyllic. Actually, the good life on the palm-rimmed holdings rose and fell with the export price of their copra. The Netherlands Indies was a major prewar supplier of copra on the world market. Indonesia, in contrast, exported in 1963 only one-fifth of the amount of 1938,[4] although the total amount grown was greater than the crop of 1938.[5] Various excuses are offered: one, that during the struggle for independence much of the rebel activity centered in the copra-producing areas (although that was a decade and a half ago), and another, the turmoil brought on by Sukarno's socialistic controls over the local economy. The *real* reason: the increased population is consuming the other four-fifths that formerly was exported.

This copra is one example out of many from the hungry nations concerning changes in the ratio of food production versus consumption. Multiply this example a thousandfold with similar illustrations of wheat in India, soybeans in China, corn in Nicaragua, beans in Chile. The reasons for the post-World War II somersault in the export-import food shipments then become clear.

### The lagging productive capacity of the land in the hungry nations

Up until 1957–1959 the world as a whole was doing pretty well regarding food. It was, in fact, increasing its agricultural production somewhat faster than the number of mouths to be fed. It managed this largely by putting new land into production throughout the undeveloped countries.

But then the increases began to falter. By 1958 these countries had run out of new land which they could farm.

The stork had passed the plow.

The undeveloped nations were failing to produce enough food for their expanding populations. Imports of food began. Something like half the net regional imports of the hungry nations were required to offset the decline in per capita output.[6]

Beginning in 1963 FAO has issued regular statements that the world's population is growing one per cent faster than its food production.

B. R. Sen, Director General of FAO, stated in a letter he sent in 1965 to Ministers and Secretaries of Agriculture throughout the world:

> While a small movement up or down in a single year in food production per head may not be significant, we are now facing something far more serious. The stark fact is that it is now no less than seven years since there was any appreciable increase in food production per head of the world's population, seven very lean years for the developing countries. The outlook is alarming. In some of the most heavily populated areas the outbreak of serious famines within the next five to ten years cannot be excluded.[7]

Then FAO disclosed that there had been *no* increase in agricultural production in 1966 even though the world population had grown that year by 70 million. In fact, Latin American, African and Asian food production had actually dropped so that there was 4 to 5 per cent less food available for each person in those hungry areas than there was the previous year. Sen summed up the situation by saying, "The world food situation is now more precarious than at any time since the period of acute shortage immediately after the Second World War."[8]

There are several ways to verify the failure of agriculture to produce food in pace with the expanding population.

For instance, if it is true that per capita production of food is decreasing one can expect the law of supply and demand to push up food prices. A recent study shows that this is exactly what is happening. Almost half of the developing nations for which data are available show food prices rising faster than the cost of living—as normally occurs when per capita food production falls.[9]

When food prices go up, then one must also expect that submarginal land, which formerly was unprofitable to farm, will be brought into production. Again there is ample evidence this has happened throughout much of the world. Look at per acre yields. Not only is agricultural production in the hungry nations falling on a per capita basis; in some it is falling on a per acre basis. Recent data developed by the Department of Agriculture reveal that corn yields per acre in Colombia, Venezuela and Ecuador were higher in 1955–1959 than in 1961–1963. In Brazil both wheat and corn per acre yields were higher in 1935–1939 than in 1955–1960. Guatemala had the greatest drop, with yields falling from 15.7 bushels to the acre in 1939 to less than 12 in 1962.[10]

The fall in acre yields in these examples may soon become more and more evident throughout the undeveloped world. Land has been put into production which simply lacks the qualities needed to *maintain* production. The rising cost of food combined with the population pressures on the land have pushed farmers farther and farther up the hillsides and farther and farther out into the jungle. They are now tilling land which should never have been farmed. This land may be able to raise a few crops successfully, but then the yields fall off because its low quality will not permit sustained production—at least not until new cultural techniques are evolved for that land through years of research.

Since World War II four-fifths of the increase in agricultural production in the undeveloped countries has resulted not from the use of fertilizers or other new twentieth-century technology, but from putting into production land which hitherto was unused. It was nothing more than extending traditional farming methods into submarginal land.[11] By 1958 virtually all of the unused, submarginal land which could be brought into production even on a forced, substandard basis was being farmed. Thus, with no new technology and no new marginal land available the race between food production and mouths to be fed—the race which until then agriculture had at least been keeping up with—now began to be lost.

Throughout much of the tropics the subsistence farmer traditionally uses a slash-and-burn technique. Every three or four years he abandons his land, moves to another plot, cuts down the brush, lets this dry and then burns it. Then he plants his corn or cassava or platanos or whatever is the staff of life in his region. The land that he moves away from is left fallow to grow weeds and brush until he returns to use it again. In the good old days he did not return to it for seven, eight or more years. Now, however, with more people pressuring to live off the land he must use the plots more and more frequently. Land that used to rest eight years between cultivations is now idle only six years. This two-year difference results in lower yields.

Whether or not one is skeptical of the accuracy of the official statistics from the undeveloped countries, the projected trends cannot be doubted. These trends add up to one conclusion:

The hungry nations have lost the capacity to feed themselves from the land available to them.

Nowhere is this more pronounced than in the tropics, where food production per capita is falling most rapidly. However, the urgency of the world food crisis stems from a few areas peripheral to the tropics where the sheer mass of humanity, as in Pakistan, northern India and China, makes any drop in per capita production a frightening figure.

Egypt is the gaudy example of the land/population treadmill on which the hungry nations now find themselves. The nub of Egypt's exploding crisis is illustrated by the steadily increasing percentage of its agricultural imports in relation to total imports, as follows:[12]

|  | *Per Cent of Total Agricultural Imports* |
|------|------|
| 1954 | 17.8 |
| 1960 | 25.2 |
| 1965 | 30.2 |

*Excluded* from these percentages is the major item of P.L. 480 shipments from the United States which, since 1954, have amounted to considerably more than a billion dollars.[13]

In 1947 Egypt's population was increasing at a rate of 340,000 additional mouths a year. This was a modest number compared to 1964 when Nasser announced his country had increased that year by 800,000 "little Egyptians." "Bless them!" he said, "but we cannot go on this way."

Egypt's farmable land, lying between the desert and the Nile, is more firmly circumscribed than any other country's. Nasser's solution to the need for increased food production is the new Aswan Dam. It is planned that this dam will increase the arable land by one-third. It is to be the great national victory over hunger. It is to bring Egypt in one jump, in one decade, from the Middle Ages into the twentieth century.

Alas! During the ten-year period of construction Egypt's population itself will have increased by one-third.

The increased food and industrial resources resulting from the enormous financial ($1.5 billion) and physical effort represented by the dam will only balance out against the population growth. Egypt will be no better fed after the dam is finished than when construction began.[14]

The one benefit that the Aswan Dam might have bought has been thrown away—time. If Nasser had started ten years ago an energetic population control program, effective results could well be under way ten or fifteen years from now. And he might have started an agricultural research program ten years ago to find out how to use more efficiently the present land and the new Aswan Dam land. He failed to do either of these things.

"Not until February [1966], under the stimulus of outside encouragement, did Egypt formally begin a nationwide campaign to check its rampant population rise"[15] (although it had officially endorsed birth control in 1962). Only now have the newspapers begun to campaign against large families with such things as a cartoon picturing two babies in a hospital nursery, with one saying, "What in God's name are you doing coming to this overcrowded country!"[16] Significantly, the campaign was not pushed into an action program by the Egyptian leadership; they remained passive and apparently disinterested in the face of the mounting statistics.[17] Only when free money was offered by such foreign organizations as the Ford Foundation and the Population Council, and by the United States and Swedish governments, were Nasser and the rest of the leadership willing to work actively for population control.

The interplay of exploding population and bogged-down food production is highlighted in Egypt for all to see and comprehend, because here the agricultural land is absolutely fixed. In Egypt the issue rings forth clear as a bell: cut down the population growth or increase food production per acre. Egypt is doing neither. The Aswan Dam is only a delusion of progress; its new lands will be farmed in the same old ways by the same old fellahins procreating as always without effective official support to curtail family size.

When a country has no new land into which to expand, it becomes dependent upon food from foreign countries. Egypt's precarious, deteriorating position is a clear example. Look at that country's growing imports for wheat and wheat flour (including P.L. 480 shipments):[18]

|      | *Metric Tons* |
|------|---------------|
| 1954 | 58,000        |
| 1960 | 1,175,000     |
| 1962 | 1,370,000     |
| 1964 | 1,586,000     |
| 1965 | 1,840,000     |

## The extent of hunger in the world today

Many observers claim that the somersault from exporter to importer is largely the result of people in those countries eating better today than before World War II. For instance, here is a statement in the same Department of Agriculture study to which I referred earlier, the one that the Secretary of Agriculture quoted so optimistically. The study states that high incomes, especially in the cities, are increasing the demand for food in most of the world's less developed countries. "Consequently, for the first time in its history, India's food shortage is not the result of crop failures and declining per capita food output, but of the increased capacity of its people to buy the food they need."[19]

Such reasoning is false, I believe, and the proof is the increasing hunger so openly evident throughout these same nations. Whatever upgrading of diet may have taken place has occurred primarily among a few favored sectors of the populace, not across the board. This change does not extend beyond a limited group in the cities.

"I'm hungry" is an elusive phrase to pin down. Obviously, it is said in different tones by the American teen-ager than by the Calcutta slum dweller. Even the nutritionists with all their charts and involuted terms cannot really draw a clean-cut line between malnutrition and starvation.

How big an area must be affected before it can be classified as famine-stricken?

What percentage of the population of the undeveloped nations should be called suffering from malnutrition?

The tourist in Lima, Singapore and Dakar possibly sees no malnutrition around him at all—if, that is, he stays in the well-to-do heart of the city, nor will he in the similar heart of Philadelphia, Savannah or London.

Perhaps when a man keels over and collapses from lack of food, then that can be accepted as the dividing line between malnutrition and starvation. Perhaps when whole families and communities keel over, then it can be called a famine. All this, unfortunately, is bad scientific terminology.

An added complication is that it is mighty hard actually to starve to death. "Starvation has to be extreme and of long duration to cause death *if adequate medical care is provided*. With the increase in quantity and quality of medical care, it seems likely that deaths from a given level of mass starvation would be much less today in a given country than would have been the case 20 or 30 years ago."[20]

If, however, I am going to predict in these pages what will happen in the world as food becomes scarcer, I ought to be able to say when a man is hungry, when he is suffering from malnutrition, when he is dying from starvation. Unfortunately, I cannot.

I like best the simple explanation of Boyd Orr, Nobel Laureate and former head of FAO: "All I have learned about calories, proteins, carbohydrates, trace-elements, vitamins and enzymes is this: If people are hungry, they need food. If they are ill-nourished they need good food."[21]

The most commonly used criterion to measure a nation's dietary level is a measuring of its food energy supply in terms of calories. Caloric requirements vary on the basis of the size of the man (or woman), the work he does and the climate in which he lives. Nevertheless, accepted estimates for calorie consumption have been established and the Department of Agriculture has devised from them a so-called world food budget. This shows:

"The share of the population . . . living in countries with average energy (calorie) supply levels below the minimum recommended was 92% for Asia, 38% for Africa and 29% for Latin America." This amounts to 79 per cent of the population in the underdeveloped regions or 56 per cent of the entire world.[22]

So three out of every four people in the developing world do not have enough calories!

A new factor regarding calories has now arisen. Recent research indicates the likelihood of a 5 to 10 per cent error in all calorie statistics regarding the tropics. Until now it has been the standard practice to state that people need less food in the tropics than in the temperate zones. Thus, FAO in its calculations recommends a 5 per cent decrease in food requirements for every 10-degree increase in environmental temperatures. However, tests by the United States Army Medical Research and Nutrition Laboratory at Denver have shown that just the opposite appears to be true.[23] This means, then, that the hotter the weather the *more* food the individual needs to perform his work. Since the hungry nations are nearly all in the tropics, it would appear as if the FAO figures should be increased by another 50 million people suffering from malnutrition—give or take a dozen million people!

During the last war there were two long sieges that ranked with just about any of the famous ones of history. One was in Leningrad and the other in Malta. In both the populace for months at a time was reduced to the last extremity before actual starvation, yet in both the fighting spirit of the people never flagged.

I lived in Moscow shortly after the Leningrad siege was broken and the Germans pushed back, and I also lived in Malta after the war. The constant stories I heard about both sieges seemed always to be centered not on the lack of food but on the great excitement whenever a load of food would somehow manage to break through the enemy lines. In Leningrad the Russians were able to keep open for one winter a workable road across a frozen lake. In Malta the successive relief convoys would be terribly battered but usually at least one ship would make it. In both places the citizens were surely suffering from malnutrition for prolonged periods, but the elated spirits of wartime action apparently counteracted the adverse physical and psychological factors. Always there was hope that next week, next month, there would be enough food.

There is no such hope among today's sufferers from malnutrition. Automatically, that makes them more liable to succumb to every passing germ or merely to waste themselves away in apathy.

The graph on page 123 illustrates that while today the gap is indeed wide between the food production of these hungry nations and their food demands, tomorrow the gap will be wider.[24]

If this graph seems unrealistic, I counter with another fearsome factor. Who has not looked in awe at the teen-ager who, having just eaten two hamburgers and a malted milk on his way home from school, settles down to a full-course meal with his family? Who eats more than teen-agers? Actually, no one. And 42 per cent of the people in the undeveloped world are under the age of fifteen.[25] Most of these children, in contrast to earlier years, will be kept alive by the new public health facilities and will grow up to adult age.

The graph[26] on page 124 shows how quickly the demand for food accelerates as a child five years old, requiring only 1600 calories a day, skyrockets to the fifteen-year-old needing 2800. If the undeveloped world cannot now feed itself, consider the difficulty when today's huge child population reaches its late teens.

Just as the food requirements of a child shoot up with the years, so will the food requirements of the hungry nations. These will skyrocket *faster* than the simple population growth percentages.

Of course, calories are only part of the health picture.

**Data for
Latin America, Far East, Near East and Africa
(The Hungry Nations)**

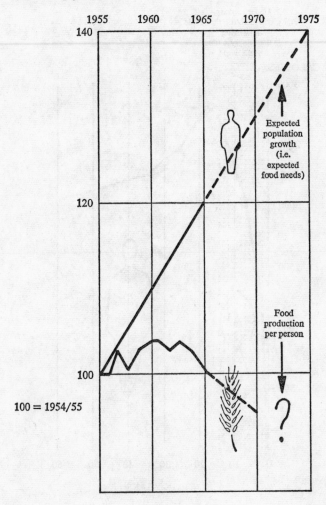

100 = 1954/55

# Calorie Requirements at Different Age Levels

Under 15 years—
Age group of HALF the people
now living
in the hungry nations
of the world

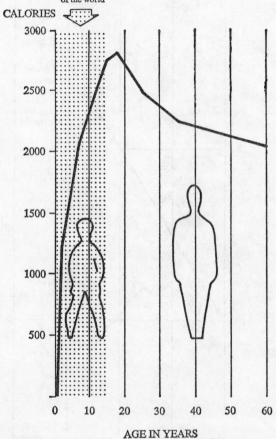

CALORIES

AGE IN YEARS

Necessary to man's energy is protein, which is an indicator of the "quality" of the diet available. Here again, over half the world lives in countries which do not have a protein intake that meets minimum acceptable standards. Also, fats are needed by man. "90 per cent of Asia's population is included in those countries with fat intake below the [recommended] standards."[27]

Hunger in its many forms, whether protein deficiency or fat deficiency or just plain empty belly, is an affliction, a scourge, a plague from one continent to another.

The crisis of population explosion versus static agriculture is indeed formed. The nations of the undeveloped world are no longer grain exporters, they are grain importers. There is no more unused land to bring into cultivation; even the deficient marginal land is by now in use. Hunger is rampant throughout country after country, continent after continent around the undeveloped belt of the tropics and subtropics. Today's crisis can move in only one direction—toward catastrophe.

Today hungry nations; tomorrow starving nations.

### 1975—the hunger becomes famine

In a 1966 seminar I attended at the Hudson Institute one of the speakers said: "People who publish population figures are propagandists. They like the extreme projections. Everyone else believes population figures will decrease sharply within a generation."

Maybe so. I hope so. Yet even a generation is too short a lead time if—always that "if"—the population figures do, after all, "decrease sharply."

For the short, ten-year span from 1965 to 1975 United Nations projections for population growth show how much additional food will be required.[28] See table on next page.

Thus, simply to maintain today's inadequate dietary levels, the hungry nations must increase their production within a single decade by 26 per cent.

Agricultural increases such as these cannot be attained by 1975. Since this is so then the diets of these nations must become considerably less than even today's level of malnutrition.

The end result for each of the affected nations will be the constant threat of catastrophe. Whenever there is too much or too little rain, whenever spring comes late or the harvest is wet, whenever civil unrest delays the plantings, whenever *anything* reduces the yield, then a portion of the population will slip over into the chasm of starvation.

### FUTURE FOOD REQUIREMENTS OF THE HUNGRY WORLD

| | Population at Current Rates of Growth | | Additional Food Production Needed Within Ten Years |
|---|---|---|---|
| | *1965* | *1975* | |
| East Asia | 867 million | 1.04 billion | 20% |
| South Asia | 975 million | 1.25 billion | 28% |
| Africa | 311 million | 404 million | 30% |
| Latin America | 248 million | 335 million | 35% |
| TOTAL | 2.4 billion | 3.0 billion | 26% |

"Famine isn't like a satellite count-down; you don't say, 'Three-two-one, it's here!' What happens is like the New York water shortage: it develops slowly; experts wring hands; public pays no attention; then, suddenly, it's headlined. That's what's happening in world food."[29] We cannot say precisely what it takes to starve a man to death. It is clear, however, that if the undeveloped world is not feeding itself today, it will feed itself even less well tomorrow.

The Swedish economist Gunnar Myrdal sees a "world calamity" in "five or ten years."[30]

Chester Bowles, Ambassador to India, says that the approaching world famine threatens to be "the most colossal catastrophe in history."[31]

Thomas M. Ware, testifying before a Senate committee, said, "Very few grasp the magnitude of the danger that confronts us."[32]

Dr. Raymond Ewell: "The world is on the threshold of the biggest famine in history. If present trends continue, it seems likely that famine will reach serious proportions in India, Pakistan and China in the early 1970's. . . . Such a famine will be of massive proportions affecting hundreds of millions."[33]

1975 will be a crucial year in the world, crucial because the world food shortage will then dominate the headlines and the results will be in full view. The present downward trends cannot be reversed, nor can they be dusted under the carpet. Those who say there are too many variables in the future to forecast food deficits ignore the present trends.

## India is the bellwether

India is the case in point. It is the bellwether that shows the path which the others, like sheep going to the slaughter, are following. The hungry nation that today refuses to heed India's history will be condemned to relive it. "The future of mankind is now being ground out in India. If no solution [is found], all the world will live as India does now."[34]

The present food crisis of India was predicted officially in 1959. In that year the Indian government, with the help of the Ford Foundation, issued a report which accurately forecast, it is now painfully realized, the serious gap that would arise by 1965–1966 between food stocks and consumption needs. Its warning of trouble and civil tensions as a result of this gap was explicit: "We have reached the inescapable conclusion that a rapid increase in production of food is India's primary problem in achieving human welfare, social justice and democracy over the next seven years. . . . The entire nation must be made aware of the impending food crisis and steps must be taken to meet it. . . . The statement has been made by Indian leaders that if the food problem is to be solved the work must be placed on a 'war footing.' . . . But an effective crusade involves more than plans. . . . 'Business as usual' will not achieve the food production targets."[35]

The Indian leadership did not do this. "Business as usual" continued with the government's emphasis on industry, its downgrading of agriculture and its insistence on socialistic controls throughout the economy.

Many of the hungry nations are, to be sure, more preoccupied today with their agricultural problems than they, or India, were eight years ago, but there is still seldom any real sense of urgency. Thus, today's troubles in India will soon become the fate of others.

India's policies on the use of fertilizers is probably as good a single example as can be found of what I mean by no real sense of urgency. India uses an amazingly small amount of fertilizer, only about three pounds of nutrients to the acre (compared with 300 in Japan, 180 in Taiwan and 100 in Korea).[36] Yet, in spite of the generally recognized need to increase the national manufacture of fertilizers, the socialistic Indian government has restricted the production of fertilizer by private industries while not making any real effort to develop the government's own small production. The government "has restricted private sales of nitrogenous fertilizer and then boosted the price of fertilizer through co-op channels in order to protect high-cost government plants; and it has not either permitted or constructed a distribution system to get fertilizer to the farmers when they need it on credit terms that are possible for the majority of farmers."[37] This favoring of government-owned fertilizer plants and harassing of privately owned plants to the detriment of the nation does, incidentally, seem to be an illustrative example of a typical weakness of the typical socialist government in the undeveloped world. It is a pertinent example of how difficult it will be for these governments to plan clearly and coolheadedly in order to prepare for the future famines.

Since the British left, India has tied its dreams to industrialization. One reason this was possible was that the country did make significant increases in agricultural production during the 1950's (a 46 per cent increase from 1951 to 1961— most of which resulted from putting new land into production),[38] and thus was not forced to think in terms of food. But then the agricultural facts of life caught up with India. For three years (1962–1964) "food-grain production in India . . . remained virtually stagnant while population during the same period . . . increased by about 33 million people." The result was a sharp rise in food-grain prices.[39] India's confidence faltered, but only for a moment. The Lord smiled again (in the form of good weather) in the crop year of 1964–1965 and India increased its agricultural production 10 per cent.[40] Confidence was great. Yet even this good production year was not enough. Whereas the Third Five Year Plan (1960–1965) had projected a production of 119 million tons of food grains (more than enough to feed the population), only 80 million tons were produced. Seven million tons of food had to be imported. Grain prices rose 30 to 40 per cent as supplies failed to meet the nation's needs.[41] When shipments were delayed a few weeks by a longshoremen's strike in the United States, food riots erupted. India was living literally "from ship to mouth."

The 1959 prediction of a food crisis in 1966, to which I referred earlier, and the Indian government's failure to heed its own warning underscore the fact that predicting civil troubles as a result of food shortages can be done with considerable accuracy. Those who found the Indian food crisis of 1966 a startling awakening may not have seen the 1959 prediction, but by 1964 the headlines clearly showed what was coming.

November 1964: "Storming mobs of angry Indians brought the southern state of Kerala to the brink of anarchy last week. Driven by hunger and prodded by the Communists, crowds looted shops and warehouses in a frantic search for food. . . . Students raced through the streets challenging the police to 'give us rice or shoot us.' "[42] The central government was able to reroute eighty thousand tons of wheat and rice into the troubled area.[43] This crisis expedient quelled—for a while —the riots which in retrospect are reported to have been caused not by direct, immediate hunger but by anger that the local rice ration had been cut to the bone while a neighboring state received a much larger ration.[44] Either way, the riots were real enough and a portent of times to come.

[The U.S. sent in] stopgap help for India. About $400 million worth of U.S. food—wheat, rice, soybean oil—is to pour into India between now and next June 30 [1965]. The Indians are as usual to pay in rupees, most of which the U.S. will immediately lend back to them. . . . In a sense, a moment of truth is upon India.[45]

Parallel with these sad statistics India came to the end of its financial rope. In 1964 it had debts which required $225 million a year just to service. Most of these debts were owed to Europeans or to the World Bank and default is a matter of time. The American suppliers of food and industrial products were not caught in this bind because they had already been paid directly by the United States government out of tax receipts. In 1964 the United States owned 12 billion rupees ($2.5 billion) derived largely from sale of U.S. food to the Indian government. "More than half the rupees now circulating in India are really owned by the U.S."[46] (by 1966 this was to be estimated at two-thirds!).

In December 1964 the all-India price index for cereal grains was 21.4 per cent higher than in December 1963.[47] The price of beans was 60 per cent higher. India made frantic efforts to procure more food. It arranged for 59,000 tons of rice from Thailand and 35,000 tons from Cambodia. A new year-end amendment of the P.L. 480 agreement provided for an extra 130,000 tons of U.S. corn and 50,000 tons of U.S. rice.[48]

Just the same, by August 1965 India was facing its greatest food crisis since the terrible Bihar famine of 1951. Riots broke out in Kilhapur, near Bombay, when an "Anti-starvation Action Committee" was formed.[49] The Indian government, in an effort to accumulate some wheat and rice reserves, reduced the people's diets from 14.4 ounces of wheat and rice a day to 12 ounces.[50]

By then food was arriving at the rate of two ships a day from the United States. And no other source of food was available. Australia and Canada had committed their wheat stocks to China.[51]

And in September war broke out between Pakistan and India. The war pacified, temporarily, the unrest arising from the food shortages, but also it obviously diverted funds into the army that otherwise might have been used in agricultural development.

By 1974 India will have increased her population by 120 million.[52] India cannot, literally cannot, feed that many more mouths. Even the United States would find it appalling to try and feed that kind of increase in numbers within its own borders within the space of eight years.

Today India totters. Tomorrow: "The most vulnerable countries include India, Pakistan, Communist China, Indonesia, Iran, Turkey, Egypt, Colombia, Peru and several other countries of Latin America. Mass starvation seems likely to hit these countries within five to ten years, or even sooner."[53] The resulting unrest will not erupt simultaneously everywhere. Like India's series of riots and disturbances, each will erupt spasmodically, but the time of quiet between eruptions will grow shorter. "[Some countries] such as Burma, Thailand, the Philippines, Nigeria, Ghana, Chile and others seem to be in relatively good shape food-wise at present, but they all have such high population growth rates that they will be in serious difficulties in a few more years [after 1980]."[54]

Vice-President Humphrey flies to India and announces a $100,000,000 loan. President Johnson decrees stepped-up food shipments. North Carolina's representative Harold D. Cooley even proposes using the United States Air Force to airlift food within India.[55] Presumably, this will be enough to save it for 1966 and perhaps for a few years to come. But when the crisis continues, what happens next? For by then other countries will be floundering with India.

Today, India is the first of the hungry nations to stand at the brink of famine and disaster. Being the first, it receives the full bounty of United States food generosity. India is today's handwriting-on-the-wall for the hungry nations in the year of 1975.

"The 'Four Horsemen of the Apocalypse'—pestilence, war, famine and death—continue to stalk the world. Although they may emerge at different times from different doors, the fact remains that they come from the same barn."[56]

The trend of export-import food statistics and the lagging productive capacity of the hungry nations show clearly that hunger is not only here today but is steadily increasing.

By 1975 civil disorder, anarchy, military dictatorships, runaway inflation, transportation breakdowns and chaotic unrest will be the order of the day in many of the hungry nations—all because hunger will turn inexorably into starvation and starvation will become widespread famine.

I opened this chapter by criticizing a 1965 speech of the

Secretary of Agriculture as falsely optimistic. It is well to close by quoting from a speech he made a year later which to me seems more realistic.

> The encouraging advances in per capita food production recorded in the developing countries during the 1950's have been reversed in many cases during the present decade. . . . Virtually all studies . . . have underestimated increases in the demand for food, largely because of underestimates of population growth, and they have overestimated increases in food production in the developing countries.
>
> If the rate of increase [of wheat imports] over the next decade should even remotely approach that of the decade just ended, world import demand for wheat will far exceed the supply capabilities of the exporting countries. . . . Unless the less developed countries sharply increase their agricultural productivity, and soon, mass famine will take place. Thus more human lives hang in the balance in the race between food and people than have been lost in all the wars of history.[57]

## Footnotes

[1] Orville L. Freeman, Secretary of Agriculture, address at the United Nations Biennial Conference of the Food and Agriculture Organization, Rome, Nov. 23, 1965.

[2] U.S. Department of Agriculture, *Changes in Agriculture in 26 Developing Nations 1948–1963,* Foreign Agricultural Economic Report No. 27 (Nov. 1965).

[3] Quentin M. West, *World Food Needs,* Foreign Regional Analysis Division, Economic Research Service, U.S. Department of Agriculture, Feb. 10, 1966, p. 10.

[4] Carl O. Winberg, "Indonesia Having Trouble Maintaining Its Copra Exports," *Foreign Agriculture,* Nov. 9, 1964.

[5] Ibid.

[6] Lester R. Brown, *Man, Land and Food,* U.S. Department of Agriculture, FAE Report No. 11 (Nov. 1963), p. 76.

[7] B. R. Sen, Director General of Food and Agriculture Organization, United Nations, Circular Letter No. 90 to Ministers of Agriculture, Aug. 1965.

[8] Bernard D. Nossiter, *Washington Post,* Oct. 13, 1966.

[9] United Nations, Food and Agriculture Organization, *The State of Food and Agriculture 1965,* p. 72.

10 A synthesis of several *Agricultural Statistics Yearbooks,* U.S. Dept. of Agriculture.

11 Brown, op. cit., pp. 53 and 56.

12 Thomas E. Street, Deputy Assistant Administrator for Export Programs, Foreign Agricultural Service, U.S. Department of Agriculture, in a letter to the author, June 27, 1966.

13 *Food for Peace 1964 Annual Report on Public Law 480,* House Document No. 130–89/1 (Washington, D.C.; Government Printing Office, Mar. 1965).

14 Paul C. Tullier, "Population Boom . . . or Boomerang," *The 1964 World Book Yearbook* (Chicago: Field Enterprises Educational Corp., 1964), p. 200.

15 *New York Times,* July 10, 1966.

16 Hedrick Smith, *New York Times,* Jan. 29, 1966.

17 *New York Times,* July 10, 1966.

18 See note 12.

19 See note 2.

20 Raymond Ewell, Vice-President for Research, State University of New York at Buffalo, in a letter to the author, July 18, 1966.

21 Ritchie Calder, *Common Sense about a Starving World* (London: Macmillan, 1962), p. 15.

22 Brown, op. cit., p. 38.

23 Frank C. Consolazio, LeRoy C. Matoush, Richard A. Nelson, Juan B. Torres and Gerhart J. Isaac, "Environmental Temperature and Energy Expenditures," *Journal of Applied Physiology* (Jan. 1963), pp. 65–68.

24 Adapted from Table II-2, United Nations, Food and Agriculture Organization, *The State of Food and Agriculture 1965,* p. 15.

25 United Nations, Department of Economic and Social Affairs, *Provisional Report on World Population Prospects as Assessed in 1963 (1964).*

26 Adapted from "Table of Recommended Dietary Allowances," National Research Council Publication No. 1146 (1964), p. vii.

27 Brown, op. cit., p. 41.

28 Calculated from figures in Robert C. Cook's "World Population Projections, 1965–2000," *Population Bull.* (Oct. 1965), pp. 96–97.

29 "Famine Is Here," *New Republic,* Sept. 18, 1965.

30 Ibid.

31 Ibid.

32 Ibid.

33 Raymond Ewell, "Famine and Fertilizer," *Chemical and Engineering News* (Dec. 14, 1964), pp. 106–117.

34 Roger Revelle, *World War on Hunger,* Hearings before the

House Committee on Agriculture, 89th Cong., 2d Sess., on H.R. 12152, H.R. 12704, and H.R. 12785, Feb. 14, 1966.

[35] *Report on India's Food Crisis and Steps to Meet It* (sponsored by the Ford Foundation but published by the Government of India, Delhi, Apr. 1959), pp. 1, 3, 14.

[36] Charles E. Lindblom, "Has India an Economic Future?," *Foreign Affairs,* Vol. 44 (1966), p. 240.

[37] Ibid.

[38] *Newsweek,* Nov. 23, 1964.

[39] Horace J. Davis, U.S. Agricultural Attaché in India, "India's Food Grain Situation," *Foreign Agriculture* (Nov. 2, 1964), p. 3.

[40] Lindblom, op. cit., p. 240.

[41] Lester R. Brown, staff economist, U.S. Department of Agriculture, in conversation with the author, Sept. 21, 1965.

[42] *Newsweek,* Nov. 23, 1964.

[43] Ibid.

[44] George K. Parman, executive secretary, Committee on Marine Protein Resource Development, Food and Nutrition Board, National Academy of Sciences, Washington, D.C., in a letter to the author, July 12, 1966.

[45] *U.S. News and World Report,* Oct. 12, 1964.

[46] Ibid.

[47] V. M. Tandon, "India's Food Outlook Brighter," *Foreign Agriculture,* Apr. 5, 1965.

[48] Ibid.

[49] Selig S. Harrison, *Washington Post,* Aug. 22, 1965.

[50] Editorial, *Washington Post,* Aug. 14, 1965.

[51] See note 41 above.

[52] See note 25 above.

[53] Raymond Ewell, *World War on Hunger,* Hearings before the House Committee on Agriculture, 89th Cong., 2d Sess., on H.R. 12152, H.R. 12704, and H.R. 12785, Feb. 16, 1966, p. 139.

[54] Ibid.

[55] Felix Belair, Jr., *New York Times,* Feb. 18, 1966.

[56] Herschel D. Newsom, testimony before the Senate Committee on Agriculture and Forestry, 89th Cong., 2d Sess., on S. 2157, S. 2826, S. 2932, S. 2933, S. 2995, and H.R. 14929, Mar. 4, 1966, p. 126.

[57] Orville L. Freeman, Secretary of Agriculture, address before the Fifth Annual High-Level Meeting of the OECD, Development Assistance Committee, Washington, D.C., July 21, 1966.

# 11. Toward a Non-Malthusian Population Policy

## JEAN MAYER

One theme of this essay is that food is only one of the elements in the population problem. Admittedly, at present, it is a major factor in some parts of the world; but there are large areas where the national food supply is a minor factor and others where it is not a factor at all. Furthermore, considering the world as a whole, there is no evidence that the food situation is worsening and there is at least a likelihood that food may at some time (20 or 30 years from now) be removed altogether as a limiting factor to population. Yet, to deny that the population problem is basically one of food for survival is not to deny that there is a population problem; it is in fact to remove the appearance of a safety valve and also to reveal the problem in its generality. For were we really to starve when the population reaches a certain magic number, this in turn would cause a drastic increase in child and infant mortality, decreased fertility, and a shortening of the average life span. In other words, it would cause the increase in population to be self-limiting. If the world can continue to feed—however badly—an ever-increasing number of people, this safety valve (however unpalatable, it *would* be a safety valve) is missing. And if lack of food is not a component of the definition of overpopulation, rich countries as well as poor ones become candidates for overpopulation—now.

Another theme is that there is a strong case to be made for a stringent population policy on exactly the reverse of the basis Malthus expounded. Malthus was concerned with the steadily more widespread poverty that indefinite population growth would inevitably create. I am concerned about the areas of the globe where people are rapidly becoming richer. For rich people occupy much more space, consume more of each natural resource, disturb the ecology more, and create more land, air, water, chemical, thermal, and radioactive pollution than poor people. So it can be argued that from many viewpoints it is even more urgent to control the numbers of the rich than it is to control the numbers of the poor.

The population problem is not new, although it has recently acquired new and dangerous dimensions. In all early treatments of the subject, considerations of population policy were not closely linked to economic concerns or the availability of food. Plato, who undertook nothing less than the projection of an ideal city-state in estimating the numbers needed for the various functions of citizenship, arrived at the figure of 5,040 citizens as the desirable size, adequate to "furnish numbers for war and peace, for all contracts and dealings, including taxes and divisions of the land." In *The Republic* he described his well-known eugenics proposal for public hymeneals of licensed breeders. His preoccupation was with the quality of man and of the state; not with the availability of food and other resources. Aristotle, who was concerned with certain of the economic consequences of overpopulation, though not specifically with food, warned in *Politics* that "a neglect of an effective birth control policy is a never-failing source of poverty, which is in turn the parent of revolution and crime," and advised couples with an excessive number of children to abort succeeding pregnancies "before sense and life have begun."

Plato and Aristotle did not go unchallenged. The Pythagoreans, in particular Hippocrates, opposed abortion. The Hippocratic oath contains the pledge: "I will not give a woman an abortive remedy." Of greater subsequent importance, the Romans, particularly Cicero, disapproved of the Greek views on population. They were not so much concerned with the quality of man as with the excellence of the Empire. Rome taxed celibacy and rewarded large families. Roman ideas, incidentally, were very similar to those of Confucius and his followers, also citizens of a large and expanding empire, and equally convinced that a numerous and expanding population should be promoted by wise rulers. The economic consequences of large populations were essentially ignored by the Romans; Confucius dealt with them by enunciating the rather intriguing formula: "Let the producers be many and the consumers few."

The Hebrews and the Fathers of the Church were similarly uninterested in the economic implications of population growth. Biblical and early Christian writers can, indeed, hardly be considered to have had a population policy, though their concepts of family life and of the dignity of man are as basic now as they were millenniums ago. Children were repeatedly designated as the gifts of God, with large families particularly blessed. The prescriptions of Saint Paul were somewhat more complex: while he stated that women could merit eternal salvation through bearing children if they continued to be faithful, holy, and modest, he praised virginity as more blessed than marriage, and dedicated widowhood as preferred above remarriage. Following Saint Paul, the position of Christians in sexual relations became variegated: from strict antinomianism, believers in all possible experiences, to fanatical ascetics who believed in self-castration to remove all possibility of temptation, with the center of gravity of Christian opinion somewhere between the traditional Roman double standard (strict virtue expected from the woman, somewhat more permissive rules for the man) and the more puritanical ideal of the Stoics.

In this ethical Babel, the absence of strict theological canons made it possible for intelligent citizens of a crowded and decaying empire to discuss the possible economic and political consequences of overpopulation. In *De Anima* Tertullian wrote: "The scourges of pestilence, famine, wars, and earthquakes have come to be regarded as a blessing to crowded nations, since they served to prune away the luxuriant growth of the human race." The position of the Church against abortion hardened in the third century, when Saint Hippolytus opposed Pope Calixtus I for showing too much leniency toward the abortionists, and reiterated the Christian position that the fetus is a person and not, as in Roman law, a part of the mother. Saint Augustine, rising from a Manichaean background and a personally unhappy sexual history, defined the purpose of Christian marriage as procreation, with abstinence permissible by mutual consent. This basis of the Christian marriage, unmodified by Thomas Aquinas or the medieval theologians, unmodified by Luther (an Augustinian, very much attached to the pattern of the order) was to survive far into the twentieth century.

In spite of theologians, Tertullian was echoed 1,300 years later in Botero, a sixteenth-century Italian writer, who held that man's productive powers are inferior to his reproductive powers, which do not diminish automatically when population increases. The population of the world, then, must be constantly checked by war and epidemics, the earth already holding as many people as it can feed. From Botero onward, concepts of optimum population size became indissolubly linked to economic considerations, but to economic considerations of the lowest order. Population limitation was advocated by writers, Malthus foremost among them, who felt they could demonstrate that population will inevitably rise to the very margin of food production capacity, with misery and vice the only consequences. The examples chosen were often unfortunate in the light of hindsight: Malthus based his prediction on an examination of the United States of the late eighteenth century. On the other side, mercantilist writers and rulers once again saw an increase in population as a guarantee of ample manpower for production and for war, and as a test of good government. Through the nineteenth century the debate continued. Malthusians saw the solution of economic problems due to overpopulation in continence and in more poverty —specifically, the repeal of the poor laws. The belief in the inevitability of starvation and the desirability of a *laissez faire* policy was in no small measure responsible for governmental inaction during the Irish famine. At the other end of the spectrum, Marx and Engels opposed Malthus as a peculiarly vicious and obsolete defender of capitalism. "Overpopulation" was a bourgeois invention designed to justify the poverty of the working classes. Improved production and distribution, not restriction of births, was the answer. A socialistic economy could thrive under all conditions of population growth, while an economy based on scarcity and high prices required birth control to mitigate its glaring deficiencies. Oddly enough, a number of modern Catholic philosophers have held a viewpoint not very different from that of Karl Marx.

The position of many Chinese leaders at present is a combination of orthodox Marxist anti-Malthusianism and traditional Chinese predilection for large families. Others, echoing Francis Place and the liberal socialists, advocate the availability of the means of birth control so as to permit the liberation of women and their participation in the edification of socialism (being careful meanwhile to avoid any Malthusian implication).

Since the mid-nineteenth century, three profound revolutions have been taking place: a technological revolution, which promises to accelerate food production still faster; a demographic explosion, which is also accelerating and places the problem of population in an even more dramatic context; and changes in human attitudes, for which Harlan Cleveland has coined the felicitous expression, "the revolution of rising expectations." It is the contention of this writer that nothing is more dangerous for the cause of formulating a sound population policy than to approach the problem in nineteenth-century terms. By continuing to link the need for population control to the likelihood that food supply will be increasingly limited, the elaboration of birth control programs of sufficient magnitude will be held up for many years, perhaps many generations. In contemporary terms, it may well be that the controversy between Plato and Cicero makes more sense than that between the neo-Malthusians and the neo-Marxists.

That the magnitude of the population problem has increased dramatically in recent years is well publicized. Scholars have estimated that after hundreds of thousands of years of slow growth, the population of the world reached the quarter billion mark some time around the beginning of this era. It doubled to 500 million by 1650. Two centuries later it reached the billion mark. The next doubling took 80 years, with a population of 2 billion in 1930. It would appear that the world is on its way to the next doubling, to 4 billion in 45 years, by 1975; and a population of 8 billion may well be reached within the following 30 or 35 years unless rates of growth are drastically decreased. The present growth rate would lead to a population of 500 billion by the year 2200, and give the surface of all continents a population density equal to that of Washington, D.C. at present!

This increase has been due not to an increase in birth rates, but to a decrease in death rates. Around 1700, life expectancy at birth of European populations was about 33 years, and had increased little in the previous three to four hundred years. By 1950, life expectancy in Western and Central Europe and in the United States had increased to 66–69 years, an increase of over 100 per cent. This decrease in mortality rates is no longer confined to populations of European stocks. In 1946, the death rate of the Moslem population of Algeria was higher than that of Sweden in 1775. In 1954, in spite of generalized guerilla war on its territory, the death rate of this population was lower than that of Sweden in 1875. A similar telescoping of the drop in death rates is going on all over the world.

From a demographic point of view it must be noted that a drop in the death rate, with birth rate unchanged, not only results in an increase in the rate of population growth, but also produces an acceleration in the rate of growth itself: a decline in age-specific mortality rates in ages prior to the end of the childbearing age has the same demographic effect as an increase in the birth rate. In the United States, 97 out of every 100 newborn white females reach the age of 20; 91 reach the age of 50. In Guatemala, only 70 reach the age of 20; 49 that of 50. If the death rate in Guatemala fell within the next decade to somewhere near the 1950 United States level, a not unlikely development, this alone would increase the number of women reaching the beginning of the childbearing period by 85 per cent. Because of the high proportion of young people in underdeveloped countries generally—a country like Costa Rica has twice the proportion of people under 15 that Sweden has—this drop in the death rate in the pre-childbearing period has now and will have in the next few years a gigantic effect on the birth rate. Brazil had 52 million people in 1950, 71 million in 1960, and 83 million in 1966. If present rates prevail it should have 240 million by the year 2000, or 14 times the 1900 population. With a drop in mortality in the young age groups, the increase could be even more spectacular.

The significance of the demographic trends within this country is not generally appreciated. The United States, with a population of 200 million, has at present one-sixteenth of the earth's population on one-sixteenth of the land area. Though a number of underdeveloped areas are piling up population faster, we are accumulating about 2.2 million people per year, more than any increase before 1946. The rate of growth seems unimpressive, 1.1 for the year 1967 (the highest rate reached was 1.8 in 1946 to 1957). If the rate prevailing over the past five years persists, the population of the United States will reach 300 million by the year 1990. What most of us have tended to ignore is that the so-called baby boom of the postwar era followed a period of depression and very low birth rates: from 1920 to 1933 the birth rate had fallen steadily from 27.7 per 1,000 in 1920 to 18.4 in 1933. The absolute decline in births was less steep, because the numerical base of women of childbearing age was still growing. When the birth rate started rising in the early forties, the increase was applied to the still large number of women born between 1916 and 1924. Since 1945, the baby boom that has been so well publicized had actually been taking place on the basis of the shrinking group of women of childbearing age born since 1924. As of 1963, the last of the undersize groups had entered the reproducing age. From 1964 (when the first girls born in the big postwar years reached the age of 18), the number of women in the childbearing age has started increasing rapidly. While in 1940 there were 32 million women 15 to 44 years of age, in 1950 34 million, and in 1960 36 million (a very slow increase), there will be 43 million in 1970 and 54 million in 1980. While the birth rate is declining (and while a better index, the age-standardized general fertility rate based upon women of childbearing age only is also declining), the sheer existence of the number of women and girls alive now means that even in the unlikely event that the fertility rate fell to the historical lows of the depression years and never departed from it, the population of the United States would still more than double in the next century. The reader will, I trust, give me credit for not minimizing the problem of total population either at home or for the world at large.

With this picture of ever-increasing numbers of people, the first reaction among a portion of the public is that we are running out of space, that the "population density" is becoming dangerously high. This concept of "population density"—number of people per unit surface—has underlain the concept of "overpopulation" in the past. It is not very useful except where the primary resources are extractive (mining) and where the most primitive types of agriculture (independent of industry for fertilizers, machines, etc., and hence essentially dependent on area) and forestry prevail. It also presupposes that there is no industry to absorb surplus manpower. It is a concept of dubious value where non-extractive industries are dominant and where trade is possible. The high density band from Boston to Washington has an area of 14,000 square miles, an aggregate population of over 30 million (or over 2,000 persons per square mile), and very limited natural resources. The median family income is $1,000 more than for the United States as a whole. Can this area be said to be overpopulated from a material standpoint? To those who object that this area is part of a larger and less densely populated whole, one might point to prosperous Holland, or Belgium, or even Hong Kong, which, although trade with its hinterland is very meagre (imports from mainland China represent only 17 per cent of total imports), not only houses 3.1 million people on 398 square miles (12,700 per square mile), but has shown an unexcelled increase in national product of 7 to 10 per cent per year—a doubling of real output within 10 years. Once one argues that a certain population density should be preserved, such as density with respect to capital for example, one is dealing with a much more complex concept. From it follows the idea that some sparsely settled countries need rapid increases in population, preferably through immigration, for optimal use of resources. The mental image of population density entertained by most people is, in any case, complicated by esthetic and social considerations, and "high density" is more likely to be ascribed to Calcutta than to Paris, to Costa Rica than to Denmark.

This leads us to the second and more popular concept, that overpopulation can best be appraised with respect to food resources and that the present rate of increase in the world's population is rapidly carrying us to the brink of or to actual starvation. It is my contention that this is not happening. Furthermore, I do not consider that my belief, which I shall now endeavor to justify, makes me an "optimist" as compared to the legions of conservationists, social scientists, etc., who have embraced a Malthusian "pessimism." If anything, this view makes me even more pessimistic about our chances of limiting the world's population at an early date: famine or the threat of famine is perhaps the worst method of limitation, but it would work.

World War II was not a Malthusian check. In spite of the horrendous numbers of soldiers and civilians killed, in spite of the massive genocide perpetrated by the Nazis, food production decreased much more than population. By 1945, intake per capita was 16 per cent lower than the 1934–38 average. The creation of the Food and Agriculture Organization, a specialized United Nations Agency that was endowed during its first years with particularly articulate spokesmen, dramatized the worldwide concern over the food situation. The difficulties inherent in getting agriculture going while industry and the means of communication were not yet rebuilt, led to a generalized feeling of pessimism. Cereals, oils, meat, dairy herds were, in succession, the objects of great attention, the conclusion being in each case that pre-war levels of production and consumption were not going to be reached for years. The chaotic state of international trade accentuated shortages, which UNRRA and various emergency agreements attempted to cope with on an *ad hoc* basis. And yet very quickly the situation improved. The oil shortage vanished first; while the gigantic ground nut scheme of the British government, which was supposed to mitigate it, was taking off to a very slow start, the reappearance in the channels of trade of adequate amounts of fats and oils eliminated the motivation for the scheme itself. United States production of cereals and animal products, which had grown during the war in spite of the lack of abundant manpower and the diversion of the chemical industry to military purposes, had to be slowed down as surpluses started accumulating, and, with their appearance, the threat of a collapse of agricultural prices loomed. By 1952–53,

the worldwide rate of per capita production of food had over-
taken pre-war rates. Since then, the average rate of increase
in the production of food for the world at large has been 3 per
cent per year, while the population has increased on the average 1.7 per cent. In document No. 8148, the Department of
State estimates that if individual consumption levels remained
at the 1955–57 level, the world at large would show by 1975
an annual surplus of 40 million tons of wheat and 70 million
tons of rice. (This estimate is based on the postulate that there
will be no increase in rice production in Europe and North
America, and no increase in wheat production in North
America.) Actually, this slight but steady gain of food production over population is part of a secular trend. E. S. and W. S.
Woytinski, in their monumental *World Population and Production,* estimate that since 1850 the increase in output has
been more rapid than the increase in population.

As chairman of the National Council on Hunger and Malnutrition in the United States I have been talking of these
evils at home for years. I have done extensive work in malnutrition in Asia and in Africa and have just returned from a
trip to Nigeria and to Biafra, where I went to study the famine
and the means to alleviate it. I am, therefore, as well aware
of the widespread character of malnutrition as anyone in the
world. Caloric undernutrition is still found in many parts of
the world, and not always as a result of war or civil disorder,
earthquakes or floods, invasions of insects and other parasites,
or abnormally prolonged droughts. Protein deficiency—
kwashiorkor where it occurs without accompanying caloric
deprivation; marasmus when both caloric and protein intakes
are inadequate—is encountered in varying degrees of prevalence among the young children of most countries of Asia and
Africa and in many of Central and South America. Vitamin A
deficiency is perhaps underestimated as a threat to the life,
and the sight, of children of most of the same areas where
protein deficiency is also seen. Riboflavin deficiency, thiamine
deficiency (beriberi in its various forms), and a number of
other deficiencies are still very much with us. Still, there is no
evidence that the situation is getting worse. The food balance
sheets on which postwar pessimism was based are imperfect
instruments. As an officer of FAO, I spent considerable time

attempting to gauge such unknowns as figures for waste at the retail level and within families, and that portion of the food supply that does not move within the channels of trade (food grown by the farmer for his family is very inaccurately known, particularly as regards fruits and vegetables which tend to be underestimated). The nutritional standards against which available supplies are gauged are themselves being refined. As the results of additional experimental and clinical work become available, it is realized that a number of such standards—those for protein and calcium among others—were probably unnecessarily high. Even without such reevaluation, the evolution of food balance sheets, the only instruments we have to judge the race between food and population, make it apparent that most regions do show the same slow increase of per capita supplies exhibited by the world at large. It must be recognized, of course, that many of the worst nutritional scourges of mankind have been historically due as much to ignorance and to callousness as to lack of nutrients as such. Thousands of children die of protein deficiency in areas where the proteins which would save them do in fact exist and are often consumed in sufficient amounts in the very households where infants and toddlers die for lack of them. A faulty understanding of a child's needs may be the main reason he is denied some of the food consumed by his father and older siblings. As for man's inhumanity to man and its contribution to starvation, it could be illustrated by thousands of examples: cereals being shipped from Ireland under the protection of naval guns during the famine; stocks being withheld during the Congo famine to keep prices up; crop destruction policies in South Vietnam; the food blockade of Biafra.

Certainly as far as food is concerned ours is not one world. The United States government rents 20 million acres from our farmers so that they will not grow food on them. A study made at Iowa State University a few years ago suggests that sixty-two and a half million acres ought to be similarly retired so that surpluses will not continue to be created in relation to the present market. Australia, Canada, New Zealand, Argentina, and France have been, or are at present, involved in similar efforts to restrict production.

Nor is this idling of food production restricted to highly

developed countries. A recent study estimates that Ghanaian farmers work only an average of two hours a day in the cocoa area, the wealthiest agricultural area of the country.

It is fair to say that in most areas of the world the race between food and population would be more favorable to the development of adequate nutrition if the rate of population growth was decreased. But I believe that there are no grounds for saying in 1969 that the nutritional state of the world is getting worse. It is not. And I believe that improvement in communication, availability of surpluses in certain countries, the existence of solid international organizations, and the gradual improvement in international morality make large-scale famines, such as the Irish or the Bengali famine, less likely to occur in this era—except perhaps in Red China because of its alienation from the two richest blocs of countries. (It appears, moreover, that the food situation in China has improved considerably in the past two years, making the recurrence of famine there, as in India, more remote.)

Bad as it is, the present is no worse than the past and probably somewhat better. But what of the future? In absolute numbers, the increase in population is likely to accelerate for some time. Can the food supply be kept up? My contention is that for better or for worse it can and will.

First, let us consider conventional agriculture. FAO's figure indicate that 3.4 billion acres are at present under cultivation. This represents less than 11 per cent of the total land area of the world. Some experts—Prasolov, Shantz, Zimmermann—estimate the area that can eventually be made arable at from 13 to 17 billion acres. Colin Clark, director of the Agricultural Economics Research Institute of Oxford, uses the figure of 19 billion acres, but counts double-cropped tropical lands twice. (He considers, incidentally, that if the land were farmed as well as the Dutch farmers work their acres today, it would support 28 billion people on a Dutch diet; if Japanese standards of farming and nutrition were used, this area would support 95 billion people.)

The biggest potential increase of food production does not, however, come from the extension of the area under cultivation, but from the increase in the use of fertilizers. The phenomenal increase in food production in this country has actually been performed with a reduction in acreage farmed. By pre-World War I standards of cultivation, it took one-and-one-half acres to support an American. If such standards prevailed today, we would need to add at least 40 million acres to our farm area every ten years, or the equivalent of an additional Iowa every decade. In fact, we use fertilizers instead. One ton of nitrogen is the equivalent of 14 acres of good farmland. The use of between two and three hundred thousand tons of nitrogen (and corresponding amounts of other necessary elements) per decade has obviated the need to discover another Iowa. And our use of fertilizer is less intensive than it is in Japan, where it is well over twice ours, or in Western Europe. (Incidentally, in spite of its already high standards of cultivation, Japan is still increasing its agricultural production at a rate of 3 per cent per year.) India, Africa, and most of Latin America use only an infinitesimal fraction of Japanese or Western amounts of fertilizer, or none at all. Garst has estimated that an expenditure of ten dollars an acre per year for fertilizers would alone add 50 to 100 per cent to the low yields in underdeveloped countries. Applying this investment to an area of 1.5 billion acres would be the equivalent to adding at least 750 million acres to the crop areas of these countries, the equivalent of a continent bigger than North America. It is interesting to note that this primacy of fertilizers was recognized relatively late. In this country, the recognition dates back only to World War II, and has accelerated since the Korean conflict. In Japan, it dates back to 1950 or thereabout. And the leaders of the U.S.S.R. only recently realized that a large-scale increase in fertilizer output would be easier and more rewarding than the extension of cultivation to the "virgin lands."

There are many other advances in agriculture that have yet to be applied on a large scale. The identification of necessary trace elements and their incorporation into fertilizers and feeds have opened vast areas to cultivation and husbandry in Australia and elsewhere. Selective breeding of plants and animals has permitted the development of species with superior hardiness and increased yields. In the greater part of the world such work has hardly begun. Advances in animal health and nutrition have permitted the mass production of milk and eggs in indoor conditioners on a scale that was unimaginable a few years ago. The city of Los Angeles, for instance, is now an important and efficient dairy area. In some large installations, computers programmed to calculate the cheapest method of providing a diet of known energy and known content in ten essential amino acids, total protein, and other nutrients, automatically set the controls that will mix basic staples providing the cheapest adequate poultry diet as they are informed of the latest commodity prices. Herbicides increase yields; pesticides prevent losses from rodents, insects, and fungi. In many underdeveloped countries one quarter of the crop is lost before it reaches the consumer. Certain methods of preservation of foods by radiation have just been approved by the Food and Drug Administration. The control of weather by seeding clouds for rain; speeding cloud formation by heating lakes by atomic energy; the desalinization of brackish water by various methods, are entering the realm of practical feasibility.

Powerful though these methods of "classical" agriculture are, I believe that they will, within the lifetime of most present inhabitants of this planet, be left far behind as methods of food production. The general public is still unaware of some new developments, their promise, and the extent of the means likely to be expended in the next decade in bringing the results of research to practical application. Large-scale manufacture of food from petro-chemicals started during World War II, when the Germans manufactured synthetic fats to feed forced labor groups. These fats did not conform to desirable standards of taste or safety (they contained a high proportion of branched-chain fatty acids not normally found in nature and probably not fully metabolized, and retained a petroleum-like odor). After the war, interest in "synthetic" fats persisted for a while during the years when it appeared that a shortage of natural fats was likely to be protracted. During the fifties, little or no work was done in this field, but recently some of the larger international oil companies have again become actively interested, and pilot plants are now in operation. Fatty acids, triglycerides (the constituents of our common oils and fats), and fully metabolizable simpler compounds, such as

1,3-butanediol, may soon be manufactured at very low cost for human food and animal feeds. While the promise of abundant and cheap atomic power, widely heralded for the morrow in the more immediate postwar period, has shown itself slow to be realized, it is coming, and it may well be that oil will be increasingly a raw material for food and plastics rather than a fuel.

As a potential source of food production, photosynthesis can be used much more efficiently in algae than in higher plants. With proper mineral fertilization and with the proper rate of removal of the finished products, one square meter may serve to support algae production sufficient to feed one man. And a large proportion of the calories produced—as much as one half—are derived from protein; vitamins are also produced into the bargain. Several universities are working with a number of species, chlorella in particular, and large industrial firms are yearly becoming more interested. The problems entailed in passing from the theoretically feasible to the economically feasible are formidable, but their solution is likely to be hastened for an unexpected reason. Interplanetary travel of long duration and the organization of distant stations require not only recycling of oxygen and waste water; they necessitate the fabrication of food and its integration into the recycling of oxygen, water, and excreta. Over the next two decades, an increasing fraction of the several billion dollars that the United States and the Soviet Union will spend every year for space travel is going to be channeled into life support systems. The money spent in the aggregate on new methods of food production will probably, during that period, dwarf the cost of the Manhattan Project. In many ways, we may have in space exploration what William James called "the moral equivalent of war." We will probably also have in it the technological equivalent of war, without the corresponding losses in men and in resources. The usable "fall-out" of such research is likely to be enormous. Certainly if economical harnessing of photosynthesis, through biological units or directly, can be realized under the hostile interplanetary, lunar, or martial conditions, it should become relatively easy to put it into effect on earth. All this is no longer science fiction. It is as much of a reality as the federal income tax. Obviously, a breakthrough in this field could for centuries altogether remove food as a limiting factor to population growth.

I hope I have said enough to show how dangerous it may turn out to link the population problem so closely to food, as so many writers have done. These have generally been conservationists and social scientists rather than agricultural or nutritional scientists, concerned—rightly—with the effects of crowding which they had observed. At the same time, not sure that the public and governments would agree with them that there was cause for concern, and action, based on these grounds, they have turned to the threat of a worldwide shortage of food as an easily understood, imperative reason for a large-scale limitation of births. Had they consulted nutritionists, agriculturists, and chemists, they might have chosen a more appropriate battleground. For if we can feed an ever-increasing number of people—even if we feed them as badly as many of our contemporaries are fed—their argument fails. And yet there is a need for the establishment as soon as possible of a sound population policy for the world at large.

There is, of course, another good reason for not tying population control to food: this tie eliminates from contention rich countries, and in particular surplus countries such as ours. Our population is increasing faster than it ever has; our major nutrition problem is overweight, our major agricultural problem is our ever-mounting excess production. Does anyone seriously believe this means that we have no population problem? Our housing problems; our traffic problem; the insufficiency of the number of our hospitals, of community recreation facilities; our pollution problems, are all facets of our population problem. I may add that in this country we compound the population problem by the migratory habits of our people: from rural farm areas to urban areas and especially to "metropolitan" areas (212 such areas now have 84 per cent of our population); from low income areas to high income areas; from the East and Midwest to the South and Southwest; from all areas to the Pacific Coast; from the centers of cities to suburbs, which soon form gigantic conurbations, with circumstances everywhere pushing our Negroes into the deteriorating centers of large cities. All this has occurred without any master plan, and with public services continually lagging behind both growth and migrations.

Let us conclude with one specific example: 4 million students were enrolled in U.S. colleges and graduate schools in 1960; 6 million in 1965. The Bureau of the Census estimates that 8 million will seek admission or continued enrollment in 1970; 10 in 1975; 12 in 1980. No one questions our ability to feed these youngsters. But are we as a nation at all prepared for a near doubling of the size of our colleges and universities in 11 years?

Let us now examine the other argument, that in certain ways the rich countries are more immediately threatened by overpopulation. A corollary of this is that the earth as an economic system has more to fear from the rich than from the poor, even if one forgets for a moment the threat of atomic or chemical warfare.

Consider some data from our own country. We have already said that "crowding" is certainly one of the pictures we have in mind when we think of overpopulation. The increased crowding of our cities and our conurbations has been referred to, but what of the great outdoors? In 1930 the number of visitor-days at our national parks was of the order of 3 million (for a population of 122 million); by 1950 it was 33 million (for a population of 151 million); by 1960 it was 79 million (for a population of 179 million); by 1967, 140 million (for a population of 200 million). State parks tell the same story: a rise in visitor-days from 114 million in 1950 to 179 million in 1960, an increase in attendance of over 125 per cent for a rise in population of less than 20 per cent! Clearly, the increase in disposable income (and hence in means of transportation and in leisure) becomes a much more important factor in crowding and lack of privacy than the rise in population.

Not only does the countryside become more rapidly crowded when its inhabitants are rich, it also becomes rapidly uglier. With increasing income, people stop drinking water as much: as a result we spread 48 billion (rust proof) cans and 26 billion (nondegradable) bottles over our landscape every year. We produce 800 million pounds of trash a day, a great deal of which ends up in our fields, our parks, and our forests. Only one third of the billion pounds of paper we use every year is reclaimed. Nine million cars, trucks, and buses are abandoned every year, and while many of them are used as scrap, a large though undetermined number are left to disintegrate slowly in backyards, in fields and woods, and on the sides of highways. The eight billion pounds of plastics we use every year are nondegradable materials. And many of our states are threatened with an even more pressing shortage of water, not because of an increased consumption of drinking fluid by the increasing population, but because people are getting richer and using more water for air-conditioning, swimming pools, and vastly expanded metal and chemical industries.

That the air is getting crowded much more rapidly than the population is increasing is again an illustration that increase in the disposable income is perhaps more closely related to our own view of "overpopulation" than is the population itself. From 1940 to 1967 the number of miles flown has gone from 264 million to 3,334 billion (and the fuel consumed from 22 to 512 million gallons). The very air waves are crowded: the increase in citizen-licensees from 126 thousand to 848 thousand in the brief 1960–67 interval is again an excellent demonstration of the very secondary role of the population increase in the new overpopulation. I believe that as the disposable income rises throughout the world in general, the population pressure due to riches will become as apparent as that due to poverty.

I trust that I have demonstrated how dangerous it is to link constantly in the mind of the public the concept of overpopulation with that of undernutrition. I believe that it is dangerous to link it necessarily with poverty. It is absurd on the basis of any criterion of history, economics, or esthetics. Some countries are poor and densely populated. A few countries are poor and so sparsely populated that economic development (e.g. road-building, creation of markets) becomes very difficult. It is easy to demonstrate that a couple with many children will be unable to save and invest. It is perhaps also true that, as the comparison to nineteenth-century France, England,

and Germany suggests, at a certain stage of development, too low a birth rate (as in France then) decreases the ambition and labor of part of the population so that the savings expected from the decreased birth rate never materialize. (Losing wars because of a smaller population and having to pay a heavy tribute, as happened to the French at the conclusion of the 1870–71 war, also nullified this advantage). The fact is that we are not yet in one world and that while in general it is true that population increases make improvement in nutrition and in delivery of social services more difficult, the relation of changes in wealth to changes in population has to be examined in each area on its own merits.

We have seen, furthermore, that there is more to the problem of population than the decrease in income consequent to overpopulation. We have seen that the increase in disposable income creates a population problem that is becoming every day more acute. The ecology of the earth—its streams, woods, animals—can accommodate itself better to a rising *poor* population than to a rising *rich* population. Indeed, to save the ecology the population will have to decrease as the disposable income increases. If we believe, like Plato and Aristotle, in trying for excellence rather than in rejoicing in numbers, we need a population policy now, for the rich as well as the poor. Excellent human beings will not be produced without abundance of cultural as well as material resources and, I believe, without sufficient space. We are likely to run out of certain metals before we run out of food; of paper before we run out of metals. And we are running out of clear streams, pure air, and the familiar sights of Nature while we still have the so-called "essentials" of life. Shall we continue to base the need for a population policy on a nutritional disaster to occur at some hypothetical date, when it is clear that the problem is here, now, for us as well as for others? Shall we continue to hide the fact that a rational policy may entail in many countries not only a plateauing of the population to permit an increase in disposable income, but a decrease of the population as the disposable income rises?

## 12. The Third Fish

### KENNETH S. NORRIS

Biologists are familiar with a "balanced aquarium." It is one with a sealed glass cover, which maintains itself for years without food being added and without being cleaned. It has plants to capture sunlight and produce energy-rich food, a rich bacteria flora in the sand, a few snails to graze. In perhaps five gallons of water, it can support only two tiny fish. If more are added, it falls into irreversible decay, the plants die, the water is fouled and the bacteria take over in massive numbers until their food, too, is depleted. Our world is that aquarium. We have too many fish in the tank, there is too much waste being produced, and the bacteria will likely reap a brief benefit if we don't act quickly.

In his State of the Union message, Mr. Nixon noted, almost as an aside, that "between now and the year 2000, over 100 million children will be born in the United States." He might well have added that we cannot assimilate 100 million new Americans in 30 years and expect to maintain anything like our present standard of living. Week after week, *Science* magazine (voice of the American Association for the Advancement of Science) predicts everything from catastrophic decay of the environment to imminent social disintegration. Nearly to the man, the nation's environmental scientists agree we are sliding into soon-to-be irreversible trouble. They only argue about the time scale. We cannot absorb a population doubling without great social disruption. Not only do we, as individuals, consume more than any other people in the world, but the social machinery necessary to keep each of us in the manner to which he is accustomed is out of all proportion to that of any other society.

Will people become so jaded with crisis talk that they will stop listening? Already the din is so great that some environmentalists fear a backlash against doom-crying. I think it has already begun. This seems especially likely now that Mr. Nixon has put before Congress a generally excellent roster of anti-pollution measures. It may not be widely appreciated that "pollution" is not the basic problem but is only a symptom. Cutting back present levels of pollution won't stop environmental decay. The Nixon environmental program is desperately needed, but it is not enough. Our population doubles in about 70 years. Taken simplistically, if we are to maintain our standard of living, we must in this time double every service, every unit of transportation, every school, every factory, every house, and we must also double every supply of raw material, all food, all waste disposal, all water supplies in that same time. Assuming no significant population dispersal, this would mean cities twice the size of Washington, New York, Los Angeles and all the rest. As society grows, it becomes more complex. Demands on facilities, goods and services rise disproportionately. Take power as an example. The Federal Power Commission estimates that in 30 years US power demand will be eight times what it is now. By then our population will have increased by about one half. At that rate, by the time we double population, power needs will be at least 16 times present levels. The environment will not stand it and our energy sources cannot support it. Remember, too, that by the time our population doubles once, the time before the next doubling will be cut drastically. Demands for everything will be accelerated. Every other natural resource need and source of pollution will increase simultaneously. Perhaps we can cut down on no-deposit, no-return beer bottles and develop edible cookie boxes, but no matter—solid and liquid wastes will increase gigantically and our present modest commitment will long since have been left behind.

Even today, we are not keeping up. One can calculate conservatively that a national expenditure of something like $100 billion a year for new facilities, housing, roads and equipment is now needed just to keep up with population growth. This figure is arrived at by calculating duplication cost of

national physical plant and service requirement in 70 years
and spreading the cost out equally by years. This figure is
obviously not enough, because old equipment and facilities
must be replaced. Cities may decay before their time because
of bad design and population thrusts that disrupt orderly
growth. Such factors might double our figure. Perhaps $200
billion a year might allow us to stay even. That is equal to the
present US budget. However, as we near the time of population doubling 70 years hence, the figure becomes orders of
magnitude too low as social complexity accelerates. Crises
can be expected to arise everywhere, from the state of our
adrenal glands, to rising sea level and reduction of oxygen
in the atmosphere as smog makes plants less able to photo-
synthesize new oxygen.

Mr. Nixon proposes a population commission. *But we
already know the facts.* We ride the crest of a technological
wave powered by nonrenewable resources of coal, oil, and
nuclear fuel as our polluting society dips ever more deeply
into its capital of minerals, biological resources and available
land and water. The Nixon program grapples with today's programs (and thank goodness it does) but not tomorrow's. The
program may save the East River which is now an open
sewer, Lake Erie, which is an algal soup, and even the parsley
in Orange County, California, which has been turning brown
from smog damage. But the basic problems of the future it
touches hardly at all.

The public has the idea that ecology (the broad relationship of organisms and their environment) and pollution, are
one. The Nixon environmental package deals with "cures" for
pollution. But we live in a *closed interacting system* in which
every action ramifies in all directions and reflects back in a
bewildering and usually unpredicted number of ways. We
must come to live with compromise in a deeply pervasive
sense, involving our ideas of property, morals and even
health. Both the public at large and our statesmen must learn
that it is no longer useful to think, "If I cause this dam to be
built, enough power to light a city of one million people will
result." Instead, we must think, "If the dam is built that
power will be generated, this downstream river will be slowed,
fish runs will be disrupted, a new increment of growth will be

allowed in the area, which will produce demands on local agriculture, transportation, etc. The dam will produce a new environmental configuration in about 20 years of this or that general character."

The Aswan Dam on the Nile is a perfect example. For the wrong reasons, we removed our support and left it to the Russians to make the ecological blunder, but never mind, we didn't understand either. The new dam did provide the water needed to expand agriculture and create power, but it also slowed the river below, caused a precipitous rise in snail populations which carry the dreadful disease schistosomiasis. Infection rates jumped between 10 and 20 percent; for the river-dwelling human population to near 70 percent. Again the slowing allowed the incursion of salt water in the rich delta, threatening that important agricultural region.

Every socio-ecologic decision acts the same way in some degree. Everyone's elbows are in everyone else's ribs. That is why another person's large family is a concern to us all, and why the foot dragging of automobile companies in producing exhaust emission controls is an affront. On the other hand, good smog suppressants will have their effect, too; cars will cost more and fuel may, also; smog-suppression may postpone the day when we control the number of cars and hence allow more and grander traffic jams. The freeways of cities, which are like the circulatory systems of animals, may develop even greater embolisms at the five o'clock rush hour.

Now what should our government be doing?

(1) *Educate itself.* The President, Congress, the regulatory agencies need a short course in ecology. I suggest a national "ecological awareness week" like that being actively designed for my own threatened paradise of Hawaii. The time scale of crisis seems not to be understood by most of our leaders; we live on the point of the population curve where it turns upward in accelerating growth and fairly rockets away *in the next 15 years.* Few men in Washington understand why it is no longer useful to think that our environmental dilemmas can be "cured" by simple applications of money.

(2) *Act with all possible dispatch to frame legislation designed to reduce population increase.* A campaign that reduces population increase by half will save the country on the

order of $100 billion a year. More important, it will buy precious time. Each new child requires more food, more highways, more schools, more police, more everything. The parent should pay commensurately, through taxes. To be sure, some may cry "racial genocide" and legislation must not discriminate against the poor or disadvantaged. We should reward people for avoiding conception. The morality of late marriage and conception needs recognition. Termination of pregnancy needs to be made socially and legally acceptable. In some ways the increasing proliferation of technology acts like a rising birth rate—each of us comes to consume more and to produce more waste products. It is certain, in the not too distant future that we must therefore *reduce* our total numbers significantly.

(3) *Continue palliative action against social and environmental decay.* Population decrease acts slowly in changing the ecological course of society, so we must expand Nixon-type proposals. Their cost will soon become prohibitive, however, without population decrease.

(4) *The nation must learn to assess the socio-ecological results of its actions.* I think, in the long run, this is our most important single task, other than population decrease. Both population increase and the explosive growth of technology are producing social and environmental change at a bewildering rate. We cannot now confidently predict the consequences of new people, machines and techniques. Our guesses are based on ever more sketchy data. Huge though the task is, however, we can learn to look at entire regions and, in some cases, at America as a whole in terms of mathematical models or other assessment systems. We can develop new computer systems, special models, for example, of river systems and a massive inventory of natural and social resources. Since we are not alone in the world, many of these studies will go beyond our borders. The sea and air are global.

The Moonshot became a worldwide team effort; we need the same application of money and talent, the same type of systems engineers here at home. NASA and the aerospace industries could be marshaled in this effort; a third of our national scientific talent and most of the systems engineers work there. The International Biological Program, under the direction of the National Science Foundation, is producing mathematical models of the grasslands that once covered so much of our central tier of states. A similar model for the desert biome, as it is called, has just been developed and studies of the eastern deciduous forest and the coniferous forest are in the planning stage.

One of the nation's top mathematical ecologists, Professor Kenneth E. F. Watts is struggling, in California, to produce a socio-ecologic model of California on a computer. Without much larger financing, he cannot produce more than a few useful submodels, but he is already doing some important things. He is showing that, given appropriate resources, an eco-technological assessment system can very probably predict where our social actions lead.

(5) *The basic science of ecology needs to be upgraded.* Excellent projects go unfinanced by the National Science Foundation. In spite of outcry about the declining quality of the environment, the Foundation had only $7.5 million to spend on environmental biology in 1969. Budding talent must turn elsewhere. It may surprise the President and his colleagues how few ecologists there are in America, 2000 to 4000, and of these only two to three hundred at best are today willing to enter public service.

(6) *Increase the protection of our basic ecological resources.* Ecologists cannot study nature without a nature to study, and it's going fast. I speak here not only of parklands and forests, but also of the unassuming salt marshes, palmetto swamps, bogs, prairie grasslands and the rest of natural America. These are the baseline, moulded by millions of years of evolution, within which the secrets of ecological balance lie. They are natural laboratories and irreplaceable. In several states natural area systems have been set aside. In the subtle interactions of their streams, in the decaying leaves and logs of their forest floors, in their water and air, we discover the secrets to our survival. While I'm at it, one of our nation's major natural resources is extremely poorly protected— the arid and semi-arid lands, nearly all within the purview of the Bureau of Land Management and amounting to something like 150 million acres. They may be our most priceless terrestrial natural resource. The undermanned, underfinanced

Bureau is manfully wrestling with what it knows must be done, but it should be expanded to become our "Forest Service of the Arid Lands."

Many Americans think anxiety over "pollution" is just a fad, the sputnik of the '70s. It's no fad; the very equilibrium of our world's balance of life is being shifted by too many people and their products. We cannot much longer throw out tin and lead and helium and mercury. Population will very likely have to drop drastically around the world before any true equilibrium can be reached. Indeed the world must be seen as a whole, like that awesome picture from the Apollo Mission with all of Africa and Europe seen at a glance beneath swirling clouds. Each of us must view himself as part of a vast intricate closed system, all of whose parts interact all of the time—as in that aquarium.

## 13. Overpopulated America

### WAYNE H. DAVIS

I define as most seriously overpopulated that nation whose people by virtue of their numbers and activities are most rapidly decreasing the ability of the land to support human life. With our large population, our affluence and our technological monstrosities the United States wins first place by a substantial margin.

Let's compare the US to India, for example. We have 203 million people, whereas she has 540 million on much less land. But look at the impact of people on the land.

The average Indian eats his daily few cups of rice (or perhaps wheat, whose production on American farms contributed to our one percent per year drain in quality of our active farmland), draws his bucket of water from the communal well and sleeps in a mud hut. In his daily rounds to gather cow dung to burn to cook his rice and warm his feet, his footsteps, along with those of millions of his countrymen, help bring about a slow deterioration of the ability of the land to support people. His contribution to the destruction of the land is minimal.

An American, on the other hand, can be expected to destroy a piece of land on which he builds a home, garage and driveway. He will contribute his share to the 142 million tons of smoke and fumes, seven million junked cars, 20 million tons of paper, 48 billion cans, and 26 billion bottles the overburdened environment must absorb each year. To run his air conditioner we will strip-mine a Kentucky hillside, push the dirt and slate down into the stream, and burn coal in a power generator, whose smokestack contributes to a plume of smoke

massive enough to cause cloud seeding and premature pre-
cipitation from Gulf winds which should be irrigating the
wheat farms of Minnesota.

In his lifetime he will personally pollute three million gallons of water, and industry and agriculture will use ten times
this much water in his behalf. To provide these needs the US
Army Corps of Engineers will build dams and flood farmland. He will also use 21,000 gallons of leaded gasoline containing boron, drink 28,000 pounds of milk and eat 10,000
pounds of meat. The latter is produced and squandered in a
life pattern unknown to Asians. A steer on a Western range
eats plants containing minerals necessary for plant life. Some
of these are incorporated into the body of the steer which is
later shipped for slaughter. After being eaten by man these
nutrients are flushed down the toilet into the ocean or buried
in the cemetery, the surface of which is cluttered with boul-
ders called tombstones and has been removed from productivity. The result is a continual drain on the productivity of
range land. Add to this the erosion of overgrazed lands, and
the effects of the falling water table as we mine Pleistocene
deposits of groundwater to irrigate to produce food for more
people, and we can see why our land is dying far more rapidly than did the great civilizations of the Middle East, which
experienced the same cycle. The average Indian citizen,
whose fecal material goes back to the land, has but a minute
fraction of the destructive effect on the land that the affluent
American does.

Thus I want to introduce a new term, which I suggest be
used in future discussions of human population and ecology.
We should speak of our numbers in "Indian equivalents."
An Indian equivalent I define as the average number of Indian citizens required to have the same detrimental effect on
the land's ability to support human life as would the average
American. This value is difficult to determine, but let's take
an extremely conservative working figure of 25. To see how
conservative this is, imagine the addition of 1000 citizens to
your town and 25,000 to an Indian village. Not only would
the Americans destroy much more land for homes, highways
and a shopping center, but they would contribute far more
to environmental deterioration in hundreds of other ways as

well. For example, their demand for steel for new autos might increase the daily pollution equivalent of 130,000 junk autos which *Life* tells us that US Steel Corp. dumps into Lake Michigan. Their demand for textiles would help the cotton industry destroy the life in the Black Warrior River in Alabama with endrin. And they would contribute to the massive industrial pollution of our oceans (we provide one third to one half the world's share) which has caused the precipitous downward trend in our commercial fisheries landings during the past seven years.

The per capita gross national product of the United States is 38 times that of India. Most of our goods and services contribute to the decline in the ability of the environment to support life. Thus it is clear that a figure of 25 for an Indian equivalent is conservative. It has been suggested to me that a more realistic figure would be 500.

In Indian equivalents, therefore, the population of the United States is at least four billion. And the rate of growth is even more alarming. We are growing at one percent per year, a rate which would double our numbers in 70 years. India is growing at 2.5 percent. Using the Indian equivalent of 25, our population growth becomes 10 times as serious as that of India. According to the Rienows in their recent book *Moment in the Sun*, just one year's crop of American babies can be expected to use up 25 billion pounds of beef, 200 million pounds of steel and 9.1 billion gallons of gasoline during their collective lifetime. And the demands on water and land for our growing population are expected to be far greater than the supply available in the year 2000. We are destroying our land at a rate of over a million acres a year. We now have only 2.6 agricultural acres per person. By 1975 this will be cut to 2.2, the critical point for the maintenance of what we consider a decent diet, and by the year 2000 we might expect to have 1.2.

You might object that I am playing with statistics in using the Indian equivalent on the rate of growth. I am making the assumption that today's American child will live 35 years (the average Indian life span) at today's level of affluence. If he lives an American 70 years, our rate of population growth would be 20 times as serious as India's.

But the assumption of continued affluence at today's level is unfounded. If our numbers continue to rise, our standard of living will fall so sharply that by the year 2000 any surviving Americans might consider today's average Asian to be well off. Our children's destructive effects on their environment will decline as they sink ever lower into poverty.

The United States is in serious economic trouble now. Nothing could be more misleading than today's affluence, which rests precariously on a crumbling foundation. Our productivity, which had been increasing steadily at about 3.2 percent a year since World War II, has been falling during 1969. Our export over import balance has been shrinking steadily from $7.1 billion in 1964 to $0.15 billion in the first half of 1969. Our balance of payments deficit for the second quarter was $3.7 billion, the largest in history. We are now importing iron ore, steel, oil, beef, textiles, cameras, radios and hundreds of other things.

Our economy is based upon the Keynesian concept of a continued growth in population and productivity. It worked in an underpopulated nation with excess resources. It could continue to work only if the earth and its resources were expanding at an annual rate of 4 to 5 percent. Yet neither the number of cars, the economy, the human population, nor anything else can expand indefinitely at an exponential rate in a finite world. We must face this fact *now*. The crisis is here. When Walter Heller says that our economy will expand by 4 percent annually through the latter 1970s he is dreaming. He is in a theoretical world totally unaware of the realities of human ecology. If the economists do not wake up and devise a new system for us now somebody else will have to do it for them.

A civilization is comparable to a living organism. Its longevity is a function of its metabolism. The higher the metabolism (affluence), the shorter the life. Keynesian economics has allowed us an affluent but shortened life span. We have now run our course.

The tragedy facing the United States is even greater and more imminent than that descending upon the hungry nations. The Paddock brothers in their book, *Famine 1975!*, say that India "cannot be saved" no matter how much food we ship her. But India will be here after the United States is gone. Many millions will die in the most colossal famines India has ever known, but the land will survive and she will come back as she always has before. The United States, on the other hand, will be a desolate tangle of concrete and ticky-tacky, of strip-mined moonscape and silt-choked reservoirs. The land and water will be so contaminated with pesticides, herbicides, mercury fungicides, lead, boron, nickel, arsenic and hundreds of other toxic substances, which have been approaching critical levels of concentration in our environment as a result of our numbers and affluence, that it may be unable to sustain human life.

Thus as the curtain gets ready to fall on man's civilization let it come as no surprise that it shall first fall on the United States. And let no one make the mistake of thinking we can save ourselves by "cleaning up the environment." Banning DDT is the equivalent of the physician's treating syphilis by putting a bandaid over the first chancre to appear. In either case you can be sure that more serious and widespread trouble will soon appear unless the disease itself is treated. We cannot survive by planning to treat the symptoms such as air pollution, water pollution, soil erosion, etc.

What can we do to slow the rate of destruction of the United States as a land capable of supporting human life? There are two approaches. First, we must reverse the population growth. We have far more people now than we can continue to support at anything near today's level of affluence. American women average slightly over three children each. According to the *Population Bulletin* if we reduced this number to 2.5 there would still be 330 million people in the nation at the end of the century. And even if we reduced this to 1.5 we would have 57 million more people in the year 2000 than we have now. With our present longevity patterns it would take more than 30 years for the population to peak even when reproducing at this rate, which would eventually give us a net decrease in numbers.

Do not make the mistake of thinking that technology will solve our population problem by producing a better con-

traceptive. Our problem now is that people want too many
children. Surveys show the average number of children
wanted by the American family is 3.3. There is little difference between the poor and the wealthy, black and white,
Catholic and Protestant. Production of children at this rate
during the next 30 years would be so catastrophic in effect
on our resources and the viability of the nation as to be beyond my ability to contemplate. To prevent this trend we must
not only make contraceptives and abortion readily available
to everyone, but we must establish a system to put severe economic pressure on those who produce children and reward
those who do not. This can be done within our system of taxes
and welfare.

The other thing we must do is to pare down our Indian
equivalents. Individuals in American society vary tremen-
dously in Indian equivalents. If we plot Indian equivalents
versus their reciprocal, the percentage of land surviving a
generation, we obtain a linear regression. We can then place
individuals and occupation types on this graph. At one end
would be the starving blacks of Mississippi; they would approach unity in Indian equivalents, and would have the least
destructive effect on the land. At the other end of the graph
would be the politicians slicing pork for the barrel, the highway contractors, strip-mine operators, real estate developers,
and public enemy number one—the US Army Corps of Engineers.

We must halt land destruction. We must abandon the view
of land and minerals as private property to be exploited in
any way economically feasible for private financial gain. Land
and minerals are resources upon which the very survival of
the nation depends, and their use must be planned in the best
interests of the people.

Rising expectations for the poor is a cruel joke foisted upon
them by the Establishment. As our new economy of use-it-
once-and-throw-it-away produces more and more products
for the affluent, the share of our resources available for the
poor declines. Blessed be the starving blacks of Mississippi
with their outdoor privies, for they are ecologically sound,
and they shall inherit a nation. Although I hope that we will

help these unfortunate people attain a decent standard of living by diverting war efforts to fertility control and job training, our most urgent task to assure this nation's survival during the next decade is to stop the affluent destroyers.

# 14. Man and His Environment

## ANSLEY J. COALE

The way our economy is organized is an essential cause, if not *the* essential cause, of air and water pollution, and of the ugly and sometimes destructive accumulation of trash. I believe it is also an important element in such dangerous human ecological interventions as changes in the biosphere resulting from the wholesale use of inorganic fertilizers, of the accumulation in various dangerous places such as the fatty tissue of fish and birds and mammals of incredibly stable insecticides. We can properly attribute such adverse effects to a combination of a high level of economic activity and the use of harmful technological practices that are inconsistent with such a high level.

The economist would say that harmful practices have occurred because of a disregard of what he would call *externalities*. An externality is defined as a consequence (good or bad) that does not enter the calculations of gain or loss by the person who undertakes an economic activity. It is typically a cost (or a benefit) of an activity that accrues to someone else. A fence erected in a suburban neighborhood for privacy also affords a measure of privacy to the neighbor—a cost or a benefit depending on how he feels about privacy versus keeping track of what goes on next door. Air pollution created by an industrial plant is a classic case of an externality; the operator of a factory producing noxious smoke imposes costs on everyone downwind, and pays none of these costs himself—they do not affect his balance sheet at all. This, I believe, is the basic economic factor that has a degrading effect on the environment: we have in general permitted economic activities without assessing the operator for their adverse effects. There has been no attempt to evaluate—and to charge for—externalities. As Boulding says, we pay people for the goods they produce, but do not make them pay for the bads.

To put the same point more simply: environmental deterioration has arisen to a large extent because we have treated pure air, pure water, and the disposal of waste as if they were free. They cannot be treated as free in a modern, urban, industrial society.

There are a number of different kinds of policies that would prevent, or at least reduce, the harmful side effects of some of our economic activities, either by preventing or reducing the volume of the harmful activity, or by inducing a change in technique. Other policies might involve curative rather than preventive steps, such as cleaning up trash along the highways, if we cannot prevent people from depositing it there.

Among the possibilities are steps that would make externalities internal. An example that I find appealing, although it is perhaps not widely practical, is to require users of flowing water to take in the water downstream of their operation and discharge it upstream. A more general measure is to require the recycling of air or water used in industrial processes, rather than permitting the free use of fresh water and clean air, combined with the unmonitored discharge of exhaust products.

Public authorities can charge for unfavorable external effects by imposing a tax on operations that are harmful to the environment. The purpose of such taxes is to reduce the volume of adverse effects by inducing a shift in technique or by reducing the volume of production by causing a rise in price. Also, the tax receipts could be used to pay for mitigating the effect. An example of a desirable tax is one imposed to minimize the use of disposable cans and bottles for soft drinks and beer. Not long ago the majority of manufacturers produced these commodities in containers that were to be returned. The producer offered a modest price for returning bottles as an inducement. It has proven cheaper to use disposable glass bottles and cans; recently aluminum cans have rapidly increased in popularity, substituting a container that lasts indefinitely for the tin cans that would sooner or later rust away. Everyone is familiar with the resultant clutter on beaches, in parks, and along the highways. If a tax of 10 cents per unit were imposed on each disposable container, it would clearly be cheaper to go back to returnables. If some manufacturers found it advantageous to pay the 10-cent tax, the receipts could be used to pay for cleaning up highways and beaches.

Another approach that would induce people to give up economic activities with harmful effects on others is to make individuals and corporations financially liable for any damage caused by their operations. The resultant litigation would be an unwarranted windfall for lawyers, but financial liability might be a very potent factor in reducing pollution.

There is general agreement that our knowledge of what affects the environment is wholly inadequate. Because of inadequate monitoring and measurement, we do not know what is happening to the atmosphere or the biosphere; we need research to keep track of what is going on as well as to develop the techniques that will produce the goods we want with fewer of the bads we do not want.

## *An economist's review of resource exhaustion*

One of the questions most frequently raised about the environmental effects of modern life is the rapid and rising rate of extraction of raw materials. Are we running out of resources?

I would first like to note that the distinction between renewable and nonrenewable resources is not a clear one. There are, of course, instances of nonrenewable resources in the form of concentrated sources of energy, such as the fossil fuels. These are reservoirs of reduced carbon embodying radiant energy from the sun that accumulated over many thousands of years. When these fuels are used, the energy that is released is to a large extent radiated into space, and we have no way of reclaiming it. The geological processes that are constantly renewing the fossil deposits of carbon are so slow compared to the rate at which we are burning the fuels that the designation "nonrenewable" is appropriate.

On the other hand, when we think of our resources of such useful materials as the metallic elements of iron, copper, nickel, lead, and so forth, we should realize that spaceship Earth has the same amount of each element as it had a million years ago, and will have the same amount a million years from now. All we do with these resources is to move them around. The energy we use is lost, but the minerals we find useful are still with us. It does not pay to recycle these minerals (that is to use them repeatedly by reclaiming scrap) because the deposits of minerals in the ground or in the ocean are still such a cheap source. It must be noted that the mining of fresh ore is cheaper than the use of scrap in part because miners are not charged for their "externalities." If harmful by-products of mining could not be discharged into streams, if mine tailings were regulated, and erosion-producing or even unesthetic practices forbidden, minerals would be more expensive and recycling more attractive. In the production of any metallic element, the easier sources are exploited first. As mining gets more difficult, the ore gets more expensive, and recycling becomes more nearly competitive. It seems wholly probable that the technology of recycling will be improved.

The surprising fact is that raw materials are not at the moment very costly, and moreover their cost relative to the cost of finished goods has not been increasing. The gross national product in the United States is more than $4500 per capita and the raw materials component per capita is less than $100. The price of raw materials relative to the price of finished goods is no higher now than at the beginning of the century, and if we were running out of raw materials, they would surely be rising in relative expensiveness. A prominent exception is saw lumber, which is substantially more expensive relative to the cost of finished wooden products than it used to be.

The reason that the future of our resource situation always seems so bleak and the past seems quite comfortable is that we can readily construct a plausible sounding estimate of the future demand for a particular raw material, but cannot form such a plausible picture of the future supply. To estimate the future demand, we need merely note the recent trends in the per capita consumption of whatever it is we are concerned about, utilize whatever plausible projection of population we are prepared to accept, multiply the two together and project an astonishingly high rate of usage 50 years in the future. If this demand does not seem overwhelming, we need only make a projection 100 years in the future. What we cannot so readily foresee is the discovery of new sources and of new techniques of extraction, and, in particular, the substitution of other raw materials or the substitution of other industrial processes which change the demand away from the raw material we are considering. Hence it can always be made to appear that in the future we are going to run out of any given material, but that at present we never have.

It is possible to set plausible limits to the stores of fossil fuels that we are likely to discover, and with the very rapid rise in the use of these fuels they will surely become more expensive in some not too distant time. It should be noted, however, that we will not suddenly "run out" of fossil fuels. Long before the last drop of oil is used, oil will have become much more expensive. If gasoline were $5 or $10 a gallon, we would utilize it much more sparingly, with small economical automobile engines, or perhaps the substitution of some non-petroleum-based fuel altogether. In fact, the principal user of our petroleum deposits may be the petrochemical industries. I have given this special attention to fossil fuels because there is no substitute in prospect for such fuels in small mobile units such as automobiles. On the other hand, the supply of overall energy seems to pose no problem. There seems to be ample fissionable material to supply rising energy needs for many centuries, if breeding reactors are perfected. If fusion proves a practical source, the supply of energy can properly be considered limitless.

Another aspect of the relation of the United States economy to resources that is much publicized today is the fact that we are consuming such a large fraction of the current annual extraction of raw materials in the world. A much quoted figure is that 6 percent of the world's population is using 30 percent of the resources. It is concluded from figures such as these that we are robbing the low-income countries of the world of the basis of their future prosperity—that we are using up not only our resources, but theirs as well. Most economists would find this a very erroneous picture of the effect of our demand for the raw materials extracted in the less developed parts of the world. The spokesmen for the less developed countries themselves constantly complain about the adverse terms of trade that they face on world markets. The principal source of their concern is the low price of raw materials and the high price of finished goods. The most effective forms of assistance that the developed countries (including the United States) give to the less developed countries are the purchases they make from the less developed countries in international trade. A developing country needs receipts from exports in order to finance the purchase of the things they need for economic development. For example, in order to industrialize, a non-industrialized country must for a long time purchase capital equipment from more advanced countries, and the funds for such purchases come from exports—principally of raw materials. Economists in the developing countries feel that the demand for raw materials is inadequate. Perhaps the most important adverse effect of slowing down the growth of the gross national product in the United States would be that it would diminish the demand for primary products that we would otherwise import from the less developed countries. After all, if a developing country wants to retain its raw materials at home, it can always place an embargo on their export. However, it would be a policy very damaging to economic progress of that very country.

Note that the effect of our high demand for raw materials is a different matter from the desirability of the domestic control of mineral resources within the developing countries. Selling oil on the world market provides immense economic advantages to a developing country. Whether foreign interests should be represented in the extraction of raw materials is another question.

## Population growth in the United States

I shall begin a discussion of population with a brief description of recent, current, and future population trends in the

United States. Our population today is a little over 200 million, having increased by slightly more than 50 percent since 1940. I think it is likely to increase by nearly 50 percent again in the 30 years before the end of the century.

This rate of increase cannot continue long. If it endured throughout the next century, the population would reach a billion shortly before the year 2100. Within six or seven more centuries we would reach one person per square foot of land area in the United States, and after about 1500 years our descendants would outweigh the earth if they continued to increase by 50 percent every 30 years. We can even calculate that, at that rate of increase, our descendants would, in a few thousand years, form a sphere of flesh whose radius would, neglecting relativity, expand at the velocity of light.

Every demographer knows that we cannot continue a positive rate of increase indefinitely. The inexorable arithmetic of compound interest leads us to absurd conditions within a calculable period of time. Logically we must, and in fact we will, have a rate of growth very close to zero in the long run. The average rate of increase of mankind from the inception of the species until the present is zero to many decimal places. If we agree that 10,000 years from now we can have no more than one person per square foot, and that the population of the world will at a minimum exceed that of Richmond, Virginia, we can say that the average annual growth of population will be within one per thousand of zero.

The only questions about attaining a zero rate of increase for any population is when and how such a rate is attained. A zero rate of increase implies a balance between the average birth and death rates, so the choice of how to attain a zero rate of increase is a choice between low birth and death rates that are approximately equal. The average growth rate very near to zero during mankind's past history has been attained with high birth and death rates—with an average duration of life that until recently was no more than 30 or 35 years. I have no difficulty in deciding that I would prefer a zero rate of growth with low rather than high birth and death rates, or with an average duration of life in excess of 70 years, as has been achieved in all of the more advanced countries of the world, rather than the life that is "nasty, brutish, and short." The remaining question then is *when* should our population growth level off.

A popular answer today is "immediately." In fact a zero rate of increase in the United States starting immediately is not feasible and I believe not desirable. The reason is the age composition of the population that our past history of birth and death rates has left to us. We have an especially young population now because of the postwar baby boom. One consequence is that our death rate is much lower than it would be in a population that had long had low fertility. That is, because our population is young, a high proportion of it is concentrated in ages where the risk of mortality is small. Therefore, if we were to attain a zero growth rate immediately, it would be necessary to cut the birth rate about in half. For the next 15 or 20 years, women would have to bear children at a rate that would produce only a little over one child per completed family. At the end of that time we would have a very peculiar age distribution with a great shortage of young people. The attendant social and economic disruptions represent too large a cost to pay for the advantages that we might derive from reducing growth to zero right away.

In fact, a more reasonable goal would be to reduce fertility as soon as possible to a level where couples produced just enough children to insure that each generation exactly replaced itself. If this goal (early attainment of fertility at a replacement level) were reached immediately, our population would increase 35 to 40 percent before it stabilized. The reason that fertility at the mere replacement level would produce such a large increase in population is again the age distribution we have today. There are many more people today under 20 than 20 to 40, and when the relatively numerous children have moved into the childbearing ages, they will greatly outnumber the persons now at those ages, and when the current population under age 20 moves into the old ages, they will be far more numerous than the people now at the old ages. Thus to move the population to replacement would be to insure approximately that the number of children under 20 will be about the same as it is today, but that the number above that age will be substantially higher. The net effect is the increase of 35 to 40 percent mentioned just above. It

is the built-in growth in our age composition that led me to
state earlier that I think an increase in the order of 50 percent of the U.S. population is not unlikely.

A sensible choice in reducing our growth rate to zero then
is between early or late attainment of fertility at the replacement level. Is there any reason that we should not attempt to
attain a fertility at replacement as soon as possible? My own
opinion is that an early move in that direction is desirable,
but for the sake of completeness, I must point out that there
is a nonnegligible cost associated with attaining a stationary
population—the population that will exist with fertility at replacement after the age distribution left over from the past
has worked out its transitory consequences.

A stationary population with the mortality levels that we
have already attained has a much older age distribution than
any the United States has ever experienced. It has more people over 60 than under 15, and half the population would be
over 37 rather than over 27, as is the case today. It would be
an age distribution much like that of a health resort.

Moreover, if we view the age pyramid in the conventional
way, with the number of males and females being drawn out
as in the branches of a Christmas tree (age representing al-
titude of the tree) the pyramid for the stationary population
is virtually vertical until age 50 because of the small number
of deaths under the favorable mortality conditions we have
attained. In contrast, the age distribution of the United States
to date has always tapered more or less sharply with increasing age. The stationary population with its vertical sides would
no longer conform in age composition to the shape of the
social structure—to the pyramid of privilege and responsibility.
In a growing population, the age pyramid does conform, so
there is a rough consonance of shape between diminishing
numbers at higher ages and the smaller number of high positions relative to low positions. In a stationary population
there would no longer be a reasonable expectation of advancement as a person moves through life. I have indicated
that sooner or later we must have a stationary population, so
that sooner or later we must adjust to such an age composition. I am pointing to this disadvantage to show that there
is a choice between moving more gradually to a stationary

population at the expense of a larger ultimate population size in order to continue to enjoy for a longer time the more desirable age distribution of a growing population.

## Connection between population and pollution

The connection between the current growth in our population and the deterioration of our environment of which we have all become aware is largely an indirect one. The problem has arisen because we are permitting the production of bads (pollution, or negative externalities) along with goods. There seems little doubt that the rapid increase in the production of goods has been responsible for the rapid increase in the production of bads, since we have made no effective effort to prevent the latter from accompanying the former. But per capita increase in production has been more important than population growth. It has been calculated that if we were to duplicate the total production of electricity in the United States in 1940 in a population enjoying the 1969 per capita usage of energy, the population could be only 25 million rather than the 132 million people there were in 1940. Population has increased by 50 percent, but per capita use of electricity has been multiplied several times. A similar statement can even be made about the crowding of our national parks. The population has increased by about 50 percent in the last 30 years—attendance in national parks has increased by more than 400 percent.

A wealthy industrial urban population of 100 million persons would have most of the pollution problems we do. In fact, Sydney, Australia, has problems of air and water pollution and of traffic jams, even though the total population of Australia is about 12 million in an area 80 percent as big as the United States. Australia is actually more urbanized than the United States, in spite of its relatively small population and large overall area.

If we have the will and intelligence to devise and apply proper policies, we can improve our environment and can do so either with the current population of 200 million, or with the population that we will probably have in another 50 years of 300 million. On the other hand, if we ignore environ-

mental problems and continue to treat pure air and water and
the disposal of trash as if they were free, and if we pay no
attention to the effects of the techniques that we employ upon
the balance of nature, we will be in trouble whether our population grows or not. There is no doubt that slower population growth would make it easier to improve our environment,
but not much easier.

### Policies that would affect the growth of population

We must, at some time, achieve a zero rate of population,
and the balance should surely be achieved at low birth and
death rates rather than at high rates. If, as at present, only
about 5 percent of women remain single at the end of the
childbearing span, and if 96 percent of women survive to the
mean age of childbearing, and if finally the sex ratio at birth
remains about 105 males for every 100 females, married couples must have an average of about 2.25 children to replace
themselves. What kinds of policies might be designed to assure such a level of fertility or, more generally, to produce
the fertility level that is at the moment socially desirable?

I begin with a set of policies that are consistent with general democratic and humanitarian principles, although a minority of the population would oppose them on religious
grounds. These are policies that would, through education
and the provision of clinical services, try to make it possible
for every conception to be the result of a deliberate choice,
and for every choice to be an informed one, based on an
adequate knowledge of the consequences of bearing different
numbers of children at different times. A component of such
a set of policies would be the development of more effective
means of contraception to reduce the number of accidental
pregnancies occurring to couples who are trying to avoid conception. These are policies that call for a substantial government role and I think that an effective government program
in these areas is already overdue. I personally believe that
education in the consequences of childbearing and in the
techniques of avoiding pregnancy, combined with the provision of contraceptive services, should be supplemented by the
provision of safe and skillful abortion upon request. It is clear

that the public consensus in favor of abortion is not nearly as clear-cut as that in favor of contraception, and I know that the extent and the strength of the moral objection to induced abortion is much greater. Nevertheless, I am persuaded by experience in Japan and eastern Europe that the advantages of abortion provided under good medical auspices to cause the early termination of unwanted pregnancies are very important to the women affected, as is evident in the fact that when medically safe abortion has been made available at low cost, the number of abortions has initially been as great or greater than the number of live births. Later there is a typical tendency for women to resort to contraception rather than repeated abortions.

The reason I favor abortion is that such a high proportion of births that occur today are unwanted, and because a large number of desperate pregnant women (probably more than half a million annually) resort to clandestine abortions today, with high rates of serious complications. In contrast, early abortion, under skilled medical auspices, is less dangerous than tonsillectòmy, and substantially less dangerous than carrying a child to full term.

In recent years the number of births that were unwanted in the United States constituted about 20 percent of the total (an unwanted birth was defined as one in which the woman said that conception occurred either as a result of a failure of contraception or in the absence of contraception but without the intent to become pregnant as soon as possible, when at the time the conception occurred the husband or wife or both did not want another child then or later). The rate at which women are having children today would lead to a completed family size of slightly under three children. If all unwanted births were eliminated, the number of children born per married woman would be about 2.4 or 2.5 on average. This is very little above replacement, and when allowance is made for the likely possibility that women understated the proportion of births that were unwanted, it is probable that the elimination of unwanted births would bring a fertility at or below replacement.

If it is true that the elimination of unwanted pregnancies would reduce fertility very nearly to replacement, it must be conceded that this outcome is fortuitous. It is highly unlikely that over a substantial period of time the free choice by each couple of the number of children they want would lead exactly to the socially desirable level of fertility. The erratic behavior of fertility in America and in other advanced industrialized countries in the last 30 or 40 years is ample evidence that when fertility is voluntarily controlled, the level of fertility is subject to major fluctuations, and I see no logical reason to expect that on average people would voluntarily choose a number of children that would keep the long-run average a little above two per couple. In other words, we must acknowledge the probable necessity of instituting policies that would influence the number of children people want. However, there is no need for haste in formulating such policy, since, as I have indicated, improved contraceptive services combined with a liberal provision of abortion would probably move our fertility at present quite close to replacement, and a gradual increase in population during the next generation would not be a major addition to the problems we already face.

Policies intended to affect people's preferences for children should be designed within the framework of our democratic traditions. They should be designed, for example, to encourage diversity and permit freedom of choice. An average of 2.25 children does not require that 75 percent of couples have two children and 25 percent three, although that would produce the desired average. Another possibility is a nearly even division of family size among zero, one-, two-, three-, four-, and five-child families. The ideal policy would affect the decision at the margin and not try to impose a uniform pattern on all. I do not think that people who prefer to have more than the average number of children should be subject to ridicule or abuse.

It is particularly difficult to frame acceptable policies influencing the number of children that people want. While it is still true that so many large families result from unwanted pregnancies, the unwanted child that is the most recent birth in a large family already faces many deprivations. The psychological disadvantages of the unwanted child cause some of our most serious social problems. In addition to these psychological disadvantages, the unwanted child in a large impoverished family faces an inadequate diet, much below average chances for schooling, and generally inferior opportunities. I hardly think it a wise or humane policy to handicap him further by imposing a financial burden on his parents as a result of his birth.

When unwanted births have become negligible in number, we could imagine trying to design a policy in which the couple is asked to pay some part of the "externalities" that an additional birth imposes on society. In the meantime, I suggest as a desirable supplement to better contraception and free access to abortion the extension of more nearly equal opportunities in education and employment for women, so that activities outside of the home become a more powerful competitor to a larger family. We should start now devoting careful attention to formulation of policies in this area—policies that could increase fertility when it fell too low as well as policies to induce people to want fewer children.

Some aspects of the deterioration of our environment appear to be critical and call for prompt action. We need to start now to frame and apply actions that would arrest the careless destruction of the world in which we live. We also need policies to reduce promptly the incidence of unwanted births. In the long run we shall also need ways to influence the number of births people want. To design policies consistent with our most cherished social and political values will not be easy, and it is fortunate that there is no valid reason for hasty action.

# PART II
*What Is the Solution to the Problem?*

# 15. U.S. Population Growth and Family Planning: A Review of the Literature

ROBIN ELLIOTT, LYNN C. LANDMAN,
RICHARD LINCOLN AND
THEODORE TSURUOKA

U.S. population growth has recently emerged as a prominent national concern. Yet 20 or even 10 years ago, when growth rates were higher than they are today, interest in the issue was negligible. During the 1930s, in fact, preoccupation was rather with a potential *decline* in the U.S. population. What, then, explains the tone of the current debate?

The interest may be traced to two general areas of concern: population pressures worldwide, and urban and environmental deterioration at home.

## World population and resources

Recent U.N. estimates of the size of the world population in the year 2000 range from 5.5 to 7.0 billion persons, up to twice its present size.[1] Present rates add to our population some 70 million persons each year, or another New York City every six weeks. Implied in these projections is that population growth continuing at present rates will conflict, perhaps critically, with the possibilities for modernization among the developing nations, and will in the long run threaten the ecology of the entire world. According to demographer Nathan Keyfitz:

If current rates of population increase do not abate, world population in 2050 could approach 18 billion people—well over half the number the world can ever hope to sustain, even at a level of chronic near-starvation for all.[2]

These grim statistics have been applied to the American scene in a number of ways. It is suggested, for example, that the United States should put its own 'population house' in order if it is to maintain international goodwill as it lends active support to population control in the developing countries. U.S. growth may be modest in relation to rates in most developing countries (less than one percent annually, compared with a world average of more than two percent), but nonetheless U.S. population may double in 70 years even as policies of control are being sponsored abroad. Thus, ecologist Paul Ehrlich writes:

> For us to succeed in persuading other people to decrease their birth rates we must be able to advocate "do as we are doing," not "do as we say."[3]

Another argument relates U.S. population growth to dwindling world resources, particularly to non-replaceable minerals and fuels. This country, with some six percent of the world's population in 1966, consumed 34 percent of the world's energy production, 29 percent of all steel production, and 17 percent of all the timber cut.[4] Such figures lead to the reasoning that each American birth contributes far more to the drain on world reserves than does, say, an Indian birth— by more than 25 times, suggests biologist Wayne Davis.[5] The problem becomes more apparent as the United States becomes increasingly dependent for its continued industrial growth upon the resources of the developing world. Since the 1930s, the U.S. has shifted from the position of a net exporter of minerals to that of a net importer, with heaviest reliance on outside sources for such basic resources as crude oil, iron ore, copper, lead and zinc.[6] Meanwhile, some geologists claim, serious shortages among certain minerals are developing. To quote the Committee on Resources and Man of the National Academy of Sciences:

> True shortages exist or threaten for many substances that are considered essential for current industrial society: mercury, tin, tungsten and helium, for example. Known and now-prospective reserves of these substances will be nearly exhausted by the end of this century or early in the next . . .[7]

Some scientists claim that American demand on foreign sources of supply will deplete resources which might otherwise be left available for industrial development and modernization in those countries at a future date,[8] and that in the longer run the developed nations themselves may find their internal and external sources of supply drying up. In this sense, the move to curb U.S. aggregate demand for primary products through population control may be seen as the first line of defense against anticipated resource shortages, the alleviation of which might otherwise have to be sought through restrictions on rising standards of living. Nutritionist Jean Mayer writes:

> The earth's streams, woods and animals can accommodate themselves better to a rising poor population than to a rising rich population. Indeed, to save the ecology the population will have to decrease as the disposable income increases.[9]

Ben Wattenberg takes issue with this position in a recent article. What, he asks, is Dr. Mayer's prescription?

> Is he against affluent people having babies but not poor people, even though the affluent have relatively few anyway? Or perhaps is it that he is just against the idea of letting any more poor people become affluent people, because they too will then consume too many resources and cause more pollution?[10]

Economist Robert Heilbroner, who supports the Mayer-Ehrlich position, draws from their analyses the conclusion that:

> . . . the underdeveloped countries can *never* hope to achieve parity with the developed countries. Given our present and prospective technology, there are simply not enough resources to permit a "Western" rate of industrial exploitation to be expanded to a population of four billion—much less eight billion—persons.[11]

Some writers, notably Frank Notestein, Joseph Fisher[12] and Harold J. Barnett, have taken issue with those who claim that we face a shortage of natural resources. Said Dr. Notestein before the Population Association of America in April 1970:

> Thanks, indeed, to the high consumption of the developed world, we have generated the knowledge and techniques that have greatly expanded both the supplies and the reserves of . . . raw materials in the world.[13]

And Dr. Barnett concludes:

> Natural resource scarcity and diminishing returns through time are not a curse that society must bear.[14]

He points to technological development as *"the* dynamic factor in the declining cost trend for agricultural and mineral commodities."

### Domestic urban and environmental problems often attributed to population growth rate

In large part the current concern with U.S. population growth may be traced to domestic issues such as environmental decay, urban blight, urban violence, crowded highways and parks and high tax levels. The literature abounds with theories which assume or attempt to establish a relationship between our social maladies and our increase in numbers. Among the problems which one finds attributed in part or in whole to the size or growth rate of our population are disruption of the ecology, the socio-psychological stresses of urban society, and economic strains, especially high taxes.

John D. Chapman defines the ecologist as one who "sees the natural world as a series of inter-related systems in a state of dynamic equilibrium into which Man intrudes as an unbalancing factor."[15] The pollution of water and air with industrial wastes, chemical fertilizers and gasoline fumes gives rise to chemical and thermal changes in the biosystem which deliver immediate injury to the environment and, in addition, set off a chain of distortions in the pattern of plant and animal life throughout the system. Such imbalances, ironically, are a direct outgrowth of Man's capacity to manipulate his environment, and are most widespread and serious in countries which are technologically most advanced. Under present conditions, a high Gross National Product tends to produce pollution, and this in turn, ironically, is likely to add further to the GNP. Writes economic historian Robert Lekachman:

> If a new pulp mill discharges chemical wastes into a hitherto clean stream, the GNP will go up, not only because of the mill's valuable output but because other enterprises and municipalities located downstream from the polluter will be compelled to invest in cleansing devices required to return the water to usable condition.[16]

The link is drawn by a number of ecologists and other bioscientists between the "ecocatastrophe" (Paul Ehrlich's description[17]) of environmental pollution and the size of population. Writes Lamont C. Cole:

> . . . there is no way for us to survive except to halt population growth completely or even to undergo a period of population decrease if, as I anticipate, definitive studies show our population to be already beyond what the earth can support on a continuous basis. Just as we must control our interference with the chemical cycles that provide the atmosphere with its oxygen, carbon and nitrogen, so must we control our birth rate.[18]

Ecologist Barry Commoner shares the concern of his colleagues with the environmental crisis, but says that the problem is *not* primarily population growth, but the failure of political institutions to assert control over the use of technology. He writes:

> My own estimate is that we are unlikely to avoid environmental catastrophe by the 1980s unless we are able by that time to correct the *fundamental* incompatibilities of major technologies with the demand of the ecosystem. This means that we will need to put into operation essentially emissionless versions of automotive vehicles, power plants, refineries, steel mills and chemical plants. Agricultural technology will need to find ways of sustaining productivity without breaking down the natural soil cycle, or disrupting the natural control of destructive insects. Sewage and garbage

treatment plants will need to be designed to return organic waste to the soil where, in nature, it belongs. Vegetation will need to be massively reintroduced into urban areas. Housing and urban sanitary facilities will need to be drastically improved. In my view, unless these actions are taken, in the 1980s large-scale environmental disasters are likely to occur, at least in the highly developed regions of the world.[19]

Among the images most frequently used by those who would call attention to the U.S. population problem is crowding—crowding of people in cities and of cars on highways, restricting freedom of movement and reducing each person's enjoyment of scarce land resources such as beaches and national parks. It is suggested that crowding creates strains and stresses for the individual which all too frequently are expressed in disruption and violence for the group. Studies of animal behavior (for example, those of rats conducted by John B. Calhoun of NIMH[20]) are cited as evidence of the debilitating effect crowding can have upon social and sexual relationships. Writes Dr. Keyfitz:

> Food riots occur in Bombay, and civil riots in Newark, Memphis, and even Washington, D.C. This ultimate manifestation of population density, which colors the social history of all continents, is a challenge that can no longer be deferred. It will not cease until population control is a fact.[21]

Suggesting in a recent article that "spiralling population growth" is responsible for "many of our tensions and failures," Representative Morris Udall gives some examples:

> The numbers of people jammed into our large cities are increasingly ominous. Crime rates soar. Freeways and airports are overloaded with traffic. Some schools are in double sessions. There is poverty, racial strife, the rotting of our central cities, the formless and ugly sprawl of urbanization.[22]

Some writers believe that such strains on our society spring not from how much population is growing, but from the way in which it is distributed. James Sundquist of the Brookings

Institution, for example, calls for a national policy of population redistribution:

> . . . [to] encourage an accelerated rate of growth in the smaller natural economic centers of the country's less densely populated regions, as the alternative to further concentrations of population in the larger metropolitan areas.[23]

In a similar vein are recent statements by Herman Miller, Chief of the Population Division of the U.S. Bureau of the Census,[24] and the Report of President Nixon's National Goals Research Staff.[25] Says Miller:

> We have serious population problems today and they are likely to intensify in the next 15 years. These problems relate to the geographic distribution and to the values of our people rather than to their numbers and rates of growth.

The White House group concludes as follows:

> . . . one decision which appears not to be urgent is that of over-all size of the population—even after the effects of a considerable amount of immigration are taken into account. The issue of population distribution is a different matter, and one to be taken seriously regardless of what may be the upper limit of population size.

Ansley Coale, Director of Princeton University's Office of Population Research, agrees and takes issue with what he sees as the simplistic link too often drawn between population growth and ecological disruption and urban stress. He writes:

> . . . it has become fashionable to blame almost every national failure or shortcoming on rapid population growth—the ugliness and hopelessness of slum life, wasteful and irritating traffic jams, unemployment and delinquency among the disturbingly large fraction of adolescents who drop out of school, the pollution of air and water and the disappearance of the natural beauty of our country behind a curtain of billboards and under a blanket of Kleenex and beer cans. . . .[26]

He decries attempts to "blame" population growth for these ills:

> Fertility in the urban ghettoes will fall if discrimination is allevi-
> ated, if educational and employment opportunities are equalized.
> . . . Pollution is caused by internal combustion engines as oper-
> ated at present and by the unrestricted discharge of noxious fumes
> from other sources into the atmosphere. Similarly, water pollu-
> tion is caused by the discharge of noxious effluents into rivers,
> lakes and oceans. A population half or three-quarters the current
> one in the U.S. could ruin the potability of our fresh water sup-
> plies and poison our atmosphere by the unrestricted discharge of
> waste. . . . In fact, most of the social and economic problems
> ascribed to our excessive population in the U.S. or to its excessive
> rate of growth are affected more by *how* our population has
> chosen to distribute itself than by its *size.* . . . The density of
> population is much higher in France, the United Kingdom and
> Netherlands. Yet pollution, traffic jams and delinquency are no
> worse in those countries than here. . . . We must attack the
> problems of pollution, urban deterioration, juvenile delinquency
> and the like directly, and if sensible programs are evolved, con-
> tinued population growth in the order of one-percent annually
> would not make the programs tangibly less effective.

### Economic costs

Most economists no longer believe that substantial population growth is essential to confident investment activity and rising per capita income.[27,28] On the contrary, population growth tends to retard economic growth in all but a very few coun- tries in special circumstances (such as Australia). Dr. Coale states the argument simply:

> In the short run, not only does a population with reduced fer-
> tility enjoy the benefit of dividing the national product among a
> smaller number of consumers; it enjoys the additional benefits of
> having a larger national product to divide.[29]

For the United States specifically, economist Stephen Enke argues:

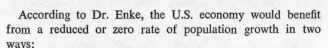

> . . . an evergrowing population is not economically desirable
> . . . in fact, per capita incomes will be higher the sooner a sta-
> tionary and stable population is attained.[30]

According to Dr. Enke, the U.S. economy would benefit
from a reduced or zero rate of population growth in two
ways:

• In the short run, it would decrease the number of young
dependents, thereby reducing private and public (i.e., tax)
expenditures for education, training, subsistence and other
support for the dependent population.

• In the longer run, it would increase capital/labor ratios
(and hence productivity), as the smaller cohorts begin to enter the labor force.

Economist Alan Sweezy adds another dimension to the argument, suggesting that some of the more undesirable con-
comitants of economic growth (e.g., pollution and congestion) are caused more by the population-increase component
than they are by economic development *per se*. He draws a
distinction between two kinds of economic development: rising per capita income under conditions of constant population, and stationary per capita income under conditions of
increasing population. He writes:

> The larger the population component in growth, the more in-
> creased output will take the form of necessities and long-
> established comforts of life. The more increased output takes the
> form of necessities, the harder it will be to gain consideration for
> ecological, aesthetic and recreational values if they stand in the
> way of expanding production.[31]

## U.S. population goals

What are the goals of those who call attention to a 'population problem' in the United States? Is there an optimum population or an optimum growth rate on which most commentators are agreed, or is the objective more generally to 'slow
down' the current rate of growth? What are the demographic
*constraints* upon achieving a given rate of growth (e.g., the
relationship between current fertility rates and future growth

rates) and what are the demographic *implications* (e.g., age structure) of a population of given size or growth rate?

One point at least is clear: the necessity for the eventual cessation of population growth worldwide. As Dr. Coale observes:

> A long-range average growth of zero will be the inevitable consequence of inevitable limits—on the one hand, standing room only, and on the other, extinction.[32]

The relevant question, then, is not if the U.S. and other nations should at some time actively support a reduced rate of growth, but when, how and at what cost this reduced rate should be achieved. The question has given rise to speculations as to the 'optimum population' for the United States.

The concept of optimum population implies the existence of independent criteria (e.g., wealth, living space, per capita income, quality of life) upon which the judgment may be based. In theory, the 'optimum' may be defined for a given society at a given stage of technological development, and will change over time. In practice, however, the concept appears elusive. Writes demographer Lincoln Day:

> So far as optimum size is concerned . . . the dependence of human well-being on the interplay of many diverse elements permits us to set only very broad limits. Recognition of the fort of ecological, resource and social limits sets the maximum number of people who can be supported and thereby narrows the range; but there remains, nevertheless, a considerable latitude within which the optimum size can be located.[33]

While most writers have shied away from assigning a specific value to optimum population, a few have claimed that present population size exceeds it. Dr. Day, for example, holds that it would have been "better" if the U.S. population had stopped growing at 150 million persons, and that such an "optimum" population would afford the individual "serenity, dignity, order, leisure, peace, beauty, elbow room . . . necessary to the cultivation of the whole person." Wayne Davis believes that "we have far more people now than we can continue to support at anything near today's level of affluence."[34]

Referring to world population, the Committee on Resources and Man suggests that "A human population less than the present one would offer the best hope for comfortable living for our descendants. . . ."[35]

The inherent problem of definition in the concept of 'optimum population' has limited its usefulness in the discussion of population goals and policy. More useful has been the notion of current and projected growth rates. Writes sociologist William Petersen:

> One is on firmer ground to contend . . . not that the United States is overpopulated, but that its population growth has been, and probably will remain, so great that the disadvantages consequent from it will become increasingly evident.[36]

It is this theme—reduction in the U.S. population *growth rate,* rather than establishment of an *optimum size*—which has been most prominent in the discussion of population goals.

## Reducing the growth rate

Of those commentators who believe that the present U.S. population growth rate is too high, some would have it reduced to a fraction of the present rate, while others would strive for a zero or even negative rate. David Lilienthal, for example, calls for "a slower rise in the size of our population rather than the present steep increase,"[37] while William H. Draper would have "the United States consider and then accept a zero growth rate as our national optimum goal here."[38] Dr. Lee DuBridge, while he was President Nixon's science advisor, urged "every human institution—school, university, church, family, government and international agency [to set reduction of our population growth rate to zero] as its prime task."[39]

Part of the reason for this sense of urgency rests in a simple demographic theorem: that a zero growth rate would be two or three generations distant even if fertility were reduced *now* to the level of the replacement. If this rate were achieved today, according to estimates prepared by Tomas Frejka,[40] a stationary population would not be reached until 60 or 70 years from now—the period of time required for the population age structure to assume a stationary pattern. Dr. Frejka warns that to achieve zero population growth immediately, it would be necessary for each family to limit itself to one child only for the next 20 years or so, with two-child families not permissible until after the year 2000. As Dr. Coale points out, this would so skew the age structure of the population as to disrupt the normal workings of the society.

Similar conclusions to those of Dr. Frejka have been reached by economist Stephen Enke; by his estimates, "the population ceiling for this country may be no lower than about 350 million and achieved no sooner than about 2065 A.D."[41]

Census Bureau projections published in 1967 assume that by the year 2000 completed family size of Americans would range from a high of 3.35 children to a low of 2.45 children, which would give the U.S. a population of from 280 to 356 million. Since 1966, these projections (mostly popularly, the "low" 300 million projection) have formed the basis upon which most writers have estimated the seriousness of the problem. In August 1970, however, the Census Bureau released a revised and considerably lower range of population projections. Explaining the revision, the Bureau commented that only the lowest of the 1967 projections (Series D) conformed with actual experiences of the succeeding three years.[42] The highest series under the earlier forecast (Series A, based on the assumption of completed fertility at 3.35 children per woman) was dropped, and a new "low" series (Series E, based on the assumption of completed fertility at replacement, or 2.11 children per woman) was added. With these assumptions, the estimated size of the U.S. population in the year 2000 ranges from 266 millions to 321 millions. Demographer Donald Bogue comments on the shift in expectations:

> Population growth is no longer a major social problem in the United States. . . . The era of zero population growth is nearly upon us. . . . This is a very different picture from that which presented itself only a few years ago [when] it looked as if the U.S. was heading into a very severe population crisis. It now appears that we have resolved it.[43]

And Dr. Notestein states:

> It is not at all beyond belief that, with contraceptives of ever increasing efficiency and legal abortion, fertility may fall below replacement level.[44]

(He adds, however, "and of course it may not.")

The ultimate age composition in a stationary population has for some writers raised questions as to its desirability. Dr. Coale, for example, notes:

> . . . a stationary population with an expectation of life of 70 would have as many people over 60 years as under 15. The median age would be about 35.[45]

He suggests that under such conditions people might be more conservative and less receptive to change. Advancement in authority for the aspiring young person would be more difficult, moreover, since there would be as many people aged 50 years as there would be aged 20. Dr. Day does not see this as a problem, and points out that the age structure of a stationary population in the United States would be similar to that of contemporary Sweden and Britain.

### *Alternative approaches to checking population growth emphasize voluntary practices or governmental coercion*

Alternative strategies recommended by those who seek a reduction in U.S. population growth range from voluntary family planning practices to coercive governmental action. The pattern of policy choices corresponds rather closely, as might be expected, to the sense of urgency with which each writer views the 'population problem.' Those who see ecological crisis nearly upon us tend to favor more draconian measures, such as putting sterilants in the water supply, while those who consider that we have not yet reached crisis levels favor building on existing motivation. For most of the measures proposed, predictions of success remain untried and speculative.

The alternative approaches to the population problem are alike in one respect: they are directed exclusively towards reducing fertility, with the assumption implicit that any policy geared to increase mortality, the second determinant of population growth, would be clearly unacceptable. The third determinant, net immigration, is rarely suggested as a target,* though it contributes an increasing portion (currently, about 20 percent) of the annual growth rate.

## *The family planning experience*

The widespread adoption by nations of policies and programs of fertility control is a phenomenon primarily of the past decade. Even voluntary family planning programs were not considered seriously as a means to lower fertility rates until the 1960s when the development of the oral contraceptive and the intrauterine device (IUD) brought new hope that unwanted fertility could be eliminated through wide dissemination of these highly effective, relatively simple and inexpensive methods.

The first few years of experience with family planning programs in some Asian countries (notably Taiwan and Korea, and based mainly on the IUD) engendered considerable optimism about the possibility of significantly reducing birth rates. Frank Notestein,[47] for example, predicted in 1967 that population growth rates in developing countries would be reduced to 1–1.5 percent by the end of the century—a level sufficiently low to enable these countries to achieve necessary modernization. He based his optimism on four factors:

- development of national policies favoring family planning,
- demonstrated public interest in limiting childbearing,
- improvement of contraceptive technology, and
- reduction of the birth rate in several Oriental countries

* One of the few who call for a net immigration rate of zero is Stephen Enke, himself an advocate of zero population growth.[46]

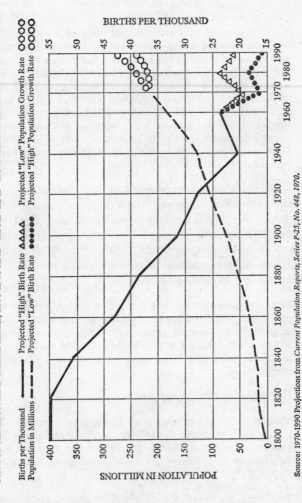

U.S. POPULATION AND BIRTH RATE, 1800–1970 AND "HIGH" AND "LOW" PROJECTIONS FOR 1970–1990

Births per Thousand ———    Projected "High" Birth Rate △△△△    Projected "Low" Population Growth Rate OOOO

Population in Millions – – –    Projected "Low" Birth Rate ●●●●●    Projected "High" Population Growth Rate OOOO

BIRTHS PER THOUSAND

POPULATION IN MILLIONS

Source: 1970–1990 Projections from *Current Population Reports, Series P-25, No. 448, 1970.*

as the result of government birth control programs (Korea, Taiwan, Hong Kong, Singapore).

He concludes:

Whatever happens, it is probable that, short of a major rise in the death rate, population growth will not be stopped for some decades. Given the necessary effort, however, it does seem likely that growth will be reduced to levels that can be coped with in a world of rapidly developing science and technology. In the long run, of course, growth must stop. Quite possibly, it will not do so even if every couple is able to limit its childbearing to the precise number of children it wants. But a world in which all couples are able to choose the size of their family will be a world in which an alteration of institutional constraints would prove rather quickly effective.

A month after the appearance of Dr. Notestein's 'optimistic' projections, Kingsley Davis published a major critique of family planning as a means to population control.[48] Davis insisted that if family planning were to remain the only means taken by governments to reduce fertility, the rate of population growth would continue at an unacceptable level, both in industrial and in developing countries:

Zero population growth [is] the ultimate goal, because *any* growth rate, if continued, will eventually use up the earth . . . at most, family planning can reduce reproduction to the extent that unwanted births exceed wanted births. . . . The elimination of unwanted births would still leave an extremely high rate of multiplication.

In another article, he declared:

Millions of dollars are being spent on the false assumption that population control can be achieved by family planning programs . . . couples can find the means to reduce their fertility if they want to do so, without any family planning programs to help them. . . .[49]

Dr. Davis, like most subsequent critics, defined family planning as a euphemism for the distribution of contraceptive devices, and charged family planners with rejecting such "voluntary" birth control measures as legalization and encouragement of abortion and sterilization and "unnatural forms of sexual intercourse."\*

He also accuses family planners of neglecting problems of motivation and of being concerned only with the numbers of women who accepted contraceptive devices. "Overlooked," he says, "is the fact that a desire for the availability of contraceptives is compatible with *high* fertility." He also insists "that the social structure and economy must be changed before a deliberate reduction in the birth rate can be achieved. As it is, reliance on family planning allows people to feel that 'something is being done about the population problem' without the need for painful social changes." It represents "an escape from the real issues," in that no country has taken "the next step" toward population control, and in that "support and encouragement of research on population policy [other than family planning]" is negligible. It is precisely this blocking of alternative thinking and experimentation that *makes the emphasis on family planning a major obstacle to population control.*"[52]

Two years following the publication of the Notestein and Davis articles, Bernard Berelson of the Population Council compiled an analysis of the various mechanisms proposed for population control.[53] Taking as his starting point voluntary contraception (family planning), which in addition to its primary mission as a socio-medical service to individuals and families is currently the only accepted method of population control in the United States, Berelson examined 29 alternative policies which governments were being urged to take beyond, or in addition to, family planning. While the scope of Dr. Berelson's review is worldwide, the examples he quotes are all relevant to the debate over U.S. population policy. His proposals are arranged according to eight categories, paraphrased below:

- *Extensions of Voluntary Fertility Control.* Institutional-

\* Male sterilization has played a central role in the Indian family planning program, female sterilization in the Puerto Rican program, and therapeutic abortion in the Japanese program. The literature does not indicate "unnatural forms of sexual intercourse" as an official component of a government-sponsored family planning program.[50,51]

ization of maternal care services,[54] legalization of abortion,[55] promotion of voluntary sterilization.

● *Establishment of Involuntary Fertility Control.* Addition of temporary sterilants to the water supply;[56] "child licenses,"[57] and "child certificates";[58] compulsory abortion of out-of-wedlock pregnancies;[59] compulsory sterilization of men with three or more children.[60]

● *Intensified Educational Campaigns.* Introducing population and family planning material in the schools;[61] use of national satellite TV.[62]

● *Incentive Programs.* Providing direct payments for delaying pregnancy,[63] for being sterilized,[64] for accepting contraception.[65]

● *Tax and Welfare Benefits and Penalties.* For example, substituting an anti-natalist system of social services for the existing pro-natalist system, by withdrawing maternity benefits or child and family allowances after Nth child,[66] or by limiting government housing, scholarships and loans to families with fewer than N children;[67] tax on births;[68] reversal of tax benefits to favor single and childless persons, and those having less than N children;[69] provision by State of N years free schooling to each nuclear family, to be allocated by family as desired;[70] pensions for poor parents with fewer than N children.[71]

● *Shifts in Social and Economic Institutions.* For example, increasing minimum age of marriage;[72] promotion or requirement of female participation in labor force;[73] selective restructuring of family in relation to the rest of society;[74] promotion of two types of marriage, one childless and the other licensed for children;[75] encouragement of long-range social trends leading toward lower fertility;[76] improved status of women;[77] continuing efforts to lower infant and child death rates.[78]

● *Approaches via Political Channels and Organization.* Insist on population control as condition of foreign aid;[79] creation of powerful super-agencies for population control;[80] promotion of Zero Population Growth as world or national policy.[81]

● *Augmented Research Efforts.* Social research to discover means of achieving lower fertility;[82] biological research toward improved contraceptive technology;[83] sex determination research.[84]

In evaluating each of the alternatives, Dr. Berelson asked a series of six questions:

• Is the scientific/medical/technological base available or likely?

• Will the Government approve?

• Can the proposal be administered?

• Can the society afford the proposal?

• Is the proposal acceptable ethically, morally, philosophically?

• Will it work?

On a time scale of 10–20 years, Dr. Berelson gave highest scores on all counts to family planning programs, intensified educational efforts and augmented research.

Dr. Berelson's paper provides a useful basis for discussion of the mechanisms proposed for population control, which are arranged below in two categories: those which aim to change fertility preferences and, if that fails, to resort to more direct means of influencing family size (e.g., the Davis position), and those which are predicated on *existing* motivation to prevent unwanted pregnancy (e.g., the Notestein position).

### 'Direct' and 'indirect' means of altering fertility behavior based on overall social needs

Measures of this type are predicated on the belief that adequate fertility reduction will depend upon changes in the motivations upon which (or in the freedom with which) people conceive and bear children. The critical point here is that current motivations and freedoms relate to *individual preferences*, and that these may bear no relation to *overall social needs*. To quote Garrett Hardin:[85]

> The sum total of personal choices about family size on the part of individual couples acting in their own self-interest may very well add up to ruinous demographic conditions for society as a whole.*

* In the short run, however, Dr. Hardin concedes the possibilities

The point has been stressed by a number of other commentators, including Paul Ehrlich,[87] Kingsley Davis,[88] and Alice Day.[89] Reference is frequently made to such sources as the 1960 Growth of American Families study,[90] in which the average family size preference of married women was reported as 3.2 children per family. This number, it is pointed out, exceeds the average completed family size which is associated with population stabilization (approximately 2.11). If a stationary population is to be achieved, it will be necessary first to motivate parents to have smaller families. Judith Blake, Chairman of the Department of Demography at Berkeley, expresses the point as follows:

> . . . the principal cause of . . . [population] growth in the United States [is] the reproduction behavior of the majority of Americans who, under present conditions, want families of more than three children and thereby generate a growth rate far in excess of that required for population stability.[91]

In attempting to change the fertility behavior of the U.S. population, these and other writers would select from a range of measures, varying from moderate (e.g., population education) to extreme (e.g., placing fertility control agents in the water supply). They are not usually posed as mutually exclusive options for a society, but rather as alternative approaches which might be tried in progression. In a recent editorial in *Science,* for example, Garrett Hardin argues as follows:

> How can we reduce reproduction? Persuasion must be tried first. Tomorrow's mothers must be educated to seek careers other than multiple motherhood. Community nurseries are needed to free women for careers outside the home. Mild coercion may soon be accepted—for example, tax rewards for reproductive nonproliferation.

---

of voluntarism. Says he: "I am sure that we can do a lot towards bringing the birth rate in this country down to a mere replacement level if we make it really possible for everybody to have birth control at the time and the place that he or she needs it."[86]

But in the long run a purely voluntary system selects for its own failure: non-cooperators outbreed cooperators . . . If parenthood is a right, population control is impossible.[92]

Kingsley Davis' pessimism is somewhat more qualified:

With indirect measures [that is, measures that leave people free to make their own reproductive decisions but which alter the conditions affecting those decisions], one hopes that compulsory measures will not become necessary. It can be argued that over-reproduction—that is, the bearing of more than four children—is a worse crime than most and should be outlawed. One thinks of the possibility of raising the minimum age of marriage, of imposing stiff penalties for illegitimate pregnancy, of compulsory sterilization after a fifth birth.[93]

Some of the more adventurous chemical approaches to involuntary fertility control, chemist Carl Djerassi points out in a recent article, are and will continue to be beyond the reach of contraceptive technology for many years. Of such "Orwellian" proposals as the addition of temporary sterilants to water or staple foods, Dr. Djerassi says:

. . . it is perfectly clear that the development of such a universal birth control agent is outside the realm of possibility in this century. . . . Immunological approaches, though probably slightly more easily implemented in an 'Orwellian' society than the addition of a sterilant to food and water, are still so far away that they do not merit serious consideration within the context of [this article].[94]

Some of the proposals would have universal impact, whereas others would have selective impact depending on the socio-economic status of the individual (see Table 1). The latter distinction may be important in terms of the anticipated political response to each program. Programs designed to restructure the family (for example, by postponing marriage or by increasing employment opportunities for women outside the home) might carry certain economic or political costs, but they would at least apply to everyone equally. They contrast with programs designed to eliminate welfare payments for

Table 1. Examples of Proposed Measures to Reduce U.S. Fertility, by Universality or Selectivity of Impact

| Universal Impact | Selective Impact Depending on Socio-Economic Status | | Measures Predicated on Existing Motivation to Prevent Unwanted Pregnancy |
|---|---|---|---|
| Social Constraints | Economic Deterrents/Incentives | Social Controls | |
| Restructure family: <br> a) Postpone or avoid marriage <br> b) Alter image of ideal family size | Modify tax policies: <br> a) Substantial marriage tax <br> b) Child tax <br> c) Tax married more than single <br> d) Remove parents' tax exemption <br> e) Additional taxes on parents with more than 1 or 2 children in school | Compulsory abortion of out-of-wedlock pregnancies <br><br> Compulsory sterilization of all who have two children except for a few who would be allowed three | Payments to encourage sterilization <br><br> Payments to encourage contraception <br><br> Payments to encourage abortion <br><br> Abortion and sterilization on demand |
| Compulsory education of children | | | Allow certain contraceptives to be distributed non-medically |
| Encourage increased homosexuality | Reduce/eliminate paid maternity leave or benefits | Confine childbearing to only a limited number of adults | |
| Educate for family limitation | Reduce/eliminate children's or family allowances | Stock certificate-type permits for children | Improve contraceptive technology |
| Fertility control agents in water supply | Bonuses for delayed marriage and greater child-spacing | Housing Policies: <br> a) Discouragement of private home ownership <br> b) Stop awarding public housing based on family size | Make contraception truly available and accessible to all |
| Encourage women to work | Pensions for women of 45 with less than N children | | Improve maternal health care, with family planning as a core element |
| | Eliminate Welfare payments after first 2 children | | |
| | Chronic Depression | | |
| | Require women to work and provide few child care facilities | | |
| | Limit/eliminate public-financed medical care, scholarships, housing, loans and subsidies to families with more than N children | | |

Source: Frederick S. Jaffe, "Activities Relevant to the Study of Population Policy for the U.S.," Memorandum to Bernard Berelson, March 11, 1969.

mothers with more than two children, to sterilize unwed mothers, or to abort all out-of-wedlock pregnancies; such measures tend to strike selectively at the poor—and in specific instances have done so. Thus, a number of bills have been introduced to sterilize *welfare mothers* who have more than one out-of-wedlock child,[95] though no legislation has been introduced to sterilize parents *in general* who have four, five or ten children. A similar judgment applies to proposals for the elimination of tax exemptions for children, or for the imposition of a "child tax," which would affect various socio-economic groups differentially.

Those methods which involve penalties and rewards for given modes of fertility behavior depend to a large extent upon a prior condition: equal access of all individuals to the means of effective birth control. In the absence of such a condition, a law of this kind would inevitably discriminate against those who were less able than others to fulfill its requirements. Economist Joseph J. Spengler draws attention to this in connection with his proposal to reward small families financially —on a deferred basis—through the social security system. He writes:

> The arrangements cannot succeed unless the means to control family size are widely available and very cheap in relation to the incomes of the masses.[96]

Many of those who advocate changing fertility behavior, whether by manipulating preferences or through coercion, are skeptical about the effectiveness of "education" or "persuasion" programs *per se*. Such programs, presumably, would need supplementing with other, more direct, legislative measures. Judith Blake, for example, writes:

> We have a compelling reason to believe that developing peoples will never be merely propagandized or 'educated' into wanting really small families. . . . It does not seem that their desires for larger families will succumb to flip-charts, flannel boards, message movies, group leaders or 'explanations' about the 'advantages' of few children.[97]

Similarly, Lincoln and Alice Day conclude that "we cannot rely on awareness of the facts of population pressure alone to provide the motivation for family limitation sufficient to stabilize our population."[98]

More optimistic projections of the possibilities of population education include a recent paper by Professors Charles B. Arnold, Roger B. Wells and Betty E. Cogswell of the Carolina Population Center. As described in the April 1970 issue of *Studies in Family Planning:*

> . . . [the paper] expresses a concept of sex education broad enough to encompass parts of the population awareness approach as well as sex and family life. . . . Arnold and his associates subdivide sex education into four areas [including] social science aspects of population (demography, human fertility, and the social determinants of population growth) . . . the Arnold group believes that educational programs . . . could lead to lower societal fertility, lower venereal disease rates, increase in the use of contraceptives [and] a rise in positive expectations regarding small family size.[99]

A number of writers have outlined entire programs of action which include measures designed to alter fertility preferences or to force changes in fertility behavior.

Kingsley Davis,[100] for example, suggests that policies be designed to de-emphasize the family "by keeping present controls over illegitimate childbirth yet making the most of factors that lead people to postpone or avoid marriage, and by instituting conditions that motivate those who do marry to keep their families small." Limiting births within marriages might be achieved by allowing "economic advantages to accrue to the single as opposed to the married individual, and to the small as opposed to the large family." Among the examples he gives are government payments for sterilization, payment of all costs of abortion, high marriage license fees, levying of a "child tax," and requiring that all out-of-wedlock pregnancies be aborted. Less "sensational" measures considered by Davis include the following: to cease taxing single persons at a rate higher than married persons; to stop giving parents special tax exemptions; to abandon income tax policies which discriminate against working wives; to reduce paid maternity leaves; to reduce family allowances; to stop awarding public housing on the basis of family size; to stop granting fellowships to married students; to legalize abortion and sterilization; to relax rules requiring medical supervision of harmless contraceptives; to require women to work outside the home or compel them to do so "by circumstances"; to pay women at the same rate as men and give them equal educational and occupational opportunities; and to organize social life around the place of work rather than around the home.

In a similar vein, though less precisely spelled out, is the proposal[101] advanced recently by the Committee on Resources and Man of the National Academy of Sciences-National Research Council. University of California geologist Preston Cloud, Chairman of the Committee, testified recently before the House Conservation and Natural Resources Subcommittee. His testimony included proposals that Congress and the President exhort, by formal declaration, all American couples to have no more than two children; that tax and welfare laws be redrafted to discourage the bearing of more than two children; that legal restraints on homosexual unions be repealed; and that abortions on request be legalized and performed free for indigent women.

The committee which he headed called for intensification "by whatever means are practicable" of efforts to control population in this country and the world, "working toward a goal of zero rate of growth by the end of the century." "Population control" for the U.S. and the world is justified on the premise "that the community and society as a whole, and not only the parents, must have a say about the number of children a couple may have. This will require," the Committee concludes, "profound modification of current attitudes toward parenthood." The Committee's recommendations were based on a paper contributed by University of California demographer Nathan Keyfitz, who declared (with Kingsley Davis) that "the essential ultimate goal of real population control will require something more effective than merely eliminating unwanted births.[102]

Carl Taylor, of Johns Hopkins University, laments what he calls "the sharpest polarization today between proponents of family planning and advocates of 'population control' [i.e., altering fertility preferences or coercing changes in fertility behavior]," and proposes a five-stage program which borrows from both approaches.[103] His suggestions are as follows:

• *Open up clinics and tell women where to go.* This, he says, can reach 15 percent of target, but will then level off. Unrealistic expectations based on rates of initial acceptance can lead to extravagant targets which will not be met.

• *Develop good technology and convenient administration.* Careful and considerate attention should be paid to quality and convenience of service, to avoid backlash. Priorities should be good follow-up care; respect for patient's privacy and dignity; and the availability of a variety of contraceptive methods.

• *Provide comprehensive health care for mothers and children.* As long as parents think their children might not survive to adulthood, they will want "extra" sons for "insurance."

• *Devise methods of economic control.* These will "alter a family's view of its own economic prospects and its understanding of the financial implications of more children" (e.g., it is better to have two educated children than six uneducated ones; hand labor of extra children is not as valuable as money to buy a new tractor, etc.). Taylor suggests eliminating a number of pro-natalist tax and welfare provisions, such as tax concessions to large families, welfare allowances, paid maternity leaves, favored housing for large families, and special educational benefits for students with children. He advocates encouraging women to work; the offering of direct dollar incentives for people to undergo sterilization or to recruit candidates for the IUD. He warns, however, that "most direct legal manipulations are politically hazardous. . . ."

• *Modify socio-cultural factors in motivation.* ". . . the most difficult to implement." We should begin now, he says, to try to postpone age at marriage, and to promote the further education of women.

*Voluntary fertility control based on individual needs*

Voluntary programs assume existing fertility aspirations as given, and attempt to maximize the freedom of each person

to fulfill his or her individual preferences. They represent a
continuation or extension of the philosophy of family planning, and may be summarized thus: to make comprehensive
birth control services, including legal abortion and sterilization, available and accessible to all persons, whatever their
socio-economic status, on a voluntary basis. Unlike the measures discussed in the last section, voluntary fertility control
measures have historically been used primarily to enhance
maternal and child health, to alleviate poverty and generally to
strengthen the health and well-being of the individual family; only secondarily has their purpose been to curb population growth. Recent and prospective advances in contraceptive
technology, combined with the wider availability of legal
abortion and sterilization, however, have raised the potential
of voluntary fertility control as a means of limiting growth.
Reductions in the net reproduction rate to below replacement
level have been achieved in four countries (Japan, Hungary,
Bulgaria, Czechoslovakia); and in all four of them the method
used was to make abortion available on demand.

Primary among the advantages of voluntary fertility control is its political and ethical acceptability:

> . . . it is a natural extension of traditional democratic values;
> of providing each individual with the information he needs to
> make wise choices, and allowing the greatest freedom for each to
> work out his own destiny.[104]

Moreover, it is the only approach which has been tried to
any degree. The very fact that it is operational stands as a
challenge to competing methods of population control. In part
because of its privileged position, the effectiveness of voluntary fertility control in reducing population growth has
become one of the central issues in the population debate.

As Kingsley Davis published the first major attack on family planning programs abroad, so his wife, Judith Blake, has
led the attack on family planning programs in the United
States. She writes:

> . . . for most Americans, the "family planning" approach, con-
> centrating as it does on the distribution of contraceptive materials

and services, is irrelevant, because they already know about efficient contraception and are already "planning" their families. It is thus apparent that any policy designed to influence reproductive behavior must . . . relate to family-size goals [rather than just to contraceptive means].[105]

### Family planning and the poor

Organized programs of voluntary fertility control, in the United States as in the developing countries, have been geared primarily to serve the poor, who can least afford the services of private physicians. Accordingly, attacks on the concept of 'voluntary family planning' in this country have been framed for the most part specifically in terms of poverty-oriented programs. In the article quoted above, Judith Blake claims:

• Publicly supported birth control services are not "appropriate to the attitudes and objectives of the poor and uneducated in matters of reproduction." In general the poor favor birth control—and particularly poverty-oriented birth control programs—*less* than do the more affluent.

• The poor not only have larger families than the well-to-do but "want larger families and consider them ideal."

• The notion that there are five million poor women who "want and need" publicly subsidized birth control help[106] is grossly exaggerated, and fails to take into account, a) the actual numbers of such women who are at risk of conception, b) the percentage who are sterile or less than normally fecund, and c) those who would object to birth control on religious or other grounds.

• The estimate of five million includes those who are already practicing effective birth control, and assumes that all poor women "need the pill and the coil." It is "fantastic" to seek to "substitute scarce medical and paramedical attention for all contraceptive methods now being used by poor couples."

• In addition to being ineffective, wasteful of funds and irrelevant both to the needs of the poor and the attainment of population stability, government-sponsored birth control programs may be actually dangerous.

• Rather than concentrating on the "irrelevant" distribution of contraceptive materials and services, she says, the government should seek to create new institutional mechanisms replacing traditional pro-natalist policies with anti-natalist policies. This would involve "basic changes in the social organization of reproduction that will make nonmarriage, childlessness, and small (two-child) families far more prevalent than they are now." This might be accomplished by lifting penalties for such anti-natalist behavior as "already exist among us as part of our covert and deviant culture, on the one hand, and our elite and artistic culture, on the other."

Oscar Harkavy, with Frederick S. Jaffe and Samuel Wishik,[107] took issue with Dr. Blake's assumptions. Responding to her article, they declared:

• Federal support of family planning programs for the poor has been based on providing for them the same opportunities to plan the number and spacing of their children as has been traditionally enjoyed by the more affluent. Government policy has also operated on the assumption that access to voluntary family planning programs will assist the poor in escaping from poverty, and will help reduce their incidence of infant and maternal mortality and morbidity.

• Dr. Blake's contention that the poor desire larger families and favor birth control less than the non-poor is based "on responses to opinion polls and ignores the three major national studies conducted since 1955, covering larger and properly structured random samples of the U.S. population." What is more, she invalidly equates 'ideal' family size with 'desired' family size.

• The three studies referred to show near-unanimous approval of birth control by *all* socio-economic groups, and reveal no significant differences in *desired* family size between the poor and the non-poor.

• The estimate of five million women who need subsidized family planning help is defended as a "reasonable approximation" based on U.S. Census Bureau tabulations of the characteristics of the poor and near-poor.

• The greater reliance of the poor on non-medical and less reliable methods of birth control cannot be attributed to their personal preferences or lack of motivation "in view of the considerable research demonstrating that the poor have little access to medical care for preventive services [and that] when access to modern family planning services, offered with energy and dignity, has been provided, the response of poor and near-poor persons has been considerable. . . . In virtually all known programs offering a variety of methods 85 to 90 percent of low-income patients voluntarily choose either pills or intra-uterine devices, the most effective methods currently known."

Oscar Harkavy and his colleagues (and Arthur Campbell, Deputy Director of the NICHD's Center for Population Research[108]) challenged Dr. Blake's assertion that desired family size among the poor was larger than among the affluent. They did not, however, confront the assertion that family planning programs, as essentially "catch-up" programs for the poor, would be insufficient to induce a zero rate of population growth (though Frederick Jaffe, with Alan F. Gutt-macher,[109] had earlier suggested that voluntary fertility control programs for all classes could have significant effectiveness in reducing fertility). This challenge has been made by Charles F. Westoff and Larry Bumpass.[110] They examine what would happen in the U.S. if "couples are able to avoid having more children than they themselves want and are also able to avoid having children before they want them." Such perfect fertility control, they say, "might well require social policies aimed at expanding research for more efficient systems for their distribution, as well as legalizing abortion on request." Summarizing his report at Planned Parenthood's 1969 Annual Meeting, Dr. Westoff declared:

> If the fertility patterns of the last decade continue, these three measures by themselves could reduce U.S. population growth considerably. They would not require any change in the number of children couples appear to want now, thus not requiring governmental policies designed to change family-size norms which in theory might be much more difficult anyway. Since no one knows of any alternative measures which can hold out the promise of this much of a reduction in U.S. population growth, it seems apparent that a major program along these lines should become the first order of business among those interested in reducing the U.S. rate of population growth.

To determine unwanted fertility, the authors analyzed responses from the 1965 National Fertility Study, and found that 22 percent of births from 1960 to 1965 were unwanted by at least one spouse, 17 percent by both (the average was 19 percent). More than one-third of non-white births were found to be unwanted. They found that the incidence of unwanted births is negatively related to education and income. Among the poor and near-poor, one-third of births were unwanted, compared with 15 percent among the non-poor; and among women with less than a high school education, unwanted fertility was more than twice as high as among women with high school education or better.

For out-of-wedlock births (the 1965 study was of married women only), the authors assumed the same proportions of wanted and unwanted children as for births which occurred in marriage. This assumption, they admitted, was "undoubtedly a bias in the direction of underestimating the extent of unwanted fertility." Another source of bias exists in that women asked retroactively about children already born have a tendency to characterize them as wanted, even though they may have been unwanted at the time of conception.

The authors estimate that in the six-year period 1960–1965 there were some 4.7 million births "that would have been prevented by the use of perfect contraception." Some two million of these births occurred to the poor and near-poor, of which half were to non-whites. For 1960–1968, they estimate that there were 6.8 million unwanted births. Their comment:

The conclusion seems inescapable that the elimination of unwanted fertility would have had a marked impact not only on our recent birth rate, but also on the life situation of millions of American women in or near poverty.

Of wanted births between 1960–1965, Drs. Westoff and Bumpass add that "two-fifths would have occurred later than they did if their timing had been controlled." Another result of such control would be a reduction in the *number* of children wanted (and, in a perfectly contracepting society, those that are born), since each delay makes it more likely that a woman will change her mind, or become sterile.

Donald Bogue[111] predicts wider availability and higher quality of voluntary fertility control in years to come, suggesting that:

> . . . by [the year 2000] the present methods of contraception, as highly effective as they are, will have been replaced by newer, more pleasant, and completely effective methods which have longer-lasting effects. These methods will be easily within the economic grasp of every citizen, and with our steadily expanding system of universal medical care, will be part of the routine medical service available to everyone, irrespective of age, marital status, or income. Abortion to avoid unwanted pregnancy will be legal and a routine part of health care.

Desired family size, Dr. Bogue suggests, is "the only supportive factor that seems capable of exerting a sustained upward thrust [on fertility rates]." He comments, however, that:

> The full impact upon the society of the dysfunctional effects of the 'baby boom' is only now beginning to be felt, and the pressures against bearing children of third or higher order may be expected to get progressively stronger as the years pass.

Voluntary fertility control composes the core of the approach to population control which is favored by Bernard Berelson.[112] Family planning programs, he claims, compare favorably with other proposals; as "soft" measures, moreover, they should be tried first before resort is taken to the "harder" measures designed to persuade or compel people to change their fertility preferences. He suggests emphasis in program implementation as follows:

> . . . on the informational side, on encouragement of commercial channels of contraception, on the use of paramedical personnel, on logistics and supply, on the training and supervision of field workers, on approaches to special targets ranging from postpartum women to young men under draft into the armed forces. If the [family planning] field did well what it knows how to do, that in itself would in all likelihood make a measurable differ-

ence—and one competitive in magnitude with other specific proposals—not to mention the further impetus of an improved contraceptive technology.

A voluntary approach, what is more, meets what Dr. Berelson (after Ansley Coale) describes as an "ideal" program of population control; this he defines as a program which:

- would permit a maximum of individual freedom and diversity,
- would help promote other goals that are worth supporting on their own merits . . . and would not indirectly encourage undesirable outcomes, e.g., bureaucratic corruption,
- would not burden the innocent in an attempt to penalize the guilty,
- would not weigh heavily upon the already disadvantaged [and] tend further to deprive the poor, and
- would be comprehensible to those directly affected . . . and subject to their response.

## Summary

This paper has drawn upon the views of some of the nation's leading scientists and social theorists and other commentators —biologists, ecologists, demographers, economists, sociologists—who have addressed themselves to the question of U.S. population growth and its consequences.

The specialists agree that world and U.S. population growth must at some time be brought to a halt (though there is considerable disagreement as to *when* this should be accomplished) if the quality of life is to be preserved, the world's finite resources to be husbanded for future generations, and the environment to be saved from irremediable pollution and degradation.

They disagree over the specific role played by U.S. population growth in creating or exacerbating such problems as environmental deterioration, urban crowding, ecological imbalances and world resource scarcity. Some believe, for example, that these problems stem from our failure to control technology; others, that the chief culprit is multiplying man with his multiplying demands for goods and services. Some social scientists fear the political and social consequences of a stationary U.S. population, with a higher median age and narrower opportunities for advancement among the young: might there not be less scientific, technological and cultural innovation with such an age distribution? Others suggest that zero population growth might be economically beneficial, reducing the tax load and possibly accelerating the rise in the standard of living.

Perhaps the sharpest division among the experts is over the methods we should employ in achieving zero growth. The main arguments are:

• Our family size preferences are innately too high, and can be reduced only through coercive means (e.g., compulsory sterilization after a certain number of illegitimate births, or temporary sterilants in the water supply).

• Family size preferences are currently (but not innately) too high, and can be reduced through public education, or through other means of persuasion (e.g., tax incentives, rewards through the social security system).

• Current family size preferences are low enough, and population growth can be sharply reduced—perhaps by half—merely by extending contraceptive, abortion and sterilization services to all who want and need them. Supporters of this argument call for more funds for research in human reproduction and contraceptive technology, and for a more rational service delivery system.

## References

1. United Nations, "World Population Prospect as Assessed in 1963," *U.N. Population Studies*, No. 41, New York, 1966.
2. Nathan Keyfitz, "United States and World Populations," in *Resources and Man*, Committee on Resources and Man, National Academy of Sciences-National Research Council, W. H. Freeman and Company, San Francisco, 1969, Chapter 3.
3. Paul R. Ehrlich, "Overcrowding and Us," *National Parks Magazine*, Vol. 43, April 1969, No. 259.
4. Luther Carter, "The Population Crisis: Rising Concern at Home," *Science*, Vol. 166, November 1969.

5. Wayne H. Davis, "Overpopulated America," *The New Republic,* January 10, 1970, pp. 13–15.

6. Joseph L. Fisher and Neal Potter, "Resources in the United States and the World," in *The Population Dilemma* (Philip M. Hauser, ed.), Prentice-Hall Inc., Englewood Cliffs, N.J., 1965, Chapter 6.

7. Committee on Resources and Man, op. cit., Introduction and Recommendations.

8. Thomas S. Lovering, "Mineral Resources from the Land," Committee on Resources and Man, op. cit., Chapter 6.

9. Jean Mayer, "Toward a Non-Malthusian Population Policy," *Columbia Forum,* Summer 1969.

10. Ben Wattenberg, "Overpopulation as a Crisis Issue: The Nonsense Explosion," *The New Republic,* April 4 & 11, 1970, pp. 18–23.

11. Robert L. Heilbroner, "Ecological Armageddon," *The New York Review of Books,* April 23, 1970, pp. 3–6.

12. Fisher and Potter, op. cit.

13. Frank W. Notestein, "Zero Population Growth: What Is It?" *Family Planning Perspectives,* Vol. 2, No. 3, June 1970; and *Population Index,* July–September 1970.

14. Harold J. Barnett, "The Myth of Our Vanishing Resources," *Transaction,* June 1967, pp. 6–10.

15. John D. Chapman, "Interactions Between Man and His Resources," in *Resources and Man,* Committee on Resources and Man, op. cit., Chapter 2.

16. Robert Lekachman, "The Poverty of Affluence," *Commentary,* Vol. 49, No. 3, March 1970, pp. 39–44.

17. Paul R. Ehrlich, "Eco-Catastrophe!," *Ramparts,* September 1969.

18. Lamont Cole, "Can the World Be Saved?" *The New York Times Magazine,* March 31, 1968.

19. Barry Commoner, "Survival in the Environmental-Population Crisis," presented at symposium: "Is There an Optimum Level of Population?" American Association for the Advancement of Science, Boston, December 29, 1969.

20. John D. Calhoun, "Population Density & Social Pathology," *Scientific American,* Vol. 206, p. 32, 1962.

21. Keyfitz, op. cit.

22. Morris K. Udall, "Standing Room Only on Spaceship Earth," *Reader's Digest,* December 1969.

23. James L. Sundquist, "Where Shall They Live?" *The Public Interest,* No. 18, Winter 1970, pp. 88–100.

24. Herman P. Miller, "Is Overpopulation Really the Problem?"

*National Industrial Conference Board Report,* Vol. 7, No. 5, May 1970, pp. 19, 22.

25. National Goals Research Staff, *Towards Balanced Growth: Quantity with Quality,* U.S. Government Printing Office, Washington, D.C., July 4, 1970, Chapter II, p. 60.

26. Ansley Coale, in *University: A Princeton Quarterly,* Winter, 1968–69, No. 39.

27. Joseph J. Spengler, "Population and Economic Growth," in *Population: The Vital Revolution* (Ronald Freedman, ed.), Doubleday & Co., Inc., Garden City, New York, 1964, pp. 59–69.

28. Alan R. Sweezy and George Varky, "Prosperity and the Birth Rate," paper presented to Planned Parenthood-World Population Board of Directors, November 1968.

29. Coale, op. cit.

30. Stephen Enke, "Is a Stationary U.S. Population Desirable and Possible?" General Electric *Tempo,* mimeograph, December 1969.

31. A. R. Sweezy, "Population, GNP and the Environment," paper delivered at the California Institute of Technology, Conference on Technological Change & Population Growth, May 7–9, 1970.

32. Coale, op. cit.

33. Lincoln H. Day, "Concerning the Optimum Level of Population," paper delivered at the 136th meeting of the American Association for the Advancement of Science, December 30, 1969.

34. Wayne H. Davis, op. cit.

35. Committee on Resources and Man, op. cit., Introduction and Recommendations.

36. William Petersen, *The Politics of Population,* Doubleday & Co., Inc., Garden City, N.Y., 1964, p. 15.

37. David E. Lilienthal, "300,000,000 Americans Would Be Wrong," *New York Times Magazine,* January 6, 1966. Reprinted PP-WP, #545.

38. William Draper, Jr., "Is Zero Population Growth the Answer?" Population Crisis Committee, mimeograph, Washington, D.C., December 2, 1969.

39. Lee A. DuBridge, quoted by William Draper, Jr., ibid.

40. Tomas Frejka, "Reflections on the Demographic Conditions Needed to Establish a U.S. Stationary Population Growth," *Population Studies,* November 1968.

41. Enke, op. cit.

42. Census Bureau Projections, U.S. Department of Commerce,

Bureau of the Census, "Population Estimates and Projections," *Current Population Reports,* Series P-25, No. 448, August 6, 1970, p. 1.

43. Donald J. Bogue, "Population Growth in the United States, 1970–2000," paper delivered to a demographers' advisory group to the U.S. Census Bureau, April 9, 1970.

44. Notestein, op. cit.

45. Coale, op. cit.

46. Enke, op. cit.

47. Notestein, "The Population Crisis: Reasons for Hope," *Foreign Affairs,* October 1967.

48. Kingsley Davis, "Population Policy: Will Current Programs Succeed?" *Science,* Vol. 158, November 10, 1967.

49. K. Davis, "Will Family Planning Solve the Population Problem?" The Victor-Bostrom Fund Report for the International Planned Parenthood Federation, Report No. 10, Fall 1968, p. 16.

50. H. B. Presser, "The Role of Sterilization in Controlling Puerto Rican Fertility," *Population Studies,* Vol. 23, p. 343, 1969.

51. P. M. Boffey, "Japan: A Crowded Nation Wants to Reduce Its Birth Rate," *Science,* Vol. 167, p. 960, 1970.

52. K. Davis, "Population Policy: Will Current Programs Succeed?" op. cit.

53. Bernard Berelson, "Beyond Family Planning," *Studies in Family Planning,* No. 38, February 1969.

54. Howard C. Taylor, Jr. and Bernard Berelson, "Maternity Care and Family Planning as a World Program," *American Journal of Obstetrics and Gynecology,* Vol. 100, 1968, pp. 885–893.

55. K. Davis, "Population Policy: Will Current Programs Succeed?" op. cit., pp. 732, 738; Paul R. Ehrlich, *The Population Bomb,* Ballantine Books, New York, 1968, p. 139; Sripati Chandrasekhar, "Should We Legalize Abortion in India?" *Population Review,* No. 10, 1966, pp. 17–22.

56. Melvin M. Ketchel, "Fertility Control Agents as a Possible Solution to the World Population Problem," *Perspectives in Biology and Medicine,* Vol. 11, 1968, pp. 687–703. See also his "Should Birth Control Be Mandatory?" in *Medical World News,* October 18, 1968, pp. 66–71; P. Ehrlich, *The Population Bomb,* op. cit., pp. 135–136.

57. Kenneth E. Boulding, *The Meaning of the Twentieth Century: The Great Transition,* Harper & Row, New York, pp. 135–136.

58. William B. Shockley, in lecture at McMaster University, Hamilton, Ontario, reported in *New York Post,* December 12, 1967.

59. K. Davis, "Population Policy: Will Current Programs Succeed?" op. cit.

60. S. Chandrasekhar, as reported in *The New York Times,* July 24, 1967.

61. K. Davis, op. cit.; Sloan Wayland, "Family Planning and the School Curriculum," in *Family Planning and Population Programs* (Bernard Berelson et al., eds.), University of Chicago Press, Chicago, 1966, pp. 353–362; Pravin Visaria, "Population Assumptions and Policy," *Economic Weekly,* August 8, 1964, p. 1343.

62. P. Ehrlich, *The Population Bomb,* op. cit., p. 162; Richard L. Meier & Gitta Meier, "New Directions, A Population Policy for the Future," University of Michigan, revised MS, October 1967, p. 11; UNESCO Expert Mission, *Preparatory Study of a Pilot Project in the Use of Satellite Communication for National Development Purposes in India,* February 5, 1968; Wilbur Schramm & Lyle Nelson, *Communication Satellites for Education and Development—The Case for India,* Stanford Research Institute, July 1968: "Family Planning," pp. 63–66.

63. Michael Young, in "The Behavioral Sciences and Family Planning Programs: Report on a Conference," *Studies in Family Planning,* No. 23, Population Council, October 1967, p. 10; Dipak Bhatia, "Government of India Small Family Norm Committee Questionnaire," *Indian Journal of Medical Education,* Vol. 6, October 1967, p. 189; Stephen Enke, "The Gains to India from Population Control," *The Review of Economics and Statistics,* May 1967, pp. 29–30; J. William Leasure, "Some Economic Benefits of Birth Prevention," *Milbank Memorial Fund Quarterly,* 45, 1967, pp. 417–425; Marshall C. Balfour, "A Scheme for Rewarding Successful Family Planners," Memorandum, The Population Council, June 1962; W. Parker Mauldin, "Prevention of Illegitimate Births: A Bonus Scheme," Memorandum, The Population Council, August 1967; Ehrlich, *The Population Bomb,* op. cit., p. 138.

64. S. Chandrasekhar, as reported in *The New York Times,* July 19, 1967; Edward Pohlman, "Incentives for 'Non-Maternity' Cannot Compete with Incentives for Vasectomy," Central Family Planning Institute, India, MS 1967?; T. J. Samuel, "The Strengthening of the Motivation for Family Limitation

in India," *The Journal of Family Welfare,* Vol. 13, 1966, pp. 11–12; K. Davis, op. cit., p. 738.

65. Julian Simon, "Money Incentives to Reduce Birth Rates in Low-Income Countries: A Proposal to Determine the Effect Experimentally"; "The Role of Bonuses and Persuasive Propaganda in the Reduction of Birth Rates"; and "Family Planning Prospects in Less-Developed Countries, and a Cost-Benefit Analysis of Various Alternatives," University of Illinois, MSS 1966–68?; Stephen Enke, "Government Bonuses for Smaller Families," *Population Review,* Vol. 4, 1960, pp. 47–54; Samuel, op. cit., p. 12.

66. Bhatia, op. cit., pp. 188–189; Samuel, op. cit., p. 14; Kingsley Davis, op. cit., pp. 738–739; Richard M. Titmuss and Brian Abel-Smith, *Social Policies and Population Growth in Mauritius,* Methuen, 1960, pp. 130–136.

67. Bhatia, op. cit., p. 190; Kingsley Davis, op. cit., p. 738.

68. Bhatia, op. cit., pp. 189–190; Samuel, op. cit., pp. 12–14; Spengler, "Agricultural Development Is Not Enough," op. cit., p. 30.

69. Bhatia, op. cit., p. 190; Titmuss and Abel-Smith, op. cit., p. 137; Samuel, op. cit., pp. 12–14; K. Davis, op. cit., p. 738; Ehrlich, *The Population Bomb,* op. cit., pp. 136–137; A. S. David, *National Development, Population and Family Planning in Nepal,* June–July 1968, pp. 53–54.

70. James Fawcett, personal communication to Bernard Berelson, September 1968.

71. Samuel, op. cit., p. 12; Goran Ohlin, *Population Control and Economic Development,* Development Centre of the Organization for Economic Cooperation and Development, 1967, p. 104; W. Phillips Davison, personal communication to Bernard Berelson, October 4, 1968.

72. David, op. cit., p. 53; Kingsley Davis, op. cit., p. 738; also, personal communication to Bernard Berelson, October 7, 1968; Young, op. cit., p. 10; Titmuss and Abel-Smith, op. cit., p. 130; Ehrlich, *The Population Bomb,* op. cit., p. 138; Bernard Berelson, Amitai Etzioni, brief formulations, 1962, 1967.

73. Philip M. Hauser, in "The Behavioral Sciences and Family Planning Programs: Report on a Conference," *Studies in Family Planning,* No. 23, Population Council, October 1967, p. 9; K. Davis, op. cit., p. 738; David, op. cit., p. 54; Judith Blake, "Demographic Science and the Redirection of Population Policy," in Mindel C. Sheps & Jean Claire Ridley, eds., *Public Health and Population Change: Current Research Is-*

*sues,* University of Pittsburgh Press, Pittsburgh, 1965, p. 62.

74. K. Davis, op. cit., p. 737.

75. Meier & Meier, op. cit., p. 9. For the initial formulation of the proposal, see Richard L. Meier, *Modern Science and the Human Fertility Problem,* Wiley, New York, 1959, Chapter 7.

76. Philip M. Hauser, " 'Family Planning and Population Programs': A Book Review Article," *Demography,* Vol. 4, 1967, p. 412.

77. United Nations Economic and Social Council, Commission on the Status of Women, "Family Planning and the Status of Women: Interim Report of the Secretary General," January 30, 1968, esp. p. 17 ff.

78. Roger Revelle, as quoted in "Too Many Born? Too Many Die. So Says Roger Revelle," by Milton Viorst, *Horizon,* Summer 1968, p. 35; David M. Heer and Dean O. Smith, "Mortality Level and Desired Family Size," paper prepared for presentation at Population Association of America meeting, April 1967. See also David A. May and David M. Heer, "Son Survivorship Motivation and Family Size in India: A Computer Simulation," *Population Studies,* 22, 1968, pp. 199–210.

79. P. Ehrlich, *The Population Bomb,* op. cit., pp. 161–166, *passim.* The author makes the same point in his article, "Paying the Piper," *New Scientist,* December 14, 1967, p. 655.

80. P. Ehrlich, *The Population Bomb,* op. cit., p. 138; S. Chandrasekhar, "India's Population: Fact, Problem and Policy," in S. Chandrasekhar, ed., *Asia's Population Problems,* Allen & Unwin, 1967, p. 96, citing a Julian Huxley suggestion of 1961; Meier & Meier, op. cit., p. 5.

81. K. Davis, op. cit., pp. 731–733.

82. K. Davis, op. cit., pp. 738–739.

83. National Academy of Sciences, Committee on Science and Public Policy, *The Growth of World Population,* 1963, pp. 5, 28–36. This recommendation has of course been made on several occasions by several people: "We need a better contraceptive." For an imaginative account of the impact of biological developments, see Paul C. Berry, *Origins of Positive Population Control, 1970–2000,* Working Paper, Appendix to *The Next Thirty-Four Years: A Context for Speculation,* Hudson Institute, February 1966.

84. Steven Polgar, in "The Behavioral Sciences and Family Planning Programs: Report on a Conference," *Studies in Family Planning,* No. 23, Population Council, October 1967, p. 10. See also the recent suggestion of research on the "possibilities

for artificially decreasing libido," in *Approaches to the Human Fertility Problem,* op. cit., p. 73.

85. Garrett Hardin, "The Tragedy of the Commons," *Science,* Vol. 162, December 13, 1968, pp. 1243–1248.

86. G. Hardin, "Multiple Paths to Population Control," *Family Planning Perspectives,* Vol. 2, No. 3, 1970, p. 24.

87. P. Ehrlich, *The Population Bomb,* op. cit.

88. K. Davis, op. cit., pp. 730–739.

89. Alice Taylor Day, "Persuasion or Coercion: Alternatives in Population Control," paper delivered at the Smith Alumnae College, "Man and His Environment: Catastrophe or Control," May 29, 1969.

90. P. K. Whelpton, A. A. Campbell and J. E. Patterson, *Fertility and Family Planning in the United States,* Princeton University Press, Princeton, 1966.

91. Judith Blake, "Population Policy for Americans: Is the Government Being Misled?" *Science,* Vol. 164, May 2, 1969, pp. 522–529.

92. G. Hardin, "Parenthood: Right or Privilege?" *Science,* Vol. 169, 1970, p. 427.

93. K. Davis, "Will Family Planning Solve the Population Problem?" op. cit.

94. Carl Djerassi, "Birth Control after 1984," *Science,* Vol. 169, September 4, 1970, p. 949.

95. Julius Paul, "The Return of Punitive Sterilization Proposals," *Law and Society Review,* Vol. III, No. 1, August 1968.

96. Joseph J. Spengler, "Population Problem: In Search of a Solution," *Science,* Vol. 166, December 5, 1969.

97. Judith Blake, "Demographic Science and the Deduction of Public Policy," *Public Health and Population Change,* eds. Mindel C. Sheps and Jean Claire Ridley, University of Pittsburgh Press, Pittsburgh, 1965.

98. Lincoln and Alice Day, *Too Many Americans,* Houghton Mifflin Co., Boston, 1964, Chapter 10.

99. Ozzie G. Simmons, *Studies in Family Planning,* No. 52, April 1970.

100. K. Davis, "Population Policy: Will Current Programs Succeed," op. cit.

101. Committee on Resources and Man, op. cit., Introduction and Recommendations.

102. Keyfitz, op. cit.

103. Carl E. Taylor, M.D., "Five Stages in a Practical Population Policy," *International Development Review,* Vol. X, No. 4, December 1968.

104. Coale, op. cit.
105. Judith Blake, "Population Policy for Americans: Is the Government Being Misled?" op. cit., pp. 522–529.
106. Office of Economic Opportunity, *Need for Subsidized Family Planning Services, United States, Each State and County,* 1968, report prepared for OEO by the Center for Family Planning Program Development, 1969.
107. Oscar Harkavy, Frederick S. Jaffe, Samuel Wishik, "Family Planning and Public Policy: Who Is Misleading Whom?" *Science,* Vol. 165, 1969, p. 367.
108. Arthur A. Campbell, "Family Planning and the Five Million," *Family Planning Perspectives,* Vol. 1, No. 2, October 1969.
109. Frederick S. Jaffe and Alan F. Guttmacher, "Family Planning Programs in the United States," *Demography,* Vol. 5, 1968, p. 910.
110. Larry Bumpass and Charles Westoff, "The Perfect Contraceptive Population: Extent and Implications of Unwanted Fertility in the U.S.," *Science,* Vol. 169, September 4, 1970, p. 1177.
111. Donald Bogue, op. cit.
112. Bernard Berelson, "Beyond Family Planning," *Studies in Family Planning,* Population Council, No. 38, February 1969.

Note: References 54–84 were taken, almost verbatim, from the excellent review of the literature prepared by Bernard Berelson ("Beyond Family Planning," *Studies in Family Planning,* Population Council, No. 38, February 1969).

# 16. Population Policy:
## Will Current Programs Succeed?
### KINGSLEY DAVIS

Throughout history the growth of population has been identified with prosperity and strength. If today an increasing number of nations are seeking to curb rapid population growth
by reducing their birth rates, they must be driven to do so by
an urgent crisis. My purpose here is not to discuss the crisis
itself but rather to assess the present and prospective measures
used to meet it. Most observers are surprised by the swiftness
with which concern over the population problem has turned
from intellectual analysis and debate to policy and action.
Such action is a welcome relief from the long opposition, or
timidity, which seemed to block forever any governmental
attempt to restrain population growth, but relief that "at last
something is being done" is no guarantee that what is being
done is adequate. On the face of it, one could hardly expect
such a fundamental reorientation to be quickly and successfully implemented. I therefore propose to review the nature
and (as I see them) limitations of the present policies and to
suggest lines of possible improvement.

## The nature of current policies

With more than 30 nations now trying or planning to reduce population growth and with numerous private and international organizations helping, the degree of unanimity as
to the kind of measures needed is impressive. The consensus
can be summed up in the phrase "family planning." President
Johnson declared in 1965 that the United States will "assist
family planning programs in nations which request such

help." The Prime Minister of India said a year later, "We must press forward with family planning. This is a programme of the highest importance." The Republic of Singapore created in 1966 the Singapore Family Planning and Population Board "to initiate and undertake population control programmes."[1]

As is well known, "family planning" is a euphemism for contraception. The family-planning approach to population limitation, therefore, concentrates on providing new and efficient contraceptives on a national basis through mass programs under public health auspices. The nature of these programs is shown by the following enthusiastic report from the Population Council:[2]

> No single year has seen so many forward steps in population control as 1965. Effective national programs have at last emerged, international organizations have decided to become engaged, a new contraceptive has proved its value in mass application, . . . and surveys have confirmed a popular desire for family limitation . . .

> An accounting of notable events must begin with Korea and Taiwan . . . Taiwan's program is not yet two years old, and already it has inserted one IUD [intrauterine device] for every 4–6 target women (those who are not pregnant, lactating, already sterile, already using contraceptives effectively, or desirous of more children). Korea has done almost as well . . . has put 2,200 full-time workers into the field, . . . has reached operational levels for a network of IUD quotas, supply lines, local manufacture of contraceptives, training of hundreds of M.D.'s and nurses, and mass propaganda . . .

Here one can see the implication that "population control" is being achieved through the dissemination of new contraceptives, and the fact that the "target women" exclude those who want more children. One can also note the technological emphasis and the medical orientation.

What is wrong with such programs? The answer is, "Nothing at all, if they work." Whether or not they work depends on what they are expected to do as well as on how they try to do it. Let us discuss the goal first, then the means.

## *Goals*

Curiously, it is hard to find in the population-policy movement any explicit discussion of long-range goals. By implication the policies seem to promise a great deal. This is shown by the use of expressions like *population control* and *population planning* (as in the passages quoted above). It is also shown by the characteristic style of reasoning. Expositions of current policy usually start off by lamenting the speed and the consequences of runaway population growth. This growth, it is then stated, must be curbed—by pursuing a vigorous family-planning program. That family planning can solve the problem of population growth seems to be taken as self-evident.

For instance, the much-heralded statement by 12 heads of state, issued by Secretary-General U Thant on 10 December 1966 (a statement initiated by John D. Rockefeller III, Chairman of the Board of the Population Council), devotes half its space to discussing the harmfulness of population growth and the other half to recommending family planning.[3] A more succinct example of the typical reasoning is given in the Provisional Scheme for a Nationwide Family Planning Programme in Ceylon:[4]

> The population of Ceylon is fast increasing. . . . [The] figures reveal that a serious situation will be created within a few years. In order to cope with it a Family Planning programme on a nationwide scale should be launched by the Government.

The promised goal—to limit population growth so as to solve population problems—is a large order. One would expect it to be carefully analyzed, but it is left imprecise and taken for granted, as is the way in which family planning will achieve it.

When the terms *population control* and *population planning* are used, as they frequently are, as synonyms for current family-planning programs, they are misleading. Technically, they would mean deliberate influence over all attributes of a population, including its age-sex structure, geographical distribution, racial composition, genetic quality, and total size. No government attempts such full control. By tacit understanding, current population policies are concerned with only the *growth* and *size* of populations. These attributes, however, result from the death rate and migration as well as from the birth rate; their control would require deliberate influence over the factors giving rise to all three determinants. Actually, current policies labeled population control do not deal with mortality and migration, but deal only with the birth input. This is why another term, *fertility control,* is frequently used to describe current policies. But, as I show below, family planning (and hence current policy) does not undertake to influence most of the determinants of human reproduction. Thus the programs should not be referred to as population control or planning, because they do not attempt to influence the factors responsible for the attributes of human populations, taken generally; nor should they be called fertility control, because they do not try to affect most of the determinants of reproductive performance.

The ambiguity does not stop here, however. When one speaks of controlling population size, any inquiring person naturally asks, What is "control"? Who is to control whom? Precisely what population size, or what rate of population growth, is to be achieved? Do the policies aim to produce a growth rate that is nil, one that is very slight, or one that is like that of the industrial nations? Unless such questions are dealt with and clarified, it is impossible to evaluate current population policies.

The actual programs seem to be aiming simply to achieve a reduction in the birth rate. Success is therefore interpreted as the accomplishment of such a reduction, on the assumption that the reduction will lessen population growth. In those rare cases where a specific demographic aim is stated, the goal is said to be a short-run decline within a given period. The Pakistan plan adopted in 1966[5] aims to reduce the birth rate from 50 to 40 per thousand by 1970; the Indian plan[6] aims to reduce the rate from 40 to 25 "as soon as possible"; and the Korean aim[7] is to cut population growth from 2.9 to 1.2 percent by 1980. A significant feature of such stated aims is the rapid population growth they would permit. Under conditions of modern mortality, a crude birth rate of 25 to 30 per thousand will represent such a multiplication of people as to make use of the term *population control* ironic. A rate of increase of 1.2 percent per year would allow South Korea's already dense population to double in less than 60 years.

One can of course defend the programs by saying that the present goals and measures are merely interim ones. A start must be made somewhere. But we do not find this answer in the population-policy literature. Such a defense, if convincing, would require a presentation of the *next* steps, and these are not considered. One suspects that the entire question of goals is instinctively left vague because thorough limitation of population growth would run counter to national and group aspirations. A consideration of hypothetical goals throws further light on the matter.

*Industrialized nations as the model.* Since current policies are confined to family planning, their maximum demographic effect would be to give the underdeveloped countries the same level of reproductive performance that the industrial nations now have. The latter, long oriented toward family planning, provide a good yardstick for determining what the availability of contraceptives can do to population growth. Indeed, they provide more than a yardstick; they are actually the model which inspired the present population policies.

What does this goal mean in practice? Among the advanced nations there is considerable diversity in the level of fertility.[8] At one extreme are countries such as New Zealand, with an average gross reproduction rate (GRR) of 1.91 during the period 1960–64; at the other extreme are countries such as Hungary, with a rate of 0.91 during the same period. To a considerable extent, however, such divergencies are matters of timing. The birth rates of most industrial nations have shown, since about 1940, a wave-like movement, with no secular trend. The average level of reproduction during this long period has been high enough to give these countries, with their low mortality, an extremely rapid population growth. If this level is maintained, their population will double in just over 50 years—a rate higher than that of world population growth at any time prior to 1950, at which time the growth in numbers of human beings was already considered fantastic. The advanced nations are suffering acutely from the effects of rapid population growth in combination with the production of ever more goods per person.[9] A rising share of their supposedly high per capita income, which itself draws increasingly upon the resources of the underdeveloped countries (who fall farther behind in relative economic position), is spent simply to meet the costs, and alleviate the nuisances, of the unrelenting production of more and more goods by more people. Such facts indicate that the industrial nations provide neither a suitable demographic model for the nonindustrial peoples to follow nor the leadership to plan and organize effective population-control policies for them.

*Zero population growth as a goal.* Most discussions of the population crisis lead logically to zero population growth as the ultimate goal, because *any* growth rate, if continued, will eventually use up the earth. Yet hardly ever do arguments for population policy consider such a goal, and current policies do not dream of it. Why not? The answer is evidently that zero population growth is unacceptable to most nations and to most religious and ethnic communities. To argue for this goal would be to alienate possible support for action programs.

*Goal peculiarities inherent in family planning.* Turning to the actual measures taken, we see that the very use of family planning as the means for implementing population policy poses serious but unacknowledged limits on the intended reduction in fertility. The family-planning movement, clearly devoted to the improvement and dissemination of contraceptive devices, states again and again that its purpose is that of enabling couples to have the number of children they want. "The opportunity to decide the number and spacing of children is a basic human right," say the 12 heads of state in the United Nations declaration. The 1965 Turkish Law Concerning Population Planning declares:[10]

> *Article 1.* Population Planning means that individuals can have as many children as they wish, whenever they want to. This can be ensured through preventive measures taken against pregnancy. . . .

Logically, it does not make sense to use *family* planning to provide *national* population control or planning. The "planning" in family planning is that of each separate couple. The only control they exercise is control over the size of *their* family. Obviously, couples do not plan the size of the nation's population, any more than they plan the growth of the national income or the form of the highway network. There is no reason to expect that the millions of decisions about family size made by couples in their own interest will automatically control population for the benefit of society. On the contrary, there are good reasons to think they will not do so. At most, family planning can reduce reproduction to the extent that unwanted births exceed wanted births. In industrial countries the balance is often negative—that is, people have fewer children as a rule than they would like to have. In underdeveloped countries the reverse is normally true, but the elimination of unwanted births would still leave an extremely high rate of multiplication.

Actually, the family-planning movement does not pursue even the limited goals it professes. It does not fully empower couples to have only the number of offspring they want because it either condemns or disregards certain tabooed but nevertheless effective means to this goal. One of its tenets is that "there shall be freedom of choice of method so that individuals can choose in accordance with the dictates of their consciences,"[11] but in practice this amounts to limiting the individual's choice, because the "conscience" dictating the method is usually not his but that of religious and governmental officials. Moreover, not every individual may choose: even the so-called recommended methods are ordinarily not offered to single women, or not all offered to women professing a given religious faith.

Thus, despite its emphasis on technology, current policy does not utilize all available means of contraception, much less all birth-control measures. The Indian government wasted valuable years in the early stages of its population-control program by experimenting exclusively with the "rhythm" method, long after this technique had been demonstrated to be one of the least effective. A greater limitation on means is the exclusive emphasis on contraception itself. Induced abortion, for example, is one of the surest means of controlling reproduction, and one that has been proved capable of reducing birth rates rapidly. It seems peculiarly suited to the threshold stage of a population-control program—the stage when new conditions of life first make large families disadvantageous. It was the principal factor in the halving of the Japanese birth rate, a major factor in the declines in birth rate of East-European satellite countries after legalization of abortions in the early 1950's, and an important factor in the reduction of fertility in industrializing nations from 1870 to the 1930's.[12] Today, according to *Studies in Family Planning,*[13] "abortion is probably the foremost method of birth control throughout Latin America." Yet this method is rejected in nearly all national and international population-control programs. American foreign aid is used to help *stop* abortion.[14] The United Nations excludes abortion from family planning, and in fact justifies the latter by presenting it as a means of combating abortion.[15] Studies of abortion are being made in Latin America under the presumed auspices of population-control groups, not with the intention of legalizing it and thus making it safe, cheap, available, and hence more effective for population control, but with the avowed purpose of reducing it.[16]

Although few would prefer abortion to efficient contraception (other things being equal), the fact is that both permit a woman to control the size of her family. The main drawbacks to abortion arise from its illegality. When performed, as a legal procedure, by a skilled physician, it is safer than childbirth. It does not compete with contraception but serves as a backstop when the latter fails or when contraceptive devices or information are not available. As contraception becomes customary, the incidence of abortion recedes even without its being banned. If, therefore, abortions enable women to have only the number of children they want, and if family planners do not advocate—in fact decry—legalization of abortion, they are to that extent denying the central tenet of their own movement. The irony of anti-abortionism in family-planning circles is seen particularly in hair-splitting arguments over whether or not some contraceptive agent (for example,

care of new human beings is socially motivated, like other forms of behavior, by being a part of the system of rewards and punishments that is built into human relationships, and thus is bound up with the individual's economic and personal interests, it would be apparent that the social structure and economy must be changed before a deliberate reduction in the birth rate can be achieved. As it is, reliance on family planning allows people to feel that "something is being done about the population problem," without the need for painful social changes.

Designation of population control as a medical or public health task leads to a similar evasion. This categorization assures popular support because it puts population policy in the hands of respected medical personnel, but, by the same token, it gives responsibility for leadership to people who think in terms of clinics and patients, of pills and IUD's, and who bring to the handling of economic and social phenomena a self-confident naiveté. The study of social organization is a technical field; an action program based on intuition is no more apt to succeed in the control of human beings than it is in the area of bacterial or viral control. Moreover, to alter a social system, by deliberate policy, so as to regulate births in accord with the demands of the collective welfare would require political power, and this is not likely to inhere in public health officials, nurses, midwives, and social workers. To entrust population policy to them is "to take action," but not dangerous "effective action."

Similarly, the Janus-faced position on birth-control technology represents an escape from the necessity, and onus, of grappling with the social and economic determinants of reproductive behavior. On the one side, the rejection or avoidance of religiously tabooed but otherwise effective means of birth prevention enables the family-planning movement to avoid official condemnation. On the other side, an intense preoccupation with contraceptive technology (apart from the tabooed means) also helps the family planners to avoid censure. By implying that the only need is the invention and distribution of effective contraceptive devices, they allay fears, on the part of religious and governmental officials, that fundamental changes in social organization are contemplated.

Changes basic enough to affect motivation for having children would be changes in the structure of the family, in the position of women, and in the sexual mores. Far from proposing such radicalism, spokesmen for family planning frequently state their purpose as "protection" of the family—that is, closer observance of family norms. In addition, by concentrating on *new* and *scientific* contraceptives, the movement escapes taboos attached to old ones (the Pope will hardly authorize the condom, but may sanction the pill) and allows family planning to be regarded as a branch of medicine: overpopulation becomes a disease, to be treated by a pill or a coil.

We thus see that the inadequacy of current population policies with respect to motivation is inherent in their overwhelmingly family-planning character. Since family planning is by definition private planning, it eschews any societal control over motivation. It merely furnishes the means, and, among possible means, only the most respectable. Its leaders, in avoiding social complexities and seeking official favor, are obviously activated not solely by expediency but also by their own sentiments as members of society and by their background as persons attracted to the family-planning movement. Unacquainted for the most part with technical economics, sociology, and demography, they tend honestly and instinctively to believe that something they vaguely call population control can be achieved by making better contraceptives available.

## The evidence of ineffectiveness

If this characterization is accurate, we can conclude that current programs will not enable a government to control population size. In countries where couples have numerous offspring that they do not want, such programs may possibly accelerate a birth-rate decline that would occur anyway, but the conditions that cause births to be wanted or unwanted are beyond the control of family planning, hence beyond the control of any nation which relies on family planning alone as its population policy.

This conclusion is confirmed by demographic facts. As I have noted above, the widespread use of family planning in industrial countries has not given their governments control over the birth rate. In backward countries today, taken as a whole, birth rates are rising, not falling; in those with population policies, there is no indication that the government is controlling the rate of reproduction. The main "successes" cited in the well-publicized policy literature are cases where a large number of contraceptives have been distributed or where the program has been accompanied by some decline in the birth rate. Popular enthusiasm for family planning is found mainly in the cities, or in advanced countries such as Japan and Taiwan, where the people would adopt contraception in any case, program or no program. It is difficult to prove that present population policies have even speeded up a lowering of the birth rate (the least that could have been expected), much less that they have provided national "fertility control."

Let us next briefly review the facts concerning the level and trend of population in underdeveloped nations generally, in order to understand the magnitude of the task of genuine control.

### Rising birth rates in underdeveloped countries

In ten Latin-American countries, between 1940 and 1959,[23] the average birth rates (age-standardized), as estimated by our research office at the University of California, rose as follows: 1940–44, 43.4 annual births per 1000 population; 1945–49, 44.6; 1950–54, 46.4; 1955–59, 47.7.

In another study made in our office, in which estimating methods derived from the theory of quasi-stable populations were used, the recent trend was found to be upward in 27 underdeveloped countries, downward in six, and unchanged in one.[24] Some of the rises have been substantial, and most have occurred where the birth rate was already extremely high. For instance, the gross reproduction rate rose in Jamaica from 1.8 per thousand in 1947 to 2.7 in 1960; among the natives of Fiji, from 2.0 in 1951 to 2.4 in 1964; and in Albania, from 3.0 in the period 1950–54 to 3.4 in 1960.

The general rise in fertility in backward regions is evidently not due to failure of population-control efforts, because most of the countries either have no such effort or have programs too new to show much effect. Instead, the rise is due, ironically, to the very circumstance that brought on the population crisis in the first place—to improved health and lowered mortality. Better health increases the probability that a woman will conceive and retain the fetus to term; lowered mortality raises the proportion of babies who survive to the age of reproduction and reduces the probability of widowhood during that age.[25] The significance of the general rise in fertility, in the context of this discussion, is that it is giving would-be population planners a harder task than many of them realize. Some of the upward pressure on birth rates is independent of what couples do about family planning, for it arises from the fact that, with lowered mortality, there are simply more couples.

### *Underdeveloped countries with population policies*

In discussions of population policy there is often confusion as to which cases are relevant. Japan, for instance, has been widely praised for the effectiveness of its measures, but it is a very advanced industrial nation and, besides, its government policy had little or nothing to do with the decline in the birth rate, except unintentionally. It therefore offers no test of population policy under peasant-agrarian conditions. Another case of questionable relevance is that of Taiwan, because Taiwan is sufficiently developed to be placed in the urban-industrial class of nations. However, since Taiwan is offered as the main showpiece by the sponsors of current policies in underdeveloped areas, and since the data are excellent, it merits examination.

Taiwan is acclaimed as a showpiece because it has responded favorably to a highly organized program for distributing up-to-date contraceptives and has also had a rapidly dropping birth rate. Some observers have carelessly attributed the decline in the birth rate—from 50.0 in 1951 to 32.7 in 1965—to the family-planning campaign,[26] but the campaign began only in 1963 and could have affected only the end of the trend. Rather, the decline represents a response to modernization similar to that made by all countries that have be-

TABLE 1.
*Decline in Taiwan's fertility rate, 1951 through 1966.*

| Year | Registered births per 1000 women aged 15–49 | Change in rate (percent)* |
|------|------|------|
| 1951 | 211 | |
| 1952 | 198 | −5.6 |
| 1953 | 194 | −2.2 |
| 1954 | 193 | −0.5 |
| 1955 | 197 | +2.1 |
| 1956 | 196 | −0.4 |
| 1957 | 182 | −7.1 |
| 1958 | 185 | +1.3 |
| 1959 | 184 | −0.1 |
| 1960 | 180 | −2.5 |
| 1961 | 177 | −1.5 |
| 1962 | 174 | −1.5 |
| 1963 | 170 | −2.6 |
| 1964 | 162 | −4.9 |
| 1965 | 152 | −6.0 |
| 1966 | 149 | −2.1 |

* The percentages were calculated on unrounded figures. Source of data through 1965, *Taiwan Demographic Fact Book* (1964, 1965); for 1966, *Monthly Bulletin of Population Registration Statistics of Taiwan* (1966, 1967).

come industrialized.[27] By 1950 over half of Taiwan's population was urban, and by 1964 nearly two-thirds were urban, with 29 percent of the population living in cities of 100,000 or more. The pace of economic development has been extremely rapid. Between 1951 and 1963, per capita income increased by 4.05 percent per year. Yet the island is closely packed, having 870 persons per square mile (a population density higher than that of Belgium). The combination of fast economic growth and rapid population increase in limited space has put parents of large families at a relative disadvantage and has created a brisk demand for abortions and contraceptives. Thus the favorable response to the current campaign to encourage use of the IUD is not a good example of what birth-control technology can do for a genuinely backward country. In fact, when the program was started, one reason for expecting receptivity was that the island was already on its way to modernization and family planning.[28]

At most, the recent family-planning campaign—which reached significant proportions only in 1964, when some 46,-000 IUD's were inserted (in 1965 the number was 99,253, and in 1966, 111,242)[29,30]—could have caused the increase observable after 1963 in the rate of decline. Between 1951 and 1963 the average drop in the birth rate per 1000 women (see Table 1) was 1.73 percent per year; in the period 1964–66 it was 4.35 percent. But one hesitates to assign all of the acceleration in decline since 1963 to the family-planning campaign. The rapid economic development has been precisely of a type likely to accelerate a drop in reproduction. The rise in manufacturing has been much greater than the rise in either agriculture or construction. The agricultural labor force has thus been squeezed, and migration to the cities has skyrocketed.[31] Since housing has not kept pace, urban families have had to restrict reproduction in order to take advantage of career opportunities and avoid domestic inconvenience. Such conditions have historically tended to accelerate a decline in birth rate. The most rapid decline came late in the United States (1921–33) and in Japan (1947–55). A plot of the Japanese and Taiwanese birth rates shows marked similarity of the two curves, despite a difference in level. All told, one should not attribute all of the post-1963 acceleration in the decline of Taiwan's birth rate to the family-planning campaign.

The main evidence that *some* of this acceleration is due to the campaign comes from the fact that Taichung, the city in which the family-planning effort was first concentrated, showed subsequently a much faster drop in fertility than other cities.[30,32] But the campaign has not reached throughout the island. By the end of 1966, only 260,745 women had been fitted with an IUD under auspices of the campaign, whereas the women of reproductive age on the island numbered 2.86 million. Most of the reduction in fertility has therefore been a matter of individual initiative. To some extent the campaign may be simply substituting sponsored (and cheaper) services for those that would otherwise come through private and commercial channels. An island-wide survey in 1964 showed that over 150,000 women were already using the traditional Ota ring (a metallic intrauterine device popular in Japan); almost as many had been sterilized; about 40,000 were using foam tablets; some 50,000 admitted to having had at least

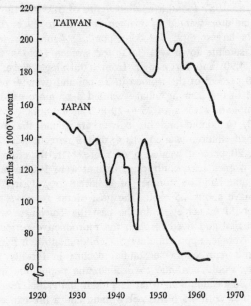

Births per 1000 women aged 15 through 49 in Japan and Taiwan.

one abortion; and many were using other methods of birth control.[30]

The important question, however, is not whether the present campaign is somewhat hastening the downward trend in the birth rate but whether, even if it is, it will provide population control for the nation. Actually, the campaign is not designed to provide such control and shows no sign of doing so. It takes for granted existing reproductive goals. Its aim is "to integrate, through education and information, the idea of family limitation *within the existing attitudes, values, and goals* of the people"[30] (italics mine). Its target is *married* women who do not want any more children; it ignores girls not yet married, and women married and wanting more children.

With such an approach, what is the maximum impact possible? It is the difference between the number of children women have been having and the number they want to have. A study in 1957 found a median figure of 3.75 for the number of children wanted by women aged 15 to 29 in Taipei, Taiwan's largest city; the corresponding figure for women from a satellite town was 3.93; for women from a fishing village, 4.90; and for women from a farming village, 5.03. Over 60 percent of the women in Taipei and over 90 percent of those in the farming village wanted 4 or more children.[33] In a sample of wives aged 25 to 29 in Taichung, a city of over 300,000, Freedman and his co-workers found the average number of children wanted was 4; only 9 percent wanted less than 3, 20 percent wanted 5 or more.[34] If, therefore, Taiwanese women used contraceptives that were 100-percent effective and had the number of children they desired, they would have about 4.5 each. The goal of the family-planning effort would be achieved. In the past the Taiwanese woman who married and lived through the reproductive period had, on the average, approximately 6.5 children; thus a figure of 4.5 would represent a substantial decline in fertility. Since mortality would continue to decline, the population growth rate would decline somewhat less than individual reproduction would. With 4.5 births per woman and a life expectancy of 70 years, the rate of natural increase would be close to 3 percent per year.[35]

In the future, Taiwanese views concerning reproduction will doubtless change, in response to social change and economic modernization. But how far will they change? A good indication is the number of children desired by couples in an already modernized country long oriented toward family planning. In the United States in 1966, an average of 3.4 children was considered ideal by white women aged 21 or over.[36] This average number of births would give Taiwan, with only a slight decrease in mortality, a long-run rate of natural increase of 1.7 percent per year and a doubling of population in 41 years.

Detailed data confirm the interpretation that Taiwanese women are in the process of shifting from a "peasant-agrarian" to an "industrial" level of reproduction. They are, in typical fashion, cutting off higher-order births at age 30 and beyond.[37] Among young wives, fertility has risen, not fallen. In sum, the widely acclaimed family-planning program in Taiwan may, at most, have somewhat speeded the later phase of fertility decline which would have occurred anyway because of modernization.

Moving down the scale of modernization, to countries most in need of population control, one finds the family-planning approach even more inadequate. In South Korea, second only to Taiwan in the frequency with which it is cited as a model of current policy, a recent birth-rate decline of unknown extent is assumed by leaders to be due overwhelmingly to the government's family-planning program. However, it is just as plausible to say that the net effect of government involvement in population control has been, so far, to delay rather than hasten a decline in reproduction made inevitable by social and economic changes. Although the government is advocating vasectomies and providing IUD's and pills, it refuses to legalize abortions, despite the rapid rise in the rate of illegal abortions and despite the fact that, in a recent survey, 72 percent of the people who stated an opinion favored legalization. Also, the program is presented in the context of maternal and child health; it thus emphasizes motherhood and the family rather than alternative roles for women. Much is made of the fact that opinion surveys show an overwhelming majority of Koreans (89 percent in 1965) favoring contraception,[38] but this means only that Koreans are like other people in wishing to have the means to get what they want. Unfortunately, they want sizable families: "The records indicate that the program appeals mainly to women in the 30–39 year age bracket who have four or more children, including at least two sons . . ."[38]

In areas less developed than Korea the degree of acceptance of contraception tends to be disappointing, especially among the rural majority. Faced with this discouragement, the leaders of current policy, instead of reexamining their assumptions, tend to redouble their effort to find a contraceptive that will appeal to the most illiterate peasant, forgetting that he wants a good-sized family. In the rural Punjab, for example, "a disturbing feature . . . is that the females start to seek advice and adopt family planning techniques at the fag end of their reproductive period."[39] Among 5196 women coming to rural Punjabi family-planning centers, 38 percent were over 35 years old, 67 percent over 30. These women had married early, nearly a third of them before the age of 15;[40] some 14 percent had eight or more *living* children when they reached the clinic, 51 percent six or more.

A survey in Tunisia showed that 68 percent of the married couples were willing to use birth-control measures, but the average number of children they considered ideal was 4.3.[41] The corresponding averages for a village in eastern Java, a village near New Delhi, and a village in Mysore were 4.3, 4.0, and 4.2, respectively.[42,43] In the cities of these regions women are more ready to accept birth control and they want fewer children than village women do, but the number they consider desirable is still wholly unsatisfactory from the standpoint of population control. In an urban family-planning center in Tunisia, more than 600 of 900 women accepting contraceptives had four living children already.[44] In Bangalore, a city of nearly a million at the time (1952), the number of offspring desired by married women was 3.7 on the average; by married men, 4.1.[43] In the metropolitan area of San Salvador (350,000 inhabitants) a 1964 survey[45] showed the number desired by women of reproductive age to be 3.9, and in seven other capital cities of Latin America the number ranged from 2.7 to 4.2. If women in the cities of underdeveloped countries used birth-control measures with 100-percent efficiency, they still would have enough babies to expand city populations senselessly, quite apart from the added contribution of rural-urban migration. In many of the cities the difference between actual and ideal number of children is not great; for instance, in the seven Latin-American capitals mentioned above, the ideal was 3.4 whereas the actual births per women in the age range 35 to 39 was 3.7.[46] Bombay City has had birth-control clinics for many years, yet its birth rate (standardized for age, sex, and marital distribution) is still 34 per 1000 inhabitants and is tending to rise rather than fall. Although this rate is about 13 percent lower than that for India generally, it has been about that much lower since at least 1951.[47]

### Is family planning the "first step" in population control?

To acknowledge that family planning does not achieve population control is not to impugn its value for other purposes. Freeing women from the need to have more children than they want is of great benefit to them and their children and to society at large. My argument is therefore directed not against family-planning programs as such but against the assumption that they are an effective means of controlling population growth.

But what difference does it make? Why not go along for awhile with family planning as an initial approach to the problem of population control? The answer is that any policy on which millions of dollars are being spent should be designed to achieve the goal it purports to achieve. If it is only a first step, it should be so labeled, and its connection with the next step (and the nature of that next step) should be carefully examined. In the present case, since no "next step" seems ever to be mentioned, the question arises, Is reliance on family planning in fact a basis for dangerous postponement of effective steps? To continue to offer a remedy as a cure long after it has been shown merely to ameliorate the disease is either quackery or wishful thinking, and it thrives most where the need is greatest. Today the desire to solve the population problem is so intense that we are all ready to embrace any "action program" that promises relief. But postponement of effective measures allows the situation to worsen.

Unfortunately, the issue is confused by a matter of semantics. "Family *planning*" and "fertility *control*" suggest that reproduction is being regulated according to some rational plan. And so it is, but only from the standpoint of the individual couple, not from that of the community. What is rational in the light of a couple's situation may be totally irrational from the standpoint of society's welfare.

The need for societal regulation of individual behavior is readily recognized in other spheres—those of explosives, dangerous drugs, public property, natural resources. But in the sphere of reproduction, complete individual initiative is generally favored even by those liberal intellectuals who, in other spheres, most favor economic and social planning. Social reformers who would not hesitate to force all owners of rental property to rent to anyone who can pay, or to force all workers in an industry to join a union, balk at any suggestion that couples be permitted to have only a certain number of offspring. Invariably they interpret societal control of reproduction as meaning direct police supervision of individual behavior. Put the word *compulsory* in front of any term describing a means of limiting births—*compulsory sterilization, compulsory abortion, compulsory contraception*—and you guarantee violent opposition. Fortunately, such direct controls need not be invoked, but conservatives and radicals alike overlook this in their blind opposition to the idea of collective determination of a society's birth rate.

That the exclusive emphasis on family planning in current population policies is not a "first step" but an escape from the real issues is suggested by two facts. (i) No country has taken the "next step." The industrialized countries have had family planning for half a century without acquiring control over either the birth rate or population increase. (ii) Support and encouragement of research on population policy other than family planning is negligible. It is precisely this blocking of alternative thinking and experimentation that makes the emphasis on family planning a major obstacle to population control. The need is not to abandon family-planning programs but to put equal or greater resources into other approaches.

### New directions in population policy

In thinking about other approaches, one can start with known facts. In the past, all surviving societies had institutional incentives for marriage, procreation, and childcare which were powerful enough to keep the birth rate equal to or in excess of a high death rate. Despite the drop in death rates during the last century and a half, the incentives tended to remain intact because the social structure (especially in regard to the family) changed little. At most, particularly in industrial societies, children became less productive and more expensive.[48] In present-day agrarian societies, where the drop in death rate has been more recent, precipitate, and independent of social change,[49] motivation for having children has changed little. Here, even more than in industrialized nations, the family has kept on producing abundant offspring, even though only a fraction of these children are now needed.

If excessive population growth is to be prevented, the obvious requirement is somehow to impose restraints on the family. However, because family roles are reinforced by society's system of rewards, punishments, sentiments, and norms, any proposal to demote the family is viewed as a threat by conservatives and liberals alike, and certainly by people with enough social responsibility to work for population control. One is charged with trying to "abolish" the family, but what is required is selective restructuring of the family in relation to the rest of society.

The lines of such restructuring are suggested by two existing limitations on fertility. (i) Nearly all societies succeed in drastically discouraging reproduction among unmarried women. (ii) Advanced societies unintentionally reduce reproduction among married women when conditions worsen in such a way as to penalize childbearing more severely than it was penalized before. In both cases the causes are motivational and economic rather than technological.

It follows that population-control policy can de-emphasize the family in two ways: (i) by keeping present controls over illegitimate childbirth yet making the most of factors that lead people to postpone or avoid marriage, and (ii) by instituting conditions that motivate those who do marry to keep their families small.

### Postponement of marriage

Since the female reproductive span is short and generally more fecund in its first than in its second half, postponement of marriage to ages beyond 20 tends biologically to reduce births. Sociologically, it gives women time to get a better education, acquire interests unrelated to the family, and develop a cautious attitude toward pregnancy.[50] Individuals who have not married by the time they are in their late twenties often do not marry at all. For these reasons, for the world as a whole, the average age at marriage for women is negatively associated with the birth rate: a rising age at marriage is a frequent cause of declining fertility during the middle phase of the demographic transition; and, in the late phase, the "baby boom" is usually associated with a return to younger marriages.

Any suggestion that age at marriage be raised as a part of population policy is usually met with the argument that "even if a law were passed, it would not be obeyed." Interestingly, this objection implies that the only way to control the age at marriage is by direct legislation, but other factors govern the actual age. Roman Catholic countries generally follow canon law in stipulating 12 years as the minimum *legal* age at which girls may marry, but the actual average age at marriage in these countries (at least in Europe) is characteristically more like 25 to 28 years. The actual age is determined, not by law, but by social and economic conditions. In agrarian societies, postponement of marriage (when postponement occurs) is apparently caused by difficulties in meeting the economic prerequisites for matrimony, as stipulated by custom and opinion. In industrial societies it is caused by housing shortages, unemployment, the requirement for overseas military service, high costs of education, and inadequacy of consumer services. Since almost no research has been devoted to the subject, it is difficult to assess the relative weight of the factors that govern the age at marriage.

### Encouraging limitation of births within marriage

As a means of encouraging the limitation of reproduction within marriage, as well as postponement of marriage, a greater rewarding of nonfamilial than of familial roles would probably help. A simple way of accomplishing this would be to allow economic advantages to accrue to the single as opposed to the married individual, and to the small as opposed to the large family. For instance, the government could pay people to permit themselves to be sterilized;[51] all costs of abortion could be paid by the government; a substantial fee could be charged for a marriage license; a "child-tax"[52] could be levied; and there could be a requirement that illegitimate pregnancies be aborted. Less sensationally, governments could simply reverse some existing policies that encourage childbearing. They could, for example, cease taxing single persons more than married ones; stop giving parents special tax exemptions; abandon income-tax policy that discriminates against couples when the wife works; reduce paid maternity leaves; reduce family allowances;[53] stop awarding public housing on the basis of family size; stop granting fellowships and other educational aids (including special allowances for wives and children) to married students; cease outlawing abortions and sterilizations; and relax rules that allow use of harmless contraceptives only with medical permission. Some of these policy reversals would be beneficial in other than demographic respects and some would be harmful unless special precautions were taken. The aim would be to reduce the number, not the quality, of the next generation.

A closely related method of de-emphasizing the family would be modification of the complementarity of the roles of men and women. Men are now able to participate in the wider world yet enjoy the satisfaction of having several children because the housework and childcare fall mainly on their wives. Women are impelled to seek this role by their idealized view of marriage and motherhood and by either the scarcity of alternative roles or the difficulty of combining them with family roles. To change this situation women could be required to work outside the home, or compelled by circumstances to do so. If, at the same time, women were paid as well as men and given equal educational and occupational opportunities, and if social life were organized around the place of work rather than around the home or neighborhood, many women would develop interests that would compete with family interests. Approximately this policy is now followed in several Communist countries, and even the less developed of these currently have extremely low birth rates.[54]

That inclusion of women in the labor force has a negative effect on reproduction is indicated by regional comparisons.[18,55] But in most countries the wife's employment is subordinate, economically and emotionally, to her family role, and is readily sacrificed for the latter. No society has restructured both the occupational system and the domestic establishment to the point of permanently modifying the old division of labor by sex.

In any deliberate effort to control the birth rate along these lines, a government has two powerful instruments—its command over economic planning and its authority (real or potential) over education. The first determines (as far as policy can) the economic conditions and circumstances affecting the lives of all citizens; the second provides the knowledge and attitudes necessary to implement the plans. The economic system largely determines who shall work, what can be bought, what rearing children will cost, how much individuals can spend. The schools define family roles and develop vocational and recreational interests; they could, if it were desired, redefine the sex roles, develop interests that transcend the home, and transmit realistic (as opposed to moralistic) knowledge concerning marriage, sexual behavior, and population problems. When the problem is viewed in this light, it is clear that the ministries of economics and education, not the ministry of health, should be the source of population policy.

### The dilemma of population policy

It should now be apparent why, despite strong anxiety over runaway population growth, the actual programs purporting to control it are limited to family planning and are therefore ineffective. (i) The goal of zero, or even slight, population growth is one that nations and groups find difficult to accept. (ii) The measures that would be required to implement such a goal, though not so revolutionary as a Brave New World or a Communist Utopia, nevertheless tend to offend most people reared in existing societies. As a consequence, the goal of so-called population control is implicit and vague; the method is only family planning. This method, far from de-emphasizing the family, is familistic. One of its stated goals is that of helping sterile couples to *have* children. It stresses parental aspirations and responsibilities. It goes along with most aspects of conventional morality, such as condemnation of abortion, disapproval of premarital intercourse, respect for religious teachings and cultural taboos, and obeisance to medical and clerical authority. It deflects hostility by refusing to recommend any change other than the one it stands for: availability of contraceptives.

The things that make family planning acceptable are the very things that make it ineffective for population control. By stressing the right of parents to have the number of children they want, it evades the basic question of population policy, which is how to give societies the number of children they need. By offering only the means for *couples* to control fertility, it neglects the means for societies to do so.

Because of the predominantly pro-family character of existing societies, individual interest ordinarily leads to the production of enough offspring to constitute rapid population growth under conditions of low mortality. Childless or single-child homes are considered indicative of personal failure, whereas having three to five living children gives a family a sense of continuity and substantiality.[56]

Given the existing desire to have moderate-sized rather than small families, the only countries in which fertility has been reduced to match reduction in mortality are advanced ones temporarily experiencing worsened economic conditions. In Sweden, for instance, the net reproduction rate (NRR) has been below replacement for 34 years (1930–63), if the period is taken as a whole, but this is because of the economic depression. The average replacement rate was below unity (NRR = 0.81) for the period 1930–42, but from 1942 through 1963 it was above unity (NRR = 1.08). Hardships that seem particularly conducive to deliberate lowering of the birth rate are (in managed economies) scarcity of housing and other consumer goods despite full employment, and required high participation of women in the labor force, or (in freer economies) a great deal of unemployment and economic insecurity. When conditions are good, any nation tends to have a growing population.

It follows that, in countries where contraception is used, a realistic proposal for a government policy of lowering the birth rate reads like a catalogue of horrors: squeeze consumers through taxation and inflation; make housing very scarce by limiting construction; force wives and mothers to work outside the home to offset the inadequacy of male wages, yet provide few child-care facilities; encourage migration to the city by paying low wages in the country and providing few rural jobs; increase congestion in cities by starving the transit system; increase personal insecurity by encouraging conditions that produce unemployment and by haphazard political arrests. No government will institute such hardships simply for the purpose of controlling population growth. Clearly, therefore, the task of contemporary population policy is to develop attractive substitutes for family interests, so as to avoid having to turn to hardship as a corrective. The specific measures required for developing such substitutes are not easy to determine in the absence of research on the question.

In short, the world's population problem cannot be solved by pretense and wishful thinking. The unthinking identification of family planning with population control is an ostrich-like approach in that it permits people to hide from themselves the enormity and unconventionality of the task. There is no reason to abandon family-planning programs; contraception is a valuable technological instrument. But such programs must be supplemented with equal or greater investments in research and experimentation to determine the required socioeconomic measures.

### References

1. *Studies in Family Planning, No. 16* (1967).
2. *Ibid., No. 9* (1966), p. 1.
3. The statement is given in *Studies in Family Planning* (*1*, p. 1), and in *Population Bull.* 23, 6 (1967).
4. The statement is quoted in *Studies in Family Planning* (*1*, p. 2).
5. *Hearings on S. 1676, U.S. Senate, Subcommittee on Foreign Aid Expenditures, 89th Congress, Second Session, April 7, 8, 11* (1966), pt. 4, p. 889.
6. B. L. Raina, in *Family Planning and Population Programs*, B. Berelson, R. K. Anderson, O. Harkavy, G. Maier, W. P.

Mauldin, S. G. Segal, Eds. (Univ. of Chicago Press, Chicago, 1966).

7. D. Kirk, *Ann. Amer. Acad. Polit. Soc. Sci.* 369, 53 (1967).

8. As used by English-speaking demographers, the word *fertility* designates actual reproductive performance, not a theoretical capacity.

9. K. Davis, *Rotarian* 94, 10 (1959); *Health Educ. Monographs* 9, 2 (1960); L. Day and A. Day, *Too Many Americans* (Houghton Mifflin, Boston, 1964); R. A. Piddington, *Limits of Mankind* (Wright, Bristol, England, 1956).

10. *Official Gazette* (15 Apr. 1965); quoted in *Studies in Family Planning* (*1*, p. 7).

11. J. W. Gardner, Secretary of Health, Education, and Welfare, "Memorandum to Heads of Operating Agencies" (Jan. 1966), reproduced in *Hearings on S. 1676* (*5*), p. 783.

12. C. Tietze, *Demography* 1, 119 (1964); *J. Chronic Diseases* 18, 1161 (1964); M. Muramatsu, *Milbank Mem. Fund Quart.* 38, 153 (1960); K. Davis, *Population Index* 29, 345 (1963); R. Armijo and T. Monreal, *J. Sex Res.* 1964, 143 (1964); Proceedings World Population Conference, Belgrade, 1965; Proceedings International Planned Parenthood Federation.

13. *Studies in Family Planning, No. 4* (1964), p. 3.

14. D. Bell (then administrator for Agency for International Development), in *Hearings on S. 1676* (*5*), p. 862.

15. *Asian Population Conference* (United Nations, New York, 1964), p. 30.

16. R. Armijo and T. Monreal, in *Components of Population Change in Latin America* (Milbank Fund, New York, 1965), p. 272; E. Rice-Wray, *Amer. J. Public Health* 54, 313 (1964).

17. E. Rice-Wray, in "Intra-Uterine Contraceptive Devices," *Excerpta Med. Intern. Congr. Ser. No. 54* (1962), p. 135.

18. J. Blake, in *Public Health and Population Change*, M. C. Sheps and J. C. Ridley, Eds. (Univ. of Pittsburgh Press, Pittsburgh, 1965), p. 41, 1195.

19. J. Blake and K. Davis, *Amer. Behavioral Scientist*, 5, 24 (1963).

20. See "Panel discussion on comparative acceptability of different methods of contraception," in *Research in Family Planning*, C. V. Kiser, Ed. (Princeton Univ. Press, Princeton, 1962), pp. 373–386.

21. "From the point of view of the woman concerned, the whole problem of continuing motivation disappears, . . ." [D. Kirk, in *Population Dynamics*, M. Muramatsu and P. A. Harper, Eds. (Johns Hopkins Press, Baltimore, 1965)].

22. "For influencing family size norms, certainly the examples and statements of public figures are of great significance . . . also . . . use of mass-communication methods which help to legitimize the small-family style, to provoke conversation, and to establish a vocabulary for discussion of family planning" [M. W. Freymann, in *Population Dynamics,* M. Muramatsu and P. A. Harper, Eds. (Johns Hopkins Press, Baltimore, 1965)].

23. O. A. Collver, *Birth Rates in Latin America* (International Population and Urban Research, Berkeley, Calif., 1965), pp. 27–28; the ten countries were Colombia, Costa Rica, El Salvador, Ecuador, Guatemala, Honduras, Mexico, Panama, Peru, and Venezuela.

24. J. R. Rele, *Fertility Analysis through Extension of Stable Population Concepts* (International Population and Urban Research, Berkeley, Calif., 1967).

25. J. C. Ridley, M. C. Sheps, J. W. Lingner, J. A. Menken, *Milbank Mem. Fund Quart.* 45, 77 (1967); E. Arriaga, unpublished paper.

26. "South Korea and Taiwan appear successfully to have checked population growth by the use of intrauterine contraceptive devices" [U. Borell, *Hearings on S. 1676* (5), p. 556].

27. K. Davis, *Population Index* 29, 345 (1963).

28. R. Freedman, *ibid.* 31, 421 (1965).

29. Before 1964 the Family Planning Association had given advice to fewer than 60,000 wives in 10 years and a Pre-Pregnancy Health Program had reached some 10,000, and, in the current campaign, 3650 IUD's were inserted in 1965, in a total population of 2½ million women of reproductive age. See *Studies in Family Planning, No. 19* (1967), p. 4, and R. Freedman *et al., Population Studies* 16, 231 (1963).

30. R. W. Gillespie, *Family Planning on Taiwan* (Population Council, Taichung, 1965), pp. 45, 18, 31, 8.

31. During the period 1950–60 the ratio of growth of the city to growth of the noncity population was 5:3; during the period 1960–64 the ratio was 5:2; these ratios are based on data of Shaohsing Chen, *J. Sociol. Taiwan* 1, 74 (1963) and data in the United Nations *Demographic Yearbooks.*

32. R. Freedman, *Population Index* 31, 434 (1965). Taichung's rate of decline in 1963–64 was roughly double the average in four other cities, whereas just prior to the campaign its rate of decline had been much less than theirs.

33. S. H. Chen, *J. Soc. Sci. Taipei* 13, 72 (1963).

34. R. Freedman *et al.*, *Population Studies* 16, 227 (1963); *ibid.*, p. 232.
35. In 1964 the life expectancy at birth was already 66 years in Taiwan, as compared to 70 for the United States.
36. J. Blake, *Eugenics Quart.* 14, 68 (1967).
37. Women accepting IUD's in the family-planning program are typically 30 to 34 years old and have already had four children [*Studies in Family Planning, No. 19* (1967), p. 5].
38. Y. K. Cha, in *Family Planning and Population Programs*, B. Berelson *et al.*, Eds. (Univ. of Chicago Press, Chicago, 1966), p. 25.
39. H. S. Ayalvi and S. S. Johl, *J. Family Welfare* 12, 60 (1965).
40. Sixty percent of the women had borne their first child before age 19. Early marriage is strongly supported by public opinion. Of couples polled in the Punjab, 48 percent said that girls *should* marry before age 16, and 94 percent said they should marry before age 20 (H. S. Ayalvi and S. S. Johl, *ibid.*, p. 57). A study of 2380 couples in 60 villages of Uttar Pradesh found that the women had consummated their marriage at an average age of 14.6 years [J. R. Rele, *Population Studies* 15, 268 (1962)].
41. J. Morsa, in *Family Planning and Population Programs*, B. Berelson *et al.*, Eds. (Univ. of Chicago Press, Chicago, 1966).
42. H. Gille and R. J. Pardoko, *ibid.*, p. 515; S. N. Agarwala, *Med. Dig. Bombay* 4, 653 (1961).
43. *Mysore Population Study* (United Nations, New York, 1961), p. 140.
44. A. Daly, in *Family Planning and Population Programs*, B. Berelson *et al.*, Eds. (Univ. of Chicago Press, Chicago, 1966).
45. C. J. Goméz, paper presented at the World Population Conference, Belgrade, 1965.
46. C. Miro, in *Family Planning and Population Programs*, B. Berelson *et al.*, Eds. (Univ. of Chicago Press, Chicago, 1966).
47. *Demographic Training and Research Centre (India) Newsletter* 20, 4 (Aug. 1966).
48. K. Davis, *Population Index* 29, 345 (1963). For economic and sociological theory of motivation for having children, see J. Blake [Univ. of California (Berkeley)], in preparation.
49. K. Davis, *Amer. Economic Rev.* 46, 305 (1956); *Sci. Amer.* 209, 68 (1963).
50. J. Blake, *World Population Conference* [Belgrade, 1965] (United Nations, New York, 1967), vol. 2, pp. 132–136.
51. S. Enke, *Rev. Economics Statistics* 42, 175 (1960); ——,

*Econ. Develop. Cult. Change* 8, 339 (1960); ——, *ibid.* 10, 427 (1962); A. O. Krueger and L. A. Sjaastad, *ibid.*, p. 423.

52. T. J. Samuel, *J. Family Welfare India* 13, 12 (1966).

53. Sixty-two countries, including 27 in Europe, give cash payments to people for having children [U.S. Social Security Administration, *Social Security Programs Throughout the World, 1967* (Government Printing Office, Washington, D.C., 1967), pp. xxvii–xxviii].

54. Average gross reproduction rates in the early 1960's were as follows: Hungary, 0.91; Bulgaria, 1.09; Romania, 1.15; Yugoslavia, 1.32.

55. O. A. Collver and E. Langlois, *Econ. Develop. Cult. Change* 10, 367 (1962); J. Weeks [Univ. of California (Berkeley)], unpublished paper.

56. Roman Catholic textbooks condemn the "small" family (one with fewer than four children) as being abnormal [J. Blake, *Population Studies* 20, 27 (1966)].

57. Judith Blake's critical readings and discussions have greatly helped in the preparation of this article.

# 17. *Multiple Paths to Population Control*

## GARRETT HARDIN

Many Americans now agree that the United States does not need more people, and that we would be better off if we could remain as we are, or even decrease our population somewhat. The problem is that we fear to face the necessity of freezing population at any particular level. We dread thinking about the alterations in our way of life that this would require.

Up to now the only method used in this country to curb population growth has been voluntary birth control. But can we make do with voluntary methods alone? The accumulated evidence of surveys taken in this country and throughout the world would indicate that we cannot, since, as Kingsley Davis[1] and others have pointed out, couples in all countries consistently express an "ideal" number of children in excess of that number required to maintain a stationary population. Recently, Larry Bumpass and Charles Westoff have completed a study which points to a possibly contradictory conclusion.[2] Their study indicates that if, in the last generation, we could have prevented *all* the unwanted births which occurred, we would have arrived very nearly at replacement levels. Dr. Westoff says "nearly," rather than "entirely." "Nearly" is not enough, since any growth at all sooner or later will get out of hand.

My contention that we will have to go beyond purely voluntary methods, however, springs from a very simple biological concept: People vary. This concept is so central to biological thinking that a biologist cannot even consider logical any argument which does not allow for human variation. We must assume, therefore, that people vary in the numbers of children they want to have. Such variation, I believe, is to a certain extent inherited—in the broadest sense of that word—not necessarily through the genes, the chromosomes, the DNA. Perhaps the inheritance is purely social, i.e., the ideas of the mother are passed down to her daughter. There is evidence, at any rate, that the daughters of women who have more children than average are themselves somewhat more likely to have more children than average.[3] Whether the inheritance is biological or social, the results are the same: In a condition of free choice, the women who have more children than the average will leave more descendants to carry on the same characteristic in the next generation. As one generation succeeds another, the fertile breeders will thus outbreed the relatively infertile, and there will be a tendency for the numbers of children to increase with each succeeding generation. This means that in the long run voluntary birth control is self-defeating; those who have low fertility will disappear from the system.

But what about the short run? How much social dislocation are we willing to put up with for the sake of attaining national objectives of zero population growth quickly? For the immediate future I would agree with those who urge that we avoid methods of coercion to attain population limitation. Let's not force people to control their breeding for the sake of national well-being; let's let them do what they want to do. I say this (although I believe that the United States is already overpopulated) because I think there is still some leeway to work out the very difficult problems involved.

### Voluntary methods that work

However, if we are going to use methods of voluntary birth control we must make them as good as we can, and that means a great deal better than they are now. Because both the pill and the IUD have obvious disadvantages, we need technologically better birth control methods. While we may never develop "the perfect contraceptive," we can, with sufficient investment of funds and personnel, produce a great variety of safe, inexpensive, effective and acceptable methods of birth control for both men and women.

But even more important than new biological techniques is the need for new techniques of a social sort. It appears that something between 20 and 35 percent of all babies born were unwanted at time of conception. This is a rate far higher than can be explained by faulty contraceptive technology alone. What else then is involved?

The fact is that we are still entrapped by Victorian hangups about the propriety of birth control. Many young people in particular share the attitude that there is something shameful about birth control and don't make use of it until after they are in trouble. Many pregnancies in young women are the result of what I would call "virginal tendencies":

Brought up by her mother to regard virginity as a precious gift to be kept as long as possible, a girl soon moves into an environment where quite conflicting and often importunate messages are heard. She is uncertain about what to do. To take precautions in advance would be to acknowledge to herself that she is going against her mother's teaching. So when the crucial night arrives she goes out unprepared. That's "all right"—she hasn't really lost her virginity, because she hasn't been cold-blooded; she's been carried away by passion. Nor is this attitude confined to girls. Both boys and girls often continue recklessly for some time until the day of reckoning does finally come. Then, and only then, is the girl ready to go to the doctor and ask for birth control.

Thus, it is not enough merely to manufacture birth control drugs and devices and distribute them to drugstores (where often, by law, they must be carefully hidden behind the counter). In a social sense, birth control methods are not really available if young women and men cannot, without hesitancy, make use of them when they need them. There is a major education job to do here, not primarily education of the young (those "at risk" as we say) but of the older people who have to deal with sexual activity of their children without embarrassment, without introduction of notions of shame and sin, so that a young person will think of using birth control naturally and unashamedly from the beginning of a sexual relationship. That is one means of making birth control truly available.

Another aspect of the problem concerns poor people, people who have a hard time latching on to anything that society offers. We certainly don't make it easy for them to get birth control. In Santa Barbara, for example, about 10 years ago, we opened a Planned Parenthood clinic. When the clinic was established with private funds it was located conveniently to where the poor lived; they could walk to the clinic and walk home. Finally, the county was persuaded that birth control was a legitimate public health function, and it took over the clinic. But after about a year the county supervisors decided that it was too expensive to maintain this separate medical facility. They decided to amalgamate it with the county hospital to save the taxpayers' money and to be more efficient. The only difficulty was that the hospital was 10 miles out of town. Now, California has been built on the assumption that man was born with an automobile between his legs. But many poor people either don't have automobiles or they have only one and the man of the house needs that to drive to work. How is his wife going to travel 10 miles to the birth control clinic? There is a bus which leaves every hour, but it sometimes skips. If she does get to the hospital, the woman will have to wait two or three hours for service because it is necessary to make "efficient" use of the doctor's time, and to hell with the patient. If she is lucky, a woman may leave her house at eight o'clock in the morning and get back home at two in the afternoon. For a poor woman who may already have several children to care for this can be a nearly impossible situation. So it has proved to be. Once afflicted by "efficiency," the whole system so discouraged patients that use dropped drastically. Thus, it isn't enough to establish birth control facilities; they must be located conveniently to where poor people live.

Similarly, to make birth control fully available to the poor we have to involve the poor in the delivery of services. There is a chain of people involved in any organized birth control effort, and direct communication must finally be with a staff person who can speak as a peer. I recall one instance where a Mexican woman had an unwanted pregnancy. She went to the Planned Parenthood group to find out if she could get an abortion, and the counselor told her that she could, but she would first have to see a psychiatrist. The Mexican woman interpreted this as an accusation that she was insane. Poor Mexicans in this community don't use psychiatrists just to pass an otherwise boring afternoon. To them, the psychiatrist is the last step on the way to the insane asylum. The Mexican woman in this case was scared speechless, would not see the psychiatrist and tried to abort herself—all because of the frightening word "psychiatrist." Now, had the counselor been a Mexican, she would have known how to explain the situation to the patient, get her to a psychiatrist and a safe medical abortion. This kind of thing also is involved in making birth control services truly available.

I am sure that we can go a long way toward bringing births down to replacement levels if we make it really possible for everybody to have birth control at the time and the place that he or she needs it. This is the important thing. This means that we must develop a national consensus that such universal availability of birth control services is so important that they should be absolutely free for everybody.

And by birth control, I should make it clear that I include abortion as a backstop method when all other methods fail. Abortions should be free too. This nation can certainly pay for abortions far more easily than it can afford unwanted children. Nor need we worry that women will have abortions for the fun of it, so there is no danger that hospitals and doctors' offices will suddenly be flooded if we make abortions available on demand. Indeed the nation will be immensely better off for having a perfect system of birth control —as it can, if abortion is available as a backstop method. This is the first priority for this country in trying to limit our numbers.

### Taxes: no economic effect

A second stage in reducing population growth would be what I call "symbolic coercion": that is, modification of the income tax laws to eliminate deductions for children after the second. I call such a move "symbolic" because economically it will not have much effect. Even under the present tax laws you don't get rich by having children. The new $625 exemption for each child is worth $125 to the taxpayer in the 20 percent bracket; and you can't raise a child on $125 a year. In the case of the poor, we would want to be careful not to penalize children who are born. So undoubtedly what was taken away from poor parents through income tax modification would be passed back to the children through their parents in the form of aid of one kind or another. That will increase—not decrease—welfare costs, so it won't save the nation money any more than it will serve as an economic incentive to parents to have less children. Such tax laws would, however, have a symbolic effect: They will indicate that the nation doesn't want parents to have more than two children; if they have more than two it is for some reason of their own. Such laws will, in short, have an educational effect, and even their introduction is important in this regard. Several such bills have been introduced. Colorado's Representative Lamm has introduced a bill which would modify that state's tax law to allow only two child deductions, and a similar bill has been introduced in the California legislature by Senator Beilenson. Neither bill would apply to adopted children or to children conceived before passage of the bill. These are important exceptions. Oregon's Senator Packwood has introduced a similar bill in the U.S. Senate which allows deductions for up to three children. Though a courageous gesture, I think this is a mistake. Since the purpose of such legislation is symbolic and its primary effect would be educational, three children on the average would be too many; it is more, in fact, than U.S. couples are now having.

Another useful step we might take is to start putting new ideas into the heads of young people, especially young girls. By young I mean first, second and third graders. We need to teach them that it is not necessary for them to become mommies when they grow up, and that if they do become mommies they need not have a lot of children. We need to introduce into the Dick and Jane readers some characters other than Jane's mommy and daddy, and the couple next door whose children are named Carol and Jack and Tom, and the neighbors across the street with their three or four children. Perhaps we need to show Dick and Jane's Aunt Debbie, a swinging single of 40, who's as pretty as a picture. Now we don't have to tell these first graders what kind of fine time she is having. They need only see her with a smile on her face, see that she likes children and is comfortable with them. Aunt Debbie isn't a sour old maid who hates kids. She loves youngsters but doesn't want them around her all the time; it's enough for her to visit her nieces and nephews. And when she isn't visiting them, she lives a different kind of life—and it's a good life.

There are too many people now who marry because they think they have to, who have children because they think they have to. Some of these people in their heart of hearts don't want to get married or don't want to have children, but they cannot resist the social pressure. So it is important to get into the schools the notion that there are alternative goals to marriage and parenthood. If we can get this message across, we not only can diminish the birth rate, but we can diminish also a great deal of heartache; because semi-reluctant parents, statistically speaking, tend to become only grudgingly reconciled parents. We want to make it possible for them to live a good life, respected by the community, that does not involve having children. While such education does not coerce the children, we may have to coerce the educators. We may have some serious battles ahead when we introduce Aunt Debbie into the first grade reader for the first time, but I think we've got to face this. I think we can win this battle.

We ought, too, to face the fact that some day in the distant future we may have to use involuntary methods of birth control—even positively coercive means. I don't know what "good" involuntary methods would be; I don't think we've invented them yet. But I think we *can* invent them, and there is time to do so. We ought not say anything foolish about coercion in the meantime.

At the present time we do not need frankly coercive measures, but let us not say that we advocate voluntary measures in order to avoid coercion, because we may not be able to avoid it. The United Nations officially proclaims that it is the right of every couple to decide how many children they will have and how they will be spaced. The primary intention of this statement is to legitimize birth control. But it also sanctions parents having as many children as they want. I think this United Nations statement is going to be the source of endless trouble in the years to come. We want to develop now all the non-coercive measures that we can, to see if we can solve the problem without coercion, but we should not close the door to coercion if it is needed in the future.

## References

1. K. Davis, "Population Policy: Will Current Programs Succeed?" *Science,* 158:730, 1967.
2. L. Bumpass and C. F. Westoff, "The 'Perfect Contraceptive' Population: Extent and Implications of Unwanted Fertility in the U.S.," *Science.*
3. F. Godley, in a master's thesis, "Relationship of Size of Family of Origin to the Fertility of Contemporary American Women," University of Maryland, 1969, unpublished.

# 18. *Unwanted Births and U.S. Population Growth*

## LARRY BUMPASS AND CHARLES F. WESTOFF

To formulate appropriate population policy, it is necessary first to evaluate the relative importance of the different components of population growth. If most U.S. population growth were due to immigration, for example, one set of remedial policies might ensue. If our growth were due mainly to wanted babies born to couples who practice modern contraception, then another set of policies might be indicated. If our growth were substantially accounted for by unwanted pregnancies among couples who practice either no contraception or inadequate contraception, then a third and quite different set of policies might be suggested.

The responses of a representative national sample of some 5,600 women interviewed for the 1965 National Fertility Study[1] has made possible an informed estimate of the extent of unwanted fertility in the period from 1960–1965. These are births described by respondents as "unwanted" at the time of their conception by either the father, the mother or both. They provide the basis for estimating the number of births that might not have occurred if the couples had access to perfect contraception.

Analysis of these data has led to a number of provocative conclusions. Most important, it is evident that a large proportion of recent births to married couples was unwanted; and that if only wanted babies had been born, the U.S. birth rate and thus, the rate of population growth would have been substantially reduced.

It can be seen from Table 1 that about one-fifth of all births and more than one-third of Negro births which occurred from 1960–1965 were unwanted. This is a "medium" estimate; the percent reported unwanted by at least one spouse was slightly higher—22 percent of all births and 41 percent of Negro births.

As would be expected, the percent unwanted increases rapidly by birth order: five percent of first births, 30 percent of fourth births and 50 percent of sixth or higher order births were reported as unwanted. For Negroes the corresponding figures are 12 percent, 44 percent and 66 percent. The high

### TABLE 1.
*Percent of Births Occurring 1960–1965 Reported as Unwanted, by Birth Order and Race*

| Race | All | Birth Order | | | | | |
|---|---|---|---|---|---|---|---|
| | | 1 | 2 | 3 | 4 | 5 | 6+ |
| **1. Unwanted by Both Spouses** | | | | | | | |
| Total | 17 | 4 | 6 | 18 | 25 | 39 | 45 |
| White | 14 | 3 | 5 | 17 | 23 | 36 | 39 |
| Negro | 31 | 9 | 17 | 24 | 37 | 51 | 61 |
| **2. Unwanted by at Least One Spouse** | | | | | | | |
| Total | 22 | 5 | 10 | 24 | 35 | 49 | 55 |
| White | 19 | 4 | 7 | 23 | 32 | 46 | 48 |
| Negro | 41 | 15 | 24 | 37 | 51 | 61 | 72 |
| **3. Medium Estimate, Average (1) and (2)** | | | | | | | |
| Total | 19 | 5 | 8 | 21 | 30 | 44 | 50 |
| White | 17 | 4 | 6 | 20 | 28 | 41 | 43 |
| Negro | 36 | 12 | 20 | 30 | 44 | 56 | 66 |
| **Number of Births in Sample** | | | | | | | |
| Total* | 4264 | 1090 | 1020 | 792 | 532 | 328 | 502 |
| White | 3091 | 839 | 779 | 602 | 397 | 215 | 259 |
| Negro | 1108 | 234 | 229 | 180 | 131 | 107 | 227 |

* The 1965 NFS double-sampled Negroes. Consequently, for measures computed for the total sample the data for non-Negroes are weighted by a factor of two. In this and all subsequent tables based on the NFS, the number of cases reported for the total are unweighted and represent the actual number of sample cases on which the statistics are based. Nonwhites other than Negroes are included in the total.

rates for Negroes underscore the magnitude of the unwanted burden of dependents that is borne by this population, although the problems of unwanted fertility are very substantial among whites as well.

As would be expected the incidence of unwanted births varies inversely with education and income. In general the proportion of births unwanted is approximately twice as high among wives with less than a high school education as among women who have attended college.

In terms of the Social Security Administration's definition of poverty, near-poverty and non-poverty, the incidence of unwanted births is very much higher among the poor and near-poor (Table 2). Fifteen percent of births to non-poor families were declared unwanted, compared to 23 percent among the near-poor and 37 percent among the poor. (Or 32 percent for poor and near-poor taken together.) Three-fifths of all sixth or higher order births among the poor were unwanted.

TABLE 2.

*Percent Unwanted Births 1960–1965 by Poverty Status, Race, and Birth Order*

| Poverty Status | Total | White | Negro | Birth Order for Total | | | | | |
|---|---|---|---|---|---|---|---|---|---|
| | | | | 1 | 2 | 3 | 4 | 5 | 6+ |
| Percent unwanted (Medium Estimate) | | | | | | | | | |
| Poor and Near-poor | 32 | 25 | 46 | 7 | 14 | 28 | 34 | 46 | 56 |
| Poor | 37 | 31 | 47 | 9 | 16 | 30 | 35 | 47 | 61 |
| Near-poor | 23 | 16 | 40 | 5 | 10 | 22 | 32 | 43 | 42 |
| Non-poor | 15 | 15 | 22 | 4 | 6 | 20 | 28 | 42 | 42 |
| Number of Births in Sample* | | | | | | | | | |
| Poor | 861 | 346 | 494 | 135 | 179 | 213 | 186 | 178 | 337 |
| Near-poor | 424 | 253 | 170 | 137 | 151 | 130 | 77 | 63 | 120 |
| Non-poor | 2979 | 2492 | 444 | 1674 | 1481 | 1061 | 670 | 308 | 320 |

* See footnote to Table 1.

Since family size is one component of the SSA definition of poverty, many couples would not have been classified as poor were it not for their fertility experience. The results, therefore, indicate the coincidence of poverty and unwanted fertility rather than any "propensity" of the poor to have unwanted births.

For the six years from 1960–1965, these proportions yield a medium estimate of 4.7 million unwanted births in all socio-

economic groups. Approximately two million of these unwanted births occurred among the poor and near-poor.

It seems clear that the prevention of unwanted fertility
would have had a substantial impact on the U.S. birth rate,
and consequently on the population growth rate over the six-
year period, 1960–1965.

The potential impact of the elimination of unwanted
fertility on our future growth rate will depend on the number
of children that women now entering the childbearing age
group will ultimately want to have. For those women who
were near the end of childbearing in 1965 (ages 35–44),
the elimination of unwanted births would have reduced their
fertility from 3.0 to 2.5 births per woman. Since to achieve a
zero rate of population growth would require an average
fertility of 2.25 children per woman, the elimination of unwanted births would not have been sufficient to establish
exact replacement, but it would have made considerable
progress toward this objective.

These estimates are likely to be too low as a result of the
reporting of originally unwanted births as wanted. It must be
difficult for a woman retrospectively to report a birth as
unwanted since such a report reflects on her ability to control
her fertility, and perhaps also on the status of the child who
is now a member of the family. Another source of underestimation is that this analysis is based on a sample of married
women living with their husbands in 1965. Births to women
not living with their husbands and most illegitimate births
are not represented.* The estimates made in this article assume that the incidence and birth order distribution of all
unwanted births is the same as those reported by wives now
living with their husbands. This undoubtedly is a bias in the
direction of underestimating the extent of unwanted fertility.

### Timing failures

It is difficult to assess the long-term effects of timing failures
(that is, births occurring before they are wanted) on popula-

* The sample design for a new national fertility study in 1970
calls for a sample of "ever married" women and will provide a
better basis for making these estimates.

tion growth. It has been suggested that the longer a "wanted" birth is delayed, the less likely a woman is to have that birth or a subsequent birth.[2] This is because the delay provides the woman time to assume roles which are not compatible with early childcare responsibility, and also increases the likelihood that she or her husband will become subfecund.

Table 3 shows the number and percent of "timing failures" from 1960–1965. More than two-fifths of "wanted" births which occurred from 1960–1965 were reported by the parents as "timing failures."

### TABLE 3.
*Percent of Wanted Births Classified as Timing Failures,\* by Birth Order and Race*

| Race | All | Birth Order | | | | | |
|---|---|---|---|---|---|---|---|
| | | 1 | 2 | 3 | 4 | 5 | 6+ |
| Percent Timing Failures | | | | | | | |
| Total | 43 | 38 | 42 | 50 | 50 | 44 | 47 |
| White | 42 | 36 | 40 | 48 | 48 | 42 | 46 |
| Negro | 56 | 50 | 61 | 59 | 62 | 57 | 50 |
| Number of Births in Sample | | | | | | | |
| Total† | 3217 | 1020 | 906 | 587 | 335 | 162 | 207 |
| White | 2513 | 805 | 722 | 466 | 269 | 116 | 135 |
| Negro | 657 | 199 | 174 | 114 | 64 | 42 | 64 |

\* A birth was classified as a timing failure when reported as wanted but not the result of the deliberate interruption of contraception.

† See footnote to Table 1.

### Policy implications

We estimate that if women near the end of childbearing in 1965 could have avoided unwanted births they would have come much closer than they did to attaining cohort replacement. It is of course possible that women now entering the childbearing ages will choose to have more children than were wanted by women of the same age in the high fertility period of the early 1950s. It is not, however, likely. The oral contraceptives have continued to be rapidly diffused since 1965, and this diffusion may well reduce the numbers of "desired" as well as unwanted children. Women may prefer smaller families as they are increasingly enabled to enter into non-familial roles (particularly employment) than they would otherwise have chosen. Indeed, there are already indications that the completed fertility of the most recent cohorts of women will be lower than that of those which preceded it.[3] It seems likely that today's young women would have a completed fertility, given the elimination of all unwanted births, below that inferred for women who were 35–44 in 1965 under the same assumption.

The elimination of unwanted fertility is an important goal in human terms as well as in terms of its potential impact on future U.S. population growth. Social policies to accomplish this would include:

• Significant expansion of research to develop more effective means of fertility control.

• Development of more efficient systems of distribution of contraceptive methods among all Americans, including those low-income couples who have not had access thus far to effective family planning.

• Legalization of abortion on request as a back-up measure in cases of failed contraception, and appropriate policies to make abortion available to all who need it, regardless of socio-economic status.

If the fertility patterns of the last decade continue, these three measures by themselves might reduce U.S. population growth considerably. They would not require any change in the number of children couples appear to want now, and thus, would not require governmental policies designed to change family-size norms. No alternative population control measures which have been proposed appear to hold out as much promise of a reduction in U.S. population growth. It seems apparent therefore, that a major program along these lines would be a significant element in any national program to reduce population growth.

## *References*

1. N. B. Ryder and C. F. Westoff, *Reproduction in the U.S.: 1965*, Princeton University Press.
2. R. Freedman, L. C. Coombs and L. Bumpass, "Stability and Change in Expectations about Family Size," *Demography* 2:267, 1965.
3. N. B. Ryder, "The Emergence of a Modern Fertility Pattern: United States, 1917–66," in S. S. Behrman, L. Corsa and R. Freedman, eds. *Fertility and Family Planning: A World View*, University of Michigan Press, Ann Arbor, 1969, p. 394.

# 19. The Case for Compulsory Birth Control

### DR. EDGAR CHASTEEN

Complete freedom is anarchy. If freedom may be thought of as the right to swing one's fist, then freedom stops where someone's nose begins. This crude but picturesque analogy serves to illustrate both the relative nature of freedom and its relationship to the population explosion. The more people there are, the less freedom there is.

Over the past 100 years, Western medicine has practically eliminated smallpox, diphtheria, scarlet fever, polio, and other mass killers. Almost all children are now inoculated against disease—in effect, life is imposed upon many who, if natural selection were allowed to operate, would not survive childhood. And when old age comes, every medical technique available is marshaled to maintain life beyond the point at which death would "naturally" occur.

The technology of death control has developed over the past century because government and medicine have deemed it good that man should live long. Governments have supported and rewarded research designed to control death, and medicine has responded as Merlin might have to King Arthur. So preoccupied with death control have government, medicine, and the biological sciences become that critics label this trinity the Health Syndicate. Over the years, its awesome efficiency has been exceeded only by the public adulation and reward heaped upon its practitioners. By contrast, those concerned with birth control have been restricted by the law and lampooned by the press.

As the technology of death control was perfected, a philosophy concerning its use was also developed. That philosophy held that it was the duty of government to ensure that all its citizens shared in these medical miracles. This was accomplished in a simple, straightforward manner—death control was made compulsory. Thus, we are not allowed to choose whether we shall be inoculated against disease; for our own and our community's well-being, we are forced to protect ourselves against epidemic and accident. Neither may we choose to die so long as the doctor or a drug can prolong life. Few people, however, see compulsory death control as an abridgment of their freedom because most want to live as long as possible. Fewer still have had the foresight or the courage to point out that we cannot forever practice compulsory death control without also practicing compulsory birth control.

We live in a finite world. Whatever the number of people it is capable of supporting, there is a limit. We do know that our world is doing a pretty poor job of supporting its present population of around 3½ billion. How long can we expect to continue to double world population every 35 years? To what end? In what ways will we be better off with 7 billion people than with 3½ billion? What possible advantages are there in even minimal population growth? Scores of disadvantages come readily to mind, but not a single benefit. The stork is not the bird of paradise.

Since man first appeared on the earth, his number has multiplied to its present level of 3½ billion. At the present rate of growth, this number will quadruple in less than 80 years. Each day now adds 325,000 babies to the world's population; 2,279,000 each week; over 118 million every year.

The number of *hungry* people in the world today is greater than the total number of people in 1900. The continents of Africa, Asia, and South America are losing the race with illiteracy, food scarcity, and political instability. With a population in excess of 200 million, America does not need any more people. Already we have too few jobs, schools, hospitals, and homes. The countryside is being gobbled up at the rate of 40 acres per mile of freeway, and still the journey to work takes longer than it did 100 years ago. The Northeastern Seaboard has become a vast and confusing megalopolis with up to 100,000 people per square mile. So contaminated is the air of Los Angeles that a sudden inversion of wind pattern could choke the life out of hundreds of people. Such a horror has stricken London twice in the past 20 years.

So desperate is the situation that an increasing number of usually placid demographers, biologists, and nutritionists have joined with conservationists and pollution critics to plead for immediate and drastic action. Georg Borgstrom's *The Hungry Planet*, Paul Ehrlich's *The Population Bomb,* Paul and William Paddock's *Famine—1975!,* and Lincoln and Alice Day's *Too Many Americans* are but four recent expressions of the climate of crisis rapidly eroding the optimism of the technocrats so dominant over the past two decades.

Just as we have laws compelling death control, so we must have laws requiring birth control—the purpose being to ensure a zero rate of population increase. We must come to see that it is the duty of the government to protect women against pregnancy as it protects them against job discrimination and smallpox, and for the same reason—the public good. No longer can we tolerate the doctrinaire position that the number of children a couple has is a strictly private decision carrying no social consequences. There is ample precedent for legislation limiting family size; for example, the law which limits a married person to only one spouse. But if we are to understand the function of law as a regulator of human conduct, we must first recall man's history.

The history of civilization is the process of translating absolute rights into conditioned privileges. Roman fathers 2,000 years ago had the power of life and death over their children. If they so chose, they could leave a child on a hillside to be stolen by animals or killed by the elements. Likewise, Chinese fathers had the right to trade female children for some needed household item. Up to the turn of this century, American parents had the right to put children to work rather than send them to school.

But all this has now changed. Laws have been passed which severely restrict the rights of parents over their own children. Compulsory-school-attendance laws, health laws, delinquency laws, housing laws—all have translated parental *rights* into *privileges*. The next logical extension of this process is to make it a privilege to have children. Such laws would serve not only to defuse the population bomb, but also to protect first-born children against too prolific reproduction by their parents. Recent studies have shown that the most crucial factor associated with the economic status of a family is its size; the larger the family, the more likely it is to be poverty-stricken. The chances of a child's acquiring an education, a healthy body, adequate shelter, and a decent job decline as the number of his brothers and sisters increases.

Some future historian will look back on the 20th century and write that in the year 19——, laws were passed which struck down forever that anachronistic practice to which we had too long adhered—the right to have as many children as one wanted. That "want," after all, is socially created and may be socially redefined. No one is born wanting a certain number of children, any more than one wants at birth to speak English or to eat with a fork. The desire to give birth to one, four, seven, or 15 children is thus exposed for what it is—an accident—conditioned by the time and place of our own birth. That future historian will consider us as uncivilized for having permitted unregulated births as we do the Romans and Chinese for their "irresponsible" behavior.

Some will object to compulsory birth control, contending that it smacks of Big Brother and *1984*. On the contrary, it would seem that such Orwellian conditions are inevitable *without* a policy of compulsory birth control. For the quality of human life is irreversibly lowered as the numbers of Homo sapiens incessantly mount. A once-virgin globe has been stripped of its beauty, contaminated beyond redemption. Wildlife has been thoughtlessly slaughtered as man has inadvertently and ominously altered his ecological environment.

Some people argue that education can solve the population problem. But even a superficial analysis shows that education cannot solve even the education problem; laws are necessary to correct deficiencies in the educational process itself. It seems naïve, then, to rely on education to persuade individual parents not to have too many children.

Even though attempts have been made to educate smokers to the dangers of cigarettes, more people are now smoking than in 1964 when the Surgeon General's report linking cigarettes to cancer was issued. Drivers continue to sit on their seat belts despite the educational campaign by the National

Safety Council, which urges us to "buckle up for safety." If such superficial behavior has not responded to education, can we expect more from our efforts to educate for "responsible parenthood"?

The argument of some religious authorities that compulsion in the face of conviction constitutes unjustified interference is less than convincing. Such reasoning was not sustained when members of the Church of God refused to pay income taxes because to do so would imply recognition of a power other than God. Neither was it upheld when the Mormons of the last century argued that plural marriages were part of their religion. The Amish have been forced to send their children to school beyond the eighth grade, and the Christian Scientist is compelled to accept medical attention for a critically ill child.

The completely effective and reversible contraceptive necessary for a policy of compulsory birth control is not yet available. Medical science is experimenting, however, with a shot and a time capsule that would inhibit fertility indefinitely. Within a few years, such contraceptives will be as available and as pleasant as the sugar-cube polio vaccine. This will make it possible to inoculate all males and females against fertility as they reach puberty. After marriage, this process could be reversed by another shot or pill designed to restore fertility temporarily.

If we can rid ourselves of outmoded values concerning laissez-faire parenthood and establish sensible and compulsory limits to family size, we shall eliminate a host of problems not otherwise soluble, and we shall expand the freedom "to be" which, after all, makes us human. If we cannot, then we must quit our practice of compulsory death control and let nature re-establish its own balance of births and deaths.

# 20. *Fertility Control Agents as a Possible Solution to the World Population Problem*

MELVIN M. KETCHEL

The world is now facing a severe problem of human over-population because the birth rate has generally remained high while the death rate has been dramatically reduced. Plans to lower the birth rate have almost invariably centered upon the concept of family planning. It is the purpose of this paper to point out that even if family planning methods become widely used they may not necessarily lower the birth rate sufficiently to provide a solution to the population problem and that other methods can and probably will be developed which could solve the population problem without relying on family planning. The use of such methods will raise moral and political questions of great importance, however, and it is my hope that this essay will provide a basis upon which a discussion of these issues can begin. Such a discussion would prepare us for making decisions concerning the implementation of these methods when they become available and may, if sufficient support for their use emerges, encourage the development of such methods.

## Family planning as a solution to the population problem

The pioneers in the family planning movement were primarily concerned with aiding families. When the natural fertility of the parents resulted in too many children for the family's welfare, family planning methods were provided to prevent unwanted pregnancies. Somewhat later the family planning movement was strengthened by the inclusion of many people whose major interest was in solving the population problem by lowering the birth rate. It was reasoned that, as more and more couples learned the techniques of limiting the size of their families, they would do so, and eventually a large percentage of the world's population would practice family planning with the result that the reduction in the number of children born to them would significantly lower the world's birth rate. No other acceptable means of solving the population problem have been available, and even partial success of the family planning approach has been of value.

Some hope has been provided by history that family planning methods might eventually dramatically lower the world's birth rate. The term "demographic revolution" has been applied to the transition of a population with a high death rate and a high birth rate to a population with a low death rate and a low birth rate. It appears that the reduction in the infant death rate which occurs as a country becomes developed makes it unnecessary for each couple to have many babies in order to raise children to maturity, that children become an economic liability rather than an economic asset, and that the aspirations of people to provide more education and other advantages for their children encourages them to have fewer children on which to concentrate their efforts. These factors, plus many others, lead to the development of the "small family ideal." The decision to have fewer children is implemented primarily by the utilization of contraceptive techniques. A demographic revolution occurred in Europe and North America following the Industrial Revolution, and in Japan following World War II, and people concerned about the growth rate of the population of the rest of the world hope that the dramatic world-wide reduction in the death rate during the past twenty-five years is the first step in a demographic revolution that will result in a rapid reduction in the world's birth rate.

Whether the conditions under which a demographic revolution can complete itself now exist in the underdeveloped countries of the world is a matter of considerable controversy. Up to the present, demographic revolutions have occurred only when a gradually declining death rate was accompanied by considerable economic and social development. It may be that the levels of education, living standard, and motivation required if family planning is to be successful cannot be attained in underdeveloped countries precisely because their high birth rates prevent the necessary economic development. On the other hand, the demographic revolution which occurred in Europe and North America took place essentially without governmental or organizational influence, whereas at present strong organizations and some governments are working strenuously to lower birth rates. How successful these efforts will be is of course a matter of conjecture, but it cannot be assumed that the demographic revolution will complete itself in the absence of considerable economic development, and it seems unlikely that the necessary economic development will occur without a decrease in the birth rate.

Even if we assume that a demographic revolution is taking place, we must also question how rapidly it will progress. The absolute numbers of people produced during a gradual reduction of the annual growth rate may provoke catastrophic upheavals as the essentials of life become increasingly scarce. Some reliable experts now believe that widespread famine will occur in the underdeveloped countries within ten years.[1,2] Of course the growth and effectiveness of the family planning movement should, like the growth of populations, be exponential, and we should be optimistic about the future of family planning. But a look at the most recent ten-year period for which data are available shows that the death rate is falling more rapidly than the birth rate, so that the annual rate of growth of the world's population is increasing. We simply do not know how rapidly the people in countries with high birth rates will accept family planning, but the slow rate at which such acceptance has occurred in the past by no means excludes the possibility that overpopulation will become overwhelming before the birth rate can be significantly lowered.

Family planning has already lowered the world's birth rate to some extent, and undoubtedly further effort will improve the results. How much improvement is required if family planning is to solve the population problem? To solve it permanently, of course, the birth rate must be lowered to the level of the death rate, for the exponential nature of the growth curve dictates that, if births exceed deaths by any amount, astronomical numbers of people will eventually be produced.

For practical purposes, however, we probably ought to be satisfied if the birth rate can be lowered enough to alleviate the problems caused by overpopulation during the next three or four generations. It would be difficult to obtain agreement among experts on how much the birth rate should be lowered, but one might ask how much the birth rate would have to be lowered if the world's population were to double only once during the next 100 years, or about four generations. The present annual growth rate of the world's population of about 1.7 per cent would then have to be reduced to about 0.7 per cent. In large parts of the world, particularly those in which the introduction of family planning is proving most difficult, the average annual growth rate now exceeds 2 per cent. The only major area of the world in which the annual growth rate is below 1 per cent is Europe.

What would be required to bring the annual growth rate of the rest of the world to below 1 per cent? Assuming that there will be no further drastic changes in the death rate, we would have to reduce the birth rate by about one-third. While at present this could not be done without family planning techniques, we must realize that even if family planning were used by everyone, the birth rate might not be sufficiently reduced. Enough people may simply choose to have large families to keep the growth rate above 1 per cent. While it is obvious that family planning can reduce only the number of unwanted children, it seems to me that discussions of family planning in relation to the population problem always have implicit in them the assumption that if we could only get enough people to use family planning techniques the population problem would be solved. This assumption cannot be accepted until we know how many children people will wish to have when they achieve the ability to regulate the numbers.

How many children could each family have if the annual growth rate is not to exceed 0.7 per cent? It is not possible to translate an annual growth rate directly into an average number of children per family, but if certain assumptions are made, a rough approximation may be calculated. For example, suppose that the average generation time, or average age of parents when their children are born, is twenty years and that all children born reach reproductive age. The average generation time varies widely and would probably be higher than twenty years in some cultures and lower in others. While all children born do not reach reproductive age, the numbers who do not are small enough to be neglected in these rough calculations. Let us assume further that 10 per cent of the couples in the population are infertile and that another 10 per cent of the population does not marry. Most estimates of infertility put the number of infertile couples at about 10 per cent, but many of these people are treatable, and probably this number could be reduced. The number of people who do not marry would probably be more than 10 per cent in some populations and less in others. Using these admittedly hypothetical conditions, a zero growth rate could be maintained if each fertile couple had an average of 2.5 children. If each fertile couple had three children, the annual growth rate would be slightly less than 1 per cent, and the population would double every eighty years. An average of 3.5 children per fertile couple would reduce the doubling time of the population to thirty-nine years. In any population in which 80 per cent of the people born marry and have children at a young age, family planning would have to reduce the average number of births to considerably less than three per family if the population were to double only once every 100 years. But an average of one-half child more or less per fertile couple makes the difference between an acceptable growth rate and a growth rate of serious consequences.

We do not have adequate information to predict how many children the average couple will want when family planning is available to everyone. It may well be less than three in some cultures, but it may also be more than three in others. In general, we have assumed that as the standard of living, educational level, and motivation of a population are increased—conditions under which family planning would be most successful—the desire of couples for large families will be decreased. But will it be decreased enough? While no statistics are available, many readers will share with me the impression that there were large numbers of couples in the United States who graduated from college and married in the years following World War II, and who used family planning methods but still had large families. Is it not possible that, even when they can easily control the size of their families, the desire for children will lead people to have more children than the earth can support?

Thus, while it is obvious that the family planning movement has been of tremendous value to the people who have used it, has lowered the birth rate when it is used, and will become increasingly valuable as the movement expands, it seems to me that the following statements should be accepted as possibilities. *The reduction in the world's death rate may not, in fact, indicate that a world-wide demographic revolution will continue to completion. If a demographic revolution is occurring, it may proceed so slowly that the increases in population which occur before its completion may be so large that they cannot be supported. And even if the demographic revolution does complete itself rapidly, the desire for children in the world's population may still be strong enough to produce an annual growth rate which will soon result in overwhelming numbers of people.*

The great interest in recent years in the study of the physiology of reproduction and in methods of contraception makes it appear to me very likely that in a relatively few years efficient methods by which the fertility of populations can be reduced without dependence upon the practice of contraception by individual couples will become available.

For the purpose of discussion, let us suppose that a compound has become available which, when administered in small doses, has no significant physiological effect except to raise the threshold requirement of some substance involved in the implantation of blastocysts. This would mean that while some blastocysts would implant in women given the compound, a percentage of blastocysts which would otherwise have implanted would not now do so. Let us further suppose that the dosage of this compound could be varied so that the reduction in the birth rate could be established at from 5 to 75 per cent less than the present birth rate. Although many problems would remain even if such an ideal compound could be found, the use of such a compound would enable a government to control the rate of growth of its population without depending upon the voluntary action of individual couples. Although a number of colleagues with whom I have discussed this differ with me in speculation about when such compounds will be developed, I believe such compounds should be available for field testing in a relatively short time, perhaps five to fifteen years.

I differentiate, then, between two methods of reducing the birth rate. One is the family planning method in which participation is voluntary. The other, which I have designated "fertility control" measures, would be carried out by governments to lower the fertility of their populations without requiring action by individual couples. Thus, part of a population may be using family planning techniques, but all of the population would be affected by fertility control measures.

## *Effects of fertility control measures*

One of the principal requirements for a contraceptive method, if it is to be useful in the family planning approach to population control, is that it be virtually 100 per cent effective. In contrast, any method developed for fertility control must not have 100 per cent effectiveness, or the population would stop having births. What would be required, then, is a method which is capable of reducing the births to any desired level.

The nature of the curve which would be obtained if a survey were made of the fertility* of couples in a population is unknown, since the data have not been collected. I have drawn curve *A* in Figure 1 as my guess as to the nature of that curve, without designating absolute units. The curve for fertility of a population would probably resemble a normal distribution curve, except that, since some couples are infertile, the curve would not become asymptotic at the left. If a compound such as the one I have hypothesized were administered to a population, it might act by slightly reducing the fertility of each couple in the population, so that there would be a shift to a lower average fertility, as shown by curve *B*. Perhaps there would be advantages if such a com-

* "Fertility" is used here to represent the relative capability to reproduce, not the amount of reproduction which actually occurs.

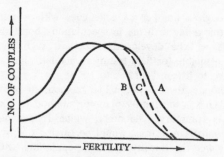

Fig. 1—Curve *A:* probable shape of the distribution curve for fertility within a population. No data are available. It would be expected that the curve would be similar to a normal distribution curve, except that, since there are a number of infertile couples in the population, the curve does not become asymptotic at the left. Curve *B:* the effect of fertility control measure which decreased the fertility of all couples in the population to an equal degree. Curve *C:* the effect of a fertility control agent which reduced the fertility of the most fertile couples in the population.

pound had the effect of selectively reducing the fertility of the most fertile couples in the population, an effect represented by curve *C*. Other possibilities exist, however, which would have to be guarded against as such agents were developed and tested. For example, some agents might selectively lower the fertility of those whose fertility is already among the lowest in the population, so that the number of infertile couples would be increased without affecting the fertility of the most fertile couples. Such an agent would deprive people of relatively low fertility of having any children at all and would not be satisfactory. Another possible effect of such a compound which would probably make it unusable is that, because of inherent variability from couple to couple of the factor affected by the agent, some couples would become completely infertile while the fertility of other couples would be unaffected. I believe that the goal in the development of fertility control agents should be to reduce the fertility of everyone equally.

It should be strongly emphasized that, although fertility control agents would be used to cause a reduction of the fertility of the population as a whole, there would still be considerable freedom of action for individual couples. Family planning methods could still be used for the purpose of limiting and spacing children within the family. Well-motivated people could probably circumvent the action of any fertility control measures that could be developed by acting to increase their chances of establishing a pregnancy, much as many couples of low fertility do at present. If too many couples circumvented the action of the fertility control agent, it would no longer be useful. However, the necessity of taking positive action would probably make such circumvention relatively unimportant.

Fertility control agents such as the hypothetical one I described would have no effect in reducing the number of unwanted children, legitimate or illegitimate, except insofar as they reduce the fertility of the population as a whole. One can, however, visualize a fertility control agent which would render everyone infertile until its action was reversed by an act of the individuals involved. Such a method might require an individual to take a pill to become pregnant, rather than to take a pill to prevent pregnancy, and would virtually eliminate the serious problem of unwanted children.

### Some requirements for a satisfactory fertility control agent

In order to be usable, a fertility control agent would need to have the following characteristics: (1) It should lend itself to being easily and unobtrusively included in the intake of everyone in the population; requiring people to receive injections, to take the agent themselves, or to submit to direct physical treatment would be unsatisfactory. In highly organized urban areas an agent might be included in the water supply, but other methods would be required in less developed areas and in areas with low population density. (2) It must be harmless. There must be no danger to the health of anyone receiving it, or to the development of fetuses or children. (3) It should be inexpensive. (4) Its effect should be easily reversible. The agent should disappear and have to be replaced fairly rapidly so that, if the fertility of the population becomes too low, there would not be too great a time lag between cessation of administration and cessation of its effect on the fertility of the population. (5) It should not interfere with the family planning activities of individual couples. (6) It should not act by affecting in any way the sexual activity of the individuals in the population.

## Fertility control as a function of government

A primary question involved in the decision to use fertility control agents is whether the control of the rate of growth of its population is a proper function of government. A recurrent theme in science fiction is the plight of couples who wish to have children but are forbidden by their government (or its computer) from doing so. Governmental intervention in the lives of individuals is often characterized either by an inflexibility which neglects individual circumstances or by a flexibility which permits discrimination and injustice. Ingle, in a discussion of the ethics of governmental intervention in reproduction, concludes that such matters should not be undertaken by governments.[3] In 1967, U Thant, secretary-general of the United Nations, issued an important statement signed by thirty heads of state in which the decision to have as many children as one desires is called a "basic human right."[4] Yet the rate of growth of the population profoundly affects the lives of all individuals within the population as well as the members of future generations. No couple may reasonably maintain that the number of children born within the family is strictly a family matter, for the quality of life of every individual in the population is changed simply by the increase in the number of people competing for the necessities of life. Few people would now maintain that the control of air pollution is outside the responsibility of government, and I would argue that allowing population growth to go unchecked is at least as serious a hazard to the welfare of people as the exhaust from automobiles and factories.

Governments already can and do influence fertility rates, although at the present time their ability to do so is primitive, and therefore the degree of control is probably small. However, governmental support or prevention of family planning activities may make it easier or more difficult for people to practice family planning. Propaganda is often used by governments to encourage people to have children. Such governmental action as giving financial rewards to couples with large numbers of children, providing housing allotments for families, giving income tax deductions for dependents, and establishing child care centers for the children of working mothers may not have as their primary purpose the encouragement of people to have children, but such actions probably tend to raise the birth rate to some degree by relieving people of some of the financial burden associated with parenthood. Traditionally, most governments, when they have acted at all, have acted to encourage a higher birth rate, but more recently some countries have made it governmental policy to encourage family planning in order to reduce the birth rate.

The function of the government in regulating the rate of growth of its population should be clearly differentiated from governmental involvement in decisions concerning who may and who may not reproduce. It would be possible for a government using fertility control agents to reduce statistically the birth rate of the population without making decisions concerning individuals, and therefore strict impartiality could be maintained. However, there would probably be great pressures exerted on the government to couple the use of fertility control agents with programs aimed at preventing reproduction among people considered "unfit" for parenthood or among geographic, racial, economic, or political groups. Such proposals would undoubtedly be made in the name of "positive eugenics." The role of government in a eugenics program should be argued on its own merits, however, because it poses a threat to individual liberty that is not involved in a program to lower statistically the birth rate of the whole population by a method that would affect everyone equally.

I believe that the question of whether the control of the rate of growth of its population is a proper function of government ultimately comes down to the question of whether it is necessary. If the rate of growth of the population presents no serious problems, the government ought not to intrude in this matter. But if the growth rate of the population is seriously affecting the welfare of the population, as a rapid growth rate surely does, and the growth rate cannot be lowered by any voluntary means, then it is, I believe, a necessary and proper function of the government to take action to slow the rate of growth.

## Possible alternatives to fertility control agents

If the control of the rate of growth of its population is a proper function of government, then a decision must be made concerning how to exercise that control. Obviously, the method of choice would be the one which is capable of accomplishing the objective of lowering the birth rate but which least interferes with the lives of the people.

It seems obvious that any government contemplating the use of involuntary methods of fertility control should lower its birth rate as much as possible by supporting family planning programs. If it becomes necessary to prevent some people from having children they want, it would be ridiculous not to try to prevent the births of children that were not specifically wanted. Also, the more the birth rate was lowered by voluntary means, the less the population would have to be affected by the use of involuntary means.

Aside from family planning programs, how can governments lower birth rates? The suggestion has often been made that there be a reversal of economic policies which encourage people to have large families. For example, dependency allowances on income taxes might be eliminated or changed to tax surcharges for each child over a specified number. Direct financial allotments to large families could be stopped. Free or inexpensive child care centers could be eliminated. Such proposals must be judged as alternatives to fertility control agents on two counts. First, how effective they would be, and second, whether they would be more onerous than fertility control agents.

Financial pressures against large families would probably be effective only in developed countries in which there are large numbers of middle-class people. In underdeveloped countries practically no financial inducements to have children now exist to be reversed, and the imposition of further taxes upon the many poor people would depress their living standards even further and probably only succeed in raising the death rates. In developed countries people in higher economic groups could still afford to have as many children as they wished, so the economic pinch associated with having children would be felt mainly by middle-class and lower-middle-class people, to whom the cost of having children, though somewhat eased by government economic favors, is still relatively high. In order to be effective, economic pressures would probably have to be severe enough to be quite painful, and when they reached a level of painfulness at which they were effective, they would probably seriously affect the welfare of the children who were born in spite of the pressures. It seems to me that the same arguments apply to the use of economic pressures to lower the birth rate as are used to argue against the issue of suppressing illegitimacy by cutting off aid to dependent children. If children become a financial burden, there will be fewer of them, but those that are born will be punished by being deprived of precisely those economic advantages they should have, both for humanitarian reasons and for their growth and development into worthwhile citizens. The same objection applies to the use of financial rewards to induce people not to have children because such programs would make the families with children the poorer families. A further objection to the use of economic pressures or rewards is that, since they would be primarily effective against certain economic groups, such methods are discriminatory.

Since there is a substantial decrease in fertility among couples as they advance in age, a delay in the age of marriage has been proposed as a means of reducing the size of families. To be effective in keeping the average family size between two and three children, the average age of marriage would probably have to be advanced by a sizable number of years. The age at which people marry is largely determined by slowly changing cultural and economic factors, however, and could probably be changed quickly in a population only by rather drastic measures. How might this be done? One can visualize raising substantially the legal age of marriage, but an inordinately severe punishment for violaters would be required. Denying housing or other requirements for married life to people below a certain age could also be used to prevent marriages. But neither of these alternatives seems attractive to me when compared to a situation in which people are allowed to marry at an age consistent with their cultural and biological desires and to have their families while they are young, and in which there is no other interference with their marriages except that the number of children they will have is reduced statistically by a fertility control agent.

A policy of allowing couples to have only a certain number of children would, of course, be effective in solving the population problem, but any conceivable way in which this could be done would, I think, be more objectionable than the use of fertility control agents. Statutory regulations of family size would be unenforceable unless the punishment for exceeding the limit was so harsh that it would cause harm to the lives of the existing children and their parents. Such possible procedures as vasectomizing the father or implanting long-acting contraceptives in the mother would require a direct physical assault by a government agent on the body of an individual that, in my opinion, would be worse to contemplate than fertility control agents. It may be argued that philosophically there is little difference between the direct physical assault of sterilization and the remote physical assault of administering a fertility control agent, but in practical terms there is obviously a great difference.

I think that, once family planning has been exploited to the degree that it can be to reduce births, further reduction, if necessary, could be accomplished only by a choice of unpleasant methods. It is my opinion that fertility control agents would be less objectionable than other solutions that can be visualized at this time.

### Moral aspects of fertility control agents

Surely the most controversial aspects of fertility control agents would be the moral issues. Is it possible to justify the affront to human dignity and privacy of forcing people to take a drug which they do not want but which may be necessary for the welfare of the society? I believe that justification for the use of fertility control agents comes from an analysis of what will happen if they are not used.

If voluntary methods of population control are not sufficiently effective, then we must either impose some involuntary method of fertility control or accept the consequences of excessive population. I attempted earlier in this paper to show that any workable involuntary methods would be more objectionable and would probably require a greater infringement on human liberty than fertility control agents. If my analysis is correct, then we may ultimately be forced to make a moral choice between fertility control agents and excessive numbers of people.

During the 1950's, discussions of the population problem often included projections of exponential growth curves which showed that the world's population would eventually become ridiculously large. One of my favorites was a projection which calculated that, if population growth were not curbed, at some future time the layer of human protoplasm which would by then be covering the surface of the earth would be expanding at the speed of light. Such dramatic projections made the problem seem so remote, however, that many people felt that population problems were really no concern of the present generation and that the relatively few children more or less that the present generation had would not be a problem. Also, such unrealistic projections invited speculation in a similar vein for dealing with the problem. For example, many people suggested that our excess population could be shipped off to other planets. More recently, when discussions have centered about problems of feeding and caring for the people that are projected for the near future, unrealistic projections of technological advances were still suggested as solutions to the problem. Farming of the sea and desert, greater utilization of farm land, and mass culture of microorganisms were proposed as solutions to the problem of feeding large numbers of people. Let the population grow, people seemed to think, somehow they will be taken care of, and we might as well have as many children as we want because what difference would our few children make in the millions that will be born.

It now appears, however, that the race between technological advances and population growth is favoring population growth and that starvation will be a major problem in the world in about ten years.[1,2] Most food surpluses in the world have been used up, and there is no indication that food production can be increased quickly enough to prevent this starvation. Laissez faire will apparently solve the population problem, therefore, simply by raising the death rate, through starvation and malnutrition, to the level of the birth rate. Large numbers of births will still occur, but so many people will die that there will be no increase in the world population until technological improvements produce a larger food supply. There seems little that can be done now to prevent starvation for millions of people in the next decade, but if we had been able to curb population growth in the last decade, this suffering probably would not be in prospect.

Massive hunger in the world, then, seems to be one alternative to reducing the birth rate. If the reduction of the birth rate requires the use of fertility control agents by governments, then the moral justification for their use must certainly be in the prevention of the agony of hunger and slow death for millions of people and a miserable level of existence for millions of others.

A laissez faire attitude toward population growth presents another prospect which seems to me to be equal in seriousness to the starvation that will occur. Unless some new technological approach to fertility control is utilized, a solution to its problem of overpopulation would require a massive effort on the part of the government of an underdeveloped country which such governments may be unable or unwilling to undertake. It would probably be far easier for a large underdeveloped country to develop a nuclear capability than it would to solve its population problem. As more and more countries acquire nuclear capability, their attempts to obtain the essentials of life may cause catastrophic upheavals in the world which will result in even greater danger and suffering than the starvation itself.

The moral question, then, resolves itself for me into a choice of alternatives. A laissez faire attitude is unthinkable because of the amount of suffering that will result. Voluntary methods are to be preferred if they will work, but if they do not, then involuntary methods must be used. Fertility control agents would seem to be the most effective and least objectionable of any methods that can be visualized.

### *Political aspects of fertility control agents*

If a perfected fertility control agent were available now, I am certain that it would not be utilized in any democratic country, for no population would be likely to vote to have such agents used on itself. This means that the effects of overpopulation are not yet acute enough for people to accept an unpleasant alternative. It seems ironic to me that, when the problems of overpopulation do become acute enough to make people willing to accept fertility control, it will only be after subjecting many individuals to great suffering which need never have occurred.

Thus, any attempt to lessen by fertility control agents the problems that will eventually occur as a result of overpopulation requires an analysis of the distastefulness of fertility control agents. The understanding gained from such an analysis would be useful in implementing governmental action.

One level of resistance to the acceptance of fertility control agents would probably be psychological. The benefits of fluorides in alleviating dental disease seem clearly to be worth the risk involved in its use, yet the acceptance of fluoride treatment of public water supplies has met extreme political resistance. Even though a primary requirement of any fertility control agent would obviously be that it have no significant effect on any physiological function other than fertility, I am sure that public resistance to fertility control agents would be far greater than the resistance to fluoride. Also, I have been surprised at the number of sophisticated and educated people who mention "saltpeter" when I suggest the possibility of using fertility control agents. They were obviously confusing the control of fertility with the control of sexual activity.

Fertility control agents will ultimately become politically acceptable when they become politically necessary. If population growth continues, people will probably be willing to accept fertility control agents as the lesser of evils. It will help people to accept them, however, if they are informed of the degree to which starvation, poverty, and other problems which ensue are related to overpopulation.

## Summary and discussion

The rate at which humans can reproduce is an evolutionary vestige remaining from an era in human history in which large numbers of offspring were required for the survival of the species, and probably includes a substantial safety factor of reproductive potential as well. The full reproductive potential of the human is probably not expressed because a variety of social, cultural, economic, and biological forces have tended to limit childbirth. These limiting forces tend to evolve very slowly, but over a sufficient period of time they can be effective in adjusting the birth rate of the population to any change in circumstances. Thus, as the death rate was gradually reduced in Europe and North America following the Industrial Revolution, a reduction in the birth rate gradually followed.

Modern technology has recently had a dramatic effect in reducing the death rate throughout the world, and it now appears that the forces which can lower the birth rate will not evolve rapidly enough to prevent widespread overpopulation and an eventual re-establishment of a high death rate. What would be required to prevent this is another significant technological advance, one which will dramatically increase the ability of the world to support the population, or one which will limit the number of people being born.

We should be actively seeking a technological advance which will increase the number of people that the earth can support, for such an advance will help us to cope with the numbers of people who will be born despite any humane action that can now be taken. However, even if such an advance were made, it could only act as a palliative because ultimately a reduction in the birth rate must occur. It is possible, however, that a technological advance which would increase greatly the food supply would provide the necessary time for the further evolution of forces which would decrease the birth rate.

Meanwhile, we should be actively seeking a revolutionary

breakthrough in methodology for reducing the birth rate. Improvements in the technology of contraception, though helpful, may not suffice, because the birth rate would still depend upon how many children people wanted rather than how many were required to stabilize the growth of the population. What is required is a method which would allow a population to control its rate of growth. I have suggested that fertility control agents would provide a practical solution to the problem. I have also attempted to show that the advantages of using fertility control agents would more than offset the considerable objections to them.

It seems clear that no single, simplistic solution to the population problem is available. Family planning has already had an effect in reducing the birth rate of the world, and our goal should be to extend its use as rapidly as is possible to the point that the only children born are those that are specifically wanted. Improved methods of contraception are important, but ways of motivating people to use them must be developed further. Food production must immediately be increased as much as is humanly possible to prevent the suffering and starvation that will inevitably occur in the next decade. But I believe we should also begin to develop and test fertility control agents seriously, to develop methods of introducing them into the intake of populations, and to arrive at a consensus which will dictate whether such agents will be utilized when they are developed.

## References

1. William Paddock and Paul Paddock. *Famine—1975! America's Decision: Who Will Survive?* Boston: Little, Brown, 1967.
2. James Bonner. *Science,* 157:914, 1967.
3. Dwight J. Ingle. *Med. Opinion and Rev.,* 3:54, 1967.
4. U Thant. *Studies in Family Planning,* no. 26, January 1968.

# 21. Population Policy for Americans: Is the Government Being Misled?

## JUDITH BLAKE

Pressure on the federal government for "action" to limit population growth in the United States has intensified greatly during the past 10 years, and at present such action is virtually unchallenged as an official national goal. Given the goal, the question of means becomes crucial. Here I first evaluate the particular means being advocated and pursued in public policy, then I present alternative ways of possibly achieving the goal.

The prevailing view as to the best means is remarkably unanimous and abundantly documented. It is set forth in the 17 volumes of congressional hearings so far published on the "population crisis";[1] in "The Growth of U.S. Population," a report by the Committee on Population of the National Academy of Sciences;[2] in a statement made by an officer of the Ford Foundation who was asked by the Department of Health, Education, and Welfare to make suggestions;[3] and, finally, in the "Report of the President's Committee on Population and Family Planning," which was officially released this past January.[4] The essential recommendation throughout is that the government should give highest priority to ghetto-oriented family-planning programs designed to "deliver" birth-control services to the poor and uneducated, among whom, it is claimed, there are at least 5 million women who are "in need" of such federally sponsored birth-control assistance.

By what logic have the proponents of control moved from a concern with population growth to a recommendation favoring highest priority for poverty-oriented birth-control programs? First, they have assumed that fertility is the only component of population growth worthy of government attention. Second, they have taken it for granted that, to reduce fertility, one sponsors birth-control programs ("family planning"). Just why they have made this assumption is not clear, but its logical implication is that population growth is due to births that couples would have preferred to avoid. Furthermore, the reasoning confuses couple control over births with societal control over them.[5] Third, the proponents of the new policy have seized on the poor and uneducated as the "target" group for birth-control action because they see this group as the only remaining target for a program of voluntary family planning. The rest of the population is handling its family planning pretty well on its own: over 95 percent of fecund U.S. couples already either use birth-control methods or intend to do so. The poor, on the other hand—at least those who are fecund—have larger families than the advantaged; they not only use birth-control methods less but they use them less effectively. The family-planning movement's notion of "responsible parenthood" carries the implication that family size should be directly, not inversely, related to social and economic advantage, and the poor are seen as constituting the residual slack to be taken up by the movement's efforts. Why are the poor not conforming to the dictates of responsible parenthood? Given the movement's basic assumptions, there are only two answers: the poor are irresponsible, or they have not had the opportunity. Since present-day leaders would abhor labeling the poor irresponsible, they have chosen to blame lack of opportunity as the cause. Opportunity has been lacking, in their eyes, either because the poor have not been "educated" in family planning or because they have not been "reached" by family-planning services. In either case, as they see it, the poor have been deprived of their "rights."[2,6] This deprivation has allegedly been due to the prudery and hypocrisy of the affluent, who have overtly tabooed discussion of birth control and dissemination of birth-control materials while, themselves, covertly enjoying the benefits of family planning.[7]

So much for the logic underlying recent proposals for controlling population growth in the United States. But what is the evidence on which this argument is based? On what em-

pirical grounds is the government being asked to embark on
a high-priority program of providing contraceptive services to
the poor? Moreover, what, if any, are some of the important
public issues that the suggested policy raises—what are its social and political side effects? And, finally, is such a policy,
even if appropriate for the poor and even if relatively unen-
cumbered by public disapproval, relevant to the problem of
population growth in America? If demographic curtailment
is really the objective, must alternative policies be considered
and possibly given highest priority?

Turning to the alleged need for government-sponsored
birth-control services, one may ask whether birth control has
in fact been a tabooed topic among the middle and upper
classes, so that the less advantaged could be said to have
suffered "deprivation" and consequently now to require government help. One may then question whether there is a
mandate from the poor for the type of federally sponsored
service that is now being urged, and whether as many as 5
million women are "in need" of such family-planning assistance.

### *Has birth control been a tabooed topic?*

The notion that the American public has only recently become willing to tolerate open discussion of birth control has
been assiduously cultivated by congressmen and others concerned with government policy on population. For example,
Senator Tydings credited Senators Gruening and Clark and
President Johnson with having almost singlehandedly changed
American public attitudes toward birth control. In 1966 he
read the following statement into the 28 February *Congressional Record*.[8]

> The time is ripe for positive action. Ten years ago, even five
> years ago, this was a politically delicate subject. Today the Na-
> tion has awakened to the need for Government action.
> This change in public attitude has come about through the
> efforts of men who had the courage to brook the tides of public
> opinion. Senator Clark is such a man. Senator Gruening is such
> a man. So is President Johnson. Because of their leadership it is

no longer necessary for an elected official to speak with trepida-
tion on this subject.

A year later, Senator Tydings reduced his estimate of the
time required for the shift in public opinion to "3 or 4
years."[9,10] Senator Gruening maintained[11] that the "ninety-
eight distinguished men and women" who testified at the
public hearing on S. 1676 were "pioneers" whose "names
comprise an important honor roll which historically bears an
analogy to other famous lists: the signers of the Declaration
of Independence, those who ratified the Constitution of the
United States and others whose names were appended to
and made possible some of the great turning points in history." Reasoning from the continued existence of old, and
typically unenforced, laws concerning birth control (together
with President Eisenhower's famous anti-birth-control statement), Stycos, in a recent article,[12] stated:

> The public reaction to family planning in the United States has
> varied between disgust and silent resignation to a necessary evil.
> At best it was viewed as so delicate and risky that it was a matter
> of "individual conscience." As such, it was a matter so totally
> private, so sacred (or profane), that no external agents, and cer-
> tainly not the state, should have anything to do with it.

Does the evidence support such impressionistic claims?
How did the general public regard government sponsorship
of birth control long before it became a subject of congressional hearings, a National Academy report, and a Presidential Committee report? Fortunately, a question on this topic
appeared in no less than 13 national polls and surveys conducted between 1937 and 1966. As part of a larger project
concerned with public knowledge and opinions about demographic topics, I have gathered together the original data
cards from these polls, prepared them for computer processing, and analyzed the results. The data are all from Gallup
polls and are all from national samples of the white, adult
population. Here I concentrate on adults under 45—that is,
on adults in the childbearing age group.

The data of Table 1 contradict the notion that Americans

## TABLE 1.

*Percentages of white U.S. men and women between the ages of 21 and 44 who, in various national polls and surveys made between 1937 and 1964,\* expressed the opinion that birth-control information should be made available to individuals who desired it.*

| Year | Men | | Women | |
|------|-----|-----|-------|-----|
|      | %   | N   | %     | N   |
| 1937 | 66  | 1038 | 70   | 734 |
| 1938 | 67  | 1111 | 72   | 548 |
| 1939 | 74  | 1101 | 73   | 630 |
| 1940 | 72  | 1127 | 75   | 618 |
| 1943 | 67  | 628  | 73   | 866 |
| 1945 | 64  | 714  | 70   | 879 |
| 1947 | 76  | 353  | 75   | 405 |
| 1959 | 78  | 301  | 79   | 394 |
| 1961 | 82  | 336  | 81   | 394 |
| 1962 | 85  | 288  | 80   | 381 |
| 1963 | 78  | 323  | 79   | 373 |
| 1964 | 89  | 324  | 86   | 410 |

\* The questions asked of respondents concerning birth control were as follows. In 1937: Do you favor the birth-control movement? In 1938, 1939, 1940, 1943, 1945, and 1947: Would you like to see a government agency (or "government health clinics") furnish birth-control information to married people who want it? In 1959, 1961, 1962, and 1963: In some places in the United States it is not legal to supply birth-control information. How do you feel about this—do you think birth-control information should be available to anyone who wants it, or not? In 1964: Do you think birth-control information should be available to anyone who wants it, or not?

have only recently ceased to regard birth control as a tabooed topic. As far back as 30 years ago, almost three-quarters of the women questioned in these surveys actively approved having the *government* make birth-control information available to the married. By the early 1960's, 80 percent or more of women approved overcoming legal barriers and allowing "anyone who wants it" to have birth-control information. The figures for men are similar. The question asked in 1964—

the one question in recent years that did not mention illegality
—brought 86 percent of the women and 89 percent of the
men into the category of those who approved availability of
birth-control information for "anyone who wants it." Furthermore, in judging the level of disapproval, one should bear
in mind that the remainder of the respondents, in all of these
years, includes from 7 to 15 percent who claim that they
have "no opinion" on the subject, not that they "disapprove."

An important difference of opinion corresponds to a difference in religious affiliation. Among non-Catholics (including
those who have "no religion" and do not attend church) approval has been considerably higher than it has been among
Catholics. Among non-Catholic women, over 80 percent approved as early as 1939, and among non-Catholic men the
percentages were approximately the same. The 1964 poll
showed that 90 percent of each sex approved. Among Catholics, in recent years about 60 percent have approved, and,
in 1964, the question that mentioned neither the government
nor legality brought opinions of approval from 77 percent of
the women and 83 percent of the men.

Clearly, if birth-control information has in fact been unavailable to the poor, the cause has not been a generalized
and pervasive attitude of prudery on the part of the American public. Although public officials may have misjudged
American opinion (and may have mistakenly assumed that
the Catholic Church "spoke for" a majority of Americans,
or even for a majority of Catholics), most Americans of an age
to be having children did not regard birth control as a subject
that should be under a blanket of secrecy and, as far back as
the 1930's, evinced a marked willingness to have their government make such information widely available. It seems
unlikely, therefore, that poorer sectors of our population
were "cut off" from birth-control knowledge primarily because informal channels of communication (the channels
through which most people learn about birth control) were
blocked by an upper- and middle-class conspiracy of silence.

What has happened, however, is that pressure groups for
family planning, like the Catholic hierarchy they have been
opposing, have been acting as self-designated spokesmen for

"public opinion." By developing a cause as righteous as that of the Catholics (the "rights" of the poor as against the "rights" of a religious group), the family planners have used the American way of influencing official opinion. Now public officials appear to believe that publicly supported birth-control services are what the poor have always wanted and needed, just as, in the past, official opinion acceded to the notion that such services would have been "offensive" to certain groups. Nonetheless, the question remains of whether or not publicly supported services are actually appropriate to the attitudes and objectives of the poor and uneducated in matters of reproduction. Is the government responding to a mandate from the poor or to an ill-concealed mandate from the well-to-do? If there is no mandate from the poor, the provision of birth-control services may prove a convenience for certain women but is likely to have little effect on the reproductive performance of the poor in general. Let us look at the evidence.

## Is there a mandate from the poor?

The notion that the poor have larger families than the affluent only because they have less access to birth-control information implies that the poor *desire* families as small as, or smaller than, those of the well-to-do. The poor are simply unable to realize this desire, the argument goes, because of lack of access to birth-control information. The National Academy of Sciences Committee on Population stated the argument very well.[2]

> The available evidence indicates that low-income families do not want more children than do families with higher incomes, but they have more because they do not have the information or the resources to plan their families effectively according to their own desires.

The committee, however, presents none of the "available evidence" that "low-income families do not want more children than do families with higher incomes." Actually, my data supply evidence that runs counter to the statement quoted

## TABLE 2.

*Mean number of children considered ideal by non-Catholic women, according to education and economic status, for selected years between 1943 and 1968.*

| Date | Age range | Level of education* | | | Income or economic status† | | | | Total respondents | |
|---|---|---|---|---|---|---|---|---|---|---|
| | | College | High school | Grade school | 1 | 2 | 3 | 4 | X | N |
| 1943 | 20–34 | 2.8 | 2.6 | 2.6 | 2.9 | 2.7 | 2.7 | 2.5 | 2.7 | 1893 |
| 1952 | 21+ | 3.3 | 3.1 | 3.6 | 3.3 | | 3.3 | 3.3 | 3.3 | 723 |
| 1955‡ | 18–39 | 3.1 | 3.2 | 3.7 | 3.2 | 3.1 | 3.2 | 3.5 | 3.3 | 1905 |
| 1955§ | 18–39 | 3.3 | 3.4 | 3.9 | 3.4 | 3.3 | 3.4 | 3.7 | 3.4 | 1905 |
| 1957 | 21+ | 3.4 | 3.2 | 3.6 | 3.3 | | 3.2 | 3.5 | 3.3 | 448 |
| 1959 | 21+ | 3.5 | 3.4 | 3.9 | 3.5 | | 3.5 | 3.6 | 3.5 | 472 |
| 1960‡ | 18–39 | 3.1 | 3.2 | 3.5 | 3.1 | 3.2 | 3.3 | 3.2 | 3.2 | 1728 |
| 1960§ | 18–39 | 3.2 | 3.4 | 3.6 | 3.2 | 3.3 | 3.5 | 3.4 | 3.4 | 1728 |
| 1963 | 21+ | 3.2 | 3.4 | 3.5 | 3.3 | 3.3 | 3.5 | 3.5 | 3.4 | 483 |
| 1966 | 21+ | 3.1 | 3.3 | 3.7 | 3.2 | 3.2 | 3.4 | 3.7 | 3.3 | 374 |
| 1967 | 21+ | 3.1 | 3.3 | 3.4 | 3.3 | 3.2 | 3.1 | 3.4 | 3.3 | 488 |
| 1968 | 21+ | 3.2 | 3.3 | 3.7 | 3.2 | 3.0 | 3.4 | 3.6 | 3.3 | 539 |

* Level of education is measured by the highest grade completed.   † Levels 1 to 4 for economic status range in order from "high" to "low."   ‡ Minimum ideal (results from coding range answers to the lowest figure).   § Maximum ideal (results from coding range answers to the highest figure).

above, both with respect to the desired or ideal number of children and with respect to attitudes toward birth control.

I shall begin with the preferred size of family. A number of national polls, conducted over some 25 years, provide data concerning opinions on ideal family size. In addition, I include tabulations of data from two national surveys on fertility (the "Growth of American Families Studies"), conducted in 1955 and 1960.[13,14] My detailed analyses of the results of these polls and surveys are given elsewhere[15] and are only briefly summarized here. Table 2 gives mean values for the family size considered ideal by white, non-Catholic women, according to education and economic status.

The data lend little support to the hypothesis that the poor desire families as small as those desired by the middle and upper classes. Within both the educational and the economic categories, those on the lower rungs not only have larger families than those on the higher rungs (at least in the case of non-Catholics) but say they want larger families and consider them ideal. This differential has existed for as long as information on preferred family size in this country has been available, and it persists. It thus seems extremely hazardous to base a major governmental effort on the notion that, among individuals (white individuals, at least) at the lower social levels, there is a widespread and deeply held desire for families as small as, or smaller than, those desired by the well-to-do. No major survey shows this to be the case.

Not only do persons of lower socio-economic status prefer larger families than the more affluent do, they also generally favor birth control less. Tables 3 and 4 show the percentages of white men and women who expressed approval of birth control in surveys made between 1937 and 1964, by educational level and economic status, respectively.

Looking at the educational differential (Table 3), one finds that, in general, the proportion of those who approve birth control drops precipitately between the college and grade school levels. As far back as the early 1940's, over 80 percent of women and 75 percent of men with some or more college education approved government action on birth control. By 1964, over 90 percent of both sexes approved. By contrast, only 60 percent of men and women with an elementary school education approved in the 1940's, and, despite a rise in approval, there is still a differential. When non-Catholics alone are considered, the educational difference is even more pronounced in many cases.

Turning to economic or income status (Table 4), one generally finds the same results. The high proportions (close to 100 percent) of women in the highest and next-to-highest economic brackets who, in recent years, have approved birth-control efforts is noteworthy, as is the fact that approximately 80 percent of women in these brackets approved such efforts as far back as the 1930's. On the other hand, men and women in lower income brackets have been slower to approve birth-control policies.

Despite the inverse relationship just described, I may have overemphasized the lesser approval of birth-control programs on the part of persons of lower economic and social status. After all, in recent years approval often has been high even among people at the lowest social levels. Among women with only a grade school education, the percentage of those favoring birth-control programs averaged 73 percent in polls taken between 1959 and 1964; among men at the lowest educational level, the corresponding average was 66 percent. Yet it is undeniably true that, throughout the period for which data are available, the people who needed birth-control information most, according to recent policy pronouncements, have been precisely the ones who were least in favor of a policy that would make it widely available.

The truth of this conclusion becomes more evident when we move to an analysis of a question asked on the 1966 Gallup Poll: Do you think birth-control pills should be made available free to all women on relief who are of childbearing age? This question presents the public with the specific issue that is the focus of current policy—namely, birth control especially for the poor. A summary of the replies to this question is given in Table 5, together with average percentages of people who, in the five surveys made between 1959 and 1964, replied that they approved birth control generally.

It is clear that the overall level of approval drops when specific reference to a poverty-oriented birth-control policy is introduced. The decline is from an average of approximately

## TABLE 3.

*Percentages of white U.S. men and women between the ages of 21 and 44 who, in various national polls taken between 1943 and 1964, expressed the opinion that birth-control information should be made available to individuals who desired it. The percentages are given by level of education\*; the numbers in parentheses are total numbers of respondents in each category.*

| Year | Men | | | Women | | |
|------|-----|-----|-----|-------|-----|-----|
| | College | High school | Grade school | College | High school | Grade school |
| 1943 | 75 (184) | 68 (284) | 56 (157) | 82 (216) | 74 (442) | 60 (207) |
| 1945 | 74 (202) | 62 (360) | 58 (140) | 83 (216) | 68 (434) | 56 (207) |
| 1947 | 91 (84) | 72 (199) | 67 (66) | 81 (89) | 74 (228) | 72 (81) |
| 1959 | 88 (89) | 76 (163) | 65 (49) | 91 (55) | 79 (279) | 68 (41) |
| 1961 | 88 (102) | 81 (188) | 67 (46) | 84 (81) | 81 (265) | 78 (50) |
| 1962 | 91 (93) | 85 (171) | 61 (23) | 84 (79) | 82 (258) | 66 (44) |
| 1963 | 86 (105) | 79 (178) | 53 (40) | 81 (80) | 78 (251) | 81 (42) |
| 1964 | 92 (107) | 88 (188) | 83 (29) | 94 (79) | 86 (293) | 74 (38) |

\* The level of education is measured by the last grade completed.

80 percent for each sex during the period 1959–64 to 65 percent for men and 71 percent for women in 1966. Of most significance, however, is the fact that the largest proportionate drop in approval occurs among members of the "target" groups themselves—the poor and uneducated. In particular, there is a remarkable drop in approval among men at this socio-economic level. There is a 42-percent decline in approval among men who have had only a grade school education and a 29-percent drop among those with a high school education. Among the college-educated men the drop in approval is only 6 percent. The results, by income, parallel those by education: there is a 47-percent drop for men in the lowest income group but only a 9-percent drop for those in the highest income bracket. Even if the tabulations are restricted to non-Catholics (data that are not presented here), the results are essentially the same.

If the ghetto-oriented birth-control policy urged on the federal government meets with limited public enthusiasm, how does the public view extension of that policy to teen-age girls? This question is of some importance because a notable aspect of the pressure for government-sponsored family-planning programs is advocacy of making birth-control information and materials available at the high school level.

The Committee on Population of the National Academy of Sciences urges early education in "family planning" in order to prevent illegitimacy.[2]

> . . . government statistics show that the mothers of approximately 41 per cent of the 245,000 babies born illegitimately in the United States every year are women 19 years of age or younger. Thus a large proportion of all illegitimate children are progeny of teen-age mothers. To reduce the number of such children born to teen-age mothers, high-school education in family planning is essential.

Katherine B. Oettinger, Deputy Secretary for Family Planning of the Department of Health, Education, and Welfare, importunes us not to "demand the eligibility card of a first pregnancy before we admit vulnerable girls to family planning services."[16] The Harkavy report states:[3]

Table 4. Percentages of white U.S. men and women between the ages of 21 and 44 who, in various national polls taken between 1937 and 1964, expressed the opinion that birth-control information should be made available to individuals who desired it. The percentages are given by economic status (levels 1–4*); the numbers in parentheses are total numbers of respondents in each category.

| Year | Men | | | | Women | | | |
|------|-----|-----|-----|-----|-------|-----|-----|-----|
| | 1 | 2 | 3 | 4 | 1 | 2 | 3 | 4 |
| 1937 | 78(112) | 70(406) | 61(520) | | 67(69) | 78(293) | 64(372) | |
| 1938 | 65(125) | 74(453) | 62(521) | | 80(51) | 73(232) | 70(259) | |
| 1939 | 78(116) | 75(432) | 73(553) | | 71(68) | 77(260) | 71(302) | |
| 1940 | 79(131) | 75(443) | 68(553) | | 80(49) | 78(258) | 71(311) | |
| 1943 | 76(80) | 72(219) | 62(330) | | 80(90) | 79(272) | 68(500) | |
| 1945 | 73(67) | 66(286) | 62(352) | | 83(75) | 77(264) | 64(531) | |
| 1947 | 86(42) | 77(123) | 72(188) | | 92(38) | 71(119) | 73(237) | |
| 1959 | 83(101) | 76(120) | 73(79) | | 83(139) | 82(152) | 72(95) | |
| 1961 | 93(42) | 85(80) | 87(103) | 69(111) | 88(41) | 80(97) | 80(76) | 81(138) |
| 1962 | 82(45) | 89(71) | 86(94) | 80(74) | 82(51) | 80(75) | 84(110) | 77(140) |
| 1963 | 88(60) | 84(79) | 76(96) | 61(97) | 87(67) | 79(107) | 79(98) | 75(100) |
| 1964 | 90(67) | 87(26) | 93(82) | 85(79) | 96(90) | 90(87) | 85(104) | 78(120) |

*Levels 1 to 4 for the years 1961-64 range from income of $10,000 and over down to incomes under $5000. Prior to 1961, levels 1 to 3 represent "upper," "middle," and "lower" income brackets.

Eligibility requirements should be liberal with respect to marital status. Such services should be made available to the unmarried as well as the married. . . . Eligibility requirements should be liberal with respect to the age of unmarried women seeking help. This will undoubtedly pose some problems, but they may not be insurmountable. Some publically supported programs are already facing them (for example, in Baltimore).

Representative Scheuer from New York has berated the federal government for not "bringing family planning into the schools." He has cited the "desperate need for family planning by unmarried 14-, 15-, and 16-year-old girls in school [which] is so transparently evident that it almost boggles the imagination to realize that nothing has been done. Virtually no leadership has come from the federal government."[9]

Obviously there is little recognition in these statements that such a policy might engender a negative public response. Yet such a possibility cannot be discounted. The results of the 1966 question "Do you think they [the pills] should be made available to teen-age girls?" suggest that a policy of pill distribution to female adolescents may be viewed by the public as involving more complex issues than the mere democratization of "medical" services. These results, tabulated by social level, are shown in Table 6.

It may be seen that, in general, a proposal for distribution of pills to teen-age girls meets with very little approval. There is more disapproval among women than among men. Even among women under the age of 30, only 17 percent approve; among men in this age group, 29 percent approve. At no age does feminine approval reach 20 percent, and in most cases it is below 15 percent. Furthermore, restriction of the results to non-Catholics does not raise the percentages of those who approve the policy. Most noteworthy is the socio-economic gradient among men. Whereas 32 percent of college-educated men approve distribution of pills to young girls, only 13 percent of men with a grade school education do. Thirty-three percent of men in the highest income bracket approve, but only 13 percent in the lowest bracket do.

Clearly, the extension of "family planning" to poor, unmarried teen-agers is not regarded simply as "health care."

Individuals may approve, in a general way, a wider availability of birth-control information without approving federal expenditure to facilitate a high level of sexual activity by teen-age girls. One suspects that explicit recognition and implied approval of such activity still comes hard to our population,

### TABLE 5.

*Percentages of white U.S. men and women between the ages of 21 and 44 who, in a 1966 poll, expressed approval of free distribution of birth-control pills for women on relief, and average percentages of individuals in this age group who, in polls taken between 1959 and 1964, expressed approval of birth control. Percentages approving and numbers of individuals interviewed are given as totals and also by education and economic status of the respondents.*

| Item | Men 1966 % | Men 1966 N | Men 1959–64 (av. %) | Women 1966 % | Women 1966 N | Women 1959–64 (av. %) |
|---|---|---|---|---|---|---|
| Total | 65 | 264 | 82 | 71 | 385 | 81 |
| Education | | | | | | |
| College | 82 | 98 | 87 | 75 | 197 | 87 |
| High school | 58 | 142 | 82 | 70 | 392 | 81 |
| Grade school | 38 | 24 | 66 | 59 | 32 | 73 |
| Economic status | | | | | | |
| 1 | 79 | 80 | 89 | 70 | 110 | 87 |
| 2 | 69 | 75 | 84 | 76 | 99 | 82 |
| 3 | 59 | 65 | 83 | 70 | 91 | 80 |
| 4 | 39 | 41 | 74 | 67 | 76 | 78 |

and that it comes hardest to the group most involved in the problems of illegitimacy and premarital conception—namely, the poor and uneducated themselves. The extreme disapproval of a policy of pill distribution to teen-age girls that is found in lower-class groups (particularly among lower-class men) suggests that a double standard of sexual behavior is operative in these groups—a standard that does not allow open toleration of the idea that the ordinary teen-age girl requires the pill, or that a part of her junior high school and high school education should include instruction in its use.

## Can "five million women" be wrong?

The most widely publicized argument favoring federal birth-control programs, and apparently the one that elected officials find most persuasive, is the claim that there are approximately "five million" poor women "in need" of publicly subsidized birth-control help.[17] I list below some of the principal assumptions upon which this estimate is based—all of which introduce serious upward biases into the evidence.

1) It is claimed that women at the poverty and near-poverty levels desire families of 3.0 children. While this may be true of nonwhite wives at this economic level, it is not true, as we have seen, of white women, who comprise a major share of the "target" group and who, on the average, desire a number of children closer to 4 (especially if Catholics are included, as they are in the "five million").

2) It is assumed by the estimators that 82 percent of all poor women aged 15 to 44 are at risk of conception (that is, exposed sexually), in spite of the fact that only 45 percent of poor women in this age group are married and living with their husbands. In arriving at the figure of 82 percent, the estimators assumed that all women in the "married" category (including those who were separated from their husbands and those whose husbands were absent) were sexually exposed regularly, and that half of the women in the "non-married" category—that is, single, widowed, and divorced women—were exposed regularly. Information is scarce concerning the sexual behavior of widows and divorced women, but Kinsey's data on premarital coitus leads one to believe that the assumption of 50 percent for single women may be high. Among the women with a grade school education in Kinsey's sample, 38 percent had had coitus at some time between the ages of 16 and 20, and 26 percent, at some time between the ages of 21 and 25. Moreover, as Kinsey emphasizes, these encounters were characteristically sporadic.[18]

3) The proportion of sterile women among the poor is assumed to be 13 percent, although the Scripps 1960 "Growth of American Families Study" showed the proportion among

white women of grade school education to be 22 percent.[14]

4) No allowance is made for less-than-normal fecundity, although the Scripps 1960 study[14] had indicated that, among women of grade school education, an additional 10 percent (over and above the 22 percent) were subnormal in their ability to reproduce.

5) It is taken for granted by the estimators that no Catholic women would object, on religious grounds, to the use of modern methods, and no allowance is made for objection by non-Catholics, on religious or other grounds. In other words, it is assumed that all women "want" the service. Yet, in response to a question concerning the desirability of limiting or spacing pregnancies, 29 percent of the wives with grade school education who were interviewed in the Scripps 1960 study said they were "against" such limitation or spacing.[14] Among the Catholic wives with grade school education, the proportion "against" was 48 percent, although half of these objectors were "for" the rhythm method. Similar objections among the disadvantaged have been revealed by many polls over a long period.

6) Perhaps most important, the estimate of 5 million women "wanting" and "in need of" birth-control information includes not only objectors but women who are already practicing birth control. Hence, in addition to all the other biases, the estimate represents a blanket decision by the estimators that the women require medical attention regarding birth control—particularly that they need the pill and the coil. In the words of the Harkavy report:[2]

> This may be considered a high estimate of the number of women who need to have family planning services made available to them in public clinics, because some of the couples among the poor and near-poor are able to exercise satisfactory control over their fertility. However, even these couples do not have the same access as the non-poor to the more effective and acceptable methods of contraception, particularly the pill and the loop. So, simply in order to equalize the access of the poor and the near-poor to modern methods of contraception under medical supervision, it is appropriate to try to make contraceptive services available to all who may need and want them.

Yet the Scripps 1960 study found that, among fecund women of grade school education, 79 percent used contraceptives.[14] The 21 percent who did not included young women who were building families and said they wanted to get pregnant, as well as Catholics who objected to birth control on religious grounds. As for the methods that women currently are using, it seems gratuitous for the federal government to decide that only medically supervised methods—the pill and the coil—are suitable for lower-income couples, and that a mammoth "service" program is therefore required. In fact, the implications of such a decision border on the fantastic—the implications that we should substitute scarce medical and paramedical attention for all contraceptive methods now being used by poor couples.

In sum, the argument supporting a "need" for nationwide, publicly sustained birth-control programs does not stand up under empirical scrutiny. Most fecund lower-class couples

TABLE 6.

*Percentages of white U.S. men and women who, in a 1966 poll, expressed approval of making birth-control pills available to teen-age girls. Percentages approving and numbers of individuals interviewed are given by age group, by education, and by economic status.*

| Item | All religions | | | | Non-Catholics | | | |
|---|---|---|---|---|---|---|---|---|
| | Men | | Women | | Men | | Women | |
| | % | N | % | N | % | N | % | N |
| Age | | | | | | | | |
| Under 30 | 29 | 86 | 17 | 149 | 34 | 65 | 19 | 102 |
| 30–44 | 19 | 172 | 8 | 238 | 20 | 133 | 7 | 169 |
| Education | | | | | | | | |
| College | 32 | 98 | 15 | 100 | 36 | 75 | 13 | 71 |
| High school | 18 | 142 | 9 | 264 | 19 | 110 | 9 | 180 |
| Grade school | 13 | 24 | 11 | 35 | 6 | 17 | 14 | 28 |
| Economic status | | | | | | | | |
| 1 | 33 | 80 | 11 | 113 | 35 | 58 | 11 | 75 |
| 2 | 20 | 75 | 13 | 105 | 24 | 58 | 14 | 72 |
| 3 | 19 | 65 | 7 | 94 | 18 | 50 | 5 | 64 |
| 4 | 13 | 41 | 16 | 82 | 15 | 33 | 14 | 66 |

now use birth-control methods when they want to prevent pregnancy; in the case of those who do not, the blame
cannot simply be laid at the door of the affluent who have
kept the subject of birth control under wraps, or of a government that has withheld services. As we have seen, opinion on
birth control has been, and is, less favorable among the poor
and the less well educated than among the well-to-do. In addition, the poor desire larger families. Although it may be argued that, at the public welfare level, birth control has, until recently, been taboo because of the "Catholic vote," most
individuals at all social levels have learned about birth control *informally* and without medical attention. Furthermore,
the most popular birth-control device, the condom, has long
been as available as aspirin or cigarettes, and certainly has
been used by men of all social classes. When one bears in
mind the fact that the poor have no difficulty in gaining access to illegal narcotics (despite their obvious "unavailability"), and that the affluent had drastically reduced their
fertility before present-day contraceptive methods were available, one must recognize and take into account a motivational
component in nonuse and inefficient use of contraceptives.
Indeed, were relative lack of demand on the part of the poor
not a principal factor, it would be difficult to explain why such
an important "market" for birth-control materials—legal or
illegal—would have escaped the attention of enterprising businessmen or bootleggers. In any event, any estimate based on
the assumption that all poor women in the reproductive group
"want" birth-control information and materials and that virtually all "need" publicly supported services that will provide
them—including women with impaired fecundity, women who
have sexual intercourse rarely or not at all, women who object on religious grounds, and women who are already using
birth-control methods—would seem to be seriously misleading as a guide for our government in its efforts to control
population growth.

Moreover, the proposal for government sponsorship takes
no account of the possible advantages of alternative means of
reaching that part of the "market" that may not be optimally
served at present. For example, competitive pricing, better
marketing, and a program of advertising could make it pos-

sible for many groups in the population who are now being counted as "targets" for government efforts to purchase contraceptives of various kinds. When one bears in mind the fact that an important reason for nonuse or lack of access to contraceptives may be some sort of conflict situation (between husband and wife, adolescent child and parent, and so on), it becomes apparent that the impersonal and responsive marketplace is a far better agency for effecting smooth social change than is a far-flung national bureaucracy loaded with well-meaning but often blundering "health workers." The government could doubtless play an initial stimulating and facilitating role in relation to private industry, without duplicating, on a welfare basis, functions that might be more efficiently handled in the marketplace.

## *Would the policy have side effects?*

The possible inadvisability of having the government become a direct purveyor of birth-control materials to poverty groups becomes more clear when we consider some of the risks involved in such a course of action.

Even if the goal of reducing family size were completely and widely accepted by the poorer and less well educated sectors of the population, we should not assume that the general public would necessarily view a policy concerned with the means and practice of birth control (in any social group) as it views ordinary medical care—that is, as being morally neutral and obviously "desirable." Birth control is related to sexual behavior, and, in all viable societies, sexual behavior is regulated by social institutions. It is thus an oversimplification to think that people will be unmindful of what are, for them at least, the moral implications of changes in the conditions under which sexual intercourse is possible, permissible, or likely. An issue such as distribution of pills to teen-age girls runs a collision course with norms about premarital relations for young girls—norms that, in turn, relate to the saliency of marriage and motherhood as a woman's principal career and to the consequent need for socially created restrictions on free sexual access if an important inducement to marriage is not to be lost. Only if viable careers alternative to marriage existed for women would the lessening of controls over sexual behavior outside of marriage be unrelated to women's lifetime opportunities, for such opportunities would be independent of the marriage market and, a fortiori, independent of sexual bargaining. But such independence clearly does not exist. Hence, when the government is told that it will be resolving a "medical" problem if it makes birth-control pills available to teen-agers, it is being misled into becoming the protagonist in a sociologically based conflict between short-run feminine impulses and long-run feminine interests—a conflict that is expressed both in relations between parents and children and in relations between the sexes. This sociological conflict far transcends the "medical" issue of whether or not birth-control services should be made widely available.

Actually, the issue of sexual morality is only one among many potentially explosive aspects of direct federal involvement in family-planning programs for the poor. Others come readily to mind, such as the possibility that the pill and other physiological methods could have long-run, serious side effects, or that racial organizations could seize on the existence of these programs as a prime example of "genocide." Eager promoters of the suggested programs tend to brush such problems aside as trivial, but the problems, like the issue of sexual morality, cannot be wished away, for they are quite patently there.[9] There *are* risks involved in all drug-taking, and it is recognized that many of the specific ones involved in long-term ingestion of the pill may not be discovered for many years. No one today can say that these are less than, equal to, or greater than the normal risks of pregnancy and childbirth. Equally, a class-directed birth-control program, whatever its intent, is open to charges of genocide that are difficult to refute. Such a program cannot fail to appear to single out the disadvantaged as the "goat," all the while implying that the very considerable "planned" fertility of most Americans inexplicably requires no government attention at all.

## Population policy for Americans

It seems clear that the suggested policy of poverty-oriented birth-control programs does not make sense as a welfare measure. It is also true that, as an inhibitor of population growth, it is inconsequential and trivial. It does not touch the principal cause of such growth in the United States—namely, the reproductive behavior of the majority of Americans who, under present conditions, want families of more than three children and thereby generate a growth rate far in excess of that required for population stability. Indeed, for most Americans the "family planning" approach, concentrating as it does on the distribution of contraceptive materials and services, is irrelevant, because they already know about efficient contraception and are already "planning" their families. It is thus apparent that any policy designed to influence reproductive behavior must not only concern itself with all fecund Americans (rather than just the poor) but must, as well, relate to family-size goals (rather than just to contraceptive means). In addition, such a policy cannot be limited to matters affecting contraception (or even to matters affecting gestation and parturition, such as abortion), but must, additionally, take into account influences on the formation and dissolution of heterosexual unions.[19]

What kinds of reproductive policies can be pursued in an effort to reduce long-term population growth? The most important step toward developing such new policies is to recognize and understand the existing ones, for we already have influential and coercive policies regarding reproductive behavior. Furthermore, these existing policies relate not merely to proscriptions (legal or informal) regarding certain means of birth control (like abortion) but also to a definition of reproduction as a primary societal end and to an organization of social roles that draws most of the population into reproductive unions.

The existence of such pronatalist policies becomes apparent when we recall that, among human beings, population replacement would not occur at all were it not for the complex social organization and system of incentives that encourage mating, pregnancy, and the care, support, and rearing of children. These institutional mechanisms are the pronatalist "policies" evolved unconsciously over millennia to give societies a fertility sufficient to offset high mortality. The formation and implementation of antinatalist policies must be based, therefore, on an analysis and modification of the existing pronatalist policies. It follows, as well, that antinatalist policies will not necessarily involve the introduction of coercive measures. In fact, just the opposite is the case. Many of these new policies will entail a *lifting* of pressures *to* reproduce, rather than an *imposition* of pressures *not* to do so. In order to understand this point let us consider briefly our present-day pronatalism.

It is convenient to start with the family, because pronatalism finds its most obvious expression in this social institution. The pronatalism of the family has many manifestations, but among the most influential and universal are two: the standardization of both the male and the female sexual roles in terms of reproductive functions, obligations, and activities, and the standardization of the occupational role of women—half of the population—in terms of child-bearing, child-rearing, and complementary activities. These two "policies" insure that just about everyone will be propelled into reproductive unions, and that half of the population will enter such unions as a "career"—a life's work. Each of the two "policies" is worth considering.

With regard to sex roles, it is generally recognized that potential human variability is greater than is normally permitted *within* each sex category. Existing societies have tended to suppress and extinguish such variability and to standardize sexual roles in ways that imply that all "normal" persons will attain the status of parents. This coercion takes many forms, including one-sided indoctrination in schools, legal barriers and penalties for deviation, and the threats of loneliness, ostracism, and ridicule that are implied in the unavailability of alternatives. Individuals who—by temperament, health, or constitution—do not fit the ideal sex-role pattern are nonetheless coerced into attempting to achieve it, and many of them do achieve it, at least to the extent of having demographic impact by becoming parents.

Therefore, a policy that sought out the ways in which coercion regarding sex roles is at present manifesting itself could find numerous avenues for relieving the coercion and for allowing life styles different from marriage and parenthood to find free and legitimatized expression. Such a policy would have an effect on the content of expectations regarding sex roles as presented and enforced in schools, on laws concerning sexual activity between consenting adults, on taxation with respect to marital status and number of children, on residential building policies, and on just about every facet of existence that is now organized so as exclusively to favor and reward a pattern of sex roles based on marriage and parenthood.

As for the occupational roles of women, existing pressures still attempt to make the reproductive and occupational roles coterminus for all women who elect to marry and have children. This rigid structuring of the wife-mother position builds into the entire motivational pattern of women's lives a tendency to want at least a moderate-size family. To understand this point one must recognize that the desired number of children relates not simply to the wish for a family of a particular size but relates as well to a need for more than one or two children if one is going to enjoy "family life" over a significant portion of one's lifetime. This need is increased rather than lessened by improved life expectancy. Insofar as women focus their energies and emotions on their families, one cannot expect that they will be satisfied to play their only important role for a diminishing fraction of their lives, or that they will readily regard make-work and dead-end jobs as a substitute for "mothering." The notion that most women will "see the error of their ways" and decide to have two-child families is naive, since few healthy and energetic women will be so misguided as to deprive themselves of most of the rewards society has to offer them and choose a situation that allows them neither a life's work outside the home nor one within it. Those who do deprive themselves in this fashion are, in effect, taking the brunt of the still existing maladjustment between the roles of women and the reproductive needs of society. In a society oriented around achievement and accomplishment, such women are exceptionally vulnerable to depression, frustration, and a sense of futility, because they are being blocked from a sense of fulfillment both at home and abroad.

In sum, the problem of inhibiting population growth in the United States cannot be dealt with in terms of "family-planning needs" because this country is well beyond the point of "needing" birth control methods. Indeed, even the poor seem not to be a last outpost for family-planning attention. If we wish to limit our growth, such a desire implies basic changes in the social organization of reproduction that will make nonmarriage, childlessness, and small (two-child) families far more prevalent than they are now. A new policy, to achieve such ends, can take advantage of the antinatalist tendencies that our present institutions have suppressed. This will involve the lifting of penalties for antinatalist behavior rather than the "creation" of new ways of life. This behavior already exists among us as part of our covert and deviant culture, on the one hand, and our elite and artistic culture, on the other. Such antinatalist tendencies have also found expression in feminism, which has been stifled in the United States by means of systematic legal, educational, and social pressures concerned with women's "obligations" to create and care for children. A fertility-control policy that does not take into account the need to alter the present structure of reproduction in these and other ways merely trivializes the problem of population control and misleads those who have the power to guide our country toward completing the vital revolution.

## References and Notes

1. *Hearings on S. 1676, U.S. Senate Subcommittee on Foreign Aid Expenditures* (the 1965 and 1966 Hearings each comprise seven volumes; the 1967–1968 Hearings, to date, comprise three volumes) (Government Printing Office, Washington, D.C.).
2. "The Growth of U.S. Population," *Nat. Acad. Sci.–Nat. Res. Council Pub. 1279* (1965), pp. 22, 10, 13; attachment A, p. 19.
3. O. Harkavy, F. S. Jaffe, S. S. Wishik, "Implementing DHEW Policy on Family Planning and Population" (mimeographed, 1967; available from the Ford Foundation, New York), p. 29.
4. "Report of the President's Committee on Population and Fam-

ily Planning: The Transition from Concern to Action" (Government Printing Office, Washington, D.C., 1968).

5. K. Davis, *Science* 158, 730 (1967); J. Blake, in *Public Health and Population Change*, M. C. Sheps and J. C. Ridley, Eds. (Univ. of Pittsburgh Press, Pittsburgh, Pa., 1965).

6. In the words of the Committee on Population, "The freedom to limit family size to the number of children wanted when they are wanted is, in our view, a basic human right . . . most Americans of higher income and better education exercise this right as a matter of course, but . . . many of the poor and uneducated are in fact deprived of the right."

7. W. J. Cohen, *Family Planning: One Aspect of Freedom to Choose* (Government Printing Office, Washington, D.C., 1966), p. 2. Cohen, former Secretary of Health, Education, and Welfare, says: "Until a few years ago, family planning and population problems were considered 'hush-hush' subjects. Public discussion was curtailed not only in polite society, but in the legislative and executive branches of the government as well."

8. *Hearings on S. 2993, U.S. Senate Subcommittee on Employment, Manpower, and Poverty, 89th Congress, Second Session, May 10* (Government Printing Office, Washington, D.C., 1966), p. 31.

9. *Hearings on S. 1676, U.S. Senate Subcommittee on Foreign Aid Expenditures, 90th Congress, First Session, November 2* (Government Printing Office, Washington, D.C., 1967), pt. 1, pp. 12, 62, 18.

10. Senator Tydings (D–Md.) said at the Hearings on S. 1676 (see 9): "As recently as 3 or 4 years ago, the idea that Federal, State or local governments should make available family planning information and services to families who could not otherwise afford them was extremely controversial. But in a brief period of time there has been a substantial shift of opinion among the moral leadership of our country, brought about in large measure by the vigorous efforts of the distinguished Senator from Alaska, Ernest Gruening, the chairman of this subcommittee."

11. E. Gruening, "What the Federal Government Is Now Doing in the Field of Population Control and What Is Needed," speech presented before the U.S. Senate, 3 May 1967.

12. J. M. Stycos, in *World Population and U.S. Government Policy and Programs*, F. T. Brayer, Ed. (Georgetown Univ. Press, Washington, D.C., 1968).

13. R. Freedman, P. K. Whelpton, A. A. Campbell, *Family Plan-*

*ning, Sterility and Population Growth* (McGraw-Hill, New York, 1959).

14. P. K. Whelpton, A. A. Campbell, J. E. Patterson, *Fertility and Family Planning in the United States* (Princeton Univ. Press, Princeton, N.J., 1966), pp. 159, 177.

15. J. Blake, *Demography* 3, 154 (1966); *Population Studies* 20, 27 (1966); *ibid.* 21, 159 (1967); *ibid.*, p. 185; *ibid.* 22, 5 (1968).

16. *Family Planner* 2, 3 (1968).

17. The estimate (by Arthur A. Campbell) under discussion here may be found in the Harkavy report (see *3*, attachment A, pp. 4–19). Another estimate has been circulated by the Planned Parenthood Federation in a brochure entitled *Five Million Women* (Planned Parenthood, New York).

18. A. C. Kinsey, W. B. Pomeroy, C. E. Martin, P. B. Gebhard, *Sexual Behavior in the Human Female* (Saunders, Philadelphia, 1953), pp. 291 and 337.

19. K. Davis and J. Blake, *Econ. Develop. Cult. Change* 4, 211 (1956).

20. I make grateful acknowledgment to the Ford Foundation for support of the research presented in this article and to the National Institutes of Health (general research support grant 1501-TR-544104) for assistance to Statistical Services, School of Public Health, University of California, Berkeley. I am also indebted to Kingsley Davis, whose critical comments and helpful suggestions have greatly advanced my thinking. The Roper Center and the Gallup Poll kindly supplied me with polling data.

## 22. Family Planning and Public Policy: Who Is Misleading Whom?

OSCAR HARKAVY, FREDERICK S. JAFFE, AND
SAMUEL M. WISHIK

Federal policies on family planning services and population research are currently under review as a result of the report of the President's Committee on Population and Family Planning.[1] Judith Blake's article, "Population policy for Americans: Is the government being misled?"[2] which is presumably intended to influence this review, contains numerous errors of fact and interpretation which it is important to clarify. To support her position, she knocks down several straw men; ignores the bulk of serious demographic research on U.S. fertility patterns in the last 15 years, as well as research on differential availability of health care and the relative effectiveness of various contraceptive methods; and cites opinion-poll data in a manner that distorts the overall picture. The article's methodological limitations alone are sufficient to suggest that the question raised in its subtitle may more appropriately be turned around and asked of the article itself.

The article is based on six principal propositions.

1) That the reduction of U.S. population growth—indeed, the achievement of "population stability"—is "virtually unchallenged as an official national goal."

2) That, in pursuit of *this* goal, the "essential recommendation" by official and private groups has been a program of publicly financed family planning services for the poor.

3) That this program of family planning for the poor will not achieve the goal of population stability.

4) That advocates of this policy contend that the poor have been denied access to family planning services because of "the prudery and hypocrisy of the affluent."

5) That the poor desire larger families than higher-income couples do and are significantly less inclined to favor birth control.

6) That the estimate of 5 million poor women as the approximate number in need of subsidized family planning services is exaggerated.

With the exception of proposition 3, each of these statements is seriously misleading or in error. Let us examine the evidence on each point.

### A consensus on U.S. population stability?

If the United States had as a national goal the reduction of its population growth and the achievement of population stability—and if the program of publicly funded family planning services for those who cannot afford private medical care had been advanced as the principal or only means of achieving population stability—Judith Blake's contention that the government is being misled would have much validity. However, neither proposition is sustained by the evidence.

We have individually and jointly been associated with the evolution of public policy in this field for more than a decade. To our knowledge, there has never been an official policy regarding the virtue or necessity of reducing U.S. population growth, much less achieving population stability. Nor has there emerged among Americans generally a "virtually unchallenged" consensus on what should constitute an official U.S. population policy.

The clearest statement of official U.S. *domestic* policy is contained in President Johnson's 1966 Health Message to Congress:[3]

> We have a growing concern to foster the integrity of the family and the opportunity for each child. It is essential that all families have access to information and services that will allow freedom to choose the number and spacing of their children within the dictates of individual conscience.

Neither in this nor in any other statement did the President cite stabilization of U.S. growth as the objective of federal

*Harkavy, Jaffe and Wishik* 327

## TABLE 1.

Number of children wanted, by education, color or race, income, and occupational status of respondents, as shown by studies made in 1960 and 1965.

| Education, income, and occupational status | 1960 White* | | | 1960 Non-white† | 1965‡ White | | | 1965‡ Negro |
|---|---|---|---|---|---|---|---|---|
| | Total | Protestant | Catholic | | Total | Non-Catholic | Catholic | |
| **Education** | | | | | | | | |
| College | 3.3 | 3.1 | 4.8 | 2.4 | 3.22 | 3.03 | 3.86 | 2.70 |
| High school (4 yr) | 3.2 | 3.0 | 3.9 | 2.7 | 3.21 | 3.01 | 3.65 | 2.89 |
| High school (1–3 yr) | 3.3 | 3.2 | 3.6 | 2.7 | | | | |
| Grade school | 3.5 | 3.1 | 4.3 | 3.5 | | | | |
| High school (1–3 yr) or grade school | | | | | 3.46 | 3.30 | 3.83 | 3.48 |
| **Husband's income§** | | | | | | | | |
| >$10,000 | 3.3 | | | | | | | |
| $7,000–9,000 | 3.2 | | | | | | | |
| $6,000–6,999 | 3.3 | | | | | | | |
| $5,000–5,999 | 3.3 | | | | | | | |
| $4,000–4,999 | 3.4 | | | | | | | |
| $3,000–3,999 | 3.4 | | | | | | | |
| <$3,000 | 3.2 | | | | | | | |
| **Occupation‖** | | | | | | | | |
| Upper white-collar | 3.3 | | | | | | | |
| Lower white-collar | 3.3 | | | | | | | |
| Upper blue-collar | 3.3 | | | | | | | |
| Lower blue-collar | 3.3 | | | | | | | |
| Farm | 3.5 | | | | | | | |
| Other | 3.0 | | | | | | | |
| Total | 3.3 | 3.1 | 4.0 | 2.9 | 3.29 | 3.11 | 3.74 | 3.21 |

* From *12*, Table 54.  † From *12*, Table 189.  ‡ From *13*, Table 4. § Unpublished data from the 1960 "Growth of American Families Studies," made available by A. A. Campbell.  ‖ From *12*, Table 71.

policy. Nor has such a goal been articulated by Congress or the federal agencies. In 1966, Secretary Gardner of the Department of Health, Education, and Welfare (HEW) stated[4] that the objectives of departmental policy are "to improve the health of the people, to strengthen the integrity of the family and to provide families the freedom of choice to determine the spacing of their children and the size of their families." In 1968 he reiterated[5] that "the immediate objective is to extend family planning services to all those desiring such services who would not otherwise have access to them."

It is clear that the federal program has been advanced, not for population control, but to improve health and reduce the impact of poverty and deprivation.

### Goals of federal family planning policy

Given this unambiguous framework for federal policy, it is inexplicable how Blake could arrive at the statement that population limitation has become our national goal and that the "essential recommendation" for reaching *this* goal has been to extend family planning services to the poor. She attributes this "misleading" recommendation to a 1965 report by the National Academy of Sciences,[6] a 1967 consultants' review of HEW programs written by us,[7] and the report of the President's Committee,[1] despite the fact that each of these reports clearly distinguishes a family planning program for the poor from an overall U.S. population control program or policy. For example, the National Academy of Sciences report stated explicitly[6] that U.S. population growth "is caused more by the preference for larger families among those who consciously choose the number of children they have than by high fertility in the impoverished segments of the population. The importance of high fertility among the underprivileged lies not so much in its contribution to the national birth rate as in the difficulties that excessive fertility imposes on the impoverished themselves."

The 1967 HEW review sought to determine how well the department's stated policy was being implemented. It found the department's efforts lagging and recommended higher priority in staff and budget for family planning services and population research programs. It also distinguished this effort from an overall U.S. population policy and program:[7]

While study should be given to the present and future implications of the growth of the Nation's population as a whole—perhaps through a series of university studies sponsored by a Presidential commission—the Federal government should at present focus its *family planning assistance* on the disadvantaged segments of the population. The great majority of non-poor American couples have access to competent medical guidance in family planning and are able to control their fertility with remarkable effectiveness. The poor lack such access and have more children than they want. It should be the goal of Federal policy to provide the poor with the same opportunity to plan their families that most other Americans have long enjoyed. Public financing of family planning for the disadvantaged is clearly justified for health reasons alone, particularly for its potential influence in reducing current rates of maternal and infant mortality and morbidity. Additionally, there are excellent humanitarian and economic justifications for a major directed program to serve the poor.

The President's Committee did not concentrate on family planning alone but made numerous recommendations for short- and long-term programs of domestic and international services, research, and education. Its recommendation on domestic family planning services again was justified, not in terms of population control, but as a health and social measure:[1]

> Excessive fertility can drive a family into poverty as well as reduce its chances of escaping it. The frequency of maternal deaths, the level of infant mortality, and the number of children who are chronically handicapped are all markedly greater among the poor than in the rest of the population. One of the most effective measures that could be taken to lower mortality and morbidity rates among mothers and children would be to help the poor to have the number of children they desire.

As for immediate programs to further reduce the incidence of unwanted pregnancy among the rest of the population, the committee recommended[1] expansion of biomedical research for improved contraceptive techniques and expansion of social research; increased education in population dynamics, sex, and human reproduction, and improved training programs for physicians and other relevant professionals. It stated explicitly[1] that these recommended programs "are only *one* of the im-

portant factors that influence population trends," and called
for a Presidential Commission on Population to, among other
things, "assess the social and economic consequences of population trends in the U.S. . . . [and] consider the consequences of alternative population policies."[1]

These reports only reiterate what has been the basic justification for publicly funded family planning services for the
poor for more than a decade. The leaders of the U.S. family
planning movement have not advanced this program as a
means of achieving population stability, because it has been
evident that the poor and near-poor, who constitute only
about one-quarter of the U.S. population, are not the major
contributors to U.S. population growth, despite their higher
fertility.

Blake believes the U.S. policy should aim toward a zero rate
of population growth, as is her right. But she has no right to
accuse family planners of misleading the public into believing
that extension of family planning to the poor would bring
about such population stability—a claim they have never made.
Of course, any reduction in births, wanted or unwanted, will
result in *less* natural increase and, other things being equal,
*less* population growth. Elimination or reduction of unwanted
pregnancies among the poor and near-poor would thus reduce
*somewhat* the rate of population growth, though not eliminate
it entirely.[8]

### *Prudery—or politics?*

Another straw man erected by Blake is the assertion that
denial of birth control services to the poor has been attributed
by advocates of family planning to the "prudery and hypocrisy of the affluent, who have overtly tabooed discussion
of birth control and dissemination of birth control materials."
As proof that this has not been the case, she cites opinion
polls going back to 1937 showing majority support for making birth control information available to those who desire it.

The proof is irrelevant in two major respects. First, the issue is not *information* about birth control, but *availability of
services* (a distinction which Blake obscures throughout her
article). And second, the operative factor in regard to the

TABLE 2.

*Percentages (by education and color of respondents) of women who favored fertility control, as shown by studies made in 1960 and 1965.**

| Education | White | | Nonwhite | |
|---|---|---|---|---|
| | 1960* | 1965† | 1960† | 1965† |
| College | 97 | 97 | 97 | 94 |
| High school (4 yr) | 95 | 97 | 90 | 94 |
| High school (1–3 yr) | 93 | 94 | 78 | 90 |
| Grade school | 82 | 82 | 67 | 84 |

* Data from *12*, Table 102.    † Data from *17a*, Table 7.

poor has not been generalized approval or disapproval, but the policies in regard to provision of contraceptive services of public health and welfare institutions on which the poor depend for medical care. As she notes, it was evident as long ago as the 1930's that most Americans approved of birth control and practiced it in some form (although it was not until the late 1950's that the mass media began to carry relatively explicit birth control material). But this public-opinion base did not control the policies of public institutions or the attitudes of political leaders. In most tax-supported hospitals and health departments there were explicit or implicit prohibitions on the prescription of contraceptive methods and materials, and many states had legislative restrictions which were enforced primarily in public agencies. To change these policies required protracted campaigns, which began in the New York municipal hospitals in 1958,[9] continued in Illinois, Maryland, Pennsylvania, and other states in the early 1960's, and culminated in legislative actions in 1965 and 1966 in at least 15 states and congressional action in 1967 in the Social Security and Poverty legislation.

The family planning movement has not ascribed the denial of birth control services to the poor to a generalized "taboo" but, rather, has ascribed it to concrete prohibitions on provision of services which stemmed from fear on the part of political leaders of the presumed controversial nature of the subject. The fears were perhaps exaggerated, but nevertheless real. The result was that very few poor women received contraceptive guidance and prescription in tax-supported agencies at times in their lives when it would have been of most importance to them—at the premarital examination and after the birth of a child, for example. It was not until the years 1964 to 1966 that several hundred public hospitals and health departments began providing family planning services, and it was not until 1967 that as much as $10 million in federal funds became available to finance identifiable family planning programs.

### *Family size desired by the poor*

Judith Blake contends that her data show that the poor desire larger families than the non-poor. She bases her assertion on responses to opinion polls and ignores the three major national studies conducted since 1955, covering larger and properly structured random samples of the U.S. population, which have probed these issues in depth. Even when the poll responses are accepted at face value, it is of interest to note that the "larger" family said to be desired by those in the lowest economic status group was larger by as much as 0.4 of a child in only 2 of the 12 years cited.[10]

Also of interest is the fact that Blake treats responses to questions on *ideal* family size as evidence of the number of children the poor *want*. At various points in the text she refers to the data she cites as demonstrating *"desired* or ideal" number of children or *"preferred* family size," or states that the poor "say they *want* larger families" (emphasis added). The dubiousness of this methodology is revealed by the very different treatment of responses on *ideal* and *wanted* family size in the 1955 and 1960 Growth of American Families Studies[11,12] and in the 1965 National Fertility Study.[13,14–16]

In the 1955 study, Freedman and his co-workers stated that the question on ideal family size "was not designed to discover the wife's personal ideal but sought a picture of her more stereotyped impressions on what family size should be."[11] "The more realistic question about desired . . . family size," they concluded, "is that regarding the number of children wanted at the time of the interview."[11] They found that the stereotyped "ideal" generally was higher than the number

TABLE 3.

*Number of children wanted by white and nonwhite wives under 30 years old, by income and farm residence of respondents, as shown by a 1965 study.**

| Residence | Family income | | | |
|---|---|---|---|---|
| | > $8,000 | $6,000–7,999 | $4,000–6,999 | < $4,000 |
| Now living on farm | 3.97 | 3.12 | 3.25 | 3.21 |
| Once lived on farm | 3.08 | 3.13 | 2.99 | 3.19 |
| Never lived on farm | 3.13 | 3.21 | 3.12 | 3.06 |

* Unpublished data from the 1965 National Fertility Study, made available by C. F. Westoff.

TABLE 4.

*Percentages (by income and farm residence of respondents) of white and nonwhite wives under 30 years old who had ever used, or expected to use, any form of contraception, as shown by a 1965 study.**

| Residence | Family income | | | |
|---|---|---|---|---|
| | > $8,000 | $6,000–7,999 | $4,000–6,999 | < $4,000 |
| Now living on farm | 84 | 100 | 85 | 89 |
| Once lived on farm | 91 | 97 | 95 | 88 |
| Never lived on farm | 95 | 96 | 93 | 92 |

* Unpublished data from the 1965 National Fertility Study, made available by C. F. Westoff.

wanted. In the 1960 study, Whelpton and his colleagues came to the same conclusion.[12] In the 1965 study, Ryder and Westoff expressed "profound reservations" about the usefulness of the "ideal" question and found that it "lacks face validity . . . is relatively unreliable and has a small variance."[13]

The poll responses cited by Blake appear to show that *ideal* family size varies inversely, among non-Catholic white women, with education and economic status. Responses to detailed surveys on *wanted* family size, however, either show insignificant differences between lower- and higher-status non-Catholic white respondents or *reverse the direction*. The data for 1960 show no difference in the number of children wanted by highest-status and lowest-status non-Catholic whites, and the data for 1965 show a very small increase in the number wanted by the group with only grade school education. (The pattern for Catholics was, of course, different.) Other measures of socioeconomic status show either no difference in the number of children wanted or, in the case of the measure of income, a smaller number for those with income below $3000 than for those with income above $10,000 (Table 1).

Judith Blake also uses opinion-poll responses, rather than the results of in-depth studies, to measure approval of birth control in the different socioeconomic groups. The result is, again, an overstatement of the differences between the highest and lowest social groups. In Table 2 are given excerpts from findings for 1960 and 1965 on approval of the practice of fertility control (including the rhythm method). The only deviation from the near-universal approval of fertility control is in the group with only grade school education, which is rapidly becoming a smaller proportion of all U.S. women and is hardly coterminous with the poor and near-poor. [Among all poor and near-poor women aged 18 to 44 in 1966, only 26.1 percent had grade school education or less; 31.9 percent had completed from 1 to 3 years of high school, and 42.1 percent had been graduated from high school; some of the latter had attended college.[17]] Even in the grade-school group, however, more than four-fifths of white women approved of birth control in both 1960 and 1965—a proportion bettered by nonwhite grade-school women in 1965—and all other groups were nearly unanimous in their approval. It is extremely difficult, in the face of these data, to conjure up the notion of great hostility to fertility control among the poor and near-poor.[17a,18]

For purposes of policy determination, the most salient questions relate, not to all poor and near-poor persons, but to those who are in their prime child-bearing years—that is, less than 30 years old. Presumably it is this group which would be most affected by public programs and whose attitudes policy makers would consider most significant. Data from the 1965 study, presented in Tables 3 and 4, permit direct comparison, for farm and non-farm women below 30 in four income groups, of the number of children wanted and the proportion of women then using, or expecting to use, some form of contraception. The conclusion is clear: younger wives in the "poor" and "near-poor" categories want as few children as wives in higher income groups—or want fewer children than the higher-income wives—and have used or expect to use some form of contraception to a similar degree.

Despite the fact that 70 percent of poor and near-poor women regarded as in need of subsidized family planning services are white,[19] Blake frequently terms the recommended federal effort a "ghetto-oriented family planning program." She also describes the charge of "genocide" which has been leveled by some black militants as "difficult to refute." However, the desire of black couples for smaller families than are desired by whites—and for smaller families than they are now having—was clearly demonstrated in the 1960 study[12] (see Table 5).

Substantially the same pattern emerges from the 1965 study, as shown in Tables 6 and 7: significantly higher percentages of nonwhites continue to prefer a family of two children or less, and the proportion of nonwhites approving and using, or expecting to use, some method of fertility control is indistinguishable from that of whites, especially in the prime childbearing ages.

### Excess fertility

Serious demographic research has thus documented the disappearance of the traditional socioeconomic and ethnic differentials in fertility aspirations and in attitudes toward fertility control. "Clearly," as Westoff and Ryder have stated, "the norm of fertility control has become universal in contemporary America."[17a] Yet within this general pattern the studies also reveal that many couples do not achieve the degree of control they wish. Some have more children than they want and can be classified in the "excess fertility" category;

others fail to have their children when they want them and are described as "timing failures." More than half of U.S. couples reported one or another type of failure in 1965; 21 percent of all respondents acknowledged that at least one of their children was unwanted.[15] (This must be regarded as an underestimate, since the questionnaire required that respondents characterize specific children already born as either wanted or unwanted.)

While excess fertility is found among all socioeconomic groups, it is more acute among the poor, among nonwhites (the majority of whom are poor or near-poor), and among those with higher parity and less education. In spite of the similarity in family-size preferences in all socioeconomic groups, the poor and near-poor had a fertility rate from 1960 to 1965 of 152.5 births per 1000 women aged 15 to 44, as compared to 98.1 for the non-poor.[20] And in spite of the expressed preference of almost all low-income parents for less than four children, nearly half of the children growing up in poverty in 1966 were members of families with five or more children under 18; moreover, the risk of poverty increased rapidly from 9 percent for one-child families to 42 percent for families with six or more children.[21] In terms of poverty, the most significant demarcation appears to be at the three-child level—the average family size wanted by low-income as well as other American couples: more than one-quarter of all families with four or more children were living in poverty, and four out of ten were poor or near-poor. Their risk of poverty was two-and-a-half times that for families with three children or less (Table 8).

The 1965 National Fertility Study provides data on the percentage of unwanted births for each birth order, ranging from 5.7 percent of first births to 56.7 percent of sixth and higher-order births. Application of these percentages to actual births, by birth order, in the years 1960 to 1965 yields an estimated average of 850,000 unwanted births annually in all socioeconomic groups. Combination of these data with Campbell's calculation of differential fertility rates shows that approximately 40 percent of births to poor and near-poor couples were unwanted by one or both parents in the years 1960 to 1965, as compared to 14 percent of births to non-poor couples.[22] [This result appears consistent with the 1960 finding of an inverse relation between education and excess fertility, with 32 percent of white, and 43 percent of nonwhite, grade-school-educated wives reporting more children than they wanted.[12]]

### Equalizing access to effective methods

It is precisely the reduction or elimination of this involuntary disparity between the poor and non-poor which has been the objective of publicly supported family planning service programs. Given the essentially similar preferences of the two groups concerning family size, programs which equalize access to modern methods of fertility control should also help to equalize the incidence of unwanted pregnancy for the two

TABLE 5.

*Number of children wanted by white and nonwhite wives, as shown by a 1960 study.**

| Couples | Number of children wanted | | Percentages wanting two children or less | |
|---|---|---|---|---|
| | Minimum | Maximum | Minimum | Maximum |
| White | 3.1 | 3.5 | 41 | 29 |
| Nonwhite | 2.7 | 3.0 | 55 | 46 |

* Data from 12, Tables 15 and 16.

groups. Blake can regard this as a "fantastic . . . blanket decision" imposed by the family planners only if she ignores (i) the evidence on the type of birth control methods on which the poor rely, (ii) the evidence on the relative effectiveness of different contraceptive methods, and (iii) the response of poor persons to organized programs which offer them a complete range of methods.

The data on contraceptive practice cited above measure the combined use of all methods, including those methods known to be least effective in preventing conception. The cited studies also show that couples of higher socioeconomic status

who can afford private medical care tend to use the more reliable medical methods, while low-income couples depend
more on less reliable, nonmedical methods. Among white
Protestants in 1960, for example, half as many wives with a
grade school education as college graduates used the diaphragm and twice as many relied on withdrawal.[12] Published
and unpublished findings for 1965 on methods employed by
whites and nonwhites reveal the same picture. Three times as
many nonwhites as whites relied on the douche[16] and on suppositories,[23] and twice as many relied on foam.[23] When the
condom is classified among effective methods and rhythm is
omitted from the analysis because of the different proportions
of whites and nonwhites who are Catholic, we find that half
of nonwhite users of contraceptives rely on the least effective
methods, as compared to about 30 percent of whites.[16]

These findings are significant in two respects: (i) the methods on which the poor rely most heavily have considerably
higher failure rates and thus would lead to a higher incidence
of unwanted fertility; and (ii) the overwhelming majority of
poor persons accept the best methods science has been able to
develop when they are given the choice.

The relative rates of failure with the different methods
range from 1 to 3 failures per 100 women-years of exposure
for pills and IUD's to 35 to 38 failures for rhythm and
douche, with the numbers for the condom, the diaphragm,
and withdrawal clustering around 15.[24]

### Response to family planning programs

It is difficult to understand how the greater reliance of the
poor on nonmedical methods can be attributed to their personal preferences in view of the considerable research demonstrating that the poor have little access to medical care for
preventive services.[25] When access to modern family planning services offered with energy and dignity has been provided, the response of poor and near-poor persons has been
considerable. The number of low-income patients enrolled in
organized family planning services under both public and private auspices has increased from about 175,000 in 1960 to
850,000 in 1968, as hospitals and public health departments

have increasingly offered services which provide the new methods not associated with the act of coitus.[22] In virtually all known programs offering a variety of methods, 85 to 90 percent of low-income patients voluntarily choose either pills or intrauterine devices (IUD's), the most effective methods currently known.

In 1965, a Chicago study found that three-fourths of patients continued to use the pills regularly 30 months after

TABLE 6.

*Desired family size, by race and by fertility planning status, as shown by a 1965 study.**

| Desired number of children | Percentages of respondents who regard their fertility as completed | | | Percentages of respondents who desire more children | | |
|---|---|---|---|---|---|---|
| | Total | White | Negro | Total | White | Negro |
| 0–2 | 36.2 | 35.4 | 44.0 | 27.1 | 25.7 | 41.0 |
| 3 | 23.6 | 24.5 | 14.8 | 28.8 | 29.2 | 24.3 |
| 4 | 40.3 | 40.2 | 41.2 | 44.2 | 45.0 | 34.8 |

* Data from 13, Table 7.

TABLE 7.

*Percentages (by age and color of respondent) of women who approved of fertility control (including the rhythm method) and were using or expected to use some form of contraceptive, as shown by a 1965 study.**

| Respondents | Percentages by age group | | | |
|---|---|---|---|---|
| | 20–24 yr | 25–29 yr | 30–34 yr | 35–39 yr |
| *Approved of fertility control* | | | | |
| White | 95 | 97 | 95 | 93 |
| Nonwhite | 92 | 93 | 90 | 87 |
| *Were using or expected to use contraceptives* | | | | |
| White | 94 | 93 | 88 | 84 |
| Nonwhite | 96 | 90 | 84 | 71 |

* Data from 17a, Tables 8 and 14.

first coming to the clinic, an astonishingly high retention rate for any procedure requiring continuous self-medication.[26]

A carefully planned program which introduced the first subsidized services in New Orleans, begun in 1967, has already enrolled nearly two-thirds of the target population, three-fourths of whom had not practiced birth control or had used nonprescription methods before attending the clinic. When given a genuine choice, 82 percent chose either pills or IUD's, while only 17 percent selected a nonprescription method.[27] In the rural Louisiana parish where this program was first tested the birth rate among the indigent decreased by 32 percent in the first year after the clinic was opened, as compared to a decrease of only 6 percent in four surrounding control counties where no organized family planning services were available. The illegitimacy ratio in the county in question dropped from 172 per 1000 live births in 1966 to 121 in 1967, as compared to an increase in the control counties from 162 to 184.[28]

TABLE 8.

*Relation of poverty to size of family, as shown by a 1966 study.**

| Number of children | All U.S. families (in thousands) | The poor | | The poor and near-poor | |
|---|---|---|---|---|---|
| | | Number of families (in thousands) | Percentage of all U.S. families | Number of families (in thousands) | Percentage of all U.S. families |
| 1 | 9,081 | 843 | 9.3 | 1,276 | 14.1 |
| 2 | 8,491 | 869 | 10.2 | 1,323 | 15.6 |
| 3 | 5,416 | 694 | 12.8 | 1,152 | 21.3 |
| Total for parity 1–3 | 22,988 | 2,406 | 10.5 | 3,751 | 16.3 |
| 4 | 2,923 | 543 | 18.6 | 904 | 30.9 |
| 5 | 1,396 | 387 | 27.7 | 593 | 42.5 |
| 6 or more | 1,286 | 541 | 42.1 | 747 | 58.1 |
| Total for parity 4+ | 5,605 | 1,471 | 26.2 | 2,244 | 40.0 |

* Data from 21, Table 4.

## Five million women

Judith Blake challenges the estimate that there are 5 million poor and near-poor women who comprise the approximate population in need of subsidized family planning services. This estimate has been arrived at independently by Campbell[20] and the Planned Parenthood Federation Research Department,[19] on the basis of Census Bureau tabulations of the characteristics of the poor and near-poor.[17] Campbell estimated a total of 4.6 million, while Planned Parenthood estimated 5.3 million. The difference stems from the use of slightly different assumptions in analyzing the data available for obtaining a "need" figure which defines all women who are (i) poor or near-poor; (ii) not currently pregnant or wanting to become pregnant; (iii) fecund; and (iv) exposed to risk of pregnancy. The differences in the assumptions and results are not regarded as significant at this point, when fewer than 1 million low-income patients are reportedly receiving family planning services.

There exists, of course, no data base from which to define precisely women who have the characteristics listed above. Both estimates have been presented as approximations which reasonably interpret available information. It is important to note that 5 million represents a residual number of potential patients at any given time, after subtraction, from the total of about 8 million poor and near-poor women aged 15 to 44, of an estimated number of those who are sterile, those who are pregnant or seeking to become pregnant (allowance being made for the fact that poor couples say they want three children, on the average), and those who are not exposed to the risk of pregnancy[20] (Table 3). The estimate does involve the policy assumption that all others should have available competent medical advice on regulating fertility—even if they choose to practice the rhythm method, or if they are less than normally fecund, or if they have sexual relations infrequently—since such advice will tend to make their family planning practice more effective. Whether or not all 5 million women would avail themselves of the opportunity remains to be seen. Until the poor are offered a genuine choice, there is no way to determine how many would actually prefer nonmedical methods. Nor is there any way to judge whether low-income Catholics will voluntarily choose methods officially proscribed by their Church to a degree equaling or possibly exceeding the 53 percent of all Catholics who reported in

1965 that they have already used methods other than the rhythm method.[23]

It is interesting to note that Judith Blake does *not* cite the one factor which might be a significant limitation on these estimates—namely, the proportion of low-income women who have been able to secure competent guidance in fertility control from private physicians. There exists no adequate information on this question, perhaps because most researchers have been singularly uninterested in the *processes* through which fertility control techniques are diffused. Fragmentary data from several state Medicaid programs suggest that, at most, the proportion of poor and near-poor persons receiving family planning services from private physicians is no higher than 10 percent of the population in need.

In sum, then, the 5-million estimate has been presented as a reasonable approximation, based on the inadequate data that are available, of those who need subsidized family planning services and for whom wise social policy would attempt to develop programs.

## Population policy

Judith Blake's article, hopefully, will stimulate responsible and dispassionate study and discussion of population policy in the United States. The scholarly community has thus far given little attention to this question, leaving the discussion largely to polemicists.

Her message is loud and clear: Our society should not waste its resources on family planning for the poor but should seek ways to restructure the family, reconsider male and female sexual roles,[29] and develop satisfying nonfamilial roles for women, if it is to achieve population stability in the long run. We regard the first part of this proposition as erroneous and misleading. The second part, however, needs thoughtful examination as to its feasibility and the costs and benefits to society. The development of voluntary family planning in the immediate future is in no way antithetical to such realistic consideration of population policy for the long run.

It would be useful if Judith Blake were to develop proposals for specific programs to advance the objective of encouraging women to seek satisfaction in careers outside the home. It would be particularly interesting to see whether those programs do not subsume, as a necessary first step, the extension of effective fertility control measures to all women who want and need them—which we believe is the immediate objective of federal policy on family planning.

## References and Notes

1. President's Committee on Population and Family Planning, *Population and Family Planning—The Transition from Concern to Action* (Government Printing Office, Washington, D.C., (1968), pp. 15–16, 37–38.
2. J. Blake, *Science* 164, 522 (1969).
3. L. B. Johnson, Message to Congress on Domestic Health and Education, 1 March 1966.
4. J. W. Gardner, Statement of Policy of the Department of Health, Education and Welfare on Family Planning and Population Programs, 24 January 1966.
5. ———, Memorandum to Heads of Operating Agencies on Family Planning Policy, 31 January 1968.
6. "The Growth of U.S. Population," *Nat. Acad. Sci. Nat. Res. Counc. Publ. 1279* (1965), p. 6.
7. O. Harkavy, F. S. Jaffe, S. M. Wishik, "Implementing DHEW Policy on Family Planning and Population—A Consultant's Report," *Dept. Health Educ. Welfare Publ.* (1967) (available from the U.S. Department of Health, Education and Welfare), pp. 23–24.
8. Calculation of data on unwanted births from the 1965 National Fertility Study yields an estimate of an annual average of about 850,000 unwanted births among all classes in the period 1960–65 [see F. S. Jaffe and A. F. Guttmacher, *Demography* 5, 910 (1968)]. This figure must be regarded, for methodological reasons, as a minimum estimate of unwanted births. It amounts to about 40 percent of the excess of births over deaths in the 6-year period under study. Prevention of unwanted births among the poor and near-poor could have reduced the overall excess of births over deaths by slightly more than 20 percent, while prevention of unwanted births among the non-poor could have reduced it by slightly less than 20 percent. These approximations show the orders of magnitude of what might be expected from the extension of modern family planning to the poor and near-poor and from improved efficiency of fertility

control for all Americans. They do not, of course, add up to a zero rate of growth, but they appear to offer the promise of more immediate progress toward reduced growth rates than any other proposed or currently feasible program of equivalent cost (or, for that matter, any cost).

9. See J. Rock, *The Time Has Come* (Knopf, New York, 1963), chap. 11; A. F. Guttmacher, *Babies by Choice or by Chance* (Doubleday, New York, 1959), chap. 8.

10. We are indebted to Dorothy Nortman of the Population Council for this observation.

11. R. Freedman, P. K. Whelpton, A. A. Campbell, *Family Planning, Sterility and Population Growth* (McGraw-Hill, New York, 1959), pp. 221, 224.

12. P. K. Whelpton, A. A. Campbell, J. E. Patterson, *Fertility and Family Planning in the United States* (Princeton Univ. Press, Princeton, N.J., 1966), pp. 37, 41, 38, 364, 281.

13. N. B. Ryder and C. F. Westoff, "Relationships among intended, expected, desired and ideal family size: United States, 1965," *Population Res.* (March 1969) (available from the Center for Population Research, National Institute of Child Health and Human Development, Washington, D.C.). Their full statement of the limitations of the "ideal" question follows: "We asked the question to correspond exactly with the wording employed in many previous inquiries, *despite profound reservations about its usefulness.* The question can be interpreted as the respondent's opinion as to what she considers to be ideal for the average American family, or what the average American family considers ideal for themselves. In the second place, the wording prompts the further question, 'Ideal for whom?' That might be answered from the standpoint of the respondent, or of the average American family, or even of the total population—since it must face the consequences of the behavior of the 'average American family.' Thirdly, the question calls for a statistical judgment of the characteristics of the average American family, a judgment probably beyond the reach of most respondents and varying in relation to their own characteristics. In the fourth place, there is ambiguity about the scope of the term 'ideal': Does it mean the ideal parity considering the circumstances as well? Finally, there would seem to be a substantial risk with a question so worded that the respondent thinks she is being asked about the actual average number of children in an American family. In our opinion, the *sole justification for including this question in our inquiry is to explore statistically*

*the validity of this very common but very dubious question* [emphasis added]."

14. Convergence is also demonstrated when actual behavior is examined, rather than attitudes. See C. F. Westoff and N. B. Ryder, in *Fertility and Family Planning: A World View*, S. J. Behrman, L. Corsa, Jr., R. Freedman, Eds. (Univ. of Michigan Press, Ann Arbor, 1969), Tables 13 and 15. In 1960 and 1965, by any measure of socioeconomic status, three-fourths to five-sixths of the lowest income groups had used or expected to use some form of fertility control (including relatively ineffective ones). As would be expected of a practice which has diffused down through the class structure, there is a lower level of practice in the lowest groups (which may also be a function of less availability of services).

15. N. B. Ryder and C. F. Westoff, "Fertility planning status of American women, 1965," paper presented before the Population Association of America, April 1968.

16. Unpublished data from the 1965 National Fertility Study, made available by C. F. Westoff.

17. Special tabulation by the Census Bureau of the characteristics of women living in poverty and near-poverty in March 1966.

17a. C. F. Westoff and N. B. Ryder, in *Fertility and Family Planning: A World View*, S. J. Behrman, L. Corsa, Jr., R. Freedman, Eds. (Univ. of Michigan Press, Ann Arbor, 1969), p. 394.

18. Blake has much to say about the responses of white men and women of lower education and economic status to a poll question. "Do you think birth control pills should be made available free to all women on relief who are of childbearing age?" She ignores the ambiguity of the question, which would appear to require of the respondents judgment on at least four issues: (i) pills; (ii) the public assistance system ("welfare handouts"); (iii) the morals of women on public assistance; and (iv) the distribution of pills without medical supervision. If we were asked the question in this form, our answer would probably also be in the negative: "Not unless the distribution was under medical supervision and the assistance recipient wanted pills."

19. G. Varky, F. S. Jaffe, S. Polgar, R. Lincoln, *Five Million Women—Who's Who Among Americans in Need of Subsidized Family Planning Services* (Planned Parenthood–World Population, New York, 1967), a publication based on the Census Bureau tabulation cited in 17.

20. A. A. Campbell, *J. Marriage and the Family* 30, 236 (1968).

21. M. Orshansky, "The shape of poverty in 1966," *Soc. Security Bull.* (March 1968).
22. F. S. Jaffe and A. F. Guttmacher, *Demography* 5, 910 (1968).
23. C. F. Westoff and N. B. Ryder, "United States: Methods of Fertility Control, 1955, 1960 and 1965," *Studies in Family Planning, No. 17* (1967), p. 2; Table 3.
24. C. Tietze, in *Manual of Contraceptive Practice*, M. S. Calderone, Ed. (Williams and Wilkins, Baltimore, 1964), Tables 3 and 4.
25. See, for example, A. F. Yerby, *Amer. J. Public Health Nat. Health* 56, 5 (1966).
26. R. Frank and C. Tietze, *Amer. J. Obstet. Gynecol.* 93, 122 (1 Sept. 1965). See also S. Polgar and W. B. Cowles, Eds., "Public Health Programs in Family Planning," supplement to *Amer. J. Public Health Nat. Health* 56 (Jan. 1966); S. Polgar, "U.S.: The PPFA Mobile Service Project in New York City," *Studies in Family Planning, No. 15* (1966); D. J. Bogue, "U.S.: The Chicago Fertility Control Studies," *ibid.*; G. W. Perkin, "A family planning unit for your hospital?" *Hosp. Practice* 2, 64 (May 1967).
27. J. D. Beasley, *Family Planning Perspectives* 1, 2 (Spring 1969).
28. ——— and V. W. Parrish, "Epidemiology and prevention of illegitimate births in the rural South," paper presented before the American Public Health Association, November 1968.
29. We confess that we do not comprehend how a society which has as much difficulty as Blake alleges ours does with regard to contraceptives for unmarried persons engaging in heterosexual activities can be expected to legitimate sexual deviancy as an antinatalist measure.

## A REPLY FROM JUDITH BLAKE

In their article Harkavy, Jaffe, and Wishik are, in effect, defending their own effort to influence the federal government regarding population policy. Harkavy and Jaffe are executives with organizations that promote "family planning" (the Ford Foundation and Planned Parenthood), and Wishik is a director of a university-based family planning program. Their past influence is not only directly visible in their consultants' report criticizing HEW's population program for not pushing family planning more aggressively, but it is indirectly evident in the authors' presence (one, two, or all) on committees and hearings concerning population, each appearing to give "independent" but somehow unanimous advice to government agencies, Congress, and the President.[1] My questioning of the alleged facts and logic supporting their advice has led them to charge me with statements I never made, nonuse of data they have carelessly overlooked in my article, and failure to include unpublished materials to which I had no access. In their anxiety to discredit my analysis, they even deny their own erstwhile goal of population control.

They begin by using over 1000 words to accuse me of claiming that there is "a consensus on U.S. population stability," or "zero population growth," as a goal. I made no such claim. I said that "action to *limit* population growth is virtually unchallenged as an official national goal," a statement implying neither zero increase nor popular consensus. If anyone doubts that population *limitation* is endorsed, and endorsed officially, he may consult President Johnson, John W. Gardner, the Republican National Platform and, recently, Senator Tydings' 8 May 1969 speech introducing S. 2108.[2] These endorsements have gone unchallenged—that is, until Harkavy *et al.* suddenly disavowed them.

Although every major proposal for federally supported family planning is phrased in terms of the need to stem population growth, my three critics now say that "the federal program has been advanced, not for population control, but to improve health and reduce the impact of poverty and deprivation." This constitutes the first explicit admission by family planning leaders that their interest in contraception is not to be equated in any way with population "planning," "control," or "policy." If this is really their view, it contradicts their past role in this field.

If the federal program is to improve health and reduce poverty, as my critics now claim, is it wanted and needed by the prospective recipients? The documents I criticized claim that the poor prefer fewer or no more children than the well-to-do, but the facts I cited show that this claim is not true and that it exaggerates the demand for birth-control services among the disadvantaged. This evidence comes principally from national polls, but it comes *also* from the only two national fertility surveys (1955 and 1960) available in print, which my critics falsely say I "ignored." In trying further to discredit the evidence, the authors' unfamiliarity with the literature leads them to cite criticisms of a question (the ideal size for the average American family) which was not asked on the polls I used. They also darkly impugn respondents' own statements of ideal family size. They prefer number of children "wanted" or "desired." Yet the National Fertility Study of 1965 shows, for whites, very close agreement among ideal, desired, and intended family size: the average "ideal" is 3.24, "desired" is 3.29, and "intended" is 3.16.[3] In further misunderstanding of the surveys the authors make the amazing statement that "almost all low-income parents" have an "expressed preference for less than four children." They confuse an *average* with a *proportion*. Actually, although the average preference is for fewer than four, approximately 40 percent of the women with incomes "under $3000" said in 1960 that they wanted four or more children.[4] As for the categorical claim that Negro couples desire smaller families than do white couples, Table 1 of the authors' own article shows that this claim is true only for well-educated Negroes. Poorly educated ones want more children than comparable whites, except for white Catholics.

Continuing to dispute the evidence, the authors object to opinion polls as against "in-depth" studies on birth control. The "in-depth" question from the 1965 study that they claim I ignored (the results were, in fact, not published) runs as follows:[5] "Most married couples do something to limit the number of pregnancies they will have. In general, would you say you are *for* this or *against* this?" If this question is superior, why are the results, tabulated by educational level (Table 2 of the Harkavy article), essentially the same as the polling data? Both sources show the least approval of birth control among respondents with only a grade school education.

Defending their idea of a great "need" for government assistance in family planning, Harkavy *et al.* turn to the overworked and ambiguous concept of "excess fertility." The concept, as applied to couples, was carefully defined when first used in the 1960 Growth of American Families Study. It was concerned with whether the respondents "really wanted" another child at the time of the last conception. If the respondent said that she, her husband, or both had not wanted another child, this was defined as "excess fertility." But the authors of the 1960 study emphasize that in 50 percent of such cases *one* spouse "really wanted" another child. The original authors also caution that "many wives who said that they had not 'really wanted' another child before the last conception also said . . . that if they could have just the number they wanted and then stop, they would have the same number they had and even more."[5] As defined in the actual studies, "excess fertility" obviously cannot be equated with "unwanted" pregnancies; yet such an equation has been a principal argument favoring a federal program.

The estimate of the five million women who "want" and "need" contraception is grossly overstated. It includes sterile women, birth control users, objectors, and women seldom or never having intercourse. Our reestimate, correcting for the errors just mentioned, shows that the number is *substantially fewer than two million*. This estimate does not imply that the women need federal services, but merely that they need contraception.

Harkavy and his colleagues are right that family planning for the poor is not a means of population control. It is not even a "first step" to that goal. But until now this has not been clear; the government has been sold a risky program as part of a population-control package. This program invites charges of genocide, dissemination of dangerous drugs, and subversion of moral standards—ironically, it now appears, for the purpose of "health" and a dubious welfare goal. The insensitivity to such risks, as well as the paradoxical confusion of goals, is exemplified by Senator Gruening's support of the statement that[6] ". . . whatever might be the long-range adverse effects of the pill . . . women prefer to take their chances. They would risk any possible ill effect rather than become pregnant."

## References and Notes

1. The principal documents under discussion are: O. Harkavy, F. S. Jaffe, and S. M. Wishik, *Implementing DHEW Policy on Family Planning and Population* (1967, mimeographed; available from the Ford Foundation, New York); *Report of the President's Committee on Population and Family Planning: The Transition from Concern to Action* (Government Printing Office, Washington, D.C., 1968); and *Hearings on S. 1676, U.S. Senate Subcommittee on Foreign Aid Expenditures* (17 volumes of testimony concerning "the population crisis").

2. Statement by President Johnson at the 20th anniversary of the United Nations at San Francisco, 25 June 1965, and swearing-in ceremony of John W. Gardner as Secretary of Health, Education, and Welfare, 18 Aug. 1965 [*Congr. Rec.* 113, 6494 (14 Mar. 1967)]. The complete text of the 1968 Republican platform appears in *Congr. Quart.*, 9 Aug. 1968; the reference to population is on p. 213. "Family planning: A basic human right," speech of Senator Joseph P. Tydings, *Congr. Rec.* 115, S. 4848 (8 May 1969).

3. N. B. Ryder and C. F. Westoff, "Relationships Among Intended, Expected, Desired, and Ideal Family Size: United States, 1965." An occasional paper published by the Center for Population Research, National Institute of Child Health and Human Development, March 1969, no pagination.

4. Tabulation from basic data cards of the 1960 study.

5. From the interview schedule used in the 1965 National Fertility Study. Kindly supplied to me by Charles F. Westoff of Princeton University, p. 236.

6. *Hearings on S. 1676, U.S. Senate Subcommittee on Foreign Aid Expenditures, 90th Congress, 1st session* (2 Nov. 1967), p. 62.

# 23. *Population Policies and Ethical Acceptability*

## ARTHUR J. DYCK

Population experts and national governments are becoming increasingly alarmed by population growth rates throughout the world, and they are calling for substantial decreases in birth rates. Active government concern with high birth rates has greatly accelerated during the past decade. Governmental programs have largely concentrated on voluntary family planning. Bolstered by the development of the loop and the pill, efforts to provide contraceptives and information concerning their use to as many people as possible, have markedly escalated.[1]

Governments and voluntary organizations can offer two very cogent justifications for such family planning programs. First, the distribution of contraceptives assists couples to have only the children they want. Hence, providing contraceptives and contraceptive information can quite properly be viewed as an extension of human freedom, and government support of family planning programs can be seen as an attempt to help those who are ignorant about contraceptives and their use and those who have difficulty obtaining them. Second, family planning programs enhance the health of individuals, particularly the health of mothers and, through rational spacing of births, the development, health, and welfare of children as well.

Many of those who have argued for family planning programs have pictured them as a means of curtailing rapid population growth.[2] Some have even argued that ready availability and clear knowledge of modern contraceptives would, in themselves, motivate people to reduce the size of their families.[3] Thus, for some family planning programs, the expectation is that they will reduce birth rates and will, therefore, contribute to the solution of problems associated with rapid rates of population increase.

Although few would dispute that family planning programs are of actual and potential benefit to individual couples and to the welfare of their children, this approach has been challenged as inadequate and largely irrelevant for the purpose of bringing down birth rates. Four arguments have been advanced against exclusive reliance upon family planning programs as an instrument of population policy.

First, some studies indicate that the introduction and acceptance of contraceptive practices have had little effect upon birth rates.[4] Second, the effect of family planning programs depends upon the family-size ideals of the culture or region into which they are introduced. Some demographers have argued that, given the family-size ideals currently prevailing, one can reduce birth rates by no more than twenty per cent in the less developed countries of the world, a reduction that would still leave these countries with growth rates high enough to double their populations every generation.[5] Such a doubling rate constitutes an increase in population rapid enough to augment or provoke economic difficulties and to impede the provision of health, education, and welfare services by the governments of these countries.

A third and quite different argument has been advanced against family planning programs as instruments of government population policy. We cannot, so this argument runs, leave the decisions of social issues to individual couples. We cannot expect couples, each pursuing their own interests, to satisfy the interests or needs of society.[6]

Still a fourth consideration has arisen. Increasingly, it is said that family planning programs are not the sole way in which governments are involved in influencing the costs and benefits of having children.[7] On the one hand, child labor laws and compulsory education have the effect of increasing the cost of having children. On the other hand, tax deductions, maternity benefits, baby bonuses, and aid to dependent children subsidize parenthood and reduce its costs.

Given these doubts concerning the efficacy of family planning as a means of implementing population policy and given also the growing realization that governments already have programs that go beyond the mere provision of contraceptives, it is not surprising to find a proliferation of population proposals that augment or supplant reliance upon family planning programs.[8]

Population policy proposals advocate ways of coping with problems associated with rapid population growth. Defining the problematic character of rapid population growth is an assessment of what is "wrong with the world," or "what is bad for people." Without a definition of what is harmful about a given demographic situation and specificity about the benefits that would follow from a given policy to change that situation, a policy recommendation would lack legitimation. Population policy proposals and population analyses alike make judgments about what is ethically acceptable and unacceptable. In assessing any given population policy recommendation, therefore, it is appropriate to ask not only whether it is likely to work and likely to be adopted, but also whether it is ethically acceptable, that is, whether it is a policy we *ought* to adopt.[9]

The purpose of this essay is to evaluate the ethical acceptability of population policy proposals and, at the same time, to suggest a framework for making such evaluations.

### The meaning of ethical acceptability

I shall use "ethical acceptability" in two ways. First, I shall use it as a normative criterion. One can ask of any given population policy whether it corresponds to what people *ought* to value and whether it resolves conflicts of value in the way that these *ought* to be resolved. These are questions for normative ethics, questions as to what things are right or wrong, good or bad. Among the most universally recognizable normative criteria identified by ethicists are freedom, distributive justice, veracity, and the calculation of benefits and harms, including at one extreme, harms that threaten survival.[10]

But normative assessments of the rightness or wrongness of given population policy proposals may differ. Where disagreements exist, it is necessary to specify criteria for adjudicating moral disputes. This brings us to the second meaning of "ethical acceptability." It can refer to what is specified by meta-ethical criteria, i.e., criteria that provide us with reasons, or a set of procedures, for preferring one moral judgment over another.

There is growing agreement among ethicists that the rationality of moral claims is to be judged by the extent to which they satisfy the following criteria: knowledge of facts, vivid imagination of how others are affected by our actions, and impartiality with respect to both our interests and our passions, so that what obtains for one person obtains for another and for ourselves as well. These criteria are derived from an analysis of moral discourse and describe the kinds of considerations that arise in the processes of formulating or reformulating our own moral judgments, and of attempting to resolve disputes.[11] They are embodied in our social and institutional practices, and appear in classical attempts to describe an ideal moral judge.[12]

Using these normative and meta-ethical criteria, I wish to explore the ethical acceptability of some major population policy proposals.

### Questions of distributive justice

The ethical acceptability of any population policy will certainly hinge on the relation it bears to distributive justice. Distributive justice refers to the way in which goods and benefits are to be divided. As used here, achieving a just distribution of goods is governed by two principles: each person participating in a practice or affected by it has an equal right to the most extensive liberty compatible with a like liberty for all, and, secondly, inequalities are justifiable only where it is reasonable to expect that they will work out for everyone's advantage and provided that the positions and offices to which they attach or from which they may be gained are open to all.[13]

Distributive justice is a strongly-held value. Gross inequalities with respect to one's share in a society's goods or one's opportunity to change a disadvantageous position, as in slavery, can prompt people to risk death. It is in the interest of society as well as individuals to satisfy the principles of distributive justice.

Population policy proposals that advocate the use of positive or negative incentives are very directly involved in questions of distributive justice. Positive incentives refer to a variety of governmental inducements that take the form of direct payments of money, goods, or services to members of the target population in return for the desired practice of limiting births. Negative incentives refer to tax or welfare penalties exacted from couples that exceed a specified number of children.

Melvin Ketchel has described very well some of the forms of injustice that would be generally perpetrated by population policies resorting to positive and negative incentives:

> In underdeveloped countries practically no financial inducements to have children now exist to be reversed, and the imposition of further taxes upon the many poor people would depress their living standards even further and probably only succeed in raising the death rates. In developed countries people in higher economic groups could still afford to have as many children as they wished so the economic pinch associated with having children would be felt mainly by middle-class and lower-middle-class people, to whom the cost of having children, though somewhat eased by government economic favors, is still relatively high. In order to be effective, economic pressures would probably seriously affect the welfare of the children who were born in spite of the pressures. It seems to me that the same arguments apply to the use of economic pressures to lower the birth rate as are used to argue against the issue of suppressing illegitimacy by cutting off aid to dependent children. If children become a financial burden, there will be fewer of them, but those that are born will be punished by being deprived of precisely those economic advantages they should have, both for humanitarian reasons and for their growth and development into worthwhile citizens. The same objection applies to the use of financial reward to induce people not to have children because such programs would make the families with children the poorer families. A further objection to the use of economic pressures or rewards is that, since they would be primarily effective against certain economic groups, such methods are discriminatory.[14]

Among the variety of specific proposals to use positive incentives is one that advocates the provision of pensions for poor parents with fewer than N children as social security for their old age.[15] This particular policy recommendation is perhaps the least unjust of all the proposals involving incentives, especially in less-developed countries where pensions are presently largely unavailable, and parents depend upon their children for social security.

If social security were provided for those parents who had no more than some specified number of children, this provision would not severely, or directly, affect the lives of children in economic conditions where it is not normally possible to save money. Similarly, it would not discriminate much against parents who exceeded the specified number of children for they would, as has been the custom, look to their children for social security.

It is true that the whole society would bear the cost of this pension plan, but such a cost could be seen as enhancing the general welfare of the society, and, therefore as a mutually advantageous burden to bear, even though it would discriminate somewhat against the grown children of large families if they were required to support their parents as well as contribute to the cost of the pension plan.

In any estimate of the benefit/harm ratio that would obtain should some policy of positive or negative incentives be initiated, it is important to consider the way in which these benefits and harms are distributed, and to take care particularly not to discriminate against the poor. Generally, the chances that the children of the poor will get a good education, that they will survive to adulthood, and that they will have a good and productive life and thus realize the hopes for the future that the parents have invested in them are not nearly as good as for the children of people at higher incomes. Having only two or three children may, from the vantage point of the poor, look precarious.

In his book, *Children of Crisis,* Robert Coles asks whether many of us understand what a new child means to many of our poverty-stricken mothers, to the men in their lives, and to their other children. To further our understanding, he cites the following very dramatic and articulate account by a black mother:

> The worst of it is that they try to get you to plan your kids by the year; except they mean by the ten-year plan, one every ten years. The truth is they don't want you to have any, if they could help it. To me, having a baby inside me is the only time I'm really alive. I know I can make something, do something, no matter what color my skin is, and what names people call me. When the baby gets born I see him, and he's full of life, or she is, and I think to myself that it doesn't make any difference what happens later, at least now we've got a chance, or the baby does. You can see the little one grow and get larger and start doing things, and you feel there must be some hope, some chance that things will get better; because there it is, right before you, a real, live, growing baby. The children and their father feel it, too, just like I do. They feel the baby is a good sign, or at least he's some sign. If we didn't have that, what would be the difference from death? Even without children my life would still be bad—they're not going to give us what *they* have, the birth control people. They just want us to be a poor version of them only without our children and our faith in God and our tasty fried food, or anything.

> They'll tell you we are "neglectful"; we don't take proper care of the children. But that's a lie, because we do, until we can't any longer because the time has come for the street to claim them, to take them away and teach them what a poor nigger's life is like. I don't care what anyone says: I take the best care of my children. I scream the ten commandments at them every day, until one by one they learn them by heart—and believe me they don't forget them. (You can ask my minister if I'm not telling the truth.) It's when they leave for school, and start seeing the streets and everything, that's when there's the change; and by the time they're ten or so, it's all I can do to say anything, because I don't believe my own words, to be honest. I tell them, please to be good; but I know it's no use, not when they can't get a fair break, and there are the sheriffs down South and up here the policemen, ready to kick you for so much as breathing your feelings. So I turn my eyes on the little children, and keep on praying that one of them will grow up at the right second, when the schoolteachers have time to say hello and give him the lessons that he needs, and when they get rid of the building here and let us have a

place you can breathe in and not get bitten all the time, and when the men can find work—because *they* can't have children, and so they have to drink or get on drugs to find some happy moments, and some hope about things.[16]

This graphic description of the feelings of one poverty-stricken mother underlines the claims of distributive justice. Within any population policy, attention must be given to the problem of poverty. This is not so much because the poor have relatively high birth rates, but rather because the conditions under which it is just and rational to expect anyone to curtail family size, do not occur in dire poverty where infant mortality rates are high enough, educational opportunities scarce enough, job opportunities uncertain enough, to undermine the usual rationale for careful family planning. Alleviating conditions of poverty and delivering better health care to the poor must be part of any population policy, if it is to be just and effective.

Clearly, population policies that employ positive and negative incentives will create injustices by discriminating against the poor and by bringing about less advantageous economic conditions, or even poverty where penalties are severe, for the children of parents who are subject to penalties or who fail to gain rewards, unless special adjustments are made for these groups. Making these adjustments may reduce the effectiveness of incentive programs. In any event, there is no direct evidence that incentives reduce birth rates and, therefore, no assurance that any injustices that might be perpetrated through the use of incentives would be worth the price.

What about the use of compulsion to secure the goals of population policy? Compulsion, on the face of it, is the most predictable and rational way to achieve the exact birth rates considered desirable or necessary for a given nation. Thus the economist Kenneth Boulding has suggested marketable licenses to have children in whatever number that would ensure a zero growth rate, say 2.2 children per couple: the unit certificate might be the deci-child, and accumulation of ten of these units by purchase, inheritance, or gift, would permit a woman in maturity to have one legal child.[17] Another proposal by Melvin Ketchel advocates mass use by government of a fertility control agent that would lower fertility in the society by 5 to 75% less than the present birth rate, as needed.[18] Such a substance is now unknown but would, he believes, be available for field testing after 5 to 15 years of research work. It would be put in the water supply in urban areas and introduced by other methods elsewhere. Variants of compulsory sterilization, both temporary and permanent, and compulsory abortions have been proposed as well.[19]

Aside from the obvious technical and administrative difficulties of all of these proposals, especially in less developed countries, the effectiveness of a policy of compulsion is directly dependent upon its ethical acceptability. Any law can be disobeyed, or subverted, and the problem of punishing offending parents is especially acute. Could it be done, for example, without inflicting suffering upon innocent children? Obviously fines and jail sentences would be a hardship for children as well as parents no matter what provision society would make for the children. Compulsory sterilizations and abortions could be used to enforce a specific quota of children per couple but these methods are ethically unacceptable for reasons that I shall note later.

Compulsion, like incentives, discriminates against the poor. Restricting the very poor to two or three children would render their lives much less joyous, much less hopeful and much more precarious. In less developed countries, such restrictions for the poor mean economic losses in the form of reductions both in labor and in security for their old age.

Suppose, however, that the gross poverty in a given population group were virtually eliminated. What other ethical objections to the use of compulsion by the government of this group would remain? The most conspicuous argument against compulsion is that it is incompatible with the freedom to pursue our own happiness and forge our own destiny. How cogent is this argument?

## Questions of freedom

Freedom refers in part to the relative absence of government interference and compulsion concerning those actions that are not harmful to the public interest. It refers also to what we sometimes call equality of opportunity, that is, the opportunity to determine and change one's economic, social and political status within one's society. Freedom in both the senses I have specified is as strong a value as survival itself. People will risk death to obtain it for themselves, and others. They will not trade it off completely for some other actual or potential benefit. Moreover, freedom serves public interests as well as private ones. Some freedom of speech, for example, is an essential component of any society; it is a necessary prerequisite to social intercourse.

But freedom is not always incompatible with compulsion. One of the ways in which freedom is secured through compulsory regulations is illustrated by the laws governing traffic. Without such laws, it is difficult to imagine how the freedom to drive private automobiles in crowded areas could be maintained. Compulsory education also guarantees and enhances freedom. Compulsion also can prevent great harms both to individuals and to society. One example is compulsory vaccinations to prevent epidemics as well as individual suffering. In all of these examples, certain choices are taken away from the individual, and yet his total freedom is increased. Would compulsion in limiting the number of one's children be comparable to any of these examples? To answer this question, one must try to characterize more nearly the kind of decision involved in choosing whether or not to have children and how many to have.

In Plato's *Symposium,* Socrates notes that there are three ways in which people can try to satisfy their deep longing for immortality.[20] One way is to have children. Another is to commit a deed or deeds noble and heroic enough to receive the attention of one's community and become a part of its collective memory. A third way is that of scholarly pursuit and authorship. Each attempt to achieve immortality depends for its success upon the receptivity and support of one's community. Children, therefore, provide a deeply gratifying link to the human community and to the future. Decisions about how we will use our reproductive powers are decisions about our own future and about our own contribution to the future of the human community, about how one's life is to count, and how far its influence is to extend.

Sexuality is at once an expression of our individuality, and a gift that each of us receives from others, his parents most immediately, but also from the wider community. Indeed, it is a gift from the human species to the human species. We owe a debt of *gratitude* to these wellsprings of our unique genetic and social individuality for the very possibility of experiencing sexual pleasure, and for the considerable rewards of child-bearing and childrearing.

As those who have been chosen to live, we incur an awesome but joyous obligation to see to it that these gifts of life, sexual expression, procreation, and childrearing, have a future. Our obligation to the larger community is particularly vital insofar as each of us has unique genetic endowments and unique talents to offer and to perpetuate. No one else can give to the species what we bring to it. Failure to reproduce is both an individual and a communal act that requires a special justification if it is to be morally responsible. Individual decisions to refrain from having children of one's own are presumably easier to justify in times of rapid population growth.

If these are the values guiding our reproductive decisions, the very dignity and identity of the person as a moral being is at stake in any decision to use compulsion in controlling reproductive behavior. There are those who believe that the dignity and autonomy associated with reproductive decisions is a human right provided for in the American Constitution. As part of its successful effort to defeat the birth control laws of Connecticut in the Supreme Court, the Planned Parenthood Federation of America argued that these laws, by forcing couples to relinquish either their right to marital sex relations or their right to plan their families, constituted a deprivation of life and liberty without due process of law in violation of the Fourteenth Amendment.[21] Earlier Supreme Court decisions were cited affirming the right "to marry, establish a home and bring up children" as among "those privileges essential to the orderly pursuit of happiness by free men" under the Fourteenth Amendment.[22] In a "Declaration on Population" presented at the United Nations in 1967, thirty nations, including the United States, affirmed their belief "that the opportunity to decide the number and spacing of children is a basic human right" and "that family planning, by assuring greater opportunity to each person, frees man to attain his individual dignity and reach his full potential."[23]

But it is precisely on this point that the battle has been enjoined. Kingsley Davis has directly challenged the right of any person to determine for himself how many children he shall have, because, on his view, the assertion of such a right conflicts with society's need to keep the number of children at some specified level.[24] In this instance, Davis, like many others, sees a conflict between individual rights and interests on the one hand, and societal necessities and interests on the other.

But has Davis correctly characterized those interests we call human rights? I am convinced that it is not correct to think of a human right as something that can come into conflict with our public interests. To identify a human value as a right is to claim that something of value is *so* valuable and *so* precious that society has a stake in it. Consider, for example, freedom of speech, which is generally considered to be a human right.[25] Freedom of speech is essential to the formation of society itself, and to the establishment and maintenance of voluntary associations.

Rights imply duties.[26] When we say that freedom of speech is a right, we imply that it is our duty, and the duty of others, to see to it that freedom of expression is generally honored and protected. In claiming that freedom of speech is a right that society should protect, we are not claiming that every utterance ought to be sanctioned regardless of its consequences. Clearly, the right to free speech is not abrogated by considering it a crime falsely to cry "fire" in a crowded theatre.[27] The important thing, however, is that the interests in encouraging certain utterances, and in discouraging others, are both public and private. It is of benefit both to individuals and to society to encourage free expression generally, and to discourage certain forms of it under special circumstances.

This is true also of decisions regarding the nature and the number of one's children. In asserting that it is the right of individual couples to make such decisions voluntarily, we are positing both an obligation and an interest of society to see to it that this right is honored. At the same time, it is in the interest both of individuals and of society to curtail the extensive expression of this choice should the consequences of rapid growth rates become too oppressive or threatening. If, therefore, society is to avoid a conflict between two public interests, namely the interest in maintaining the quality of life, as against the interest in maintaining the right voluntarily to decide the number of one's children, every effort must be made to provide the information, materials, and conditions that will assist individuals voluntarily to limit their births for their own welfare and for the common good.

For the sake of argument, let us imagine a hypothetical situation in which a particular government had conscientiously implemented every possible and conceivable program designed to bring down its population growth rates and these had failed. As a result, this nation was required to attain nothing short of zero growth rates very quickly or face consequences that the government and its people feel they must avoid, even at great cost. Under these circumstances, compulsory measures to curb birth rates might be justified as a last resort.

What I wish to argue is that *not every compulsory measure can be justified even as a last resort*. The continuation of human life depends upon the exercise of our reproductive powers. To maintain a population at a replacement level requires slightly more than two children per couple at the death rates now prevailing in affluent nations. In principle, every couple in this world could be granted the right and privilege to have at least two children of their own.[28] The threat of overpopulation is not in itself a sufficient argument for singling out any given type of individual for compulsory sterilizations or compulsory abortions. The suggestion by Kingsley Davis[29] that abortions be required in cases where the child would be illegitimate not only dries up the most important source of children for sterile couples but also denies the unwed woman any right to a moral decision regarding either the fate of her fetus or the physical risks to which she will be subjected.

The right to exercise one's procreative powers is not identical with the right to have as many children as one wants through the use of those powers. In a situation of last resort, societies might very well decide to ration the number of children per family and try to provide some just means, like a lottery, for deciding who will be permitted to reproduce more than two children. This limits the right to choose how many children one will have but not the right to choose to have one or two children of one's own. Ketchel's proposal threatens this right since by the use of sterilants that reduce everyone's fertility some people are unvoluntarily rendered infertile. Of course, if Ketchel can prevent or offset such mishaps, his proposal could be used as a method of rationing.

The right to have a choice regarding the exercise of one's procreative powers and to be able to retain the capacity to procreate is as fundamental as the right to life.[30] Choosing to have a child of one's own is a choice as to one's own genetic continuity. One should be free to express one's gratitude to one's parents and to honor their desire for continuity in the human community; one should be free to seek a place in the memory of future generations. If our lives are to be deprived of any choices in establishing these links to the past and the future, we have lost a great deal of what life is all about and, indeed, we have lost the most predictable way known to us of extending our lives on this earth. Only very few people achieve immortality on earth in other ways. Compulsory, irreversible sterilization, I would contend, is not an ethically acceptable method of curbing birth rates.

Our draft system is often used as an analogy for justifying the use of compulsion to meet the needs of society. A just war, fought with just means, as a last resort, and in self-defense, would seem to justify conscription. But even in this situation, conscientious objectors are exempted from military service. Population policies should make a similar provision for those who cannot in good conscience submit to sterilization, or have an abortion, or stay for other reasons within a given rationing scheme. Presumably, where population problems are a clear and present danger, most people will wish to limit the number of their children. Precedents in human history are now well known; hunter-gather societies presently being studied in the deserts of Africa keep their populations at levels that guarantee them ample food and leisure for what they regard as the good life.[31] They have what modern societies will need to develop, namely, a very keen appreciation of the limits of their environment and of their own technical capacities to benefit from it without harming it.

Although I believe it is wise to sort out in advance what forms of compulsion would be least evil as last resorts, I consider any compulsory control of birth rates unjustifiable now and in the indefinite future for at least three reasons. First, famines and environmental deterioration are not exclusively a function of population growth rates; secondly, more practical and ethically acceptable alternatives to compulsion exist and have not yet been sufficiently tested; and thirdly, there are distinct benefits associated with small families which can be facilitated and the knowledge of which can be more widely disseminated.

### Questions of benefits and harms

Nutritional deficiencies and ecological imbalances will not be eradicated simply by reducing or even halting growth rates. To overcome these harms, agricultural development and pollution abatement will be necessary even if zero growth rates were to be immediately achieved throughout the world. The reasons for this are thoroughly discussed elsewhere.[32]

Rapid population growth rates do make it more difficult to feed people, to prevent environmental deterioration, and to maintain the quality of life in other ways.[33] Are there population policies that are more beneficial than harmful and which do not involve injustices or serious threats to human freedom? I wish to suggest some.

In a country like the United States, birth rates have been dropping for the past decade. We have time to see how much more can be done by extending voluntary family planning,[34] by providing the health services where needed to improve infant and maternal care, by educating people to the bad consequences of continued population growth for the nation as well as the individual family, and by improving educational and job opportunities for everyone, especially blacks, women, and other currently disadvantaged groups.

What about the situation in less developed countries? On

the basis of intensive research over a period of 7 years in the Punjab region of India, Gordon and Wyon hypothesize that people in such an area would be motivated to reduce their birth rates if: mortality rates for infants and children were sharply decreased; local social units were stimulated to measure their own population dynamics and to draw inferences from them concerning their own welfare and aspirations; and efficient methods of birth control were introduced.[35] Initiating these conditions would substantially increase the opportunities to reduce family size without undue fear, to assess more precisely how fertility affects families and their community, and to plan family size more effectively. Whether birth rates would be markedly lowered by bringing about these conditions alone would depend not simply upon the extent to which people in that region stand to benefit from a reduction in fertility but also upon the extent to which they actually perceive such benefits, both social and economic, and believe they are attainable.

The gathering and dissemination of information is, therefore, a crucial aspect of this proposal. Without accurate information, a sense of group responsibility cannot exist on a rational basis, and will have no perceptible dividend to the individual members. The proposal of Gordon and Wyon assumes that rational and purposeful behavior exists already to some degree and can be modified in the direction of lower fertility by certain modifications in the environment which make small families beneficial and more attainable.

Looking at the total ecological context within which population problems arise in the less developed countries, especially the factors of undernourishment, poverty, and lack of opportunity, some writers have suggested that nothing less than substantial technological, social, and economic changes would provide the conditions under which birth rates can be sufficiently reduced.[36] These changes include industrialization, urbanization, and modern market agriculture. In the demographic history of the West such an environment certainly has been associated with sharp declines in birth rates. Urbanization and industrialization, accompanied as they are by rising levels of literacy, better communications, increased economic opportunities, improved health care, lower infant mortality rates, higher status for women, and higher costs of bearing and rearing children, may be necessary to provide the incentives and the means to control population growth. In these terms, a population policy is an overall social and economic development policy.

These two policies would not violate any of our ethical criteria. They would enhance human freedom and encourage responsible community behavior. Indeed, they do not on the face of it violate any of the normative or meta-ethical criteria we have introduced in this essay. Both would increase the elements in the decision-making processes of individual couples that contribute to making the morally best decision. They would increase knowledge of the facts, stimulate the imagination of people concerning the effects of reproductive decisions, and encourage impartiality by fostering more universal loyalties that go beyond one's own interests and passions, and those of one's own group.

Gordon and Wyon's proposal has the advantage of introducing a minimum of disruption into a culture. It may, by the same token, be inadequate to induce the requisite behavior without further transformations of the social and economic lot of the people involved. Each of these ethically acceptable population policy proposals relies upon the voluntary decisions of individual couples. Several writers have contended recently that population policies *cannot* rely upon individual couples pursuing their own benefits to satisfy the needs of society.[87]

Garrett Hardin, for example, has argued that in matters of reproduction individual interests are definitely incompatible with collective interests and, therefore, population growth rates will have to be regulated by society.[38] How cogent is this argument?

His argument rests on what he calls "the tragedy of the commons." He notes that where a finite amount of grazing land is available to a number of sheepherders, each sheepherder will add sheep to his own flock, ultimately amassing a larger total number of sheep than the land will sustain. Although each individual sheepherder is aware of this fact, his immediate decisions are determined, nonetheless, by the profit he contemplates from adding another sheep to his flock. The knowledge that the commons will at some point be over-grazed, if everyone does this, does not suffice to deter him.

All of this seems reasonable enough when one is talking about sheep. But does the analogy extend to decisions of parents regarding the number of their children? Are the benefits of adding a child to our own families even roughly comparable with the benefits that come from enhancing our economic status?

In discussing freedom, I took the view that children are one means of extending our own selfhood into the future, of obtaining some kind of personal continuity. Children are also a way of replenishing the human community in which we hope to live on as a cherished memory. One child surviving into adulthood and having children of his own will suffice to maintain our own continuity. If our self-interest is extensive enough to embrace a concern for the continuation of society and of the species, two or three children will be enough.

However, in some circumstances we may feel disquieted about limiting ourselves to two or three children. When, for example, we live under conditions where infant mortality is high, we may very well want to have one or two extra children to be sure that two will survive us, or at least will live to have children of their own.

A second set of satisfactions and opportunities is associated with childbearing and childrearing. To the extent that having a child is a quest for the experience of rearing a child, it is not clear that relatively large families are best. For those satisfactions that come from the quality and frequency of one's contacts with one's own children, small families are preferable to large families. In very large families, the older children, not the parents, obtain most of the satisfactions of playing, of training, and of other forms of intimate interaction with the younger ones. Parental contacts with children in a large family are more likely to occur as disruptions for a busy mother than as opportunities for a show of affection and an exchange of ideas.

The benefits of bearing children are somewhat more ambiguous. At present there is no sure knowledge as to the strength of the drive to bear a child and what role this plays in the number that people have. The desire to have the experience of giving birth may be satisfied with the birth of one child. Some women, however, may covet the repetition of this kind of experience.[39] One psychoanalyst has expressed his amazement that the desire to bear children is so easily and quickly satiated.[40] Such satiation may result from the long period of dependency typical of human offspring as well as from the physical exertion, pain, and risks of childbirth itself. Whatever joys may be associated with our children, there are also lifelong concerns and anxieties.

Spacing the interval between births is good for both children and parents.[41] It enhances the intellectual development of children and the health and tranquillity of mothers. Even in societies where average family size is relatively large, spacing is extensively practiced.[42]

A fourth element in reproductive decisions, not present in decisions to add a profit-making sheep to our flock, has been observed by Rainwater.[43] In his intensive studies of working-class parents, he found that among those who had more children than they professed to want there were parents who reported that they had exceeded their own family-size ideals because they did not wish to be seen as selfish by their neighbors. This desire to be seen as an unselfish, kind, and public-spirited person could be used to bring about a wider acceptance of small family-size ideals. In view of the social problems generated by rapid rates of population growth, generous impulses can now best be exhibited by having only the children that society considers desirable or necessary.

Of course, Hardin might contend that the shepherd who adds to his flock is not deterred by the possibility that such additions will be seen as selfish by other shepherds using the same grazing land. In his case, however, *selfishness* and profit are linked; but in childbearing and childrearing, *unselfishness* is linked with benefit.

Where children serve to provide a substitute for a social security system or where they bring economic profit through their labor the situation begins more nearly to approximate the one depicted by Hardin. Nevertheless, the constraints that we have cited obtain even in the rural villages of less developed countries where children are often economic assets. There are some recent indications that in areas where agricultural productivity is increasing, birth rates are coming down.[44] Given the history of the demographic transition in developed nations, this should hardly come as a surprise. If adding children were like adding sheep to one's flock, however, birth rates should be going up. Surely Hardin's analogy is at best an uncertain one, and, at worst, inappropriate.[45]

Davis and Blake have also expressed the belief that individual couples will not voluntarily provide for the collective interests of society but will, given the strongly positive public attitude toward parenthood and especially toward motherhood, persist in having relatively large families.[46] Like Hardin, they do not take into account any of the four constraining factors we have cited.

One could argue, contrary to Davis and Blake, that we would do well to think of motherhood even more positively and to emphasize the tremendous responsibility entailed by it. If, much more than they now do, societies came to measure the quality of parenthood and motherhood by the achievements and the quality of life of children, the constraints of which we have spoken would operate even more effectively. If the concern of parents is for the best possible development of their children, then it is important to space children widely, to expose them as much as possible to the stimuli and warm support of parental interaction, and to be a model of unselfish restraint in keeping down the size of one's family. Responsible parenthood of this kind would include living in accord with whatever national fertility goals may become morally desirable or necessary to maintain the quality of human life, and guarantee a future for the human species.

Davis and Blake have stressed the need to improve the status of women by providing better and more extensive opportunities for employment, and for contributions to society in ways other than through childbearing and childrearing. Employment for women and opportunities to make a variety of contributions to the human community extend the freedom of women. Better and more extensive education for women also has the effect of contributing to the quality of mothering as well as to other forms of self-realization.

It would seem to be a shortsighted policy to attack the institution of motherhood and parenthood generally. Stressing the quality of mothering and parenthood and, at the same time, providing women with alternative forms of vocation and self-realization would appear to be a morally and demographically superior policy.

To claim, as I have, that individual couples and their children benefit in certain ways from keeping families small, is not to claim that these benefits will necessarily suffice to off-set other forces that presently keep many families large enough to maintain rates of population growth rapid enough to be troublesome to certain countries. I am maintaining, however, that to mitigate these latter forces, it is helpful to study, facilitate and make known the benefits associated with small families, and to expose some of the fallacies of assuming that individual couples who actively seek the satisfaction of childbearing and childrearing will generally benefit most by having relatively large families or even as many children as they can afford.

## *Veracity and meta-ethical criteria as practical guidelines*

There are certain practical guidelines that should be part of the formulation and implementation of population policies. Generally, these guidelines draw in a special way upon the norm of veracity, i.e. truth-telling, and promise-keeping, and the meta-ethical criteria specified earlier.

## *Knowing the facts*

An ideal program that would evoke the voluntary response of the people affected by it would make an honest case for the reproductive behavior called for in the policy. Parents need to know what benefits will accrue to them from limiting the number of their children. Evaluations of population policy recommendations, therefore, must include specific designations of what counts as a population problem and of what interests individuals and societies have in their children. Research is definitely needed to explore more fully the significance and meaning of children to parents in a wide variety of circumstances.

Often, in discussions of population policy, there are allusions to the use of propaganda. This word threatens to create a credibility gap. If by propaganda we mean trying to persuade people that a certain policy is in their interest, without giving them the facts that will allow them to decide whether it *is* actually in their interest, we violate the canons of veracity. Moreover, we do not satisfy the criterion of giving people as many of the facts as possible, and hence do not respect their potential to make a morally correct decision and to act upon it.

### Vividly imagining how others are affected by our actions

In some of the literature, there is a distinct elitist strain, implying that only certain people are in a position to formulate population policy and that the rest of mankind must be propagandized, won over by incentives, or compelled to act in ways considered to be desirable by the experts. In contrast to such elitism, ethically acceptable population policies should be based on sympathetic understanding of the conditions of life and of the aspirations of the people who will be affected. To guarantee this, many voices must be heard.

Black people in the United States are among those who are making apparent the value of wide and diverse participation in the planning process and thereby extending the actualization of democratic ideals and the humanization of social institutions. Ways must always be sought to assure that vivid images of how people live, and of what they feel and desire, will guide and shape the planners and their work.

### Universalizing loyalties: impartiality

To strive for impartiality or universal loyalties is to strive to discount the influence upon our moral judgments of particular interests and passions. For example, we demand of a judge that he not try his own son and that he disqualify himself in an antitrust suit involving a company in which he is a significant shareholder. Similarly, both our constitutional provisions for separate branches of government and our continuing quest for fair judicial process are attempts to minimize the effect of particular interests or passions by providing representation of diverse interests, while at the same time assuring equitable checks and balances.

Problems of rapid population growth make the need for impartiality, our third meta-ethical criterion, concretely explicit. Though survival values within our species are strong and tenacious, they are usually individualized and tied to relatively small interest groups representing one's social, ethnic, and national identity. For the survival of such groups many would, under certain circumstances, make sacrifices and even die. But population policies, though they must attend to the needs and interests of particular regions and population groups, should endeavor to ascertain and foster the best interests of the entire human species in its total ecological setting, a task that embraces attention to other species and material resources as well. The goals of population policies go beyond the boundaries our societal and national interests set for us.

In defining these goals, population policies would fail utterly to improve the human condition and enlist its deepest loyalties, were they to diminish, rather than augment, the extent to which beneficence, freedom, distributive justice, and veracity are realized on the earth. These are not moral luxuries: our survival, and the worth of that survival, depend upon their effective implementation. As the demographer Ansley Coale has so sagely observed, "preoccupation with population growth should not serve to justify measures more dangerous or of higher social cost than population growth itself."[47] It would be the ultimate irony of history if through our population policies we should lose precisely what we seek to save, namely, human rights and welfare.

### Footnotes

[1] See, for example, Bernard Berelson, *et alia* (eds.), *Family Planning and Population Programs*. Chicago: University of Chicago, 1966, Bernard Berelson (ed.), *Family Planning Programs: An International Survey*. New York: Basic Books, 1969, and Dorothy Nortman, "Population and Family Planning Programs: A Fact Book," *Reports on Population/Family Planning* (Population Council), December 1969.

[2] See the essays by Harvey Leibenstein, T. Paul Schultz, and J. D. Wray in *Rapid Population Growth: Some Consequences and Some Public Policy Implications* (Baltimore: Johns Hopkins Press, 1971).

[3] A staunch proponent of this view is Donald J. Bogue. For his most complete statement of it, see *Principles of Demography*. New York: John Wiley and Sons, 1966, Chapter 20.

[4] See, for example, John C. Cobb, Harry M. Raulet, and Paul Harper, "An I.U.D. Field Trial in Lulliani, West Pakistan" (paper presented at the American Public Health Association), October 21, 1965, and John B. Wyon and John E. Gordon, "The Khanna Study," *Harvard Medical Alumni Bulletin* 41 (1967), 24–28.

[5] See Harvey Leibenstein, "Population Growth and the Development of Underdeveloped Countries," *Harvard Medical Alumni Bulletin* 41 (1969), 29–33.

[6] See, for example, Kingsley Davis, "Population Policy: Will Current Programs Succeed?" *Science* 158 (1967), 730–739, and Garrett Hardin, "The Tragedy of the Commons," *Science* 162 (1969), 1243–1248.

[7] An extensive discussion of this appears in the chapter on population policy in Vol. I of the two volume study by the National Academy of Sciences of the "Consequences of Population Growth and Their Policy Implications."

[8] See Bernard Berelson, "Beyond Family Planning," *Studies in Family Planning* 38 (1969), 1–16, for an extensive review and evaluation of 29 such proposals.

[9] *Ibid.* In this essay, Berelson delineates ethical acceptability as one of six criteria by means of which he evaluates population policy proposals. Berelson does not restrict ethical acceptability to its normative meaning but uses it in a purely descriptive way by asking whether a given proposal is congruent with the values of those who will be affected whatever those values may be.

[10] See W. D. Ross, *The Right and the Good*. Clarendon, Oxford, 1930, for a more complete list, one which is widely used and referred to among professional ethicists. Ross calls these norms *"prima facie* duties." *Prima facie* duties specify recognizable right and wrong—making characteristics of actions. Specific actions or policies will be right or wrong insofar as they exhibit one or the other of these characteristics. For example, the act of telling a lie to save a friend violates the *prima facie* duty of truth-telling but satisfies the *prima facie* duty of not harming others. To decide the rightness or wrongness of particular actions or policies will usually involve a process of weighing conflicting moral claims upon us.

The normative criteria I have specified are to be understood as *prima facie* claims.

[11] See, for example, Kurt Baier, *The Moral Point of View*. Ithaca: Cornell University, 1958, Richard B. Brandt, *Ethical Theory*. Englewood Cliffs: Prentice-Hall, 1959, Roderick Firth, "Ethical Absolutism and the Ideal Observer," *Philosophy and Phenomenological Research* 12 (1952), 317–345, William Frankena, *Ethics*. Englewood Cliffs: Prentice-Hall, 1963, R. M. Hare, *Freedom and Reason*. Clarendon: Oxford, 1963, and Maurice Mandelbaum, *The Phenomenology of Moral Experience*. Glencoe: The Free Press, 1955.

[12] See Roderick Firth, *ibid*.

[13] This formulation appears in John Rawls, "Justice as Fairness," *The Philosophical Review* LXVII (1958), 164–194.

[14] Melvin M. Ketchel, "Fertility Control Agents as a Possible Solution to the World Population Problem," *Perspectives in Biology and Medicine* 11 (1968), 687–703.

[15] See, for example, Goran Ohlin, *Population Control and Economic Development*, Development Centre of the Organization for Economic Co-operation and Development (1967), 104, T. J. Samuel, "The Strengthening of the Motivation for Family Limitation in India," *The Journal of Family Welfare* 13 (1966), 12–14, and Joseph Spengler, "Population Problem: In Search of a Solution," *Science* 166 (Dec. 5, 1969).

[16] Robert Coles, *Children of Crisis*. Boston: Atlantic-Little Brown, 1964, 368–369.

[17] Kenneth Boulding, *The Meaning of The Twentieth Century: The Great Transition*. New York: Harper and Row, 196, 135–136.

[18] Melvin Ketchel, *op. cit.*

[19] Kingsley Davis, "Population Policy: Will Current Programs Succeed?" *Science* 158 (1967), 730–739, and Paul Ehrlich, *The Population Bomb*. New York: Ballantine, 1968.

[20] B. Jowett (tr.), *The Dialogues of Plato*. New York: Random House, 1937, Vol. I, 332–334.

[21] The Connecticut law was judged to be in violation of the rights guaranteed by the Fourteenth Amendment, specifically of the right to privacy. See *Griswold v. Connecticut*, 381 U.S. 479 (1965).

[22] See *Meyer v. Nebraska*, 262 U.S. 390, 399 (1923); cf. *Skinner v. Oklahoma*, 316 U.S. 535 (1942), and "Universal Declaration of Human Rights," Article 16, adopted by the General Assembly of the United Nations, in: Richard Brandt, *Value and Obligation*. New York: Harcourt, Brace and World, 1961, 494.

[23] See *Studies in Family Planning*, 26 (1968), 3.

[24] Kingsley Davis, *op. cit.*

[25] See "Universal Declaration of Human Rights," *op. cit.*, Article 19.

[26] See, for example, E. F. Carritt, *Morals and Politics*. Clarendon: Oxford, 1935, Chapter 13, and A. C. Ewing, *The Individual, the State, and World Government*. London: Macmillan, 1947. I would abstractly define a right much in the way Ewing does to refer to powers or securities that an individual or group can rightly demand of other individuals or groups that they should not normally interfere with them.

[27] "The most stringent protection of free speech would not protect a man in falsely shouting 'fire' in a theatre and causing a panic." Oliver Wendell Holmes, Jr., *Shenkwin v. United States* (1919).

[28] In the United States, there are sterilization laws in some states that permit the sterilization of certain classes of people. In North Carolina, for example, the mentally ill, the feeble-minded, and epileptics can be sterilized. (See Moya Woodside, *Sterilization in North Carolina*. Chapel Hill: University of North Carolina, 1950.) Presumably these are voluntary sterilizations in the sense that the consent of guardians is required but the state can appoint such guardians. The constitutionality of this procedure in the case of the feeble-minded was upheld in *Buck v. Bell*, 274 U.S. 200 (1927). This North Carolina law and others like it, are ethically very questionable. In *Skinner v. Oklahoma, op. cit.*, the Supreme Court did declare a law permitting the sterilization of "habitual criminals" to be unconstitutional.

[29] Kingsley Davis, *op. cit.*

[30] To say a right is fundamental means, in this context, that it is the kind of right that is universally recognized and has a *prima facie* claim upon us.

[31] Harold Thomas, unpublished manuscript.

[32] See, for example, Roger Revelle, "International Cooperation in Food and Population," *International Organization* XXII (1968), 362–391, and Grace Goldsmith, *et alia*, "Population and Nutritional Demands," *The World Food Problem, Report of the Panel on the World Food Supply*, Vol. II. A Report of the President's Science Advisory Committee, the White House, May 1967, 1–135. On environmental deterioration, see Roger Revelle's testimony in *Effects of Population Growth on Natural Resources and the Environment*. U.S. Government Printing Office, Washington, 1969 (Hearings before the Keuss Subcommittee on Conservation and Natural Resources).

[33] See the appropriate essays in this volume.

[34] Liberalized abortion laws are among the methods now being

advocated. For a thorough discussion of the wide variety of ethical issues raised by abortion, see Ralph B. Potter, Jr., "The Abortion Debate," in: Donald Cutler (ed.), *The Religious Situation: 1968.* Boston: Beacon Press, 1968, 112–161.

[35] See Wyon and Gordon, *op. cit.*

[36] Roger Revelle, *op. cit.*

[37] See, for example, Judith Blake, "Population Policies for Americans: Is the Government Being Misled?" *Science* 164 (1969), 522–529, Kingsley Davis, *op. cit.*, Paul Ehrlich, *op. cit.*, and Garrett Hardin, *op. cit.*

[38] Garrett Hardin, *ibid.*

[39] Some women seem to have a strong unconscious urge to bear children even while practicing birth control. Dr. Hilton Salhanick has observed that some women practicing the rhythm method will break or lose their thermometers at the critical juncture in their menstrual cycle.

[40] Frederick Wyatt, "Clinical Notes on the Motives of Reproduction," *The Journal of Social Issues* XXIII (1967), 29–56.

[41] See the essays by Harvey Leibenstein, T. Paul Schultz, and J. D. Wray, *op. cit.*

[42] Wyon and Gordon, *op. cit.*

[43] See Lee Rainwater, *And the Poor Get Children.* Chicago: Quadrange Books, 1960, see also *Family Design,* Chicago: Aldine Publishing Co., 1965, particularly Chapters 5 and 6, where the concern for unselfish parenthood is documented for the middle class as well as the working class.

[44] For example, in certain areas of India. See John Wyon, "Population pressure in rural Punjab, India, 1952 to 1969," paper presented at the Seventh Conference of the Industrial Council for Tropical Health, October 1969, at Harvard School of Public Health, Boston, Massachusetts.

[45] This is not to deny the existence of interests that may in the long run keep family size just high enough to prove troublesome.

[46] Kingsley Davis, *op. cit.*, and Judith Blake, *op. cit.*

[47] Ansley Coale, "Should the United States Start a Campaign for Fewer Births?" Presidential Address to the Population Association of America, 1968.

# Notes on Contributors

MARSTON BATES is Professor of Zoology at the University of Michigan.

JUDITH BLAKE is Chairman of the Department of Demography, University of California, Berkeley.

DONALD J. BOGUE is Professor of Sociology and Director of the Community and Family Study Center of the University of Chicago. He is a former president of the Population Association of America.

LARRY BUMPASS is Assistant Professor of Sociology at the University of Wisconsin.

EDGAR CHASTEEN is a Board Member of Zero Population Growth (ZPG), and teaches Sociology at William Jewell College.

ANSLEY J. COALE is Director of the Office of Population Research, Princeton University.

KINGSLEY DAVIS is Professor of Sociology and Director of International Population and Urban Research, University of California, Berkeley.

WAYNE H. DAVIS teaches in the School of Biological Sciences at the University of Kentucky.

ARTHUR J. DYCK is Mary B. Saltonstall Professor of Population Ethics, School of Public Health, Harvard University.

PAUL R. EHRLICH is Professor of Biology at Stanford University.

ROBIN ELLIOTT is Coordinator of Population Activities for Planned Parenthood-World Population.

GARRETT HARDIN is Professor of Human Ecology, Department of Biological Sciences, University of California, Santa Barbara.

OSCAR HARKAVY is Program Officer in charge of the Population Office, the Ford Foundation.

JOHN P. HOLDREN is affiliated with the Lawrence Radiation Laboratory, Berkeley, California.

FREDERICK S. JAFFE is Director of the Center for Family Planning Program Development and Vice President of Planned Parenthood-World Population.

MELVIN M. KETCHEL is Professor of Physiology at the Tufts University School of Medicine.

LYNN C. LANDMAN is Associate Editor of *Family Planning Perspectives*.

RICHARD LINCOLN is Editor of *Family Planning Perspectives*.

JEAN MAYER is Professor of Nutrition, lecturer on the History of Public Health, and member of the Center for Population Studies at Harvard University.

LAWRENCE A. MAYER is a member of the Board of Editors of *Fortune*.

KENNETH S. NORRIS is Director of the Oceanic Institute in Hawaii.

FRANK NOTESTEIN is President Emeritus of the Population Council, and a member of the Planned Parenthood-World Population Board of Directors.

WILLIAM AND PAUL PADDOCK are, respectively, an agronomist and plant pathologist, and a retired foreign service officer.

FRANK POLLARA is the Assistant Director of the AFL-CIO Department of Research.

THEODORE TSURUOKA is Program Planning Analyst for Planned Parenthood-World Population.

MORRIS K. UDALL is United States Representative from Arizona.

BEN WATTENBERG is the co-author (with Richard Scammon) of *This U.S.A.* and *The Real Majority*.

CHARLES F. WESTOFF is Executive Director of the Commission on

Population Growth and the American Future, and Professor of Sociology at Princeton University.

SAMUEL M. WISHIK is Director of the Division of Program Development and Evaluation, Columbia University Institute for the Study of Human Reproduction.

# The Power of Networked Teams

# The Power of Networked Teams

*Creating a Business Within a Business*
*at Hewlett-Packard in Colorado Springs*

———

Pamela Shockley-Zalabak

Sandra Buffington Burmester

OXFORD
UNIVERSITY PRESS
2001

# OXFORD

UNIVERSITY PRESS

Oxford   New York

Athens   Auckland   Bangkok   Bogotá   Buenos Aires
Calcutta   Cape Town   Chennai   Dar es Salaam   Delhi
Florence   Hong Kong   Istanbul   Karachi   Kuala Lumpur
Madrid   Melbourne   Mexico City   Mumbai   Nairobi
Paris   São Paulo   Shanghai   Singapore   Taipei   Tokyo   Toronto   Warsaw

*and associated companies in*
Berlin   Ibadan

Library of Congress Cataloging-in-Publication Data is available

ISBN 0–19–513448–6

1 3 5 7 9 8 6 4 2
Printed in the United States of America
on acid-free paper

# Contents

Foreword     vi

Preface     vii

Acknowledgments     xi

1   The Birth of a New HP Way     3

2   Business Goals Do the Driving     15

3   Core Culture Driving Change: Networked Teams     31
Look Like the Answer

4   Educate, Educate, Educate: Designing Networked Teams     49

5   Role Shifting: Teams Learn to Cope with Ambiguity     73

6   Growing Pains: Teams That Worked and Some That Didn't     99

7   Networked Teams Prove Themselves     143

Epilogue:     173
HP and Agilent Technologies Leaders Talk about the Future

Appendix 1: 
CSFSC Facilitator Position Plan/Ranking Criteria, 1992     181

Appendix 2: 
Colorado Springs Financial Services Center     185
FOM Feedback Form

Appendix 3:     187
Self-Directed Team Responsibilities and Parameters,
June 17, 1999

Notes     197

Research Notes     205

Index     225

# *Foreword*

This book vividly describes the birth and development of a new culture within an existing culture. Hewlett-Packard is known for its legendary corporate culture, which we have come to call the "Hewlett-Packard Way." It emphasizes decentralization and the empowerment of individuals at all levels. At first glance the story seems to fly in the face of that culture because it describes how the company centralized an important part of its corporate service function.

But the new organization, HP's Colorado Springs Financial Services Center, has provided the perfect incubator for the self-directed network team structure that has evolved within it. This was not the first self-directed team at Hewlett-Packard, but it has become one of the most successful and longest sustained use of teams in the company. The transition was not easy, and the book documents the problems that were encountered and solved along the way. In the final analysis, self-directed teams have proved to be a powerful means of nurturing, empowering, and directing our people. I have always felt that the success of the new center has been the result of the confidence our people have in the concept and their consistent desire to continuously improve the services they provide to their customers—who are, after all, other HP divisions.

I hope you enjoy the story and find ideas that can help you manage your organization more effectively.

—Kemp Bohlen

HP Worldwide Financial Services Manager
January 2000

# Preface

This is a book about one of the world's most respected companies, the Hewlett-Packard Company. Listed at or near the top in almost all studies of high-performing organizations, HP is heralded for its leadership, creation of a unique culture known as the HP Way, superior products, and sustained financial performance. Although our story certainly supports this view of Hewlett-Packard, we take you where other stories have not gone—into the trenches of financial transaction processing. We find in these trenches an unusual success with application to virtually every industry and organization regardless of size. Our story is about HP's experience with creating both a new organization and a new organizational form—networked teams—to provide shared financial transaction processing for its U.S. factory locations. In just a little over nine years this unique and wildly successful organization is processing transactions of over $19 billion annually while reducing transaction costs as a percentage of revenue by a factor of four from .36 percent to .09 percent, which is significant for a $47 billion company. Employee satisfaction ranks among the highest in all of HP, and more than 90 percent of the new organization's customers give the organization the highest possible ratings for excellent service.

But the story is about more than shared services and financial transaction processing. It is about the often overlooked potential of transforming routine organizational processes to new and creative forms capable of generating major contributions to the bottom line. It is a story about compelling goals and the high-risk (even for HP) participation of line workers. It is about creating a new organizational form born of technological and process advances coupled with the self-directed team concept popular in manufacturing areas of many companies. It is a story about changing from a cost center to a service business. It is about creating and growing a world-class organization within a huge company. But most importantly it is a success story created in the trenches without strong top management support. It is a story that CEOs and CFOs will find compelling but also a story that line managers and professionals responsible for day-to-day organizational life will find useful and encouraging.

Two of us are writing this book. Although both of us have been involved from the very beginning of the organization, we bring divergent vantage points born of our differing professional backgrounds and HP responsibilities. Pam Shockley-Zalabak is a university professor and twenty-year consultant to Hewlett-Packard, having worked in more than twenty-five divisions and operations. She was asked by the initial management team (four members) of the shared services organization to assist with organizational design and training. She has conducted research and consulted continuously with this organization since 1991. Sandra Burmester became the sixth member of the management team six weeks after Shockley-Zalabak began work. Burmester participated in making the original decision to use self-directed teams supported by process and technology changes—a decision that ultimately resulted in a new organizational form. Coming to this project in 1991 from another HP division, Burmester is the manager responsible for training and organizational development.

Both of us care deeply about this organization. Shockley-Zalabak brings the view of the academic who draws contrasts between this organization and others and is particularly interested in the application of creativity and innovation to routine organizational processes. She also provides the perspective of a consultant who has had the privilege of staying on a project long enough to see whether her involvement in map making was worth anything or not. Burmester is a "trench manager" who has lived and continues to live the reality—both frustrations and triumphs—associated with designing and growing this success story.

Our shared conviction is that this story is worth telling. We believe that you will come to agree with us that the creation of a shared transaction processing center at HP both departs from and supports conventional wisdom about the Hewlett-Packard Company. We also believe that you will come to understand the power of generating new organizational types and transforming routine organizational processes into genuine businesses. The gyroscope is the symbol closely associated with the organization in our story. In a very real sense, we want this book to be about a new twenty-first century gyroscope.

## Plan of the Book

In the first chapter you will learn why and how this unique organization came into being. You will discover the seven critical lessons that have been learned over the last nine years. And you may be surprised to learn that almost no one seriously believed that this bold vision could actually work. In chapter 2 we describe the business goals on which the organization was founded and explain how these goals drove early organizational decisions. In chapter 3 we take a close look at HP's culture in terms of decisions to change and create new processes and organizational forms. The people we talk to in chapter 3 discuss the culture of the Colorado Springs Financial Services Center and relate this new organization to HP's future. The networked teams organizational form, which we discuss extensively throughout this book, receives special emphasis in chapters 4 and 7. In particular we describe networked teams, which focus the organization on customers more than transactions with a unique blend of both centralized and decentralized decision making. Also in chapter 4 we describe the type of training curriculum HP developed with its unique blend of team and technical skills. In chapters 5 and 6 we look at how leadership avoided quick fixes and took the strategic long-term view despite enormous pressures for fast results. In chapters 5 and 7 we debunk the myth that team structures only benefit the organization. You will discover how important it is for individuals to contribute to their teams' successes as well as their own career potential. In chapter 7 we describe networked partnerships as they apply to the new organizational form and the basics of customer service. Volumes have been written about customer service, but the Colorado Springs Financial Services Center (CSFSC) approach provides new ideas and opportunities to examine notions of what service really means and where service contributes to achieving outstanding productivity. Finally, in the epilogue, we ask HP leaders to begin again—to speculate about the massive changes under way at HP and about what comes next not only for the organization in our story but for HP in general. The answers they gave us will surprise and stimulate you.

# Acknowledgments

I am extremely grateful to Greg Spray, who released HP's interests and materials in this book, and to Kemp Bohlen, who spent many hours reviewing the book when he could least afford the time. Many thanks to the people who shared their time and experiences and made this book possible: Rick Hobbs, Mike Waterlander, Diana Morgan, Reed Breland, Kathy Jones, Ray Cookingham, Jim Luttenbacher, D'Ann Darling, Joyce Conger, Tammy Biggs, Bill Brown, Bill Kritz, Sharon Botti, Barb Edwards, Mike Cookson, Harland Baker, Nancy Brennan, Mia Taherkhah, Scott Beetham, Kent Young, Carmen Fuller, Carol Douglas, John Knudsen, Don Whitelaw, and Mike Hostetler. Pam Shockley-Zalabak has been an incredible partner in this endeavor and someone from whom I have learned a great deal. Lastly, without the unwavering support of my husband, Douglas D., I could not have "hung in for the fourth quarter."

—Sandra Buffington Burmester

This book would not have been possible without Sandra Buffington Burmester. I want to thank those whom Sandy has recognized, along with the literally hundreds of HP people who have helped me understand the living nature of the HP Way over the past twenty years. I am particularly grateful to the leadership and team members of the CSFSC. I owe a special debt to Karen Norris for her unfailing assistance with the details—assistance going way beyond the call of duty. Herb Addison at Oxford is, simply, the best editor with whom we have ever worked. And, most importantly, the never-failing support that my husband, Charles, gives provides meaning to the lesson that "individuals thrive when working collaboratively."

—Pam Shockley-Zalabak

# The Power of Networked Teams

# 1
---

## The Birth of a New HP Way

[The HP Way] is the policies and actions that flow from the belief that men and women want to do a good job, a creative job, and that if they are provided the proper environment they will do so.

—Bill Hewlett[1]

In 1990, despite fifty years of remarkable growth and achievement, storm clouds were forming on Hewlett-Packard's horizon. HP stock dropped to a price below book value for the first time in the company's history (and the only time as of the writing of this book). Mandates for change permeated the company, with specific emphasis on reducing overhead costs. Managers and employees felt pressured to increase sales, decrease costs, and reverse what some considered the erosion of the HP Way. Increased competitiveness was the order of the day.[2] The decision to form a new financial organization—one that seemingly would violate the HP Way—came during this turbulent period in the company's history.

The changes made in 1990 produced dramatic results. By 1999, 36,000 products accounted for $47 billion in annual revenues, HP (prior to its 1999 split into two companies: Hewlett-Packard Company and Agilent Technologies) was listed among Fortune 500 companies as fourteenth in the United States and forty-seventh globally. Six hundred sales and support offices and distributors were home to over 124,600 employees worldwide. By any standards it has been tremendous growth from the beginning days of a company started by two friends in a garage in Palo Alto, California, on January 1, 1939.[3]

Bill Hewlett and Dave Packard used a coin toss to decide the name of their company. They began their business with the notion of creating innovative products that would be respected by their peers in the engineering and scientific community. The 1940 revenues for the unincorporated partnership were $34,000, produced by three employees and a total of eight products. This modest beginning led to growing respect and years of success. The year 1957 saw HP's first public stock offering. In 1968 the rapidly growing company introduced the world's first desktop scientific calculator, a forerunner of HP's current high-performance workstations. HP made the engineer's slide rule obsolete in 1972 with the first handheld calculator. In the 1980s it became a major player in the emerging computer industry with a full range of desktop computers, minicomputers, and inkjet and laser printers. By 1990 major business segments included computer products, service, and support; test and measurement products and services; medical electronic equipment and services; electronic components; and chemical analysis and service.

From the very beginning everyone in the company was on a first-name basis. Employees who have never met either Hewlett or Packard refer to them as Bill and Dave; a sense of the company's history is evident despite the growing numbers of employees. The culture has been established with highly valued decentralized structures in which general managers have been expected to run divisions as mostly stand-alone entities. HP's stated core values include innovation and flexibility, high levels of achievement and contribution, teamwork, trust and respect for individuals, and uncompromising integrity.[4]

Prior to 1990, HP's financial transaction processing was highly decentralized, as were other support functions. This practice was very much in keeping with the pervasive organizational culture. Services such as general accounting, human resources, and information technology (IT) were duplicated at each HP site and in some cases at each major division within a multiple division site. The redundancies inherent in the significant number of sites performing similar general accounting functions contributed to the high costs for finance. All transaction processing was performed on a single-entity basis housed within the entity's general accounting function. The complexity of dealing with multiple entities with differing state and local requirements was not considered. Employees performing accounting transaction processing referred problems to a supervisor, and if employee input was provided the manager/supervisor typically was the decision maker for problem resolution. Employees were not expected to become actively involved in identifying opportunities for process improvements. During this period, independent studies by Price Waterhouse, Touche Ross, and Ernst and Young all identified HP transaction processing costs as two to three times that of companies with similar revenues. The need to reduce transaction processing costs as a percentage of revenue was obvious. With shrinking profit margins, HP began to examine alternatives to maintaining these expensive decentralized support structures.

Early in 1990 a group of controllers representing the major organizations in HP (factory, field, and group) was formed to chart a vision for the future of HP accounting transaction processing. Based on their work, a now prophetic August 2, 1990, memo from Bob Wayman, HP CFO, announced to all U.S. controllers that HP was going to centralize general ledger and accounting transaction processing for two primary reasons: (1) to achieve lower costs due to economies of scale and process improvements from reengineering and (2) to achieve higher service levels due to the creation of a dedicated team with a high level of expertise. No one responsible for the 1990 decision envisioned the genuinely unique organization that would develop.

Colorado Springs was selected as the host location, and an entrepreneurial manager, Jim Luttenbacher, was chosen to lead the development of this counter–HP culture organization. Luttenbacher and his initial team were charged with the ambitious goal of reducing transaction processing costs by 50 percent. Some HP insiders and observers thought that the goal could be achieved, whereas others were openly skeptical. The organization born in August 1990, the HP Colorado Springs Financial Services Center (CSFSC), quickly evolved from a centralized organization to a new organizational form not found elsewhere in HP. In telling our story, we will talk about this form—the networked teams organization—describing how technology, geographically dispersed organizational partners, and self-directed teams worked in combination to create an unprecedented success.

## A Business within a Business

The purpose of the HP Colorado Springs Financial Services Center was to provide innovative and cost-effective shared business services. The services to be offered were relatively standard and included what the former decentralized functions had provided: accounts payable, general ledger, travel accounting, fixed asset accounting, information access, intracorporate accounting, and customer support. Although important, the stated purpose, in and of itself, was not unique. Early leadership decisions to create a business within a business and then to continually change every aspect of the business in response to market-driven challenges and opportunities were unique. Prior to HP's 1999 split into two companies—HP and Agilent Technologies—this unique environment was annually processing more than $19 billion in accounts payable flowthrough, working with over 73,000 external vendors, tracking 101,400 assets, processing an intracorporate flowthrough of $170 billion, processing over 176,000 travel expense reports, handling 219,881,000 annual general ledger audit details, responding to over 132,000 customer requests, and maintaining an information warehouse of 150 gigabytes. A total of 296 people made this happen serving twenty-eight customer sites and directly supporting 57,000 U.S. employees. *The cost results speak for themselves—transaction processing costs as a percentage of revenue are 75 percent lower than they were in 1990.*

The exciting part of this story is figuring out why and how this unique organization succeeded. What caused experienced HP managers to consciously choose a different path? What happens when you realize you are creating a new and uncharted future? How do individuals react to a totally new work environment—a new organizational form? What accounts for the tremendous results? What is going to happen next? In the next several chapters you will learn the answers to these questions and more. Additionally, you will have an opportunity to think along with us about how the lessons learned at the HP Colorado Springs Financial Services Center can be applied in other organizations and other circumstances. But first we want to describe what we believe are the seven most important lessons learned in our story. We believe these lessons literally gave birth to a new way of doing business at HP and a concept of organization that has broad application to other organizations regardless of size.

### Lessons Learned: The Birth and Maturing of Change

From day one the gyroscope has been the symbol displayed at every introductory team training session for this project—representing a combination of change, rapid movement, flexibility, balance, and stability. Inspired by the movement of the gyroscope, we will explore what we have learned and what HP has learned. Some of the lessons are tied directly to the larger HP environment, but some speak directly to changing our thinking about traditional overhead operations, organizational structures, innovation, and what constitutes service. Among the many lessons learned during these several years, seven critical factors deserve special consideration. Although all these factors will be explained in detail (some in full chapters), we want to provide a brief overview of them before we continue our story. We believe these factors account for the success of the Colorado Springs Financial Services Center, and we are convinced that they have the potential to guide innovation and organizational transformation in many types and sizes of organizations.

### Lesson 1: Business Goals Do the Driving

The directions for the new organization could not have been more clear: Cut the cost of transaction processing by 50 percent while improving customer satisfaction. Stop operating as decentralized cost centers and become a service business. Contribute to the changes HP needs to make to improve its overall competitive position. Become an HP strategic advantage. And the goals were published—not just within the new organization but throughout HP and to its customers and vendors. The clarity of the initial goals became the foundation of what emerged as a business within a business. The driving imperative of these ambitious goals set the stage for the innovation and high-risk thinking that characterized early stages of our story.

### Lesson 2: Core Culture Drives Change

The Hewlett-Packard Company has a famous culture that is envied by many. Bill Hewlett and Dave Packard are generally credited with building a quality company noted for producing excellent, highly competitive products. Based on a unique valuing of individuals, a strong commitment to HP, and a vigorous entrepreneurial spirit, the "HP Way" is the term coined to describe a strong, enduring culture that most consider the bedrock of HP's success. Management is expected to develop and lead day-to-day practices that support the basic values which underlie corporate objectives. Stated core values are expected to result in an environment that fosters intense individual creativity and community commitment and involvement.[5]

On the surface, centralizing and standardizing transaction processing appeared to be genuinely counterculture. And when the decision was announced, some voiced the opinion that the Colorado Springs Financial Services Center was not in line with the HP Way. A closer examination, however, suggests that the new organization has evolved into the very type of organization that supports the basic core of HP values. Although the new organization breaks HP tradition in terms of organizational structure and form (i.e., practices), its entrepreneurial spirit and creative utilization of people is a close fit with the bedrock of HP's culture.

### Lesson 3: Networked Teams Require World-Class Processes, People, and Technology

One of the most important lessons from the HP Colorado Springs Financial Services Center story is the emergence of the networked teams organization. The term "networked teams" is not a play on words, and it is not the virtual organization of today's popular press. We have coined this term to describe an organization form with elements of the virtual organization, self-directed work teams, unique relationships with partners, and state-of-the art processes and technologies. The organization, by design, is networked with organizational partners, is networked through technology, is networked with new and innovative processes, and is networked internally with the structure of self-directed work teams. This form focuses the organization on service more than transactions and functions with a unique blend of both centralized and decentralized decision making. To date, HP's networked teams significantly outstrip the performance of the more hierar-chically structured accounting industry. Indeed, the results speak for themselves—in 1998 HP costs for accounting transaction pro-cessing were 27.4 percent lower in real dollars (unadjusted for inflation) than in 1990. During that period HP grew from a $16.4 billion to a $47 billion company.

### Lesson 4: Hang In for the Fourth Quarter

As already noted, the decision to form the Colorado Springs Financial Services Center was made during a turbulent period for HP. Temptations to look for quick fixes were everywhere. Early CSFSC leadership viewed these temptations as dangerous, realiz-ing that what they were attempting was going to take a consider-able amount of time—no ninety-day wonders in this venture. From the very beginning, announced plans included a five-year timetable with no guarantees of significant financial return prior to 1995. Early savings were to be invested in new processes and technologies and in building the team structure itself. Responsi-bilities given to teams were increased slowly and deliberately, with ample time allocated for team development. Pushed to make more rapid progress, management resisted admirably, knowing the organization was moving as fast as possible and needed time to mature. Management committed to tough goals and simultane-ously argued against self-funding too quickly. This hardly sounds like a corporation based in the United States in the late 1980s and early 1990s. But looking at what the organization has accom-plished compels us to argue that this "staying power" contributed to the overwhelming success in Colorado Springs.

### Lesson 5: Educate, Educate, Educate

Almost any review of corporate expenditures reveals that when profits are tight, training budgets are among the first to be slashed.

At the beginning of 1992, the new HP CSFSC certainly had one of the most challenging financial goals in all of HP. Despite this challenge and the conventional wisdom of how to construct a lean budget, Jim Luttenbacher and Rick Hobbs, two of the early leaders, approved record training expenditures for the start-up year. Beginning with top management and including every member of the organization, self-directed work team training and technical training were top priorities. During year one, team members spent a record fifty days in the classroom. And the training continues. As this book is being written, all new hires receive the same introductory training that was provided to the initial employees. This commitment far exceeds that of competitor organizations as well as other parts of HP.

### *Lesson 6: Individuals Thrive in a Team-Based Organization*

The downsizing of the 1990s and the flattening of many organizations have created a well-publicized crisis for individual career management. In addition to the basic problem of less vertical mobility, critics of self-directed work teams contend that team structures provide little incentive for individuals to truly excel because they simply have nowhere to go beyond the team. Numerous reports indicate that employees asked to participate in self-directed teams complain that the broader organization within which they are employed does not utilize teams, making their new skills of limited value. Our story provides a different view. Several years' experience in teams shows that employees and managers at HP thrive both within the networked teams and after leaving the organization. CSFSC employee satisfaction ratings are among the highest in HP, a company generally known for high employee morale. Both individual team members and managers have moved from the CSFSC to other positions of significant responsibility and career growth both within HP and outside the company. Their experiences simply debunk the myth that team structures only benefit the organization.

Leadership continues its commitment to teams and believes the networked teams organization is a part of the twenty-first century for both HP and Agilent Technologies. Simply put, we have learned that the networked teams organization supports aggressive business goals because individuals thrive in the organization.

### Lesson 7: The Product Is Service

The final lesson from the CSFSC experience centers around customers. How do people who formerly controlled transaction processing within their own business operation become both customers and genuine organizational partners? How do you meaningfully involve customers in organizational design? What accounts for superior customer satisfaction despite increased standardization and centralization of service? The product that matters most to the achievement of outstanding productivity is service. Service encompasses quality, volume, accuracy, rapid response, innovation, cost-effectiveness, and customer satisfaction.

The CSFSC demonstrates a subtle but important distinction between transaction processing as product and service as product. Service encompasses literally all aspects of partner interactions—certainly transaction processing but also very importantly cost, technology, quality and timeliness of assistance, and commitment to adding value. We have come to believe that service, in the broadest of terms, is what contributed to the productivity of this organization. Sound processes are important but did not, in and of themselves, stimulate the excellence that is evidenced in the results in our story. Although volumes have been written about customer service, the CSFSC approach provides new ideas and opportunities to examine notions of what service really means and where service contributes to achieving outstanding productivity.

We believe that these seven lessons were fundamental for the birth and maturing of significant change. They aren't fancy lessons and some will say they are common sense. Actually, they are common sense—but uncommon practice. And practice is what generates results. In the next several chapters, we pay specific attention to where the seven factors we have been discussing take not only HP but other organizations as well. We ask questions and propose tentative answers about what we believe this story means for innovating and transforming almost any organization. We also make proposals about how this organization fits within the broader theory and research on dynamic change in organizations. In the next chapter you will learn specifically what we mean when we say that business goals do the driving.

# 2

## *Business Goals Do the Driving*

> Maybe I had a gut feeling that it sounds like one of those good programs on paper, but in practice it would never work.
>
> —Joyce Conger

In 1990 a major directive was announced—cut the cost of transaction processing in half by consolidating all processing for U.S. factory locations. Half of the announcement was welcome; the other half went counter to the HP culture. Cost reductions were more than welcome, but centralizing and reducing individual division autonomy generated at best a cool and in some cases an openly hostile reaction.

Anyone who peruses the business shelves of major bookstores knows that volumes have been written about establishing business goals, particularly aggressive ones such as Hewlett-Packard's "cutting the cost of transaction processing in half."[1] We seem to know that people need compelling goals but do not know why most goals fail to compel and what, if anything, can be done about it. We now look at the chain of events that the HP transaction processing goals set in motion.

Controllers throughout HP knew that changes had to be made. Thus few were surprised early in 1990, when Bob Wayman, HP's chief financial officer, formed a task force charged with the job of developing a new vision for accounting transaction processing. Wayman took personal responsibility for seeking ideas from the experiences of others. Wayman discussed the experiences of General Electric and Digital Equipment Corporation with Ray Cookingham, HP's corporate controller. Digital especially interested Wayman because DEC had taken a centralization approach to transaction processing, opening four centers in the United States.

After months of fact-finding and debate, the vision group responded to Wayman with two compelling challenges: (1) centralize the general ledger and accounting transaction processing (ATP) to achieve lower costs and (2) achieve higher service levels by creating a dedicated group of people with a high level of expertise. They presented both regional processing centers and one-site options. In the meantime, Cookingham learned in discussions with his Digital counterpart that if DEC could do it over again, they would go to one center as opposed to four. Based on the vision task group report and the Digital experience, Cookingham boldly recommended the single-site plan to Wayman.

Wayman made it official with his August 2, 1990, memo to all U.S. controllers. U.S. general accounting for all factories was moving to a single site in Colorado Springs, with the leader of the new organization reporting directly to the corporate controller. The entire U.S. financial organization was impacted—HP was changing its fundamental approach to basic accounting operations.

HP tradition had little in common with the organization Wayman proposed. Historically, HP had established extensive financial functions, including accounting transaction support with each new management entity. Prior to 1990, there were forty-six ledgers in the United States, with each ledger supporting a product, distribution, sales, or headquarters organization. Local entity management controlled the finance function, frequently developing highly specialized processes for a specific site.

By 1990 tradition was on a collision course with mounting competitive pressure that forced consideration of any and all means to reduce costs. HP was struggling to diversify from its powerful position in the test and measurement business to become a major force in the turbulent computer industry, and the finance function was pressured to adjust. At the beginning of 1990, consolidations of general ledgers for HP locations with multiple divisions or operations reduced the overall ledger number from forty-six to thirty-six. Wayman's vision task force faced the fact that access to HP financial information was complex and inefficient. Advances in computer network technology meant that customer and service provider no longer had to occupy the same physical location. In using decentralized approaches to a variety of support functions, HP was not only increasingly in the minority, but transaction costs were two to three times those of other companies of similar size. The time had come to reengineer processes for dramatic improvements in performance. Those involved in the decision to create the new organization knew they were making changes but could not have known the fundamental transformation they were setting in motion.

Jim Luttenbacher was not a member of the group charged with creating the new vision. An energetic, entrepreneurial manager with eleven years at HP, Luttenbacher was immediately attracted to the opportunity of creating a new organization. He and a handful of other internal candidates applied for the openly posted position to lead the Colorado Springs Financial Services Center. His interview with Ray Cookingham, HP corporate controller, Bob Wayman, and task force members responsible for crafting the vision led to a quick decision. Luttenbacher, the risk taker and excellent manager, would lead HP's accounting transaction processes into a new era. More importantly, although he did not know it when he accepted the job, he would begin transforming accounting processes into a business and new organizational form capable of world-class performance.

Luttenbacher recalls his decision to take the job:

> This provided an opportunity to do something with the finance
> function that was more line management. Very often I have pri-
> vately and publicly thanked the people who were on the task force
> that studied the opportunity to consolidate accounting transaction
> processing services. The task force basically built in their recom-
> mendation a fairly detailed outline for what they thought this
> would look like, what they thought the opportunity would be in
> terms of cost reduction, how long they thought it would take in
> terms of calendar time, and what they thought the investment
> would need to be. I really felt that HP was seriously committed to
> this activity and committed to doing it right. I felt that I was being
> set up to be successful.[2]

Coming to Colorado from Palo Alto, California, where he was
PC group controller, Luttenbacher saw Colorado Springs as a
desirable site for four reasons: (1) HP had space in the Colorado
Springs facility, (2) the time zone permitted work across the United
States within a reasonable number of operating hours, (3) qualified staff were available, and (4) the area was not as earthquake
prone (did not have the same potential for critical data interruption as a result of seismic activity) as the San Francisco Bay area.

Beginning in late October 1990, Luttenbacher set about to
assemble his initial management team. He hired three HP veterans—Rick Hobbs, Mike Hostetler, and Greg Spray. Despite solid
HP experience, none of the team had faced the challenge of creating a new organization. Hobbs was named head of operations and
was charged with addressing issues of organizational structure.
Hostetler was to engineer the development effort, and Spray
assumed the overall information technology effort. Hobbs, who
owned the organizational structure responsibility, was attracted to
the CSFSC because, as he is fond of saying,

it was a start-up. It had the feeling of a green field. It was a corporate organization away from corporate with the majority of the organization not in place at the time. It was a new business. That was appealing. The other thing that was appealing was the way Jim described the approach he wanted to use—running it like a business, earning the business from internal HP even though it was somewhat of a mandate from the CFO, marketing it and having development plans—your typical triad of manufacturing, R&D and marketing. That was appealing.[3]

Hobbs, in particular, liked the initial goal of reducing costs from $60 to $30 million in five years and often explained that

> what was neat about it [the goal] was that it was simple and compelling and everybody recognized it and understood it, and it was very measurable. That made it fun. First of all I bought into the idea. Secondly, I also knew from working in general accounting organizations before that we don't invest in these processes. We don't have the bandwidth in the divisions to do it. I knew that a central organization with funding from corporate to get it started would be able to invest in things that no individual department could do. I felt like we had a huge competitive advantage over the current model based on the way it was going to be done. Our sponsors funded it. We asked for the $30 million, over five years and we got it.

Luttenbacher and his team rapidly developed launch strategies for the new organization. In a culture that prized a decentralized structure, Luttenbacher's managers were acutely aware that the initial reaction of the U.S. factory divisions was anything but favorable. One division manager, in an open meeting, reportedly said, "HP shouldn't imitate others—centralize and give financial guys control—this is dangerous—it is not the HP Way." Others agreed but were less vocal.

Corporate mandates are rarely issued at HP. Instead, a management-of-change approach that focuses on the merits of a project or program for organizational change is used to win support. Jim, Rick, Mike, and Greg knew they had to come up with a strategy to make the concept of shared services for accounting transaction processing palatable to the factory divisions. Jim decided early on that joining the Financial Services Center should be a voluntary act. According to Jim,

> It [joining CSFSC] was not mandated, and that decision put me in a position of dancing a tightrope, as it were. I sold Wayman and Cookingham on that idea, but not thoroughly sold them. They would put up with me with respect to that philosophy as long as we were meeting our milestones and making progress according to the agreed upon plan. I knew for sure that if we had started to slip and/or, for whatever reason, not been able to attract customers, that philosophy would have really been tested.

Within the first ninety days of operation the management team crafted a straightforward and simple strategy: CSFSC would operate as a for-profit business unit and attract divisions as customers based on reduced costs and improved services. This strategy and the decisions that followed launched the new organization of networked teams and set HP on a course that, as of the writing of this book, continues to exceed all expectations.

In November 1990, twenty-seven employees were transferred from other Colorado Springs responsibilities to create the CSFSC. The initial group consisted of experienced HP employees who were located in accounting functions in three Colorado Springs divisions, had financial transaction backgrounds, and had worked with significant variations of processes and computer systems within the separate functions.

Two months after the first twenty-seven began work, Luttenbacher and his managers announced their strategy to all U.S.

factory locations. CSFSC would operate as a customer-focused service business rather than a mandated "corporate service." A remote support organization would remain at each local entity site, acting as customer liaisons and providers of customized local services. These remote support organizations were to be known as Accounting Services Centers (ASCs). Finally, cost reductions would be partially passed on to customers and partially used to fund process development activities. The new organization would take an evolutionary approach to the consolidation of processes. New services would be offered as the organization matured. It sounded good, but no one was sure what it was going to take to pull it off.

## HP People: New Roles, Responsibilities, and Challenges

Everyone who joined the CSFSC—all thirty-four people including management—came from divisions with local autonomy and on-site customers or from corporate finance not charged with directly supporting customers. Not one person had worked with self-directed teams or extensively networked processes, or viewed the people they supported as both partners and customers. They were accustomed to evaluations based on performance within a division and from individuals who knew them personally. They were highly competent individuals who had no reference points to understand the dynamics of taking transaction processing from a routine over-head operation to a high-performing business. They were in good trenches but trenches nevertheless. Above all, they needed to believe the goal was possible. Joyce Conger was one of the most senior of the Colorado Springs HP employees assigned to the CSFSC. She remembers her initial response:

My first reaction was disbelief. I just couldn't believe that HP would think of going that direction. That was at a time when there were

so few self-directed teams. You just didn't hear much about the concept. HP had been a hierarchy for so long. I was totally shocked. I
think another thing was that I was very apprehensive. Maybe it was
that I had a gut feeling that it sounds like in theory one of those
good programs on paper, but in practice, it would never work. I
thought it would be very short-lived.[4]

Joyce was not alone in this reaction. Many in Colorado Springs
and throughout HP shared her pessimism. It is a different story
today. According to Joyce, "I think the team concept is really a very,
very powerful thing. I think another thing that is far superior in a
team concept is the development of work skills. We all had different skills and it was really good to learn from each other."

Sandy Burmester was applying for a voluntary severance package from HP when CSFSC jobs were posted on the company-wide
job system. She recalls,

I was in Fort Collins [with HP] as a financial analyst. HP was offering voluntary severance packages, [and] I was considering getting
a Ph.D. in plant pathology. Everyone taking the severance package
had to take a class called Accepting Personal Responsibility. In that
class you had to write your perfect job description. A person who
had taken the class with me and knew what I had written saw the
job posted for training and development and told me my "perfect"
job had just been created. I looked at it and said to myself I had to
give this opportunity a go. I contacted Rick Hobbs and then interviewed. It really sounded like a good fit. I have odd credentials for
an HP finance person—biology/chemistry and electrical engineering with an M.S. in accounting. I wanted a job that would let me
challenge ways of doing things—and this certainly was the case.[5]

Rick Hobbs was attracted to the challenge of creating major
change when he interviewed and was hired as operations manager
for the CSFSC. "The job was made known to me by my boss. I was

in Colorado Springs at Logic Systems Division and my job was winding down. I liked the idea of running CSFSC as a business and not being in the Palo Alto area. I believed we could meet the goals. I knew we could not micromanage and would need a different approach." Hobbs credits the compelling cost-reduction goal with helping management think creatively and take risks not previously associated with the transaction processing function.

## HP Productivity: New Processes, New Technologies, New Organizational Structure

The goal of cutting transaction processing costs by 50 percent in five years was not open for debate, and the management team came to CSFSC knowing they were expected to execute to meet this objective. What they didn't have was a business plan. The goal had to translate into operations. A. T. Kearney, an independent consulting firm, was retained to conduct goal validation studies to determine potential savings. Their report, based on studies of several U.S. and Japanese companies, supported the viability of the goal, identifying important savings potential from consolidation, standardization, and reengineering. In early 1991, Jim Luttenbacher and his team set out to develop a plan that would achieve the desired results without mandating anyone to use CSFSC services. The success of the plan rested with attracting customers who could see the value in cost reductions from centralized and standardized processes.

The business plan, first published in June 1991, identified the purpose of the Colorado Springs Financial Services Center as (1) performing standardized accounting transactions that are business independent and (2) providing access to general ledger data. The strategy was straightforward: simplify the consolidation process, standardize accounting transaction processes, opportunistically reengineer processes, improve linkages to nonaccounting processes, and maximize economies of scale. The value to be delivered: a 50 percent reduction in transaction cost, simplified processes, and improved customer access to general ledger data.

Planning for the initial organizational structure included determining what services would be provided by CSFSC and what would remain with each local entity—the Accounting Services Center. The original business plan described four general categories of work—two managed by the CSFSC and two remaining at local sites. The two CSFSC categories of work were a front-end response center and a back-end operations activity. The response center was developed to provide training to local entity staff, develop process expertise, and provide source document collection. The operations activity would provide the actual transaction processing. Business decision support would remain with each HP entity but would be enhanced by the availability of consolidated information and improved tools for information access. Local entities (ASCs) would continue to provide accounting services that required a local physical presence, for example, physical asset control and preliminary transaction document review. The published plan sounded good but virtually nothing was ready. The pressure to make it happen was intense.

Typical cost centers organized like the CSFSC allocate all costs across customer divisions. Instead of meeting customer wants and needs, the typical cost center uses what Burmester describes as a "here you go, use this and be happy" approach. Luttenbacher and his managers began with the notion that the financial goal was to break even—expenses equal revenue. Customer divisions were to be billed for their level of usage through fees established for each major cost driver. For example, a specific fee is charged for each line item on an invoice. The majority of the fee covers the cost of processing the transaction plus a small add-on for the research and development costs for reengineering processes or creating new computer tools. In general CSFSC must provide the kinds of services that motivate the customer to pay for the service offered. No buyer means that CSFSC doesn't do a project unless the costs can be covered in the transaction processing rates or billed directly to the user organizations.

The challenges were obvious. Each factory site had its own computer systems and processes that fit the site's particular ways of doing business. Each site was responsible for accounts payable, travel, fixed assets, general ledger, and intracorporate accounting, among other responsibilities. Every month each site would close the books, and the site information technology group would send general ledger information to corporate, where all the information was rolled together. It was cumbersome and expensive but it worked. Jim and his team had to determine what initial services they could offer and what type of structures and technology were going to be required.

The cost reduction goal influenced the decision to select accounts payable, travel accounting, fixed assets, general ledger, and intracorporate accounting as the initial set of services. Accounts payable services would include paying invoices for those goods and services that Hewlett-Packard acquired from outside the company. Travel accounting became responsible for reimbursing HP employees for expenses incurred for travel-related expenses while on company business. Fixed assets would record the acquisition, transfer, retirement, or disposal of HP capital assets, with intracorporate accounting recording transactions generated for goods and services acquired from within HP. Finally, the new general ledger services included maintaining integrity of data in the general ledger, that is, ensuring that all accounting computer subsystems book to the general ledger correctly while supporting tools designed to access general ledger information. All of these services were to be supported by a customer response center handling inquiries related to the basic functions. CSFSC management quickly realized that consolidated detailed information was even more valuable if it could be easily accessed. A portion of the funds billed to the sites was invested in the development of computer applications that provided user-customizable expense reports to any manager via a personal computer.

The goal had come with a timeline of five to six years. The 1991 business plan called for all U.S. general accounting transactions to be managed by the CSFSC by the end of 1995. The schedule was ambitious, especially for an organization planning on attracting customers without a corporate mandate. To meet the goal, the CSFSC initially would need to streamline the consolidation process from twelve to eighteen months to less than six months. The new organization was gearing up to add one new entity per month. The plan was aggressive even by HP standards.

Key process solutions had to come on line quickly. The existing information systems would not work in the highly centralized model that was evolving. Luttenbacher had two very different options: (1) develop new applications and integrate the existing processes or (2) patch the existing systems, build really good processes, and then automate. He selected the latter.

> We were aided in that regard by Michael Hammer [author of *Reengineering the Corporation*],[6] this famous IT consultant who was getting a fair amount of exposure around HP at the time. He was preaching in a very emphatic manner that the failure of office automation in general had a lot to do with the fact that if you looked at the strategy for automating processes and using information technology, we often found companies trying to automate existing manual processes. If the process happened to be very good, the results weren't too bad. If the processes themselves were not in good shape then you ended up with the classic garbage in, garbage out. That struck a cord with me and I felt very strongly about that. We decided to get some experience at running consolidated services before we built a computer system that would accommodate our needs.

The information technology decision was the first major example of the staying power important for the success of this organization (which will be discussed later). The leadership team was moving rapidly and slowly all on the same issues.

The most notable of the early systems to be developed was the "payables solution" known as MEPS: multi-entity payables system. Built around an existing accounts payable system, MEPS provided the functionality needed to process invoices for multiple rather than single entities. Many more processes and systems would follow during the next five years.

Potential customer entities were told to plan on keeping 30 percent of their existing personnel for the start-up phase, with a long-term goal of local entities needing only 10 percent of their existing accounting organizations. Ninety percent of the work defined in 1991 as general accounting would eventually be done at the CSFSC. The published plan sounded good, but virtually nothing was ready. The pressure to make it happen was intense.

## HP Relationships: New Ways of Servicing Customers

The CSFSC was a new business without customers. Leadership was charged with starting a centralized service that few really wanted. The business plan would take control away from entity management while asking them to become supportive partners. Jim Luttenbacher claims that one of his biggest initial problems was accomplishing the goals for consolidation without mandating divisions to participate:

> I think one of the most important things was really convincing our customer base that they were customers and that this was not simply a "we're here from corporate, and we're here to help" kind of program. We early on developed a marketing function, and John Knudsen [a former HP site controller hired to become the first

customer services manager] had a lot to do with developing the marketing for the Financial Services Center. We held seminars with prospective customers and went out to visit prospective customers. All along we were very much into selling the quality of our services—developing a value proposition that would cause people to want to be part of the Financial Services Center as opposed to having to join by edict.

Most HP observers were amazed at this market-driven approach. Cost-effectiveness and quality became the basis of the sales pitch— the divisions had to listen. Many entity managers were skeptical about working remotely while maintaining a local staff, but as one manager put it, "If you make an honest appraisal of the cost savings, there is no way you can walk away from the table."

In August 1991 the consolidations began. The first three entities to become CSFCS customers were located in Colorado Springs, and all of the first CSFCS employees had come from these customer divisions. There were challenges to the first consolidations, but the challenges were with three local customers. In November 1991 the Cupertino site in California became the first customer outside Colorado. Cupertino's experience would be important in convincing others to join the CSFSC. Luttenbacher remembers fearing that the next one or two consolidations following Colorado Springs might fail. His fears were unfounded. Based on the early success, a new model emerged—selling the new business, training the customer, helping the customer reorganize local functions, and then providing the services.

## What We Learned When "Business Goals Do the Driving"

The world-class goal of cutting transaction processing by 50 percent was clear, specific, and measurable, and it presented a major challenge. Everyone involved knew what the goal was and would know whether or not it was achieved. Less obvious is the importance of the thoughtful development of the goal. The imperative for change actually drove initial visioning. The vision team, the A. T. Kearney studies, and the imperative to cut costs all contributed to understanding the business need and translating that business need into a compelling goal. The goal was developed with input but did not depend on consensus. The goal preceded the organization and it incorporated high-level strategic direction. The goal drove hiring and initial decisions. The goal attracted the type of leaders who wanted to risk enough to make it happen. Finally, the goal not only was compelling for the new organization but had measurable customer benefits. We believe the driving imperative of this goal and the way it was developed were critical success factors in our story. The goal was big enough to force large-scale change.

## What This Means for Others

We believe the lessons learned in our HP story have implications for organizations of all sizes and for both leaders and individual/team contributors. The *goals do the driving* lesson encourages everyone involved with establishing goals to put them to the test of some tough questions. (1) Are the goals big enough to force thinking about large-scale change or can they be achieved with only minor alterations to the status quo? What is needed? How do you know? Goals that fail to propel organizations to the future often are achievable, are safe, and protect the status quo. (2) Are the goals challenging business goals or are they "imitation goals" following the latest industry trends and management fads? (3) Are the goals truly business goals or are they driven by the need to solve other organizational problems? (4) Finally, are the goals clear to everyone in the organization and are they used as a fundamental basis for day-to-day decisions? Leadership needs to understand the goals, but when both leadership and individual/team contributors understand that they are accountable to big, clear, realistic goals, results happen.

## The Move to Teams

The early success was important. But it quickly became obvious that the pace of change required even more reengineering to stay on target and meet the goal. The CSFSC had to look for an improved way of doing business. Rick Hobbs came to believe that teams might be the answer. Rick is an avid reader, which had a lot to do with what happened next. Charged with designing the organizational structure, Hobbs knew the cost reduction goals could not be met with traditional ratios of managers to employees. He began to read. Self-directed work teams were "hot" in the popular and trade press literature of the early 1990s. Hobbs was impressed by reported productivity and quality gains in self-directed work team organizations and he wanted to know more. He realized that he needed help in evaluating this concept, in deciding whether or not to pursue this type of organization, and in defining the processes for hiring and training a new workforce. Sandy Burmester was hired as an internal development specialist to work directly with Rick. Six weeks earlier Luttenbacher and Hobbs had selected Pam Shockley-Zalabak as the external consultant for organizational design, research, and training. Sandy and Pam were introduced to each other in a meeting to discuss moving the CSFSC to a self-directed work team model.

In chapter 3 you will discover what Rick and Sandy learned about teams and how the decision was made to use the self-directed work team concept for internal CSFSC networking. You also will learn that the decision to move to teams received only skeptical support from key people responsible for CSFSC's future.

# 3

## Core Culture Driving Change: Networked Teams Look Like the Answer

The hierarchy of this thing was horrendous.

—Jim Luttenbacher

When Rick Hobbs accepted the job of accounting operations manager, he knew that the organization would need to grow rapidly with tight cost controls. He also knew that Hewlett-Packard tradition and practices challenged this approach. HP had always believed in close contact between supervisors and employees. In fact, when the HP Colorado Springs Financial Services Center began, the typical span of control in HP's general accounting function was one supervisor for every six to eight employees. For the new organization to meet its aggressive cost control goals, the span of control would need to increase to twenty to thirty employees for every manager. Most agreed that traditional hierarchy was not going to work, yet no one had a better idea.

Rick's early experiences led him to think about a radical departure from past practices:

First of all we had three different groups that came from different cultural backgrounds, HP cultural backgrounds, and they were different with different processes and somewhat different systems.

We continued to work kind of colloquially in those separate systems, so it was very difficult to merge them and turn them into a
team without a set of processes that were standardized, that they
all used, that they could help each other on, and a set of systems
that they all worked on together as well. That is one thing that I
found that was different. The other thing, too, is that it was
twenty-five people versus ten. I had ten before when I was general accounting manager at Logic Systems. I could go in and do
somebody's job if I had to. Then when you get twenty-five doing
different things with systems, you don't have the bandwidth anymore to be able to know that much. So if you got by as a manager
being able to micromanage, you couldn't do that. That was one
of the key differences and one of the early signs that I would have
to have a different approach to management than the one that I
was raised with in HP.[1]

Jim Luttenbacher and his initial team of managers had no intention of creating a team-based structure when they began the
CSFSC. But the cost-reduction driver was powerful and stimulated
looking for alternatives to hierarchy. Rick remembers, "I think realistically, the driver of the idea (teams) at first was the need to
reduce costs. We were talking about reengineering processes all
along, and Jim asked me to take ownership for reengineering the
organization structure because he felt that also needed to be
reengineered."

Luttenbacher was trying to figure out how best to build an
organization that would grow to 400–500 people. Jim credits the
cost-reduction goal with providing the stimulus for moving to a
new structure: "We were aware that if you just looked at the
model of a hierarchical structure for 500 people doing transaction processing, for every six to ten people you would have a
supervisor and then for every six supervisors you would have a
manager. And so on and so on and so on. The hierarchy of this
thing was horrendous."[2] The hierarchical structure did not fit

what Jim needed to achieve. Jim and his managers found creative examples of alternative organizational structures in some of HP's manufacturing and service areas. They also looked at what other companies were experiencing.

The more Rick and Jim read and talked with others, the more convinced they became that self-directed work teams made sense for the new organization. Jim asked the Colorado Springs HP human resources department to recommend potential consultants to assist with the new structure. Jim and Rick interviewed Pam Shockley-Zalabak, a professor at the University of Colorado and long-time HP consultant. She had recently begun work with team-based organizations and was intrigued by the opportunity to work with a team-based structure during its initial start-up phase. Pam was hired to provide an external view and work with a yet-to-be identified organizational development person whose responsibility would be to shepherd the fledgling start-up.

Sandy Burmester found her perfect job and Rick knew from her enthusiasm that she was the person he wanted to lead the development effort. Early discussions among Jim, Rick, Pam, and Sandy focused on what others had learned from self-directed team environments and what were the truly unique characteristics of a team structure. Jim recalled,

> As we were doing our research and we got beyond the surface of those organizations that really seemed to be doing something different, it was very intriguing to me and to our team that these people seemed to have more energy and success. It was clear that self-directed teams can be simply redrawing the organization chart and declaring that we now have self-directed teams. Or you can really try to do something different. We chose the route of really doing something different.

Rick Hobbs agrees that the research provided optimism that went beyond the cost reduction goal:

We found that there are also a lot of issues around quality and productivity that you can deal with as well. In addition, we felt like there needed to be something more in the work environment for individuals in a general accounting shop. It's a big transaction, nuts-and-bolts sort of thing, and our belief is that traditionally in HP people try to enter HP in those jobs, but they would get out as quickly as they could. So we wanted to create an environment where they could be motivated and grow with that kind of a job. One way is to give them more say on how it was done. They could exercise more creativity at work and that would be more fun. They would feel more valued. And that was also part of it. As we dove into it, cost turned out to be the least compelling reason to do it, but that was the spark that caused us to look at it.

Jim, Rick, and Sandy took a hard look at the environment into which a new organizational structure would be introduced. They were concerned that HP had tried several programs such as total quality management and process of management (POM) that were only marginally successful, leaving many skeptical about structural change. Sandy recalls an attitude that "if I wait around it will go away—programs roll in and out. This isn't real; if I lag enough it will go away."[3] Additionally, the HP finance function was rebounding from a series of what many HP managers considered poorly designed projects. These experiences, at least in part, fueled the opposition to the centralization of transaction processing. Jim and Rick knew they would face some tough questions if they added a team-based structure to the already questionable notion of centralized processing. Manufacturing areas of HP were using teams successfully, but teams in the financial service sector were nonexistent.

Despite the potential opposition, Jim, Rick, and Sandy believed similarities between transaction processing and product manufacturing were significant, making gains found in manufacturing possible for CSFSC. They began to talk about the major challenges.

Their research highlighted three significant problems in creating team-based structures: negotiating with unions about team responsibilities, developing customer acceptance, and accounting for savings and productivity increases important for competitive positioning. The first issue, negotiating with unions, did not apply to the nonunion HP. But customer acceptance and competitive positioning were critical.

Prior to making a final decision, Jim, Rick, and Sandy made site visits to Bob Shultz and his HP Eastern Sales Region and to AT&T in New Jersey. Rick was excited:

> We talked to an AT&T team-based organization about the pitfalls and the upside and that sort of thing, so we got a sense of how involved the employees could get at this level. We were pretty impressed. I remember walking away thinking, "Wow, these folks really have their heads screwed on straight!" It is the same feeling that I think companies that visit us now have when they talk to our people. They say, "Wow, these people are really mature compared to our folks, you know, professionally." I think we had that feeling when we went to Paramus [HP New Jersey site] and talked to Bob's folks. Observing it was far more powerful than anything we read. That does stick out in my mind. I can still remember some of the conversations with those folks.

Sandy recounts a particular AT&T conversation:

> We got into a discussion with their teams who had a manager who was poor quality and was terminated following input from the teams. It was a strong concept. One person could perform all of the processes from beginning to end. People had an unbelievable level of ownership—those were characteristics we wanted. People were articulate and excited about their jobs. We would choose this environment any day.

Pam recalls her first meeting with the team following the East Coast trip:

> They were excited, they had seen what they wanted, and they were ready to go for it. I kept asking the question, "Are you in it for the long haul?" The yes response was unwavering. They wanted to change the basic structure. But how and who made the final decision to move to teams is not completely clear to me.[4]

Rick will tell you,

> It is a typical HP decision when you don't know who made it! Jim liked the whole concept of a totally different, flatter organization. So I would say that Sandy and I made the decision that we should go, but with Jim's full support. Ultimately, Jim had to sell it upward because it was not well supported by Ray [Jim's immediate boss and corporate controller]. It was something that Ray was going to close his eyes and hope that we didn't screw it up.

And Jim says,

> We decided to go for it in a very serious way. We wanted to make self-directed teams more than a self-declared name on an organization chart, something that was really part of our culture and part of the processes and services that we were going to build and provide.

## Skeptical Support

Jim Luttenbacher was excited about the potential for creating a self-directed work team structure. His immediate staff agreed, but beyond that the champions were few and far between. Kemp Bohlen, who would follow Jim as the second manager of the CSFSC, was head of the HP Americas Geographic Operations

Financial Services Center in Atlanta when discussions of a new structure began to surface. Kemp remembers,

> To be honest with you, I was somewhat skeptical, but I wasn't skeptical of the concept itself. I was more skeptical of the management of change and how much change the organization could really take. There were also a bunch of naysayers out there. I think a lot of people thought that centralization in Hewlett-Packard just doesn't make any sense whatsoever. Ninety-five percent of the community didn't think this concept was going to work anyway, and then if they heard that this crazy "warm and fuzzy thing" was going on out there as well, a natural reaction was, "What's this thing going to look like? What are they doing out there?" I talked to Jim about that. He knew the kind of image it had but he prevailed and the results speak for themselves. I always felt that Ray deep down really felt this was too much of a touchy-feely approach. I think he has grown to not only accept it, but I think he really embraces it now. I think he has spent enough time with the people that he has seen the kind of maturity and growth, and he has been able to watch this thing all the way through. I don't think that Ray felt that it would be a disaster if it didn't work, but if you really nailed his feet to the ground he would probably sit there and tell you he didn't think this was going to make it.[5]

Ray Cookingham remembers a more moderate reaction to self-directed work teams than is generally attributed to him:

> I think that the first reaction was that this was a concept which would have great potential. The idea of the workplace environment being more collaborative, more of a partnership inherently had a lot of appeal, but at the same time I had a certain amount of reservation, just recognizing how different that would be from the traditional environment in which we had done general accounting and transaction processing. Recognizing that this was going to be

experimental, anytime that you are experimental, there are some natural reservations.[6]

Ray does not recall making the statement widely attributed to him, "This sounds like a warm and fuzzy free-for-all."

> I honestly don't remember saying that, but it is possible that I did. I would hope my initial reaction was a bit more balanced than that. The reservations that I have expressed—recognizing that it was experimental—but I do recall thinking that this was an idea that had great potential if it worked and that the historic environment that we had for processes was not all that stimulating—all that rewarding in many cases, and so I think I related to the thought that we can have a much more stimulating, creative environment.

Cookingham based his decision to sponsor the new organizational structure on two fundamental principles, first, the potential for the concept and, second, the confidence he had in the leadership of the CSFSC to execute and follow through. Luttenbacher felt supported. Jim knew there was pressure to make the new organization successful but he claims it was not overwhelming.

From the beginning both Bob Wayman and Ray Cookingham were told by CSFSC leadership it would take five years to get the organization fully operational and profitable. Wayman did not believe it would take that much time but the message he continued to get was clear. According to Jim Luttenbacher,

> We never changed the answer to Bob that it was going to take five years and we were going to end up with 500 people. He was always supportive. He never wavered in terms of trying to make us do short cuts or anything like that. So I think they were pretty darned good sponsors in retrospect. We delivered so it was a good partnership between the sponsors and the team.

## Communicating the Change

Once the team structure had been decided, Jim set about the task of selling the benefits. His first presentation, of course, was to Cookingham and Wayman. Following their agreement, Luttenbacher, Hobbs, and Burmester gathered affected employees and announced the plan. Most employees were stunned—they thought they had already gone through unprecedented change with the centralization. A few were excited but more were vocally resistant. The leadership team, however, was determined to forge ahead.

Jim quickly began working with Pam to form groups responsible for developing and implementing the team-based structure. A steering committee (composed of Jim's direct managers) would provide overall direction and oversee the work of a design team. The design team would literally design the team-based structure in conjunction with process and technology changes. Potential design team members were informed of the new structure and of their role in shaping the reengineering processes. Most expressed excitement coupled with concern about what they really were going to do.

Luttenbacher added the team structure to his overall marketing presentation. The already skeptical financial organizations were only mildly surprised. The CSFSC was changing everything they had ever known about general accounting. If this was the HP Way, it certainly didn't look like it.

## The HP Way and the New Organization

The HP Way, the bedrock that many credit for HP's sustained success, is perhaps Bill Hewlett and Dave Packard's most creative invention. A philosophy of management emerging from Hewlett and Packard's values about innovation, contributions, people, and community, the HP Way fosters individual responsibility, creativity, entrepreneurial activity, community involvement, and fundamental respect for people. The HP Way is so important to the company that it has become a formal written document supported by extensive training for all who are charged with making it a living reality. More than forty years after its formal introduction into the company, employees evaluate decisions as to their fit with the famous HP Way. The CSFSC decision is an excellent example.

Codified in 1957 at the company's first ever managers' retreat (led personally by Dave Packard and Bill Hewlett) and updated again in 1966, the HP Way describes core objectives for profit, customers, field of interest, growth, employees, organization, and citizenship. The organizational objective is of particular interest, with its specific mandate to create an environment that "fosters individual motivation, initiative and creativity, and a wide latitude of freedom in working toward established objectives and goals."[7] Based on these objectives, HP has grown and prospered over the years with a highly decentralized divisional structure with extraordinary local autonomy. The creation of the CSFSC as a shared transaction processing center appeared to be countercultural.

Jim Luttenbacher describes the CSFSC fit within HP:

> What we were doing was very nontraditional, and in a sense it went exactly against the grain of the independent business unit structures of HP. Essentially we were going to take this responsibility away from individual operating units and provide back a centralized service. Individual units would no longer directly control the activities of the transaction processing part of their business. This was absolutely counter to the HP culture of independence.

Centralization, standardization, and removing local division autonomy clearly were not part of the HP Way; but what about a team-based structure? After all, HP prided itself on exceptional levels of teamwork. In some respects the creation of a team-based operating structure was less countercultural than the creation of the CSFSC itself. The team concept supported notions of individual responsibility and accountability, but the structure that Luttenbacher and his managers proposed challenged the core of HP's practices with regard to management involvement in day-to-day decision making. Luttenbacher was proposing a ratio of one manager to every thirty employees. HP research and development labs were well-known for project teams but with a team leader (project manager) for every six to eight engineers. Historically, the six to one ratio was considered desirable throughout most functions in HP, including finance. Luttenbacher and Hobbs were claiming that traditional management approaches were both unnecessary and too expensive.

The context in which HP was operating in the late 1980s and early 1990s helps us understand the complexity of creating a seemingly countercultural organizational form while attempting to maintain HP's core values and mission. In the mid-1970s, HP had begun its move into the computer business. John Young, who became president in 1977, quickly realized that the decentralized, autonomous divisions were hard to coordinate and that few incentives existed to manage cooperation. Furthermore, so much information was fed into the executive committee charged with establishing overarching objectives that decision making was slow and cumbersome. Although highly participative, the decision-making processes within HP were no match for the fast-paced rambunctious computer world. A 1990 *Wall Street Journal* article characterized HP as a "bureaucratic morass."[8] It was at this point that HP stock prices fell below book value. Industry observers questioned the future of the respected giant. Young knew that massive changes had to occur. David Packard, the seventy-eight-year-old chairman of the board, returned to work on a daily basis. Packard and Young began to remove layers of management and look for opportunities to energize the company. The reduction of transaction processing costs was but one of many such "opportunities."

## The Perils of Centralization

Dave Packard was well-known for what he calls in his book, *The HP Way*, the "perils of centralization":

> It has been my experience that most business executives are quick to praise the concept of decentralization. But when it comes to their own organization, many are reluctant to adopt it. Perhaps the idea of turning over a portion of their authority to others is too unsettling. From personal experience I've learned that even widely decentralized companies should be alert to signs of cumbersome centralization.[9]

HP's entry into the computer business turned out to be a real test of this philosophy. Packard tells an important story of changes:

> Prior to entering the computer field, the HP organization was structured for the instrument business, with decentralized divisions responsible for well-defined product lines and operating with a good amount of independence. This structure had worked very well for instruments, and some thought it could be applied with equal effectiveness to computers.
>
> But working against the idea were two principal characteristics of the computer business. One, new to HP, was the whole area of software. How do you organize to produce software? ... Second, the computer business is a systems business. It requires many elements—software, mainframes, peripherals, operating systems—to be combined into salable products supported by strong service and maintenance. Good coordination is essential.
>
> HP responded to these challenges by trying various forms of organization. There were divisions, group structures, then various task forces, councils, and committees intended to improve coordination. Over time these efforts began to create a complicated

bureaucracy. Problems needing prompt and intelligent decisions were being referred through level after level of management with unwieldy committees. Decisions were often postponed for weeks or even months.

By 1990, we faced a crisis. Committees had taken over the decision-making process at HP, and decision cycle times had ballooned. For example, one central committee, the Computer Business Executive Committee, was intended to achieve a better focus and coordination for computer activities. Instead, it was slowing vital decisions just as our company entered the lightning-fast competitive world of computers in the 1990s. In fact, the paralysis was spreading to areas of the company that had nothing to do with computers. That we were struggling was no secret; our stock had fallen to $25.

... Thanks to the company's long-standing open door policy, we (Hewlett and Packard) were receiving visits from troubled HP managers as well as an increasing number of letters from concerned employees. After a while, Bill and I actually began systematically to visit several HP facilities and meet with employees at all levels of the organization to find out what, really, was going on.

Eventually, we knew what we needed to do. Too many layers of management had been built into the organization. We reduced them. We brought a gifted younger manager, Lew Platt, into the executive committee as chief executive. His predecessor, John Young—the skilled executive who had managed the company's explosive growth through the late 1970s and 1980s—was part of the group that selected Lew.... Needless to say, the Computer Business Executive Committee was disbanded, as was much of the bureaucracy. Most important, computer operating units were given greater freedom to create their own plans and make their own decisions, resulting in a much more flexible and agile company.... HP systems increasingly include products from different groups and divisions, and even though an organization is highly decentralized, its people should be regularly reminded that cooperation between individuals and coordinated efforts among operating units are essential to growth and success. Although we minimize corporate direction at HP, we consider ourselves one single company, with the flexibility of a small company and the strengths of a large one—the ability to draw on corporate resources and services; shared standards, values, and culture; common goals and objectives; and a single worldwide identity.[10]

## Core Culture Driving Change

Packard's leadership signaled the imperative for change and his unwavering belief in the core of the HP Way. Although many questioned the wisdom of creating the CSFSC with its team-based structure, virtually everyone agreed HP was at a turning point and change was inevitable. In most respects the CSFSC is a good example of the difference between core values and practices. HP practice had placed the finance function under the control of autonomous divisions. The practice was no longer cost competitive and, as a result, detracted from the basic mission of individual divisions. HP core values support entrepreneurial spirit with significant individual autonomy in decision making. The leeway Jim and his managers received to create a for-profit business approach was very much in concert with the HP Way. Challenging the ratio of managers to employees, while certainly breaking a common practice, was in line with what was happening throughout the company in late 1991 and 1992. In 1992 John Young, reflecting on HP's changes, observed, "Our basic principles have endured intact since our founders conceived them. We distinguish between core values and practices; the core values don't change, but the practices might."[11] The CSFSC was created on this distinction. Although Luttenbacher understood the countercultural aspects of the new CSFSC, he also saw a clear fit with the core culture. According to Jim Luttenbacher,

What I hoped to bring to this organization was spirit of entrepreneurial activity and, to a great extent, that fit the culture of HP very, very well in that HP is in essence an organization that is built on a structure where independent or autonomous business units are encouraged and nurtured. People are encouraged to go off and figure out how to develop new businesses and run them and grow them and so forth. We really wanted to stress that was what we were all about in the Financial Services Center. I think that fit the HP culture very well. That is a very strong underpinning and was the major theme of what we were trying to do and as a result of that entrepreneurial philosophy for the organization, that put us into a very good fit with HP.

Kemp Bohlen, who would become closely linked to the new organization, remembers a conversation with Dave Packard about the CSFSC:

I can remember talking to Dave Packard about it at a general managers' meeting three or four years ago and he had heard about it. He was asking about it and seemed to be very interested. He asked me this very question, "How do you think this plays with the HP Way?" And I said, "It is made for it." At the time I invited him to come and take a look, and I was really sorry that he didn't get here before he died. We could have put the teams in with Dave and he would have just gone nuts.

## What We Learned When Core Culture Drives Change

We learned two major lessons about the HP Way and organizational change. First, the core of the HP culture is not synonymous with traditional practices, no matter how long they have been in place. Second, the HP value of trust and support for people enabled risk and change that, on the surface, appeared counter-cultural. The decision to centralize and standardize transaction processing certainly broke tradition with local division autonomy. However, centralization took on a particularly HP look—running the centralized service as a for-profit business and contributing to bottom-line profitability by returning savings to the divisions. In a real sense, the CSFSC was extending HP's entrepreneurial spirit to what normally had been considered routine overhead opera-tions. Top management supported the team-based structure despite misgivings about the "experiment." And that support was given despite the stated five-year timetable to realize returns. This fundamental trust in leadership to do the right thing was even more remarkable because many did not agree with the decision. The CSFSC illustrates that waiting for total agreement limits the magnitude of real change. The decision to centralize and use a team-based structure underscored the importance of taking risks even with routine organizational processes. Finally, the early mar-keting strategy of selling the customers on benefits, including the value of a team-based structure, provides evidence that continu-ous communication during disagreement is fundamental to support genuine innovation.

### What This Means for Others

The lesson that *core culture drives change* applies to both new and mature organizations. Core culture identifies the values leaders and the entire organization want to support and clear identifica-tion of those values helps distinguish between values and organizational habits, traditions, and practices. When culture is defined from the history of events as contrasted to the history of values, change can be slow and often occurs only in response to serious crisis. For new organizations this distinction suggests that leaders must pay attention to what values they foster and, from the very beginning, distinguish those values from the day-to-day practices they put in place. For mature organizations the task is often more difficult. The "way we have always done things" becomes individual and collective security and is confused with what might be called the core value of security. Practices that stay in place too long can actually contribute to insecurity and failure more than risk-laden change. But it is hard for people to believe and understand that to "stay the same we must change."

Changing practices is not about consensus. Creative and productive change is about fundamental trust in people and is based on the underlying assumption that people can find ways to energize literally all aspects of organizations.

## The Beginning of Networked Teams

There was no turning back. The CSFSC was launched during a period of rapid change. Resistance was evident, yet most agreed that change had to occur. The team structure was something of an unknown, causing less concern than the shift from division autonomy to centralized services. Luttenbacher and his managers had to move quickly and their decision list was staggering. Little did they know that in the next several months the form of the organization would change even more.

In the next chapter we will take you step-by-step through the early formation of the CSFSC. You will learn about forming the teams, a myriad of training issues, the early hiring processes, and the struggle to define the parameters of roles and responsibilities for literally everyone. You will witness the beginnings of the networked teams concept.

# 4

## *Educate, Educate, Educate: Designing Networked Teams*

I am sure I will survive this, it might even be fun; but oh, boy, I don't think my accounting professor would believe this.

—Training participant

Everything had to be done at once. The decisions had been made, and now it was time to make it happen. On June 14, 1991, Jim Luttenbacher and his staff published the first organization chart for the Colorado Springs Financial Services Center (see fig. 4.1). Most people looking at the chart described it as a traditional hierarchy. Although at the beginning it certainly looked that way, ultimately they would be proven wrong. Jim had three major functions reporting directly to him—process development, operations, and customer services. Two additional dotted-line relationships were identified. Greg Spray represented an organization within Hewlett-Packard named CAIS (Corporate Administrative Information Systems), which provided information technology support for many HP units, divisions, or operations. CSFSC decided to buy information technology management from CAIS, and Greg came to Colorado Springs to head the effort. The Cupertino site controller also joined the initial team as a representative of all remote sites, which would eventually consolidate their transaction processing within the CSFSC. Although the organization chart looked traditional, the concept of linking customers directly to the management team and placing service providers on the team was the unrecognized but embryonic beginning of the networked teams concept.

A Remote Processing Steering Committee was formed to guide the organization's development. Local CSFSC management was joined by representatives from corporate, Cupertino, Stanford Park, Vancouver, Lake Stevens, and Corvallis sites to regularly review plans and progress for the new organization. The representative from Stanford Park, D'Ann Darling, recalls,

> We became the overseeing body. We met about once a month, or more often if we needed, to oversee the decisions. We set up process

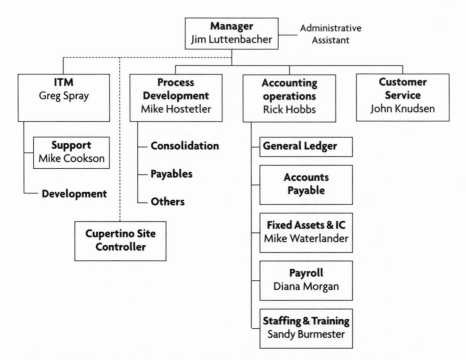

**Figure 4.1. Colorado Springs Financial Services Center Organizational Structure, May 1991**

committees that looked at each process to figure out what could be centralized, what should stay local. We looked at what the hiring policies should be. And we were actually the decision-making body. There were only about six or seven of us so we just made lots of decisions and I am totally amazed at how many of those very early decisions are still in effect today.[1]

From the very beginning the desire to create a truly unique organization was apparent. One of the authors, Pam Shockley-Zalabak, recalls,

I had worked with a large number of management teams, both within HP and other organizations, by the time I began to work with the CSFSC. I can recall only a handful that spent so much time discussing how to build their organization. They were task focused but they also really wanted to create a new way of doing business. I am not sure why they were so committed to challenging taken-for-granted assumptions about service organizations but they were. It was fascinating to watch and to participate in their discussions. They were certain they had to function like a profit-making operation.[2]

### Christmas at the Cheyenne Mountain Inn

Jim, Rick, Sandy, and Pam spent many hours discussing how to launch a team-based organization. Pam was responsible for bringing the experiences of others to the group while Rick and Sandy had primary responsibility for thinking through the needs of the emerging CSFSC. In the fall of 1991, Rick, Sandy, and Pam recommended a major off-site retreat for all CSFSC managers (the number had grown from the initial group of four to twelve). The purpose of the December 1991 retreat was to begin designing the organization based on the goals and objectives of the CSFSC and the experiences of other team-based organizations.

Pam arrived at the Cheyenne Mountain Inn early on the first morning of the retreat. Lavish Christmas decorations and festive music made her smile. Although she and her training partners felt well prepared to facilitate the two-day meeting, the large boxes under the massive Christmas tree reminded her of the potential for surprises—both good and bad. She would leave the retreat two days later with her instincts confirmed. The CSFSC managers would struggle with many of the new concepts but would leave the Cheyenne Mountain Inn with a sense that transforming a set of routine overhead processes into a for-profit-minded business was urgently needed.

Pam and her training team opened the retreat with a presentation of the gyroscope as a metaphor for organizational change and stability. The metaphor, illustrated by actual gyroscopes, appealed to the assembled group; one person voiced the opinion that they (the managers) would need to look like a gyroscope if they were to build a creative yet stable organization. Others joked that the gyroscope reminded them of the upcoming holidays. They needed to get moving in all directions at once if Jim was going to give anyone any time off. Humorous introduction notwithstanding, the gyroscope stuck as a way to think about the project. Managers began to talk about building a new gyroscope to chart the future. To date, all new hires are introduced to the gyroscope as a symbol of the guiding philosophy of the team-based organization. (Interestingly enough, the 1995 HP *Annual Report* compared HP to a gyroscope: "Gyroscopes have been used for almost a century to guide ships, airplanes, and satellites. A gyroscope does this by combining the stability of an inner wheel with the free movement of a pivoting frame. In an analogous way HP's enduring character guides the company as we both lead and adapt to the evolution of technology and markets.")[3]

After reviewing a variety of perspectives on team-based organizations, the assembled managers began to envision a team structure for the CSFSC and HP in general. Sandy recalls,

We were all over the place. Most saw the potential but clearly some felt we didn't have time to add this team stuff with everything else on our plates. We did an exercise to identify our hopes, concerns, and fears for the project. It was interesting—we all wanted the same things but were concerned whether we could make it happen. At the extreme most of us just didn't want to be associated with a failure. We were a competitive bunch—we feared failure even though we knew we had a good chance to succeed.[4]

The training team and the managers discussed success requirements for a team-based organization. Top-level commitment was a major issue, and Jim made it clear he was not going to waver. Management–employee trust was less certain. Many of the managers expressed concern that the individual contributors assigned to the CSFSC were skeptical about teams, not trusting the motivation behind the move to a new organization form. The group concluded that they would need a strong communication plan to help individual contributors understand both the business imperative and the rationale for a team structure. Other success factors discussed were risk taking, shared information, time and resources, training, help and support, and appropriate operations. Each generated often heated conversation. No one doubted that the entire organization was engaged in risk taking that required shared information. Many, however, were genuinely concerned whether HP would provide the time and resources necessary to make the new concept work. Jim assured the group that he would buy time and that top management (Wayman and Cookingham) already agreed. The concern remained for many, especially those not who had not met with Cookingham. The rumor mill about skeptical support had taken a toll.

The training issue was less controversial. The need for training was a given; however, the need to do everything at once made the training requirements seem overwhelming. Help and support was a huge question mark: many within HP had not wanted the change;

rumor had it that top management was skeptical; and who, including the consultants, really knew how to help? Everyone agreed that no one had a blueprint showing what appropriate operations would look like. At one point, a member of the group who was growing impatient with the high anxiety levels (none of us present can remember exactly who it was, although we collectively remember the exchange) said something like, "Wait a minute, we are questioning everything, although we have all accepted this challenge to make it happen. We need to get a grip." Discussion stopped, and then the group laughed and began to move forward. They definitely "got a grip." Their concerns and fears were on the table but they would not block the changes to come.

Pam recommended a process of forming steering and design teams to become the architects and builders of the new organization. These two groups were to be separate from the Remote Processing Steering Committee, although they would work closely with the recommendations from that group. The steering committee, composed of Luttenbacher, Hostetler, and Hobbs, would continually clarify the mission of developing the new organization, establish general parameters for the design team, adopt an overall framework for planning, provide resources, deal with policy and system issues, and communicate change and results. The design team would analyze current systems, develop visions of redesigned approaches, deal with issues of team structure, tasks, results, training, and rewards, review planning with the steering committee, communicate with stakeholders, and manage the implementation process. They were not being asked to buy a preexisting model of a team-based organization. They were challenged to design and build their own. Jim, Rick, and Sandy immediately bought the recommendation. (They, of course, had known what Pam was going to propose.) Many of the others were enthusiastic but several were thoughtfully silent. The extent to which everyone genuinely agreed remains unclear to this day. Jim, Rick, and Mike became the steering team. The design team consisted of all of the other managers. Rick, with his overall responsibility to guide the development of the team-based structure, was a member of both the steering and design teams with specific accountability for linking the needs of both groups. Jim assumed responsibility for connecting the work of the steering and design groups to the Remote Processing Steering Committee.

## Designing Networked Teams:
## Processes, People, Technology

A number of authors have talked about the concept of synchronous innovation, making simultaneous changes throughout an organization. The concept of synchronous innovation stands in stark contrast to the incremental, sometimes plodding change processes in which many organizations engage.[5] Pam remarks,

> I think the CSFSC design phase was one of the best examples of synchronous innovation with which I have personally worked. They were designing technical transaction processes, rethinking hardware and software solutions, creating customer consolidation templates, and organizing workflow into a team-based structure. All of that was happening at once and they deliberately chose that strategy. The energy level was extremely high.[6]

### Designing Processes and Technology

Jim and his managers created the Solutions Center to drive the reengineering of transaction processes. The first process selected for reengineering was accounts payable. Don Whitelaw, a process engineer and an early recruit to the Solutions Center, headed the MEPS project for designing a multi-entity capability for accounts payable processing. The multi-entity accounting system would take entity-specific transactions from remote divisions and still generate a general ledger for each entity. This enabled team members in Colorado Springs to enter transactions for multiple divisions using standardized processes. Additionally, this information needed to be instantaneously available to decentralized divisions, which valued having their accounting information accessible on-site. Other major CSFSC processes were consolidated and then reengineered following Jim's early decision to ensure the quality of the processes before standardizing and automating them. Over time, the Solutions Center became the permanent home for large reengineering projects. Solutions Center personnel are expected to work with customers and with the teams responsible for implementing the processes. In turn the teams are expected, through total quality management efforts, to make important contributions to Solutions Center projects. Two of the best examples of this collaborative approach to reengineering have been (1) efforts on imaging and work flow for accounts payable and (2) raising the dollar limits for capitalization on assets for the entire company. The goal has always been to eliminate the frequently occurring criticism that process engineers don't understand what people in the trenches know about potential improvements in work flow.

Technology decisions also had to move quickly. A member of Greg Spray's group led the effort to determine the types of hardware and software products most appropriate for networking among teams and with customers. UNIX workstations were selected for processing because of their speed and multiwindow capability. LANs were installed and new PC software products for word processing, graphics, and spreadsheets were selected. Each team had one PC in their work area. None of the existing workforce had familiarity with any of the new products, let alone the new processes. No one questioned the need for comprehensive training.

*Designing Customer Relationships*

Although the CSFSC would ultimately form partnerships with their customers, the initial form was much more closely aligned to a traditional client–vendor relationship. The managers of the local Accounting Services Centers (ASCs) generally viewed themselves as customer representatives more than as a link in the service delivery chain. The ASC managers reported through managers at each customer site rather than to the CSFSC manager. The customer perspective was healthy and important during the early consolidation phases, although the model fostered questioning and criticism that could be challenging, especially during customer meetings.

Processes for working with customers required extensive planning and design. Rick explains,

> As we built our customer base, we did road shows constantly. We visited every division every year. We would get in a room where we had targets on the board, we had hostile customers out there throwing questions at us. We would take them and we would not get defensive. When we had the quarterly customer meetings, which brought all the representatives of the customer base to us, we would go over what we had done and how we had addressed concerns that had been expressed. I think that gained us all kinds of support because there wasn't a focus on what wasn't working, there was much more of a focus on how responsive we were and how we were going to get to where the customer needed us to be. We didn't consolidate all customers in one year. We said, "You don't have to come." We made it a sort of free market approach. Nobody really believed in their heart of hearts that they could get away with staying out of the FSC, but it wasn't from pressure from us. They came when they were ready— when they had a team in place. We also had a world-class consolidation process. It is still a model in HP that has never been met and is the envy of everybody that tries to consolidate.[7]

John Knudsen and Mike Hostetler owned the consolidation process, a two-phase process, to which Rick refers. Templates were function specific, for example, travel accounting, intracorporate accounting, accounts payable, fixed-asset accounting. The first-phase template was used by sites to get processes such as account reconciliation or chart of accounts usage and systems in shape (standard configuration) for consolidation. In preparation for the start of the second phase, each site received a set of documents that included a timeline and description of steps to be taken weekly and issues to be considered. The template was used as a reference at checkpoint meetings to get a feel for how well each site was using the tool. Consolidation progress was tracked using a red light–green light approach. When too many signals were red, concerns or issues were escalated for new approaches and solutions. Additionally all consolidation sites relied on site procedures and the HP Accounting and Finance Manuals. Constant communication was the strategy. Everyone involved kept reminding one another that nondefensive behavior was the key. This positive approach could be wearing at times but the end result was worth it.

### Designing the Teams

Shortly after the Cheyenne Mountain retreat, the design team for the team-based structure began to meet, meet, and meet. In addition to the four CSFSC operations managers, Sandy and three representatives from the Solutions Center joined the design team. Not one person had previously attempted to design an organization. They were smart, capable, and lost—all at the same time. But they did not remain lost for long.

Working with Rick, this group of eight set about to answer tough questions about team structure. That the teams would report to Rick in his role as accounting operations manager was a given. How to structure the teams, how to organize their work, and how they were to be managed and manage themselves was less clear. The term "self-directed teams" was adopted and the "gyroscope" journey began in earnest.

Meeting at least once a week and often more frequently, the design team spent the first quarter of 1992 formulating their design and implementation plan. Six central questions had to be addressed: (1) How should existing middle management be accommodated? (2) How should teams be composed? (3) What is an appropriate team size? (4) How much autonomy should be given to teams? (5) What responsibilities should teams own? and (6) Over what time frame should team responsibilities be assumed by the teams?

## Creating the Facilitator Role

From the early stages of the project Rick had recognized that a traditional HP span of control, or ratio of managers to employees, would not produce the potential cost reductions necessary for the new organization. Guided by Rick's research, the design team composed of mostly middle managers had to tackle the reality that some of their jobs would need to go away. Not only would the numbers be different, but the actual job content required a major transformation. Working with Pam and reviewing the experiences of others, the design team literally created the HP facilitator role. Rick explains that

> in a self-directed team environment, middle management moves from a hierarchical-supervisory position to one of a coach of SDT (self-directed team) members. Their job becomes not to tell workers what to do, but rather how to teach team members to lead themselves. However, supervisor resistance to such change is great. Middle managers tend to feel they are being pushed out of the firm and struggle to protect their turf. It is to everyone's benefit if the

firm provides a safety net to existing middle management not interested in participating in the SDT program. Allowing these
individuals to make a lateral move within the firm can substantially
increase the chances of success for the SDT program.

One of the early design team members decided his personality
and work approach were not suited to what he was hearing. He left
the project, openly admitting that "I would not be comfortable
giving up a high level of control while still having responsibility for
the results of the process."[8] His honest assessment set an important tone for the project and his lateral transfer was treated as a
success. Stimulated by the departure of a capable individual, both
CSFSC management and design team members candidly discussed
the importance of self-awareness in assessing the new balance of
skills needed to make the organization a success. Sandy recalls,

> We sat down and took a look at the skill set. In retrospect we did
> not spend enough time doing that. The role and responsibilities
> would have been easier to deliver if we had spent more time. There
> is an old approach that says managing is managing. Well it isn't and
> we did not offer enough training to make the transition easier.

The design team formalized the purpose of the facilitator role—
develop and continually promote high-performing, self-directed
teams within the FSC who process accounting transactions while
meeting/exceeding customer expectations. Key responsibilities
were outlined and they represented a fundamental shift in thinking. HP is a technical company and accounting is a technical field.
Amazingly, technical and administrative skills composed only 20
percent of the new key responsibilities. Facilitation and leadership
skills accounted for 50 percent of the responsibilities, with communication and interpersonal skills making up the remaining 30
percent. Eighty percent of the new job was coaching, instructing,
training, visioning, dealing with conflict, listening, providing feed-

back, and empowering. The words sounded good but making it happen would be the challenge.

The change was swift. One day people were managers and the next day a group of four became facilitators. Diana Morgan, one of the first middle managers to transition to a facilitator role, remembers,

> Major responsibilities in the beginning had to do with helping the teams form, understanding their purpose and role, and helping them answer why do we exist. I think this was real important because we had so many outside hires [new to HP]. We had to help them learn HP culture, understand our policies and guidelines, and clarify roles. One of my major responsibilities was to coach and advise on responsibilities, work load balancing, etc. Things like conflict management, customer service and communication, we spent a great deal of time on because they needed to know how to work together as team members and what that meant, and how to resolve conflict instead of, in a traditional environment, coming to a manager and saying, "Sally is mad at me, and it's your problem. Fix it." One of the biggest changes for me was guiding instead of directing. There is a big difference when you start giving people coaching to get them to think through the answer, what alternatives to consider, and doing research to get the answer. I have always said that if someone asks you a question and you answer yes or no, you are directing, not guiding. Really the biggest difference is changing your mind-set to help the team members so they can do the research on their own to answer their questions and run the business that they are involved in.[9]

Initially the facilitator role was scoped for compensation at an HP supervisory level. The hiring of a new facilitator quickly put the issue of technical versus facilitation skills squarely on the table. An individual with extensive technical skills was hired to fill a technical role but was shifted to a facilitator position on arrival. However, his technical (higher than supervisor) pay scale remained. The original facilitator team challenged management on this issue. According to Sandy,

> They clearly said to management you have to show us that these interpersonal skills you are requiring of us are just as important as technical skills. I think what the facilitators wanted was an action that demonstrated that there really was support for this concept. To them the evidence was the scoping of the job—the really long-term commitment. Rick Hobbs was very instrumental in making the change to a higher level job scope. It was not hard for the other managers to do this. They were supportive. Looking back, this was a critical decision—to make the facilitator an important player in the overall design.

### Creating the Teams

The design team turned their attention to structuring the teams. Classic discussions over customer or functional assignments consumed hours. Sandy comments, "I got bloody over this one. I wanted cross-functional, customer-focused teams. We ended up with functional teams with a primary customer base." Teams were to process transactions for one or more of the five processing areas: accounts payable, fixed assets, intracompany, general ledger, and travel expense. Teams also staffed the Customer Response Center. The size of the teams had to be decided. Sandy and Rick reviewed the professional literature and determined that most research supported a range of sizes from four to no more than ten members per team. The design team chose to recommend no fewer than four individuals on a team and a maximum team size of eight. They wanted critical mass while remaining small enough to avoid subgroup formations.

The toughest issue of all for design team members was determining how much autonomy should be given to the teams. Some of the former managers (now facilitators) had concerns about surrendering managerial control with teams that were not yet trained and had not worked together. Others argued that it was necessary to start from the very beginning with high expectations for mature behavior and responsibility. In the end, design team members decided to empower teams to balance work loads, review time cards, and schedule vacation/sick time. Additionally, team members were expected to participate in interviewing new hires and to conduct team meetings, write system requests (SRs—requests to make changes to computer systems), develop team expectations, and learn to track performance metrics.

In mid-January 1992, the twenty-seven original employees, along with Sandy, Pam, and an HP human relations liaison, Diane Pugh, returned to the Cheyenne Mountain Inn to formally communicate the decision to move to a team environment and discuss the initial design team decisions. One of the first questions asked was, "So what is the backup plan if this team thing doesn't work?" The reply shocked many—there was no plan B. This was intentional. For change to be believable, change had to occur and it had to have staying power.

All involved believed it was extremely important to follow the announcement with action. The design team had detailed what responsibilities made sense for the new teams. Sandy asked the assembled employees to determine where they wanted to start with their new responsibilities. It was unanimous—the pioneer team members wanted to be involved in hiring their peers. Sandy and Diane quickly put together instruction on interviewing and the teams were officially launched.

Over the next several years, the initial responsibility list expanded dramatically to include such difficult issues as peer and facilitator performance feedback and input for formal appraisals. In later chapters we will describe this expanding empowerment as we follow the evolution of the teams.

(It is important to remember that no one on the original steering or design teams knew that the organization would evolve beyond a team-based structure to a form we are calling networked teams. The beginnings were there—the close relationship with customers, the technology, the new processes, and the self-directed team structure—but the network relationships and influence processes were not embedded in daily organizational practice. That would come later as the CSFSC evolved and grew.)

## Hiring for Teams

Early on Jim and his staff had decided that HP employees in accounting functions throughout the country would have the option of transferring to Colorado Springs if and when their jobs were affected by the CSFSC. Rick and Sandy knew that few probably could or would take that option, making it important to develop a comprehensive recruitment and hiring plan to staff the new organization. Like everything else in the CSFSC, the plan was aggressive.

Sandy devised a three-step process that would apply to both external and internal candidates: "We would resume screen for compliance with minimum requirements, conduct a set of technical assessments, and interview for the important interpersonal skills. Candidates had to meet the assessment requirements in order to progress to the interview."

In January 1992, ads ran in the Colorado Springs and Denver papers describing the new organization and qualifications for potential team members. Over 600 individuals applied for approximately fifty open positions. During the first two weeks of February 270 individuals were given written assessments, with 154 people being interviewed during the last week of February and first two weeks of March. The interview schedule was grueling. Five interview teams (Alpha, Bravo, Charlie, Delta, and Echo) each conducted six one-hour interviews each day. Interview panels consisted of a CSFSC manager, a human resources representative, and a team member from the original group transferred to the CSFSC. Ques-

tioning focused on how individuals would handle a variety of interpersonal and customer situations. All applicants were made aware
of the envisioned responsibilities a team structure would bring.
Fifty-one new hires emerged from the applicant pool of 600. Stag-
gered start dates began in April and extended through June.

The process for screening current HP employees ran concur-
rently with external recruitment. Interested individuals in consolidating divisions or other HP employees completed a work sample
assessment, and successful candidates were interviewed with the
same set of scripted questions used with external applicants. Eighteen internal candidates interviewed, with ten employees actually
transferring.

The hiring schedule throughout 1992, 1993, and 1994 continued
at a rapid pace. Hiring occurred again in late October 1992, and
ten separate times during 1993 and 1994. Not only was the initial
workforce unfamiliar with teams and consolidated processes, but
in a two and a half year period, 144 new hires joined their ranks.
The 144 were new to teams, new to HP technology and processes,
and new to the HP culture. For any given day, chaos and confusion
would be a polite way to describe the activity level.

### Educate, Educate, Educate

It was time to put the gyroscopes in motion. Literally everyone
needed a solid introduction to the team concept as well as extensive technical training. Jim and Rick approved a record training
budget for 1992, putting everyone through more than fifty days of
classroom instruction (see box 4.1). Sandy was responsible for the
education and training plans which she describes as two separate
approaches:

> Training involves teaching someone how to complete a task, such
> as what steps must be completed to enter invoice information into
> the MEPS systems. Education, on the other hand, instills the fun-

damental skills needed to perform in a position. Education includes, for example, problem solving or managing conflict. CSFSC uses both; however, our real emphasis is on education rather than just training.

And educate (and train) they did.

---

**Box 4.1. New Employee Training Checklist**

Training for new team members should include all of the items listed below. A separate checklist is provided for the functional area technical training. Training is provided by team members, FSC management, consultants, and individual self-paced efforts.

Orientation/Health and safety checklist
CSFSC and site tour
Review CSFSC Web site
Meet with operations manager
Accounting theory pretest
PC training
Phone and voice mail training
E-mail training
Accounting theory (if needed)
Technical training
Tax training (accounts payable and fixed assets)
Abilene Paradox video
Meeting management training/Meetings
Bloody Meetings video
Team training
Performance, evaluation, and pay
Review self-directed team responsibilities
Peer input process
Giving and receiving feedback videos
Total quality management
General ledger
Design team function and history
Accounting theory posttest (if needed)
End-of-training review
Submit completed training checklist

All new hires were introduced to teams in a two-day team workshop designed and presented by Pam and her group. The now familiar gyroscope was used to introduce each session. Team members first were asked to make the gyroscope work and then describe why gyroscopes were a metaphor for the type of organization CSFSC wanted to become. Many new hires had never seen a gyroscope, making them dependent on their fellow team members as well as the instruction sheet. Once the gyroscopes were up and running, however, descriptions flowed. Answers frequently reflected an understanding of the need for rapid movement, teamwork, the concept of maintaining balance only when moving, and the notion of not getting set on moving in one direction.

Participants were told that the team structure was selected and implemented to support compelling business goals. Creativity and productivity gains were expected because teams provided an excellent opportunity for a mature treatment of the workforce. Research about other team structures was presented and team members were introduced to the notion of dual competency—team and technical. Like the managers before them, all new hires identified their hopes, fears, and concerns for the new organization. Prominent among the responses were hopes for being accepted by other team members, having fun, finding job satisfaction, making a difference, and building knowledge and effective skills. Fears commonly centered around not fitting in, inability to handle conflicts, failing, and not meeting team expectations. Concerns were more diffuse, frequently relating to dealing with people who don't buy into the team idea, managing workload, and using new and unfamiliar tools and processes. All team members completed the Myers-Briggs Type Inventory and a series of conflict preference instruments. Three team processes were stressed: problem solving and decision making, conflict management, and meeting management. Team members identified team values and behavior norms that subsequently were posted in team work areas. Upon completing the training, one participant said, "I am sure I will survive this, it might even be fun; but oh, boy, I don't think my accounting professor would believe this."

Mike Hackman, one of the trainers in Pam's group and also a professor at the University of Colorado, describes the reactions of participants to team training,

> Like so many of the groups with whom I work, the employees in the team training at HP are often anxious about the experience of working in teams. Many wonder if they can be successful in this organizational structure and how a team-based environment will differ from what they have encountered in the past. Participants in the training generally respond very positively when they begin to understand how teams operate. Of course, change, even change for the better, creates uncertainty. HP is unique, however, because there is such strong support for the use of teams from top-level management. Although many of the organizations I have worked with have demonstrated a strong commitment to the use of teams, few have been as consistent as HP in reinforcing the value of teams. This cannot be overlooked in explaining the success of teams within the FSC at HP. Support from above is a critical determinant of success in the implementation of a team-based organizational structure. Without visible, vocal, long-term support from senior management, the kind of success that has been enjoyed by the teams at HP is not possible.[10]

Following their introduction to teams and throughout their first year, all new hires had extensive technical training on HP processes and software programs as well as additional work on conflict management, communication, and interviewing. And this support for education and training continues today. The CSFSC routinely makes financial and time commitments to education that far exceed most competitor organizations. Sandy believes this continuous commitment to development models the very essence of a learning organization.[11]

## What We Learned When Designing
## and Educating Networked Teams

We quickly learned that the process of designing and building a great organization does not come with map, compass, or prepackaged blueprints. There is no one right answer, and when you come to accept this as normal, true ownership and creativity are unleashed. Research and the experiences of others can and should assist designing, but excellence comes from unleashing the talents of people who, as designers and builders, must live in their own creation. We again saw the importance of business goals to the design phase. It was tough for managers to become facilitators, but the numbers were clear. Business goals could not be achieved with a typical HP span of control. We learned the benefits of synchronous innovation when designing accounting processes, selecting technology, structuring teams, and building customers' processes all occurred at once. No one function of the organization drove the way it had to be in other areas. We also learned that, unlike the construction of a physical structure, there is no distinct beginning and ending to good design and implementation. The CSFSC is simultaneously in design, implementation, evaluation, and revision. We came to understand that in the midst of the start-up and design the designers frequently did not know exactly where they were headed. And we have come to believe this was a strength of their work. A new organization form does not emerge from old blueprints; the gyroscope truly provides a better model.

We learned that education is more important than training for a team-based organization. Investing in developing critical thinking, problem solving, decision making, conflict resolution, and communication skills builds for the future. Training for a specific skill set gets the job done today and requires retraining when the job changes. We also learned that working in a team-based organization is not an experience many bring with them. Unlearning old habits takes time and support because personal and team development reinforce change. Finally, the CSFSC debunks the myth that learning takes away from doing. CSFSC members at all levels spent and continue to spend more time in educational and training activities than competitor organizations. They also continue to outdistance these competitors in terms of productivity.

## What This Means for Others

The lessons "designing networked teams" and "educate, educate, educate" blend together in ways that are often hard to internalize, although they both call for a lot of hard work. Simply put, the road to an excellent organization does not come with many shortcuts. It requires leaders and numerous others to commit long hours to thinking through what is needed and what is not. Designing a team-based organization can be facilitated by what others have experienced, but the one-size-fits-all model rarely maximizes the opportunities in a specific organization. We also believe careful consideration should be given to creating simultaneous changes throughout the organization. The HP experience provides an example of the energy that was unleashed when change was occurring in literally all aspects of the new organization. Additionally, the small size of the start-up venture made large-scale change even easier to implement.

Gaynelle Winograd, one of the original CSFSC trainers and a member of the current team responsible for new-hire team training, describes what she believes the emphasis on design and education can mean for others:

> Many team-based initiatives fail when there is a lack of emphasis on creating a shared model or understanding regarding what constitutes an effective team. Because of a variety of backgrounds and experiences, team members come preset with different images as to what is an effective team. At the CSFSC, there has been a deliberate attempt to create a common vision and language for what an

effective team is to look, feel, and sound like. The socialization processes of new members into a team-based environment are more complex than a traditional organization with a traditional structure. It cannot be left to chance or best wishes.[12]

## The First 18 Months

By the end of 1992, a pattern was emerging. The reengineering effort was under way. Consolidation was progressing and the pace was quickening. The teams were beginning. The customers were still skeptical, but many liked the continuous communication with an emphasis on listening and responding. Although costs were high and no major productivity gains had been achieved, the managers were enthused, believing gains were just around the corner. Then the unexpected happened. Jim Luttenbacher resigned. The visionary leader, the individual charged with buying time for the organization to succeed, was leaving HP. In the next chapter you will learn why Jim left and how his leaving affected the CSFSC. We will also describe the complex management challenges involved in transitioning embedded hierarchical management roles to a networked teams organization. Finally, you will learn what happens when the wrong manager gets hired.

# 5

## Role Shifting:
## Teams Learn to Cope with Ambiguity

I can imagine what the customer calling in thought—egad, what is going on in Colorado Springs.

—Diana Morgan

### Changes at the Top

Jim Luttenbacher's announcement that he had taken a position outside Hewlett-Packard shook the organization and raised all sorts of questions. Did he think the Colorado Springs Financial Services Center was going to fail? Were his bosses about to pull the plug on the business plan? What was going on? Oddly enough, even though his leaving created a high degree of internal anxiety, the offer that lured him away—joining Mentor Graphics for a position in finance and later becoming the division manager for the advanced verification and interconnect division—ame precisely because the financial world external to HP was beginning to take notice of what was happening in Colorado Springs. Others wanted innovative leadership. Jim recalls his decision to leave:

I got to a point with the Financial Services Center where I knew it was going to work.... once I knew it was going to work there was something in me that it wasn't quite as exciting anymore. Seeing it through was something I really wanted to do, but on the other hand, we always got calls from the outside and opportunities to look at different positions. As those calls started to come in, I found myself answering them and starting to look at what else was out there. I guess I was assessing also what I wanted to do in the long term and how my long-term career goals would be met inside of HP. I started to convince myself that in order to be a really well-rounded financial executive it would take me a very, very long time to get all the exposure to all the different things and all the different processes that a CFO-type person needed to have if I had stayed with HP. I was just kind of antsy, bottom line. I got enamored with this idea of being a bigger fish in a smaller pond and I decided to make that change.[1]

Insiders agreed that the selection of Jim's successor would signal whether the CSFSC model would survive. Ambiguity increased in November 1992, when Kemp Bohlen, the Americas geographic controller, was selected to replace Luttenbacher. Kemp had headed a fast ramp up of the Atlanta FSC field support organization but in a traditional hierarchical model. Although he had not criticized the CSFSC, no one had heard him express strong support for a team-based structure. Kemp describes his arrival in Colorado Springs: "Everyone quizzed me the first day I was here, 'Did I believe in this concept?' I think quite frankly I had a hard time convincing them that I did, having come from Atlanta where we weren't in that construct."[2] But Kemp quickly became known for supporting the founding business plan. Cookingham and Wayman were staying the course. The CSFSC had just cleared a major hurdle—a change at the top.

Kemp came to the CSFSC in a time of intense growth and consolidation. Immediately prior to his appointment, Lake Stevens, Stanford site, and Vancouver had become CSFSC customers. Corporate joined the month Kemp arrived, and in 1993 new customers included Loveland, Scientific Instrument, WCSO, San Jose, Fort

Collins, San Diego, ICON, New Jersey, and part of Chelmsford. Forty-eight new employees were hired and trained to handle increased volumes from consolidations. Kemp's responsibilities broadened beyond Colorado Springs when he was asked to become the owner of HP Worldwide Financial Services. This group would lead the implementation of a new computer platform for the finance function worldwide. Juergen Rottler left CSFSC's information technology group to assume leadership of the worldwide financial transaction processing project with reporting responsibility to Kemp (see fig. 5.1). The organization was changing before it had been fully formed.

The year 1993 became known as the year of the new platform phase.[3] The initial consolidations had illustrated the pain involved with the current systems. Some sites had systems that were vastly different from others, and there were real questions about the ability of the legacy systems to handle the volumes that the CSFSC

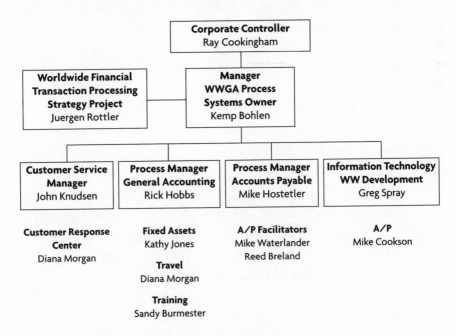

**Figure 5.1. Colorado Springs Financial Services Center Organizational Structure, January 1993**

would require. And the customers were moving to a hot new product, SAP. SAP was touted as capable of integrating business functions typically requiring multiple systems and interfaces to meet needs.

The worldwide project added pressure to the already chaotic pace of the CSFSC. The new worldwide strategy included a vision that boldly embraced one financial transaction organization, one budget, and one set of objectives. A worldwide business plan was to be developed with one overall SAP installation strategy. The German FSC was identified as the initial target, and SAP was selected as the new platform. The CSFSC was barely under way, with the HP centralization concept developing a head of steam all its own.

The year also began with what was to become a steady stream of visits to the CSFSC from other companies. Cargill, the agricultural business leader with some 82,000 employees in fifty-nine countries, came first, and by fall 1993, so many wanted to visit that the CSFSC scheduled the first of many open houses. The early open houses provided interactions that surprised the visitors—team members talking about their experiences directly to top managers without any HP leadership present. The openness of the approach bothered some even as it intrigued others. Jim Villamana, director of Americas Financial Services for J.D. Edwards, describes his visits:

> The HP FSC is a first-class operation. As you walk through their facility and talk to their organization, you get a real sense that they are proud of, and should be proud of, what they have accomplished. Although I have been to the HP service center on several occasions, every visit brings a new learning experience.[4]

Most agree, and attendance at the open houses has, to date, brought over 150 companies to learn about the Colorado Springs experience.

The decision and strategy changes that were made in 1993 were substantial but only part of the changes important for our story. The role shifting required for leading the team-based organization was creating difficult challenges as well as opportunities.

## Who Changed the Rules?

The old HP rules about excellent management were a thing of the past. A one-on-one relationship with a small group of subordinates was simply too expensive. Experienced managers who were accustomed to delegating a set of well-defined responsibilities and assessing each individual's ability to contribute to the workload found the magnitude of needed change somewhat staggering. The old rules were gone but no one had written the new rules. Pam recalls:

> I had numerous conversations with the initial set of facilitators about their role. Sometimes they just wanted someone to tell them what to do; we would have to step back and assess why that was not possible. If the teams were to mature into high-performing groups, the art and science of facilitation would have to mature as well. The facilitators needed to become their own high-performing team by learning how to grow and evolve their roles. I often likened their experiences to the protean concept of shapeshifting[5] [the continual seeking of new forms and shapes] or to the gyroscope metaphor of fluid change as the ultimate stability mechanism.[6]

### Facilitative versus Directive Management

Everyone involved was accustomed to directive management. But providing direction and directing are two very different processes. The leadership of CSFSC came to know and respect the distinction. Kemp Bohlen explains,

You have to change your management style, and you have to learn to operate in this environment. The key operating word is patience. Your inclination is to jump right into the fray, particularly in the start-up environment. You have to learn how to keep from providing team members with the answer and encourage them to come up with the answer on their own. The other key thing is you have to be willing to let people make mistakes. Because of your managerial experience you can see it coming. I think the key is to set the environment so the teams can make the mistake and it doesn't become lethal. In the traditional model, if you are in there telling everybody exactly what to do and something goes wrong, you only have one person to blame. In this environment you spread the overall decision making and consequently some of the risk management. I guess if you believe in the concept of synergy, you get a better decision with the spread. At the end of the day, I always felt that I was responsible for the organization and if something went south, it was my fault one way or another. It does cause you to change your managerial style if you want the organization to be successful.[7]

Mike Waterlander, Diana Morgan, Reed Breland, and Kathy Jones were among the first individuals to assume the facilitator role and actually grow and evolve the role for the future.[8] All four had mixes of HP and accounting experience but, similar to the management team, they had no real experience in start-up organizations or with team-based structures. Reed remembers his response to an ad in HP's job listings for the CSFSC: "It said the job seeker must enjoy coaching, working with people, and bringing about improvement through hands-off guidance and leadership. And this was for an accounts payable position. It was unlike any job listing I had ever seen." Breland, who has an MBA in finance and had a goal of becoming a controller, flew to Colorado Springs for an interview. Part of the interview process included meeting with some of the team members he would lead if hired:

> Some of them were twenty- or twenty-one-year-olds doing clerical-level accounting, so I'm thinking, How hard is it going to be to impress them? But I was amazed at how well prepared they were. They wanted to know about things like how I handled conflict, what kind of time-management skills I had, and how I felt about delegating. It was the strangest interview I've ever had.[9]

In an August 1998 meeting, the four facilitator pioneers and Sandy Burmester[10] reflected on the defining characteristics and challenges of leading in a team-based structure. They began by talking about important distinctions between facilitation and supervision. Mike Waterlander explains,

> Facilitation is steering versus controlling, leading, coaching, focus on development, listening—more a partner role. You're just a voice in decision making, whereas in supervision you are the decision maker. Leadership can be authority-based or based on expertise. In the case of self-managed teams, leadership comes from expertise in facilitation skills.

According to Diana Morgan,

> There is an element of ego difference between the two. Supervision—you're in control. You know everything and if someone comes up to you, you have an answer, and you just pop it off. But I think ego in facilitation is wanting others to be successful and relying on them to be the experts. One of the biggest things you want to do is help your teams communicate—learn how to develop good communication skills with each other and with other people outside the organization so they can get things done without you.

Kathy Jones adds that

> in the supervisory role you're looked at more as a technical expert. But I think one of the responsibilities of a facilitator, if you have a new group and it's a new area, is ensuring that you share that technical base so they all inherit your knowledge. It is really knowledge transfer to the people you're facilitating.

### Letting Go: Letting Mistakes Happen

The discussion turned to the tough subject of letting mistakes happen. As Mike recalls,

> I thought it was really hard. We didn't let them drive off the cliff. We kind of helped them avoid the big monumental mistakes but let them make some mistakes and develop trust in their own judgment. That was hard. And I think one of the things that made it especially hard was the unknown repercussions to our own performance evaluation. How the teams performed and whether they were succeeding or failing was a direct reflection on us and so, given this new management environment, I wasn't sure how hard I could let them crash when they went off the cliff without feeling the pain myself. It was more difficult to know when to let them crash versus stepping in and helping them avoid a potentially disastrous crash.

Mike describes the strategies he used to navigate the potential mistake:

> I think it was just a coaching step. It's not stepping in and swooping down—it's not that kind of take control, but you're asking questions. Have you thought about x? Have you thought about y? What will your customers think about that if everyone is taking FTO [leave] on Friday? It's that kind of thing. So I think it's still the facilitation, really, not deviating from that, but it's a little bit more

proactive versus waiting for something to blow up. You can see something bad coming down the road—you're going to have this problem, but in more of a coaching way you ask questions—probing questions. I think that's the most effective way because then people can learn from the questions. It is not just yes or no.

Diana remarks that

sometimes you don't know how big the mistake is until later on. And the example I had is one the teams still share with other teams. It was a hiring situation where they could not agree on the best candidate so they picked a candidate that was a compromise. You don't know at the time that the person may not be the best choice, but sometimes you have this feeling gnawing at the back of you that this could be a mistake. Sure enough, ten months down the road it did not work out. So instead of the team working out the issues of why they were so separated on their choice, they went with someone totally different, and it did not work.

Kathy agreed that hiring is an area where potential mistakes happen:

When it comes to hiring decisions made by the team before they have really had enough experience to think of all the attributes, they sometimes take the perspective of my best friend versus what are the skill sets we need for our team to be successful.

Reed describes how dealing with mistakes

requires understanding that every team has a different personality and a different maturity. Some teams, right from the get go, are really professional—thinking about what skills we need on this team—other teams are not. Working with the differences as a facilitator included being flexible enough to change your style with this teams versus that team. So I could be more hands-off with one team that came in like gang busters, whereas another team needed all kinds of nudging and coaching and that kind of stuff. It is really pretty dynamic from that standpoint.

Sandy provides an additional example of team member growth based on mistakes that the facilitators knowingly allowed to happen:

A learning opportunity occurred around our early reward and recognition process. In an effort to get teams used to setting goals, striving to meet them, and determining if the goals had been met, we developed an R&R [reward and recognition] program that asked the teams to set quarterly goals and, at the end of the quarter, determine whether or not the goals were met. If the goals were met, the team got a small cash award and a hot air–style balloon for their team area. Even though we stressed the need for the goal to be a stretch goal, over time, the award became more important than setting challenging goals. This tendency became very obvious to the facilitators early on. However, the facilitators deciding to cancel the program versus the teams making that decision would not have been the right answer. As we had hoped, the teams eventually became irritated with what was perceived as rewards for doing work that met day-to-day expectations instead of reaching for a stretch goal. The teams, themselves, made the decision to cancel the program.

### Channeling Energy: Focusing on Business Needs

Without a doubt the team members were energetic. The real challenge was to focus that energy on business needs. And the concept of business needs required specific articulation for everyone, team members and management alike. Once the broad concepts of facilitation versus direction were identified, those concepts had to translate into parameters for the teams—parameters that shifted traditional roles and responsibilities. The discussions around the specifics challenged the support for the core values of self-direction. What did self-direction mean? What was too much too soon? What would contribute to substantive change? The initial parameters list was basic but challenging for individuals not accustomed to role shifting. Managers were no longer solely responsible for interviewing, time cards, team meetings, or workload balancing. Team members would participate in interviewing, review their own time cards, run their own meetings, and manage the work. Teams would write system requests (SRs), develop their own group expectations, performance metrics, and, in general, become their own coordinators. Team members said they were ready. One facilitator wondered aloud how long he would have a job. Although his peers laughed at him, others may have felt the same. Reed remembers the early facilitator role as being extremely hard: "I would go home every night and rethink what I did, how I did it, and whether I should change it."[11]

Although all of the teams began with the same set of parameters, the concept of differential development came into play. Realistically, not all teams could be expected—based on a combination of personal factors, technical experience, and skills—to progress at the same rate. If role shifting and the evolution of self-direction were to be genuinely meaningful, it would be necessary to devise a strategy to move teams on a team-by-team pace as long as overall business needs were met. In other words, the design team and the facilitators had to devise a plan for individual team development acknowledging that not all teams would move in lockstep through both development activities or the assumption of increasing responsibilities.

Another canon of management—equal treatment and equal expectations for all—was challenged. Team development plans had to focus on the needs of the specific team with the end result that all teams would be expected to support business goals. There would be general target dates for all teams to assume responsibilities, but individual team differences were to be treated as normal and not a problem. Furthermore, team members were expected to collaborate with the facilitators to identify their specific needs and to identify opportunities to meet those needs. It was different for everyone and it required more skill. It wasn't just end-product thinking. Facilitators and team members both were expected to utilize critical thinking and creativity to assess needs and identify formal and informal opportunities for growth and development. The desired end product did not come with map and compass. As one team member told Pam, "I should have paid more attention to that darned gyroscope."

### Team Member Laments: "You Aren't Doing Your Job!"

Although most supported the changes at least verbally, the role shifting was tough. Team members wanted responsibility, but they had spent most of their work lives in traditional authority structures. The facilitators were often perceived as not doing their job. In conversations with both Sandy and Pam and directly with the facilitators, team members contended that the facilitators were paid to help more than they were helping. Pam notes,

> It seemed to me at this point in the development of the organization we were observing an important dynamic in the practical aspects of change. We had seen how important core values were to driving the new organization. I had observed throughout the hiring process the search for individuals who could commit to this type of environment. Discussion at all levels focused on attitudes of flexibility and willingness to change. Then came the day-to-day work realities. Teams wanted autonomy and control most of the time. But when there were serious conflicts, they wanted the facilitators to take over. I considered it critical that the facilitators learned to push back at the very time the teams seemed to need them most.

This tension illustrated the importance of sustained behavior change. It would have been very easy to literally flip the organization back to a more traditional structure to avoid working through this period.[12]

Sandy recognizes that

even today, new team members have a difficult time with internalizing that managing conflict is the team member's responsibility. Most teams still struggle with when to hand a conflict over to the facilitator. The balance will always be a difficult one. Some teams will work with a conflict way too long before handing it to the facilitator. Other teams want to give it to the facilitator before exerting much effort to correct the situation. Once a conflict is handed to the facilitator, the three-step HP corrective action process is used that mandates confidentiality between the facilitator and the team member. Since discussion of the status of the situation with other team members is not allowed, this can be perceived as "nothing is happening." HP's three-step process includes verbal warning, written warning, and probation. If the performance or behavior is not changed as a result of probation, termination occurs. Only then do other team members see "results."

The company requirement that corrective action processes are handled by a manager is a good example of where preexisting hierarchical structure forces a compromise with established team responsibilities. Ideally, teams handling the formal corrective action process would be an indication of strong self-management. HP's existing requirements place limitations on the degree to which teams can evolve in this area.[13]

## Team Managers as a Team

Greg Spray had come to Colorado Springs to head the information technology effort and to serve on the initial leadership team. Later he would follow Kemp Bohlen and John Knudsen as head of the CSFSC. When he began to work directly with the facilitators and the teams, he quickly saw the importance of the facilitator team:

> It is my insistence and my belief, sometimes against other people's beliefs, that the facilitator team is the key to success—make or break. The organization leader role is fairly easy as long as you're willing to put 100 percent into the communication. Facilitator is a make-or-break role. You need not only to have numbers of the four sigma empowering type people (Greg refers to HP's description of a statistically small number of people who are extremely strong performers), but you also need to have them be team players and you need to have them work as a high-performing team and model those behaviors. You can really see how the teams pick up on that or don't pick up on that.

Greg responds to those within HP and others who don't see the necessity of the facilitators as a team:

> That's absolutely not true. Also there is an echo of critics who say that facilitators—that role which is more people than technical— should not be as valued as the technical roles and maybe that's an HP response but I think that's exactly opposite. It's fairly easy, I think—natural to be good at technology, good at project work. It's very hard, I think, to be an effective facilitator. And yet your lever-age on facilitation is so high that you can't afford not to have your best people there and reward them accordingly.[14]

### Managing Up, Down, and Sideways

Although Mike, Reed, Diana, Kathy, and Sandy agreed with Greg that valuing and rewarding the facilitator role was critical, they unanimously believed that the role initially was ambiguous, with most not really understanding the potential contribution. Mike explains:

People really didn't understand the role. People viewed the role somewhat suspiciously. The role wasn't always respected or it didn't always feel like it was respected because it was viewed as very touchy-feely. [Later the CSFSC would change the role title from facilitator to finance operations manager—FOM.] I think that was difficult because in many respects we had traditional responsibilities, and we were trying to execute them within a very traditional organizational structure [the larger HP environment]. I never felt like the responsibilities changed. You still have responsibility for metrics, performance, and everything else—quality—but you're trying to deliver that in a very nontraditional way.

According to Reed,

We had that one diagram depicting the movement of the gears. I always remember that pace of change. Something moving slowly high up in the organization but the bottom wheels are really turning. And we were in the middle trying to keep that in sync in a time when change was incredibly fast paced, with the consolidations and the new systems. You get sandwiched in the middle. The traditional higher management [external to the CSFSC and managers above the facilitators] sometimes would just come down with decisions, although your team environment is used to participating and giving input on the decision. There you are with the decision trying to make them think they are participating.

As Mike points out, "To try to push back on that senior manager saying—well, we need to go and involve the teams. That did not always work. The manager might say, no, we are going to do this. Let's go."

Reed describes facilitator responses when customers attempted to escalate problems to managers:

> In our role, you couldn't do that because that would undermine the teams and potentially really destroy progress from a team perspective. That was really challenging as external issues and people tried to force their style into the team environment. As Mike pointed out, we were sort of the intermediary that had to deal with that—let them know that yes we are working on the problem. We recognize the individual may not be performing to the level that you see as satisfactory, but the team is working on it and we're getting through this process. That was a difficult response for some people to swallow.

Diana recalls one story in particular. Customer Response Center team members had a customer who wanted to escalate a complaint to a supervisor. "The customer was told, 'We don't have managers here. This is a self-directed team environment. We do things ourselves.' I can imagine what the customer calling in thought—egad, what is going on in Colorado Springs."

### Walking the Talk: Maintaining Consistency

Early facilitators struggled with not only an undefined role but also the sheer volume of daily interactions. Most were working with upward of thirty team members, and balancing people and technical issues could be difficult. They quickly learned that not everyone was going to like them. Unlike their experience in managing six or seven people, facilitators came to know each individual less well, which contributed to potential misunderstandings about personal styles or the rationale for decisions.

Collaborative decision making was a real test of "walking the talk" in a self-directed environment. Reed recalls,

My personal style is very much action oriented and I've got a real tendency to jump into an issue and try to come up with solutions immediately. As a facilitator I had to really work very, very hard not to do that and to allow all of the participants from a team to provide their input and become a part of the problem-solving process. I think the more the input you get the better the solution. It is more thorough and tested. The collaborative effort in and of itself is very powerful from a management of change perspective. Because if two solutions were provided and one were to have been devised by me independently, and I said here is the solution, go make it work—it would take a lot of management of change to work with the teams to accept that and go through whatever was necessary to implement it. If they came up with the exact same solution, they would already be bought into the fact that the change is good.

Reed had just identified a critical success factor for the evolving organization. The teams and their ultimate networking with partners provided continuous opportunity for participation in decisions—even hard decisions. This ownership of decisions moved the organization more rapidly through change than organizations with seemingly more *efficient* decision-making processes.

Sandy recalls that early on the facilitators did not always check with one another to talk through how to maintain consistency in their overall decision making. She tells the story of the multiplying refrigerators:

One team asked their facilitator if they could purchase a small refrigerator for their team area with their team budget. Although the organization provides large refrigerators in central locations, the team claimed having a small one in their area would mean fewer trips to the large refrigerators. The facilitator agreed without consulting with other facilitators. Of course, when one team has something that other teams don't have, the other teams set out to equalize the playing field. Before long, all teams were wrangling for their own small refrigerator. When the facilitators challenged them to justify the purchases based on business need, all kinds of creative justifications were forthcoming. The issue had to be resolved by Rick Hobbs. He simply stated that purchasing refrigerators was not what the organization wanted to do. The one that was already purchased was turned into an organizational model and placed in a central location. By not thinking about the consistency issue, a whole series of actions were set in motion that did not benefit the organization. It was a bit of a humorous example but a good learning [experience] for the facilitators.

Diana points out that

it is really important in the areas of administration of policies and guidelines for the facilitators to be consistent. It is not as important for setting stretch goals for individual teams. You should encourage them to do different things depending on where they are in their development. Consistency has been an issue for us around administrative issues. It is important to be consistent in team building and efforts to gain new skills. We as a FOM team need to be doing the same types of training as we ask our teams to do and remember that people will imitate what they see done.[15]

### Taking Feedback

The facilitator discussion turned to the subject of feedback. In Diana's experience,

You get it from your teams. You get it from your peers. You get it from your manager. I think the feedback is really important in this environment. It's kind of like walking the talk. You have got to get feedback. The teams are involved in peer evaluations and they do give feedback to the facilitators. For the most part my experience has been that it's somewhat valuable. The teams will point out if you are starting to get overly busy with more technical issues. They will tell you whether or not you are missing out on team meetings or things that are important to them. You will get a little bit of everything. You will get the ones that will take the feedback opportunity to beat you with a bat over the head for something you did once. But that's probably no different from anybody else's evaluation. We try to encourage the teams not to do that, but I would rather get the feedback than not get it at all.

Mike adds that

in addition, you throw on the ambiguity of how you are performing. You have four teams and two teams are really strong, maybe going toward that high-performing team spectrum and two are caught in mistrust and name-calling: how do you rate that? How are we judged? I think that was a question that came up a lot. How do you know if you are doing a good job? I think the team feedback usually is helpful and most of it was delivered in the ways we coached them—direct, specific, and nonpunishing. I had one team give me direct feedback when I did something that showed that I was not trusting an individual on the team. The individual was a strong performer. The team was emotionally upset about this. We had a special meeting and the team was in tears and people were very upset. My behavior was perceived as a breach of trust to one of the team members. They all gave me feedback and I wanted to make sure I modeled receiving the message and did not overreact, did not discount the team's feedback, and handled it professionally. That helps the team deal with their own intrateam questions and issues. It was a valuable experience and the team went from there and we had a really good relationship.

Initially, the feedback to the facilitators was informal although strongly encouraged. In 1996, the informal became a specific process with teams evaluating the performance of individual facilitators and the facilitator team as a whole. By this time the term "facilitator" had been replaced by the finance operation manager title, although many continue to refer to the FOMs as facilitators. The formal individual FOM evaluation is based on coaching and mentoring, leadership, job development, functional area knowledge, and communication. The FOM team as a whole is evaluated for consistency in policies and guidelines, open door practices, support for self-directed team initiatives, and communication.[16] The feedback from the teams is reviewed by the FOM manager, and needs or opportunities that are identified become part of individual and team development plans. Evaluation results are not swept under the rug but are discussed, often in great detail. Team members agree that facilitator (FOM) feedback is important. Tammy Biggs, a former member of the AP 1-I Mountaineers (all teams select their own team names) who started with the CSFSC in 1997, explains, "It's a good process to give feedback. But I also think it is important to give regular feedback—ongoing feedback to your facilitator. Especially if there are issues, communication problems, or anything we feel that they are not doing or should be doing, or if they are doing it right. You should let them know, otherwise, how would they know."[17]

## Career Issues in a Team-Based Organization

Resistance to team-based structures is based in part on concerns held by managers and team members alike that their individual careers will be adversely affected by team versus individual evaluations and the lack of promotional opportunity in flat organizational structures. The career experiences of the early leaders and facilitators in our story provide key evidence to the contrary. Jim, of course, was lured from HP to Mentor Graphics. In the next chapters you will learn about the career experiences of Kemp, Greg, Rick, and Sandy. Diana has chosen to stay within the

CSFSC and is currently the senior member of the FOM team; Kathy has moved as a team member to HP's Americas Financial Services SAP team. Reed was first promoted to Americas Financial Services new business manager role and then to the Americas IT controller position. (A controller role was Reed's initial goal.) Mike went from the facilitator position to an SAP lead, and then to Worldwide Financial Operations manager. Following that, he was promoted to Worldwide Financial Services process manager. Additionally, you will learn about the contributions that Mike and Reed are making to Agilent's future. All the early facilitators are recognized as outstanding contributors with excellent futures.

Mike explains how the facilitator experience has contributed to his career: "I found it [the facilitator role] was excellent training in how to deal with ambiguity." Reed adds,

> For me, because of the way the role is structured with upward of twenty-five to thirty folks on the teams, it forced you to be involved in lots of things that were not necessarily traditionally part of the management role. I think it really brought an increased exposure into all of the aspects of management and leadership that you typically don't get unless you go through many years of it in many different positions. So we were drinking from a fire hose, and I think that having that opportunity to learn very quickly has certainly made subsequent jobs down the road easier.

As the senior facilitator (FOM), Diana has the most experience with the role transition:

> I think today, we [the FOMs] have more operational and strategic responsibility for business teams, process convergence, and running the operation. Our role has escalated to a higher level. It is not that change is bad; the organization has changed. Facilitating new people with veteran people who have been here for a while rather than all new teams is very challenging. There are different levels of

skills and training and that creates an issue. A difference between the beginning and now is the span of control over the number of teams and team members has doubled, along with the other changes.

Diana continues to believe in the team environment:

> We make better decisions with enormous buy in. We certainly have larger spans because some of the managing has been delegated to the teams. We have eliminated a complete layer. I think there is greater job satisfaction for employees who have a say in how their job is done. We have a more promotable pool of candidates for the next job. Team members make management presentations. They manage a budget and resolve conflicts, do peer evaluations, inter-view, and hire. We track the data to capture the number of people who have been promoted. When I look at the last six years and the number of people who have left the areas I facilitate, they have almost all been promoted to really nice jobs.

Two of the later facilitators, Bill Kritz and Sharon Botti, have developed a series of descriptions of the facilitator role which include advice for others (See box 5.1).

### What We Learned When "You Hang In for the Fourth Quarter"

The key lesson from this period was that it is possible to stay on target in regard to goals while letting mistakes happen and evolv-ing a leadership structure. We saw a leadership change at the top shake the organization, and then we saw the organization become even stronger because that leadership change did not alter the com-mitment to the founding goals. We saw the facilitators change behaviors long before they were comfortable with whether or not the behaviors would actually result in desired team responses. We saw the meaning of trust take on an entirely new dimension. A somewhat unexpected learning was the importance of continually talking about the desired behavior changes for facilitators and team members alike. For about two years this "talking the walk" occurred in most meetings and was part of evaluation processes. We believe the talk was the self-defining process important for role definition. We also believe the talk brought needed definition to the ambiguity of role shifting—definition from those filling the roles, not from any top-down notion of what the roles should be. Top management held to the long-term goals. Customers learned it was a different environment. The middle and bottom of the organization (from an old hierarchical point of view) drove the shape shifting.

---

**Box 5.1.   What Facilitators Say to Others**

**Bill Kritz on facilitation:**

- Facilitation is the hardest yet most rewarding job I have had in my ten-plus years at HP.

- Working with peers on our own self-directed team taught me to "walk the talk" with regard to teamwork and self-directedness.

- Until you truly empower individuals and teams, you will not fully tap into the power, enthusiasm, and creativity self-directed teams possess. When you do tap into their power, enthusiasm, and creativity, the resulting effect is an adrenaline rush likened to that of winning the Super Bowl.

- Facilitation is not about managing, supervising, and directing; it is about supporting, coaching, and mentoring. It is about desiring above all else the successful progression of team development—from storming to norming.

- My greatest comfort was knowing that a team knows why they are doing what they do instead of simply knowing how.

- The greatest rewards were the sheer number of people I have had the opportunity to work with and influence, the number of people who developed their own skills and abilities and promoted their way to other positions, and the camaraderie and rapport developed within teams and between teams as we all worked together toward achieving the common goal of excellent customer service.

## Box 5.1. What Facilitators Say to Others (continued)

**Sharon Botti's Pearls of Wisdom: Advice for Others**

- It was the best job and the worst job all in one day (I think Diana Morgan said this but I loved it because it was so true).

- Have clear objectives and expectations for the team and team members. Periodically review them so that everyone is in agreement.

- The most effective metrics or goals are those established together with the team and the facilitator.

- Fairness is critical to teams and team members.

- You [as a facilitator] are the conduit to the teams for the mood of the organization. Keep a positive attitude even when times are difficult. Be realistic and acknowledge difficult times but keep the team and team members focused on what needs to be done.

- Keep the teams informed of your schedule.

- Be visible.

- Wander through the team areas just to visit. Don't just go to the team area when there is a problem.

- Use team meetings to share information.

- Allow team members to come to you for advice about the team or team members but direct them back to the team area to resolve the issue.

- Giving and receiving feedback effectively is critical to overcoming conflict and team growth in general.

- Use your peer facilitators to share ideas, discuss problems, and voice frustrations. This will not only keep you sane but will leverage techniques and tools that have worked or not worked with other teams in the same environment.

- It is hard work to be a successful team. It is easy to focus on the difficulties, but the facilitator needs to help the team find ways to talk about, celebrate, and reinforce the positive aspects of teams.

*Note:* Descriptions and advice developed by Bill Kritz on August 18, 1999, and by Sharon Botti on August 17, 1999.

We learned that change is both rapid and slow. Utilizing a sports metaphor common to the organization, we learned that what happens in the fourth quarter comes from sticking to a sustained game plan and not prematurely returning to an old style of play.

## What This Means for Others

The *hang in for the fourth quarter* lesson is complex in its application for others. Our HP experience illustrates the staying power needed to define new relationships (i.e., the facilitator role) and to learn to sustain new behaviors over time. A leader in a Fortune 50 organization attempting to move to a team-based structure illustrates our point. The leader in question went through a fairly exhaustive facilitator training, visited several team-based organizations, and believed she was ready to proceed. She and her peers never had meetings, she continued to respond to top management requests without involving team members, and she denied team member requests to "brief" the customers on the internal changes, including who was responsible for decisions at what level. She also asked team members to provide a ninety-day report showing their progress so she could tell top management most of their goals were being met. She was not requiring herself to change, even though all around her had the potential for enormous change. She was not exhibiting the staying power it takes to make new behaviors (in this case facilitative versus directive management) a natural way of being. Thus she was retarding the very change that we believe she sincerely wanted. You can call staying power a variety of things (i.e., game plans, concertos, strategic direction) but you don't get excellence without it.

We have learned that seeming paradoxes need careful examination. For example, successful large-scale change must be fast and slow simultaneously. Mistakes contribute to quality. Changed attitudes are not necessary for changed behaviors. All involved have to take personal responsibility for their own abilities to execute a sustained course of action.

## Moving On

In 1993–1994 the pace of consolidations was rapid as the form of the self-directed team environment took shape. But the team environment had many specifics yet to be addressed and the worldwide strategy would drive the organization to even more change. The potential and early results from the teams, coupled with an expanded organizational vision, would move the CSFSC to what we describe as the networked teams form. In the next chapter you will learn about the growing organization, the shift in vision and philosophy, and the massive reengineering and technical changes that created the networked teams organization. You will also learn about the toughest team and organizational problems.

# 6

---

## *Growing Pains:*
## *Teams That Worked and Some That Didn't*

Because one day you have total control and the next day you want the teams to do everything and they don't know what is what!

—Mike Waterlander

The start-up period was over and the results were becoming visible to everyone. From 1990 to 1993 Hewlett-Packard's general accounting headcount was reduced by 127 (17 percent) and the supervisors/managers/IT headcount was reduced by 98 (44 percent), for a total savings of $6 million. Even some of the early skeptics were impressed. But more change was on the way. Early on, Kemp had been assigned responsibility for the initial worldwide SAP project. No one was really surprised when, in January 1994, he was named the Worldwide Financial Services manager (see fig. 6.1). But unlike Jim, who left HP, Kemp would remain part of our story. The Colorado Springs Financial Services Center would report directly to him and then to Ray Cookingham. John Knudsen would remain as Customer Services manager and assume the CSFSC leadership role. Greg Spray would become the Worldwide Financial Services information technology manager. The Colorado Springs IT function would report directly to Kemp and have dotted-line responsibility to John Knudsen. These dual responsibilities and Kemp's continuing involvement were the beginnings of a future that would look very different from the initial start-up days.

In 1994, the aggressive consolidation pace continued. Fifty-seven additional operations people were hired from among 820 applicants. New customers included Boise Printer, Santa Clara, Corvallis, part of Chelmsford, Sonoma County, Disk Memory, Pacific Technology Park, two Roseville divisions, part of Support Materials Organization, and Little Falls (except accounts payable). The consolidations would finish in early 1995 with the additions of Andover/Waltham, Spokane, the remainder of Little

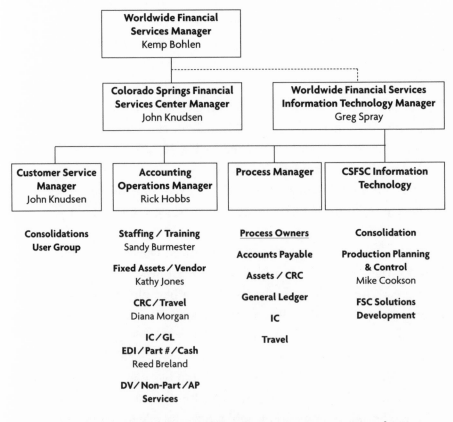

**Figure 6.1. Colorado Springs Financial Services Center Organizational Structure, July 1994**

Falls, McMinnville, Greeley, and the Finance and Remarketing Division. It was fitting that John Knudsen, who had responsibility for the initial consolidations, would oversee their completion— six months ahead of the original schedule. Sixteen additional employees were hired during early 1995, just in time to become part of a major postconsolidation celebration that occurred on April 22, 1995. The CSFSC was ahead of schedule and poised for even more change.

## Growing the Organization

John Knudsen remained as manager of the CSFSC until March 1995. His experience with the entrepreneurial nature of the CSFSC led him, like Jim Luttenbacher, to move to an entirely different type of operation. John left HP after a total of twenty-five years for Telectronics. Greg Spray replaced him in May 1995. Greg had been with the CSFSC from its early months. His history with the development of the CSFSC and his ability to think strategically about large-scale change made him an obvious choice. Greg would move the organization through a major reengineering phase, including a new vision and the convergence with HP's Atlanta Financial Services Center. (We describe this convergence more fully in chapter 7.)

Greg frequently talked about key lessons from the organization's founding and growth. In his open house presentations, Greg would tell others what he believed the CSFSC experience meant and how it could stimulate thinking for many other types of organizations. Greg's consolidation phase lessons help us understand the need for challenging the status quo, moving rapidly, involving customers, and not attempting to do more than is possible (see box 6.1). In particular, Greg emphasized the hard work necessary for consolidations and the need for the best people to be involved, since they represent the front line of significant customer contact. Greg also stressed the importance of understanding best practices, learning both from within HP and

---

**Box 6.1.    Consolidation Phase: Key Lessons**

• **Consolidations**
  Dedicated consolidation teams
  Expect division to work hard during consolidation
  Standardize as much as possible
  Make sure the division is clean before consolidation
  Minimize ASC size
  Put best people on consolidation—first customer contact

• **Projects**
  Don't overestimate ability to do reengineering while consolidated
  Create skunk works teams

• **Solutions**
  Find out and leverage best practices (internal, external)
  Rebel against current processes and policies
  Start early on capacity planning and management

• **Other**
  Invest in cost accounting
  Celebrate successes
  Market yourself like crazy! Old perceptions die hard

---

from others. He believed the CSFSC had rebelled against current processes and policies while at the same time not overestimating its ability to do reengineering while consolidating. He reiterated the underlying theme of creating a new business within a business and the need to market yourself vigorously.

The first customer and partner satisfaction survey was conducted in 1995. Pam worked with a task force of CSFSC facilitators and process engineering and IT professionals to develop the survey with the purpose of creating an ongoing measure of customer satisfaction in order to help identify high-priority focus areas for improvements and new services. The 1995 results were extremely positive. Across nine different customer and partner populations and with over 1,000 people responding, only eleven individuals gave the CSFSC a low satisfaction rating. Fifty-six percent gave the new organization the highest possible ratings.

Also between 1995 and 1997, the distinctions between customers and partners became more focused. Originally, anyone with whom a CSFSC employee had contact was a customer. This approach was too broad and diluted the differences among real customers, partners, and other important relationships. It was difficult to distinguish who should drive change, who beyond the CSFSC should hold what types of responsibilities, and, most importantly, which were the key relationships to define the future. After considerable discussion, the customer was defined as the "economic buyer" who negotiates on behalf of any organization for CSFSC goods and services. Strong service support is provided to all those with whom employees come in contact, but these contacts (users) are not customers. Contacts (users) are defined as a myriad of relationships that are important to the CSFSC. Finally, the term "partner" is reserved for organizations having a key role in helping the CSFSC deliver services, such as the Accounting Services Center personnel located at each customer site. These ASC partners are service providers, communication leaders, and contributors to setting both strategic and tactical direction. We say more about these important distinctions and how they relate to the networked teams organizational structure in chapter 7.

Shortly after Greg assumed the CSFSC leadership, a program to replace UNIX workstations with PCs was implemented, and a major organizational change created the CSFSC Solutions Center combining financial process engineering and IT. Rick Hobbs assumed the business development manager role formerly held by John Knudsen, the facilitator team reported directly to Greg, and the Americas SAP program manager and Solutions Center manager also were direct reports (see fig. 6.2). By March 1996, with the addition of nineteen new operations employees, the hiring to support consolidations ended. In May over thirty companies came to see what was happening in Colorado Springs. The start-up phase was over. It was successful by almost anyone's standards. But could it be sustained?

**Figure 6.2. Colorado Springs Financial Services Center Organizational Structure, August 1995**

Greg, Rick, and Sandy had been with the organization from its early months. Instead of breathing a sigh of relief and resting on the successful completion of the consolidations, they knew more change needed to occur. Greg led that change based on his somewhat unusual value equation designed to create delight. "Delight" is not a word commonly used to describe bottom-line organizational results. Greg did not hesitate—he wanted to capture attention, both internally and externally. The value equation he created for the CSFSC served as the basis for the *count on us* theme that defined the major reengineering phase the organization was about to enter—the phase that would result in the networked teams structure. Greg describes how he developed the equation:

> The origins of the value equation actually happened really before I took the FSC management job. I had the opportunity to visit a lot of other companies and listen to what they were doing and for some reason the things that intrigued me were their people investments and their people projects. In particular, the community delight[1] part of the equation added value. So all these elements together were really effective. And it wasn't just to make the people feel better about themselves. It was a very bottom-line benefit in that we had better skilled employees—more experienced people [who were] able to do more things.[2]

Greg's value equation was the first published view of the networked relationships that formed the core of the CSFSC (see fig. 6.3). He distinguished between partners and customers, sponsors and employees, and he included the broader community. He wanted everyone to be delighted. The concept was both simple and unusual. When there is a close relationship between the CSFSC and their partners, genuinely new and improved processes will emerge. Employees who feel effective and empowered (delighted) gain skills by community volunteerism and the community benefits (is delighted). Innovative and capable people produce more innovative and cost-effective services and products, and the customers are delighted. Results produce sponsor delight, which in turn sustains sponsorship and funding. The *count on us* themes that supported the vision defined "delight" (see box 6.2). Transaction processing was important but only as a means to an end. The real product was service and high-quality financial products. Greg reflects on the equation: "It wasn't a technical vision. It wasn't necessarily a vision of what we do. It was really how we were putting this all together, and that is really timeless."

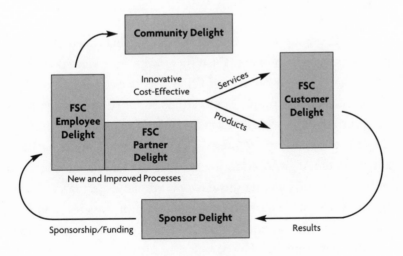

**Figure 6.3    Value Equation**

---

### Box 6.2   Count on Us Themes

**Customer**

Our customers can count on us to deliver value by providing innovative, cost-effective products and services, engineered to anticipate their ever-changing business needs.

Our customers can count on us to provide exceptional service through excellence in execution and personal ownership of their requests, problems, and issues.

**Employee**

CSFSC employees can count on each other to help make HP the best place to work. We work with the best people in an inclusive environment that is diverse, challenging, rewarding, and full of opportunity.

**Partner**

Partners can count on us to cooperatively pursue opportunities that provide mutual benefit and expansion of each other's potential through proactive communication and shared goals.

**Community**

Our community counts on us to contribute our resources, experience, and energy; to provide employment opportunities; and to make environmentally conscious decisions.

**Sponsors**

Sponsors can count on us to meet our commitments and delight our customers, employees, partners, and community.

*Note:* Prepared from Greg Spray's open house presentation, December 8, 1997.

---

The vision supported clarifications that had been emerging during the start-up phase. Customers were now viewed as those individuals who negotiated for CSFSC services on behalf of their divisions and operations. Transactions supporting literally thousands of HP employees and vendors were processed for this more limited set of customers. Greg sought to form a genuine partnership with the ASCs (Accounting Services Centers), involving them in both visioning and day-to-day operational decisions. The ASC partners became responsible for gathering information and providing that information to the CSFSC in order to guide future product development. The partners, in turn, were responsible for representing CSFSC products and services within the divisions and operations. Daily virtual communications supported the growing interdependence.

Greg began to describe the uniqueness of the CSFSC as a business within a business, a team-based organization, an efficient user of technology, and a genuine ASC partnership.[3] His business within a business description included manufacturing/service, research and development, marketing, staffing/training, customer service, and finance functions—not the traditional functions found in most transaction processing organizations (see fig. 6.4). Greg believed the concept was responsible for attracting and retaining talent. The approach stimulated valued behaviors and broad participation in decision making. Importantly, the business within a business concept was designed to instill a competitive sense of urgency within the organization, an urgency often lacking in large support organizations. Greg contended that the business within a business strategy improved customer perceptions of value, clarified roles and responsibilities (as well as expectations), and was more fun and rewarding. In describing the approach to

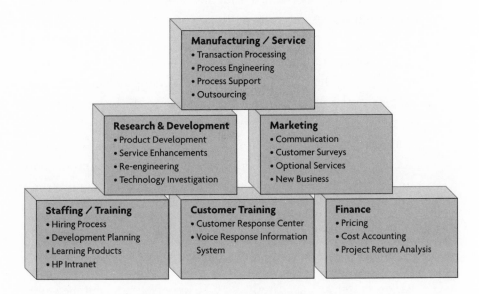

**Figure 6.4.    Business Within a Business**

visiting companies, Greg also acknowledged potential disadvantages: less integration with company strategy and hard-to-reengineer end-to-end processes with an arm's length relationship could lead to outsourcing or spin-off; shared service business goals could be inconsistent with overall company goals; a reduced feeling of being part of the company could lead to the development of separate cultures; and less employee movement between the company and shared service center.[4] But he firmly believed that the advantages outweighed the potential problems.

The original reasons for creating the team-based environment—cost savings and job enrichment—also had evolved. By the end of the start-up phase, Greg, as well as other members of the leadership team, believed the team-based environment had generated increased ownership of customer problems, increased creativity and improvement ideas, higher morale, and greater teamwork resulting in less need for onerous business controls. Less management of change efforts were required and more people were helping with projects. Team members no longer wanted the traditional model; in fact, Greg claimed team members would no longer accept a hierarchical organization.

In 1996, the CSFSC offered more services to customers. Cash disbursement functions such as employee and customer rebates were among the most prominent. Leadership began to explore opportunities for expansion, capitalizing on the expertise developed in transaction processing. The thinking was to look for transactions that might not be financial in nature but would require skills like those developed in the CSFSC. This approach to growing the business required even broader involvement in defining strategies.

In HP, as in most large organizations, top management is typically responsible for strategy development. Greg and his team believed it was time to consistently involve all levels of the organization as well as the customers and partners. Leadership began to coordinate strategy development with a process of broad input.

Volunteer teams were created to develop responses to employee survey data, and focus groups contributed to vision, mission, and purpose revisions. Rick Hobbs had worked himself out of a job. The early operations manager role was eliminated, with the facilitator team reporting directly to Greg. Rick's new business development role was very different from the early consolidation role with the same title. Both roles were concerned with attracting business to the CSFSC, but Rick's responsibilities were to find opportunities not yet under consideration for the CSFSC.

Major work flow reengineering to accommodate imaging began in 1996. These changes required accounts payable teams to become more production-line structured. Previously each individual had handled an invoice from beginning to end. The introduction of scanning technology into transaction processing reduced paper, made images available electronically, and permitted a new flow for processing within the teams. Self-service transactions also benefited. The user could enter information for reimbursements directly into the computer with user-friendly software. Electronic forms for nonwage compensation were also added. These advances eliminated major process components and thus contributed to productivity. The teams were ready for the challenge. Change was viewed as a normal, sometimes inconvenient part of the CSFSC culture.

During the start-up phase the marketing effort had been intense. By 1996, Greg and his managers faced a very different marketing challenge. The memory of doing general accounting in the divisions had begun to fade. The centralization versus decentralization issue belonged to the distant past. The downside of the success became evident—out of sight, out of mind. There was no incentive to use more services. The new marketing function had to remind parts of HP that the CSFSC existed and that it wanted to expand its services. The irony of meeting goals, providing high-quality service, and becoming invisible was not lost on the leadership team.

The challenges during this growth period were different from those of the start-up days but represented some of the toughest problems the organization would face: leadership communication, changing technology, empowerment, dealing with conflict, evaluating performance, defining parameters, compensation, reward and recognition, and fairness and consistency. Facing these issues and others would determine whether or not a great beginning could be sustained.

### Leadership Communication: The Major Responsibility

Greg describes his greatest management challenge in leading a team-based organization:

> There is only one answer. I actually thought about it and then it was so obvious that I crossed out my other ideas. And that was the tremendous, unbelievable need and desire for communication— almost to the point where one person can't do enough. In my previous jobs where I had had between five and ten managers, you would allocate a portion of your time and you would give each of those people 10 to 15 percent of your time to talk through things. When you come into a team-based environment you end up having, in a way, 200 managers and they all expect, deserve about the same amount of time you used to give to eight people. I was really the communication leader in trying to make sure that people knew what was going on, knew what was expected, had a chance to give inputs and decisions because they knew more than any of the managers did.

Employee satisfaction surveys routinely gave Greg high marks for communication. Although appreciative of the positive feedback, Greg contends that

It wasn't just me. It takes a commitment by all levels of the organization and, most importantly, the employees. They have to want to communicate—it is not usually a problem—but in some cases you sometimes had to drag some of the teams to talk. Once you got them over the fear of it or the feeling that maybe there was some work involved, then they wanted to come back. But they had to be a part of it.

Communication reactions were not always positive and productive. Greg recalls losing sleep:

Sometimes it was lots of sleep. One thing that I always worried about was the numbers of people and very qualified people, very thoughtful people, who would abandon the teams in a heartbeat. I just couldn't reconcile what I saw as the power of the teams in terms of customer delight and clearly in employee morale and all those things with the adamant rejection of the concept by, I would guess, about 20 percent of the population. I always wondered why that was. Even to the point where I was wondering if it would be more effective to have a way for those people to opt out of teams, become more productive in a nonteam environment that would allow the remaining population to be in an environment where everyone wanted to be on the team. I tinkered with that idea. Didn't do it. Don't know if it would have sent the wrong signal. I think from the earliest days there was always a concern about the viability of the management's commitment to teams, so any crack would probably have been not worth it. That still puzzles me to this day. I think it might be human nature and cultural as well. That was one thing. And the other thing, which was probably more pragmatic, was the very, very razor-thin line between effective teams and a quick drop in morale, quick drop in positiveness. Anything can happen within one meeting.

Leadership communication remains a continuous challenge. The evolution of the networked teams structure, changing technology, virtual relationships, and an increasingly diverse customer and user base, as well as a myriad of other issues, underscore the importance of providing ample, current information while creating a continuous listening environment.

## Changing Technologies: The Pepper Strategy

From the very beginning high-quality processes supported by advanced technology were key to the success of the CSFSC. Unlike many organizations, however, CSFSC introduced technological change slowly and with a strange combination of centralized and decentralized decision making. The CSFSC had started with UNIX workstations because of their multiwindow capability, speed, and reliability. Harland Baker, a CSFSC IT engineer who is informally known as the sole hardware guru for the organization, remembers that "the workstations were really great for our environment. They were very reliable and they did what we needed them to do but what started to happen was that most of the new applications that were being developed were for the PCs."[5] An increasing demand for software applications (word processing, spreadsheets, etc.) prompted the organization to consider a PC platform. (This period was early 1994.) After numerous alternatives were examined, the decision was made to change from UNIX workstations to the PC platform. The "pepper strategy" management of change approach was utilized for project implementation. Harland explains,

> We picked volunteers from different areas of the organization to make sure that a PC showed up almost everywhere in the CSFSC. I didn't want to go in and change a whole team because that would cause a huge amount of disruption. We peppered them through the organization. At that time I believe we had about 200 people or so that we had to convert. So every month, we would roll out fifteen new PCs and every month I had at least fifteen new volunteers. I actually never had the position where I did not have a volunteer to

fill a slot. The change occurred naturally and slowly. I think it had to do with that "pepper strategy" where people could actually look and see what happens. At one point, I had more volunteers than I had PCs to roll out. I never had to go to someone and say, "You will change now." It was completely voluntary all the way.

Later decisions to change software were approached in much the same way. In late 1997 HP converted from one suite of software products for graphics, word processing, and spreadsheets to another product. Harland explains, "It is not like you have to make an instant cutoff or a decision to go from one to the other. Typically, things that we change here are pretty well thought out, so that we know if people change to it, they will like it better than where they were." Harland sums up the CSFSC approach to technological change, "It just takes some time to change in this big of an organization. But things are changing so fast now. What we think is fast today, tomorrow will be three times as fast."

The selection of SAP software with its powerful order management functions was a major decision not only for CSFSC but for others in HP. Traditionally, HP had created their own systems. By the early 1990s a myriad of systems were in place in all areas of financial processing. Sandy recalls, "Our home-grown systems were not providing HP with the integrated picture that the company needed, especially to streamline order fulfillment."[6]

Mike Cookson, a member of the Americas IT group, rejoined the CSFSC and assumed responsibility for SAP in early 1997. Mike recalls that as early as 1992 Greg and others believed that HP's extensive legacy systems would get the CSFSC started but would need to be quickly replaced. The first consolidations had convinced them that additional interfaces would become complicated and that massive integration capacity was desirable. Mike recalls,

We decided we needed to do something fundamentally different, and that raised the issue of another platform. We eventually found

another way to deal and it kept us moving along and delayed the
need to do a real quick implementation of the enterprise, third
party package.[7]

(As of this writing, the CSFSC still is using some of its legacy systems with SAP implemented for travel and fixed assets. Implementation has been affected by the split into two companies and the numbers of HP organizations adopting SAP. The CSFSC continues to provide extensive SAP consulting to the businesses they support.) Mike describes some of the history of HP's SAP project:

> TMO (Tests and Measurement Organization) selected it, CSO
> (Computer Systems Organization) selected it, Financial Services
> selected it. I heard the smaller divisions or smaller businesses saying
> there is no way I am going to get stuck on the legacy systems. So
> once you have pushed the domino over, then everybody else starts
> to grab on there and try to make it happen.

Mike refers to cautions that have arisen over time about the SAP project. "A pendulum has centered itself now. We have found that SAP is not going to solve all of our problems in our culture or in our environment. So some are not going to go that way and really have cut back the scope of SAP." The SAP project, although not an overt "pepper strategy," has worked in much the same way as the earlier introduction of PCs. Although much of HP adopted the SAP platform, no corporate-wide integration program was developed. Each organization interested in the platform began its own SAP initiative. Mike recalls,

> I'll never forget one of the first meetings I went to with an SAP consultant. CSO was talking to them and saying we were going to have
> a project in the Americas and in Europe and in Asia and in Puerto
> Rico. The consultant just shook his head and said, "You don't get
> it. This is an integrated system. You have one for the company." And

my comment was, "We're not just doing CSO. We're talking about a piece of HP. Recognize that TMO, MPG (Medical Products Group), CAG (Chemical Analysis Group), PSO (Professional Services Organization), Financial Services, and everybody else—we are not the same. By the way, it is not that we don't get it. It's that you don't get it. In a company this size, this distributed, there is no way you can get CSO to agree on a business model within CSO, much less try to deal with the distribution operation, etc." So SAP has had an interesting migration over the last couple of years from this idea that one single integrated system runs your whole business to adding features to let us have more capability that allows us to integrate across implementations.

The organization-specific versus corporate-wide SAP program will result in CSFSC supporting both SAP and legacy systems with a myriad of interfaces. HP's approach to SAP is an excellent example of simultaneous centralization and decentralization enabled by sophisticated technologies. The integration capability of SAP and the ability to standardize processes worldwide is increasingly important as HP moves to global shared services. Yet the expectation is plain—support those who reject the SAP platform.

Mike talks about the major challenges faced in this massive change:

There is a technology perspective, there is a process perspective, and there is a people perspective. The people perspective is the toughest one. The technology one is the interfaces. We spend our time trying to figure out how we interface with SIDO (Software and Information Delivery Organization), how you interface with CLF (Channel Logistics and Fulfillment) business models, how you interface with the legacy business models, and how we feed this information downstream to our legal and management reporting. From a procedural standpoint, the challenge is to get existing processes, which were put in place for good reasons and evolved over time, to map to this new process model that you have. That is tough. At the 40,000-foot level you can say these are the worldwide standard processes. But when you get down to actual implementation, how do you boil that down to recognizing what our credit exposure is to a specific customer? For millions of good reasons you adjust your processes to match the software: for upgrades, for integration with anything outside of SAP, you want to keep SAP as vanilla as possible.

Mike continually helps others understand that the competitive advantage is not from HP's uniqueness in paying bills or accepting credit but in its ability to reduce overall support costs.

It is Mike's belief that

the toughest one [challenge] is the cultural one, and I think that is true for just about any SAP implementation. If you have a centralized, hierarchical, strong decision-making business, it is quicker to implement than it is within a distributed business model and decision making. And I think the distributed model is HP's strength. But when you try to implement a package that says, "No, you don't get to choose what your process is, no, you don't get to choose how this is going to work," that is just not a good fit. Next we add the difference between the Colorado Springs self-directed teams and Atlanta's (Atlanta Financial Services Center) hierarchical organization, one system, one set of processes, multiple decision makers. That is a very difficult change. SAP is going to require a different skill set. You are changing how people do the work day in and day out. That brings a whole set of training and management of change issues.

In Sandy's view,

SAP shifts the people who are doing transaction processing work from a skill-based, data-input type of job to more knowledge-based work because a much larger percentage of their time is devoted to problem solving. For example, the procurement process is initiated in the system and provides one piece of data that finance will need to match and pay AP or IC invoices. Only those transactions where there is not a match will "fall out," requiring that a processor intercede, investigate the problem, and resolve the issue.[8]

Even before SAP is fully functional, changes with worldwide uses of the Internet for non–SAP related functions and the company split are impacting the future. Mike predicts that when all of the systems are put together, a new type of consolidation phase will take place. "When we get all the functionality put together, we are going to have to have a consolidation-type environment that allows us to do three to four implementations a month to meet the 2001 goals." The CSFSC experiences with legacy systems, multiple interfaces, PCs, SAP, and the growing use of the Internet illustrate the ongoing evolution and challenges associated with increased networking and are examples of what is to come.

### Defining Parameters

During the CSFSC start-up phase the steering and design teams, along with the facilitators, engaged in lengthy discussions of responsibility parameters for teams—parameters on which empowerment would be based. Pam advocated moving in stages with team responsibilities increasing over time and not necessarily with all teams in lockstep:

I thought it was important for teams to have overall target dates for assumption of increasing responsibilities. Realistically, however, not everyone is ready at the same time. The process the design team and the facilitators put in place had overall goals for team empowerment but provided room for each team to work with its facilitator in designing team development and assessing readiness for new responsibilities. This approach is more complex but, in the end, produces better results.[9]

The initial design called for phasing responsibilities over a four-year period (see box 6.3). Team responsibilities ranged from basic coordination and meeting management to performance feedback and managing rotations and promotions. (A descriptive list of team parameters is included in the appendix.) Although the list is relatively short, identifying these parameters took over 200 hours of discussion and planning time.

The degree of self-directedness the CSFSC wanted was an issue generating considerable disagreement and debate. Pam had urged the design team to be careful in their identification of parameters. The danger rested not in the specifics of the list but in giving teams a parameter and then taking it back for managerial control. The concept of self-direction and empowerment is ambiguous at best, and for teams to believe in the expected changes, change must occur with a high degree of consistency. To decide that teams should do workload balancing, for example, and then change that parameter because balancing is not occurring as desired sends a powerful negative message about the staying power of the environment.

Diana Morgan describes the role of parameters within the larger organizational context:

> The teams don't have absolute authority to make all decisions. The CSFSC reports to a traditional management so sometimes business decisions are made at a higher level. Most of the customers we deal with are traditional and that plays a role in influencing the parameters. A lot of the new responsibilities need to be consistent since there needs to be training and new skills—you can't roll those responsibilities out without parameters. We are dual-purpose: we promote an enriched environment for the employee in order to complement business goals.[10]

---

**Box 6.3     Team Responsibilities/Parameters**

**1992**

Interviewing
Time cards
Workload balance
Meetings
Write system change requests
Group expectations
Metrics
Coordinators

**1993**

Design team membership
Peer evaluations
SR coordinators
Training budgets
On-the-job training
Reconciliation review
Consolidation visits
Conflict management
Presentations to managers
Documentation
Reward and recognition
Manage rotations

**1994**

Team budget management
Improved conflict resolution and communication
Improved customer service
TQM emphasis

**1995**

Performance feedback process
Manage rotations and promotions
Sign and approve journal vouchers
Schedule training
Evaluate facilitators
New hire training

---

Greg Spray has told many visiting organizations it is important to focus on the degree of desired self-directedness and then set well-defined parameters.

Parameters and the timeline for their assumption help establish training schedules, are useful as a measure of team development, and provide an overall plan to transition managers from supervision to more strategic responsibilities. When working optimally, the cycle flows through stages of identifying team parameters, providing coaching and training for teams to assume parameters, team assumption of parameters, facilitator coaching, decreasing facilitator involvement, team responsibility for parameters, and facilitator assumption of new responsibilities. Parameter setting provides the opportunity for both teams and managers to assume new responsibilities. Although a great deal of attention has been focused on the growth and development of team members through the assumption of additional responsibilities, less visible are the opportunities for management to assume more strategic roles as they manage less of the day-to-day activity. In fast-paced, changing environments this opportunity to devote leadership to what is coming versus what exists now can be a significant advantage in almost all organizations.

## Dealing with Empowerment

Many call "empowerment" the most overused term of the 1990s. Others contend that empowerment is the cornerstone of the twenty-first century workplace. Regardless of what perspective they take, most agree that empowerment is a thorny issue. Early on the CSFSC struggled to understand what the concept meant in a team-based environment.

Once parameters had been set, the teams expected changes and leadership expected changes. But how to make meaningful change was less certain. The early facilitators concluded that empowering people was an art and a science that required new thinking and behaviors from everyone. Empowerment is an issue that continues to require vigilance as the organization matures. Empowerment simply does not come with a clear definition, although virtually everyone at the CSFSC can say whether they are empowered or not.

Mike Waterlander provides his personal description:

I always view it as you work with a team to set a high-level objective. It might be a shared vision process or it could be kind of guiding, "We want to go in this direction." Giving that kind of parameter and then stepping back and letting the team decide the best path to get to that goal and manage themselves through that process—that's true empowerment. Resisting the temptation of every time there is a little bit of a hiccup to swoop down and take over control of the situation with classic management, crisis management tactics. I think empowerment is all of those things to me. It's being willing to step back and let people find the right path to get to that end point, whatever that is. The biggest risk to that empowerment model is the yo-yo effect. Because one day you have total control and the next day you want the team to do everything and they don't know what is what.

Reed Breland adds to Mike's comments:

For me, it was very simple. A team was empowered when they were unafraid to make a decision after they had all the information to make an informed decision. Teams are not empowered when they can't make decisions. They are either afraid to because someone will shoot them, they think that a manager/supervisor is going to come in and undercut a decision that they make, or they are going to be reprimanded for trying to make a decision. That's an unempowered team or individual. So, when you see people making decisions after having enough facts to make informed decisions, then that's empowerment.

One of the early parameters in support of empowerment was team member responsibility for interviewing and contributing to hiring decisions. None of the team members previously had participated in interviewing, to hire either peers or managers. The assumption of the parameter required training, including the legalities of the hiring situation, and the development of meaningful questions to determine skills and individual fit within a team-based organization. Team members developed questions that required interviewees to talk about what they have actually done rather than what they would do. Questions asked for descriptions of handling an extremely angry customer over the telephone, working with a difficult individual, or solving the toughest problem the individual ever faced. Learning to listen to the answers and distinguish among candidates also is part of the challenge. Team members are expected to provide assessments of each candidate and contribute to the hiring decision. Today teams interview and hire their own new members from among internal candidates without management oversight.

Team members Bill Brown and Tammy Biggs[11] both joined the CSFSC through the panel interview process. Tammy says,

> I remember it well. It was very intimidating. The first half hour I said I am doing great. Then they started to counter every question I answered. I thought, you know, I just can't answer these questions good enough. I thought this was tough. I walked out of here and I said, "Well, there went that." But the weird thing is, I put my notice in at my previous job. I don't know why. Went ahead and did that. Got the call the next day, and I said, "well, this is some tough stuff."

Bill got lost on the way to his interview and, after arriving twenty minutes late, could not believe the group would even talk to him:

> I now see how the interview questions are developed from the skills that are identified as being the ones that are most needed. So I see why the questions are what they are and why a lot of the follow-up questions that Tammy was talking about are used. The follow-up questions really are meant to help you demonstrate the behaviors that they are looking for. They are not meant to put you on the spot

or get you—mark you down. They are meant to give you more chances to get marked up.

Tammy remarks:

> I still think [new interviewees] are waiting for those "tell us your strengths and weaknesses" questions. It's like you want to tell them straight out—forget it. I was waiting for that question for forty minutes before I finally figured out it was not going to happen. And I thought, why do they keep asking me these silly questions? And they keep re-asking me—they never did ask me about my strengths and weaknesses. It is very intimidating.

Interviewing is an excellent example of how empowerment develops. Team members acquire another skill and participate in a process new to them. But the process comes with considerable responsibility. They are contributing to making decisions, not only about individual future employment but about those with whom they will work on a day-to-day basis. No one can say, "Who in the world hired that person? They should have known better." Although mistakes are made, the shift is to "we should have known better."

Bill Brown describes an additional example of his experiences with empowerment:

> I had been here about three weeks. Our team was having a real struggle because an account reconciliation that one of our team members owned was a real mess. The whole team took responsibility. We were up against a month-end deadline and I think about two nights in a row, the four of us stayed here until about 8 or 8:30 at night and just worked together to get the thing done. We had evaluated the overtime impact and the expenses and the customer needs to get it done, and we just together kind of took all of those things into account and decided that we had to do this no matter

how long it took us. The perception, I think, was that because we were a self-directed team we had to take it upon ourselves. We couldn't buck it upstairs to a supervisor and say, "Well, it's over to you boss." So, I guess it was really the sense of responsibility of the team in getting the job done. When we were pretty much at the end, maybe around 7 P.M., it started getting lighter instead of harder.

Bill and Tammy agree that empowerment brings team responsibilities that are both difficult and rewarding. Bill enjoys "working together, communicating with each other about what needs to be done and how to go about doing it. Trying to reach consensus. It's not always easy, but it is fun." Tammy identifies some of the more difficult problems:

> Finding time to train a new person coming on. Sometimes you are short staffed and under a lot of stress. It is very, very difficult to train that person correctly and spend enough time with them. Another issue is dealing with the low performer on your team; I think that is very, very difficult because the team has to take responsibility to work it out. The manager is there for guidance, but it is the team's responsibility.

Bill says that he agrees with Tammy

> about dealing with a teammate who maybe has performance problems or when you have to give constructive feedback and try to help them get the job done better. That can be really, really tough.

Other team members who asked not to be identified said empowerment was necessary in the environment because "they [managers] don't know how to do the stuff we do." Team members generally agreed that managers were willing to be helpful but were not going to solve problems for them. Empowered teams work on their own within a set of business parameters.

## Dealing with Conflict: Team
## and Facilitator Breakdowns

Regardless of organizational structure, dealing with conflict consistently rates at or near the top of difficult managerial challenges. Add to the general difficulty of managing conflict an environment in which teams are expected to manage their own conflicts, and the potential for navigating rough waters escalates. Within the first year of the beginning of the CSFSC, Sandy and the facilitator team identified conflict management as a training priority for all teams. Sandy described what was needed—not immersion but a periodic dose of information. Sandy believed, and others agreed, that team members were more likely to internalize the information when it was presented over a period of months. With Pam and her team in consultation, the decision was made to put a year-long emphasis on building conflict skills. Pam and Mike Hackman developed a seven-session set of modules that could be facilitated during team meetings by either a team's primary facilitator or other facilitators. The facilitators had observed that often team members could work more productively on conflict issues if the primary facilitator who would later participate in their evaluations was not present. Facilitators working across teams to assist with developing skills for dealing with conflict proved to be a positive alternative. All facilitators participated in a train-the-trainer session prior to delivering modules. The modules were designed to have teams work on specific issues within their teams as they were building more general skills. The facilitators planned to deliver the modules over a twelve-month period with the potential for repetition of several modules to improve specific skill building. The training continues today when new staff members are hired and when teams are experiencing conflict. All new employees are scheduled to begin the conflict modules after they have been on the job for six months. But, as most would expect, training does not solve all of the problems. Our facilitators provide examples of challenging team conflicts, ones that were resolved and some that were not. For Mike Waterlander,

> it was the big issue with the vendor team. We had one long-term HP employee who moved into the FSC environment and really never was comfortable with peer feedback, peer input. I think there may have been some male–female dynamics involved, and he had some bad work habits. We also had some team members that were too much into the police mode of teams and really watching and timing each other and coming to me with lists that he was gone from this time to this time with very specific minutes. There was a three- or four-month process of trying to stop the bad behavior and focus on what was positive. We used some of the materials from the employee assistance provider training we received. We would get some progress and some behavior change, but then people mistrusted one another so much that they did not really trust that the behavior was genuine. I had to make the point that it did not really matter as long as the right things were being done. You can't really control thoughts. It was a very, very distrustful environment. It was improved but I would never say all the way back to a healthy family. We were still dysfunctional. That was the hard part. There are some things you can correct and help and some things that probably the best thing to do is dissolve a team where certain players are really not the right fit. The person left the team and went back to a more traditional environment. That was probably the right thing for HP and everyone involved but it was hard because we never really felt as if we were able to turn the corner.

Diana Morgan remarks that

> I have had several [team breakdowns]. In fact some of the most recent ones are categorized into communication issues. A lot of it has to do with personal information. Team members become like a family and they are very close, often doing activities outside of

work. They share information that normally would not be shared in a workplace environment. Some of that gets muddled and they start using that information in a teasing way and pretty soon trust deteriorates and you have a major conflict. What I have found works best is to use a process for managing conflict situations—I still go back to the conflict modules and use the problem-solving approach. I think another key is to take some time. Don't jump too quickly to resolution. That is a very traditional approach. In a traditional manager's role it is problem fix, problem fix, the sooner the better. Team members need to do a lot of self-analysis of the issue and that takes time. The role I play is true facilitation—help them get the meeting together, help them define what we are going to talk about, have them do some thinking and research. They are the ones who are going to solve it, not me.[12]

Kathy Jones experienced

a similar situation where a team member came to me and alleged sexual harassment, however, without any details. After I talked with legal counsel, there was not anything I could do to move through the problem—I could not talk with the other individual because there were not any details to share. So, for me that was very frustrating. It felt like the issue was brought up but cut off short and we were not able to work through a resolution both for the complaining individual or the person about whom the issue was raised.

Reed Breland was the facilitator of the first team to be dissolved because of an inability to work through conflict. It was a critical decision, not only for the team involved but for the precedent it would set about conflict management expectations. Reed[13] describes the situation:

The team had been together for probably about six months when it was up to a full eight-person team with the normal growing pains of a team coming together. After they had been together for a period of six, seven, eight months, there was a recurring problem, a theme that continued to surface at team meetings, at TQC sessions, and just in general—certain individuals could not work with other individuals and there appeared to be a very serious, or at first a very underlying, personality conflict. There was a lot of talk about different styles and different work ethics and different values. So over the course of nine months the team tried to address it by going through and setting team guidelines and ground rules and what the team values and expectations were. Over this nine-month period, there were peaks and valleys in terms of successes.

By the end of the nine-month period, the team got into a position where they were completely polarized. The team had split into two separate groups, and the two groups would not even talk to each other. Because of the physical layout they did not have to cross paths. Actually, the joke was, they had renamed their two subteams because they saw themselves as being that different. Some very petty things were happening—one person would not get the other person's printouts off the printer if they were printing. These were just indicators that this thing had really come to a grinding halt.

Finally, when there were some serious performance concerns both at the individual and team level, the total team productivity and effectiveness was seriously compromised. I decided that something needed to be done. The team and I had worked for a number of months trying to address it. They were not making progress. I felt that they had become so polarized there was no turning back. So I had a conversation with a number of the other facilitators, with some of the CSFSC management staff, with the site HR manager, and with Pam. We talked about the option of dissolving a team. That notion was not terribly appealing to me, given what we were trying to do. I wasn't sure what kind of precedent that would set. The feedback from all of those people was clear—support for dissolving this team. I learned that regardless of whether they were a team performance was something that we could not compromise and we had to address performance issues. Pam provided me information about the numbers of teams that succeed and the numbers that fail. As a team-based organization we had been very successful and having one or more teams that did not gel was not unusual at all—the best thing to do was to start from scratch again and move on.

So with that feedback, I went into a team meeting and told them the unilateral decision has been made that you are no longer a team. This had a very interesting effect—actually rallied the team together. They complained, both as a team saying they wanted another chance and then individually. They would say, "You know I think we can work through this if we can get through this or that." But it was clear that the underlying issues had not been addressed and that the individual personality conflicts were still there. So I held firm and over the course of the next two months all of the individuals were placed into existing teams or were part of a new team because we were still growing this organization.

Reed describes the process of individuals getting new assignments:

These individuals were all free agents, so to speak. They were not placed on any teams. Other teams had to interview them and choose to accept them if they wanted. The only intervention I participated in was when three of the individuals decided they wanted to be part of a new start-up team. I told them that three was too many. They potentially had too much influence over the new group, and it was three from one of the polarized subgroups. So I felt that that was not appropriate and told them that the most that could be together on a single team would be two from the prior group. There was a little resistance with that decision, but again, the goal overall was to get the personalities split back out and give everyone a fresh start. The result was that all of the individuals went on to new teams or a different team and were very, very successful in a short period of time.

In hindsight the people think the decision was absolutely the right thing to do. As they look back at it they remember how painful a process it was. They laugh at how dysfunctional they were and how they ever thought they could have gotten through it.

Pam remembers this conflict situation as leading to

a tough decision. It would set a tone for the entire organization, not just the team in question. The decision to dissolve was based on quantifiable performance issues and was highly visible throughout the organization. In the short term other teams were anxious about what was happening. Over time, however, the results have been clear and positive. Teams that don't perform don't stay intact simply because it is a team-based environment. But team members are given the opportunity to learn from the conflicts. All of the team members in question were successful on other teams. I think everyone learned a valuable lesson about conflict management and change. In fact, this example has become an important organizational story within the CSFSC. It helps us think about short-term versus long-term benefits from conflict resolution. All too often the long-term is sacrificed with short-term thinking.

Team members were not the only ones who experienced difficulty and conflicts. Greg Spray describes the difficult task of removing a facilitator who was not doing a good job:

That was hard. It was particularly hard in this case because it was hard to determine exactly what the issues were. But once I started digging in, I knew right there that this person had to be removed from the job. This person's skills were not a good match for the skill sets we needed. Damage was being done every day in terms of the team model and trust of the entire facilitator team. In fact, I think that damage still persists years later, so it is not something to take lightly.

Team members were saying that they would never have an open door conversation again with any facilitator—it is a crime to allow that perception to happen. And once you lose that trust, one person tells about twenty other people.

Greg operated with numerous organizational constraints during the removal period:

One of the typical corrective action processes is that you create a plan for people to get back on track. Once I realized the damage, there was no way that the person could continue in the role. So the constraint was needing to go through a corrective action process and at the same time not allowing the person to practice or to do that role. So that was tough. It also was hard for others—the other facilitators—to understand that we needed to allow this person to understand the impact of his or her actions. This individual did not do enough wrong that I would have considered immediate termination, so it was kind of a unique situation where the person had to be pulled from the role, yet still allowed to develop and become a better employee.

I think there was more knowledge about this individual's issues than the individual was told, either by his or her own team or by his or her peers. I think there should have been more direct coaching and feedback. I really believe that the person was not doomed to fail in this role. I do think that this person was inclined to fail, but I think that with the right kind of early coaching and early feedback the manager would have been a successful facilitator.

Based on this experience and others, Greg believes that organizing the facilitators into a team is key:

If I had to do it all over again, I think I would have treated the facilitator team as a team with all of the same responsibilities (including peer feedback), all of the same tools, all of the same expectations of any other team.

## Building the Yardstick: Fairness, Performance Evaluation, Compensation, and Rewards

It was obvious that the yardstick of overall evaluation had to change. Leadership and team members alike understood that if team behaviors were to be expected, then team behaviors would have to be evaluated, compensated, and rewarded. Consistency and fairness in evaluation and rewards were complicated by the approach that teams would move to high performance at different rates. Moving from understanding to building the yardstick was difficult. HP, like most organizations, has an elaborate evaluation and compensation system. The steering and design teams set out to think about what needed to change. And they did not move quickly.

One of the first issues the facilitators faced was how to be fair and consistent even though teams were expected to develop with different pacing and with differing maturity levels. Reed addresses some of the early issues:

I think consistency is a very, very important component of facilitation. And it is not consistency, necessarily in decision making, but consistency in treatment of others, consistency in how you run meetings or whether you attend a meeting or not, consistency in the treatment of individuals during performance evaluations or ranking sessions. The team members share a lot of information. They share salary and wage information. They share ranking information. They share everything. And so consistency is critical.

Kathy remarked,

I would agree that it is very important because not only do team members talk with each other but they talk with other teams. For an example—they talk about quarterly feedback one-on-one sessions. A real consistency among facilitators that this is occurring is just critical, otherwise, questions come up about why isn't this happening.

Diana addresses the need for consistency and the reality that teams do not progress at the same rate:

> We [facilitators] are not robots. And teams are at different stages and facilitators should have the leeway to make decisions on what some teams can do. We are currently trying to educate the team members that we are going to be consistently inconsistent when it comes to what kind of things teams are doing depending on what stage they are in their development. Sometimes that gets misconstrued or misunderstood that the facilitator is doing something that another facilitator absolutely does not allow. It is a fine line because we are not clones of each other and we don't do everything perfectly the same day in and day out. So it is an ongoing struggle.

The issues of individual and team performance evaluation were even more difficult. Following the first two years of CSFSC operation, the team member role had differentiated to the extent that the single pay range was no longer adequate. Additional pay ranges were created to recognize the multiple skills required in a team-based environment. But how to evaluate the role was much more difficult. The standard HP employee evaluation process had been used from the beginning of the CSFSC. In 1993 the peer input process (PIP) was initiated, with peers actively involved in evaluating one another. In 1998 the team part of the peer evaluation and ranking process was begun.

The PIP process begins in August of each year, the timing driven by HP salary and wage administration cycles. Each team member's performance is evaluated by other team members. A self-evaluation is encouraged but not required. Ground rules are established by each team around the process. An example of a ground rule common to most teams is requiring the feedback to be shared verbally before it appears on the PIP form—no surprises. Each team member must prepare a PIP form for each of the other team members to help prevent groupthink. Once the forms are prepared, the team is free to decide how the feedback captured on the PIP will be given to the individual team member. Less mature teams might elect to provide the feedback one-on-one, while others get together as a team and everyone provides a certain team member the feedback at the same meeting.

Along with the written feedback, the team members initially provide input to the facilitator on ranking the individual's overall performance with respect to HP's five performance rank bands. Recent changes have been made to the process, which no longer requires an overall ranking but instead requires the evaluation of several skill set areas. A team evaluation is also done by each team. The team examines how well they have performed as a team with regard to goals set and team development. There is also a comparison to the performance of other teams. This input also is provided to the facilitator, who weighs the team portion, the individual portion, and any other information (customer feedback or feedback from other sources in the organization) and assigns a final ranking that determines the employee's pay increase. Although the PIP initially required an evaluation of each individual's contribution to the team, the team evaluation focuses on the performance of the team as a unit versus the individuals on the team, and it looks at a set of skills that are team-based versus individual.

Facilitators quickly learned that the yardstick is not motivating if it is only a formal process of evaluation and compensation. Not a surprising finding given years of research which suggests that money can lead to work dissatisfaction but genuine satisfaction is much more complex.[14] In 1996, the CSFSC established a formal Award and Recognition Program (nonsalary based) that relies on be doomed to failure. Finally, the HP experience demonstrates the importance of training and on-going evaluation of teams.[15]

Gaynelle recognizes that

it is easy to cut corners with assessment and feedback. The CSFSC, from the beginning, has embraced these processes at three levels: for customer satisfaction, team performance, and individual performance. On a regular basis they finance the collection of customer satisfaction surveys, team performance surveys, and individual performance assessments. Most importantly, these data do not sit in a drawer. Instead, they play a critical role on a team's platter of responsibilities. The team reviews the overall data for the CSFSC, as well as for their team and customers, allowing these data to help them in setting new goals for performance improvement. As a result, assessment and feedback serve to foster ownership and commitment to goals and change.[16]

Sandy sums up our concept of staying power with the advice she gives those considering a team-based structure:

There is no recipe, no roadmap, no template. Each team environment is as unique as the people in the teams are unique. Visit others to observe their environments and steal and adapt what you can use for your particular situation. But be prepared for the long haul. It took the CSFSC at least three years to develop a strong team environment. If you are looking for a quick fix, teams are not it. Roll up your sleeves because establishing a strong team environment takes a whole lot of work. Processes have to be designed and redesigned as the environment changes. Getting team members to take risks and make their own decisions takes urging and patience. Work on strengthening trust as teams are developed. If trust issues are present in a team model and are not quickly resolved, the productivity impact is enormous. Get people with the right skill set in the facilitator role. The impact on a whole organization when the wrong person is placed in this position is significant and long lasting. Leadership in a team-based organization is demonstrated differently than in a traditional organization, so make sure the people in leadership positions in your organization are evidencing the team type of leadership. Consider Greg Spray's recommendation to form the facilitators into a self-managing team from day one.

Getting the right people also applies to the teams. Develop hiring processes to more accurately predict whether applicants have the interpersonal skills to be successful team members. But also take the time to enjoy the satisfaction that stems from watching people grow and develop.[17]

Our story illustrates that, even with well-developed goals and processes, tough challenges call for persistence and risk taking in making difficult yet innovative decisions. Not everyone will be convinced of the merits of change, and even competent individuals may continue to disagree. The question is not whether serious issues will occur but what is the commitment to the vision and the original goals? We are not saying that goals and plans should never change, but in the absence of staying power they are often changed for the wrong reasons.

## Americas Financial Services: CSFSC and Atlanta

Issues of leadership, technology, parameter setting, empowerment, conflict, and building effective yardsticks do not get solved or go away. The CSFSC experience underscores the dynamic and continual challenges presented by these issues and the quality of leadership required to move an organization forward while treating tough problems as expected and normal. The changes that were about to happen in 1997 illustrate this point.

In January 1997, Kemp Bohlen announced a more formal convergence between the Colorado Springs and Atlanta Financial Services Centers—one a team-based organization and one a traditional hierarchy. (Greg Spray had been informally involved in pioneering efforts between the two organizations prior to the announcement.) The two organizations would become Americas Financial Services with Colorado Springs and Atlanta locations (see figs. 6.5 and 6.6).

The worldwide strategy was gaining momentum. The concept of financial services as a business within a business was expanding. The purpose, mission, vision, and products of Americas Financial Services were succinct and clear (see box 6.4). The CSFSC vision certainly was in alignment, but no one believed that more change would not occur. The days of the CSFSC as its own business within a business seemed limited, and further evolution of the networked teams organization was under way. In the next chapter we will examine what these changes meant to the CSFSC and how they contributed to the networked teams organization form.

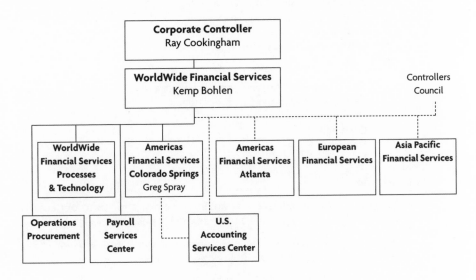

**Figure 6.5. Worldwide Financial Services Organization Structure, September 1997**

### Box 6.4 Americas Financial Services

**Purpose:**

We add value to HP by providing efficient, innovative financial services enabling the businesses to focus on their objectives.

What is our business? Financial services.

What products or services do we produce? Transaction processing, collection, access to and reporting of financial data, business controls, consulting.

Who are our customers? HP businesses.

What do our customers expect? Focus on core competencies, allow customers to focus on primary job (not accounting), add value, cost-effectiveness, quality, enable corporate/business financial reporting.

How do we contribute to the objectives of HP? Process innovation and improvement, application of technology.

**Vision:**

Hands-off transaction processing

Hands-on customer service

What does "hands-off transaction processing" mean?
>    Reduction of effort required to process transactions
>    Automation (electronic processing)
>    Flexible services
>    Cost-effective
>    Fewer people and different skill sets

What does "hands-on customer service" mean?
>    Exceeding expectations—going the extra mile
>    Services adapted to customer's needs
>    Flexibility
>    Ownership
>    Delivery
>    Personalized attention

**Mission:**

We will excel in the delivery of quality financial services to our customers while supporting the evolution of HP's business models.

We will do this by focusing on customer service intensity and on excellence in execution, technology, and processes.

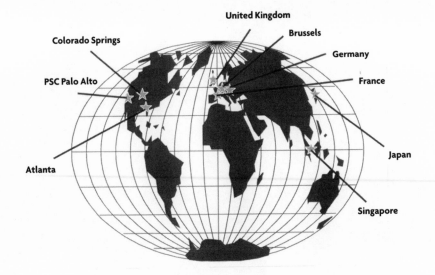

**Figure 6.6. Financial Services Centers Locations**

# 7

---

## *Networked Teams Prove Themselves*

Come on, you have just been staged to come in here and tell this. This sounds way too good to be true.

—CFO of visiting company

### The Evolving Organization: Networked Teams

By 1997 two constants characterized the Colorado Springs Financial Services Center—change and the team-based structure. The needs of Hewlett-Packard had been in flux from the organization's beginning, and even the early leadership could not have known how advances in technology would impact worldwide transaction processing. Business challenges, self-directed work teams, and changing technologies combined to create what we are describing as the networked teams organizational structure. No single individual or group of individuals created all aspects of this design. It literally evolved in response to complex, changing circumstances. We have come to believe that the design evolved because both leadership and team members were willing to rebel against tradition and reject the concept that a service support organization, although necessary, was destined to be expensive overhead. The business within a business philosophy had made a significant impact. By early 1997, the CSFSC was networked with self-directed work teams, customers, partners, and other organizations within HP. The CSFSC joined with the Atlanta FSC (responsible for field sales and marketing transactions) to form Americas Financial Services and was part of the growing worldwide transaction processing strategy. Decision making was simultaneously centralized and decentralized, with hundreds of networks—both human and technological—reflecting complex patterns of interactions.

Everyone was on a team. Greg and his managers were responsible for the Colorado Springs operation, for joining the leadership efforts for Americas Financial Services, and for contributing to HP's emerging worldwide strategy.

Through Americas Financial Services Colorado Springs was formally linked to the Atlanta FSC, a traditional hierarchy. Both organizations were required to think collaboratively about standardization of processes across service centers as well as new uses of technologies. Both were charged with innovating for the future.

Colorado Springs was internally and externally networked with the self-directed work team structure that had been with the organization from the very beginning. Team members were tightly networked to one another for workload balancing, problem solving, new idea generation, conflict management, and a host of other responsibilities. Teams were expected to solve complex issues with either their assigned facilitators or any member of the facilitator team. (The facilitator team by now was called the FOMs—financial operations managers—in keeping with their Atlanta counterparts.) Often teams worked problems directly with partners or customers. Extensive strong and weak network relationships permeated the organization.[1]

ASCs (Accounting Services Center representatives in local operations) had become true partners with well-defined service and communications responsibilities. Early on, ASCs and division controllers had attended face-to-face meetings in Colorado Springs to review CSFSC future plans and provide input. The early interactions cast the ASCs mostly in a customer rather than partner mode. Over time the ASCs became involved in establishing priorities and providing the communication necessary for change and innovation. Although geographically dispersed throughout the United States, the ASCs have become a regular part of the CSFSC planning network. Today the ASCs participate in developing strategy to address issues identified in the customer satisfaction survey, have significant responsibilities in new process and product development, and are the key communication link to the controllership in all customer divisions. The ASCs are the partners and all division or operation employees and vendors are the contacts/users. (The survey is called a customer satisfaction survey because this is how users would most likely characterize themselves. Internally, the CSFSC continues to use the term "customer" for the economic negotiator/buyer of services and "users/contacts" for all those for whom transactions are processed.)

Although face-to-face gatherings continue, ASC meetings are often telemediated with voice and Web interactivity. Today there are fewer CSFSC team presentations and more ASC presentations. There has been a definite shift from the CSFSC taking feedback to discussions of how the ASCs and CSFSC can jointly lead the general accounting function. The focus on projects, however, has not changed. Recent meetings, for example, have discussed SAP implementation implications, Web and chart of accounts updates, and the travel reengineering project. Meetings are also characterized by discussions of changes such as the formation of the Americas Financial Services, the worldwide strategy, and the split of HP into two companies. Barbara Edwards, the ASC manager in Fort Collins, Colorado, sums up her experiences as a CSFSC partner:

My experience as an ASC manager has been interesting and mixed. The best experience I have had has been getting to know my colleagues at the partners meetings. There are things that I found out from other ASC managers that I did not know and my people did not know. I think the biggest challenge has been to really push the envelope of "same old way" thinking. This has not always gone over well with my staff or with our customers. If there is going to be "pain," as there always is, when you change a system, processes, and so on, it is best to get the pain over with as quickly as possible.... this really goes against the HP grain with consensus management, participative management. That has been my biggest challenge—convincing my manager, my staff, and so on, to "just do it," endure the pain of the change, and get on with it![2]

Prior to 1997, CSFSC organizational charts made no reference to the ASCs. A September 1997 organization chart linking the ASCs to management illustrates just how important the ASCs have become (see fig. 7.1). The ASC involvement in decision making and priority setting is an excellent example of a centralized, standardized product (CSFSC transaction processing) designed and developed through decentralized participation. The ASCs are the most tightly linked geographically dispersed members of the networked teams design.

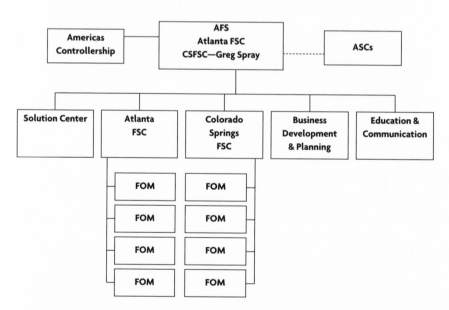

**Figure 7.1  Americas Financial Services Organization, September 1997**

Users, now defined as all HP employees and vendors, also have frequent interactions with the CSFSC. Increasingly user transactions are Web based and are facilitated through information systems. For most, the interactions rarely require a human voice. These are the weaker links in the networked teams organization. They frequently provide important information not readily available from other sources. Problems with processing time, use of computer systems, accuracy, and quality and ease of use of process documentation can surface in telephone conversations with service center personnel. Often the problems that users raise individually are addressed before they impact larger numbers of people. Additionally, users provide extensive amounts of performance data in the customer satisfaction survey conducted every other year. These "weak ties"[3] are critical for the identification of new needs or emerging problems. CSFSC leadership, teams, and ASCs all utilize these data for process improvements and to measure the ongoing quality of services provided.

The CSFSC is linked to top HP management through a traditional hierarchical chain of command. Results in terms of dollars expended and work produced remain appropriate mechanisms for evaluating the performance of the organization. The links, however, have been known to manifest themselves in somewhat unusual ways. Team members, for example, present results directly to Ray Cookingham as well as to CEOs and CFOs from other companies. Team member visibility and access to top management rivals that of generally more prominent research and development engineers.

Although empowered people are the foundation of the networked teams design, none of the design would be possible without sophisticated networked technologies. The networked teams design is based on the technical capacity to standardize functions and processing without regard to geography. SAP, imaging, Web-based processing, and a host of legacy systems all combine to create a spiderweb of technological networks necessary for processing huge volumes of transactions. These technical networks literally eliminate the geographical imperatives of previous years.

We believe that the unique combination of the sheer computing power of the technical networks and the human networking of the CSFSC is the basis of the success of this organization. The CSFSC people design is not based on a deskilled[4] workforce but, in fact, a workforce that is expected to execute a complex variety of problem solving and communication responsibilities. This approach maximizes the utilization of the technology and prepares the way for the increasing complexity of SAP and Web-based applications.

The networked teams design is a fluid mix of centralization and decentralization, weak and strong network ties, interdependence and responsibility. The design calls for more trust among participants than do more hierarchical models. Traditional hierarchical controls are simply not in place. We believe hierarchical controls have been replaced by far more powerful controls, controls established by a committed workforce that demonstrates ownership for results. D'Ann Darling, a member of the original FSC Remote Processing Steering Committee and the manager of the largest ASC located in the Bay Area, sums up her reaction today:

> The customers of all the different centralizations that HP has done, whether it is HR or accounting or whatever, the customers in general view this one [the CSFSC] as being the most successful of all of them. I think one of the reasons is the business connection is still there. We have a local advocate [the ASCs]. When you get people in the much more self-directed mode where they feel they can affect their processes and their destiny, they want to improve things. They don't want things to be the same old way. You hire people with that mind-set and they continue to grow. That has nothing but positive implications all the way down the line.[5]

## Key Lessons about Networked Teams

By late 1997, Greg Spray had identified what he considered key lessons from a networked teams organization.[6] He described these lessons in open house presentations and in a variety of management meetings. The early planning stages received particular attention. Greg believed that the use of an external consultant had provided a third-party view and discipline important for designing the new organization. He concluded that the often laborious work of the steering and design teams had made worthwhile contributions to not only the start-up phase of the CSFSC but the mature organization as well. He stressed the importance of determining how much self-directedness was desirable and then identifying responsibility parameters to support self-direction. Greg also reflected on the need to clearly define roles and responsibilities while attempting to understand employees' perception of success as contrasted to management's view of it.

In a variety of public settings in late 1997, Greg talked about the importance of effective communication and the expectation that criticism would occur and could become a positive for the organization. He continually reiterated the concept that the CSFSC must be able to work on team ideas or the organization would teach the teams not to think. Education and development were key and included not only individual team members but the facilitators and other non–team based parts of the organization. Greg believed that the CSFSC had developed a culture in which teams expected stretch goals, and thus it was important to not let a gap develop between achieving one goal and communicating the next goal. Success, no matter how small, was to be celebrated. Greg also acknowledged the importance of the efficient use of technology. Cost-effective networking, mail-enabled workflow, Web-based transactions, imaging and process workflow, high-performance access to information, and implementing next generation systems such as SAP all contributed to the networked teams' success. Staffing the Solutions Center with financial process and information technology experts provided worldwide leverage.

During this period, Greg also talked extensively about leadership priorities for teams. He believed the very best people should be facilitators. He told the FOMS and others that facilitators must schedule an incredible amount of communication. On a slide presented at an open house he declared, "Prepare and schedule incredible amounts of Communication, Communication, Communication, Communication, Communication, Communication, Listening, Listening, Listening, Listening, Questioning, Communication."[7]

Greg identified helping teams understand organization culture, purpose, vision, directives, issues, initiatives, parameters, goals, and customer needs as a leadership priority. Leadership also was responsible for understanding and addressing team needs. Greg thought managers and other leaders should study teams by actually sitting down and doing the work, experiencing what it is like to work on a team. Using a distinction Pam had made in the initial team training, Greg concluded that it was important to respect the differences between teamwork and self-directed work teams. Teamwork was needed in a variety of structures, including the structure of self-directed work teams. But the process of teamwork did not fully capture the responsibilities and capabilities required for effective high-performing teams. Greg believed that facilitators and leadership in general should concentrate on leadership skills as opposed to in-depth technical expertise. He was fond of saying that you must lead people toward a direction, not an answer. He specifically encouraged the use of humor, symbolism, analogies, and urgency. Leadership was responsible for building the self-esteem of the teams. Greg's final imperative for leaders was to know more about customer needs than anyone else in the organization.

## Team Successes

The numerical successes are stunning, and we will discuss them when we describe CSFSC efforts to meet business goals. But the teams have had successes that cannot be described in metrics alone. They have influenced the entire company and numerous other organizations as well. For example, one of Diana Morgan's teams literally changed corporate policy with their proposal for a variable work schedule. The team did all of the research on the pros and cons, talked with human resources, worked with legal, and developed a presentation for an alternative work schedule to support both business and individual needs. Their presentation was persuasive and resulted in the first HP-wide sanctioned four ten-hour-day schedule. Their work has been used as the model from which other similar work alternatives have been designed.

Reed Breland describes watching a team become genuinely high performing:

My definition of a high-performing team is one that has outstanding team communication, increased total performance, a much broader perspective of information gathering, and support of other teams beyond their own group. One of my teams really got together and gelled. They were able to significantly out-perform other teams, demonstrate some phenomenal team work and team behaviors, and I think they all walked away from it very, very energized. It is a state of performance you can't achieve permanently.[8] So I think that that experience was the most enjoyable because you were able to finally put all of the readings and all of the work and all of the observation in the background and just look at it and say, "Wow!" This team has done a phenomenal job and they recognize it. And you don't need to congratulate them because they achieved that themselves and they recognized it and they were doing it for each other. That is when my facilitation was no longer needed. That was really, really exciting.[9]

Team successes often were best captured during HP open houses. Reed explains:

We saw open houses as our opportunity to showcase our center in terms of the people, the processes, and the technology. Originally, I think when we created the open houses we were really impressed with ourselves from a technology perspective. But I think what we started to learn through the course of giving open houses, we started hearing from the companies that they wanted to learn more about what we were doing with teams than with technology. So this was a shift for us when these visitors would come in: we would set them up with team members in a variety of settings. In some cases the team members would just get up and present some of the project improvement activities that the teams were owning. We would set them up during lunches where the visitors would get a chance to sit down in a somewhat informal setting and just ask open questions to team members. The visitors would get to sit in the team areas and observe team members working and then ask them questions as it went on. So it was really very much an interactive process—very free form. From my perspective and from a lot of the managers' perspectives it was quite scary because it was an open forum for any type of complaining by the team members. If they wanted to voice their concerns, whether it was teams or technology or workload or whatever, they had these typically very high ranking senior officials who were visiting to lay this out and to complain. One story that started out to be very, very scary, was a lunch. It was the CFO of a Fortune 50 company and several others who had an opportunity to have lunch with an intact team of about six people. So this group of twelve went off, had their lunch, and they were in a private conference room with no other participants from the FSC facilitators or managers or anyone else.

Typically questions are asked, "What do you like about teams, what don't you like about teams, how long have you been doing teams, what do you think are the benefits?" I wasn't there but the story says the CFO said, "Come on, you have just been staged to come in here and tell this. This sounds way too good to be true." And one of the team members said, "No, no, not at all. We can say or do anything we want. We are telling you the truth. This is what it is like." The individual pressed harder, saying, "No, I don't buy into it. I just know that if I were to go back to my company and have individuals talk to an outsider and they could say anything they wanted, they certainly would not be saying all these good things about their work environment and their management structure and things like that." So after probably two or three probes of really trying to get the "dirt" on the organization, one individual who had been pretty quiet through the whole lunch finally spoke up and, I was told, said, "Well, I have been with HP for more than fifteen years and most of that career has been in a very traditional organization with supervisors and managers and whatnot. I have been here for a couple of years and I can tell you that I would not go back to the way it was for twice the money." Either the sincerity or the honesty or whatever of this person came through loud and clear such that the CFO then relayed this story back to the CSFSC managers after the lunch was over. So we probed a bit and asked about the individual and some physical characteristics to try to determine who it was. We believe, although we are not sure, that this was one of the individuals who was probably one of the most vocal detractors to teams in the first few months, even upwards of the first year that the person was part of the organization. Over the course of two years and really working through teams, the individual had come to embrace the whole team concept to such a point that he or she would make a statement that at twice the price they would not go back. This speaks very highly of what we are doing and I think it leaves a very strong, lasting impression on the companies that come through here.

## Individuals in a Networked Teams Environment

The satisfaction ratings reported from the HP corporate employee survey tell the story. In a company known for employee satisfaction, the CSFSC ranks among the most satisfied of all HP divisions and organizations. Table 7.1 presents CSFSC results for 1994 and 1996 and compares the organization's results to the overall controllership and to all of HP in the United States. In every category overall

**Table 7.1   Employee Satisfaction Ratings:
Improved Favorable Ratings in 17 of 18 Categories**
(in percent)

| | FY96 CSFSC | FY94 CSFSC | FY96 Controller | FY96 U.S. |
|---|---|---|---|---|
| Management | 83 | 73 | 78 | 66 |
| Supervision | 70 | 54 | 72 | 67 |
| Communication | 73 | 64 | 72 | 65 |
| Relationships | 80 | 76 | 83 | 76 |
| Work Environment | 76 | 66 | 73 | 61 |
| Performance | 67 | 49 | 66 | 61 |
| Development | 80 | 75 | 77 | 71 |
| Promotions | 47 | 29 | 53 | 43 |
| Recognition | 61 | 56 | 65 | 59 |
| Job | 82 | 79 | 83 | 77 |
| Corporate Management | 84 | 70 | 85 | 68 |
| Pay | 48 | 36 | 46 | 43 |
| Benefits | 91 | 86 | 91 | 75 |
| Quality | 88 | 77 | 82 | 68 |
| Survey | 74 | 47 | 71 | 56 |
| HP Way | 85 | 70 | 83 | 67 |
| Diversity | 80 | 74 | 77 | 69 |
| Pay Addendum | 62 | 66 | 65 | 56 |
| Total Compensation | 73 | Insuf. | 65 | 51 |
| Work / Life | 81 | Insuf | 81 | 69 |

satisfaction is higher for the CSFSC than for HP U.S., and the CSFSC exceeds the controllership group in all but six categories. Importantly, the 1994 and 1996 CSFSC ratings demonstrated improvement in seventeen of eighteen category areas. The results support the conclusion that individuals thrive in a networked teams environment.

Most employees believe their abilities are better utilized in a team-based structure and they have more control over their work and their future. Box 7.1 provides a cross section of team member comments about their experiences. The issue of the value of a team-based structure for individual careers has all but disappeared. Team members and managers alike have experienced career growth, and most credit experience in the team environment as pivotal to their success. Team members Tammy Biggs and Bill Brown, who earlier described their experiences with the team structure, are typical examples. Tammy moved from an accounts payable process specialist to a professional position on a support desk as a member of the IT technical staff in Americas Information Technology Group. Bill is expanding his knowledge base with lateral transfers from a fixed assets process specialist to an intra-corporate accounting process specialist, and to an accounts payable process specialist position. Lateral transfers are common as individuals work to broaden their process expertise. Others use their experiences to move vertically. As Sandy describes it,

Many people move through a progression that begins with a higher-level (pay scale based on competence and contributions) nonexempt specialist position supporting the teams to an entry-level exempt position focusing on analysis of the current processes to an exempt process engineer focusing on reengineering processes. A number of team members have moved to cost accounting positions. A few have moved to entry-level buyer positions in procurement. Those leaving the CSFSC routinely find good positions within HP and some are recruited to other companies.[10]

### Box 7.1   Team Members Talk

Imagine a job where you have the empowerment to share leadership roles, where teams set their own goals and schedules, where you have equal input, perform interviews, and make hiring recommendations, plus review overall process performance … this is my job as a team member. It has been an awesome learning experience!

—Carmen Fuller, fixed assets team

A key to the success of the self-directed teams is the utilization and implementation of the self-initiated and mandatory training and materials that are offered to us. Again, it is the "utilization and implementation" of those tools to be put into practice in our day-to-day business that allows us to succeed.

—Kent Young, AP cash management team

A team can use each team member's expertise to do projects. A team learns what a valuable tool communication is to become a high-performing team. My greatest reward is knowing that I contributed to a team member's training and development to become a strong team member.

—Carol Douglas, AP team

One of my best experiences in being a member of a team has been that I have developed much more than I would have as an independent contributor. I appreciate the fact that within the cohesiveness of my team, we have continual sharing of information and best practices. This allows each of us to become better employees and to further our development as individuals.

—Mia Taherkhah, intracorporate accounting team

Working in the team environment has given me the opportunity to pursue my career development goals while being a strong team member. Through the peer input process, I am able to give and receive feedback on strengths and opportunities that I or team members may have.

—Nancy Brennan, travel team

Since my team members are committed to the team's performance, low performers are encouraged to raise their own standards of excellence but are not chastised for a lack thereof.

Accounts payable would be very clerical and boring if it were in a traditional environment. The CSFSC team environment allows me to break up the monotony of the job by allowing me to put on the hats of management, project management, and consultant.

—Scott Beetham, customer response center

Kemp Bohlen sums up what most team members say about their CSFSC experience: "The litmus test is, and I ask it every so often, 'Would you go back to working the other way?' And I have not yet had one person tell me that they would do that." (Later you will learn about the career progress of the early leaders who are taking HP and Agilent into the twenty-first century.)

## Partner/Customer Satisfaction

Beginning in 1995 and continuing to the present, serious efforts have been undertaken to survey partners, customers, and vendors with the goal of utilizing broadly generated input for strategic planning. Unlike many organizations conducting customer satisfaction surveys, CSFSC leadership wanted the survey to meet acceptable methodological and statistical standards for survey design, collection, and interpretation. They planned on using the data and they wanted it to be reliable and valid. Pam was asked to work with the task team responsible for the survey to identify appropriate questions and sampling procedures and to analyze the data. ASC contacts, administrative assistants, managers, customer response center callers, procurement specialists, travelers, vendors, EER/SST (electronic employee reimbursement/self-service transaction) users, and ASC walk-ups (individuals working in a face-to-face mode with ASCs) were all treated as separate survey populations. The idea was to determine overall satisfaction with CSFSC services, to use these various populations to target areas for improvement, and to determine where to focus energies on new products and process improvements. Survey topics included ease of contact and ease of use of information, documentation and communication information, teamwork, quality and accuracy of transaction processing, quality and availability of systems, ownership of issues, overall satisfaction, and ideas for process and product improvements. A rating scale of one to six (one being the lowest rating) has been used across all three survey administrations

(1995, 1997, 1999). The results confirm the success of the CSFSC from a customer and user perspective. Extremely satisfied responses (a rating of five or six) have ranged from 55 to 64 percent of everyone responding for all three survey years (1,400 to 1,600 respondents per year). Less than 7 percent of all respondents have ever given the organization an unsatisfactory (one or two) rating. The professionalism of team members in working with vendors, customers, and partners routinely receives outstanding marks as well as written comments. Professionalism scores frequently exceed 5.0 on the one to six scale. Pam remarks,

> Over the years of my professional career, I have worked with or reviewed similar customer satisfaction data from approximately five hundred organizations. These results consistently are the best I have seen. The professionalism scores are not just good, they are unusually good. The written comments often ask how the CSFSC has been able to achieve this level of competence. I believe this is a perfect example of what can happen when individuals are given good training, are in a results-oriented organizational structure, and are supported by a culture with high expectations. Customers do see the difference. Unfortunately, although we generally have high expectations for volume of work produced, we often don't create environments that foster the quality of interactions that contributes to high customer satisfaction. The CSFSC has done both—focus on volume and quality service. In fact, that focus is what has contributed to the cultural concept that the *product is service.*[11]

### Meeting Business Goals

The answer is yes. The business goals have been met. Transaction processing costs have been sharply reduced and customer satisfaction is high. Employees enjoy working at the CSFSC and the results show. But the organization is not static. The culture is capable of supporting both technological and organizational change. Unlike many other success stories, however, the results from the CSFSC have been sustained over a long period of time (nine years as of this writing) and there is more to come. In the epilogue you will learn that both HP and Agilent have selected the networked teams organizational form for their future.

By 1998 transaction processing costs had been cut 27.4 percent (in real dollars unadjusted for inflation) from 1990 costs (see table 7.2). During that time HP revenue tripled from $16.4 to $47 billion. Twenty-eight HP factory sites plus corporate headquarters formed the customer base. The customers were coast-to-coast with a total of 56,678 employees supported by the CSFSC. CSFSC headcount was 296 people—252 permanent employees and 44 temporary workers. The breakdown by function was 53 IT employees; 21 process engineers; 194 operations processing and administration personnel; 11 managers/facilitators; and 17 people devoted to special projects and new business. Eleven managers and facilitators were running the entire organization. If the old ratios of managers to transaction processing personnel had been maintained, there would have been thirty-two managers devoted to transaction processing alone.

The sheer work produced exceeds industry standards in virtually every category. A typical processing month is described in table 7.3. Additionally, 2,600 pieces of mail are processed each day, 16 million audit detail records are created each month, 101,400 active

**Table 7.2    Fiscal Year 1998 Accounting Transaction Processing Survey Results ($M)**

|                 | FY90   | FY98   | Δ       | Δ%      |
|-----------------|--------|--------|---------|---------|
| Wages/Salary    | $25.8  | $20.9  | ‹ $4.9  | −19.0%  |
| IT              | $15.8  | $8.8   | ‹ $7.0  | −44.5%  |
| Other           | $9.4   | $7.3   | ‹ $2.0  | −21.6%  |
| **Total**       | **$51.0** | **$37.0** | **‹ $13.9** | **−27.4%** |

Note: Between FY90 and FY98 HP tripled in size.

**Table 7.3    CSFSC Processing in a Typical Month**

144,000 Invoices

65,000 Payments ($1.5B/month)

38,000 Checks

25,000 Direct Deposits

18,000 Quick Card Transactions

15,000 Travel Expense Reports

32,000 Electronic Employee Reimbursements

11,000 Customer Response Center Cases

400 Wire Payments

assets are managed, $14 billion in intracorporate transactions flow through monthly, 150 gigabytes are stored in the information warehouse, and approximately 75 different report jobs are launched to each of 30 HP entities.

Table 7.4 provides annual volume figures. Figure 7.2 provides an analysis of cost savings for the CSFSC and ASC model, and figure 7.3 projects what costs would have been without the new organizational form using sales and general administrative growth rates. The numbers speak for themselves. The volume of work produced is high, the quality is high, the customers are satisfied, and CSFSC employees are thriving. The CSFSC has become a successful business within a business.

**Table 7.4    Fiscal Year 1998 CSFSC Volumes**

| | |
|---|---|
| AP $ Flowthrough (annual) | $19 Billion |
| External Vendors | 73,000 |
| Assets Tracked | 101,432 |
| IC $ Flowthrough (annual) | $170 Billion |
| TERs Processed (annual) | 176,323 |
| GL Audit Details (annual) | 219,880,696 |
| CRC Cases (annual) | 132,000 |
| Information Warehouse | 150 Gigabytes |

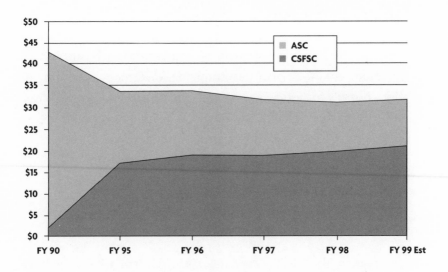

**Figure 7.2    Total U.S. Factory Accounting Transaction Processing
Cost Envelope**

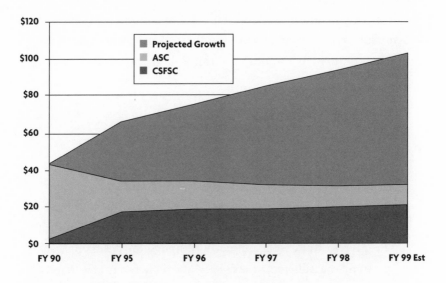

**Figure 7.3    Total U.S. Factory Accounting Transaction Processing
Projected Costs Without New Organizational Model**

In 1997 a disaster recovery plan was tested and it worked effectively. Both internal and external auditors gave the CSFSC a clean bill of health. The Price Waterhouse audit found no business control issues. Auditors' main recommendations were to continue to relax controls for efficiency. An HP internal audit identified four problem invoices in all of the 1995 data, with auditors commenting that the CSFSC was "the cleanest shop they have found of this size—it was like finding a penny (the 4 invoices) in the Federal Reserve."[12]

## Industry Reactions

Others view the CSFSC as a success and adapt what they have learned to their own particular needs. Fran Bengtson, director of business development for Lockheed Martin Shared Services, became involved after a senior vice president of Lockheed Martin Shared Services attended a Gunn Partners workshop in Colorado Springs and visited the CSFSC. (Gunn Partners is a leading consulting organization working with global companies that need to generate increasing effectiveness in their administrative functions.) Bengtson attended the next workshop and was pleased with her HP visit:

> Very impressive! Well organized, well managed, very strong employee pride and ownership of the processes. We had the service center director, Greg Spray and his director of process improvements, Reed Breland, come to Valley Forge and address the VF directors and our high-involvement work team coordinators on the methodology and concepts used by HP Colorado Springs in their self-directed work team approach. Although our team approach was somewhat different at Lockheed Martin, we were able to learn some nuances from HP regarding team organization, management and training, especially training.[13]

Jim Villamana, director of J.D. Edwards Americas Financial Services, describes what he has learned from the CSFSC:

> Migrating to shared services involves technology and dynamics surrounding the organization and processes. Although we have been successful with technology utilizing our own software, we need to focus more on the organization and key drivers. As a result, we are rolling out performance measurements by functional area and are developing a formal communication strategy. We feel that a disciplined communication strategy centered around the issues, wants, and needs of the organization will be key to keeping the momentum. We are also evaluating a customer service desk to provide "one-stop shopping" for internal and external customers. Finally, we plan to evaluate self-directed work teams to help us achieve better results. Organizations who are considering shared services should make it a point to see the HP way.[14]

Kelly D. Klute, senior manager of business consulting for Arthur Andersen LLP, identified the CSFSC as one of four "world-class" self-directed work teams organizations:

> There is a widely varying definition of what constitutes a self-directed work team. On one end of the spectrum, there were teams that were in reality hierarchical in lines (i.e., clerical, supervisor, manager, etc.). And communications were expected to follow those same organizational lines. Communication was consistent with a traditional hierarchical organization, but poor in comparison to truly effective SDWT organizations. Direction came from the top down. And autonomy, creativity, individuality, team cohesiveness, proactivity, etc. [some of the fundamental attributes required for successful SDWTs] were hard to find. The other end of the spectrum was where a vision was set by leadership and it was up to the respective teams and coaches to determine the specific actions they

would take to achieve the vision. The teams were truly self-suffi-cient and self-policing, up to and including HR functions such as hiring, firing, and evaluating. HP definitely was on the latter end of the spectrum.... Second, there was a wide range of success in implementing and operating SDWTs.... HP was definitely at or near the top in both implementation and operational effective-ness.... SDWT concepts in general have been incorporated into the planned operations of our shared services center. And having a suc-cessful implementation and operation of SDWT concepts by an organization as admired as HP to point to has dramatically helped to sell the SDWT concept internally within AA.[15]

Bob Gunn, founder of Gunn Partners, has encouraged many of his clients to visit the CSFSC:

HP is at the very top of financial service centers. What distinguishes HP is not specifically their productivity but that they are one of the few truly global shared services organizations. They are at the top in putting in place their team-based model. They are really "walk-ing the talk" and are in a class by themselves. They have hit a home run because of the global organization with all of the cultural dif-ferences.[16]

Gunn goes on to explain that no large company has grown up in a team-based model. Putting teams in place surfaces assumptions around teamwork, collaboration, and decision making. Gunn con-tends that team-based models generally are the best structures for staff and administrative organizations. When asked what he believes has contributed to the HP experience, Gunn concludes, "Kemp's leadership has provided continuity. He was willing to change his stripes and change from his past experience. The recruiting of quality people who wanted to work in a collaborative model also was key." Gunn supports team-based structures so strongly that Gunn Partners has migrated to a shared leadership model without a CEO. Gunn, in affirming the importance of taking ownership for change and organizational structure, contends, "Organizations must own their own improvements; they must trust their own wisdom and common sense." Although not specifically directed to the organization in our story, Gunn was summarizing much of what has happened at the CSFSC.

## What We Learned When the Product Is Service

Creating a profit-like organization generates ongoing questions about product development. From the beginning, the CSFSC began to think about the products of transaction processing as contrasted to thinking about transaction processing as support. In an organization attempting to voluntarily attract customers with centralized processes that few really wanted, the competitive advantage came from developing a broad concept of service. Just as the business within a business philosophy and the compelling goals of cutting transaction processing by 50 percent had stimulated the team-based design, the broad concept that the most important product is service literally drove how decisions were made, who was involved, and the timing of almost all process changes. Service as product came to mean high volumes of work produced, quality and accuracy in transaction processing, timeliness, low cost, professionalism in all interactions, regular input from customers, involvement of partners in priority setting, and flexibility. The service-as-product approach created an imperative for managers and team members alike to ask themselves what high-quality service would look like in any situation prior to engaging in problem solving and decision making.

We learned that when the product is service, people must be able to make rapid decisions in the interests of the customer and they must not be slowed down by the organizational structure. Not only must individuals respond, but the organizational structure must be flexible and fluid to meet changing needs. But those internal to the organization cannot define the characteristics (feature sets) of high-quality service. We learned early on that regular, in-depth input from customers was essential to understanding what constitutes high-quality service. Once the understanding is in place, managers and team members could set about to build the product of service with the desired feature sets. Finally, we learned that the service product must be supported by continual change. The changing needs of the transaction processing environment require the introduction of new product features on a regular basis. In other words, capturing the essence of high-quality service is a fleeting illusion. Meeting ongoing needs requires continual involvement with customers, empowerment of those in the first line of customer contact, and a willingness to change just as things are working smoothly.

## What We Learned When Individuals Thrive in a Networked Teams Organization

The CSFSC experience taught us that only when individuals thrive can organizations sustain the type of performance evidenced in our story. Individuals may be expendable in short-term gains, but you don't win at the end of the fourth quarter without a high-performing team. Individuals in the CSFSC thrive personally, professionally, and in support of business goals. Personal goals, professional goals, and business goals, when working synergistically, support sustained performance. We do not claim, of course, that everyone who ever worked at the CSFSC thrived with the experience. But the overwhelming majority seem to say they have. Satisfaction ratings, analyses of career progressions, low attrition rates, and a host of less visible measures support the conclusion that the networked teams design is a good place to learn and utilize a growing set of skills and abilities.

The issue of fully utilizing human abilities is an ongoing problem in most organizations. We believe the CSFSC experience provides an important lesson in developing human potential by learning what to control and where control should be located. The CSFSC with clear business goals learned to control for outcomes but not to control people. The culture of the organization, the high expectations, the extensive training, and the involvement of customers and partners prepared individuals and entire teams to control themselves. The results have exceeded even the most ambitious of goals. Controlling for outcomes means letting go for individuals to thrive in a culture that supports change and fosters high expectations. Controlling people is easier, but it doesn't work as well and it blurs leadership accountability for outcomes. The CSFSC experience teaches us that letting go can be the ultimate form of control.

## What This Means for Others

The lesson that the product is service helps us ask questions about whether an organization should be providing services or developing a product of service. In many ways the approach to service as product is based on the establishment of a business within a business concept which differs from units which provide routine overhead services. Making the decision to become a for-profit like business (with an overhead service) influences not only organizational form but how products are developed, who is involved, and how the outcomes are measured. We believe the business within a business concept is the future because it moves the necessary (overhead services) from an expense to an operation capable of making measurable contributions to the bottom line.

The fact that individuals thrive in a networked teams organization provides two key lessons for those considering a team-based model: (1) the model won't work if individuals don't thrive and (2) excellence comes from tapping the brain power of literally everyone. Although this is common sense, it is uncommon practice, contributing to mediocre results or outright failure. Teams are different; they do challenge assumptions about what constitutes good management but they work. And when they work, they do so because of the ownership collectively exhibited throughout the organization. For that ownership to be sustained over a long period of time, individuals must see themselves and others achieving recognition, personal satisfaction, and career progress. That has happened in our story and it can happen for others as well.

## The Constant of Change

By 1998 the CSFSC was considered a highly successful organization by almost any standard. But the constant challenge of change was about to test the strength of the networked teams design and the people who had guided the organization from its early years. In February 1998, based in large measure on the success of the CSFSC, Greg Spray was asked to lead a corporate project called 5x5x5, which was associated with the Power of One, Best of Many program championed by HP CEO Lew Platt. Greg was charged with determining both processes and new organizational forms that could reduce costs in operations procurement by 5 percent. Kemp Bohlen, while continuing with his worldwide responsibilities, became the acting CSFSC manager. Pat Robison, a twenty-year HP veteran working as a cost accounting manager in Convex (one of HP's recent acquisitions), was hired to become CSFSC operations manager. The FOMs were worried. They had been reporting directly to Greg, and Pat's arrival appeared to some to be adding a layer to the organization. The magnitude of the changes to come would soon put this issue in perspective.

## HP and Agilent Technologies

The announcement made on March 2, 1999—that HP would become two companies—changed literally everything and called into question not only the future of the networked teams design but the very existence of the CSFSC. The new company, Agilent Technologies, would be home to the products of the original HP—

test and measurement, health care, chemical analysis, and the semi-conductor businesses. The new HP would focus on computers, printers, and scanners. Ned Barnholt, a long-time HP executive, was named CEO of Agilent. HP CEO Lew Platt had submitted his resignation to be effective as soon as a replacement could be selected for the businesses that would retain the HP name. In July 1999, Carleton "Carly" Fiorina became the first outsider to head HP since its founding. The new era was under way. What did this unprecedented change mean for the CSFSC?

The answers to questions about the future of the CSFSC came rapidly. In July 1999, Kemp Bohlen's role as Worldwide Financial Services manager for HP was significantly expanded. HP's Americas Financial Services plus Asia and Europe would report directly to him, with the goal of finally moving the worldwide strategy into one cohesive organization. Americas Financial Services would be managed by a relative newcomer to Colorado Springs, Pat Robison. Part of the workforce would remain in Atlanta, but all operations would report directly to Pat. Kemp, the early firm supporter of teams, emphatically announced that the teams were here to stay and that the networked teams organization was the future. The Agilent organization made decisions just as rapidly. Mike Waterlander, one of the original facilitators, was named manager of the new Agilent FSC. Agilent would build its FSC in Colorado Springs with some of the team members from the former CSFSC. Agilent would not retain any Atlanta presence. As Kemp did, Mike quickly declared that Agilent business goals could only be met with the continuation of the team-based structure. Reed Breland, also an early facilitator, was named controller for the Agilent Americas Information Technology Group. Greg Spray assumed the role of director of HP Operations Procurement and Rick Hobbs was named director of Agilent's Operations Procurement. The early CSFSC leadership was positioned to lead both HP and Agilent into the future of transaction processing, information technology, procurement, and the shared services organizations of the future (see figs. 7.4, 7.5).

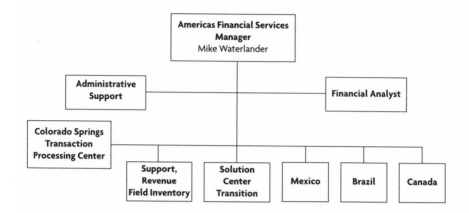

**Figure 7.4    Agilent Technologies Financial Services Center, August 1999**

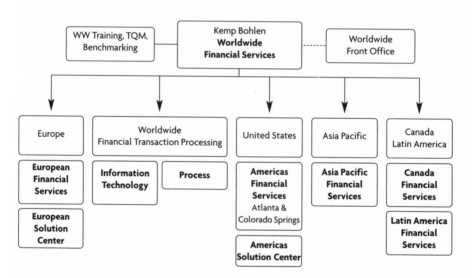

**Figure 7.5    Hewlett-Packard Worldwide Financial Services, August 1999**

With this surprising turn of events, our story ends where it began—with the beginning of a new organization—only this time it is two organizations growing out of the experiences of the last nine years. As 1999 ended, the CSFSC that is described in our story ceased to exist, having become part of HP's Americas Financial Services. HP's Americas Financial Services and Agilent's CSFSC are the new organizations evolving from the old and adapting to the needs of the future. They both have a culture of change, a network of teams, and the entrepreneurial spirit that characterized the beginning of our story. They have leaders who are experienced with teams and team members who don't want to work any other way. They face challenges ahead, since change is the constant. They are the gyroscopes of the twenty-first century.

In the epilogue, Kemp Bohlen, Greg Spray, Mike Waterlander, Reed Breland, and Pat Robison talk about the future of HP and Agilent, the future of the networked teams designs, and what they think our story means for others.

# Epilogue

---

# HP and Agilent Technologies Leaders Talk about the Future

The organization described in our story is now two organizations: HP Americas Financial Services with new relationships to HP Worldwide Financial Services, and Agilent Financial Services Center. The leaders of both HP and Agilent are CSFSC veterans who are committed to continuing the networked teams structure and vision a future increasingly dependent on the power of teams.

Kemp Bohlen, with his global HP responsibilities, talks about the road ahead:

> I think for both companies [HP and Agilent] the focus on individual businesses is going to be heightened. Speaking for the HP side of the house, I sense that we are going to see these businesses [HP is now organized into four businesses: enterprise computing solutions, inkjet imaging, laser-jet imaging systems, and computer products] start to diverge. They will cater to their own customer bases. So, if you take the computing products organization, which is basically our PCs, they are competing in a really tough marketplace. It is a very cost-competitive world. And so it would not be surprising for me to see the group controller and the CEO of that business come to us and say, "We need a much lower-cost model." If you look at the philosophy of how we got started and where we

have been, we have done a one-size-fits-all model because the major thrust of what our customer base wanted was the lowest-possible-cost model they could get. And, obviously for us, that was standardization.

I think where the group controllers and the CEOs are starting to go with these businesses, particularly in the HP area, they are starting to say, "Maybe low cost is not exactly what I want. Maybe a more tailored approach to fit my business needs might be worth some more money." That is a good and a bad news story. The issue we will face is that there are four major businesses and if we deviate for one of those businesses, that can mean some higher costs for some of the other businesses. So I think the real balancing act for us is how to determine what is absolutely standard and stays the same for everybody—that is probably going to be general ledger and expense reporting. I think the new HP tends to view the financial services organization as a strategic partner.

Cost is still clearly an element and a lot of what we do with technology will continue to drive those costs down. But I see a major shift in the next two or three years. We probably will move our outsourced processing to Bangalore, India. [Bangalore has been an HP location for just over ten years.] The technology allows us through imaging and work flow to basically load the data any place in the world. Currently this work is done in the Philippines. We will transfer that data to India, they will do the processing, and the data will be ready for us when people get in here [Colorado Springs] in the morning. I think you will see this organization turn into more of a research and development, process engineering, and problem-solving organization as opposed to a processing organization. I think the same thing will be true in Europe and, obviously, Asia Pacific. So I see a major shift both in the type of work that we do here and in the skill sets that are going to be required. Because I really see at the end of the day that people who are working here in Colorado Springs are fairly high-level problem solvers and are R&D and process engineering technologists.... I'm really energized. I think our whole organization is understanding that we are really coming together as a global team for the first time. We have talked that talk but we really weren't operating that way.[1]

Mike Waterlander, manager of Agilent Financial Services Center, describes what he sees ahead:

Agilent has some large challenges. We are splitting the financial services organization between HP and Agilent in several countries but not in all countries. The volume of work being split is disproportionately higher [in Agilent] than the revenue being split out for the new company. Therefore, there is a significant loss in the economies of scale associated with financial services. From a sponsor's standpoint we have done a good job of educating them on this situation. I think we will have to look at a more aggressive consolidation strategy on a geographic basis. At HP we reached a certain point where we had big centers in Brussels, France, Germany, the UK, Atlanta, Colorado Springs, Japan, and Singapore. I think there will be additional pressure in Agilent to continue to consolidate those activities into one center for all of Europe and likewise in the Americas, where we really have not gotten very far outside of the U.S. with respect to a shared services model for financial services.

I think the question now is, How do we recover from this split? One logical thing is to consolidate the additional transaction volumes in Canada and Latin America. That is something we are including in our strategy and can implement down the road. We first have to consolidate Agilent transactions processed in our Atlanta center by HP personnel and really create a U.S.–wide processing center here in Colorado Springs for Agilent. We will regain some economies of scale from just that consolidation alone. That will help costs here in the Americas. The other opportunity is to look at other processes that historically have not been part of the shared services model in HP.[2]

We asked Pat Robison, newly named manager of HP Americas Financial Services, his view of the future for teams and for HP. Pat replied,

> Teams have found a solid home in the Financial Services Center and will be an integral part of our plans going forward. The future direction of self-directed teams will depend on several factors influencing our environment. These factors include different locations, virtual workforces, outsourcing, e-commerce, and the total customer experience. With the increase of automation and electronic services, it has become easier to introduce the concept of the virtual team. The challenge we face is creating a work environment that enables team members to make decisions when the teams are distributed across different locations. Maintaining team synergy and effectiveness will be key.
>
> Both outsourcing and e-commerce will change the type of work that is required of teams. Much of the pure transaction processing work will be outsourced or will be input by the original requestor using tools such as the Internet. This will change the work environment, the type of work we do, and the skills that are required within financial services. Our focus will be on exception processes, managing supplier relationships and process improvements. As a result, the ability for teams to engage in continuous process improvement will be heightened. Finally, managing the total customer experience for the services we provide will drive how the teams are organized. "One-size-fits-all" does not work anymore. We have a combination of customers, suppliers, and employees that generate different requirements. Forming teams that concentrate on our various customer segments will help us adjust to each of their unique needs.[3]

We returned to the veterans of the entire HP experience, Kemp Bohlen and Mike Waterlander, and asked them for their perceptions of the future of networked teams. Kemp responded, "Will we stay in teams? Yes, because of the success that we have had with the teams."[4] Kemp is planning on introducing self-directed employee teams in India and seeking other opportunities to expand team responsibilities. Mike felt that

> there is no change in terms of the stance. The self-directed teams are a hugely important part of how we organize ourselves here in the U.S. I have gone on record here pretty early on after the split was announced that, yes, we will have a team-based organizational model. There was a question about that. Did Agilent want to keep that model knowing there are things that are not perfect with that model? In my opinion, there is no perfect organizational model and I will take the pluses of a team-based organization even though there are challenges. We want to do some additional investment in the training of teams. The challenge now is where do we go next with self-directed teams. The company split is probably good from the standpoint that it allows both companies to reevaluate, reassess, develop new strategies and plans. I think if both companies look at what teams provide, they will realize there is a tremendous opportunity that can be tapped further. I am optimistic about the future of self-directed teams in both companies.[5]

Greg Spray, once such a powerful influence for the CSFSC and now the director of HP operations procurement, agrees that teams are part of the future: "I see more responsibility for teams, even pushing the envelope further in terms of self-management, self-directed features. I also see the need for teams to be more independent and entrepreneurial."[6] Greg predicts many internal infrastructure services will be outsourced to commercial e-services suppliers:

> In this new model, the self-directed teams will need to serve multiple customers and interact with the user over the Internet. Teams have already proven a level of quality and professionalism that will be required in this new model. The expectations for teams will be

higher. We will see constant changes in the services provided and in expectations and responsibilities for the teams. Teams that have outstanding teamwork and the ability to learn and change quickly will be a great asset, one that can differentiate an e-service in a very competitive marketplace.[7]

Greg endorses team-based structures, saying,

> If I ever get a chance to build another organization, there is no question I would use teams. And, if I were building an organization with no legacy requirements, I would build teams across the exempt/nonexempt boundary as well. Because I think the power is there.[8]

Reed Breland, the former facilitator and new controller for Agilent Americas Information Technology Group, talks about what he would advise others:

> I think what Colorado Springs has done with self-directed teams is much more than mainstream corporate America will potentially do—team members are involved in some very, very detailed day-to-day management activities. I think we are further down the continuum than many other companies. Certain company styles and culture don't fit. But I do think that collaborative work will continue to become more and more common. I think we will see more teams and more teamwork. I don't see one best model of teams for all companies. I think teams are going to be the mechanism that continues to propel collaborative efforts to provide better solutions. I think the days of the hierarchical organization—very autocratic—are leaving us more and more and that twenty, thirty, or forty years down the road they will be in the minority.[9]

In describing what he would say to those considering teams, Mike Waterlander concluded,

I would not paint an overly rosy picture of self-directed teams. There are some tremendous challenges that come with this model. So, if an organization is really going to this model it has to understand what it means to make this happen. I think a lot of people see the benefits, or the perceived benefits, of the team-based organizational model and want to go directly to the benefits and skip the hard part. I would clearly sell them on the benefits of teams. I am a strong advocate of teams and will continue to be. But I would also make sure people are aware of the investment level that is needed. Investment not only for the management team but also for the team members themselves. It is not just a one-time investment in training but an ongoing focus on development. On the surface I think some people oversimplify teams. I think what we have experienced here is the need for ongoing investment, ongoing education, and sometimes resetting the teams. How far do you take teams? I don't think people understand, myself included, what is the end point we should be targeting. Maybe there is no logical end point and it is up to us to define that for ourselves.[10]

Kemp sums up much of the sentiment from many who are a part of our story and a part of the future for HP and Agilent:

Well, I think at the end of the day, when I look back on my career at HP, I view my involvement with the self-directed work teams as one of the achievements of which I am most proud. Not because I had all that much to do with it, but I think it grew me as a person and it is not something that is easy to understand. You have to invest some time. You have to do some reading. And then you have to go listen to the people.

I will tell a story about a guy who will remain anonymous. When we were having the open houses, we were bringing companies here. And one of the things that we do is put a team in with a group of visitors. No management, no anybody. And a corporate comptroller came up to me after the session and told me, "I can't believe it. I would no more let my people loose with this level of people without somebody around than fly to the moon." I almost told him but did not have the guts to tell him, "Maybe that is part of your problem." I practically cried on the way home that night. That said more to me about the development of our organization, of our people, the strengths and characteristics of these people. That is the reason this place has been as successful as it is. People say, "Kemp, you have been doing this for nine years now. Aren't you bored?" It is challenges like this. Go pull together a worldwide organization. We are the only ones in the world besides American Express that is doing this. Go start a self-directed work team in India. That is pretty cool stuff. I would like to turn this into the hallmark of the organization.[11]

# Appendix 1

---

## CSFSC Facilitator Position Plan/Ranking Criteria, 1992

Purpose: Develop and continually promote high-performing, self-directed teams within CSFSC who process accounting transactions while meeting/exceeding customer expectations.

### Key Responsibilities:

*Facilitation Skills—25% percent*

Facilitators will utilize coaching, instructing, and training as well as supporting, encouraging, and empowering to meet the established performance measures.

**Performance Measures:**
- Development of operations teams to mature self-directed teams as demonstrated by the adoption of responsibilities from the Design Team two-year plan
- Effective transition management for operations teams to maturity
- Effective transition for facilitator from traditional supervisory role to self-directed team environment
- Degree to which operations teams use appropriate judgment in making decisions, managing conflict resolution and solving problems
- Results of organizational audit in facilitation areas

- Provide high quality training on problem analysis, communication processes and conflict management
- Results of facilitator evaluation from operations teams and peers

## 2. Leadership Skills—25% percent

Visionary with respect to the self-directed team environment, which challenges the status quo and is inspiring and passionate about the CSFSC purpose. Demonstrates credibility and consistency, and learns from experience by not repeating mistakes. Demonstrates commitment to customer service. Creates an atmosphere of trust and encourages risk taking by operations teams. The facilitator should also be willing to take risks on team development opportunities.

### Performance Measures:
- Results of team development toward self-directed maturity
- Model the self-directed team way
- Know your team members by paying attention to people more than technical details
- Work with teams to remove dragon eggs (hurdles)
- DO THE RIGHT THING versus doing things right
- Work with management to achieve overall CSFSC goals
- Demonstrate commitment to the self-directed environment
- Use innovative techniques for operations team development
- Demonstrate good judgment when being assertive
- Results of organizational audit in leadership areas
- Results of facilitator evaluation from operations teams and peers

## 3. Communication Skills—15% percent

Demonstrates communication skills by effectively utilizing conflict resolution techniques. Provides open and honest feedback in a direct, specific, and nonpunishing manner. Employs effective listening skills in interactions with CSFSC management, customers, and operations team members.

**Performance Measures:**

- Provide timely and clearly stated responses to customer and team issues
- Results of organizational audit in communication areas
- Results of facilitator evaluation from operations teams and peers

## 4. Interpersonal Skills—15% percent

Observes and offers perceptions on individual and team behavior. Is patient with individuals and operations teams as they learn and grow in the self-directed team environment. Draws ideas and input from facilitator and operations teams and demonstrates respect for all team members.

**Performance Measures:**

- Results of organization audit in interpersonal skills
- Results of facilitator evaluation from operations teams and peers
- Consistent, professional interaction with all CSFSC staff and customers

## 5. Technical Skills—10% percent

Acts as a technical resource for teams on operational issues and monitors and ensures key business metrics are met. Understands HP's policies and guidelines for hiring and staffing. Develops operations teams understanding of Accounting and Finance Manual policies. Provides coaching on general accounting principles, helping operations staff to find the answers themselves.

**Performance Measures:**

- Effectively utilizes and coaches teams on problem-solving methodologies such as TQM
- Demonstrates understanding of process and related technical issues

- Understands impact of team actions and decisions on other CSFSC operational processes
- Results of organizational audit in technical skills areas
- Results of facilitator evaluation from operations teams and peers
- Monitors key business controls

## 6. Administrative Skills—10% percent

Completes performance evaluations and performs ranking and salary administration. Acts as contact for individual and/or team performance issues. Participates in recruitment, selection, and training of new employees. Provides regular one-on-one feedback to all operations team members. Oversees completion of and monitors progress on team and individual development plans.

### Performance Measures:

- Timely completion of performance evaluations
- Complete development plans for both individual team members and operational teams
- Appropriately utilize HP performance, evaluation, and pay guidelines and CSFSC ranking criteria and process
- Results of facilitator evaluation from operations teams and peers
- Results of organizational audit in administrative skills areas

# *Appendix 2*

---

**Colorado Springs  Financial Services Center FOM Feedback Form**

Date:  _____

Completed By:  _____

FOM Feedback For:  _____

1. In what way does your FOM provide coaching/mentoring?

    * Team (e.g. team meetings; resolution of issues; encourages involvement in projects)

    * Individual (e.g. career coaching; quarterly reviews; corrective action; one-on-ones)

2. Give examples of how your FOM demonstrates leadership regarding the future of your team and process area. (e.g. consistent in policy/ guidelines; information flow to operations; promotes oneness between CS & ATL)

3. Explain how your FOM promotes job development. (e.g. training; business objectives; encourages advancement)

4. Convey how your FOM demonstrates an understanding of the functional area. (e.g. review team metrics; problem solving/TQM; conforms to business controls)

5. In what manner does your FOM provide effective *communication?* (e.g. evaluation/ranking; open door policy; approachable)

Please provide any additional comments, strengths, and opportunities below:

Comments:

Strengths:

Opportunities:

## Team Member Evaluation of FOM Team as an Entire Team
## (1999 FOM Team Placement Model)

|  | Consistent in Policy and Guidelines | Open Door Policy | Supportive of Self-Directed Team Initiatives | Communication |
|---|---|---|---|---|
| **Examples** | Administering decisions across the board; IPP/leave; rotational/ promotional procedures | Confidentiality; approachable; trustworthy | Pilot projects; annual events; task forces; off-sites | Direction of FSC/HP; FOM Team meetings / off-sites/projects; business climate |
| **Excellent** |  |  |  |  |
| **Good** |  |  |  |  |
| **Fair** |  |  |  |  |
| **Needs Improvement** |  |  |  |  |

Please place an "X" in each category and include comments below, to support each placement.

_____

_____

_____

_____

_____

# Appendix 3

———

# Self-Directed Team Responsibilities and Parameters, June 17, 1999

The Colorado Springs Financial Services Center (CSFSC) empowers employees with a goal of continual improvement to both transaction processes and team and individual development.

## Hiring Processes

### (1) Fill an open position
*Team Parameter:* Offer input to the FOM on need to fill vacant position.

*Financial Operations Manager (FOM)/Facilitator Parameter:* Decide if and when to fill position. Own the requisition process.

### (2) Manage team rotational openings
*Team Parameters:* Team with rotational opening—advertise openings, prepare interview questions, conduct the interview, make the hiring decision with hiring FOM and communicate the team's hiring decision, provide specific feedback to the candidate(s), have a thorough understanding of the CSFSC Operations Rotation Process to determine eligibility of interested candidates, offer input to FOM on start date, establish a training plan. Team whose member is rotating—administer Peer Input Process per CSFSC guidelines.

*Hiring FOM/Facilitator Parameter:* Enforce eligibility criteria for team rotation, determine start date using input from current FOM, hiring team, and current team.

### (3) Participate in external hiring process

*Team Parameters:* Complete behavioral interviewing class, demonstrate thorough understanding of knowledge, skills, and abilities required to be successful in CSFSC team environment, review interview packets for existing "make offer" candidates, prepare for and serve on three-person interview panel, make hiring decision (make offer decision) and communicate to interview panel, participate in project groups for rewriting scripted interview questions and making hiring process improvements.

*FOM/Facilitator Parameters:* Complete behavioral interviewing class, serve on three-person interview panel, make offer to successful candidate, determine start date, seek input from team on existing "make offer" candidates.

## Guidelines for Performance (Team, Individual)

### (4) Establish team expectations (ground rules)

*Team Parameters:* Adhere to CSFSC/HP Policy currently in place when establishing expectations, agree to standard expectations for all members, publish and make expectations readily available for all members, make changes when necessary (e.g., when new members join the team), involve every team member in the change process.

*FOM/Facilitator Parameters:* Review ground rules as appropriate.

### (5) Set team goals (team development plan)

*Team Parameters:* Set, document, review, and revise clearly defined and measurable goals that are shared by all team members.

*FOM/Facilitator or Management Staff Parameter:* Review team goals as appropriate. Check for alignment with organizational objectives. Provide assistance/coaching on development areas.

### (6) Maintain team accomplishments list

*Team Parameter:* Maintain an annual, cumulative list of team accomplishments which should include those significant team activities that go beyond day-to-day expectations.

*FOM/Facilitator Parameter:* Review periodically.

### (7) Set individual goals (individual development plan)

*Team Parameters:* Individuals within the team set, document, review, and revise clearly defined and measurable goals for themselves, may be reviewed by members of individual's team.

*FOM/Facilitator Parameter:* Review goals periodically. Provide assistance/coaching on development areas.

### (8) Maintain individual accomplishments list

*Team Parameter:* Communicate the need to each team member for maintaining an annual, cumulative list of individual accomplishments which should include those significant individual activities that go beyond day-to-day expectations.

*FOM/Facilitator Parameter:* Review periodically.

## Team Administrative Duties

### (9) Determine training needs and schedule training classes

*Team Parameters:* Identify areas where training is needed; provide on-the-job technical training when classroom training is not provided, ensure all required training is completed.

*FOM/Facilitator Parameters:* Identify areas where training is needed; conduct classes that are provided and/or sponsored by FOMs or Facilitators.

### (10) Provide/monitor new team member training

*Team Parameters:* Plan and provide items noted as "Team" on New Employee Training Checklist, determine who will provide new employee technical training, seek help from other teams and/or functional areas to complete new hire training if needed, monitor new employee's progress on completing New Employee Training Checklist.

*FOM/Facilitator Parameters:* Plan and provide items noted as "FOM/Facilitator" on New Employee Training Checklist, monitor progress of new employee.

### (11) Manage team budgets

*Team Parameters:* Spend within budget limit, adhere to established spending guidelines for members of CSFSC, manage team budget for the purpose of team/individual development, tailor budget to conform to the current business situation, track actual to target by team or team members.

*FOM/Facilitator Parameter:* Review periodically, actual to target for team budgets.

*Management Staff:* Determine availability of funds for team budgets. Coach on appropriateness of spending.

### (12) Maintain team coordinator role definitions

*Team Parameter:* Make available in each team area written definitions and descriptions of the coordinator roles.

*FOM/Facilitator Parameter:* Review roles with team periodically for workload balance input.

### (13) Monitor changes in responsibilities

*Team Parameter:* May initiate the JSE process for their functional area when job responsibilities have significantly changed.

*FOM/Facilitator Parameter:* Apply criteria for activation of JSE by team, seek human resources liaison involvement.

## Time Management

### (14) Review, collect, and submit time cards

*Team Parameters:* Establish time card coordinator to review time cards for accuracy and compliance with HP and CSFSC policies and guidelines; collect, sign and submit in accordance with established processes and deadlines; obtain FOM's/Facilitator's signature for guideline exceptions; determine specific process for managing time card review, flextime, time shifting, and time flexing.

*FOM/Facilitator Parameters:* Sign time cards with any guideline exceptions, manage time reporting abuse and use of earned vs. available FTO.

### (15) Balance workload

*Team Parameters:* Maintain an even distribution of workload between the members of a team to ensure that business needs are met, initiate and apply workload balance across teams within functional area, ask for help when it is needed and offer assistance when other team members need it, keep list of team members and their basic responsibilities up-to-date, communicate changes across CSFSC and externally as needed.

*FOM/Facilitator Parameter:* Assist in workload balancing across teams when needed.

### (16) Schedule backup coverage

*Team Parameters:* Schedule vacation with enough notice to allow team members time to ensure team job functions remain effective, efficient and the customer needs are met, handle any planned or unplanned absence of a team member in an equitable manner within the team and make sure the absence is invisible to the customer.

*FOM/Facilitator Parameter:* Intercede when adequate backup coverage is not provided and/or business needs or hours are not being met.

## Technical Responsibilities

### (17) Set, collect, and report process performance data

*Team Parameters:* Use management by objectives approach. Set process metric goals (working with the appropriate FOM/Facilitator or Solution Center resources) and any additional goals selected by the team that will track team efforts and functional area efforts by quantity and quality, gather accurate data and compile data into a graphical format, use data gathered to identify problem areas where TQM can be applied.

*FOM/Facilitator Parameter:* Assist teams with process metric goal setting; ensure alignment with organizational goals.

### (18) Comply with fundamental business controls

*Team Parameters:* Follow the business controls that are defined by the AFM, management staff, auditors, and the customers, create and update reports to ensure compliance, track and resolve all aged items (e.g., recons, inventory, CRC cases, etc.), escalate as appropriate, provide input on the timing and frequency of internal audits.

*FOM/Facilitator Parameter:* Provide periodic checks to ensure that business controls are Company compliant.

### (19) Manage documentation procedures

*Team Parameters:* Define and document procedures for each functional area, as appropriate, per HP policy, schedule periodic process meetings to recommend changes and update procedure documentation.

*FOM/Facilitator Parameter:* Sponsor documentation assignments for training internal/external customers/partners/team members.

## Process Improvements, Projects, and Customer Service

### (20) Prioritize projects

*Team Parameters:* Initiate, implement, and prioritize projects in accordance with HP/CSFSC business needs.

*FOM/Facilitator Parameter:* Evaluate, approve, or disapprove proposed projects. Sponsor big project initiatives.

### (21) Provide high-quality customer service

*Team Parameter:* Provide timely, high-quality service that meets and exceeds customer's expectations and business needs, track ongoing customer issues, follow up on problems through resolution, share expertise to improve partnerships.

*FOM/Facilitator Parameter:* Provide timely feedback as appropriate.

### (22) Resolve process problems

*Team Parameters:* Use effective problem solving processes to resolve job-related issues; recognize, document and resolve operational problems; utilize process improvement forms, FSC support groups, cross-functional communications and research; see problems through to closure.

*FOM/Facilitator Parameter:* Assist team if necessary and provide additional resources as appropriate.

### (23) Initiate and handle TQM process implementations— excludes SR process

*Team Parameters:* Identify improvement opportunities and potential approaches to be evaluated within the team and functional area, research the opportunities by gathering input from the appropriate resources (may include all affected areas) and conducting a pilot prior to approval, seek appropriate approval, design the process improvement and scheduled for implementation, document and file the appropriate paperwork, track results of the improvement.

*FOM/Facilitator Parameter:* Provide periodic checks and provide resources as appropriate.

### (24) Participate on cross-functional teams

*Team Parameters:* Provide team members to initiate temporary or new cross functional task force teams when the need is identified or participate on existing CSFSC task force teams such as the Design Team, Comm Link, Delight Teams, Day Care, Family Work Life, etc., may limit an individual's or the team's role if daily business operations would be compromised, make sure representation of team is adequate and participation in the cross-functional teams, such as the Comm Link, Design Team and ART, is rotated.

### (25) Propose AFM changes

*Team Parameters:* Identify and initiate changes to the Accounting and Finance Manual (AFM) by presenting a proposal to the appropriate decision-making team or individual.

*FOM/Facilitator Parameter:* Provide sponsorship for appropriate changes.

### (26) Submit systems requests (SRs)

*Team Parameter:* Utilize processes as stated by the SR and documentation resources for initiating, submitting, and prioritizing systems SRs, monitor associated documentation changes.

### (27) Implement new systems

*Team Parameters:* Participate in testing of databases, providing feedback and making suggestions for added features and changes, participate in the training of co-workers and site personnel on new system, provide documentation for the new system if the new system is to be used within the team's functional area.

*FOM/Facilitator Parameter:* Ensure appropriate resources are utilized to transition smoothly; overall owner of MOC.

## Communicate, Communicate, Communicate

### (28) Use 10-Minute Team concepts

*Team Parameter:* Use as is or modify 10-Minute Team concepts as a communication tool. (*The Ten Minute Team Book* written by Thomas Isgar.)

*FOM/Facilitator Parameter:* Provide feedback on team use of process.

### (29) Administer team meetings

*Team Parameter:* Utilize rotating meeting management roles (e.g., facilitator, scribe, timekeeper) to conduct effective, formal team meetings, publish the results of the meetings in a timely manner. (Formal team meetings are scheduled, ongoing meetings versus the informal, ad hoc meetings conducted in team areas.)

*FOM/Facilitator Parameter:* Attend team meetings; provide feedback on effectiveness of meeting management.

### (30) Give and receive feedback

*Team Parameter:* Give feedback in a timely and constructive manner, receive feedback which is given appropriately in a gracious manner, use periodic one-on-ones to communicate exceptional performance or identify development opportunities or resolve problems.

### (31) Establish efficient communication

*Team Parameter:* Establish efficient communication with CSFSC personnel, ASC personnel, Corporate Financial Reporting (CFR), and internal and external customers using telephone, teleconferences, fax, e-mail, large and small group presentations, formal and informal team meetings, Coffee Talks, one-on-ones, whiteboards, etc.

### (32) Give presentations within/between work groups

*Team Parameter:* Give effective verbal presentations to own team, functional areas, cross-functional areas, management and customer divisions as appropriate (e.g., for communication of process changes, reviews with management staff).

## Manage Conflict

### (33) Resolve interpersonal problems

*Team Parameter:* Deal with conflicts that arise in a timely manner, minimize the effect of conflict on productivity, complete the Conflict Management modules to improve skills in using the models, concepts, and techniques for resolving conflict (e.g., Ten Minute Team, problem-solving approach, principled negotiation, giving and receiving feedback), review the material from the Conflict Management modules as needed.

*FOM/Facilitator Parameter:* Provide conflict management training; may need to facilitate conflict resolution sessions with team members.

## Evaluate Performance (Individual, Team, FOM)

### (34) Administer Peer Input Process

*Team Parameters:* Provide a written evaluation, highlighting key strengths and development opportunities for individuals and the team as ranking input to team FOM/Facilitator, use the process and forms in the PIP Guide, attend PIP Process training.

*FOM/Facilitator Parameter:* Use PIP information as input to individual/team ranking.

### (35) Administer and provide FOM feedback

*Team Parameter:* Prepare feedback and deliver to the FOM/Facilitator, using the defined process.

*FOM/Facilitator Parameter:* Provide follow-up on any development opportunities.

# Notes

## Chapter 1

1. This Bill Hewlett quote is heard throughout HP. Greg Spray used Hewlett's concept of the HP Way in his open house presentation, December 8, 1997.

2. For an in-depth discussion of this period and the subsequent steps HP took to increase competitiveness, see Bruce R. Scott, "Competitiveness: 23 Leaders Speak Out," *Harvard Business Review,* July-August 1987, 106–123; Peter Wilsher, "The Source of HP's Success," *Management Today,* October 1992, 52–56; and Daniel Levine, "Justice Served," *Sales and Marketing Management,* May 1995, 52–61.

3. For a comprehensive history of the founding of Hewlett-Packard Company see David Packard, *The HP Way: How Bill Hewlett and I Built Our Company* (New York: HarperBusiness, 1995).

4. Greg Spray used this values description in his open house presentation, December 8, 1997. HP values are widely published throughout HP.

5. Greg Spray made this relationship between core values and individual creativity and community involvement in his open house presentation, December 8, 1997.

## Chapter 2

1. For an expanded discussion of the importance of organizational goals, see Carl Larson and Frank LaFasto, *Teamwork* (Newbury Park, Calif.: Sage, 1989); James C. Collins and Jerry I. Porras, *Built to Last: Successful Habits of Visionary Companies* (New York: HarperBusiness, 1994); James C. Collins and Jerry I. Porras, "Building Your Company's Vision," *Harvard Business Review,* September-October 1996, 65–77; and Dale E. Yeatts and Cloyd Hyten, *High-Performing Self-Managed Work Teams: A Comparison of Theory and Practice* (Thousand Oaks, Calif.: Sage, 1998).

2. All Jim Luttenbacher quotes are from an interview by the author, September 12, 1997.

3. All Rick Hobbs quotes are from an interview by the author, September 12, 1997.

4. All Joyce Conger quotes are from an interview by the author, March 12, 1998.

5. Personal recollections of the author.

6. For a discussion of Michael Hammer's ideas and recommendations, see Michael Hammer and James Champy, *Reengineering the Corporation: A Manifesto for Business Revolution* (New York: HarperBusiness, 1993); Michael Hammer and Steve A. Stanton, *The Reengineering Revolution: A Handbook* (New York: HarperBusiness, 1995); and Michael Hammer, *Beyond Reengineering: How the Process-Centered Organization Is Changing Our Work and Our Lives* (New York: HarperBusiness, 1996).

## Chapter 3

1. All Rick Hobbs quotes are from an interview by the author, September 12, 1997.

2. All Jim Luttenbacker quotes are from an interview by the author, September 12, 1997.

3. Personal recollections of the author.

4. Personal recollections of the author.

5. All Kemp Bohlen quotes are from an interview by the author, April 2, 1998.

6. All Ray Cookingham quotes are from an interview by the author, March 11, 1998.

7. For a detailed description of the HP Way, see David Packard, *The HP Way: How Bill Hewlett and I Built Our Company* (New York: HarperBusiness, 1995).

8. Stephen Kreider Young, "A 1990 Reorganization at Hewlett-Packard Already Is Paying Off," *Wall Street Journal,* July 22, 1991, A1.

9. David Packard, *The HP Way: How Bill Hewlett and I Built Our Company* (New York: HarperBusiness, 1995), 148.

10. David Packard's discussion of centralization is found on pages 148–151 in Packard, *The HP Way: How Bill Hewlett and I Built Our Company.*

11. James C. Collins and Jerry I. Porras first published this interview with John Young in their book, *Built to Last: Successful Habits of Visionary Companies* (New York: HarperBusiness, 1994), 46.

## Chapter 4

1. All D'Ann Darling quotes are from an interview by the author, March 24, 1999.

2. Recollections of the author.

3. See James C. Collins and Jerry I. Porras, *Built to Last: Successful Habits of Visionary Companies* (New York: HarperBusiness, 1994), xv.

4. Recollections of the author.

5. Synchronous innovation generally is defined as mutually supportive simultaneous changes in technology, organization, jobs, and people and is proposed as an action-oriented approach to organizational change. For a comprehensive discussion of the concept see J. Ettlie, *Taking Charge of Manufacturing* (San Francisco: Jossey-Bass, 1988).

6. Recollections of the author.

7. All Rick Hobbs quotes are from an interview by the author, September 12, 1997.

8. Authors' recollection of private conversation.

9. All Diana Morgan quotes are from an interview by the author, January 7, 1998.

10. All Mike Hackman quotes are from an interview by the author, August 2, 1999.

11. For a discussion of learning organizations, see Gareth Morgan, *Images of Organizations* (Thousand Oaks, Calif.: Sage, 1997); and Peter Senge, *The Fifth Discipline* (New York: Doubleday/Currency, 1990).

12. Gaynelle Winograd, interview by the author, August 15, 1999.

## Chapter 5

1. All Jim Luttenbacher quotes are from an interview by the author, September 12, 1997.

2. All Kemp Bohlen quotes are from an interview by the author, April 2, 1998.

3. This material is adapted from Greg Spray's open house presentation, December 8, 1997.

4. Jim Villamana, director, America's Financial Service Center for J.D. Edwards, interview by author, August 16, 1999.

5. For the psychological concept of protean shapeshifting, see Robert J. Lifton, *The Protean Self* (New York: Basic Books, 1993). For a discussion of organizational shapeshifting, see Pamela Shockley-Zalabak, "Protean Places: Teams Across Time and Space," presentation before the

International Communication Association Convention, San Francisco, May 1999. For a contrast between Silicon Valley and Route 128 industries with regard to protean concepts, see AnnaLee Saxenian, *Regional Advantage* (Cambridge: Harvard University Press, 1994).

6. Recollections of the author.

7. Kemp Bohlen, interview by author, April 2, 1998.

8. See CSFSC facilitator position plan in appendix, pages 181–184.

9. See Reed Breland, interview in *Fortune*, February 20, 1995, 98.

10. All quotes from Mike Waterlander, Diana Morgan, Kathy Jones, and Sandy Burmester unless otherwise noted are from a group discussion taped on August 25, 1998.

11. See Reed Breland, interview, 98.

12. Recollections of the author. For a comprehensive discussion of the congruity principle and cognitive dissonance, see C. Osgood and P. Tannenbaum, "The Principle of Congruity in the Prediction of Attitude Change," *Psychological Review* 62 (1955): 42–55; L. A. Festinger, *A Theory of Cognitive Dissonance* (Evanston, Ill.: Row Peterson, 1957); and K. K. Reardon, *Persuasion: Theory and Context* (Beverly Hills, Calif.: Sage, 1981).

13. Recollections of the author.

14. All Greg Spray quotes are from an interview by the author, August 18, 1998.

15. Diana Morgan, interview by author, January 7, 1998.

16. For a complete set of the FOM performance evaluation forms, see appendix, pages 185–186.

17. All Tammy Biggs quotes are from an interview by the author, February 25, 1999.


## Chapter 6

1. The concept of community delight, and indeed much of the design of the organization, is based on cooperation and collective action. These concepts are related to what Robert Putnam and others refer to as social capital, or features of social organization such as trust, norms, and networks that can improve the efficiency of society by facilitating coordinated action. For a discussion of social capital and its important relationships to trust, see Robert Putnam, *Making Democracy Work* (Princeton: Princeton University Press, 1993). For a discussion of social capital and value creation, see Wenpin Tsai and Sumantra Ghoshal, "Social Capital and Value Creation: The Role of Intrafirm Networks," *Academy of Management Journal* 41, no. 4 (1998): 464–476.

2. All Greg Spray quotes are from an interview by the author, August 18, 1998.

3. This material was part of Greg Spray's open house presentation, December 8, 1997.

4. Ibid.

5. All Harland Baker quotes are from an interview by the author, May 11, 1999.

6. Sandy Burmester quotes are from a discussion with Harland Baker, taped on May 11, 1999.

7. All Mike Cookson quotes are from an interview by the author, February 12, 1999.

8. Recollections of the author.

9. Recollections of the author.

10. All Diana Morgan, Mike Waterlander, Reed Breland, and Kathy Jones quotes are from an interview by the author, taped on August 25, 1998.

11. All Bill Brown and Tammy Biggs quotes are from interviews by the author, February 25, 1999.

12. Some of Diana Morgan's examples are from an interview by the author, January 7, 1998. The examples were repeated in the August 25, 1998, facilitator discussion.

13. Reed Breland's discussion of dissolving a team is from an interview by the author, August 13, 1998, and is described in *Fortune*, February 10, 1995, 93–100.

14. For the foundational discussion of distinctions between workplace satisfaction and dissatisfaction, see Frederick Herzberg, *Work and the Nature of Man* (Cleveland: World, 1966).

15. Mike Hackman, interview by author, August 2, 1999.

16. Gaynelle Winograd, interview by author, August 15, 1999.

17. Recollections of the author.

## Chapter 7

1. The network property of strength refers to the frequency and length of interactions among linked individuals. Strong links communicate more frequently than weak links and usually have longer periods of interaction. The stronger the communication link among people the greater the chances of linked individuals influencing each other's behavior. For a broad discussion of communication networks, see Pamela Shockley-Zalabak, *Fundamentals of Organizational Communication*, 4th ed. (New York: Addison-Wesley Longman, 1999).

2. Barbara Edwards, interview by author, August 24, 1999.

3. The term "weak ties" refers to communication links that are less developed and are generally more limited in space, place, time, and strength of emotional bonding. The notion of weak ties in organizations is important because individuals with many weak ties have increased access to information primarily because of the diverse nature of those links. In other words, individuals who are closely linked have the potential to all end up with the same information. Information coming from diverse sources provides the potential for different perspectives and new ideas. For a more complete discussion of the concept of weak ties, see Mark Granovetter, "The Strength of Weak Ties," *American Journal of Sociology* 78 (1973): 1360–1380.

4. Deskilling refers to the reduction of skill requirements for jobs through mechanization or automation. For a comprehensive discussion, see Joseph Straubhaar and Robert LaRose, *Communications Media in the Information Society* (Belmont, Calif.: Wadsworth, 1996).

5. D'Ann Darling, interview by author, March 24, 1999.

6. Adapted from Greg Spray, open house presentation, December 8, 1997.

7. Greg Spray, open house slide presentation, December 8, 1997.

8. For a description of the concept of jamming, see Eric M. Eisenberg, "Jamming: Transcendence through Organizing," *Communication Research* 17, no. 2 (1990): 139–164.

9. Reed Breland, interview by author, August 13, 1998.

10. Sandy Burmester, interview by author, August 3, 1999.

11. Recollection of the author.

12. Greg Spray, open house slide presentation, December 8, 1997.

13. Frances Bengtson, interview by author, August 31, 1999.

14. Jim Villamana, interview by author, August 16, 1999.

15. Kelly D. Klute, interview by author, August 8, 1999.

16. Bob Gunn, interview by author, September 10, 1999.

## Epilogue

1. Kemp Bohlen, interview by author, July 30, 1999.

2. Mike Waterlander, interview by author, August 17, 1999.

3. Pat Robison, interview by author, December 6, 1999.

4. Kemp Bohlen, interview by author, July 30, 1999.

5. Mike Waterlander, interview by author, August 17, 1999.

6. Greg Spray, interview by author, August 18, 1998.

7. Greg Spray, interview by author, August 26, 1999.

8. Greg Spray, interview by author, August 18, 1998.

9. Reed Breland, interview by author, August 13, 1998.

10. Mike Waterlander, interview by author, August 17, 1999.

11. Kemp Bohlen, interview by author, July 30, 1999. *Final note:* In January 2000 Kemp Bohlen informed the organization that after twenty-three years he was leaving Hewlett-Packard to pursue an opportunity with Exult, a start-up business process outsourcing firm headquartered in California. As director for shared services, Bohlen expects to continue his use of networked teams. In February, Ray Cookingham named Bob Shultz (we first met Shultz when we visited his HP team-based organization in New Jersey) director of worldwide financial services and began a new chapter in the leadership of the Financial Services Center.

# Research Notes

---

For chapters 2–7, the following research notes provide a variety of perspectives for further exploration of the experiences we have been describing. We have concluded that no single theoretical perspective or model adequately explains this HP success, and thus we will present a web of theories and research findings to help us understand what has happened over the nine years since the founding of the CSFSC. The research notes do not examine all theories or research that might apply but highlight some of what we consider the more interesting and provocative concepts that relate to our story. The concepts discussed are designed to stimulate thought and provide you with additional sources to explore what this HP experience can mean for others.

## Chapter 2: Business Goals Do the Driving

Compelling evidence exists that supports the importance of establishing challenging goals. In their pioneering study of high-performing teams, Carl Larson and Frank LaFasto[1] identify eight common characteristics of the exceptional teams in their study: a clear, elevating goal, results-driven structure, competent team members, unified commitment, collaborative climate, standards of excellence, external support and recognition, and principled leadership. Larson and LaFasto conclude that the unambiguous stretch goal contributes not only to outstanding results but also to the day-to-day commitments and processes which generate the results. James Collins and Jerry Porras,[2] in their research on long-term successful companies, describe visionary companies as using bold missions (what the authors refer to as BHAGs, "Big Hairy Audacious Goals") to stimulate progress. They contend that a clear and compelling goal becomes a unifying focal point of effort, is consistent with organizational core ideology, engages people, falls well outside the comfort zone, requires little or no explanation, serves as a stimulus to commitment and risk, and does not depend solely on the charismatic nature of leadership or even the same individuals remaining in leadership. Collins and Porras identify an inherent danger of the driving goal: when it is achieved, an organization can drift into what they call the "we've arrived" syndrome and fail to establish bold new goals for the future. In a comparison of theory and practice for self-directed work teams, Dale Yeatts and Cloyd Hyten[3] support the importance of clear, compelling goals for team performance. Yeatts and Hyten found that teams without challenging goals often are conflicted over the rationale for team decisions and become dissatisfied with team decision-making processes.

Although the evidence is clear that compelling goals contribute to high performance, less is known about how and why individuals and particular organizations are stimulated to establish the types of goals that truly propel action while others set achievable goals that fail to inspire or at best maintain the status quo. The differences in the way goals are developed and communicated, as well as the results they stimulate, are of continuing theoretical and practical interest. These important differences point to the need for leadership self-awareness coupled with continuing examination of an organization's visioning and goal-setting processes.

### Notes

1. Carl Larson and Frank LaFasto, *Teamwork* (Newbury Park, Calif.: Sage, 1989).

2. James C. Collins and Jerry I. Porras, *Built to Last: Successful Habits of Visionary Companies* (New York: HarperBusiness, 1994).

3. Dale E. Yeatts and Cloyd Hyten, *High-Performing Self-Managed Work Teams: A Comparison of Theory and Practice* (Thousand Oaks, Calif.: Sage, 1998).

## Chapter 3: Core Culture Driving Change

A plethora of cultural approaches to organizational theory attempt to describe how organizational members collectively interpret the organizational world around them in order to both create and define organizational happenings. Cultural research attempts to identify how a unique sense of the place (culture) contributes to individual behavior and organizational effectiveness. Terrance Deal and Allen Kennedy in their book, *Corporate Cultures: The Rites and Rituals of Corporate Life*,[1] identify five basic elements of organizational culture: business environment, values, heroes, rites and rituals, and the cultural network. Deal and Kennedy suggest that the business environment is the single greatest influence in shaping a corporate culture. What companies do in their competitive environments shapes the reality of how organizations manage activity and whether or not they are successful. Values emerge that help individuals determine where the emphasis of their efforts should be placed. In other words, organizational values help people become dedicated to a cause, which in turn guides decisions about all types of behaviors.

In their famous best-seller, *In Search of Excellence,* Thomas Peters and Robert Waterman[2] report the results of their efforts to understand how large companies adapt to changing environments. Based on data from sixty-two successful U.S. companies, Peters and Waterman identify a series of cultural themes that most nearly characterize excellent, innovative companies. Two have special relevance for our HP experience: a bias for action and hands-on, value-driven. Their bias for action theme suggests that excellent companies make decisions. They are analytical but not paralyzed by information. When there is a problem, they take action. The hands-on, value-driven theme is directly related to the importance of organizational culture. Peters and Waterman contend that the basic philosophy and values of the organization contribute more to achievement than any specific technology or material resource. Values are described as influencing behavior and are considered the core of excellence.

Edgar Schein[3] provides a model of organizational culture with three distinct levels: (1) artifacts and creations, (2) values, and (3) basic assumptions. Artifacts and creations are the most visible level of culture consisting of the physical and social environment created by organizational members. Values refer to both individual and group preferences for the way it should be in the organization, whereas basic assumptions are the core of what individuals believe to be true about the world and how it works. Based on the concepts and models of Schein and others, Shockley-Zalabak and her colleagues[4] have conducted extensive work relating organizational values and culture to a variety of organizational outcomes, including perceptions of effectiveness and overall belief in goal attainment. Their findings suggest that the more similar individual and organizational values are, the more likely it is that individuals will have positive perceptions of the organization and will support adaptation and change. The degree of value congruence between individual values and organizational cultural norms and practices is predictive of perceptions of organizational communication, teamwork, satisfaction with peers and leadership, and estimations of organizational survival and growth. It is important to note, however, that perceptions of organizational effectiveness also can be described as influences for behavior, not just outcomes of organizational experiences. In other words, core values and cultural ideology simultaneously influence organizational perceptions and are shaped by perceptions of organizational effectiveness.

James Collins and Jerry Porras[5] describe companies that sustain high performance over many years as having a fervently held core ideology. They suggest that this adherence to the core can appear almost cultlike, with tightly held values driving literally every aspect of the business. The important distinction in their research, however, is that core ideology and values should not be confused with practices. Practices change but the values are much more enduring and stable.

In sum, a large body of research supports the importance of culture for organizational functioning. The findings do not identify an "ideal type" of culture but help us understand the relationships among the organization's environment, core organizational values, individual values, and an organization's ability to adapt and change over time.

## Notes

1. Terrance Deal and Allen Kennedy, *Corporate Cultures: The Rites and Rituals of Corporate Life* (Reading, Mass.: Addison-Wesley, 1982).

2. Thomas Peters and Robert Waterman, *In Search of Excellence* (New York: Harper & Row, 1982).

3. Edgar Schein, *Organizational Culture and Leadership* (San Francisco: Jossey-Bass, 1985).

4. The work described in this section can be found in Pamela Shockley-Zalabak and Donald D. Morley, "Adhering to Organizational Culture: What Does It Mean, Why Does It Matter?" *Group and Organization Studies* 14 (1989): 483–500; Donald D. Morley and Pamela Shockley-Zalabak, "Setting the Rules: An Examination of the Influence Of Organization Founders' Values," *Management Communication Quarterly* 4 (1991): 442–449; Pamela Shockley-Zalabak and Donald D. Morley, "Creating a Culture: A Longitudinal Examination of the Influence of Management and Employee Values on Communication Rule Stability and Emergence," *Human Communication Research* 20, no. 3 (1994): 334–355; and Donald D. Morley, Pamela Shockley-Zalabak, and Ruggero Cesaria, "Organizational Communication and Culture: A Study of Ten Italian High-Technology Companies," *Journal of Business Communication* 34 (1997): 253–268. See also Bradley L. Kirkman and Debra L. Shapiro, "The Impact of Cultural Values on Employee Resistance to Teams: Toward a Model of Globalized Self-Managing Team Effectiveness," *Academy of Management Review* 22, no. 3 (1997): 730–757.

5. James C. Collins and Jerry I. Porras, *Built to Last: Successful Habits of Visionary Companies* (New York: HarperBusiness, 1994).

## Chapter 4: Educate, Educate, Educate

Two concepts—synchronous innovation and protean shapeshifting— are particularly relevant for understanding this period in the development of the CSFSC. Introduced by J. Ettlie[1] in 1988, synchronous innovation suggests that change will be most productive when simultaneously occurring in interacting systems within and without the organization. According to Ettlie, "The theory of synchronous innovation predicts that firms will be most successful when they match the degree of radicalness in their administrative experiment with the degree of radicalness in the technologies they adopt" (p. 51). The concept is grounded on the belief that simultaneous change in many or most parts of the organization will bring about the most potential gain. Linear change in one area at a time, while easier to implement, does not have the potential for creativity and growth or the synergistic force that multiple simultaneous changes provide.

As in our HP story, many different types of organizations in diverse industries are redistributing influence throughout the organization. Hierarchies are abandoned for flatter and more horizontal designs. Decision making is dispersed throughout the organization, with self-managing teams assuming responsibilities previously reserved for managers in areas as diverse as planning, scheduling, work design, and rewards. Engineer/blue-collar teams, shared services organizations, and cross-functional teams are common examples of organizational approaches to close coupling of top management with the line activities of the organization. Downsized and delayered organizations reject economies of scale for minimal inventories, subcontracting, fast changeovers, just-in-time manufacturing, and quick response.[2] Hitt, Hoskisson, and Harrison,[3] in their description of strategic competitiveness, support the concept of synchronous innovation based on restructuring organizations while cultivating an organizational culture based on entrepreneurial spirit, global focus, and high-quality products and services.

Like the concept of synchronous innovation, protean shapeshifting[4] is about change. Protean shapeshifting differs from research focusing on change from one state to another with its emphasis on continual shifting and the associated underlying structures and processes. Lifton, who introduced the concept of the protean self, utilizes Homer and Euripides' mythology of Proteus to describe human resilience in an age of fragmentation. In Homer's *Odyssey,* Proteus was the Greek sea god of many forms who was only capable of prophecy if seized and chained to be held to his original shape. Proteus' shapeshifting from lion to serpent to leopard to great boar to sousing water, and then to a green tree, was equated with wisdom, whereas his prophecy came only when he was held to his original shape against his will. Euripides depicted Proteus as an Egyptian king who was a pillar of strength and a preserver of values. Lifton utilizes the protean concept as "a metaphor sufficiently rich to suggest the blending of radical fluidity, functional wisdom, and a quest for at least minimal form."[5] Lifton utilizes three basic concepts to describe proteanism: sequentiality (shapeshifting), simultaneity (the balancing of contrasts and direct oppositions), and sociality (the development of a sense of place during shapeshifting). When applied to the organizational setting, sequentiality, or shapeshifting, represents the emergence and continual shaping of new organizational forms in response to rapidly changing environmental circumstances; simultaneity is evidenced in the balancing of contrasts such as centralization and decentralization; and the concept of sociality represents the need to maintain the known or the core ideology as a mechanism to support change and the evolution of a new sense of place. Taken as a whole, the concept of protean shapeshifting suggests that change and innovation are about the simultaneous disruption of place and the seeking of a new sense of place. Shapeshifting is about the simultaneous occurrence of chaos and order. Finally, shapeshifting is about simultaneously maintaining core values while supporting continually changing practices.

Synchronous innovation and protean shapeshifting challenge taken-for-granted assumptions about change and innovation. Both concepts suggest that what has been considered polar opposites, such as order and chaos or centralization and decentralization, should be viewed not only as occurring simultaneously but as compatible processes. Both concepts embrace radical fluidly as organizational reality and both require new ways of thinking about strategy, structure, and human resilience during change.

### Notes

1. For a developed discussion of the concept of synchronous innovation, see J. Ettlie, *Taking Charge of Manufacturing* (San Francisco: Jossey-Bass, 1988).

2. Based on a compilation of research reported in Pamela Shockley-Zalabak, *Understanding Organizational Communication* (New York: Longman, 1994).

3. For a discussion of strategic competitiveness and change, see M. Hitt, R. Hoskisson, and J. Harrison, "Strategic Competitiveness in the 1990s:

Challenges and Opportunities for U.S. Executives," *The Executive* 5, no. 2 (1991): 7–22.

4. See Robert J. Lifton, *The Protean Self* (New York: Basic Books, 1993); and Pamela Shockley-Zalabak, "Protean Places: Teams Across Time and Space" (address presented to the International Communication Association convention, San Francisco, May 1999).

5. Lifton, *The Protean Self*, 5.

## Chapter 5: Role Shifting

The new leadership and management challenges are not without internal contradictions. On the one hand, the imperative is to move to group and team self-leadership; on the other hand, leaders are exhorted to singularly risk the future to motivate follower commitment if necessary. Leadership is described as both a lonely and a highly participative endeavor. The increasing complexity of an information society places new demands on leaders and managers. Rosabeth Moss Kanter concludes that "as work units become more participative and team oriented, and as professionals and knowledge workers become more prominent, the distinction between manager and non-manager begins to erode.... [Managers] must learn to operate without the crutch of hierarchy. Position, title, and authority are no longer adequate tools, not in a world where subordinates are encouraged to think for themselves and where managers have to work synergistically with other departments and even other companies. Success depends increasingly on tapping into sources of good ideas, on figuring out whose collaboration is needed to act on those ideas, on working with both to produce results. In short, the new managerial work implies very different ways of obtaining and using power."[1] Kanter goes on to explain that these changes will require leaders to inspire people to believe in the importance of their work, to give people more opportunity to set agendas and exert personal control, to share with employees in value creation (including new compensation practices), to provide opportunities for continual learning, and to contribute to the creation of a positive public and professional recognition.

Research overwhelmingly supports the concept that fast-paced change is the order of the day and a fundamental leadership challenge.

Warren Bennis explains, "The organizations of the future will be networks, clusters, cross-functional teams, temporary systems, ad hoc task forces, lattices, modules, matrices—almost anything but pyramids."[2] Many describe the organizations of the twenty-first century as borderless and boundaryless. The "middleless" organization gains attention as the new organizational design for the twenty-first century. Fewer managers with larger spans of control characterize organizational hierarchies in almost all industries. Work teams are given higher degrees of autonomy and control over immediate work situations. The goals are to increase competitiveness and improve employee morale. The traditional responsibilities of managers are replaced as power and control are passed to lower levels in the organization. Managers become facilitators, coaches, teachers, and experts, whereas previously they may have been controllers, directors, planners, and rewarders. The new responsibilities are roles, not new organizational positions. Advances in communications technology give rise to the concept of networked teams; leaders and managers must learn how to contribute to teams of people who may not be in the same geographic location and only work face-to-face on rare occasions if at all. For the most part, educational background and past work experiences do not prepare leadership for the magnitude of these organizational changes.[3]

Based on the magnitude of change virtually all are experiencing, organizational trust has become a primary leadership issue and challenge. Roderick Kramer and Tom Tyler, in their research-based discussion of trust in organizations, conclude, "We believe it is possible to predict rather precisely the trust requirements of alternative forms (organizational forms), the point of impact of trust failures, and their relative costs. Comparatively, in functional forms, trust failures reduce efficiency; in divisional forms, they reduce effectiveness and raise costs; in matrix forms, they cause the form to fail; and in networks, they cause the firms to fail."[4] Charles Handy suggests, "It is easy to be seduced by the technological possibilities of the virtual organization, but the managerial and personal implications may cause us to rethink what we mean by an organization. At it simplest, the managerial dilemma comes down to the question, How do you manage people whom you do not see? The simple answer is, By trusting them, but the apparent simplicity disguises a turnaround in organizational thinking. The rules of trust are both obvious and well established, but they do not sit easily with a managerial tradition that believes efficiency and control are closely linked and that you can't have one without a lot of the other."[5]

The challenges described by Kanter, Bennis, Kramer and Tyler, Handy, and others are transforming a variety of leadership and managerial processes. Donald Cushman and Sarah King have termed some of these new processes high-speed management.[6] Its goal is the achievement and maintenance of sustainable competitive advantage through innovative, flexible, adaptive, efficient, and rapid response to environmental change. Cushman and King describe a high-speed management system: "Innovative management refers not only to product development, but to innovation in corporate structure, human resources utilization, outsourcing, inventory control, manufacturing, marketing, servicing, and competitive position. Adaptive management refers to an organization's appropriate adjustment to change in employee values, customer tastes, investor interests, government regulations, the availability of global economic resources, and the strategic position of competitors. Flexible management refers to the capacity of an organization to expand, contract, and shift direction on products and competitive strategy; to assimilate acquisitions, joint ventures, and coalitions; and to excise unproductive or underproductive units. Efficient management refers to maintaining the industry lead in world-class products, productivity, investors' equity, return on investment, employee satisfaction, customer support, product quality, and serviceability. Rapid response management refers to setting and maintaining the industry standard in speed of response to environmental change."[7]

The work of Margaret Wheatley attempts to synthesize many of the previous concepts. Wheatley describes the natural organizing phenomena in the physical world and suggests that the power of guiding principles or values is the natural organizing phenomenon of the organizational world. She links these concepts to leadership: "These ideas speak with a simple clarity to issues of effective leadership. They bring us back to the importance of simple governing principles: guiding visions, strong values, organizational beliefs—the few rules individuals can use to shape their own behavior. The leader's task is to communicate them, to keep them ever-present and clear, and then allow individuals in the system their random, sometimes chaotic-looking meanderings."[8] Using the concept of the strange attractor from quantum physics, Wheatley identifies meaning as a powerful strange attractor for organizations. She concludes that when purpose is clear and compelling, although behaviors among individuals will differ, trust can be placed in behaviors staying within the bounds of supporting the purpose of the organization. Wheatley describes her view of leadership derived from concepts of new science: "Leadership skills have also taken on a relational slant. Leaders are being encouraged to include stakeholders, to evoke followership, to empower others. Earlier, when we focused on tasks, and people were the annoying inconvenience, we thought about 'situational' leadership—how the situation could affect our choice of styles. A different understanding of leadership has emerged recently. Leadership is always dependent on the context but the context is established by the relationships we value. We cannot hope to influence any situation without respect for the complex network of people who contribute to our organizations. Is this a fad? Or is it the web of the universe becoming felt in our work lives?"[9]

## Notes

1.  Rosabeth Moss Kanter, "The New Managerial Work," *Harvard Business Review,* November-December 1989, 85–92.

2.  Warren Bennis, "Leading Change," *USC Business,* Winter-Spring 1992, 47–51.

3.  For an expanded discussion of the research supporting this section, see Pamela Shockley-Zalabak, *Fundamentals of Organizational Communication,* 4th ed. (New York: Addison-Wesley Longman, 1999).

4.  For a research-based discussion of organizational trust, see Roderick M. Kramer and Tom R. Tyler, *Trust in Organizations* (Thousand Oaks, Calif.: Sage, 1996), 26.

5. Charles Handy, "Trust and the Virtual Organization," *Harvard Business Review,* May-June 1995, 40–50.

6. For an expanded discussion of high-speed management, see Donald Cushman and Sarah King, "High-Speed Management: A Revolution in Organizational Communication in the 1990s," *Communication Yearbook* 16, ed. S. Deetz (Newbury Park, Calif.: Sage, 1993), 209–236.

7. Cushman and King, "High-Speed Management," 215–216.

8. Margaret Wheatley, *Leadership and the New Science* (San Francisco: Berrett-Koehler, 1992), 133.

9. Wheatley, *Leadership,* 144–145.

## Chapter 6: Growing Pains

The challenges during this period in the development of the CSFSC are diverse and complex. Three receive particular attention in this research note—leadership communication, empowerment, and changing technologies.

Literally hundreds of studies describe various dimensions of leadership communication. The lack of consensus as to effective approaches, needs, impacts, or processes is striking, although considerable agreement exists that leadership communication is integral to organizational life. One of the more stimulating current approaches to leadership comes from Howard Gardner, who uses case studies from important twentieth-century leaders to develop an anatomy of leadership that includes what he calls six constants of leadership.[1] The first constant—the story—refers to the central story or message that the leader brings to a variety of audiences. The story is fundamental to excellent leadership because stories create identity, provide background, and frame future options. The second constant—the audience—refers to the interactive relationships between the leader and those he or she attempts to influence. Stories and messages should be developed in nuanced language to account for subtle but important differences in relationships and in understanding by diverse audiences of the central story. The organization itself is a constant inextricably linked to all leadership processes both framing and restraining opportunities. The fourth constant—embodiment—refers to the need for the leader to literally embody the story, that is, walk the talk and model the message and the future. Embodiment is related to questions of authenticity and credibility. The fifth constant depicts leadership as both direct and indirect, with Gardner contending that movement between the two is more easily accomplished when the stories and messages are similar, regardless of formal or informal influence processes. The final constant—the issue of expertise—refers to the domain of expertise the leader possesses. Gardner contends that the more involved one becomes in direct leadership (formal leadership/managerial roles) the more difficult it is to retain technical expertise. Gardner suggests that leadership encompasses a series of paradoxes with tensions between the need for technical expertise and the necessity for broad-based communication skills to carry the story or message across many different audiences. Leaders are challenged to communicate stories that speak to many individuals and help achieve individual and group identity. Finally, leaders must come to understand that stories have the potential to both broaden and strengthen or fragment a sense of community. In other words, stories become the substance of both successful and failed leadership.

Closely related to the processes of leadership communication are a variety of complex empowerment processes. Empowerment is related to defining role and responsibility parameters, evaluating performance, dealing with conflict, and many aspects of creativity and change. Michael Hackman and Craig Johnson provide a comprehensive review of research on the concept of empowerment and how empowerment and leadership processes intersect. Hackman and Johnson suggest, "There is no leadership without power, and some forms of power are more effective for leaders than others. However, a leader will frequently want to distribute rather than to maintain power. Reducing power differentials often enhances group performance and may be the key to organizational survival. Paradoxically, leaders gain more power by empowering others."[2] Hackman and Johnson go on to provide five major research-based reasons why leaders choose to share power: increased task satisfaction and task performance, greater cooperation among group members, collective survival, personal growth and learning, and preventing power abuses. Hackman and Johnson (referencing the work of Albert Bandura and J. A. Conger and R. N. Kanungo) conclude:

> One way to empower followers is by giving them access to the funds, materials, time and organizational support they need to do their jobs. However, empowerment also means helping followers to believe in their own abilities.... Followers who believe that they can deal with the people, events and situations in their environments— who have a sense of self-efficacy or personal power—are more likely to take initiative, set and achieve higher goals, and persist in the face of difficult circumstances.... Leaders empower followers when they: provide positive emotional support, particularly during times of stress and anxiety; express confidence; model successful performance themselves or provide opportunities to observe others who are successful ... and structure tasks so that followers experience initial success. Initial victories build expectations for future triumphs. Effective leaders structure tasks so that they become increasingly complex. Completing one part of the job is followed by training and then greater responsibilities. The same strategy can be used to introduce large-scale change [in the CSFSC case the pepper strategy for technology]. A new marketing strategy or billing system can be started in one region or plant and then adopted by the organization as a whole.[3]

The sheer potential from new technical capability and capacity influences rethinking leadership, employee empowerment, and the various forms in which work can and should be performed. Janet Fulk and Geraldine DeSanctis identify key forces of change in organizational life that currently affect the technology-organization relationship: (1) migration toward greater complexity; (2) global presence; (3) severe economic pressures; (4) desires to enhance innovation; (5) increased entrepreneurial activity; (6) incorporation of social values for more participative, learning-oriented, and diverse management practices; and (7) replacing managing form with managing relationships.[4]

Sophisticated technical networks make possible new organizations for all types and sizes. The small organization or the giant corporation can work locally, regionally, nationally, multinationally, or globally. Peter Monge and Janet Fulk identify communication issues associated with network forms of organizations: extensive geographic distances, asynchronicity across time zones, and diverse national and regional cultures.[5] All organizational processes are influenced by the types of information architecture chosen and the flexibility and efficiency of information flow across network nodes. Specific challenges include leveraging and interfacing with public information resources, building applications and databases around global customer relationships, protecting personal freedom and privacy, and understanding the boundaries and limitations of information technology.

Few question the spiderweb of relationships among leadership communication, empowerment, and rapidly changing technologies. Most agree that the challenges are identified more readily than appropriate and effective responses are determined. The research, however, is clear that these profound changes make fixed organizational structures, hierarchical control, and stable, slowing changing work processes obsolete.

### Notes

1. For a complete development of Howard Gardner's frameworks for leadership, see Gardner, *Leading Minds: An Anatomy of Leadership* (New York: Basic Books, 1995).

2. For development of the concept of empowerment and other aspects of leadership communication, see Michael Hackman and Craig E. Johnson, *Leadership: A Communication Perspective* (Prospect Heights, Ill.: Waveland, 2000).

3. Hackman and Johnson, *Leadership*, 150–151.

4. For a comprehensive discussion of the relationship between emerging communications technologies and organizational processes, see Janet Fulk and Geraldine DeSanctis, "Electronic Communication and Changing Organizational Forms," *Organization Science* 6, no. 4 (1995): 337–349.

5. For a discussion of the communication issues associated with global network organizations, see Peter Monge and Janet Fulk, "Global Network Organizations," a presentation made before the International Communication Association convention, Albuquerque, N.M., May 1995.

## Chapter 7: Networked Teams Prove Themselves

The research that describes changing organizational forms traces three broad eras beginning in 1850 and projecting through approximately 2050: the era of standardization, the era of customization, and the era of innovation. The era of standardization was represented by hierarchical forms such as the functional organization and, as markets became more demanding, the divisional form allowing companies to serve related markets with differentiated goods and services. The era of customization gave rise to the matrix organization with a dual focus on both stable and emerging market segments and customers. The 1980s pull toward customization was intensified by the advent of an increasingly deregulated global marketplace. The era of innovation had begun and a new organizational form was needed. According to Miles, Snow, Mathews, Miles, and Coleman, "The key contribution of the network form was not just its ability to rapidly respond to market demands for differentiated products and services, but to do so efficiently by extending the customization process backward and forward along the entire industry value chain.... Increasingly, firms turned to network structures in which empowered teams managed not only their internal work processes, but also external relationships with upstream and downstream partners.... In the future complete cellular firms will achieve a level of know-how well beyond that of earlier organizational forms by combining entrepreneurship, self-organization, and member ownership in mutually reinforcing ways. Each cell will have an entrepreneurial responsibility to the larger organization."[1] Sirkka Jarvenpaa and Blake Ives describe dynamic network organizations as spiders' webs spun from small, globally dispersed, ad hoc teams or independent organizational entities performing knowledge or service activities.[2] They reshape themselves dynamically as customer requirements change or as the environment evolves. Network nodes are added to the web when they can add value and are disengaged as they are no longer required.

These emerging organizational forms are characterized by fluidity, equifinality (more than one way or approach) in problem identification and solving, the presence of simultaneously loose and tight operating properties, extensive use of technology, extensive and diverse information sources established through geographically dispersed weak ties (see Granovetter cited in chapter 7, note 3), rapid response, and a variety of team-based structures. They are confronted with the ever-present challenges of working with people through constant change and the realities of the team-oriented work world.

One of the fastest growing of all contemporary organizational changes is the move to team-based structures.[3] The growing number of team-based organizations is a direct response to increased global competitiveness requiring reduced overhead and increased productivity. A by-product of this need to improve competitive position is the potential inherent in the team-based structure (but not necessarily the reality) for the workforce to be treated in a more mature way. In other words, the opportunity to work in self-managing teams and team-based organizations replaces close supervision by hierarchies with individuals and groups who self-monitor, innovate, and produce quality work with little or no supervision.

Over 70 percent of major corporations today have team-based structures in parts of their operations. Many small organizations also utilize team organizational forms. Research indicates that team-based organizations generally outperform more hierarchically organized structures in terms of product and service output, less absenteeism, fewer industrial accidents, more worker flexibility, quality improvements, and overall employee job satisfaction. Some estimate by the year 2010 over 75 percent of the workforce will participate in some form of a team-based structure.

The team-based organization is not without issues and concerns. Working in a team-based organization requires a complex mix of competencies, both technical and communicative. Many technically capable people report difficulty adapting to providing and receiving peer feedback. Additionally, career advancement is less well understood than it is in more traditional structures. The question of who gets credit for what is an issue, as well as whether team members are adequately compensated for their contributions to increased competitiveness. Critics also charge that team structures have a potential for exploitation based on continual pressures to increase productivity.

In recent work relating financial performance and people-management practices, Jeffrey Pfeffer and John Veiga identify seven practices associated with successful financial practice: employment security; selective hiring, self-managed teams, and decentralization as basic elements of organizational design; extensive training and comparatively high compensation contingent on organizational performance; reduction of status differences; and sharing information.[4] Pfeffer and Veiga identify some of the salient arguments for the seven practices:

> The idea of providing employment security in today's competitive world seems somehow anachronistic or impossible and very much at odds with what most firms seem to be doing. But employment security is fundamental to the implementation of most other high performance management processes.... Companies serious about obtaining profits through people will expend the effort needed to ensure that they recruit the right people in the first place.... Second, the organization needs to be clear about what are the most critical skills and attributes needed in its applicant pool.... Perhaps one of the greatest payoffs from team-based organizations is that teams substitute peer-based control for hierarchical control of work. Team-based organizations also are largely successful in having all of the people in the firm feel accountable and responsible for the operation and success of the enterprise, not just a few people in senior management positions. This increased sense of responsibility stimulates more initiative and effort on the part of everyone involved. In addition, and perhaps most importantly, by substituting peer for hierarchical control, teams permit removal of layers of hierarchy and absorption of administrative tasks previously performed by specialists, avoiding the enormous costs of having people whose sole job it is to watch people who watch other people do the work.... It is often argued that high compensation is a consequence of organizational success, rather than its progenitor.... Obviously, successful firms can afford to pay more, and

frequently do so, but high pay can also produce economic success.... Training is often seen as a frill in many U.S. organizations,
something to be reduced to make profit goals. Knowledge and skill
are critical—and too few organizations act on this insight.... Training can be a source of competitive advantage.... The fundamental
premise of high performance management systems is that organizations perform at a higher level when they are able to tap the ideas,
skills, and effort of all of their people.[5]

The Pfeffer and Veiga research was published in May 1999. Our
story began in 1990. The companies Pfeffer and Veiga studied do not
include the CSFSC, but the comparisons are striking. The culture of
HP and CSFSC has supported employment security. Hiring practices
are highly selective and the base organizational structure is self-managed teams. The organizational design is both centralized and
decentralized. The compensation systems are comparatively high, and
extensive training opportunities have been provided without interruption since the founding of the organization. Status differences are
minimal, information is broadly shared, and conscious efforts continue to tap the ideas, skills, and effort of all organizational members.
The results speak for themselves.

### Notes

1. For a broad discussion of emerging organizational forms over time,
see R. E. Miles, C. C. Snow, J. A. Mathews, G. Miles, and H. J. Coleman,
"Organizing in the Knowledge Age: Anticipating the Cellular Form," *The
Academy of Management Executive* 11, no. 4 (1997): 7–12.

2. Sirkka Jarvenpaa and Blake Ives, "The Global Network Organization
of the Future: Information Management Opportunities and Challenges,"
*Journal of Management Information Systems* 10, no. 4 (1994): 25–57.

3. For comprehensive research citations examining team-based
structures, see Pamela Shockley-Zalabak, *Fundamentals of Organizational
Communication,* 4th ed. (New York: Addison-Wesley Longman, 1999).

4. Jeffrey Pfeffer and John Veiga, "Putting People First for
Organizational Success," *The Academy of Management Executive* 13, no. 2
(1999): 37–48.

5. Pfeffer and Veiga, "Putting People First," 40–43.

# Index

Accounting Services Centers (ASCs), 21, 57, 103, 106–7, 144–45
accounts payable, 58
  imaging and work flow, 56
Agilent Technologies, 3, 168–71
  future of, 173, 175
America's Financial Services, 138, 140
  Colorado Springs and Atlanta, 139
  convergence, 139
A.T. Kearney, 23
A.T. & T., 35

Baker, Harland, 112–13
Barnholt, Ned, 169
Bengtson, Fran, 162
Biggs, Tammy, 92, 122–24, 155
Bohlen, Kemp, 36–37, 45, 74, 77–78, 86, 92, 99–100, 139, 157, 164, 169, 173–77, 179–80
Botti, Sharon, 94, 96
Brown, Bill, 122–24, 155
business,
  for-profit, 20
  plan, 23
Breland, Reed, 78–79, 81–82, 86–89, 93, 121, 127–30, 132, 151–53, 169, 178
Burmester, Sandy, 22, 30, 33–35, 39, 51–54, 58, 62, 64–65, 79, 82, 85–86, 89–90, 92, 104, 116–17, 125, 137, 155
bureaucratic, 41
Business within a business, 6, 107–8

capitalization, 56
careers,
  progress, 92–94, 155
  resistance to teams, 92
centralization, 5, 40, 42
change, 7, 112, 116, 168, 218
chapter notes, 197–203
Colorado Springs Financial Services Center,
  accounts payable, travel accounting, fixed assets, intracorporate accounting, general ledger, customer response center, 25
  growth, 110
  history, 18–30
  services, 24, 108
  visitors, 76
communication, 39, 110–12, 150
  plan, 53
  virtual, 107
compensation, 132
computer business, 43
conflict,
  approach, 125
  dissolving a team, 127–30
  experiences, 126–27
  modules, 125
  removing a facilitator, 130–31
  training, 125
Conger, Joyce, 21–22
consolidations, 74–75
  process templates, 58
  pace of, 74–75, 100–102
Cookingham, Ray, 16–17, 37–38, 53

Cookson, Mike, 113, 115–16
competitiveness, strategic, 210
Corporate Administrative Information Systems, 49
cost centers, 24
costs, 19
count on us themes, 104, 106
culture,
    artifacts and creations, 208
    basic assumptions, 208
    change, 116
    core, 8, 44, 207–8
    value congruence, 208
customers, 27–28, 57, 103

Darling, D-Ann, 50–51
decision quality, 94
delight,
    community, 104–5
    customer, 105
    employee, 105
    sponsor, 105
Digital Equipment Corporation, 16

education, 10–11, 65–66
Edwards, Barbara, 145–46
empowerment, process of, 120–21, 124, 217–18

facilitation,
    business needs, 82
    corrective action, 85
    development plan, team, 83–84
    definition, 79–80
    decision ownership, 89
    feedback, 90–91
    maintaining consistency, 88–90
    mistakes, 80–82
    parameters, team, 83
    team, 86–87
facilitator, 59
    advice for, 94–96
    compensation, 61–62
    directive management, 77
    facilitative management, 77
    formal appraisals, 63
    performance feedback, 63

position plan, 181–84
ranking criteria, 181–84
role,
    ambiguity, 86–87, 91
    definition and development, 60–61, 77
    shifting, 83–85
    skill set, 60
    team, 131
financial operations managers (FOMS), 92, 144
    evaluations, 92
    feedback form, 185
    FOM Team Placement Model, 186
Fiorina, Carleton, 169
fixed assets, 58

General Electric, 16
goals,
    business goals, 8, 15, 28
    compelling, 205–6
    HP Financial Services Center, 5–6, 23–26, 38
    stretch, 149
    transaction processing, 16
Gunn, Bob, 164–65
gyroscope, 7, 52, 59

Hackman, Mike, 68, 125, 136
Hammer, Michael, 26
Hewlett, Bill, 3–4, 40, 43
hiring,
    for teams, 64–65, 122
    interview process, 122–23
Hobbs, Rick, 18–19, 22, 31, 33–36, 39, 51, 54, 57–59, 64–65, 103–4, 169
HP
    future of, 173–80
history, 4, 41
    rules, 77
    split into two companies, 168–69, 171
Way, 3, 19, 39–40
Worldwide Financial Services, 75
Hostetler, Mike, 18, 54, 58

ideology, core, 208

imaging and work flow, 56
implications for others, 29, 46–47,
    70–71, 97–98, 136–38, 167–68,
    177–79
individuals, 11–12
industry reactions, 162–65
    Arthur Anderson LLP, 163–64
    Gunn Partners, 164–65
    J.D. Edwards, 163
    Lockheed Martin, 162
information technology, 27
intracorporate accounting, 58

Jones, Kathy, 78, 80–81, 86, 93, 127,
    132–33

Klute, Kelly, 163
Knudsen, John, 27, 58, 86, 99, 101,
    103
Kritz, Bill, 94–95

leadership,
    changing, 73–74, 101, 212
    challenges, 112
    constants of, 216
    priorities, 110, 150, 213
    reactions, 111
lessons learned, 8–13, 28–29, 45–46,
    69–70, 94–97, 101–102, 135–36,
    149, 165–67
Luttenbacher, Jim, 17, 18–20, 26,
    31–36, 39–41, 44–45, 49, 51–54,
    56, 64–65, 71, 73–74, 92

management, high-speed, 214
managers, operations, 58
marketing, 109
meaning, as strange attractor, 215
Morgan, Diana, 61, 78–79, 81, 86,
    88, 90–93, 118, 126–27, 135, 151
multi-entity payables system, 27, 56

networked teams, 6, 9–10, 149
    beginning, 47
    centralization, 148
    decentralization, 148
    definition, 147

evolving, 143–45
    human networking, 148
    technical networking, 148, 219

organizational forms,
    history, 221
    21st century, 213
organizational growth, 101
organizational structure, 50, 75, 100,
    104, 139, 141, 146, 170
organizational success factors,
    222–23

Packard, Dave, 4, 40–44
partner, 103, 106
performance evaluation,
    consistency, 133
    individual, 133
    peer input process (PIP), 133–34
    ranking bands, 134
    team, 132–33
platform phase, new, 75
Platt, Lew, 43, 169
presentations,
    open house, 149
process design, 55
proteanism,
    sequentiality, 211
    shapeshifting, 209
    simultaneity, 211
    sociality, 211
Pugh, Diane, 63

reengineering, 55–56, 109
Remote Processing Steering
    Committee, 50, 54–55
research notes, 205–23
results,
    audit, 162
    business goals, meeting, 158
    cost comparisons, 99, 161
    costs, 159
    corporate policy change, 151
    customer satisfaction, 157–58
    disaster recovery, 162
    employee satisfaction, 152–57
    high performance, 151

results *(continued)*
    HP Financial Services Center, 7
    metrics, 159–60
    partner satisfaction, 157–58
    volumes, 160
rewards, 132, 134–35
Robison, Pat, 168–69, 176
role shifting, 212
Rottler, Juergen, 75

SAP, 76, 93, 103, 113–16, 150
service,
    as product, 12
Shockley-Zalabak, Pam, 30, 33, 36,
    51–52, 54–55, 59, 67, 77, 84,
    117–18, 128, 130, 136, 157–58
Shultz, Bob, 35
Solutions Center, 55–56, 58, 103, 150
span of control, 31, 77
Spray, Greg, 18, 49, 56, 85–86, 92,
    101, 103–111, 119, 130, 144, 149,
    169, 177–78
standardization, 40
staying power, 10
strategy development, 108
survey,
    customer satisfaction, 102, 145
synchronous innovation, 55, 209

travel accounting, 58
team structure, 52
    autonomy, 62
    benefits, 108
    Customer Response Center, 62
    processing areas, 62
    size, 62
    status of, 221
teams, 30
    design, 54–55, 58, 60, 62
    facilitator, 131
    formal appraisals, 63
hiring, for 64–65
    hiring responsibilities, 63
    parameters, 63, 117–19, 120–21,
        187–95

performance feedback, 63
    responsibilities, 63, 117–19,
        187–95
    self-directed, 59–60
    steering, 54
teamwork,
    distinctions from team structure,
        150
technology design, 55
    change, 103, 112, 115
    legacy systems, 114, 117
    Pepper Strategy, 112–13
    technology consolidations, 117
training, 65–66,
    conflict management, 67
    decision making, 67
    dual competencies, 67
    hopes, fears, concerns, 67
    meeting management, 67
    Myers-Briggs Type Inventory, 67
    problem solving, 67
    team skills, 67
    technical, 68
transaction processing,
    history, 5
trust, 213–14

UNIX workstations, 56
users, 147

values,
core, 4, 207–8
    equation, 105
Villamana, Jim, 76, 163
vision, 105–6

Waterlander, Mike, 78, 80, 86–87,
    91, 93, 121, 126, 169, 175–76,
    178–79
Wayman, Bob, 16–17, 38, 53
Whitelaw, Don, 55
Winograd, Gaynelle, 70, 136–37

Young, John, 41, 43–44